the HISTORY of SEXUALITY
SOURCEBOOK

the HISTORY of sexuaLIty SOURCeBOOK

edited by Mathew Kuefler

UNIVERSITY OF TORONTO PRESS

LIBRARY AND ARCHIVES CANADA CATALOGUING IN PUBLICATION

The history of sexuality sourcebook / edited by Mathew Kuefler.

Includes bibliographical references and index.

ISBN: 978-1-55111-738-6

     1. Sex—History—Sources. I. Kuefler, Mathew Stephen, 1961–
HQ12.H58 2007   306.709   C2006-906020-7

We welcome comments and suggestions regarding any aspect of our publications—please feel free to contact us at news@utphighereducation.com or visit our Internet site at www.utppublishing.com.

Cover & Interior Design by Michel Vrána, Black Eye Design.

10 9 8 7 6 5 4 3

North America
5201 Dufferin Street
North York, Ontario, Canada, M3H 5T8

2250 Military Road
Tonawanda, New York, USA, 14150

Orders Phone: 1–800–565–9523
Orders Fax: 1–800–221–9985
Orders E-mail: utpbooks@utpress.utoronto.ca

UK, Ireland and continental Europe
NBN International
Estover Road, Plymouth PL6 7PY, UK
Orders Phone: 44 (0) 1752 2023001
Orders Fax: 44 (0) 1752 202333
Orders E-mail: enquiries@nbninternational.com

To Bob Martel

contents

acknowledgements

I began this project after teaching the history of sexuality for the first time at San Diego State University when I realized that there were few collections of historical sources on the history of sexuality at all, and none that covered the whole of human history. I started collecting my own sources, here and there, using them in my classes, abandoning some and gathering others. I continued to ask publishers: is there such a sourcebook for the history of sexuality?

Eventually I began to ask: would you be interested in publishing such a sourcebook for the history of sexuality? What you have in your hands is the result.

I want to begin by thanking my history of sexuality students at San Diego State University. They have challenged me to teach them history in a way that changes their lives. I want to thank all of the folks at Broadview Press who worked so hard on my behalf during the publication process, including Don LePan, Mical Moser, Natalie Fingerhut, Amy Nimegeer, Jen Elsayed, Tammy Roberts, Indrani Roy, Crescent McKeag, Judith Earnshaw, and Judith Brand—and I am sure that there are several others working behind the scenes whose names I never learned. I thank Oliva Espin, retired professor of women's studies, and Frank Nobiletti, lecturer in history, for taking the time to read a huge manuscript. I am also grateful to my research assistants over the past few years—Padraic Benson, Kelli Black, Susanne Hillman, and Darin Neufeld—who helped me fill in so many of the gaps in this collection, tracked down the obscurest of references, and carted books by the armload from the library to my office and back. I continue to be thankful for Brian's and Joe's presence in my life. This book is dedicated to Bob Martel, one of my oldest and dearest friends, with whom I have engaged in many conversations over the years—about sexuality, history, and just about every other subject—and who has helped to change my life.

preface

The History of Sexuality Sourcebook brings together samples of the entire vast array of histori-cal documents that describe just how central sexuality is in history. From diaries and letters to laws and sacred writings; texts written by central and marginal figures, men and women, the old and the young; these readings—or sources, as historians usually call them—trace the rele-vance of the history of sexuality from the earliest human societies to the present day.

The study of the history of sexuality is not only one of the fastest growing areas of history but also touches on some of the most central issues of the human experience: an individu-al's relationship to society; the organization of marriage, family, and kinship; and the role of the state and religion in regulating human behavior or social customs. While this source-book will be of greatest use to students of the history of sexuality, its insights and informa-tion should also interest students of history more generally. This is especially true for students of world history, since the sources contained in this collection cover the range of human experience from prehistory to the present day and include examples drawn from all regions of the world. I would encourage instructors of world history as well as instruc-tors of the history of sexuality to use this book as part of a new perspective on the past, and one that is frequently ignored by world his-tory textbooks. Sexuality has also become an important focus of study in many other fields, and students of sociology, psychology, women's studies, cultural studies, and other academic disciplines may find much that is helpful here, especially in providing a historical outlook on modern-day concerns.

The samples included here will, of course, only scrape the surface of the richness of the historical writings that deal with sexuality. After all, it would be impossible to address in a comprehensive way human history in all places and times. While I tried to find sources that reflected broad human concerns, I mostly had to choose one time and place in which to demonstrate the issues included here. In a few places, I included clusters of sources, representing different voices from the same society—for example, in first-century Rome, seventeenth-century Japan, or the nineteenth-century United States—but this was impossible to do too often without making the source book too unwieldy. In the end, I chose sources that were roughly typical of a body of similar writings or were particularly influential. In many cases, I have been able to provide only a small excerpt of a much larger and more detailed work. In the notes at the back of each chapter, I have mentioned when more of the same source could be read with benefit in a history of sexuality. Additional related primary sources are listed for those instructors who will want to incorporate longer readings with these excerpts or create their own clusters of readings.

Many current instructors of the history of sexuality will already have their own favorite sources to supplement this collection. Others will want to combine the use of this sourcebook with those that are more specific or include only modern sources. This sourcebook's many premodern sources (about half of the collection) is intended to demonstrate that a history of sexuality must not necessarily be a modern history or one centered on one region but can be truly comprehensive and cross-cultural. To help those instructors who want to expand their range of vision in the history of sexuality, there are suggestions for further readings from recent scholarship on the themes, times, and places for each of the sources. These would also be helpful to advanced students for supplemental information. The bibliography of other sourcebooks on the history of sexuality—most of which specialize in one place or time—is for those who would like to use this book in combination with others.

The organization of the sourcebook is thematic rather than chronological, regional, cultural, or topical, and I had important reasons for my choice. The main drawback to a chronological arrangement, especially for pre-modern history, is that sources are often only roughly datable, including, for example, forgeries attributed to much earlier writers and later manuscript versions of older documents. Sometimes sources were written down after centuries of oral circulation. So it would be impossible to know precisely how to arrange most of the first half of the sources, and in addition, the importance of an early source was often the influence it exerted on later generations. The weakness of a regional arrangement is that it must assume that the societies that exist in one area of the world share features that make them distinct from other societies of their time and features that are inherited from one era to another, an assumption that hardly seems tenable (and one immediately recognizable to instructors of world history, who have worked hard to avoid it). The disadvantage of a cultural arrangement is similar: Separating the past into discrete cultures erases the differences that exist within the same societies—differences of gender, class, ethnicity, and so on—even while it ignores the boundaries or influences between societies. The drawback to a narrowly topical arrangement, finally, is that most writers included in this collection touch on a few topics in one passage, so it would have seemed somewhat arbitrary to choose one topic under which to list it.

Instead, the readings have been divided into three broad parts, and then subdivided into thematic chapters, albeit with concessions made to the other approaches. Each part, for example, moves roughly chronologically through history, using ancient sources in the first, late ancient and medieval sources in the second, and early modern and modern sources in the third, although the arrangement of individual sources within these units is not chronological. Likewise, within each chapter, groups of sources from the same regions and cultures have often been included together, so that differences within societies or changes through time might be immediately apparent. Finally, since chapters represent a thematic series of related topics, the sources contained in each chapter often demonstrate several examples of writings on these topics as well as the relationship of some topics to others.

The themes of the parts will be described in more detail in the introduction, but can be briefly described here as reflecting three major ways of looking at sexuality. The first part examines sexuality as social custom; the second, sexuality as ideology; and the third, sexuality as identity. This arrangement allowed me to talk about the insights of other academic disciplines into the history of sexuality, especially anthropology, philosophy, and psychology, and also permitted me to outline the contributions of these main schools of thought to the nature of human sexuality, which I have labeled Darwinist, Marxist, and Freudian (as well as to summarize critiques of these three schools). Individual instructors may prefer one of these approaches and be very critical of the others, but it seemed best to me to present each of them and allow students to think about the strengths and weakness of each perspective.

Within these parts, each of the chapters addresses a different aspect of these three broader themes. For example, in the unit dealing with sexuality as social custom, one chapter discusses marriage customs, while another discusses alternative sexual arrangements to marriage. The sources for each chapter have been selected to highlight different aspects of its perspective, but there is nothing that inherently links a particular time or place with a particular perspective. Rather, the readings are intended to provide insight into a perspective that could be applied to just about any source, from any region or era. Chapter 12, for example, looks at social forces, their impact on sexuality, and people's awareness of that impact. Because of its position in this collection, I've selected eighteenth-, nineteenth-, and twentieth-century sources to highlight those issues. But social forces are at work throughout history, to be sure, and the issues raised in that chapter could be applied with benefit to many of the other readings in the history of sexuality. The purpose of such an organization was so that ideas about the history of sexuality could work hand in hand with the sources, and as students work through the sources in the collection, they would also learn essential skills for studying the history of sexuality, such as distinguishing between public and private sexualities (chapter 4) or seeing how sexuality is often used to define The Other in history (chapter 10).

Again, I have tried to make this sourcebook as useful as possible to the greatest number of instructors and students. For those who would prefer to arrange the sources differently in their classes, I have included a chronological and regional index as well as a topical index at the back of the book. All of the sources have been chosen because they offer a glimpse into the fascinating field of human sexuality in history. I hope that they inspire not only a greater awareness of the past but also a greater sympathy for it.

THREE (OR MORE) WAYS OF LOOKING AT THE HISTORY OF SEXUALITY

Sexuality, one might say, is history's biggest secret. Long shunned by historians as not a proper subject for study and as too private or even too obscene for legitimate research, sexuality lies nonetheless at the core of much of history. Indeed, if history is meant to inform us about the lives of people who lived in the past, then sexuality must form an integral part of history, a part that more and more historians are now willing to recognize. To help in this recognition is the purpose of this book.

Some historians have claimed, in contrast, that there is no history of sexuality. Their argument is sometimes made in economic terms: It was not until the financial separation of the individual from the family and the community, made possible by modern capitalism with its urbanization and wage labor, that we in the modern world were free to develop sexualities distinct from the demands of our societies. This argument is sometimes made in psychological terms: It was only recently that individuals thought of sexuality as something important about ourselves, something that identified us and set us apart from others. I talk in more detail about the modern social and economic changes to sexual-

ity in the introduction to chapter 12, and more on the "social constructionist" ideas, which reject similarities drawn between the past and the present in the history of sexuality, in the introduction to chapter 15. Despite the undeniable changes between modern and premodern sexuality, similarities still remain, and discovering what links us to the past as well as what separates us from it lies at the heart of history itself. Since past individuals *did* make sexual choices that went against the grain of their societies (see, for example, the sources in chapter 8, "Dissenting Voices"), individualism in matters sexual is clearly not only a modern reality. Since even the distant past provides evidence for a variety of sexual lifestyles (see, for example, the sources in chapter 3, "The Varieties of Sexual Expression"), it seems too simplistic to imply that there was one model of sex before the advent of capitalism. In short, it seems better not to assume that the past had no sexuality but rather to investigate how sexuality has changed through time. That is also what this sourcebook is intended to do.

Each of the book's three parts reflects a broad perspective on the history of sexuality and uses the insights of different academic fields and schools of thought in order to get at this question of what the history of sexuality means. The first part looks at sexuality as social custom. This is the perspective of anthropologists whose methods have enriched historians' viewpoints, notably in the history of sexuality. Anthropologists seek to examine the patterns of interactions in human societies and to understand them as having important social purposes. Historians of sexuality have benefited greatly from this approach. Why do certain sexual customs arise, maintain themselves, or disappear? Why do we see similar sexual customs among otherwise disparate cultures, or conversely, why do some sexual customs differ so widely among cultures? These are the sorts of questions that anthropologists have asked. They also use cross-cultural comparison to help understand the answers more completely. Historians interested in sexuality as social custom ask similar questions. Since historians cannot interview living members of past societies, they must get their information from those written sources that have survived from the past. They also gain real advantages from cross-cultural comparisons between historical societies and between them and modern societies.

Seeing sexuality as social custom was a common perspective in the ancient world, and so it becomes a helpful organizing theme for his book's first part that contains mostly ancient sources. Members of ancient societies—at least, most members who were able to leave us a written record of their thoughts—thought of their own society as having evolved certain sexual customs for their utility or overall benefit, or even because they were "natural," that is, in accordance with human nature or the nature of the world. They thought their society did things in a certain way because that way "made sense" or because it was "the normal way" of doing things. There were usually elaborate legends or myths that explained how customs had developed, sexual and otherwise. These ancient writers frequently saw alternative arrangements as illogical or abnormal, even bizarre, and often condemned them as such, either when seen in their own society or if they visited other societies with different customs. Whether talking about their own customs or those of foreign cultures, though, they left us a valuable record of the past.

The idea that some sexual customs were "normal" or "natural" to human beings resurfaced in a new way in the nineteenth century with the writings of Charles Darwin. A botanist by training, Darwin didn't seem much interested in the history of sexuality, at least from what he wrote. But his ideas on human evolution prompted a whole new school of thought that viewed all human interactions, sexual and social, as determined by basic animal nature. If human beings were related to and descended from other animal species, then our behavior, whether behind closed doors or out in the open, should resemble in the broadest terms the sexual behavior of other animals. Indeed, since we are most closely related to other primates, our instinctive sexual behavior should be much like theirs.

When Darwin was formulating his ideas about human evolution, another Englishman,

Herbert Spencer, was formulating his own ideas about social evolution, what he called Social Darwinism. He believed that human societies evolve in much the same way that individuals do: as adaptations to environments and for "the survival of the fittest" (a phrase that Spencer coined). This form of Darwinism has been especially popular with anthropologists, who typically look at social customs as adaptations intended to ensure the success of a society and tend to understand extinct societies as failures to adapt to changing environments. And sexual customs are often closely linked to a society's chances for survival.

The more biological or individual form of Darwinism did not disappear, however. One sees the evidence for such a Darwinist approach in some of the modern explanations for sexual customs, especially within the sociobiology movement founded by Edward O. Wilson. Polygamy among human beings, for example, is said to be only the "alpha-male" or natural leader of the human pack asserting his dominance over the other females in the group, as do other animals like lions or elephants. Monogamy among human beings is claimed to be the human equivalent of the pair bonding and mating for life that occurs in so many animals, from swans to gray wolves. As this one example shows, it is possible to explain contradictory human sexual behaviors by pointing to the parallels with animal behavior, so diverse is the animal kingdom.

A close parallel to the Darwinist school can be seen in those recent writers who maintain that various hormonal differences determine human sexual behavior. If men are sexually aggressive and sometimes commit rape, it is because of male testosterone levels. If women nurture children born to them, it is caused by female estrogen levels. These ideas about hormones and behavior have usually relied on scientific experimentation on animals and assumed roughly equivalent responses in humans, although the recent medical ability to manipulate human hormone levels is providing new data for study. Sometimes similar arguments are made based on physiological differences between men and women or the expanding knowledge about human genetics.

In the end, it is difficult to say how much of human sexual behavior is caused by "nature" rather than "nurture." Biologists and anthropologists certainly haven't resolved the debate, which should not be too surprising. No human being is raised in a vacuum, and throughout our lives we respond to an array of cultural values and models as well as react to hormonal or genetic impulses in making our sexual choices. So it seems impossible to separate out which of our behaviors are caused by our biological makeup and which are caused by our environment, let alone which result from a combination. Moreover, Darwinist ideas are all too often used to excuse sexual misconduct as beyond our control or to reinforce moral customs about sexuality as "natural" to human beings.

The importance of social environment and cultural values brings us to the book's second part, sexuality as ideology. "Ideology"—by which I mean a network of connecting ideas, beliefs, and values—is a term coined by philosophers, who remind us of the importance of ideas to history generally, including to the history of sexuality. Sexual customs change, after all: They fall out of favor or are revised, according to the ideas of social critics and reformers or when the social conditions that gave rise to them change. What kinds of ideas are promoted about sex and by whom? What justification do the promoters of those ideas offer in order to persuade others to follow them? And what happens to those who refuse to obey the "rules" about sex? Are they tolerated, condemned, or eradicated? These are the sorts of questions that philosophers have asked about sexuality. When historians ask these questions, they must frequently do so by examining legal, religious, and philosophical codes where good and bad behavior are most clearly spelled out and where the rewards for the one and punishments for the other are also clarified.

Because the ideology of sexuality was greatly emphasized in the late ancient and medieval worlds, insofar as we can see from historical documents, I use sources mostly from these eras to illustrate this theme. The world's major religions took shape in the Middle Ages. If ancient writers mostly supported sexual customs they considered "logical" or "natural" and rejected ones they considered "illogical" or "unnatural," medieval writers tended to approve of sexual customs they thought of as "moral" or "enlightened" or "divinely decreed" and to disapprove of ones they thought of as "immoral" or "spiritually dangerous" or even "demonically inspired." And whether they were describing their own society as following the rules or not, or giving advice to others about how to follow a moral code more precisely, we learn a lot about the sexual ideologies that these medieval writers espoused.

In the nineteenth century, Karl Marx developed a method and a terminology for talking about the relationship between those attempting to maintain the social status quo, those subject to it, and those attempting to subvert, reform, or overthrow it. These Marxist ideas have proved popular among historians, especially those studying the history of sexuality. For Marx, those who have power are always interested in keeping it from those who have little or no power. To gain power, the powerless must use their collective strength to combat the powerful. Sometimes the powerful use physical force to keep the powerless in check and to demonstrate their superiority in mili-

tary might. In such cases, rebellion against the powerful must take the form of armed revolution. At other times the powerful use ideas to support their dominance, especially about their own superiority and the inferiority of the powerless, ideas often supported by appealing to "the way things have always been" or even to a divine decree. For Marx, religion was the opium of the masses, making the powerless docile and passive through the force of ideas. Rebellion against such oppressive ideas must take the form of a counterideology, a set of new ideas that rejected the old and replaced them. Out of such intellectual rebellions came legal, religious, and philosophical revolutions, as well as revolutions that rejected the authority of law, religion, or philosophy altogether.

Marx wasn't much interested in the history of sexuality. His friend and associate, Friedrich Engels, did try to transpose Marx's ideas onto the history of sexuality, showing how traditional marriage and the family unit was a means by which those with power (husbands) attempted to keep it from those without it (their wives and children). In recent decades, French philosopher and historian Michel Foucault has expanded upon Marx's ideas in formulating his own theories about the history of sexuality. For Foucault, rebellion against oppressive ideas has always been difficult, even impossible, because the web of forces that oppress is all around: The institutions of state, religion, law, and custom all work to keep the individual in check. In fact, the forces that dominate us are even within us: We are so oppressed that we act as our own monitors, our own internalized oppression keeping us from acting as we would want to. Even when we manage to rebel and think we are finally free of oppression, we are only deluding ourselves, since new types of oppressions arise to replace the old ones.

Marx's and Foucault's ideas have been criticized for their rather pessimistic view of human nature. Is it inherent in human beings to try to oppress each other? Isn't it possible that human beings might act out of altruistic motives, including in the area of sexual desire, especially when that desire is connected to love and affection? Likewise, is change only possible through revolution, whether by force or by ideas? Is there no possibility that human beings can opt to change their own ideas or behavior, rather than having changes forced upon them? In other words, critics of a Marxist approach argue that power relations may not be the sole or even primary type of social or sexual relations, and that the human personality incorporates much more than one basic relationship of dominance and oppression.

This book's third part draws upon these insights about the human personality, using sexuality and identity as its organizing theme and including sources mainly from the modern world. Here the insights are largely borrowed from psychologists, who have been at the forefront of the study of sexuality and whose work has also greatly impacted historians of sexuality. How do we, as individuals, compare to others? How do we differ from others? What does sexuality tell us about ourselves or about others? These sorts of questions, influenced by psychology, have also substantially shaped the ways historians look at sexuality.

Such ways of looking at sexuality seem quintessentially modern. If ancient writers looked for "natural" customs in sexuality and medieval writers for "moral" guidance in sexual values, then modern writers are often said to look to sexuality to help us know "who we are." Somehow we think we will comprehend ourselves and others better if we see sexuality as part of those identities. We look to sexuality to set us apart from the identities of others, to determine an "us" versus "them": "righteous" versus "perverse" desires, "repressed" versus "liberated" ideas, or "normal people" versus "freaks"—depending, of course, on our perspectives. Here, the very categories that we create for our own identities and for those of others are important for the study of sexuality.

An early champion of such an approach was Sigmund Freud, another nineteenth-century thinker (who continued to live and write in the early twentieth century). He became famous even in his own day for suggesting that sexuality provided the key to understanding ourselves. According to Freud, human sexuality develops as a gradual narrowing from a wide range of sexual potential—what he called "polymorphous perversity"—to appropriate sexual desire, at least in most individuals. Freud described the process as he understood it, beginning with the infant's affectional bond with its mother and the mother's sexual bond with her husband. In other individuals, sexual desire was channeled in different directions that resulted in various "sexual aims"—Freud's term for sexual activities that individuals want to do—and various "sexual object choices"—his term for who or what they want to do them with.

Freud's ideas were extended by other psychologists who came after him. Jacques Lacan, for example, suggested that our identities are shaped not only by who we discover ourselves to be but also by who we discover others to be. We identify ourselves as being not somebody else, whom we identify as the "Other" (the term is usually capitalized to highlight it). And in establishing the parameters of the Other's identity, we are able to establish our own identity more precisely.

The ideas of Freud and other psychologists have been criticized for their assumptions about human development. We don't know whether all human beings develop and mature in the same ways, nor do we know that the same sort of environment must always produce the same sort of person. Freud also made many assumptions about the environment into which children are born: He assumed that all children had a mother and a father, for example, something that was not universally true of the late nineteenth century and is even less true today. Freud—and Lacan after him—also felt that girls grow up with a profound sense of loss at not having been born male, the basis of their theories about women's development, an assumption that may say more about their own sense of themselves as men than about general human development.

These three schools of thought—Darwinist, Marxist, and Freudian—have nonetheless deeply shaped all of modern knowledge, including the history of sexuality. Note that all three thinkers were nineteenth-century European men. That in itself says something about who had access to higher education, who had money and leisure to write, and whose voices have been heard in modern universities and, as a result, become mainstream. Their ideas have been criticized over the years, but their influence remains, and their ideas reflect larger patterns of thought about sexuality, patterns that proved useful in shaping the themes in this book.

Recently, it is important to note, there have been attempts to offer alternative ways of looking at sexuality. One that I find intriguing is a model of sexuality as "performativity" proposed by the philosopher Judith Butler. She borrows this metaphor from the theater: In sex as in acting, there are scripts that have to be memorized, but there are also impromptu performances. In both, some actors perform these scripts better than others, according to their inclinations (since they are drawn to some roles rather than to others), their abilities (since they differ in how well they are able to perform roles), and their interests (since some don't want to follow the script word for word, while others do). And just like actors, sexual performers are judged in their performance by a variety of audience members, who use diverse criteria for making their judgments.

Such a performative model of sexuality is an attractive one, since it reduces the moral associations that other models imply: This model has no "natural" or "unnatural," "moral" or "immoral," "normal" or "abnormal." But it might be criticized for the same reason: It offers no basis for an ethics of sexuality. In other words, there is no justification for approving or disapproving of anyone's performance of sexuality, since it is all about the actor's interests and abilities and the audience's judgment is seen as arbitrary. There might be compelling reasons to object to some types of sexual performances, though, for example, ones based on compulsion rather than consent.

Perhaps there is no single overarching way of looking at sexuality. It is, after all, one of the most universal of human activities, and one likely shaped by a combination of social, ideological, and personal factors. And because sexuality contains layers of biology, culture, and individuality, it is both fascinating and vital to see it at work in history.

PART I
sexuality as social custom

CHAPTER 1
Patriarchy

Early human history is overwhelmingly a record of men's domination of women. Feminist scholars, who were the first to study and appreciate this imbalance in history, described male-dominated societies as patriarchies. The word "patriarchy" comes from the Greek, and means "rule by the father," since in male-dominated societies a woman's life is usually controlled first by her father, then by her husband, and lastly by her son or sons. The term, however, has come to mean the whole range of values and behaviors associated with a belief in the superiority of men and the inferiority of women.

Insofar as we know, most early human societies were patriarchal. There are some clues that perhaps there were ancient peoples either dominated by women (matriarchal) or egalitarian, but the evidence is scanty. The Minoans of ancient Crete in the eastern Mediterranean, for example, have been suggested as one such egalitarian or matriarchal society, yet we know so little about the Minoans, except what can be seen about their art and architecture in the archeological remains of the palace at Knossos and at other sites. We don't even know the Minoans' name for themselves: "Minoan" is a modern scholarly designation for the culture.

In recent years, scholars have tried, with only limited success, to determine why patriarchy was so prevalent in the ancient world. A Darwinist might suggest that the biological differences between men and women explains this fact. Women's biological destiny meant that they were the ones who gave birth to children and nursed them in their early years. Women, therefore, more often remained close to home, looking after children and gathering and preparing food, and they lost their positions in public life. Other physiological differences might also contribute to this Darwinist explanation. Men, who tend to have greater upper body strength than women, took advantage of their abilities as hunters and as warriors, eventually using force to seize control of early societies. This argument, however, has a serious flaw: If women were the food gatherers, then they were likely the ones who discovered and developed agriculture, which gradually became the dominant food source. If they had controlled the production of food, however, why didn't women use this knowledge or their control of the food from agriculture to gain power over men?

Here a Marxist approach might be offered. As hunters and warriors, men came into contact more regularly with other tribal groups and competed with them for dominance. At first they killed their competitors, but eventually they enslaved them. Then, as men learned to benefit from the forced labor of others, they decided to do the same with the women in their own groups. They divided their own societies into the powerful and the powerless and created a gendered hierarchy of men over women. This sort of power-based explanation, however, also contains a flaw: Even if it helps to explain "how" a gender imbalance might have occurred, it does not really explain "why" men should have been interested in enslaving women.

Here Freudian explanations have been offered. Freud believed that girls grow up jealous of their brothers, especially their freedom in a male-dominated society, and that in childhood they attribute it to anatomical differences, what he called "penis envy." Psychologist Nancy Chodorow believes that the opposite is true, that boys are jealous of their sisters. All infants, she suggests, begin life with a deep bond to their mothers. As children find out about themselves, boys discover that they are different from their mothers in anatomical ways, while their sisters are not. To establish a sense of themselves as male,

boys must break with their mothers and forfeit that sense of intimacy that girls retain from their identification with their mothers. Men's resulting resentment of women translates into attempts at social oppression.

There are difficulties with any one of these theories, to be sure, but all of them point to the problems of attempting to reconstruct the origins of human society and sexuality. After all, modern homo sapiens evolved perhaps 200,000 years ago, but the first writing systems were invented only about 5,000 years ago. By the time written records came into existence, patriarchy was well established, so its starting point lies in the long prehistory of humanity. There are only ambiguous clues in the past that offer the possibility of other social arrangements.

One of these clues is worth noting, though: the myths and legends of many ancient peoples, which often describe female deities with far more rights and freedoms and a much greater social presence than enjoyed by the women who lived in those societies. How do we explain an ancient people who worshipped a powerful goddess while simultaneously keeping in subordination the actual women around them? Here is one possible explanation: The earliest human beings, it must be assumed, did not understand reproduction. Like animals, they simply had sex because they desired it and did not connect sex to birth. In such a society, women's ability to give birth would likely have been highly valued, since it contributed to the continuation of the group. Women's fertility would not have been understood and might have seemed mysterious and even supernatural, possibly connected to the fertility of the earth and the growth of new plants every year. The worship of a female divinity as representing the power of fertility seems to have been common among ancient peoples, perhaps reflecting the remnants of this awe for women's fertility. Eventually, of course, human reproduction was linked to sex, and men recognized their own role in the process. To this era might be dated the many myths of creation as a great cosmic act of sex, where the sky and the earth join together to produce life. Also at this time, perhaps, the many fertility goddesses and earth mothers acquired husbands or consorts in new myths developed to spiritualize the power of sexuality. As men's role in reproduction became better understood, they sought to limit women's sexuality, especially through seclusion from public life, which made it easier to determine who had fathered children. These myths and legends remained, though, even after patriarchy was firmly rooted.

Without enough early evidence, most of this discussion of patriarchy's origins is conjecture, but it demonstrates how central the study of sexuality's history is to understanding human origins and the earliest civilizations. It also demonstrates another important point: History becomes interesting if it connects to issues that are important to us today. Because the changing gender roles of men and women are clearly a central issue of modern society, investigating those past roles and their changes becomes all the more relevant. The sources contained in this chapter deal with various aspects of the question of patriarchy in ancient societies.

1. THE SO-CALLED VENUS OF WILLENDORF

Time: about 25,000 BCE
Place: modern Austria
Artist: unknown

Scattered throughout several regions of the world, especially in Europe and western Asia, are the so-called Venus figurines, sculpted objects of varying sizes depicting the female form, like this one found at Willendorf in Austria. Some are more abstract and some more realistic in an array of body shapes, often with breasts, hips, and vulvas emphasized and facial features de-emphasized, but their purpose is unknown. Were they talismans meant to encourage fertility, as is commonly thought? Were they images of deities? Were they erotic art? Were they children's dolls? Without supporting evidence to demonstrate their use, it is difficult to say with any certainty what function they served. These are the sort of tantalizingly obscure evidence of gender relations from the earliest human societies.

Questions for Reflection and Discussion

What do you think was the likeliest purpose for this figurine? Might it have served more than one function? What evidence might this figurine provide for ideas about women's bodies or for ideals of beauty among ancient peoples? Why might there be so many of these female figurines and so few male ones?

2. AKKADIAN HYMN TO ISHTAR

Time: sixteenth century BCE
Place: Mesopotamia (modern Iraq)
Author: unknown

Ishtar was the name given to a fertility goddess by the Akkadians, an ancient Semitic people who inhabited the lands along the Tigris and Euphrates rivers. Temples of enormous size—indeed, some of the largest of the permanent buildings erected in the ancient world—were erected in honor of Ishtar in the various towns ruled by the Akkadians. Vast temple compounds included living spaces for numerous attendants, including priests and priestesses, and serve as monuments to the reverence given to her. Such was the respect with which heavenly women were treated in antiquity.

Praise the goddess, the most awesome of the goddesses.
Let one revere the mistress of the peoples, the greatest of the great gods of heaven.
Praise Ishtar, the most awesome of the goddesses.
Let one revere the queen of women, the greatest of the great gods of heaven.
She is clothed with pleasure and love.
She is laden with vitality, charm, and voluptuousness.
Ishtar is clothed with pleasure and love.
She is laden with vitality, charm, and voluptuousness,
In lips she is sweet; life is in her mouth.
At her appearance rejoicing becomes full.
She is glorious; veils are thrown over her head.
Her figure is beautiful; her eyes are brilliant.
The goddess—with her there is counsel.
The fate of everything she holds in her hand.

At her glance there is created joy,
Power, magnificence, the protecting deity and guardian spirit.
She dwells in, she pays heed to compassion and friendliness.
Besides, agreeableness she truly possesses.
Be it slave, unattached girl, or mother, she preserves her.
One calls on her; among women one names her name.
Who—to her greatness who can be equal?
Strong, exalted, splendid are her decrees.
Ishtar—to her greatness who can be equal?
Strong, exalted, splendid are her decrees.
She is sought after among the gods; extraordinary is her station.
Respected is her word; it is supreme over them.
Ishtar among the gods, extraordinary is her station.
Respected is her word; it is supreme over them.
She is their queen; they continually cause her commands to be executed.
All of them bow down before her.
They receive her light before her.
Women and men indeed revere her.
In their assembly her word is powerful; it is dominating.
Before Anum their king she fully supports them.
She rests in intelligence, cleverness, and wisdom.
They take counsel together, she and her lord.
Indeed they occupy the throne room together.
In the divine chamber, the dwelling of joy,
Before them the gods take their places.
To their utterances their attention is turned....
By her orders she has subjected to him

The four world regions at his feet;
And the total of all peoples
She has decided to attach them to his
yoke.

Questions for Reflection and Discussion

Which qualities that belong to Ishtar as a
deity also belong to her as a woman? What
sort of relationship exists between Ishtar and
humanity? What role is played by Ishtar's male
consort, called here, Anum. Why might a patriarchal society have linked Anum to Ishtar?

3. THE LEGEND OF ADAM AND EVE

Time: written down between the tenth and
    fifth centuries BCE, from oral traditions
Place: Israel
Author: unknown

*Among the most famous stories from the
sacred books of the ancient Israelites known
as the Bible is that of the Garden of Eden and
its inhabitants, the first human beings, Adam
and Eve. The legend also contains an explanation for the existence of patriarchy, listed
alongside such human miseries as the need for
work, the necessity of clothing, and the inevita-
bility of death. Here the bad choices made by the
original human pair are believed to have had
consequences for all humans since.*

When the Lord God made the earth and the
heavens ... the Lord God formed the man
from the dust of the ground and breathed into
his nostrils the breath of life, and the man
became a living being. Now the Lord God
had planted a garden in the east, in Eden; and
there he put the man he had formed. And the
Lord God made all kinds of trees grow out of
the ground—trees that were pleasing to the
eye and good for food. In the middle of the
garden were the tree of life and the tree of the
knowledge of good and evil.... The Lord God
took the man and put him in the Garden of
Eden to work it and take care of it. And the
Lord God commanded the man, "You are free
to eat from any tree in the garden; but you
must not eat from the tree of the knowledge
of good and evil, for when you eat of it you
will surely die."

The Lord God said, "It is not good for the
man to be alone. I will make a helper suitable
for him." Now the Lord God had formed out
of the ground all the beasts of the field and all
the birds of the air. He brought them to the
man to see what he would name them; and
whatever the man called each living creature,
that was its name. So the man gave names to
all the livestock, the birds of the air and all the
beasts of the field. But for Adam no suitable
helper was found. So the Lord God caused
the man to fall into a deep sleep; and while
he was sleeping, he took one of the man's ribs
and closed up the place with flesh. Then the
Lord God made a woman from the rib he had
taken out of the man, and he brought her to
the man. The man said, "This is now bone of
my bones and flesh of my flesh; she shall be
called 'woman,' for she was taken out of man."
For this reason a man will leave his father and
mother and be united to his wife, and they
will become one flesh. The man and his wife
were both naked, and they felt no shame.

Now the serpent was more crafty than any
of the wild animals the Lord God had made. He
said to the woman, "Did God really say, 'You
must not eat from any tree in the garden'?" The
woman said to the serpent, "We may eat fruit
from the trees in the garden, but God did say,
'You must not eat fruit from the tree that is in
the middle of the garden, and you must not
touch it, or you will die.'" "You will not surely
die," the serpent said to the woman. "For God

knows that when you eat of it your eyes will be opened, and you will be like God, knowing good and evil." When the woman saw that the fruit of the tree was good for food and pleasing to the eye, and also desirable for gaining wisdom, she took some and ate it. She also gave some to her husband, who was with her, and he ate it. Then the eyes of both of them were opened, and they realized they were naked; so they sewed fig leaves together and made coverings for themselves. Then the man and his wife heard the sound of the Lord God as he was walking in the garden in the cool of the day, and they hid from the Lord God among the trees of the garden. But the Lord God called to the man, "Where are you?" He answered, "I heard you in the garden, and I was afraid because I was naked; so I hid." And he said, "Who told you that you were naked? Have you eaten from the tree that I commanded you not to eat from?" The man said, "The woman you put here with me—she gave me some fruit from the tree, and I ate it." Then the Lord God said to the woman, "What is this you have done?" The woman said, "The serpent deceived me, and I ate."

So the Lord God said to the serpent, "Because you have done this, cursed are you above all the livestock and all the wild animals! You will crawl on your belly and you will eat dust all the days of your life. And I will put enmity between you and the woman, and between your offspring and hers; he will crush your head, and you will strike his heel." To the woman he said, "I will greatly increase your pains in childbearing; with pain you will give birth to children. Your desire will be for your husband, and he will rule over you." To Adam he said, "Because you listened to your wife and ate from the tree about which I commanded you, 'You must not eat of it,' cursed is the ground because of you; through painful toil you will eat of it all the days of your life. It will produce thorns and thistles for you, and you will eat the plants of the field. By the sweat of your brow you will eat your food until you return to the ground, since from it you were taken; for dust you are and to dust you will return." Adam named his wife Eve, because she would become the mother of all the living. The Lord God made garments of skin for Adam and his wife and clothed them. And the Lord God said, "The man has now become like one of us, knowing good and evil. He must not be allowed to reach out his hand and take also from the tree of life and eat, and live forever." So the Lord God banished him from the Garden of Eden to work the ground from which he had been taken.

Questions for Reflection and Discussion

What might it mean to those who believe in the sacredness of this legend that gender inequality is construed as punishment for sin? Does its placement together with the requirement for toil and the wearing of clothing put it among the evils of civilization? What might it mean that knowledge of one's nakedness is the first type of new knowledge that Adam and Eve are said to have gained?

4. SATAKATRAYA

Time: fifth century CE
Place: north India
Author: Bhartrihari

The poet Bhartrihari described the appeal of women of his day and what he considered to be the dangers of that appeal for men. It is meant to be playful in tone, but its attitude reflects an underlying patriarchal ideology that valued women for what they offered to men and resented women for any sort of power they exercised. We know little about the historical person of Bhartrihari, but it is not difficult to imagine that his views were shared by other men in his

When men behold the beauty of women
with exotic flashing eyes,
youthful pride in voluptuous breasts,
creepers of beauty-creases
twining above their slender bellies,
those few are fortunate whose minds
are still unperturbed.
With smiles, affection, modesty, and art;
hostile looks and ardent glances;
eloquence, jealous quarrels, and play
with all her emotions woman enchains us.
With the striking of their slipping
bangles,
the jeweled sounds of their girdles,
and their ringing anklets,
they shame the call of the royal goose.
With the trembling eyes of frightened
does,
whose mind will girls not destroy?
I do indeed speak without bias;
this is acknowledged as truth among men.
Nothing enthralls us like an ample-
hipped woman;
nothing else causes such pain.
Women's gestures are naturally
charming,
seductive only in a fool's infatuated heart.
The lotus's passionate red is natural too,
and still bees hover there bewitched....
In this vapid, mundane world,
wise men take two courses:
they spend some time with minds
submerged in the fluid elixir of wisdom,
the rest with tender women
whose breasts and hips enjoy the pleasure
of hiding men's eager hands
in their laps of ample flesh....
There is no ambrosia or poison
except in the love of an ample-hipped
woman;

enamored, she is an ambrosial vine,
indifferent, a poisonous creeper.
Glances cast with dancing brows and
downcast eyes,
tender words and modest smiles,
dallying languor in posture and gait—
all are woman's ornament and her
weapon....
The culprit unlocking the door to the city
of hell
is fair-eyed woman's key, her graceful
creeper-brow.
Like waves three furrows of beauty encir-
cle her waist,
a pair of wild geese in flight are her lusty
breasts,
a radiant blooming lotus is her face....
Surely poets are mistaken
who call amorous women weak.
When their tremulous wanton glances
captivate heroic gods like Indra,
how can they be weak? ...
It is strange and perverse that men
indulge erotic passion in old age,
and that round-hipped women do not
stop
living or loving when their breasts sag.
I prefer being bitten by a terrible serpent,
long, wanton, tortuous, gleaming like a
black lotus,
to being smitten by her eye.
Healers are everywhere to cure one of a
serpent bite,
but there is no spell or remedy for me;
I was struck by the glance of a beautiful
woman! ...
Renunciation of worldly attachment
is only the talk of scholars,
whose mouths are wordy with wisdom.
Who can really forsake the hips
of beautiful women bound
with girdles of ruby jewels?

What ideals for women in appearance and behavior are described in this poem? In what ways does men's erotic desire for women fit easily within a patriarchal context? In what ways is it a challenge to patriarchy?

5. THE LAWS OF MANU

Time: fifth century BCE, from earlier oral
   traditions
Place: north India
Author: unknown

The Laws of Manu are an ancient law code that belongs to the early Hindu or Vedic tradition of north India. In that tradition, Manu was the original human being. In its entirety, The Laws of Manu describe the early caste system and the duties of various key players in ancient Indian society, such as kings and priests, as well as providing guidance on the performance of rituals and the punishment of crimes. They also describe the role of women in ways that would have been familiar to many ancient societies.

I will tell the eternal duties of a man and wife who stay on the path of duty both in union and in separation. Men must make their women dependent day and night, and keep under their own control those who are attached to sensory objects. Her father guards her in childhood, her husband guards her in youth, and her sons guard her in old age. A woman is not fit for independence. A father who does not give her away at the proper time should be blamed, and a husband who does not have sex with her at the proper time should be blamed; and the son who does not guard his mother when her husband is dead should be blamed.

Women should especially be guarded against addictions, even trifling ones, for unguarded women would bring sorrow upon both families. Regarding this as the supreme duty of all the classes, husbands, even weak ones, try to guard their wives. For by zealously guarding his wife he guards his own descendants, practices, family, and himself, as well as his own duty. The husband enters the wife, becomes an embryo, and is born here on earth. That is why a wife is called a wife, because he is born again in her. The wife brings forth a son who is just like the man she makes love with; that is why he should guard his wife zealously, in order to keep his progeny clean.

No man is able to guard women entirely by force, but they can be entirely guarded by using these means: he should keep her busy amassing and spending money, engaging in purification, attending to her duty, cooking food, and looking after the furniture. Women are not guarded when they are confined in a house by men who can be trusted to do their jobs well; but women who guard themselves by themselves are well guarded. Drinking, associating with bad people, being separated from their husbands, wandering about, sleeping, and living in other people's houses are the six things that corrupt women. Good looks do not matter to them, nor do they care about youth; "A man!" they say, and enjoy sex with him, whether he is good-looking or ugly. By running after men like whores, by their fickle minds, and by their natural lack of affection these women are unfaithful to their husbands even when they are zealously guarded here. Knowing that their very own nature is like this, as it was born at the creation by the Lord of Creatures, a man should make the utmost effort to guard them. The bed and the seat, jewelry, lust, anger, crookedness, a malicious nature, and bad conduct are what Manu assigned to women. There is no ritual with Vedic verses for women; this is a firmly established point of law. For women, who have no virile strength and no Vedic verses, are false-hood; this is well established.

Questions for Reflection and Discussion

Why is the guarding of women so important in a patriarchal society? How do the stereotypes about women's sexuality help to support a patriarchal system? Since this is a law code, it describes ideal rather than typical behavior. Is there any evidence within the source itself that suggests that women did not always act as they were supposed to act?

6. LESSONS FOR A WOMAN

Time: first century CE
Place: north China
Author: Ban Zhao

Ban Zhao (whose name is also spelled Pan Chao) was born into a famous family highly placed in the Han Dynasty of early imperial China. Her brother, for example, was an army general and later historian to the Imperial Court. The Han Chinese government promoted an ideology based on the teachings of Confucius, who had lived centuries earlier. Confucius was a great believer in social order and in the importance of education for teaching everyone his or her proper place in that order. Nonetheless, he said little about women. So Ban Zhao decided to write a treatise to educate women about their proper role and duties and, in doing so, gave us a rare glimpse at an ancient woman's understanding of patriarchy.

I, the unworthy writer, am unsophisticated, unenlightened, and by nature unintelligent, but I am fortunate both to have received not a little favor from my scholarly father, and to have had a cultured mother and instructresses upon whom to rely for a literary education as well as for training in good manners. More than forty years have passed since at the age of fourteen I took up the dustpan and the broom in the Cao family [through marriage].… Being careless, and by nature stupid, I taught and trained my children without system.… I do grieve that you, my daughters, just now at the age for marriage, have not at this time had gradual training and advice; that you still have not learned the proper customs for married women. I fear that by failure in good manners in other families you will humiliate both your ancestors and your clan.… I wish every one of you, my daughters, each to write out a copy for yourself. From this time on every one of you strive to practice these lessons.…

Let a woman modestly yield to others; let her respect others; let her put others first, herself last. Should she do something good, let her not mention it; should she do something bad, let her not deny it. Let her bear disgrace; let her even endure when others speak or do evil to her. Always let her seem to tremble and to fear.… Let a woman retire late to bed, but rise early to duties; let her not dread tasks by day or by night. Let her not refuse to perform domestic duties whether easy or difficult. That which must be done, let her finish completely, tidily, and systematically.… Let a woman be correct in manner and upright in character in order to serve her husband. Let her live in purity and quietness of spirit, and attend to her own affairs. Let her love not gossip and silly laughter.…

The Way of husband and wife is intimately connected with *Yin* and *Yang* [these are the two basis elements of Daoism that represent all opposites: male and female, hard and soft, hot and cold, and so on].… If a husband be unworthy, then he possesses nothing by which to control his wife. If a wife be unworthy, then she possesses nothing with which to serve her husband. If a husband does not control his wife, then the rules of conduct manifesting his authority are abandoned and broken. If a wife does not serve her husband, then the proper relationship between men and women and the natural order of things are neglected and destroyed....

Now examine the gentlemen of the present age. They only know that wives must be controlled, and that the husband's rules of conduct manifesting his authority must be established. They therefore teach their boys to read books and study histories. But they do not in the least understand that husbands and masters must also be served, and that the proper relationship and the rites should be maintained. Yet only to teach men and not to teach women—is that not ignoring the essential relation between them? According to the *Rites* [a book of the Confucian tradition] it is the rule to begin to teach children to read at the age of eight years, and by the age of fifteen years they ought then to be ready for cultural training. Only why should it not be that girls' education as well as boys' be according to this principle?

As *Yin* and *Yang* are not of the same nature, so man and woman have different characteristics. The distinctive quality of the *Yang* is rigidity; the function of the *Yin* is yielding. Man is honored for strength; a woman is beautiful on account of her gentleness. Hence there arose the common saying: "A man though born like a wolf may, it is feared, become a weak monstrosity; a woman though born like a mouse may, it is feared, become a tiger."...

If husband and wife have the habit of staying together, never leaving one another, and following each other around within the limited space of their own rooms, then they will lust after and take liberties with one another. From such action improper language will arise between the two. This kind of discussion may lead to licentiousness. Out of licentiousness will be born a heart of disrespect to the husband. Such a result comes from not knowing that one should stay in one's proper place.... If wives suppress not contempt for husbands, then it follows that such wives rebuke and scold their husbands. If husbands stop not short of anger, then they are certain to beat their wives. The correct relationship between husband and wife is based upon harmony and intimacy, and conjugal love is grounded in proper union. Should actual blows be dealt, how could matrimonial relationship be preserved? Should sharp words be spoken, how could conjugal love exist? If love and proper relationship both be destroyed, then husband and wife are divided....

To guard carefully her chastity; to control circumspectly her behavior; in every motion to exhibit modesty; and to model each act on the best usage, this is womanly virtue. To choose her words with care; to avoid vulgar language; to speak at appropriate times; and not to weary others with much conversation, may be called the characteristics of womanly words. To wash and scrub filth away; to keep clothes and ornaments fresh and clean; to wash the head and bathe the body regularly, and to keep the person free from disgraceful filth, may be called the characteristics of womanly bearing. With whole-hearted devotion to sew and to weave; to love not gossip and silly laughter; in cleanliness and order to prepare the wine and food for serving guests, may be called the characteristics of womanly work....

Whenever the mother-in-law says, "Do not do that," and if what she says is right, unquestionably the daughter-in-law obeys. Whenever the mother-in-law says, "Do that," even if what she says is wrong, still the daughter-in-law submits unfailingly to the command. Let a woman not act contrary to the wishes and the opinions of parents-in-law about right and wrong; let her not dispute with them what is straight and what is crooked. Such docility may be called obedience which sacrifices personal opinion. Therefore the ancient book, *A Pattern for Women*, says: "If a daughter-in-law who follows the wishes of her parents-in-law is like an echo and shadow, how could she not be praised?"

Questions for Reflection and Discussion

How supportive is Ban Zhao of the patriarchal system? How critical is she of it? What do we learn about family structures in ancient China from Ban Zhao's treatise? What is Ban Zhao's own relationship to the ideas she expressed in her treatise?

7. THE PEOPLE OF EARLY JAPAN

Time: third century CE
Place: north China
Author: unknown

The Wei Chih *was the official history of the Wei Dynasty in ancient China. Among its contents is this record of a Chinese traveler to Japan. There are no Japanese written records that go back this far, so we only have this outsider's viewpoint on what Japanese society was like so long ago. There are indications that the relationships between men and women were organized quite differently in Japan than in China and elsewhere in the ancient world. While these sorts of accounts are rare, they provide some evidence that not all ancient societies were patriarchal, or at least, not all to the same extent.*

The people of Wa [Japan] dwell in the middle of the ocean.... The land of Wa is warm and mild. In winter as in summer the people live on raw vegetables and go about barefooted. They have [or live in] houses; father and mother, elder and younger, sleep separately.

They smear their bodies with pink and scarlet, just as the Chinese use powder. They serve food on bamboo and wooden trays, helping themselves with their fingers....

In their meetings and in their deportment, there is no distinction between father and son or between men and women. They are fond of liquor. In their worship, men of importance simply clap their hands instead of kneeling or bowing. The people live long, some to one hundred and others to eighty or ninety years. Ordinarily, men of importance have four or five wives; the lesser ones, two or three. Women are not loose in morals or jealous. There is no theft, and litigation is infrequent. In case of violation of law, the light offender loses his wife and children by confiscation; as for the grave offender, the members of his household and also his kinsmen are exterminated. There are class distinctions among the people, and some men are vassals of others....

The country formerly had a man as ruler. For some seventy or eighty years after that there were disturbances and warfare. Thereupon the people agreed upon a woman for their ruler. Her name was Pimiko. She occupied herself with magic and sorcery, bewitching the people. Though mature in age, she remained unmarried. She had a younger brother who assisted her in ruling the country. After she became the ruler, there were few who saw her. She had one thousand women as attendants, but only one man. He served her food and drink and acted as a medium of communication. She resided in a palace surrounded by towers and stockades, with armed guards in a state of constant vigilance....

When Pimiko passed away, a great mound was raised, more than a hundred paces in diameter. Over a hundred male and female attendants followed her to the grave. Then a king was placed on the throne, but the people would not obey him. Assassination and murder followed; more than one thousand were thus slain. A relative of Pimiko named Iyo, a girl of thirteen, was then made queen and order was restored.

Questions for Reflection and Discussion

What type of society does ancient Japan seem to be: patriarchal, matriarchal, or egalitarian? How well-informed does the author seem to be about Japan? How well-informed does he seem to expect his audience to be? How reliable could any outsider's view of another society be?

8. HERODOTUS ON THE PEOPLES OF NORTH AFRICA

Time: fifth century BCE
Place: Greece
Author: Herodotus

Herodotus is often called the father of history, but he could just as easily be considered the father of anthropology. He is certainly one of the earliest writers to try to record the major peoples of his day and their customs, especially those that differed from his own Greek ones. In this excerpt from his Histories, *Herodotus describes how sexual relations between men and women might vary from one people to another, in this case, among the peoples living along the coast of North Africa. It is difficult to know how informed Herodotus was about these peoples and, in consequence, how accurate was their depiction. This is a problem for the accounts of many ancient travelers that sometimes, as in the examples that follow, provide the only written evidence for some ancient peoples.*

The following is a description of the Libyan tribes in their order: starting from Egypt, the first are the Adyrmachidae, whose way of living is more or less Egyptian in character. They dress like the rest of the Libyans. Their women wear a bronze ring on their persons, and grow their hair long; when they catch a bug on their persons, they give it bite for bite before throwing it away. They are the only Libyan tribe to follow this practice, as also that of taking girls who are about to be married to see the king. Any girl who catches his fancy, leaves him a virgin no longer....

Still proceeding in a westerly direction, one comes next to the Nasamones, a numerous tribe, who in the summer leave their cattle on the coast and go up to a country to a place called Augila for the date harvest.... These people also catch locusts, which they dry in the sun and grind up fine; then they sprinkle the powder on milk and drink it. Each of them has a number of wives, which they use in common, like the Massagetae—when a man wants to lie with a woman, he puts up a pole to indicate his intention. It is the custom, at a man's first marriage, to give a party, at which the bride is enjoyed by each of the guests in turn; they take her one after another, and then give her a present—something or other they have brought with them from home....

Next come the Gindanes. The women of this tribe wear leather bands round their ankles, which are supposed to indicate the number of their lovers: each woman puts on one band for every man she has gone to bed with, so that whoever has the greatest number enjoys the greatest reputation for success in love.

Questions for Reflection and Discussion

How might Herodotus's views be verified or challenged in the absence of other documents about these peoples? Would it help to know the sexual customs of his own people? What possible information might these stories provide, even if we cannot determine their truthfulness?

SOURCES AND FURTHER READING

On the origin and nature of patriarchal societies in history, one of the best accounts for nonspecialists is historian Gerda Lerner's *The Creation of Patriarchy* (New York: Oxford University Press, 1986). For a discussion of the role of sexual difference in human evolution, see R. Meredith Belbin's *Managing Without Power: Gender Relationships in the Story of Human Evolution* (Oxford: Butterworth-Heinemann, 2001); or Linda Fedigan's "The Changing Role of Women in Models of Human Evolution," *Annual Review of Anthropology* 15 (1986): 25-66. A great series of questions about gender relations in early human societies are posed by Riane Eisler in *The Chalice and the Blade: Our History, Our Future* (Cambridge, MA: Harper and Row, 1987), although her answers are a bit too speculative. Examples of Darwinist-influenced explanations of gender roles can be found in David Barash and Judith Lipton's *Making Sense of Sex: How Genes and Gender Influence Our Relationships* (Washington, DC: Island, 1997), revised as *Gender Gap: The Biology of Male-Female Differences* (New Brunswick, NJ: Transaction, 2001); or David Herlihy's "Biology and History: The Triumph of Monogamy," *Journal of Interdisciplinary History* 25 (1995): 571-83. Examples of a Marxist-influenced approach include Marilyn French's *Beyond Power: On Men, Women, and Morals* (New York: Summit, 1985); or Carolyn Fluehr-Lobban's "A Marxist Reappraisal of the Matriarchate," *Current Anthropology* 20 (1979): 341-59. Nancy Chodorow's *The Reproduction of Mothering: Psychoanalysis and the Sociology of Gender* (Berkeley: University of California Press, 1978) describes her theories (see an excerpt of it in source 128); she also further

criticizes traditional Freudian concepts in her *Feminism and Psychoanalytic Theory* (New Haven: Yale University Press, 1989) and *Feminities, Masculinities, Sexualities: Freud and Beyond* (Lexington, KY: University of Kentucky Press, 1994).

1. "The So-Called Venus of Willendorf" is taken from Johannes Maringer and Hans-Georg Bandi, *Art in the Ice Age: Spanish Levant Art, Artic Art*, Robert Allen, trans. (New York: Frederick A. Praeger, 1953), 28.

More information on the Venus figurines may be found in the useful overview by Catherine Hodge McCoid et al., "Toward Decolonizing Gender: Female Vision in the Upper Paleolithic," in *American Anthropologist* n.s. 98 (1996): 319-26, as well as in general discussions of prehistoric art. Issues relevant to a history of gender and sexuality can be found in Timothy Taylor's *The Prehistory of Sex: Four Million Years of Human Sexual Culture* (New York: Bantam Books, 1996) and in several essays in *Representations of Gender from Prehistory to the Present*, Moira Donald and Linda Hurcombe, eds. (New York: St. Martin's Press, 2000) or in *Archeologies of Sexuality*, Robert Schmidt and Barbara Voss, eds. (New York: Routledge, 2000); and, even if mostly about later periods and more sophisticated artifacts, in several essays in *The Role of Gender in Precolumbian Art and Architecture*, Virginia E. Miller, ed. (Lanham, MD: University Press of America, 1988). Interesting comparisons might be made with images of male figures from early human cultures, which also survive in abundance but which have not received nearly as much scholarly attention. On this larger issue, see Uli Linke's "Manhood, Femaleness, and Power: A Cultural Analysis of Prehistoric Images of Reproduction," *Comparative Studies in Society and History* 34 (1992): 579-620.

2. "Akkadian Hymn to Ishtar" is taken from *The Ancient Near East*, vol. 1, *Texts and Pictures*, James Pritchard, ed. and Ferris Stephens, trans. (Princeton, NJ: Princeton University Press, 1958), 231-33, with slight changes.

For more information on the religious beliefs of ancient Mesopotamia, see Jean Bottero's *Religion in Ancient Mesopotamia*, Teresa Lavender Fagan, trans. (Chicago: University of Chicago Press, 2001), or Jeremy A. Black's *Gods, Demons, and Symbols of Ancient Mesopotamia: An Illustrated Dictionary* (Austin: University of Texas Press, 1992). Additional primary sources that discuss Ishtar's role at greater length include *The Epic of Gilgamesh* (available in numerous translated editions) and *The Epic of Izdubar*, Leonidas Hamilton, trans. in *Babylonian and Assyrian Literature* (New York: Colonial Press, 1901). Other hymns to goddesses survive from ancient Egypt, another ancient society with a good historical record, and may be found in Barbara Lesko's *The Great Goddesses of Egypt* (Norman, OK: University of Oklahoma Press, 1999); or in Louis Zabkar's *Hymns to Isis in Her Temple at Philae* (Hanover, NH: University Press of New England, 1988). For a specific example of the relationship between ancient myth and women's social status, see Susan Tower Hollis's "Women of Ancient Egypt and the Sky Goddess Nut," *Journal of American Folklore* 100 (1987): 496-503.

3. "The Legend of Adam and Eve" is taken from *The Holy Bible: New International Version* (Grand Rapids, MI: Zondervan Bible, 1978), 2-4 (Genesis 2:4b, 7-9, 1-25 and 3:1-23).

The literature on issues of gender and sexuality in the Bible is extensive. A useful summary of traditions of interpretation of the Adam and Eve legend can be found in the several essays in *Eve and Adam: Jewish, Christian, and Muslim Readings on Genesis and Gender*, Kristen E. Kvam et al., eds. (Bloomington, IN: Indiana University Press, 1999); or in *The Creation of Man and Woman: Interpretations of Biblical Narratives in Jewish and Christian Traditions*, Gerard Luttikhuizen, ed. (Leiden, NLD: E.J. Brill, 2000). A readable account is Pamela Norris' *Eve: A Biography* (New York: New York University Press, 1999) that looks at interpretations of the legend in history and literature.

4. "Satakatraya" is taken from *The Hermit and the Love-Thief*, Barbara Stoler Miller, ed. and trans. (Harmondsworth, UK: Penguin, 1967), 59-60, 62, 63-64, 67, 73, 76, 82.

For information on gender and sexuality in ancient India, see the annotated references on "Women in Ancient India" by Karen Lang in *Women's Roles in Ancient Civilizations: A Reference Guide*, Bella Vivante, ed. (Westport, CT: Greenwood Press, 1999). See also the first few essays in *Faces of the Feminine in Ancient, Medieval, and Modern India*, Mandakranta Bose, ed. (New York: Oxford University Press, 2000). Miller has translated other Bhatrihari's poems, also of note for a history of sexuality, and provided some biographical information on the poet, in *Bhartrihari's Poems* (New York: Columbia University Press, 1967). There is also a biography: Harold Coward's *Bhartrhari* (Boston: Twayne Publishers, 1976). See also notes 5 and 14.

5. "The Laws of Manu" is taken from *The Laws of Manu*, Wendy Doniger and Brian K. Smith, trans. (London: Penguin, 1991), 197-98.

See also notes 4 and 14. For information on legal custom in ancient India, see Rajendra Nath Sharma's *Ancient India according to*

Manu (Delhi: Nag Publishers, 1980); on women and law, see Dwarka Nath Mitter's *The Position of Women in Hindu Law* (New Delhi: Inter-India Publications, 1984). The whole of the chapter in *The Laws of Manu* from which this excerpt was taken deals with issues of marriage and the family and could be used for a history of sexuality. For more legal sources from ancient India, see *The Dharma Shastra or The Hindu Law Codes: A Literal Prose English Translation*, Mammatha Nath Dutt, trans. (Varanasi: Chaukhamba Amarabharati Prakashan, 1977); or *The Naradasmrti*, Richard Lariviere, ed. and trans. (Philadelphia: University of Pennsylvania Press, 1989).

6. "Lessons for a Woman" is taken from Nancy Lee Swann, *Pan Chao: Foremost Woman Scholar of China* (New York and London: Century, 1932), 82-88.

Note that in this and other Chinese sources, all Wade-Giles transliterations have been changed to Pinyin.

For references to works on gender and sexuality, see the essay "Women in Ancient China" by Anne Behnke Kinney in *Women's Roles in Ancient Civilizations: A Reference Guide*, Bella Vivante, ed. (Westport, CT: Greenwood Press, 1999). A good summary is Bret Hinsch's *Women in Early Imperial China* (Lanham, MD: Rowman & Littlefield, 2002). On Ban Zhao, see Swann's biography, from which the excerpt was taken, or the more recent "Pan Chao: Poet, Historian, and Moralist," in Bettina L. Knapp's *Images of Chinese Women: A Westerner's View* (Troy, NY: Whitson Publishing, 1992). For more on the traditions of Confucianism regarding gender and sexuality, see the essays in *The Sage and the Second Sex: Confucianism, Ethics, and Gender*, Chenyang Li, ed. (Chicago:

Open Court, 2000), or in *Confucianism and the Family*, Walter H. Slote and George A. De Vos, eds. (Albany, NY: State University of New York Press, 1998). For other sources on women in traditional China, see Robin Wang's *Images of Women in Chinese Thought and Culture: Writings from the Pre-Qin Period through the Song Dynasty* (Indianapolis: Hackett, 2003).

7. "The People of Early Japan" is taken from *Sources of Japanese Tradition*, vol. 1, Ryusaku Tsunoda et al., eds. (New York: Columbia University Press, 1958), 4-5.

General histories of early Japan can provide information on what is known of social or political culture. For many references to works on women in early Japan, see Michiko Y. Aoki's "Women in Ancient Japan" in *Women's Roles in Ancient Civilizations: A Reference Guide*, Bella Vivante, ed. (Westport, CT: Greenwood Press, 1999). On knowledge of early Japanese rulers, see especially Joan Piggott's "Chieftain Pairs and Co-Rulers: Female Sovereignty in Early Japan" in *Women and Class in Japanese History*, Hitomi Tonomura et al., eds. (Ann Arbor, MI: University of Michigan Press, 1999); or Michiko Aoki's two essays in *Heroic with Grace: Legendary Women of Japan*, Chieko Irie Mulhern, ed. (Armonk, NY: M.E. Sharpe, 1991). Information on the Wei kingdom of China can be found in any general histories of early China, under the traditional "Three Kingdoms Period"; see also note 6.

8. "Herodotus on the Peoples of North Africa" is taken from Herodotus, *The Histories*, Aubrey de Selincourt, trans. (Harmondsworth, UK: Penguin, 1954), 328-30, with slight changes.

The literature on women in ancient Greece is extensive, but it must be kept in mind that social and sexual customs were localized and differed dramatically from one region of Greece to another. See Bella Vivante's "Women in Ancient Greece" in *Women's Roles in Ancient Civilizations: A Reference Guide*, Bella Vivante, ed. (Westport, CT: Greenwood Press, 1999). Herodotus was from the coast of Asia Minor; he was familiar with Athens and ended his life in a Greek colony in southern Italy. For biographical details as well as excellent essays on the historical context to his writings, see *Brill's Companion to Herodotus*, Egbert J. Bakker et al., eds. (Leiden: Brill, 2002), especially Josine Blok's "Women in Herodotus' Histories" and Klaus Karttunen's "The Ethnography of the Fringes." A recent biography is James S. Romm's *Herodotus* (New Haven, CT: Yale University Press, 1998). There is little scholarship on ancient North Africa apart from Egypt, but see Donald White's "An Archeological Survey of the Cyrenaican and Marmorican Regions of Northeast Africa," in *Africa and Africans in Antiquity*, Edwin Yamauchi, ed. (East Lansing, MI: Michigan State University Press, 2001).

marriage

Marriage, it is often said, is one of the building blocks of society. Those who say so often assume that it has always more or less meant the same thing. In fact, while a core definition of marriage might be possible—individuals who are joined together for sexual, companionate, reproductive, economic, social, and/or political reasons—that is not much of a definition, since it must take into account all of the variations that have existed in marriage throughout history and in different cultures. How many individuals can be involved in a marriage? How unrelated must they be or conversely, how related must they be? How freely, how formally, and how permanently are they joined together? Exploring some of these variations in the history of marriage is the goal of this chapter.

The different schools of thought could suggest varied purposes behind marriage. A Darwinist might say that it is human instinct to form bonded units for the purpose of companionship, cooperative work, and the rearing of offspring and that we are not much different than many other animals in this regard. A Marxist might add that the formalities of marriage provide for guaranteed sexual rights as well as important labor: someone to raise children, someone to support the family unit financially, and someone to inherit property. A Freudian might expand on these ideas by adding that the ritual of marriage functions as a rite of passage from childhood to adulthood and that by participating in the creation of a new family, individuals ensure for themselves the continued security of the family unit and even the continued dynamics of the family relationship beyond the deaths of their parents and the dissolution of their birth families. Perhaps all three schools of thought have some part of the answer.

There is another way of looking at the history of marriage, though, a perspective that historians, assisted by anthropologists, can provide. Here the insights of functionalism, a branch of anthropology that was championed in the early twentieth century by scholars such as Bronislaw Malinowski and A.R. Radcliffe-Brown, are helpful and have been applied by historians to the past. One of the things that historians must learn when studying past societies is that social customs usually make sense, at least to those who perpetuated them. It is essential that historians try to place themselves in the mindset of these past inhabitants and try to understand why a social custom arose and became established. What social purpose did it serve? How did that custom provide a good solution to a particular problem, or the best option among several choices, given the larger context of that society, its values and behaviors? Such speculations do not mean that historians must always agree with that logic, since they will always have their own values and ideas about what is proper and improper behavior. Social customs, however, usually have an internal logic, and if we are truly to understand a past society, then seeing that logic is of the utmost importance.

Marriage arose in early human societies because it "made sense" on some fundamental level and seemed a practical solution to a particular problem or set of problems: maybe the economic cost of the rearing of children, the financial support of women in patriarchal societies after their fathers' deaths, the assurance of paternity, or the indisputable transition of property and other inheritances to children. Quite possibly it was a combination of these factors. Gradually, customs around marriage evolved to deal with these problems, if not perfectly, at least well enough that a society could function relatively smoothly.

Because each society had its own problems and needs, marriage evolved in different ways. Some societies allowed polygamy (marriage with more than one person at a time), endogamy (marriage of related persons), and child marriage. Some societies permitted only monogamy (marriage with only one person at a time), exogamy (marriage of unrelated persons), and marriage only after puberty. Parents chose their children's marriage partners in some societies; individuals chose their own marriage partners in others. In some societies formal procedures to establish the marriage were necessary, such as a payment or a public ritual, and in other societies simple cohabitation was sufficient. Divorce and remarriage were permitted in some societies; others required lifelong vows and perpetual widowhood after a spouse's death. What were the reasons for these differences? Maybe it was an imbalance in the numbers of men and women in a society where men died young in continual warfare (as has been suggested for polygamy), or it was a desire to keep wealth and lands within the larger family unit (as has been suggested for endogamy). It may have been a reluctance to complicate inheritance with half-siblings (as has been suggested for a ban on remarriage), or an attempt to encourage the compatibility of married couples by raising them together (as has been suggested for child marriage). Although different historians will suggest various explanations, according to what makes the most sense to them, we can assume that there was some logic to the tradition.

The best explanations take into consideration that the sexual customs that evolved in past societies also reflected their values. Because most ancient societies that we know anything about were patriarchal, marriage generally favored men. Typically, wives were expected to confine their sexual activity to their husbands alone, while their husbands had rights of sexual access to many women, with additional wives, concubines, slaves, or prostitutes. Marriage payments, if made at the start of the marriage, usually passed from the bride's family to her new husband or to his family in what was known as a "dowry." (Less commonly, marriage payments were passed from the groom or his family to his new wife or her family; these payments were traditionally called a "brideprice," but more recently "reverse dowry," a more neutral term.) If divorce was permitted, it was often only the husband who had the sole right to initiate it. If perpetual widowhood was required, it was mostly only required of a wife after her husband's death. Trying to understand the logic behind these social customs does not preclude seeing them as inherently unequal.

The best explanations also keep in mind the social and economic conditions in which certain sexual customs took root. For example, there were usually great differences in age between husbands and wives in the ancient world; men were sometimes 20 or more years older than their wives. Why would such a custom arise? Well, most ancient societies were agricultural, where wealth came from inheritance of land rather than from wages earned. A son, who would inherit most of his father's wealth, would not have been financially independent until after his father's death. His marriage, then, might well be delayed until then. If the upper life expectancy for men in the ancient world was 70, say, then the son would not marry until he was in his midthirties. A daughter, in contrast, would be an economic burden on her parents until she was married and transferred to another household, since patriarchal societies did not permit women to contribute in many ways except through childbearing. It was in the family's interest, then, to marry their daughter as soon as she reached childbearing age, if not before. So a woman in her midteens would typically be married to a man in his midthirties. (These differences in ages at marriage also explain the frequency of widowhood in the ancient world; a woman might also outlive her husband by 20 years or more.) The pattern makes sense, given the social context and values of the ancient world, even if it seems odd or even offensive to us.

The following sources provide glimpses into the features of ancient marriages. Look for common and distinguishing features, such as rights of men and women within marriage, existence of formal procedures and payments for marriage, consent to marriage, and dissolubility of marriage.

9. THE CODE OF HAMMURABI

Time: eighteenth century BCE
Place: Mesopotamia (modern Iraq)
Author: Hammurabi

The Code of Hammurabi is one of the oldest law codes in human history. It begins with a declaration by the king of Babylon, Hammurabi, that he had received the laws from the god of wisdom and was promulgating them on Earth. How much Hammurabi improvised in his laws and how much he was merely putting into writing existing social custom is hard to say; that is a difficulty with many ancient law codes. We don't even know whether Hammurabi himself was responsible for these laws, or whether some administrator wrote them up without his involvement. Despite these uncertainties, it is clear from the laws excerpted below that regulating marriage was among the primary concerns in the law code.

117. If a man has become liable to arrest under a bond and has sold his wife or his son or his daughter or gives them into servitude, for 3

years they shall do work in the house of him who has bought them or taken them into servitude; in the fourth year their release shall be granted.

119. If a man has become liable to arrest under a bond and sells his slave-girl who has borne him sons, the owner of the slave-girl shall pay the money which the merchant has given for her and shall redeem his slave-girl.

128. If a man has taken a woman to wife, and has not drawn up a contract for her, that woman is not a wife.

129. If a married lady is caught lying with another man, they shall bind them and cast them into the water; if her husband wishes to let his wife live, then the king shall let his servant live.

131. If the husband of a married lady has accused her but she is not caught lying with another man, she shall take an oath by the life of a god and return to her house.

133a. If a man takes himself off and there is the necessary maintenance in his house, his wife so long as her husband is delayed, shall keep herself chaste; she shall not enter another man's house.

133b. If that woman has not kept herself chaste but enters another man's house, they shall convict that woman and cast her into the water.

134. If the man has taken himself off and there is not the necessary maintenance in his house, his wife may enter another man's house; that woman shall suffer no punishment.

135. If the man takes himself off and there is not the necessary maintenance in his house, and before his return his wife enters another man's house and then bears sons, if her husband afterward returns and regains his city, that woman shall return to her first husband; the sons shall follow their respective fathers.

136. If a man has abandoned his city and flees and after his departure his wife enters another man's house, if that man returns and finds his wife, because he has hated his city and has fled, the wife of the fugitive shall not return to her husband.

137. If a man sets his face to divorce a lay-sister who has borne him sons or a priestess who has provided him with sons, they shall render her dowry to her and shall give her a half-portion of field plantation or chattels and she shall bring up her sons; after she has then brought up her sons, they shall give her a share like that of a single heir in anything that has been given to her for her sons, and a husband after her heart may marry her.

138. If a man wishes to divorce his first wife who has not borne him sons, he shall give her money to the value of her bridal gift and shall make good to her the dowry which she has brought from her father's house and so divorce her.

141. If a married lady who is dwelling in a man's house sets her face to go out of doors and persists in behaving herself foolishly wasting her house and belittling her husband, they shall convict her and, if her husband then states that he will divorce her, he may divorce her; nothing shall be given to her as her divorce-money on her journey. If her husband states that he will not divorce her, her husband may marry another woman; that woman shall dwell as a slave-girl in the house of her husband.

142. If a woman has hated her husband and states "Thou shall not have the natural use of me," the facts of her case shall be determined in her district and, if she has kept herself chaste and has no fault, while her husband is given to going about out of doors and so has greatly belittled her, that woman shall suffer no punishment; she may take her dowry and go to her father's house.

144. If a man has married a priestess and that priestess has given a slave-girl to her husband and she has then brought sons into the world, if that man sets his face to marry a lay-sister, they shall not allow that man to do this; he shall not marry a lay-sister.

145. If the man has married a priestess and she has not provided him with sons and so he sets his face to marry a lay-sister, that man may marry a lay-sister and take her into his house; that lay-sister shall not then make herself equal to the priestess.

146. If a man has married a priestess and she has given a slave-girl to her husband and she bears sons, if thereafter that slave-girl goes about making herself equal to her mistress, because she has borne sons her mistress shall not sell her; she may put the mark of a slave on her and may count her with the slave-girls.

147. If she has not borne sons, her mistress may sell her.

148. If a man has married a wife and ague attacks her, and he sets his face to marry another woman, he may marry her. He shall not divorce the wife whom ague has attacked; she shall dwell in the house which he has built, and he shall continue to maintain her so long as she lives.

149. If that woman does not consent to dwell in the house of her husband, he shall make good to her her dowry which she brought from the house of her father and so she shall go away.

150. If a man has bestowed a field, a plantation, a house, or chattels on his wife and has executed a sealed tablet for her, after the death of her husband her sons shall not bring a claim for it against her; the mother shall give the charge of the estate to her son whom she loves. She shall not give it to another person.

153. If a woman has procured the death of her husband on account of another man, they shall impale that woman.

154. If a man carnally knows his daughter, they shall banish that man from the city.

155. If a man has chosen a bride for his son and his son has carnally known her, and if thereafter he himself lies in her bosom and they catch him, they shall bind that man and shall cast him into the water.

156. If the man has chosen a bride for his son and his son has not carnally known her and he himself lies in her bosom, he shall pay her one-half *maneh* of silver and further shall make good to her anything that she has brought from the house of her father, and a husband after her heart may marry her.

157. If a man after the death of his father lies in his mother's bosom, they shall burn both of them.

158. If a man after the death of his father is caught in the bosom of his chief who is the mother of sons, that man shall be expelled from his paternal estate.

162. If a man has taken a woman to wife and she has borne him sons, and that woman has then gone to her fate, her father shall not bring a claim against him for dowry; her dowry belongs to her sons.

163. If a man has married a wife and she has not provided him with sons, and that woman has then gone to her fate, if his father-in-law renders to him the bridal gift which that man has brought to the house of his father-in-law, her husband shall bring no claim for the dowry of that woman; her dowry belongs to her father's house.

167. If a man has taken a wife and she has borne him sons and that woman goes to her fate, if after her death he marries another woman and she bears sons, after the father goes to his fate, the sons shall not make a division according to mothers; they shall take the dowry of their mothers and shall divide the property of the paternal estate in proportion to their number.

170. If the first wife of a man has borne him sons and his slave-girl has borne him sons, and the father in his life-time states to the sons whom the slave-girl has borne him "You are my sons," he shall count them with the sons of his first wife. After the father goes to his fate, the sons of the first wife and the sons of the slave-girl shall take proportionate shares in the property of the paternal estate; an heir, being a son of the first wife, shall choose and take the first share at the division.

171. Or, if the father in his lifetime does not state to the sons whom the slave-girl has borne him "You are my sons," after the father goes to his fate, the sons of the slave-girl shall not take shares in the property of the paternal estate with the sons of the first wife; the release of the slave-girl and her sons shall be granted, and the sons of the first wife shall make no claim to the sons of the slave-girl for slavery....

175. If either a slave of a palace or a slave of a villein has married a lady and she bears sons, the owner of the slave shall make no claim to the sons of the lady for slavery.

177. If a widow whose sons are infants sets her face to enter another man's house, she shall not enter without the knowledge of the judges. When she enters the other man's house, the judges shall determine what is the estate of her former husband's house and shall entrust her former husband's house to the charge of her latter husband and of that woman and shall make them execute a tablet; they shall keep the house and shall bring up the infants. They shall not sell any utensils; the buyer who buys any utensil of the widow's sons forfeits his money, and the property shall revert to its owners.

183. If a father has bestowed a dowry on his daughter who is a lay-sister, has given her a husband and has written a sealed tablet for her, after the father goes to his fate, she shall at the division not take anything out of the property of the paternal estate.

184. If the man has not bestowed a dowry on his daughter who is a lay-sister and has not given her to a husband, after the father goes to his fate, her brothers shall bestow a dowry on her according to the capacity of the paternal estate and shall give her to a husband.

Questions for Reflection and Discussion

How do the rights of wives compare to those of husbands? How do the rights of daughters compare to those of sons? What seem to be the major problems relating to marriages in this society that are being corrected by this legislation? In other words, in what historical context might these laws have "made sense" to solve certain social needs?

10. CREON'S SPEECH
FROM *ANTIGONE*

Time: fifth century BCE
Place: Greece
Author: Sophocles

Among the most poignant descriptions of marriage in the ancient world are those from the Greek plays, performed in ancient Athens during religious festivals—probably to a male-only audience—and intended to commemorate various myths and legends. In this excerpt, Creon, mythical king of Thebes, must withdraw his consent to his son's marriage to Antigone, since she has committed a foul deed and a treasonous crime. What was her crime? To have properly buried her father, the king whose throne Creon had stolen. Ancient plays usually provide a more vivid sense of marriage than can be provided by law codes, even if the characters are fictional.

Creon: Son, you have heard, I think, our final judgment on your late betrothed. No angry words, I hope? Still friends, in spite of everything, my son?

Haemon: I am your son, sir; by your wise decisions my life is ruled, and them I shall always obey. I cannot value any marriage tie above your own good guidance.

Creon: Rightly said. Your father's will should have your heart's first place. Only for this do fathers pray for sons obedient, loyal, ready to strike down their fathers' foes, and love their fathers' friends. To be the father of unprofitable sons is to be the father of sorrows, a laughing-stock to all one's enemies. Do not be fooled, my son, by lust and the wiles of a woman. You'll have bought cold comfort if your wife's a worthless one. No wound strikes deeper than love that is turned to hate. This girl's an enemy; away with her, and let her go and find a mate in Hades. Once having caught her in a flagrant act: the one and only traitor in our State—I cannot make myself a traitor too; so she must die. Well may she pray to Zeus, the God of Family Love. How, if I tolerate a traitor at home, shall I rule those abroad? He that is a righteous master of his house will be a righteous statesman. To transgress, or twist the law to one's own pleasure, presume to order where one should obey, is sinful, and I will have none of it. He whom the State appoints must be obeyed to the smallest matter, be it right or wrong. And he that rules his household, without a doubt, will make the wisest king, or, for that matter, the staunchest subject. He will be the man you can depend on in the storm of war, the faithfullest comrade in the day of battle. There is no more deadly peril than disobedience; states are devoured by it, homes laid in ruins, armies defeated, victory turned to rout. While simple obedience saves the lives of hundreds of honest folk. Therefore, I hold to the law, and will never betray it—least of all for a woman. Better be beaten, if need be, by a man, than let a woman get the better of us.

Questions for Reflection and Discussion

How does the father-son relationship compare to the husband-wife or the father-daughter relationship in this passage? How do the metaphors of war or the comparisons with politics that the playwright uses help us to understand attitudes about marriage?

11. ANDROMACHE'S SPEECH FROM *THE WOMEN OF TROY*

Time: fifth century BCE
Place: Greece
Author: Euripedes

Euripedes, another of the greatest of the ancient Athenian playwrights, is often judged differently from his contemporaries for his interest in and sympathetic approach to women, although this assessment is hotly debated by scholars. In this excerpt, taken from the legend of the Greek conquest of Troy, one of the most famous of ancient Greek legends, Euripedes placed the woes of marriage in the mouths of two women of the Trojan royal household, who had seen the destruction of their city and who were awaiting their fates as slaves to the Greeks. Numerous historical sources indicate how common it was for women to suffer sexual violence in ancient wars: rape, enslavement, or marriage without their consent to their captors.

Hecabe: There is always more. My sorrows are without end; and each is sharper than the last.

Andromache: Your daughter Polyxena is dead. They killed her at the tomb of Achilles, as a gift to his dead body…. I saw her myself. I left the chariot, and covered her with a robe, and shed the tears that were due for her.

Hecabe: O my child, my child! What blasphemous murder! How terrible to die like this—O my daughter!

Andromache: It was terrible; but she is dead now; and being dead she is happier than I who am left alive.

Hecabe: No, no. To be dead is worse. In life there is hope; but in death, nothing.

Andromache: Listen, Hecabe—you are my mother, as you are hers: let me comfort your heart with welcome truth. I believe that to be dead is the same as never to have been born, and far better than living in misery. The dead have no feeling; so evil can bring no pain. But one who has known prosperity, and falls from happiness to unhappiness, wanders bewildered in an unknown world. It is for Polyxena as though she had never been born; in death she remembers nothing of all that she suffered. For me it is different. I aimed at high repute, and was successful; now I have lost all that I aimed at. As Hector's wife I studied and practiced the perfection of womanly modesty. I gave up all desire of visiting my neighbors and stayed in my own house—where a woman must stay, however blameless her reputation, unless she means to invite slander; and I refused to admit into my house the amusing gossip of other women. Having by nature a sound mind to school me, I was content; before my husband I kept a quiet tongue and a modest eye; I knew in what matters I should rule, and where I should yield to his authority. It seems that report of me reached the Greek camp, and was the cause of my present fate; for when I was captured Achilles' son asked for me as his wife. What could that be but slavery, in the house of the man who killed my husband? What am I to do? Must I forget my beloved Hector and open my heart to my new husband, and be known as a betrayer of the dead? But if I am faithful to Hector's love I shall earn my master's hate. And they say one night is enough to dispel a woman's dislike of any husband! How I despise the woman who in a new marriage forgets her first husband and loves the second! Why, even a horse will refuse to pull in harness, when separated from its stable-companion; yet a beast is an inferior creature with neither speech nor mind! Dearest Hector! You had all that I could ask for in a husband: wisdom, birth, wealth, and manliness, all in abundance. You took me untouched from my father's house, and my virginity was given to you. Now you are dead; and I must sail, a prisoner and a slave, to Hellas. Hecabe, you weep for Polyxena; but do you not feel that her death is a lesser evil than what I have to bear? I have not even the common human blessing of hope; I cannot delude myself with the pleasant dream of any imaginary happiness in the future.

Questions for Reflection and Discussion

How does Euripedes present the mother-daughter relationship? The husband-wife relationship? What patriarchal values are being questioned by these women's words? How is marriage in particular being criticized? How might an ancient audience of patriarchal men have reacted to such words?

12. THE MARRIAGE OF ISAAC AND REBEKAH

Time: written down between the tenth and
   fifth centuries BCE, from oral traditions
Place: Israel
Author: unknown

The legends of the ancient Israelites, as recorded in the Bible, provide all kinds of fascinating details about their customs surrounding marriage. In this excerpt, Abraham—considered an early ancestor of the Israelites—arranged the marriage of his favorite son and primary heir, Isaac, by sending a servant to find a suitable wife from among Abraham's relatives. Elsewhere, the Bible also relates that Abraham himself had married his sister Sarah and also had a son by Sarah's maidservant, Hagar.

Abraham was now old and well advanced in years, and the Lord had blessed him in every way. He said to the chief servant in his household, the one in charge of all that he had, "Put your hand under my thigh. I want you to swear by the Lord, the God of heaven and the God of earth, that you will not get a wife for my son from the daughters of the Canaanites, among whom I am living, but will go to my country and my own relatives and get a wife for my son Isaac." The servant asked him, "What if the woman is unwilling to come back with me to this land? Shall I then take your son back to the country you came from?" "Make sure that you do not take my son back there," Abraham said. The Lord, the God of heaven, who brought me out of my father's household and my native land and who spoke to me and promised me on oath, saying, 'To your offspring I will give this land'—he will send his angel before you so that you can get a wife for my son from there. If the woman is unwilling to come back with you, then you will be released from this oath of mine. Only do not take my son back there." So the servant put his hand under the thigh of his master Abraham and swore an oath to him concerning this matter.

Then the servant took ten of his master's camels and left, taking with him all kinds of good things from his master. He … made his way to the town of Nahor. He had the camels kneel down near the well outside the town; it was toward evening, the time the women go out to draw water. Then he prayed, "O Lord, God of my master Abraham, give me success today, and show kindness to my master Abraham. See, I am standing beside this spring, and the daughters of the townspeople are coming out to draw water. May it be that when I say to a girl, 'Please let down your jar that I may have a drink,' and she says, 'Drink, and I'll water your camels too'—let her be the one you have chosen for your servant Isaac. By this I will know that you have shown kindness to my master."

Before he had finished praying, Rebekah came out with her jar on her shoulder. She was the daughter of Bethuel son of Milcah, who was the wife of Abraham's brother Nahor. The girl was very beautiful, a virgin; no man had ever lain with her. She went down to the spring, filled her jar and came up again. The servant hurried to meet her and said, "Please give me a little water from your jar." "Drink, my lord," she said, and quickly lowered the jar to her hands and gave him a drink. After she had given him a drink, she said, "I'll draw water for your camels too, until they have finished drinking." So she quickly emptied her jar into the trough, ran back to the well to draw more water, and drew enough for all his camels.… When the camels had finished drinking, the man took out a gold nose ring weighing a *beka* and two gold bracelets weighing ten shekels. Then he asked, "Whose daughter are you? Please tell me, is there room in your father's house for us to spend the night?" She answered him, "I am the daughter of Bethuel, the son that Milcah bore to Nahor." And she added, "We have plenty of straw and fodder, as well as room for you to spend the night." …

The girl ran and told her mother's household about these things. Now Rebekah had a brother named Laban, and he hurried out to the man at the spring. As soon as he had seen the nose ring, and the bracelets on his sister's arms, and had heard Rebekah tell what the man said to her, he went out to the man and found him standing by the camels near the spring. "Come, you who are blessed by the Lord," he said. "Why are you standing out here? I have prepared the house and a place for the camels." So the man went to the house, and the camels were unloaded. Straw and fodder were brought for the camels, and water for him and his men to wash their feet. Then food

was set before him, but he said, "I will not eat until I have told you what I have to say." "Then tell us," Laban said.…

[When they heard all that had happened,] Laban and Bethuel answered, "This is from the Lord; we can say nothing to you one way or the other. Here is Rebekah; take her and go, and let her become the wife of your master's son, as the Lord has directed." When Abraham's servant heard what they said, he bowed down to the ground before the Lord. Then the servant brought out gold and silver jewelry and articles of clothing and gave them to Rebekah; he also gave costly gifts to her brother and to her mother. Then he and the men who were with him ate and drank and spent the night there.

When they got up the next morning, he said, "Send me on my way to my master." But her brother and her mother replied, "Let the girl remain with us ten days or so; then you may go." But he said to them, "Do not detain me, now that the Lord has granted success to my journey. Send me on my way so I may go to my master." Then they said, "Let's call the girl and ask her about it." So they called Rebekah and asked her, "Will you go with this man?" "I will go," she said. So they sent their sister Rebekah on her way, along with her nurse and Abraham's servant and his men. And they blessed Rebekah and said to her, "Our sister, may you increase to thousands upon thousands; may your offspring possess the gates of their enemies." Then Rebekah and her maids got ready and mounted their camels and went back with the man. So the servant took Rebekah and left.

Now Isaac … was living in the Negev. He went out to the field one evening to meditate, and as he looked up, he saw camels approaching. Rebekah also looked up and saw Isaac. She got down from her camel and asked the servant, "Who is that man in the field coming to meet us?" "He is my master," the servant answered. So she took her veil and covered herself. Then the servant told Isaac all he had done. Isaac brought her into the tent of his mother Sarah, and he married Rebekah. So she became his wife, and he loved her; and Isaac was comforted after his mother's death.

Questions for Reflection and Discussion

What customs exist regarding the initiation of a marriage, according to this source? What rights do individuals have regarding their marriages, and what rights do their families have? What makes Rebekah a suitable wife for Isaac?

13. A FATHER'S ADVICE

Time: second century BCE
Place: Israel
Author: Jesus, son of Sirach

This excerpt is from a book, known as Ecclesiasticus, considered by some Jews and Christians as part of the Bible, although not by others. Its canonical status is irrelevant to its importance as a historical document. It was probably composed during the later Greek occupation of Israel, since it betrays Greek cultural influences in language and content. It takes the form of advice from a father to his son about marriage and family life, especially advice about the proper wife and raising daughters.

Any wound rather than a wound of the heart!
Any spite rather than the spite of woman!
...
I would sooner keep house with a lion or a dragon
than keep house with a spiteful wife.
Do not be taken in by a woman's beauty,
never lose your head over a woman.

Bad temper, insolence and shame hold sway
where the wife supports the husband.
Low spirits, gloomy face, stricken heart:
such the achievements of a spiteful wife.
Slack hands and sagging knees
indicate a wife who makes her husband wretched.
Sin began with a woman, and thanks to her we all must die.
Do not let water find a leak,
do not allow a spiteful woman free rein for her tongue.
If she will not do as you tell her, get rid of her.
Happy the husband of a really good wife;
the number of his days will be doubled.
A perfect wife is the joy of her husband,
he will live out the years of his life in peace.
A good wife is the best of portions,
reserved for those who fear the Lord;
rich or poor, they will be glad of heart,
cheerful of face, whatever the season....
A bad wife is a badly fitting ox yoke,
trying to master her is like grasping a scorpion.
A drunken wife will goad anyone to fury,
she makes no effort to hide her degradation.
A woman's wantonness shows in her bold look,
and can be recognized by her sidelong glances.
Keep a headstrong daughter under firm control,
or she will abuse any indulgence she receives.
Keep a strict watch on her shameless eye,
do not be surprised if she disgraces you.
Like a thirsty traveler she will open her mouth
and drink any water she comes across;

she will sit in front of every peg,
and open her quiver to any arrow.
The grace of a wife will charm her
husband,
her accomplishments will make him the
stronger.
A silent wife is a gift from the Lord,
no price can be put on a well trained
character.
A modest wife is a boon twice over,
a chaste character cannot be weighed on
scales.
Like the sun rising over the mountains of
the Lord
is the beauty of a good wife in a well-kept
house.
Like the lamp shining on the sacred
lampstand
is a beautiful face on a well-proportioned
body.
Like golden pillars on a silver base
are shapely legs on firm-set heels.

Questions for Reflection and Discussion

What qualities make an ideal and a not-so-ideal wife, and how might those qualities "make sense" in a social context? How might the stereotype of women's wantonness, seen here and in other sources, reinforce the values of the ancient world? How do the qualities of a wife fit with those described in the previous source, which comes from the same cultural tradition?

14. THE RAMAYANA

Time: unknown
Place: India
Author: traditionally ascribed to Valmiki

One of the best known of the legends of ancient India, the Ramayana tells the story of Rama, an exiled king, and his beloved wife, Sita. She is captured by the demon Ravana, and much of the poem describes Rama's efforts to free her. There is another layer to the legend, however, that may be a later interpolation: Rama, it turns out, is the human incarnation or avatar of the god Vishnu, and Sita herself may be a goddess, since she was born from the earth and at the end of her life, returns to it. So the legend mixes human and divine realities, even while it offers a model of marriage chosen by the gods.

Several excerpts from the lengthy legend are included, showing the wealth of detail about marriage in the story.

[In this first excerpt, Sita's father, King Janaka, gives her in marriage to Rama and her sisters to Rama's brothers.]

Bringing Sita richly adorned with ornaments and jewels, and placing her before Rama and the sacrificial fire, king Janaka said, "O Rama! Sita is my daughter and from this day she becomes your partner in life. Take her by the hand; good betide you. Let her be chaste and devoted, and she will follow you like your own shadow." Saying this, Janaka spread holy waters sanctified by *mantras* upon Rama's hand. The Gods and saints praised the union. Kettle-drums began to be played and flowers were profusely showered. After conferring Sita on Rama, addressing Lakshmana, Janaka said, "Come forward, O Lakshmana, accept Urmila and take her by the hand." Then addressing Bharata, Janaka said, "O Bharata, you accept Mandavi," and to Satrughna he said, "You take Srutakirty. Do not delay and be united with your wives." … King Janaka then gave many thousand cows and a number of fine blankets, heaps of silken cloths, well-adorned elephants, horses, infantry as guards of honor, and profuse gold, silver, pearls, rubies as dowries to his daughters. He also gave hundreds of servants and maids of honor to each of his daughters.

[Soon after, Rama is sent into exile as a result of palace intrigues, and Sita must choose to go with him or remain at court.]

Kausalya [Rama's father] then after embracing Sita and kissing her head said: "My daughter, the woman, though she may be the object of everyone's affection, who fails to serve her husband in adversity, is reckoned as unchaste. The nature of such a false woman is that she enjoys happiness at the time of her husband's prosperity, but in adversity she accuses the husband of many things, nay more, even deserts him. She is untruthful, and gets irritated even at trivial things, because her mind is not attached to her husband. Fickle-minded women do not care for rank or lineage; they are won over by ornaments or dress; they are ungrateful, and have little regard for righteousness, and they never acknowledge their faults even when pointed out. But those who are obedient, to their superiors, truthful and pure, regard their husbands as the supreme agents for moral and spiritual wellbeing. Now, though Rama has been sent into exile, do not neglect him. Whether he be rich or poor, you must always revere him as a God." Sita then replied in clasped palms, "I shall surely obey your words. I know how one ought to behave with her husband. I am inseparable from righteousness as the brightness from the moon. A woman can never be happy even with a hundred sons without the husband. Her life is then like a lyre without the strings, or a chariot without its wheels. The gifts of the father, mother and the son are limited. It is only the husband's gifts that are unlimited; nobody can give so much. Who will not serve her husband? Why should I slight my husband? Husband is the highest God to a woman." Kausalya was mightily pleased at Sita's words.

[Much later in the legend, after Sita has been captured and returned to Rama, her husband begins to have doubts—groundless though they may be—about whether Sita had been faithful to him, or if she had been seduced or forced into sex by her captor, and expresses those doubts to his brother, Lakshmana.]

Then Rama with a dry countenance observed, "Just hear what the citizens say about Sita, but do not be sorry. Much evil is said about me both in the city and in the country. I have been greatly mortified by that report. You see, I am born in the family of the great Ikshvaku. Sita too is born of noble Janaka. Lakshmana, you know that I have slain Ravana because he abducted Sita from the Dandaka forest. At the time it occurred to me that Sita was long imprisoned in Ravana's harem—how could I accept her again as my wife? Then Sita for my satisfaction in the presence of all entered into a fire as a proof of her purity. Then all the gods and saints declared her to be absolutely stainless and pure; then Indra offered her to me because she was chaste and pure. I did also know in my heart of hearts that Sita is chaste and pure. Then I have brought her back to Ayodhya. But this infamous report has greatly pained my heart. He lives in hell about whom evil reports are spread. Everybody hates ill-fame and worships fame. Every noble man aspires after fame. Not to speak of Sita, I can even give up my life for fear of infamy. I have been plunged into an ocean of sorrow for this piece of ignominy. I have not suffered greater pain in the past. So, my brother, take Sita tomorrow morning in the chariot driven by Sumantra and leave her in some other country.... Go and leave there Sita in some secluded place. Don't make any request about Sita. Just do as I say. Go now; there is no need of discussing good or evil. I shall be greatly offended if you want to dissuade me from this. Swear by my feet not to speak to me anything about it. I do entreat to consider, that whoever will speak anything about it, will be reckoned by me as my great enemy for standing in the way of my wishes. If you be one with me, keep my request, go and abandon Sita in some deserted place, and thereby keep my prestige."

[Lakshmana must tell Sita of her fate.]

Sita fainted at these terrible, cruel words of Lakshmana. After some time, when she regained her consciousness, she said with tears, "Lakshmana! God has created me for suffering. I have been suffering and meeting with sorrows ever since the beginning of my life. I don't know what great sin I committed in my prior birth, or to whom I caused pangs of separation, that my lord has abandoned me, though I am chaste and devoted to him. Formerly, I could bear all the hardships of a forest life because Rama was by my side. But how shall I live alone in this asylum? To whom shall I speak my sorrows? … O Lakshmana! Certainly I would have drowned myself in the Ganges, if Rama's child was not within my womb. Now, do what you have been asked to do. Leave this miserable woman and obey the royal command. But let me tell you a few words, just listen to them. Convey my respects to my mothers-in-law, then after due greetings tell my royal lord that I am thoroughly devoted to him and my character is stainless. I have great respect for him and I know that he has abandoned me in fear of public odium. He is the highest goal of my life and it is my duty to purge him from all stains of ignominy. Tell also the virtuous king that he should look upon his people as he does, with affection as to his brothers. It is his noble duty, and that he should rule justly over the people. I shall not grieve even for a moment even if I lose my life. He should act in the manner by which he may be free from all calumny. Her husband to a woman is her highest lord, friend and preceptor. A woman should even sacrifice her insignificant life for the good of the husband."

[Sita gives birth to twin sons in the forest, and returns to Rama only when her sons have reached adulthood.]

Sita clad in red, with downcast look, and with joined palms, said, "If I have never thought of any person but Rama, then let mother Earth be divided and let me enter into it. If I have adored Rama with my body and soul, let mother Earth be divided and let me enter into it. If this be true that I do not know anybody besides Rama, let mother Earth be divided and let me enter into it." When Sita was taking this solemn vow, a magnificent throne rose from the bowels of the earth. Goddess Earth took Sita in her embrace and disappeared below. Flowers were showered from above and the gods sang her praise. When Sita disappeared below the ground, Rama leaned against a wooden pole and began to weep with a downcast look…. After Sita's disappearance, Rama grew very sad and dismissed the gathering of the princes and people. He always thought of Sita and did not take a second wife, but passed his days in thinking of her, and the golden statue of Sita supplied the place of his wife at the time of sacrifice.

Questions for Reflection and Discussion

In what sense does love triumph in this legend? And in what sense does duty overcome or replace love? What lessons might husbands and wives in ancient India have taken from this legend for their own married lives?

15. POEM BETWEEN A HUSBAND AND WIFE

Time: third century CE
Place: China
Author: Lu Yun

Ancient poetry sometimes preserves feelings between married couples better than law codes, which deal with crime, or even legends, which usually require some sort of dramatic crisis. Lu Yun, who lived at Loyang, the capital of the Western Jin Dynasty of China, believed that poetry should be concise but also poignant. He wrote this letter-like poem between a distant and lonely husband and his loving wife. The pole-star mentioned in the poem, because it was a fixed astronomical phenomenon, often served as a symbol of faithfulness. We don't know how autobiographical this poem is.

> *Husband*
> I live in Three Rivers [of Loyang] sunshine,
> You live in Five Lakes [of the Wu district] shade.
> Mountains, seas, a gulf so vast,
> Like the gulf between fliers and divers.
> My eyes imagine your clear kind face,
> My ears hold echoes of your good sweet voice.
> I sleep alone with many distant dreams,
> Then waken, caressing your empty collar.
> Oh beautiful heart of my heart!
> My love is only for you.
>
> *Wife*
> Far, far away you journey on,
> Alone, all alone I stay still.
> How to cross mountains and rivers?
> Forever cut off, road of ten thousand leagues.

Mansions in the capital are full of pretty charms,
Brilliant, brilliant city women.
Elegant footsteps, soft waists slender,
Bewitching smiles show white teeth.
Their loveliness is so enviable.
My ugliness hardly worth a mention.
I received your fond words from a distance,
I cherish the kind thought unexpected.

> *Husband*
> … Great love wed us in the past,
> Vows of fidelity bound us to the Three Gods.
> I keep my heart metal and rock firm—
> How would I be lured by mere fashion?
> Lovely eyes may pass, I don't look!
> Slender waists are nubile in vain!
> How shall I pledge my deep affection?
> I look up and point at that pole-star!

Questions for Reflection and Discussion

How is ancient Chinese court life described in this poem? What is implied about domestic life? How accurately do you think Lu Yun captures a wife's anxieties about her marriage? How accurately does he portray a husband's feelings?

16. EGYPTIAN MARRIAGE CONTRACTS

Time: fourth and first centuries BCE
Place: Egypt
Author: various, unknown

Most historical sources on marriage provide either generalized comments or fictionalized ideals. The arid climate of Egypt, though, has meant that actual marriage contracts have survived on fragments of papyrus, although the individu-

alized details that they contain may have been mixed together with formulaic phrases by the scribes who wrote them. The depictions of marriage revealed in these two examples, though, are fascinating. The first comes from the fourth century BCE *and the second from the first century* BCE. *Both were written during the Greek occupation of Egypt, so it is unclear how marriages as described here might compare to those from earlier periods of Egyptian history.*

In the seventh year of the reign of Alexander, son of Alexander, the fourteenth year of Ptolemy's administration as *satrap*, in the month of Dius. Contract of marriage of Heraclides of Temnos and Demetria. Heraclides takes as his lawful wife Demetria of Cos from her father Leptines of Cos and her mother Philotis. He is free; she is free. She brings with her to the marriage clothing and ornaments valued at 1,000 *drachmas*. Heraclides shall supply to Demetria all that is suitable for a freeborn wife. We shall live together in whatever place seems best to Leptines and Heraclides, deciding together. If Demetria is caught in fraudulent machinations to the dishonor of her husband Heraclides, she shall forfeit all that she has brought with her. But Heraclides shall prove whatever he charges against Demetria before three men whom they both approve. It shall not be lawful for Heraclides to bring home another woman for himself in such a way as to inflict contumely on Demetria, nor to beget children by another woman, nor to indulge in fraudulent machinations against Demetria on any pretext. If Heraclides is caught doing any of these things, and Demetria proves it before three men whom they both approve, let Heraclides return to Demetria the dowry of 1,000 *drachmas* which she brought, and forfeit 1,000 *drachmas* of the silver coinage of Alexander. Demetria, and those representing Demetria, shall have the right to exact payment from Heraclides and from his property on both land and sea, as if after a legal action. This contract shall be decisive in every respect, wherever Heraclides may produce it against Demetria, or Demetria and those helping Demetria to exact payment may produce it against Heraclides, as though the agreement had been made in that place. Heraclides and Demetria shall each have the right to keep a copy of the contract in their own custody, and to produce it against one another. Witnesses: Cleon of Gela, Anticrates of Temnos, Lysis of Temnos, Dionysius of Temnos, Aristomachus of Cyrene, Aristodicus of Cos.

In the twenty-second year of the reign of Ptolemy also called Alexander, the god Philometor, the priesthood of the priest of Alexander and the other priests as listed in Alexandria, the eleventh of the month Xandicus which is the eleventh of the month Mecheir at Cerceosiris in the district of Polemon in the Arsinoite *nome*. Philiscus, son of Apollomus, Persian of the Epigone, acknowledges to Apollonia (also known as Cellauthis), daughter of Heraclides, Persian, with her brother Apollonius as guardian, that he has received from her 2 *talents* and 4,000 *drachmas* in copper coinage as her dowry agreed to by him. Apollonia is to remain with Philiscus, obeying him as a wife should her husband, owning their property in common. Philiscus is to provide everything necessary, both clothing and whatever else is appropriate for a wedded wife, whether he is at home or away, according to the standard of their common resources. It shall not be lawful for Philiscus to bring home for himself another wife in addition to Apollonia nor to maintain a female concubine nor a little boyfriend nor to beget children by another woman while Apollonia is alive, nor to dwell in another house over which Apollonia has no rights, nor to throw her out, nor insult her or treat her badly, nor to alienate any of their common property to defraud Apollonia. If he is shown to be doing any of these things, or not to be providing her with necessities and clothing and other things as written, Philiscus is to pay the dowry of 2 *talents* and 4,000 *drachmas* of copper in full to Apollonia, immediately. In the same way it shall not be lawful for Apollonia to be absent for a night or a day from the house of Philiscus without the knowledge of Philiscus, nor to have intercourse with another man nor to ruin the common household nor to dishonor Philiscus in whatever brings dishonor to a husband. And if Apollonia of her own free will wishes to separate from Philiscus, Philiscus is to return the dowry unaltered within ten days from the day the demand is made. If he does not return it, as written, he is to forfeit one and a half times the amount of the dowry to her immediately. Witnesses: Dionysius, son of Patron, Dionysius, son of Hermaiscus, Theon, son of Ptolemy, Didymus, son of Ptolemy.

Questions for Reflection and Discussion

Do these marriages seem egalitarian? What rights and responsibilities do the husbands have? What rights and responsibilities do the wives have? What sense of a family life in ancient Egypt does one get from these contracts?

17. AN EGYPTIAN MARRIED COUPLE

Time: twenty-sixth century BCE
Place: Egypt
Artist: unknown

While our knowledge of Egyptian marriage is much better for the later periods of its long

history, especially during the era of Greek and Roman influence, it is uncertain how much marital customs had changed from earlier times. Among the most ancient of Egyptian records are sculpted and painted images of married couples that perhaps shed some light on these earliest traditions. This example, from the Fourth Dynasty (the same period in which the pyramids at Giza were built), shows the pharaoah Menkaura and his queen, Khemernebty. Here she embraces him, but similar images some-

times show the husband embracing his wife or both embracing each other.

Questions for Reflection and Discussion

What does this image tell us about relations between husband and wife in ancient Egypt? Or does it say more about political status? How much do you think the relationship was idealized, and if so, what can such ideals tell us about real marriages?

18. AUGUSTINE'S *CONFESSIONS*

Time: fourth century CE
Place: north African coast, part of the
    Roman Empire
Author: Augustine of Hippo

In this memoir of sorts, Augustine looks back on his life from his childhood until his conversion in adulthood to Christianity. Once he became a Christian, he decided to give up sex altogether, but before that he probably lived a life typical for Roman men of his day and for generations before that. The informal sexual relationship that Augustine describes was the only legal type of cohabitation permitted in Roman law for individuals who came from widely differing social classes. Augustine was from the lower ranks of the Roman nobility; presumably his mistress (or "concubine," the more usual term for an informal wife) was from the lower classes, perhaps even his slave. He later abandoned this informal wife, because he planned a formal marriage with a woman of more equal social standing, although this later marriage never took place. Also included below is a passage in which Augustine describes the marriage of his parents, Patricius and Monica.

I went to Carthage, where I found myself in the midst of a hissing cauldron of lust. I had not yet fallen in love, but I was in love with the idea of it, and this feeling that something was missing made me despise myself for not being more anxious to satisfy the need. I badly wanted to love something.... In those days I lived with a woman, not my lawful wedded wife but a mistress whom I had chosen for no special reason but that my restless passions had alighted on her. But she was the only one and I was faithful to her. Living with her I found out by my own experience the difference between the restraint of the marriage alliance, contracted for the purpose of having children, and a bargain struck for lust, in which the birth of children is begrudged, though, if they come, we cannot help but love them....

[Some years later, Augustine moved to Milan in Italy to study philosophy. He brought his mistress with him, but set up a household with his mother and a friend, Alypius.]

It was Alypius who prevented me from marrying, because he insisted that if I did so, we could not possibly live together in uninterrupted leisure, devoted to the pursuit of wisdom, as we had long desired to do. As for himself, even as a grown man, he was quite remarkably self-controlled in matters of sex. In early adolescence he had had the experience of sexual intercourse, but it had not become habitual. In fact he had been ashamed of it and thought it degrading and, ever since, he had lived a life of the utmost chastity.... [But] I was bound down by this disease of the flesh. Its deadly pleasures were a chain that I dragged along with me, yet I was afraid to be freed from it....

I was being urged incessantly to marry, and had already made my proposal and been accepted. My mother had done all she could to help; ... the plans for my marriage were pushed ahead and the girl's parents were asked for their consent. She was nearly two years too young for marriage, but I liked her well enough and was content to wait. Meanwhile I was sinning more and more. The woman with whom I had been living was torn from my side as an obstacle to my marriage and this was a blow which crushed my heart to bleeding, because I loved her dearly. She went back to Africa, vowing never to give herself to any other man, and left me with the son whom she had borne me. But I was too unhappy and too weak to imitate this example set me by a woman. I was impatient at the delay of two years which had to pass before the girl whom I had asked to marry became my wife, and because I was more a slave of lust than a true lover of marriage, I took another mistress, without the sanction of wedlock....

[As he recounts his mother's death, Augustine pauses to reflect on her life.]

My mother was brought up in modesty and temperance ... and when she was old enough, they gave her in marriage to a man whom she served as her lord.... He was unfaithful to her, but her patience was so great that his infidelity never became a cause of quarrelling between them.... Though he was remarkably kind, he had a hot temper, but my mother knew better than to say or do anything to resist him when he was angry. If his anger was unreasonable, she used to wait until he was calm and composed and then took the opportunity of explaining what she had done. Many women, whose faces were disfigured by blows from husbands far sweeter-tempered than her own, used to gossip together and complain of the behavior of their men-folk. My mother would meet this complaint with another—about the women's tongues. Her manner was light but her meaning was serious when she told them that ever since they had heard the marriage deed read over to them, they ought to have regarded it as a contract which bound them to serve their hus-

bands, and from that time onward they should remember their condition and not defy their masters. These women knew well enough how hot-tempered a husband my mother had to cope with. They used to remark how surprising it was that they had never heard, or seen any marks to show, that Patricius had beaten his wife or that there had been any domestic disagreement between them, even for one day. When they asked her, as friends, to tell them the reason, she used to explain the rule which I have mentioned. Those who accepted it found it a good one: the others continued to suffer humiliation and cruelty.

Her mother-in-law was at first prejudiced against her by the tale-bearing of malicious servants, but she won the older woman over by her dutiful attentions and her constant patience and gentleness. In the end her mother-in-law complained of her own accord to her son and asked him to punish the servants for their meddlesome talk, which was spoiling the peaceful domestic relations between herself and her daughter-in-law. Patricius, who was anxious to satisfy his mother as well as to preserve the good order of his home and the peace of his family, took the names of the offenders from his mother and had them whipped as she desired. She then warned them that anyone who told tales about her daughter-in-law, in the hope of pleasing her, could expect to receive the same award. After this none of them dared to tell tales and the two women lived together in wonderful harmony and mutual goodwill.

Questions for Reflection and Discussion

What do we learn about Augustine's reasons for becoming involved in an informal marriage, and his reasons for ending it? What does he think about his relationship, looking back at it from a very different perspective about sex? How does his parents' relationship compare to other ancient marriages as seen in this chapter?

SOURCES AND FURTHER READING

Surprisingly, there are few general histories of marriage. The classic text, now unfortunately out of date, is Edward Westermark's *The History of Human Marriage*, 3 vols. (London: Macmillan, 1903). More recent surveys are Gladys Robina Quale's *A History of Marriage Systems* (New York: Greenwood, 1988) and, very readable though mostly modern, are Stephanie Coontz's *Marriage, A History: From Obedience to Intimacy, Or How Love Conquered Marriage* (New York: Viking, 2005) and Marilyn Yalom's *A History of the Wife* (New York: HarperCollins, 2001). Probably the best comparative scholarly works are the many books by historically minded anthropologist Jack Goody, especially *The Oriental, the Ancient, and the Primitive: Systems of Marriage and the Family in the Pre-Industrial Societies of Eurasia* (New York: Cambridge University Press, 1990). These must be supplemented by more specialized histories of marriage, which are numerous.

9. "The Code of Hammurabi" is taken from *The Babylonian Laws*, vol. 2, G.R. Driver and John C. Miles, eds. and trans. (Oxford: Clarendon, 1955), odd pages 47-75.

For information on the Code of Hammurabi, see Driver and Miles's collection, from which the excerpts are taken. The first volume is a lengthy legal commentary by subject, the second, the text and a philological commentary. On ancient Babylonian law, see Claus Wilcke's *Early Ancient Near Eastern Law* (Munich: Bayerischen Akademie der Wissenschaften, 2003), or Russ VerSteeg's *Early Mesopotamian Law* (Durham, NC: Carolina Academic Press, 2000). On women in ancient Mesopotamia, see Zainab Bahrani, *Women of Babylon: Gender and Representation in Mesopotamia* (New York: Routledge, 2001); "Love and Sex in Babylon" and "Women's Rights" in Jean Bottero's *Everyday Life in Ancient Mesopotamia*, Antonia Nevill, trans. (Baltimore, MD: Johns Hopkins University Press, 2001); many more references can be found in Karen Rhea Nemet-Nejat's "Women in Ancient Mesopotamia" in *Women's Roles in Ancient Civilizations: A Reference Guide*, Bella Vivante, ed. (Westport, CT: Greenwood Press, 1999). Interesting comparisons with ancient Israel are found in Victor Matthews et al.'s *Gender and Law in the Hebrew Bible and the Ancient Near East* (Sheffield, UK: Sheffield Academic Press, 1998).

10. "Creon's speech from *Antigone*" is taken from Sophocles, *The Theban Plays*, E.F. Watling, trans. (Harmondsworth, UK: Penguin, 1947), 143-44.

A good analysis of women in ancient Athens, despite its tendentious tone, is Eva Keuls's *The Reign of the Phallus: Sexual Politics in Ancient Athens* (New York: Harper and Row, 1983; revised 1993). See also the many references by Bella Vivante, "Women in Ancient Greece," in *Women's Roles in Ancient Civilizations: A Reference Guide*, Bella Vivante, ed. (Westport, CT: Greenwood Press, 1999); and the recent collection, *Sex and Difference in Ancient Greece and Rome*, Mark Golden and Peter Toohey, eds. (Edinburgh: Edinburgh University Press, 2003). For a discussion of Sophocles' works, see James C. Hogan, "Antigone" in *A Commentary on the Plays of Sophocles* (Carbondale, IL: Southern Illinois University Press, 1991); on issues of gender and sexuality in Sophocles, see Kirk Ormand's *Exchange and the Maiden: Marriage in Sophoclean Tragedy* (Austin,

TX: University of Texas Press, 1999). Any of Sophocles' plays could be read with benefit in a history of sexuality.

11. "Andromache's speech from *The Women of Troy*" is taken from Euripedes, *The Bacchae and Other Plays*, Philip Vellacott, trans. (Harmondsworth, UK: Penguin, 1954), 103-04.

See note 10 for readings on women and sexuality in ancient Athens. On Euripedes, see David Kovacs, *Euripedea* (Leiden, NLD: E.J. Brill, 1994); on issues of gender and sexuality in Euripedes, see Nancy Sorkin Rabinowitz, *Anxiety Veiled: Euripedes and the Traffic in Women* (Ithaca, NY: Cornell University Press, 1993); or the various essays in *Euripedes, Women, and Sexuality*, Anton Powell, ed. (New York: Routledge, 1990). The most frequently discussed play of Euripedes is *Medea*, which could be read with great profit in a history of sexuality, as would for that matter any of his plays.

12. "The marriage of Isaac and Rebekah" is taken from *The Holy Bible: New International Version* (Grand Rapids, MI: Zondervan Bible, 1978), 23-25 (Genesis 24:1-20, 22-25, 28-33, 50-67).

The literature on women in the Bible is extensive; less well studied are Biblical marriage customs. See Naomi Steinberg's *Kinship and Marriage in Genesis: A Household Economics Perspective* (Minneapolis, MN: Fortress Press, 1993); or Carol Meyers' "The Family in Early Israel," in *Families in Ancient Israel*, Leo G. Perdue et al., eds. (Louisville, KY: Westminster John Knox Press, 1997); or Shunya Bendor's *The Social Structure of Ancient Israel: The Institution of the Family (Beit Ab) from the Settlement to the End of the Monarchy* (Jerusalem: Simor, 1996). See also *Genesis*, Athalya Brenner, ed. (Sheffield, UK: Sheffield Academic Press, 1998),

on women and marriage in the Biblical book of Genesis specifically. See note 13 for more on women in ancient Israel. Other excellent and brief books of the Bible for describing the nature of marriage and the status of women, albeit in very different historical circumstances, are Ruth and Esther.

13. "A Father's Advice" is taken from *The Jerusalem Bible* (New York: Doubleday, 1966), 932-33 (Ecclesiasticus 25: 13-26 and 26: 1-18).

For more information on this source and its relation to a history of sexuality, see especially Warren C. Trenchard's *Ben Sira's View of Women: A Literary Analysis* (Chico, CA: Scholars Press, 1982). For more general information on women in ancient Israel, see Carol Meyers's *Discovering Eve: Ancient Israelite Women in Context* (New York: Oxford University Press, 1988). See note 12 for more on marriage and the family in ancient Israel. For more information on the source itself, which is part of the modern Catholic and Orthodox Bible but not of the modern Jewish or Protestant Bible, see John G. Snaith, *Ecclesiasticus, or the Wisdom of Jesus Son of Sirach* (London: Cambridge University Press, 1974), or generally, in Otto Kaiser's *The Old Testament Apocrypha: An Introduction* (Peabody, MA: Hendrickson, 2004).

14. "The Ramayana" is taken from *The Ramayana*, Makhan Lal Sen, trans. (Calcutta: Oriental Publishing Co., no date), 1: 94-95, 187-88, 3: 422-23, 427-28, 459-60, with slight changes.

See notes 4 and 5 for further readings on women in ancient India. On marriage in ancient India, see several essays in *Changing Patterns of Family and Kinship in South Asia*, Asko Parpola and Sirpa Tenhunen, eds.

(Helsinki: Finnish Oriental Society, 1998); or Heramba Nath Chatterji's *Studies in the Social Background of the Forms of Marriage in Ancient India* (Calcutta: Sanskrit Pustak Bhandar, 1972). See also Johann Jakob Meyer's *Sexual Life in Ancient India* (London: Kegan Paul, 2003; orig. publ. 1930), which draws heavily from the Ramayana. On the influence of the legend, see Jonah Blank, *Arrow of the Blue-Skinned God: Retracing the Ramayana through India* (Boston: Houghton Mifflin, 1992; reprinted New York: Grove Press, 2000); or J.L. Brockington, *Righteous Rama: The Evolution of an Epic* (New York: Oxford University Press, 1985). On the influence of Sita as a role model for women, see Sally Sutherland's "Sita and Draupadi: Aggressive Behavior and Female Role-Models in the Sanskrit Epics," *Journal of the American Oriental Society* 109 (1989): 63-79. Finally, on the social and historical context of the legend, see Shantikumar Nanooram Vyas, *India in the Ramayana Age: A Study of the Social and Cultural Conditions in Ancient India as Described in Valmiki's Ramayana* (Delhi: Atma Ram, 1967); or Ananda Weihena Palliya Guruge, *The Society of the Ramayana* (Maharagama, Ceylon: Saman Press, 1960).

15. "Poem between a Husband and Wife" is taken from Anne Birrell, *New Songs from a Jade Terrace: An Anthology of Early Chinese Love Poetry, Translated with Annotations and an Introduction* (London: George Allen & Unwin, 1982), 94-95.

Birrell's book is a good place to start to learn more about ancient Chinese love poetry. For more on ancient Chinese marriage, see Hugh Baker's *Chinese Family and Kinship* (New York: Columbia University Press, 1979), or H.P. Wilkinson's *The Family in Classical China* (Arlington, VA: University Publications of America, 1976), or more recently, Patricia

Buckley Ebrey's *Women and the Family in Chinese History* (New York: Routledge, 2002). See note 6 for more on women in ancient China. Insofar as I know, there is no English language biography of Lu Yun or of the other men of his family, who were also poets.

16. "Egyptian Marriage Contracts" is taken from Sarah Pomeroy's *Women in Hellenistic Egypt: From Alexander to Cleopatra* (Detroit, MI: Wayne State University Press, 1990), 86-88.

Pomeroy's book is the best place to start for more information on the marriage contracts and their context. Further readings on marriage in ancient Egypt include William Edgerton's *Notes on Egyptian Marriage Chiefly in the Ptolemaic Period* (Chicago: University of Chicago Press, 1931). On women in ancient Egypt, including rights in marriage, there is much more available, including Joyce Tyldesley's *Daughters of Isis: Women of Ancient Egypt* (London: Penguin, 1995); Gay Robins's *Women in Ancient Egypt* (Cambridge, MA: Harvard University Press, 1993); and Barbara Watterson's *Women in Ancient Egypt* (New York: St. Martin's Press, 1991). On Egyptian women and writing, see Jennifer Sheridan's "Not at a Loss for Words: The Economic Power of Literate Women in Antique Egypt," *Transactions of the American Philological Association* 128 (1998): 189-203. Other fascinating written sources, such as love poems, may be found in *Ancient Egyptian Literature: An Anthology*, John Foster, ed. and trans. (Austin, TX: University of Texas Press, 2001). Keep in mind that ancient Egyptian civilization spanned two millennia of recorded history, and modern writers are not always as careful as they should be about distinguishing between the different periods of Egyptian history.

17. "An Egyptian Married Couple" is taken from *Mistress of the House, Mistress of Heaven: Women*

in Ancient Egypt, Anne Capel and Glenn Markoe, eds. (New York: Hudson Hills, 1996), 27.

See note 16 for further readings on women and marriage in ancient Egypt. There is much available on Egyptian art generally, although little specifically on marital images; on women in ancient Egyptian art, see the catalog for an exhibition organized by the Cincinnati Art Museum, from which the image was taken, noted above, or that for an exhibition at the Metropolitan Museum of Art in New York City, *The Women of Amarna: Images of Beauty from Ancient Egypt*, Dorothea Arnold, ed. (New York: Metropolitan Museum of Art, 1996). The art associated with the Amarna period of ancient Egypt is particularly interesting, since the rigid poses of traditional art were abandoned for more relaxed poses, including ones of familial affection. See *Akhenaten and Nefertiti* (New York: Brooklyn Museum, 1973), or *Pharaohs of the Sun* (Boston: Museum of Fine Arts, 1999).

18. "Augustine's *Confessions*" is taken from *Saint Augustine: Confessions*, R.S. Pine-Coffin, trans. (Harmondsworth, UK: Penguin, 1961), 55, 72, 128, 129-30, 131, 194-95.

On marriage in the later Roman Empire, there is an abundance of literature. On legal aspects, see Judith Evans Grubbs's *Law and Family in Late Antiquity: The Emperor Constantine's Marriage Legislation* (Oxford: Clarendon Press, 1995); or Antti Arjava's *Women and Law in Late Antiquity* (Oxford: Clarendon Press, 1996). On social aspects, see Gillian Clark's *Women in Late Antiquity: Pagan and Christian Lifestyles* (Oxford: Clarendon Press, 1993); or Brent Shaw's "The Family in Late Antiquity: The Experience of Augustine," *Past and Present* 115 (1987): 3-51, which focuses on the source in question. See, however, Dale Martin's "The Construction of the Ancient Family: Methodological Considerations," *Journal of Roman History* 86 (1996): 40-60, for an alternative point of view. On concubinage or informal marriage in the Roman cultural tradition, see Thomas McGinn's "Concubinage and the *Lex Iulia* on Adultery," *Transactions of the American Philological Association* 121 (1991): 335-75. There is also an abundant literature on Augustine's *Confessions*; see, for example, Margaret Miles's *Desire and Delight: A New Reading of Augustine's Confessions* (New York: Crossroad, 1992). The classic biography of Augustine is Peter Brown's *Augustine of Hippo: A Biography* (Berkeley, CA: University of California Press, 1967). See notes 32 for more on women in ancient Rome, 33 on marriage in ancient Rome, and 66 on Augustine and sexuality.

CHAPTER 3
the varieties of sexual expression

If one of the chief benefits in studying the history of sexuality is to understand better the evolution of sexual institutions like marriage that still shape our modern world, surely another is to appreciate how differently societies have organized sexual behaviors. When we try to figure out what sexuality means to us today, it is useful to see what was important to past societies: what behaviors were praised or condemned, tolerated or criticized, assumed as natural or rejected as unnatural.

All past societies, it would seem, created categories of sexuality. They wanted to encourage some sexual behaviors and discourage others, and we must presume that they did so because such behaviors either fit or did not fit with overall goals or values of that society. Societies that wanted to increase their population typically encouraged childbearing, for example and might have encouraged early ages of marriage so that individuals would begin reproducing as soon as possible. They might have discouraged frequent or easy divorces, so that individuals would be obliged to remain married and thus be likelier to produce children. As the last chapter suggested, sexual customs usually arise or are retained for logical or sensible reasons, at least according to past standards.

It might be possible, then, to work backwards from this assumption and, in viewing social attitudes to certain behaviors in historical societies, to learn important things about their overall values. We might find interesting differences between our own society and those of the past and wonder why we praise or condemn certain behaviors, and how our own values are reflected in those larger attitudes toward sexuality. When doing so, we must be careful, however, not to assume that we share their same categories of thinking about sex. This open-mindedness of thought about sexuality in the past is crucial. The idea that societies need to be studied without judgment and respecting their uniqueness was also borrowed from anthropology, first outlined by Franz Boas and extended by his students, including Ruth Benedict, Alfred Kroeber, and Margaret Mead. In anthropology it is known as the principle of cultural relativism, a principle that historians have also adopted.

The subject of pederasty is a perfect example of the importance of respecting the differences of the past. When we hear about pederasty in the modern media, it is used to refer to child assault and molestation and always spoken of in definitely negative terms. The individuals who practice pederasty, it is assumed, are a small minority of "predators" who are drawn to commit such actions with young children, often with both boys and girls without differentiation. To an audience of Athenians in ancient Greece, pederasty had widely different meanings. (The word itself comes from the Greek and means "boy-love.") First, it was socially sanctioned; second, the types of relations associated with it were quite different. As the term suggests, it involved boys, probably only adolescents , and mutual love typified the relationship rather than predation. Third, since pederasty was sanctioned, there were no "pederasts," so to speak, because it was a normalized behavior and all men were expected to participate in it. If pederasty in ancient Athens had a social function, it was probably to encourage the early participation of adolescent boys in the life of politics in the Athenian democracy, by creating strong and intimate ties with established public figures. That this mentorship would include a sexual component was thought natural, since it was assumed that most adult men, even while they were married and fathering children, would want to have sex with adolescent boys.

These ideas, it hardly needs saying, are not much like the ideas of our modern age. Notice also that not only are the attitudes toward the behaviors different, but the categories for understanding the behavior are equally different. The adult men of ancient Athens were not pederasts as we would use the term unless we qualify that definition quite a bit. Nor are they homosexuals, since there is no exclusive choice of same-sex partners, which is fairly basic to our modern perceptions of homosexuality. Just as the ancient Greeks had no concept corresponding to our "pederast," they also had no word meaning "homosexual." It was not that the ancient Greeks would not have understood our definitions of homosexuality or heterosexuality—they noted when someone had an exclusive interest in one sex or the other—but they just didn't think it significant enough to create categories or terms for the behaviors. In the same way, we have no modern terms for individuals who are attracted only to individuals with certain hair, skin, or eye colors, although we can understand the categories easily enough. In sum, our ideas about sexual categories must be challenged when we study the history of sexuality. (Evidence from other ancient societies is mostly not as detailed as for ancient Athens, but the pattern of adult men's sexual interest in both women and boys seems common enough elsewhere.)

Incest is another area where ancient societies sometimes differed from our own. Brother-sister marriages were practiced by the ancient Egyptians, at least in later periods of their history, although perhaps only among their nobility. Such marriages were encouraged probably for very practical reasons: In an age when noble marriages were accompanied by payments, especially of land, brother-sister marriages did not alienate land from the family holdings, and that was probably particularly important in ancient Egypt where everyone lived on a thin strip of fertile land alongside the Nile. In other cultures, cousin marriages did the same thing, keeping land holdings within the extended family, and in still other cultures, uncle-niece marriages were permitted. But in ancient Egypt, sex between a brother and his sister was distinguished in thought and in attitude from other forms of what we would call incest, like father-daughter or mother-son sexual relationships. These relationships were condemned, even while brother-sister marriages were seen as normal and natural. (Did the peoples of the ancient world understand that marriage between persons too closely related led to offspring with increased chances of fatal or chronic genetic disorders? Probably not. Rates of child mortality were so high that parents expected that many if not most of their children would die in infancy. The difference between deaths due to genetic causes as opposed to infections was probably not apparent.)

Prostitution is a third example of the variety of sexual expression in the past. It is claimed that prostitution is the oldest profession in the world, and while this is doubtful, its antiquity is not in question. From what we already know about marriage customs in past societies, we can assume that prostitution was common in societies that were patriarchal, that had slavery, and where ages of marriage were delayed for men—and that means most ancient societies. Becoming a prostitute provided women without families with a livelihood when they were excluded from other areas of public life. Slaves of both sexes would also be made to work as prostitutes. Visiting a prostitute was seen as one of the privileges of being a man, providing him with a sexual outlet between puberty and marriage, which might not take place until he reached his midthirties. He might prefer female prostitutes or male ones or both, without it being considered unusual.

The need to conceptualize prostitution differently when studying the history of sexuality is especially true when looking at the social custom known as sacred prostitution (sometimes also called temple prostitution or cultic prostitution). It must be said that the sources for this custom give us radically different and even conflicting details, so some modern scholars question the very existence of the practice, as well as its nature and function. If it existed, sacred prostitution seems to have been connected with the widespread fertility cults of the ancient world. As part of worshipping these fertility goddesses and their consort gods, men engaged in ritual sex with priests and priestesses who acted as surrogates for the deities. The practice may seem odd, but many religions take everyday activities and ritualize them: eating, bathing, dressing. Peoples of the ancient world—at least those living around the Mediterranean and in southwest and south Asia, where there is evidence for the practice—might have spiritualized the act of sex in ritual observances. If such a custom existed, the meanings associated with being a prostitute would necessarily have been radically different from our own understandings.

Castration was yet another commonplace sexual practice in parts of the ancient world that shows how differently ancient peoples thought about sex. Slaves could be made eunuchs in order to guard the chastity of women, especially in the households of the wealthy. Again, it has an internal logic: neither women nor other men could be trusted to guard women, so castrated men did it. (Modern studies done on men castrated in adulthood suggest that only a minority retain their sexual drive afterward, and most ancient slaves were castrated well before puberty, so probably even fewer did.) Castrated slaves also sometimes serviced their masters sexually. Again, the practice makes sense in context: If most men were assumed to be attracted to adolescent boys, then castration would prolong those qualities—no body or facial hair, higher voice—that puberty undid in boys. Castration has also been linked to the fertility cults and sacred prostitution. In this case, the sacrifice of one's own genitals in rites of castration may have been felt to ensure the overall fertility of the community, and eunuchs may have also served as sacred prostitutes.

One final sexual custom of antiquity deserves mention, if only for the fact that it is still widely practiced and partly institutionalized today. It is the practice of circumcision. The origins of male circumcision (removal of the foreskin of the penis) are obscure. It might have been as a hygienic measure, albeit a drastic one, and it might have begun as a lesser form of symbolic castration, reducing personal sexual pleasure in sacrifice to a deity. The ancient Israelites, who are most closely identified with the custom and who legitimized it for modern Jews and Muslims, saw it as a personal marker of dedication to one god. As a marker, though, it only identified men. There is no evidence for female circumcision (removal of the clitoris and/or labia) in antiquity, although modern cultures that practice it often refer to ancient custom to legitimize it. The modern social logic used to justify female circumcision is a longstanding and patriarchal one. A circumcised woman is more attractive to men, must remain a virgin before marriage, and is less likely to stray sexually from her husband, since the pleasure she derives from sex is greatly reduced by her circumcision.

Again, the variety of sexual expressions in antiquity alerts us to the fact that the attitudes we hold about sexuality are linked to the time and place in which we live. We need only look at the past and its customs and prohibitions about sex, to see how bound up in culture sexuality is.

19. ARISTOPHANES' SPEECH FROM THE *SYMPOSIUM*

Time: fifth century BCE
Place: Greece
Author: Plato

Plato is one of the great thinkers of the ancient world, and his Symposium *is one of his most famous works. It is set at an imaginary dinner party, where the guests are some of the key public figures of Plato's day, and all are asked to give their opinions about what love is. In this excerpt, Aristophanes, a writer of comedic plays, gives what we can assume was meant to be a funny description of the origin of love, imagining how different sexual practices and sexual tastes began. It provides an example of how an ancient writer categorized sexual desires.*

First of all, you must learn the constitution of man and the modifications which it has undergone, for originally it was different from what it is now. In the first place there were three sexes, not, as with us, two, male and female; the third partook of the nature of both the others and has vanished, though its name survives. The hermaphrodite was a distinct sex in form as well as in name, with the characteristics of both male and female, but now the name alone remains, and that solely as a term of abuse. Secondly, each human being was a rounded whole, with double back and flanks forming a complete circle; it had four hands and an equal number of legs, and two identically similar faces upon a circular neck, with one head common to both the faces, which were turned in opposite directions. It had four ears and two organs of generation and everything else to correspond. These people could walk upright like us in either direction, backwards or forwards, but when they wanted to run quickly they used all their eight limbs, and turned rapidly over and over in a circle, like tumblers who perform a cart-wheel and return to an upright position. The reason for the existence of three sexes and for their being of such a nature is that originally the male sprang from the sun and the female from the earth, while the sex which was both male and female came from the moon, which partakes of the nature of both sun and earth. Their circular shape and their hooplike method of progression were both due to the fact that they were like their parents.

Their strength and vigor made them very formidable, and their pride was overweening; they attacked the gods…. So Zeus and the other gods debated what was to be done with them. For a long time they were at a loss, unable to bring themselves either to kill them by lightning, as they had the giants, and extinguish the race thus depriving themselves for ever of the honors and sacrifice due from humanity—or to let them go on in their insolence. At last, after much painful thought, Zeus had an idea. "I think," he said, "that I have found a way by which we can allow the human race to continue to exist and also put an end to their wickedness by making them weaker. I will cut each of them in two; in this way they will be weaker, and at the same time more profitable to us by being more numerous. They shall walk upright upon two legs. If there is any sign of wantonness in them after that, and they will not keep quiet, I will bisect them again, and they shall hop on one leg." With these words he cut the members of the human race in half, just like fruit which is to be dried and preserved, or like eggs which are cut with a hair. As he bisected each, he bade Apollo turn round the face and the half neck attached to it towards the cut side, so that the victim, having the evidence of bisection before his eyes, might behave better in future. He also bade him heal the wounds. So Apollo turned round the faces,

and gathering together the skin, like a purse with drawstrings, on to what is now called the belly, he tied it tightly in the middle of the belly round a single aperture which men call the navel. He smoothed out the other wrinkles, which were numerous, and molded the chest with a tool like those which cobblers use to smooth wrinkles in the leather on their last. But he left a few on the belly itself round the navel, to remind man of the state from which he had fallen.

Man's original body having been thus cut in two, each half yearned for the half from which it had been severed. When they met they threw their arms round one another and embraced, in their longing to grow together again, and they perished of hunger and general neglect of their concerns, because they would not do anything apart. When one member of a pair died and the other was left, the latter sought after and embraced another partner, which might be the half either of a female whole (what is now called a woman) or a male. So they went on perishing till Zeus took pity on them, and hit upon a second plan. He moved their reproductive organs to the front: hitherto they had been placed on the outer side of their bodies, and the processes of begetting and birth had been carried on not by the physical union of the sexes, but by emission on to the ground, as is the case with grasshoppers. By moving their genitals to the front, as they are now, Zeus made it possible for reproduction to take place by the intercourse of the male with the female. His object in making this change was twofold; if male coupled with female, children might be begotten and the race thus continued, but if male coupled with male, at any rate the desire for intercourse would be satisfied, and men set free from it to turn to other activities and to attend to the rest of the business of life. It is from this distant epoch, then, that we may date the innate love which human beings feel for one another, the love which restores us to our ancient state by attempting to weld two beings into one and to heal the wounds which humanity suffered.

Each of us then is the mere broken tally of a man, the result of a bisection which has reduced us to a condition like that of flat fish, and each of us is perpetually in search of his corresponding tally. Those men who are halves of a being of the common sex, which was called, as I told you, hermaphrodite, are lovers of women, and most adulterers come from this class, as also do women who are mad about men and sexually promiscuous. Women who are halves of a female whole direct their affections towards women and pay little attention to men; Lesbians belong to this category. But those who are halves of a male whole pursue males, and being slices, so to speak, of the male, love men throughout their boyhood, and take pleasure in physical contact with men. Such boys and lads are the best of their generation, because they are the most manly. Some people say that they are shameless, but they are wrong. It is not shamelessness which inspires their behavior, but high spirit and manliness and virility, which lead them to welcome the society of their own kind. A striking proof of this is that such boys alone, when they reach maturity, engage in public life. When they grow to be men, they become lovers of boys, and it requires the compulsion of convention to overcome their natural disinclination to marriage and procreation; they are quite content to live with one another unwed. In a word, such persons are devoted to lovers in boyhood and themselves lovers of boys in manhood, because they always cleave to what is akin to themselves.

Whenever the lover of boys—or any other person for that matter—has the good fortune to encounter his own actual other half, affection and kinship and love combined inspire in him an emotion which is quite overwhelming, and such a pair practically refuse ever to be separated even for a moment. It is people like these who form lifelong partnerships, although they would find it difficult to say what they hope to gain from one another's society. No one can suppose that it is mere physical enjoyment which causes the one to take such intense delight in the company of the other. It is clear that the soul of each has some other longing which it cannot express, but can only surmise and obscurely hint at. Suppose Hephaestus with his tools were to visit them as they lie together, and stand over them and ask: "What is it, mortals, that you hope to gain from one another?" Suppose too that when they could not answer he repeated his question in these terms: "Is the object of your desire to be always together as much as possible, and never to be separated from one another day or night? If that is what you want, I am ready to melt and weld you together, so that, instead of two, you shall be one flesh; as long as you live you shall live a common life, and when you die, you shall suffer a common death, and be still one, not two, even in the next world. Would such a fate as this content you, and satisfy your longings?" We know what their answer would be; no one would refuse the offer; it would be plain that this is what everybody wants, and everybody would regard it as the precise expression of the desire which he had long felt but had been unable to formulate, that he should melt into his beloved, and that henceforth they should be one being instead of two. The reason is that this was our primitive condition when we were wholes, and love is simply the name for the desire and pursuit of the whole.

Questions for Reflection and Discussion

What are the different categories of sexual desire, according to this story, and how closely do they resemble our own categories? What stereotypes are associated with each category of sexual person? How is pederasty described? What are the advantages and disadvantages to pederasty, as implied in this story?

20. PEDERASTY IN GREEK ART

Time: fifth century BCE
Place: Greece
Artist: unknown

Numerous images from ancient Athenian art make it clear how widespread and common-place was the custom of pederasty. Images such as this one were placed on drinking cups, used at all male social gatherings called symposia, *occasions where men might meet and court boys. (Plato's* Symposium, *excerpted in the previous source, takes place at one of these gatherings.) Some images show individuals of widely vary-ing ages, as above; others show individuals of roughly equivalent age. In ancient Athens, as elsewhere in the ancient world, art that has sur-vived can help to expand our knowledge about sexual practices such as pederasty.*

What conventions of age and sexual posi-tion does this image reflect? How is the man's sexual interest and the boy's sexual interest differently represented? What meaning might the display of such activities on pottery used at banquets have conveyed?

21. POEM OF THEOCRITUS

Time: third century BCE
Place: Egypt
Author: Theocritus

Theocritus lived about a century after Plato, after Alexander had conquered his vast empire and Greek-influenced cultures (called Hellenistic) existed in Egypt, throughout the eastern Mediterranean, and beyond. Pederasty was still part of the social conventions of the Hellenistic societies but notice how differently the relationship is expressed. Theocritus, a Greek who lived in Egypt, tries to show us what the pederastic relationship meant for him—or at least, for the personality in his poem.

"Sincerity comes with the wine-cup," my dear:
Then now o'er our wine-cups let us be sincere.
My soul's treasured secret to you I'll impart;
It is this: that I never won fairly your heart.
One half of my life, I am conscious, has flown;
The residue lives on your image alone.
You are kind, and I dream I'm in para-dise then;
You are angry, and lo! all is darkness again.

Is it right to torment one who loves you?
Obey
Your elder; it were best; and you'll thank
me one day.
Settle down in one nest on one tree (tak-
ing care
That no cruel reptile can clamber up
there);
As it is with your lovers you're fairly
perplext;
One day you choose your bough, another
the next.
Whoe'er at all struck by your graces
appears,
Is more to you straight away than the
comrade of years;
While he's like the friend of a day put
aside;
For the breath of your nostrils, I think, is
your pride.
Form a friendship, for life, with some
likely young lad;
So doing, in honor your name shall be
had.
Nor would Love use you hardly; though
lightly can he
Bind strong men in chains, and has
wrought upon me
Till the steel is as wax—but I'm longing
to press
That exquisite mouth with a clinging
caress.
No? Reflect that you're older each year
than the last;
That we all must grow gray, and the wrin-
kles come fast.
Reflect, ere you spurn me, that youth at
his sides
Wears wings; and once gone, all pursuit
he derides:
Nor are men over keen to catch charms as
they fly.
Think of this and be gentle, be loving as I.

When your years are more mature, we
two shall be then
The pair in the Iliad over again.
But if you consign all my words to the
wind
And say, "Why annoy me? You're not to
my mind,"
I—who lately in quest of the Gold Fruit
had sped
For your sake, or of Cerberus guard of the
dead—
Though you called me, would ne'er stir a
foot from my door,
For my love and my sorrow thenceforth
will be o'er.

Questions for Reflection and Discussion

What are Theocritus's complaints with this boy,
and what is perhaps the real reason Theocritus
is so unhappy? What does this poem tell us
about the mutual feelings in pederastic relationships in Theocritus's day? How do these
compare to the feelings described a century
earlier in source 19?

22. THE CHINESE EMPERORS' MALE FAVORITES

Time: late second or early first century BCE
Place: China
Author: Sima Qian

*The most famous of early Chinese historians,
Sima Qian (also spelled Ssu-ma Ch'ien) took
earlier accounts and legends and wove them
into a series of histories on various themes from
earliest times to his own day. He also sprinkled
his stories liberally with moral lessons, as he did
in this excerpt, and as most ancient historians
did. Sima Qian lived during the later part of the
Han Dynasty, and his work was sponsored by
the ruling Han emperor, so these emperors were*

his patron's ancestors and we can assume that he was trying to cast them in a positive light.

Yet it is not women alone who can use their looks to attract the eyes of the ruler; courtiers and eunuchs can play at that game as well. Many were the men of ancient times who gained favor in this way. When the Han arose, Emperor Gaozu, for all his coarseness and blunt manners, was won by the charms of a young boy named Ji, and Emperor Hui had a boy favorite named Hong. Neither Ji nor Hong had any particular talent or ability; both won prominence simply by their looks and graces. Day and night they were by the ruler's side, and all the high ministers were obliged to apply to them when they wished to speak to the emperor. As a result all the palace attendants at the court of Emperor Hui took to wearing caps with gaudy feathers and sashes of seashells and to painting their faces, transforming themselves into a veritable host of Jis and Hongs….

The gentlemen who enjoyed favor in the palace under Emperor Wen included a courtier named Deng Tong and the eunuchs Zhao Tan and Beigong Bozi. Beigong Bozi was a worthy and affectionate man, while Zhao Tan attracted the emperor's attention by his skill in observing the stars and exhalations in the sky; both of them customarily rode about in the same carriage with Emperor Wen. Deng Tong does not seem to have had any special talent…. Once Emperor Wen was troubled by a tumor, and Deng Tong made it his duty to keep it sucked clean of infection. The emperor was feeling depressed by his illness and, apropos of nothing in particular, asked Deng Tong, "In all the empire, who do you think loves me most?" "Surely no one loves Your Majesty more than the heir apparent!" replied Deng Tong. Later, when the heir apparent came to inquire how his father was, the emperor made him suck the tumor. The heir apparent managed to suck it clean, but it was obvious from his expression that he found the task distasteful. Afterward, when he learned that Deng Tong had been in the habit of sucking the tumor for the emperor, he was secretly filled with shame….

Emperor Jing did not have any particular favorites among the officials at his court. There was one man, a chief of palace attendants named Zhou Wenren, who enjoyed rather more favor than ordinary men, but even so it was nothing very extraordinary. Among the favorites of the present emperor were the courtier Hann Yan, the great grandson of Xin, the king of Hann, and the eunuch Li Yannian.

Questions for Reflection and Discussion

How does Sima Qian contrast pederastic and familial relationships in this story? What do we learn about the practice of pederasty in ancient China? Can we assume that men other than the emperors were also involved in it?

23. THE STORY OF A EUNUCH AND THE QUEEN DOWAGER

Time: late second or early first century BCE
Place: China
Author: Sima Qian

In patriarchal societies, eunuchs often served as guardians of the sexual modesty of women. Contemporaries invariably wondered, however, whether men were completely trustworthy in such roles, as in this story told by the most famous of early Chinese historians, Sima Qian. Although Sima Qian lived in the Han era, in this excerpt he recalled a time a century and a half earlier, when the King of Qin conquered the other Chinese states and became China's First Emperor. Sima Qian was hostile generally to the memory of the First Emperor, as this passage implies. The Queen Dowager here is the First Emperor's mother; her lover's name, Lao Ai, means something like "lustful misdeed" in Chinese, and his "large penis" could also mean "great conspiracy," both plays-on-words that fit well with the moralistic tone of the story. Sima Qian records elsewhere his opinion that the First Emperor was not the son of the King from whom he inherited his throne but, instead, of Lu Buwei, the Prime Minister of Qin. It is worth noting that Sima Qian was himself a eunuch, castrated for an unknown crime.

The [future] First Emperor was growing into manhood, but the Queen Dowager's licentiousness was ceaseless. Lu Buwei feared that if this became known, misfortune would reach him. So he privately found a man with a large penis named Lao Ai and made him his retainer. At times he would indulge in song and music, making Lao Ai walk around with his penis stuck through a wheel of wood. He had the Queen Dowager hear of this, in order to entice her. When the Queen Dowager heard, as expected, she wanted to have him in private. Lu Buwei then presented Lao Ai and conspired to have someone accuse him of a crime for which he should be castrated. Buwei then addressed the Queen Dowager secretly, saying: "If you permit this trumped-up castration, then you can have him in your apartment." The Queen Dowager then secretly gave rich gifts to the official in charge of castrations, instructing him to pluck out Lao Ai's beard up to the eyebrows, making him a "eunuch" so that he could serve the Queen Dowager. The Queen Dowager had congress with him in private and loved him very much. She became pregnant by him, and fearing that someone would come to know of it, she produced a sham divination saying that she should avoid an inauspicious period; she moved her palace and lived in Yung. Lao Ai often visited her; she rewarded him with very rich gifts, and all the affairs in the house were decided by Lao Ai....

In the ninth year of the [future] First Emperor [238 BCE], someone reported that Lao Ai was not really a eunuch; that he often privately fomented chaos with the Queen Dowager; that she had given birth to two sons; and that they had concealed everything. He had conspired with the Queen Dowager, saying: "Once the king is dead, we will make one of these sons his successor." Therefore the King of Qin handed this matter down to his officials to investigate; they grasped the truth of the situation, and the affair was linked to the Prime Minister, Lu Buwei. In the ninth month, the king exterminated Lao Ai's clan to the third degree of relation, killed the two boys that the Queen Dowager had borne, and banished the Queen Dowager to Yung. All of Lao Ai's henchmen had their families' wealth confiscated and were banished to Shu.

Questions for Reflection and Discussion

What do these events imply about the roles of women at the early Chinese courts? How might the suggestion that Lao Ai was not really a eunuch be related to other men's concerns? Sima Qian liked to tell stories with moral lessons. What is this story's lesson?

24. THE HOLINESS CODE

Time: perhaps the seventh century BCE, from
    earlier oral traditions
Place: Israel
Author: unknown, traditionally ascribed to
    Moses

Leviticus is the Biblical book of instructions for ancient Israelite priests. In this excerpt from it, the prohibitions for incest and other sexual transgressions are given. The passage is taken from a larger section known to scholars as the Holiness Code, and reflects an attitude that sexual morality is essential for the general well-being of the Israelite community. Questions remain: To what extent were these priests trying to change social customs with their prohibitions, and to what extent were they cementing into written law what were already existing social customs?

The Lord said to Moses, "Speak to the Israelites and say to them: 'I am the Lord your God. You must not do as they do in Egypt, where you used to live, and you must not do as they do in the land of Canaan, where I am bringing you. Do not follow their practices. You must obey my laws and be careful to follow my decrees. I am the Lord your God. Keep my decrees and laws, for the man who obeys them will live by them. I am the Lord.

"'No one is to approach any close relative to have sexual relations. I am the Lord. Do not dishonor your father by having sexual relations with your mother. She is your mother; do not have relations with her. Do not have sexual relations with your father's wife; that would dishonor your father. Do not have sexual relations with your sister, either your father's daughter or your mother's daughter, whether she was born in the same home or elsewhere. Do not have sexual relations with your son's daughter or your daughter's daughter; that would dishonor you. Do not have sexual relations with the daughter of your father's wife, born to your father; she is your sister. Do not have sexual relations with your father's sister; she is your father's close relative. Do not have sexual relations with your mother's sister, because she is your mother's close relative.

"'Do not dishonor your father's brother by approaching his wife to have sexual relations; she is your aunt. Do not have sexual relations with your daughter-in-law. She is your son's wife; do not have relations with her. Do not have sexual relations with your brother's wife; that would dishonor your brother. Do not have sexual relations with both a woman and her daughter. Do not have sexual relations with either her son's daughter or her daughter's daughter; they are her close relatives. That is wickedness. Do not take your wife's sister as a rival wife and have sexual relations with her while your wife is living.

"'Do not approach a woman to have sexual relations during the uncleanness of her monthly period. Do not have sexual relations with your neighbor's wife and defile yourself with her. Do not give any of your children to be sacrificed to [the god] Molech, for you must not profane the name of your God. I am the Lord. Do not lie with a man as one lies with a woman; that is detestable. Do not have sexual relations with an animal and defile yourself with it. A woman must not present herself to an animal to have sexual relations with it; that is a perversion.

"'Do not defile yourselves in any of these ways, because this is how the nations that I am going to drive out before you became defiled. Even the land was defiled; so I punished it for its sin, and the land vomited out its inhabitants. But you must keep my decrees and my laws. The native-born and the aliens living among you must not do any of these detestable things, for all these things were done by the people who lived in the land before you, and the land became defiled. And if you defile the land, it will vomit you out as it vomited out the nations that were before you. Everyone who does any of these detestable things—such persons must be cut off from their people. Keep my requirements and do not follow any of the detestable customs that were practiced before you came and do not defile yourselves with them. I am the Lord your God.'"

What is the exact relationship between sexual morality and community identity? How does the Levitical definition of incest differ from our own? Why are some sexual relationships— for example, sexual relationships between women—not mentioned among those condemned? Should one infer ignorance of these relationships or tolerance of them? What do these differences say about these ancient categories and our own?

25. PROSTITUTION AS METAPHOR

Time: seventh century BCE
Place: Israel
Author: traditionally ascribed to Ezekiel

The writings of the prophets in the Bible claim to be the words of God transmitted through human mouthpieces. In this excerpt, the prophet Ezekiel was using the metaphor of prostitution to explain to his audience the fouled relationship between God and humanity. Of course, the use of the metaphor assumes that his audience was familiar enough with the social practice of prostitution—described here in considerable detail—to understand his analogy. Note also that the references to high places and a mound may indicate that this is in part a critique of sacred prostitution. And the mention of finding an infant who would be raised as a prostitute may be understood as another widespread ancient custom: that of abandoning babies in the open, especially girls, if they were unwanted by the family, after which they might be taken by someone else and made slaves, even slaves used as prostitutes.

The word of the Lord came to me: "Son of man, confront Jerusalem with her detestable practices and say, 'This is what the Sovereign Lord says to Jerusalem: Your ancestry and birth were in the land of the Canaanites; your father was an Amorite and your mother a Hittite. On the day you were born your cord was not cut, nor were you washed with water to make you clean, nor were you rubbed with salt or wrapped in cloths. No one looked on you with pity or had compassion enough to do any of these things for you. Rather, you were thrown out into the open field, for on the day you were born you were despised. Then I passed by and saw you kicking about in your blood, and as you lay there in your blood I said to you, "Live!" I made you grow like a plant of the field. You grew up and developed and became the most beautiful of jewels. Your breasts were formed and your hair grew, you who were naked and bare.

"'Later I passed by, and when I looked at you and saw that you were old enough for love, I spread the corner of my garment over you and covered your nakedness. I gave you my solemn oath and entered into a covenant with you, declares the Sovereign Lord, and you became mine. I bathed you with water and washed the blood from you and put ointments on you. I clothed you with an embroidered dress and put leather sandals on you. I dressed you in fine linen and covered you with costly garments. I adorned you with jewelry: I put bracelets on your arms and a necklace around your neck, and I put a ring on your nose, earrings on your ears and a beautiful crown on your head. So you were adorned with gold and silver; your clothes were of fine linen and costly fabric and embroidered cloth. Your food was fine flour, honey and olive oil. You became very beautiful and rose to be a queen. And your fame spread among the nations on account of your beauty, because the splendor I had given you made your beauty perfect, declares the Sovereign Lord.

"'But you trusted in your beauty and used your fame to become a prostitute. You lavished your favors on anyone who passed by and your beauty became his. You took some of your garments to make gaudy high places, where you carried on your prostitution. Such things should not happen, nor should they ever occur. You also took the fine jewelry I gave you, the jewelry made of my gold and silver, and you made for yourself male idols and engaged in prostitution with them. And you took your embroidered clothes to put on them, and you offered my oil and incense before them. Also the food I provided for you—the fine flour, olive oil and honey I gave you to eat—you offered as fragrant incense before them. That is what happened, declares the Sovereign Lord. And you took your sons and daughters whom you bore to me and sacrificed them as food to the idols. Was your prostitution not enough? You slaughtered my children and sacrificed them to the idols. In all your detestable practices and your prostitution you did not remember the days of your youth, when you were naked and bare, kicking about in your blood.

"'Woe! Woe to you, declares the Sovereign Lord. In addition to all your other wickedness, you built a mound for yourself and made a lofty shrine in every public square. At the head of every street you built your lofty shrines and degraded your beauty, offering your body with increasing promiscuity to anyone who passed by. You engaged in prostitution with the Egyptians, your lustful neighbors, and provoked me to anger with your increasing promiscuity. So I stretched out my hand against you and reduced your territory; I gave you over to the greed of your enemies, the daughters of the Philistines, who were shocked by your lewd conduct. You engaged in prostitution with the Assyrians too, because you were insatiable; and even after that, you still were not satisfied. Then you increased your promiscuity to include Babylonia, a land of merchants, but even with this you were not satisfied. How weak-willed you are, declares the Sovereign Lord, when you do all these things, acting like a brazen prostitute! When you built your mounds at the head of every street and made your lofty shrines in every public square, you were unlike a prostitute, because you scorned payment. You adulterous wife! You prefer strangers to your own husband! Every prostitute receives a fee, but you give gifts to all your lovers, bribing them to come to you from everywhere for your illicit favors. So in your prostitution you are the opposite of others; no one runs after you for your favors. You are the very opposite, for you give payment and none is given to you.

"'Therefore, you prostitute, hear the word of the Lord! This is what the Sovereign Lord says: Because you poured out your wealth and exposed your nakedness in your promiscuity with your lovers, and because of all your detestable idols, and because you gave them your children's blood, therefore I am going to gather all your lovers, with whom you found pleasure, those you loved as well as those you hated. I will gather them against you from all around and will strip you in front of them, and they will see all your nakedness. I will sentence you to the punishment of women who commit adultery and who shed blood; I will bring upon you the blood vengeance of my wrath and jealous anger. Then I will hand you over to your lovers, and they will tear down your mounds and destroy your lofty shrines. They will strip you of your clothes and take your fine jewelry and leave you naked and bare. They will bring a mob against you, who will stone you and hack you to pieces with their swords. They will burn down your houses and inflict punishment on you in the sight of many women. I will put a stop to your prostitution, and you will no longer pay your lovers. Then my wrath against you will subside and my jealous anger will turn away from you; I will be calm and no longer angry....'"

What do we learn about the actual practice of prostitution in ancient Israel from this passage? What does the hostile tone used in this passage tell us about attitudes toward prostitution? What does the use of sexuality as a metaphor for religion—here, God as the spurned lover—tell us about the connection between these two facets of human life?

26. HERODOTUS ON
SACRED PROSTITUTION

Time: fifth century BCE
Place: Mesopotamia (modern Iraq)
Author: Herodotus

The Greek historian Herodotus offers a glimpse into the practice of sacred prostitution in Babylon. Yet notice how vague the historian is: He implies that some customs have changed, others have disappeared. These sorts of oddities have led some historians to conclude that he was inventing the whole concept as a comment on the Greek women of his day. Many other ancient writers mention sacred prostitution, but all are similarly unclear in what they say, and they usually contradict each other on specific parts of the custom.

The dress of the Babylonians consists of a linen tunic reaching to the feet with a woolen one over it, and a short white cloak on top, they have their own fashion in shoes, which resemble the slippers one sees in Boeotia. They grow their hair long, wear turbans, and perfume themselves all over; everyone owns a seal and a walking stick specially made for him, with a device carved on the top of it, an apple or rose or lily or eagle or something of the sort; for it is not the custom to have a stick without some such ornament. I will say no more about

dress and so forth, but will go on to describe some of their practices.

The most ingenious in my opinion is a custom which, I understand, they share with the Eneti in Illyria. In every village once a year all the girls of marriageable age used to be collected together in one place, while the men stood round them in a circle; an auctioneer then called each one in turn to stand up and offered her for sale, beginning with the best looking and going on to the second best as soon as the first had been sold for a good price. Marriage was the object of the transaction. The rich men who wanted wives bid against each other for the prettiest girls, while the humbler folk, who had no use for good looks in a wife, were actually paid to take the ugly ones, for when the auctioneer had got through all the pretty girls he would call upon the plainest, or even perhaps a crippled one, to stand up, and then ask who was willing to take the least money to marry her—and she was knocked down to whoever accepted the smallest sum. The money came from the sale of the beauties, who in this way provided dowries for their ugly or misshapen sisters. It was illegal for a man to marry his daughter to anyone he happened to fancy, and no one could take home a girl he had bought without first finding a backer to guarantee his intention of marrying her. In cases of disagreement between husband and wife the law allowed the return of the purchase money. Anyone who wished could come even from a different village to buy a wife. This admirable practice has now fallen into disuse and they have of late years hit upon another scheme, namely the prostitution of all girls of the lower classes to provide some relief from the poverty which followed upon the conquest with its attendant hardship and general ruin....

There is one custom amongst these people which is wholly shameful: every woman who is a native of the country must once in her life go and sit in the temple of Aphrodite and there give herself to a strange man. Many of the rich women, who are too proud to mix with the rest, drive to the temple in covered carriages with a whole host of servants following behind, and there wait; most, however, sit in the precinct of the temple with a band of plaited string round their heads—and a great crowd they are, what with some sitting there, others arriving, others going away—and through them all gangways are marked off running in every direction for the men to pass along and make their choice. Once a woman has taken her seat she is not allowed to go home until a man has thrown a silver coin into her lap and taken her outside to lie with her. As he throws the coin, the man has to say, "In the name of the goddess Mylitta"—that being the Assyrian name for Aphrodite. The value of the coin is of no consequence; once thrown it becomes sacred, and the law forbids that it should ever be refused. The woman has no privilege of choice—she must go with the first man who throws her the money. When she has lain with him, her duty to the goddess is discharged and she may go home, after which it will be impossible to seduce her by any offer, however large. Tall, handsome women soon manage to get home again, but the ugly ones stay a long time before they can fulfill the condition, which the law demands, some of them, indeed, as much as three or four years. There is a custom similar to this in parts of Cyprus.

Questions for Reflection and Discussion

How does Herodotus suggest that the practice of sacred prostitution arose? Does Herodotus appear to approve or disapprove of this custom? If he did invent this practice, what was he trying to say by describing it in the ways he did?

27. PSEUDO-LUCIAN ON RITUAL CASTRATION

Time: second century CE
Place: Syria
Author: ancient writer once mistakenly identified as Lucian

The anonymous author known to scholars as Pseudo-Lucian has left us an interestingly detailed account of castration and its relationship to ancient rites of fertility. As with Herodotus, however, the details seem vague, or contradictory, or even unbelievable, making it difficult to know how reliable an account it is. The term Galli *(used for the eunuch priests) is also of uncertain origin.*

I did see, however, in Byblos, a great sanctuary of Aphrodite of Byblos in which they perform the rites of Adonis, and I learned about the rites. They say, at any rate, that what the boar did to Adonis occurred in their territory. As a memorial of his suffering each year they beat their breasts, mourn, and celebrate the rites. Throughout the land they perform solemn lamentations. When they cease their breast-beating and weeping, they first sacrifice to Adonis as if to a dead person, but then, on the next day, they proclaim that he lives and send him into the air. They also shave their heads, as do the Egyptians when Apis dies. The women who refuse to shave pay this penalty: For a single day they stand offering their beauty for sale. The market, however, is open to foreigners only and the payment becomes an offering to Aphrodite. There are some inhabitants of Byblos who say that the Egyptian Osiris is buried among them and that all the laments and the rites are performed not for Adonis but for Osiris.…

There is another sacred account, which I heard from a wise man, that the goddess is Rhea, and the sanctuary is a creation of Attis. Attis was a Lydian by birth, and he first taught rites pertaining to Rhea. All the rites which Phrygians, Lydians and inhabitants of Samothrace perform, they learned from Attis. When Rhea castrated him, he ceased his male lifestyle. He took on instead a feminine form and donned female clothing. He went out into every land, performed the rites, related his sufferings and sang the praises of Rhea. On these journeys he came to Syria. Since the men beyond the Euphrates accepted neither him nor the rites, he established the sanctuary in this place. Here is the proof: The goddess is similar in many ways to Rhea, for lions carry her, she holds a tympanum and wears a tower on her head, just as the Lydians depict Rhea. The wise man also said about the *Galli* who are in the temple, that *Galli* never castrate themselves for Hera, but they do for Rhea and they also imitate Attis....

This custom, once it began, has remained even to the present and each year in the sanctuary many castrate themselves and become womanish either as a consolation for Combabus or as an honor to Hera. In any case, they are castrated. These people no longer wear male clothing. Instead, they don feminine garments and do the work of women. As I heard it, the reason for this, too, is attributed to Combabus. For it once happened to him that a foreign woman came to a festival, saw him, handsome and still wearing male clothing, and fell madly in love. But when she later learned that he was not a whole man, she slew herself. As a result of this, Combabus, depressed because he was unlucky at love, donned female clothing, so that no other woman would be likewise deceived. This is the reason for the female garment of the *Galli*....

On appointed days, the crowd assembles at the sanctuary while many *Galli* and the holy men whom I have mentioned perform the rites. They cut their arms and beat one another on the back. Many stand about them playing flutes, while many others beat drums. Still others sing inspired and sacred songs. This ceremony takes place outside the temple and none of those who performs it enters the temple. On these days, too, men become *Galli*. For while the rest are playing flutes and performing the rites, frenzy comes upon many, and many who have come simply to watch subsequently perform this act. I will describe what they do. The youth for whom these things lie in store throws off his clothes, rushes to the center with a great shout and takes up a sword, which, I believe, has stood there for this purpose for many years. He grabs it and immediately castrates himself. Then he rushes through the city holding in his hands the parts he has cut off. He takes female clothing and women's adornment from whatever house he throws these parts into. This is what they do at the Castration.

Questions for Reflection and Discussion

How does Pseudo-Lucian understand the origins of ritual castration? How might religious mythology have helped to legitimize these sexual practices? Does the sexual category of *Galli* seem at all like any modern sexual category?

28. APULEIUS ON EUNUCHS

Time: second century CE
Place: north Africa in the Roman Empire
Author: Apuleius

Apuleius, a Roman author of medical and religious treatises, has also left us an entertaining story about the adventures of a man turned into a donkey. In this excerpt, the donkey—who still has the consciousness of a man—is sold to one member of a group of Galli, *the eunuch priests of the fertility cult.*

Taking delivery of this new member of the family he led me off home, where as soon as he got indoors he called out: "Look, girls, at the pretty little slave I've bought and brought home for you." But these "girls" were a troupe of queens, who at once appeared jumping for joy and squealing untunefully in mincing effeminate tones, in the belief that it really was a human slave that had been brought to serve them. When they saw that this was not a case of a hind substituting for a maiden but an ass taking the place of a man, they began to sneer and mock their chief, saying that this wasn't a servant he'd brought but a husband for himself. "And listen," they said. "You're not to gobble up this nice little nestling all on your own we're your little dovvies too, and you must let us have a share sometimes." Exchanging badinage of this sort they tied me up next to the manger. They also had in the house a beefy young man, an accomplished piper, whom they had bought in the market from the proceeds of their street collections. Out of doors he tagged along playing his instrument when they carried the goddess around, at home he was the regular "boy-toy" to the whole establishment. As soon as he saw me joining the household, without waiting for orders he served me out a generous ration of food and welcomed me joyfully. "At last," he said, "here's somebody to spell me in my loathsome duties. Long life to you! May you please our masters and bring relief to my exhausted loins!" When I heard this I began to picture to myself the ordeals that lay ahead of me.

Next day they all put on tunics of various hues and "beautified" themselves by smearing colored gunge on their faces and applying eyeshadow. Then they set forth, dressed in turbans and robes, some saffron-colored, some of linen and some of gauze; some had white tunics embroidered with a pattern of purple stripes and girded at the waist; and on their feet were yellow slippers. The goddess, draped in silk, they placed on my back, and baring their arms to the shoulder and brandishing huge swords and axes, they capered about with ecstatic cries, while the sound of the pipes goaded their dancing to frenzy. After calling at a number of small houses they arrived at a rich man's country estate. The moment they entered the gates there was bedlam; they rushed about like fanatics, howling discordantly, twisting their necks sinuously back and forth with lowered heads, and letting their long hair fly around in circles, sometimes attacking their own flesh with their teeth, and finally gashing their arms with the weapons they carried. In the middle of all this, one of them was inspired to fresh excesses of frenzy; he began to gasp and draw deep labored breaths, feigning madness like one divinely possessed—as if the presence of a god sickened and enfeebled men instead of making them better!

Anyway, let me tell you how heavenly Providence rewarded him. Holding forth like some prophet he embarked on a cock-and-bull story about some sacrilegious act he accused himself of having committed, and condemned himself to undergo the just punishment for his crime at his own hands. So, seizing a whip such as these effeminates always carry about with them, its lashes made of twisted wool ending in long tassels thickly studded with sheep's knucklebones, he laid into himself with these knotted thongs, standing the pain of the blows with extraordinary hardihood. What with the sword-cuts and the flogging, the ground was awash with the contaminated blood of these creatures. All this worried me a good deal: seeing all these wounds and gore all over the place I was afraid that, just as some men drink asses' milk, this foreign goddess might conceive an appetite for asses' blood. Finally, however, exhausted or sated with lacerating themselves, they gave over the carnage, and started to stow away in the roomy folds of their robes the coppers, indeed the silver money, that people crowded round to bestow on them— and not only money but jars of wine and milk and cheeses and a quantity of corn and wheat; and some presented the bearer of the goddess with barley. They greedily raked in all this stuff, crammed it into the sacks that they had ready for these acquisitions, and loaded it on my back, so that I was carrying a double load, a walking barn and temple combined.

In this way they roved about plundering the whole countryside. In one village they enjoyed a particularly lavish haul and decided to celebrate with a banquet. As the price for a fake oracle they got a fat ram from one of the farmers, which they said was to be sacrificed to appease the hungry goddess. Having made all the arrangements for dinner they went off to the baths, whence having bathed they brought back with them to share their dinner a robust young peasant, finely equipped in loin and groin. Dinner was hardly begun and they had scarcely started on the *hors d'oeuvre* when the filthy scum became inflamed by their unspeakable lusts to outrageous lengths of unnatural depravity. The young man was stripped and laid on his back, and crowding round him they made repeated demands on his services with their loathsome mouths.

Questions for Reflection and Discussion

Would you consider Apuleius' tone toward the eunuchs as teasing or hostile? Does this passage shed light on the eunuchs' gendered sense of themselves? Or on others' view of the eunuchs' gender identity?

29. LACTANTIUS ON SEXUAL DIFFERENCE

Time: fourth century CE
Place: Greece, in the Roman Empire
Author: Lactantius

In this treatise, Lactantius, who was tutor to the sons of the Roman Emperor Constantine the Great, was trying to explain how sexual difference worked, and why it worked differently in some individuals than in others. He was not a physician, but he seems to have known something about the medical ideas of his day, mentioning two ancient authorities; perhaps he wrote down what most educated persons of his day believed. Lactantius was a Christian, but his ideas about human gestation are derived entirely from ancient Greek and Roman medical writings.

Something must be said also about the uterus and conception…. The vessel in males which contains the semen [that is, the testicles] is two-fold…. The right one contains the male seed, the left one the female (and in the entire body on the whole the right side is the masculine, the left, feminine)…. Likewise in women, the womb is divided into two parts and these, spread apart and bent back, are folded around like the horns of a ram. The part which twists to the right is the masculine part, that which is on the left, feminine. Varro and Aristotle think that conception takes place thus. They say that the seed is not in males only, but also in the females…. They think that the likenesses to parents are brought about in the bodies of children in this way. When the seeds which have been mixed among themselves coalesce, if those of the male are in the ascendancy, then the offspring, whether male or female, will be like the father; if the woman's prevail, the offspring of either sex will resemble the mother…. Hence, it generally comes about that the features of the one only stand out. If there has been an equal mixing of even semen, the features are also mingled so that the offspring is common, or it seems to resemble neither parent, because it does not have all from the one of the two entirely, since it has borrowed part from each....

Different natures also are thought to come about in this way. When it chances that a seed from a male parent falls into the left part of the uterus, the opinion is that a male is begotten, but since it is conceived in the female part, it suffers some female characteristics to hold sway in it more than its masculine splendor: either a beautiful figure, or exceeding whiteness or lightness of the body, or delicate limbs, or short stature, or a soft voice, or a weak mind, or several of these characteristics. Likewise, if seed of a feminine stock flows into the right part, a female is, of course, begotten, but, since it is conceived in the masculine part, then some characteristics of maleness hold sway more than the usual sex classification would permit: either strong limbs, or excessive height, or a ruddy complexion, or a hairy face, or an unlovely countenance, or a heavy voice, or a daring spirit, or several of these. If, however, a masculine seed comes into the right part and a feminine into the left, the two fetuses come forth rightly, so that for the feminine the beauty of its nature holds throughout all things, and for the masculine manly strength is preserved both as to the mind and the body.

Questions for Reflection and Discussion

Why might it be that the masculine is associated with the right and the feminine with the left? Why was it important for Lactantius to explain sexual ambiguity? Why should it have been believed that the testes are said to determine sexual difference but the womb is said to determine only sexual ambiguity?

SOURCES AND FURTHER READING

Much has been written on the varieties of sexual expression in antiquity; indeed, most of this scholarly literature has emphasized the distinctiveness and dissimilarity of ancient from modern forms. The further readings for the sources listed below provide numerous examples of this approach. Nonetheless, it is often useful to compare ancient societies and modern ones, even while respecting the individuality of their sexual customs. A good introduction is D.L. Davis and R.G. Whitten's "The Cross-Cultural Study of Human Sexuality," in *Annual Review of Anthropology* 16 (1987): 69-98. The anthropological school of Cultural Relativism began with a critique of the comparative approach. See Franz Boas, "The Limitations of the Comparative Method in Anthropology," in his *Race, Language, and Culture* (London: Macmillan, 1948).

A combination of anthropological and historical literature can shed light on the specific practices of antiquity. On institutionalized pederasty, reference is often made to a classic work by anthropologist Gilbert Herdt on a people of New Guinea (referred to as the Sambia, although that is not their actual name) entitled *Guardians of the Flutes: Idioms of Masculinity* (New York: McGraw-Hill, 1981; revised 1994). These people are now the subject of a BBC film, also called *Guardians of the Flutes*. See note 19 on ancient Athenian pederasty, notes 27 and 28 on ritualized castration, and note 126 for a comparison with the *hijras* of India. On prostitution in history, numerous general works exist. Among the most readable for nonspecialists is Vern Bullough's *The History of Prostitution* (New Hyde Park, NY: University Books, 1964), revised as *Prostitution: An Illustrated Social History,* with Bonnie Bullough (New York: Crown, 1978); and George Ryley Scott's *A History of Prostitution from Antiquity to the Present* (New York: AMS, 1976). Theoretically sophisticated is Shannon Bell's *Reading, Writing, and Rewriting the Prostitute's Body* (Bloomington, IN: Indiana University Press, 1994). On incestuous marriage, only localized studies exist; recent ones include M.K. Hopkins, "Brother-Sister Marriage in Roman Egypt, *Comparative Studies in Society and History* 22 (1983): 303-55; Brent Shaw, "Explaining Incest: Brother-Sister Marriage in Graeco-Roman Egypt," *Man* 27 (1992): 267-99; and William Davenport, *Pi'o: An Enquiry into the Marriage of Brothers and Sisters and Other Close Relatives in Old Hawai'i* (Lanham, MD: University Press of America, 1994). On circumcision, general studies exist: David Gollaher's *Circumcision: A History of the World's Most Controversial Surgery* (New York: Basic Books, 2000); an interesting study of the practice in antiquity is Lawrence Hoffman's *Covenant of Blood: Circumcision and Gender in Rabbinic Judaism* (Chicago: University of Chicago Press, 1996).

19. "Aristophanes' Speech from the *Symposium*" is taken from *Plato: The Symposium*, Walter Hamilton, ed. and trans. (Harmondsworth, UK: Penguin, 1951), 59-64.

On pederasty in ancient Athens, the best is Kenneth Dover's *Greek Homosexuality* (Cambridge, MA: Harvard University Press, 1978); see also the debates on the social approval of the practice by David Cohen, "Law, Society, and Homosexuality in Classical Athens," *Past and Present* 117 (1987): 3-21, and Clifford Hindley's "Law, Society, and Homosexuality in Classical Athens (in Debate)," *Past and Present* 133

(1991): 167-83, followed by Cohen's reply (184-94). Aristophanes' speech is analyzed by David Halperin in "Sex Before Sexuality: Pederasty, Politics, and Power in Ancient Athens" in *Hidden from History: Reclaiming the Gay and Lesbian Past*, Martin Duberman et al., eds. (New York: New American Library, 1989) and reprinted in *Same Sex: Debating the Ethics, Science, and Culture of Homosexuality*, John Corvino, ed. (Lanham, MD: Rowman & Littlefield, 1997). See also Bernard Sergent's *Homosexuality in Greek Myth* (Boston: Beacon, 1986) for pederasty in other ancient legends. The whole of Plato's *Symposium* could be read to benefit in a history of sexuality, as it provides different perspectives on same-sex love. Commentaries on the *Symposium* are numerous, but see Robert Mitchell's *The Hymn to Eros: A Reading of Plato's Symposium* (Lanham, MD: University Press of America, 1993); or several of the essays in *Feminist Interpretations of Plato*, Nancy Tuana, ed. (University Park, PA: Pennsylvania State University Press, 1994). As with other aspects of ancient Greek society, different city-states had very different sexual traditions.

20. "Pederasty in Greek Art" is taken from Kenneth Dover, *Greek Homosexuality* (Cambridge, MA: Harvard University Press, 1978).

See note 19 on ancient Greek pederasty. On sexuality in Greek art, see Martin Kilmer's *Greek Erotica on Attic Red-Figure Vases* (London: Duckworth, 1993). Eva Keuls's *The Reign of the Phallus: Sexual Politics in Ancient Athens* (New York: Harper & Row, 1985) also includes many erotic images, mostly of men and women together.

21. "Poem of Theocritus" is taken from *The Idylls of Theocritus*, Charles Stuart Calverley,

trans. (Boston: Houghton Mifflin, 1906), 150-51, with slight changes.

See notes 19 and 20 for more on homoeroticism in ancient Greece. Daniel Garrison's *Sexual Culture in Ancient Greece* (Norman, OK: University of Oklahoma Press, 2000) includes a chapter on changes to sexual customs in the Hellenistic era, in which Theocritus lived. On Theocritus, see Joan Burton's *Theocritus's Urban Mimes: Mobility, Gender, and Patronage* (Berkeley, CA: University of California Press, 1995). On sexuality in the eastern Mediterranean's Hellenistic societies, and the blending of Greek, Egyptian, Syrian, and other customs, there is not yet much scholarly literature, except about Hellenistic Judaism. See Kathy Gaca's "The Reproductive Technology of the Pythagoreans," *Classical Philology* 95 (2000): 113-32, on the development of a procreation-based sexual morality in the Hellenistic era; or Michael Satlow's *Tasting the Dish: Rabbinic Rhetorics of Sexuality* (Atlanta, GA: Scholars, 1995); and Daniel Boyarin's *Carnal Israel: Reading Sex in Talmudic Culture* (Berkeley, CA: University of California Press, 1993), for examples on Hellenistic Judaism.

22. "The Chinese Emperors' Male Favorites" is taken from Sima Qian, *Records of the Grand Historian: Han Dynasty II*, Burton Watson, ed. and trans. (Hong Kong/New York: Renditions/Columbia University Press, 1961), 419-21.

On pederasty in Chinese history, a good book for nonspecialists is Bret Hinsch's *Passions of the Cut Sleeve: The Male Homosexual Tradition in China* (Berkeley, CA: University of California Press, 1990). On the historian Sima Qian, see Burton Watson's *Ssu-ma Ch'ien, Grand Historian of China* (New York: Columbia University Press, 1958). In general, Sima Qian was much more interested in politics than in sexuality in his writings. See also note 23.

23. "The Story of a Eunuch and the Queen Dowager" is taken from Paul Goldin's *The Culture of Sex in Ancient China* (Honolulu: University of Hawai'i Press, 2002), 82-83.

Goldin's book, from which the excerpt is taken, is a sophisticated discussion of sexuality in early Chinese writings, although not easy for nonspecialists to read. On castration in Chinese history and the political role of eunuchs, a readable overview is Taisuke Mitamura's *Chinese Eunuchs: The Structure of Intimate Politics*, Charles Pomeroy, trans. (Rutland, VT: CE Tuttle, 1970). For another legendarily powerful empress, albeit for a much later (Tang) period, see Dora Shu-fang Dien's *Empress Wu Zetian in Fiction and in History* (Hauppauge, NY: Nova Science, 2003).

24. "The Holiness Code" is taken from *The Holy Bible: New International Version* (Grand Rapids, MI: Zondervan Bible, 1978), 124-25 (Leviticus 18: 1-30).

There are numerous general commentaries on Leviticus, as on all books of the Bible. Most interesting for a history of sexuality might be the anthropological approach by Mary Douglas's *Leviticus as Literature* (Oxford: Oxford University Press, 1999); see also *Reading Leviticus: A Conversation with Mary Douglas*, John Sawyer, ed. (Sheffield, UK: Sheffield Academic Press, 1996). On the incest prohibitions specifically, see Calum Carmichael's *Law, Legend, and Incest in the Bible: Leviticus 18-20* (Ithaca, NY: Cornell University Press, 1997); or the essays in *The Book of Leviticus: Composition and Reception*, Rolf Rendtorff and Robert Kugler, eds. (Leiden, NLD: Brill, 2003). On the prohibition of sex between men, see Saul Olyan's "'And With a Male You Shall Not Lie the Lying Down of a Woman': On the Meaning and Significance of Leviticus 18:22 and 20:13," *Journal of the History of Sexuality* 5 (1994): 179-206.

25. "Prostitution as Metaphor" is taken from *The Holy Bible: New International Version* (Grand Rapids, MI: Zondervan Bible, 1978), 901-3 (Ezekiel 16: 1-42).

There are many commentaries on Ezekiel, as on all of the books of the Bible; perhaps an interesting one is the psychological approach by David J. Halperin, *Seeking Ezekiel: Text and Psychology* (University Park, PA: Pennsylvania State University Press, 1993). On this passage in particular, see M.G. Swanepoel's "Ezekiel 16: Abandoned Child, Bride Adorned or Unfaithful Wife?" in *Among the Prophets: Language, Image and Structure in the Prophetic Writings*, Philip R. Davies and David Clines, eds. (Sheffield, UK: JSOT, 1993). Generally on the metaphor of the unfaithful wife in the Bible, see the essays in *A Feminist Companion to the Latter Prophets*, Athalya Brenner, ed. (Sheffield, UK: Sheffield Academic Press, 1995). On sacred prostitution in ancient Israel, there is much debate, but a recent contribution is Phyllis Bird's "'To Play the Harlot': An Inquiry into an Old Testament Metaphor," in *Gender and Difference in Ancient Israel*, Peggy Day, ed. (Minneapolis: Fortress, 1989), reprinted in *Missing Persons and Mistaken Identities: Women and Gender in Ancient Israel* (Minneapolis, MN: Fortress, 1997). See also note 26.

26. "Herodotus on Sacred Prostitution" is taken from Herodotus, *The Histories*, Aubrey de Selincourt, trans. (Harmondsworth, UK: Penguin, 1954), 120-22.

There is much debate on the nature, extent, and even existence of sacred prostitution. For some of the debates, see Eugene Fisher's "Cultic Prostitution in the Ancient Near East? A Reassessment," *Biblical Theology Bulletin* 6 (1976): 225-36; Joan Westenholz's "Tamar, *Qedesa*, *Qadistu*, and Sacred Prostitution in Mesopotamia," *Harvard Theological Review* 82 (1989): 245-66; Mayer Gruber's "The Hebrew *Qedesah* and Her Canaanite and Akkadian Cognates," in *The Motherhood of God and Other Studies* (Atlanta, GA: Scholars, 1992); Richard Henshaw's *Female and Male: The Cultic Personnel: The Bible and the Ancient Near East* (Allison Park, PA: Pickwick, 1994); Mary Beard and John Henderson's "With This Body I Thee Worship: Sacred Prostitution in Antiquity," in *Gender and the Body in the Ancient Mediterranean*, Maria Wyke, ed. (Oxford: Blackwell, 1998); or Julia Assante's "From Whores to Hierodules: The Historiographic Invention of Mesopotamian Female Sex Professionals," in *Ancient Art and its Historiography*, A. A. Donahue and Mark Fullerton, eds. (Cambridge: Cambridge University Press, 2003). See note 25 for more on prostitution in ancient Israel, note 27 on male sacred prostitutes, and note 8 for more on Herodotus.

27. "Pseudo-Lucian on Ritual Castration" is taken from Pseudo-Lucian, *The Syrian Goddess (De Dea Syria)*, Harold Attridge and Robert Oden, trans. (Missoula, MT: Scholars/University of Montana Printing Department, 1976), 13, 15, 23, 37, 39, 55.

On the practice of ritual self-castration in the ancient Mediterranean, see Will Roscoe, "Priests of the Goddess: Gender Transgression in Ancient Religion," *History of Religions* 35 (1996): 195-230, which provides a nice overview; for more scholarly details, see Maarten J. Vermaseren, *Cybele and Attis: The Myth and the Cult* (London: Thames and Hudson, 1977); or the various essays in *Cybele, Attis and Related Cults: Essays in Memory of M.J. Vermaseren*, Eugene Lane, ed. (Leiden, NLD: E.J. Brill, 1996). Connected to this practice is the possibility of male sacred prostitution, an even more hotly debated subject than female sacred prostitution. For denials of the practice in ancient Israel, see Phyllis Bird's "The End of the Male Cult Prostitute: A Literary-Historical and Sociological Analysis of Hebrew *qades-qedesim*," in *Supplements to Vetus Testamentum*, vol. 66, J.A. Emerton, ed. (Leiden, NLD: E.J. Brill, 1997); and Mayer Gruber's "The *qades* in the Book of Kings and Other Sources," *Tarbiz* 52 (1983): 167-76.

28. "Apuleius on Eunuchs" is taken from Apuleius, *The Golden Ass*, E.J. Kenney, trans. (London: Penguin, 1998), 143-45, with slight changes.

See note 27 on ritual self-castration and male sacred prostitution. On eunuch priests in the Mediterranean in the Roman era, see Mary Beard's "The Roman and the Foreign: The Cult of the 'Great Mother' in Imperial Rome," in *Shamanism, History, and the State*, N. Thomas and C. Humphrey, eds. (Ann Arbor, MI: University of Michigan Press, 1994). Much of *The Golden Ass* provides an entertaining glimpse into Roman sexuality; it includes, for example, the legend of Cupid and Psyche. See Fergus Millar's "The World of *The Golden Ass*," *Journal of Roman Studies* 71 (1981): 63-75. For other interesting fictional tales from antiquity, most of what are called the Ancient Greek Romances, would be entertaining and informative reading; for an introduction to these texts, see Thomas Hägg's *The Novel in Antiquity* (Oxford: B. Blackwell, 1983).

29. "Lactantius on Sexual Difference" is taken from *Lactantius: The Minor Works*, Mary Francis MacDonald, ed. and trans. (Washington, DC: Catholic University of America Press, 1965), 38-41.

The most thorough analysis of theories of gender difference in the ancient Mediterranean is Prudence Allen's *The Concept of Woman: The Aristotelian Revolution, 750 B.C.—A.D. 1250* (Montreal: Eden, 1985). See also Lesley Dean-Jones's *Women's Bodies in Classical Greek Science* (Oxford: Oxford University Press, 1994); or Helen King's *Hippocrates' Woman: Reading the Female Body in Ancient Greece* (New York: Routledge, 1998). For the Roman era, see the first chapters of Aline Rousselle's *Porneia: On Desire and the Body in Antiquity*, F. Pheasant, trans. (Oxford: Basil Blackwell, 1988); or Rebecca Flemming's *Medicine and the Making of Roman Women: Gender and Authority from Celsus to Galen* (Oxford: Oxford University Press, 2000). Many Roman medical ideas depended on earlier Greek ones, as would later Christian and Islamic ones. Comparative information must be sought through general scholarly works on ancient Egyptian, Chinese, or Indian medicine. Some ancient specialized works survive and have been translated, such as Soranus of Ephesus's *Gynecology*, Owsei Temkin, trans. (Baltimore, MD: Johns Hopkins Press, 1956), but most ancient medical texts are dry, of a general nature, and would be difficult to incorporate into a history of sexuality.

CHAPTER 4

PUBLIC AND PRIVATE SEXUALITY

One thing is essential to keep in mind when studying the history of sexuality: We can never know exactly what goes on behind closed doors. There is always a difference between the sexuality that is visible, open, and public and the sexuality that is invisible, hidden, and private. A careful look at primary sources can demonstrate how central a feature this difference can be and how it changes the way we read historical writings about sex.

Most of us are familiar with the discrepancy between public and private sexuality from the modern gay rights movement. Being "in the closet," first used to describe gay men and lesbians who refuse to acknowledge their sexual orientation to themselves or to others, has become such a cliché that it is used in a variety of situations, in part because it is such a useful shorthand for talking about a hidden part of oneself or someone else. But this difference between a public persona and the private self is a crucial concept for the history of sexuality because no matter what we can learn about past individuals and their lives, including their sex lives, a part of them will always remain concealed, and we can never be certain that we understand them fully or clearly.

This discrepancy can be imagined in a variety of ways. We might know that certain historical figures were married and perhaps even some facts associated with their marital relationship: how they met, for how long and how many times they were married, whether they had children, and if so, how many. But we will never be able to know some things: why they decided to get married, how happily married they were, whether their children were planned or accidental, and whether childlessness was the result of a choice or not. This sort of information is not likely to be retained in the historical record for even the most famous of public figures, especially those who lived in the distant past. Even if we have a diary or letters from those persons, we cannot be sure that they told the truth when describing these personal facts or if they themselves understood the real reasons for their actions. Likewise, even if some aspects of their private sexuality leaked out in rumors or innuendoes or were thrown open in scandals or exposés, with details that get preserved in historical accounts, we still cannot be certain that such historical gossip is accurate.

Just because these aspects of an individual's private sexuality are difficult to know and impossible to know definitively, it does not mean that they are not worth exploring. In some ways, these hidden parts are often the most fascinating, and that is perhaps why historians often like to speculate about them, even if they have only the slimmest of facts. Having learned about the actions performed by individuals in the past, we would often like to know more about their motivations and feelings about them. We have to be prepared, however, to leave such questions unanswered or allow room for a range of possible answers. That may not be a satisfactory result to some, but it is at least an honest one.

The discrepancy between public and private sexuality is especially important when thinking about the relationship between the individuals who lived in the past and their societies. Given that all societies have organized sexuality into categories of licit and illicit behaviors, there are serious social pressures that attempt to channel the individual's sexual interests and expressions in approved directions. Those who differed from the norm, whose actions were not approved, may have sought to assume a more respectable public persona. Social pressure may have been enough to make those individuals stop acting in disapproved ways, but their illicit desires remained even if they did not act on them.

Again, there may not be much of a historical record of such dissent from the norm. Individuals who are seeking to hide actions from the public eye are unlikely to publicize their behaviors or desires, unless their dissent is important enough to them or if they feel they might allude to it indirectly. Others may note that dissent, casually, approvingly, or in hostile denunciation. This sort of commentary we might see in the historical record, but perhaps the best sources for such dissent are the prohibitions of legal or religious codes, since no prohibition exists unless someone wants to do what is prohibited.

The concept of honor, central to the sexual customs of many ancient societies, is very much related to this discussion of public and private sexuality. If dissent from social and sexual norms brings dishonor, then honor can be found in compliance to those norms. In other words, an honorable person, at least in sexual terms, is one whose private sexuality matches the public sexuality that is expected. We can see this concept of honor at work especially in patriarchal societies in the lives of women, who were often deemed honorable if they followed closely the ideals set for them by men. Men's honor in patriarchal societies not only stemmed from their own compliance with society's sexual rules but also can be seen in their willingness and ability to force the women under their control to be honorable. According to a patriarchal understanding, then, a woman's dishonor reflected badly not just on her but on the man who was responsible for her. The work of anthropologist Julian Pitt-Rivers, who pioneered the use of honor as a determining value in the study of societies, especially in gender relationships, is often cited by historians working in this field.

Recognizing the individual's relationship to sexual norms is crucial in studying the history of sexuality. Understanding why sexual customs developed and how they differed from one society to the next is important, as is how individuals responded to those customs. The following sources all address aspects of this essential relationship between the individual and his or her society.

30. FRAGMENTS OF SAPPHO'S POEMS

Time: seventh century BCE
Place: Greece
Author: Sappho

Only fragments of Sappho's poems survive; most were destroyed by later intellectuals who condemned her association with sexual dissent, especially lesbianism. (Indeed, it is from the island of Lesbos, where Sappho lived, that the word "lesbian" is derived and "Sapphic," a less common synonym.) It is difficult to interpret Sappho's poems definitively, especially since so few pieces of them survive and virtually nothing is known about her life. The fragments excerpted below do express a strong love for women—such as the fragment to Atthis. Some poems may even have described eroticism directly, including the fragment from "The Virgin," in which some have interpreted the "sweet apple" as the clitoris.

Love—bittersweet, irrepressible—
loosens my limbs and I tremble.
Yet, Atthis, you despise my being.
To chase Andromeda, you leave me.

May you find sleep on a
soft girlfriend's breast.

"The Virgin"

Like a sweet apple reddening on the high
tip of the topmost branch and forgotten
by the pickers—no, beyond their reach.
Like a hyacinth crushed in the mountains

by shepherds; lying trampled on the earth
yet blooming purple.

All the while, believe me, I prayed
our night would last twice as long.

Safe now. I've flown to you
like a child to its mother.

I will never find again honey or the honey
bee.

Questions for Reflection and Discussion

What indications exist in the poems as to the nature of Sappho's desire? Is that desire sexual or affectionate? Could it be both? Would the existence of erotic poems written to men preclude Sappho's erotic interest in women?

31. AUGUSTINE'S DENUNCIATIONS IN *THE CITY OF GOD*

Time: fifth century CE
Place: north Africa in the Roman Empire
Author: Augustine of Hippo

The City of God was an attempt in writing to persuade the pagan Romans to convert to Christianity. In this work, Augustine ridiculed and condemned various features of the pagan religions, including sacred prostitution and religious self-castration. He complained especially about the public nature of these sexual rites when, in his opinion, the behaviors should not even be committed in private.

The fact is that there comes a time when the vilest of women grow tired of the crowds of lovers they have acquired to gratify their sensuality; and in the same way the debauched soul which has prostituted itself to filthy spirits takes the greatest delight in the multiplicity of gods before whom to fall and offer itself for defilement; but in the end comes disgust.… The Great Mother has for servants the mutilated *Galli*, to signify that those who lack seed should devote themselves to the earth. Is that so? Was it not rather the devotion to her service that robbed them of seed? Do they acquire seed by attending on this goddess because they lack it? Or do they rather lose the seed they have by reason of that attendance? … The same applies to the effeminates consecrated to the Great Mother, who violate every canon of decency in men and women. They were to be seen until just the other day in the streets and squares of Carthage with their pomaded hair and powdered faces, gliding along with womanish languor, and demanding from the shopkeepers the means of their depraved existence.… The Great Mother of the gods introduced eunuchs even in the temples of Rome. And she kept up this savage custom, since it was supposed that she increased the virility of the Romans by depriving these men of their manhood.

Questions for Reflection and Discussion

What is it about sacred prostitutes and the eunuchs known as *Galli* that so angers Augustine? How is the critique of their sexual morality related to a critique of their sexual ambiguity? Does it seem that Augustine expects support for his opinions?

32. THE RAPE OF LUCRETIA

Time: first century CE
Place: Italy in the Roman Empire
Author: Livy

In his historical account of Rome, Livy included several episodes that, if their historical basis is sketchy, at least provided him with an opportunity to portray old-fashioned Roman values. A famous episode is the rape of Lucretia, which Livy *described as the beginning of the overthrow of the Roman kings and the establishment of democracy in Rome, and so there is a definite critique of a government that would allow sexual crimes to take place. There is an equal emphasis, however, on personal honor, which must attempt to integrate public and private sexuality.*

They were drinking one day in the quarters of Sextus Tarquinius—Collatinus, son of Egerius, was also present—when someone chanced to mention the subject of wives. Each of them, of course, extravagantly praised his own; and the rivalry got hotter and hotter, until Collatinus suddenly cried: "Stop! What need is there of words, when in a few hours we can prove beyond doubt the incomparable superiority of my Lucretia? We are all young and strong: why shouldn't we ride to Rome and see with our own eyes what kind of women our wives are? There is no better evidence, I assure you, than what a man finds when he enters his wife's room unexpectedly."

They had all drunk a good deal, and the proposal appealed to them; so they mounted their horses and galloped off to Rome. They reached the city as dusk was falling; and there the wives of the royal princes were found enjoying themselves with a group of young friends at a dinner party, in the greatest luxury. The riders then went on to Collatinus' house, where they found Lucretia very differently employed: it was already late at night, but there, in the hall of her house, surrounded by her busy maidservants, she was still hard at work by lamplight upon her spinning. Which wife had won the contest in womanly virtue was no longer in doubt.

With all courtesy Lucretia rose to bid her husband and the princes welcome, and Collatinus, pleased with his success, invited his friends to sup with him. It was at that fatal supper that Lucretia's beauty and proven chastity kindled in

Sextus Tarquinius the flame of lust, and determined him to debauch her. Nothing further occurred that night. The little jaunt was over, and the young men rode back to camp.

A few days later Sextus, without Collatinus' knowledge, returned with one companion to Collatia, where he was hospitably welcomed in Lucretia's house, and, after supper, escorted, like the honored visitor he was thought to be, to the guest chamber. Here he waited till the house was asleep, and then, when all was quiet, he drew his sword and made his way to Lucretia's room determined to rape her. She was asleep. Laying his left hand on her breast, "Lucretia," he whispered, "not a sound! I am Sextus Tarquinius. I am armed—if you utter a word, I will kill you." Lucretia opened her eyes in terror; death was imminent, no help at hand. Sextus urged his love, begged her to submit, pleaded, threatened, used every weapon that might conquer a woman's heart. But all in vain; not even the fear of death could bend her will. "If death will not move you," Sextus cried, "dishonor shall. I will kill you first, then cut the throat of a slave and lay his naked body by your side. Will they not believe that you have been caught in adultery with a servant—and paid the price?" Even the most resolute chastity could not have stood against this dreadful threat.

Lucretia yielded. Sextus enjoyed her, and rode away, proud of his success.

The unhappy girl wrote to her father in Rome and to her husband, who were away, urging them both to come at once with a trusted friend and quickly, for a frightful thing had happened…. They found Lucretia sitting in her room, in deep distress. Tears rose to her eyes as they entered, and to her husband's question, "Is it well with you?" she answered, "No. What can be well with a woman who has lost her honor? In your bed is the impress of another man. My body only has been violated. My heart is inno-

cent, and death will be my witness. Give me your solemn promise that the adulterer shall be punished—he is Sextus Tarquinius. He came last night as my enemy disguised as my guest, and took his pleasure of me. That pleasure will be my death—and his, too, if you are men."

The promise was given. One after another they tried to comfort her. They told her she was helpless, and therefore innocent; that he alone was guilty. It was the mind, they said, that sinned, not the body: without intention there could never be guilt. "What is due to *him*," Lucretia said, "is for you to decide. As for me I am innocent of fault, but I will take my punishment. Never shall Lucretia provide a precedent for unchaste women to escape what they deserve." With these words she drew a knife from under her robe, drove it into her heart, and fell forward, dead.

Questions for Reflection and Discussion

In what sense does Lucretia's honor depend on ensuring that the public and private aspects of her sexuality mirror each other? What else contributes to her honor? How is the honor of men affected by the rape of Lucretia? What criticisms are implied about other women in this story and the discrepancies between public and private sexuality?

33. SUETONIUS ON AUGUSTUS AND CALIGULA

Time: second century CE
Place: Italy in the Roman Empire
Author: Suetonius

The historian Suetonius composed his historical accounts of the early Roman emperors also in part as models of good and bad behavior. In his life of Caesar Augustus, the first emperor, Suetonius contrasted the public sexuality of the

[First, some excerpts from the life of Augustus.]

He revised existing laws and enacted some new ones, for example, on extravagance, on adultery and chastity, on bribery, and on the encouragement of marriage among the various classes of citizens. Having made somewhat more stringent changes in the last of these than in the others, he was unable to carry it out because of an open revolt against its provisions, until he had abolished or mitigated a part of the penalties, besides increasing the rewards and allowing a three years' exemption from the obligation to marry after the death of a husband or wife. When the [men of the lower nobility, called] knights even then persistently called for its repeal at a public show, he sent for the children of Germanicus and exhibited them, some in his own lap and some in their father's, intimating by his gestures and expression that they should not refuse to follow the young man's example. And on finding that the spirit of the law was being evaded by betrothal with immature girls and by frequent changes of wives, he shortened the duration of betrothals and set a limit on divorce....

In his youth he was betrothed to the daughter of Publius Servilius Isauricus, but when he became reconciled with Antony after their first quarrel, and their troops begged that the rivals be further united by some tie of kinship, he took to wife Antony's stepdaughter Claudia, daughter of Fulvia by Publius Clodius, although she was barely of marriageable age; but because of a falling out with his mother-in-law Fulvia, he divorced her before they had begun to live together. Shortly after that he married Scribonia, who had been wedded before to two ex-consuls, and was a mother by one of them. He divorced her also, "unable to put up with her shrewish disposition," as he himself writes, and at once took Livia Drusilla from her husband Tiberius Nero, although she was with child at the time; and he loved and esteemed her to the end without a rival.

By Scribonia he had a daughter Julia, by Livia no children at all, although he earnestly desired issue. One baby was conceived, but was prematurely born. He gave Julia in marriage first to Marcellus, son of his sister Octavia and hardly more than a boy, and then after his death to Marcus Agrippa, prevailing upon his sister to yield her son-in-law to him; for at that time Agrippa had to wife one of the Marcellas and had children from her. When Agrippa also died, Augustus, after considering various alliances for a long time, even in the equestrian order, finally chose his stepson Tiberius, obliging him to divorce his wife, who was with child and by whom he was already a father. Mark Antony writes that Augustus first betrothed his daughter to his son Antonius and then to Cotiso, king of the Getae, at the same time asking for the hand of the king's daughter for himself in turn.

From Agrippa and Julia he had three grandsons, Gaius, Lucius, and Agrippa, and two granddaughters, Julia and Agrippina.... In bringing up his daughter and his granddaughters he even had them taught spinning and weaving, and he forbade them to say or do anything except openly and such as might be recorded in the household diary. He was most strict in keeping them from meeting strangers, once writing to Lucius Vinicius, a young man of good position and character: "You have acted presumptuously in coming to Baiae to call on my daughter." He taught his grandsons reading, swimming, and the other elements of education, for the most part himself....

But at the height of his happiness and his confidence in his family and its training, Fortune proved fickle. He found the two Julias, his daughter and granddaughter, guilty of every form of vice, and banished them. He lost Gaius and Lucius within the span of eighteen months, for the former died in Lycia and the latter at Massilia. He then publicly adopted his third grandson Agrippa ... but he soon disowned Agrippa because of his low tastes and violent temper, and sent him off to Surrentum.... He informed the senate of his daughter's fall through a letter read in his absence by a *quaestor*, and for very shame would meet no one for a long time, and even thought of putting her to death.... After Julia was banished, he denied her the use of wine and every form of luxury, and would not allow any man, bond or free, to come near her without his permission, and then not without being informed of his stature, complexion, and even of any marks or scars upon his body. It was not until five years later that he moved her from the island to the mainland and treated her with somewhat less rigor. But he could not by any means be prevailed upon to recall her [to Rome] altogether, and when the Roman people several times interceded for her and urgently pressed their suit, he in open assembly called upon the gods to curse them with like daughters and like wives. He would not allow the child born to his granddaughter Julia after her sentence to be recognized or reared.

[Next, a few excerpts from the life of Caligula.]

He lived in habitual incest with all his sisters, and at a large banquet he placed each of them in turn below him, while his wife reclined above. Of these he is believed to have violated Drusilla when he was still a minor, and even to have been caught lying with her by his grandmother Antonia, at whose house they were brought up in company. Afterwards, when she was the wife of Lucius Cassius Longinus, an ex-consul, he took her from him and openly treated her as his lawful wife; and when ill, he made her heir to his property and the throne.... The rest of his sisters he did not love with so great affection, nor honor so highly, but often prostituted them to his favorites; so that he was the readier at the trial of Aemilius Lepidus to condemn them, as adulteresses....

It is not easy to decide whether he acted more basely in contracting his marriages, in annulling them, or as a husband. At the marriage of Livia Orestilla to Gaius Piso, he attended the ceremony himself, gave orders that the bride be taken to his own house, and within a few days divorced her; two years later he banished her, because of a suspicion that in the meantime she had gone back to her former husband.... When the statement was made that the grandmother of Lollia Paulina, who was married to Gaius Memmius, an ex-consul commanding armies, had once been a remarkably beautiful woman, he suddenly called Lollia from the province, separated her from her husband, and married her; then in a short time he put her away, with the command never to have intercourse with anyone....

He respected neither his own chastity nor that of anyone else. He is said to have had unnatural relations with Marcus Lepidus, the pantomimic actor Mnester, and certain hostages. Valerius Catullus, a young man of consular family, publicly proclaimed that he had violated the emperor and worn himself out in his dealings with him…. There was scarcely any woman of rank whom he did not approach. These as a rule he invited to dinner with their husbands, and as they passed by the foot of his couch, he would inspect them critically and deliberately, as if buying slaves, even putting out his hand and lifting up the face of anyone who looked down in modesty; then as often as the fancy took him he would leave the room, sending for the one who pleased him best, and returning soon afterward with evident signs of what had occurred, he would openly commend or criticize his partner, recounting her charms or defects and commenting on her conduct.

Questions for Reflection and Discussion

What might Suetonius's point have been in damning the memory of Augustus and Caligula? What might the relationship be between sexual irregularity and the exercise of political power? Did absolute authority create sexual excess or did the dislike of political authority find expression in accusations of sexual crimes?

34. MARTIAL'S EPIGRAMS

Time: first century CE
Place: Italy in the Roman Empire
Author: Martial

Martial was famous around Rome—or infamous is probably better—for his scathing and yet humorous poems of the type known as epigrams. Martial loved to point out the hypocrisy of both men and women who acted one way in public and another in private. There is a playful tone to Martial's poems, however, and he mocked himself almost as often as he mocked others.

We all know Galla's services as a whore
Cost two gold bits; throw in a couple more
And you get the fancy extras too. Why, then,
does your bill, Aeschylus, amount to ten?
She sucks off for far less than that. What is it
You pay her for? Silence after your visit.

Either get out of the house or conform to my tastes, woman.
I'm no straitlaced old Roman.
I like prolonging the nights agreeably
with wine; you, after one glass of water,
Rise and retire with an air of hauteur.
You prefer darkness: I enjoy lovemaking
With a witness—a lamp shining or the dawn breaking.
You wear bedjackets, tunics, thick woolen stuff,
Whereas I think no woman on her back can ever be naked enough.
I love girls who kiss like doves and hang round my neck:
You give me the sort of peck
Due to your grandmother as a morning salute.
In bed, you're motionless, mute—
Not a wriggle,
Not a giggle—
As solemn as a priestess at a shrine
Proffering incense and pure wine.
Yet every time Andromache went for a ride
In Hector's room, the household slaves used to masturbate outside;
Even modest Penelope, when Ulysses snored,
Kept her hand on the sceptre of her lord.
You refuse to be buggered; but it's a known fact

That Gracchus', Pompey's and Brutus'
wives were willing partners in the act,
And that before Ganymede mixed Jupiter
his tasty bowl
Juno filled the dear boy's role.
If you want to be uptight, all right,
By all means play Lucretia by day. But I
need a Lais at night.

I wouldn't like you with tight curls
Nor yet too tousled. Both a girl's
Complexion and a gypsy's tan
Are unattractive in a man.
Beards, whether Phrygianly short
Or wild like those defendants sport,
Put me off, Pannychus, for I hate
The butch and the effeminate
Equally. As it is, your trouble
Is that despite the virile stubble
That mats your chest and furs your leg
Your mind's as hairless as an egg.

He favours drab, dark cloaks, he has a
passion
For wearing Baetic wool and grey; the
fashion
for scarlet he calls "degenerate,"
"un-Roman,"
And, as for mauve, that's "only fit for
women."
He's all for "Nature"; yet, though no one's
duller
In dress, his morals sport a different
color.
He may demand the grounds of my
suspicion.
We bathe together, and his line of vision
Keeps below waist level, he devours
With his eyes the boys under the showers,
And his lips twitch at the sight of a lus-
cious member.
Did you ask his name? How odd, I can't
remember!

Glossary of Terms

Andromache and Hector: characters from
   Homer's *Iliad*
Penelope and Ulysses: characters from
   Homer's *Odyssey*
Gracchus, Pompey, and Brutus: characters
   from Livy's Roman history
Ganymede, Jupiter, and Juno: Roman gods;
   according to myth, Zeus, who was mar-
   ried to Hera, snatched the mortal boy
   Ganymede to serve him sexually
Lucretia: a character from Livy's Roman his-
   tory, known for her sexual honor
Lais: a character from several Roman plays,
   who was a prostitute
Phrygian: refers to a region of the Roman
   Empire (in modern Turkey)
Baetic: refers to a region of the Roman
   Empire (in modern Spain)

Questions for Reflection and Discussion

What can be learned about the sexual tastes
of Martial and the aristocrats of Rome from
these poems? Is Martial really trying to reform
the Romans' sexual behavior? If not, what purpose did his epigrams serve?

35. SHAKUNTALA

Time: fifth century CE
Place: India
Author: Kalidasa

The Shakuntala *is an example of drama that
flourished in India in antiquity. Like ancient
Greek drama, it was drawn from mythology and
attempted to evoke strong emotions in its audience. This example is the story of a king who,
wandering in a forest while hunting, meets a
beautiful peasant girl named Shakuntala, who
is being raised by hermits at their* ashrama *(her-
mitage). He promises her marriage as his queen*

if she will love him, and she accepts, but when she travels back to the court to meet him, he does not remember her or at least pretends that he does not. Clearly, as this scene demonstrates, one of the character's honor is at stake.

The hermits, Sarngavara and Saradvata, enter, bringing Gautami and Shakuntala with them. The Chamberlain and a Priest attached to the royal household follow. Gautami places Shakuntala in front of her. At first the group stands at some distance from the King.

Sarngavara: This king is a fine man, Saradvata, and very gifted. The meanest of his subjects are well behaved. But I feel like a fish out of water with so many people around.

Saradvata: All hermits do in a city. I'm not very happy here myself. I've a trick though: I look on the people as the pure look on the impure, the waking on the sleeping, the free on the enslaved.

Shakuntala: I have a feeling it's not going to turn out right, Mother Gautami.

Gautami: There's nothing to worry about, Shakuntala.

Priest: The king is ready to receive you, O hermits. He will hear you standing.

Sarngavara: You honor us, sire. We are grateful to you, but your courtesy doesn't surprise us. Trees bend with fruits, the clouds with rain, and wealth brings humility to a good man.

Guard: You look happy, hermits. I hope your news is pleasant.

The King looks at Shakuntala and speaks in an aside to the Female Guard.

King: Who is that veiled lady? She stands out like a glistening bud among brown leaves.

Guard, aside: I couldn't say, sire. But she is very lovely.

King, aside: Hold your tongue. She may be married.

Shakuntala, aside: I must keep calm. I know he loves me.

Priest, advancing toward the King: They carry a message from their father, sire.

[They exchange pleasantries before the message is revealed.]

Sarngavara: "You fell in love with my daughter and married her," he says. "I approve of it, for you are known to be a man of honor, and she is devoted to you. When two excellent persons are brought together, there can be no blame. Take her now, for she is with child."

Gautami: I can add nothing to the message, sire. You are aware of the exceptional circumstances of the case. She kept her love to herself; you didn't tell us either. It's difficult for a third person to interfere with a private arrangement.

Shakuntala, aside: What can he possibly say to that?

King: I don't understand.

Shakuntala, aside: There is anger in his voice.

Sarngavara: We don't either. You know the custom, sire. We cannot keep her in the ashrama. We know she is pure, but what will people say? A wife must stay with her husband.

King: Are you implying that I'm married to her?

Shakuntala, aside: I was afraid of this.

Sarngavara: You may have made a mistake, but duty comes first to a king.

King: You're presumptuous.

Sarngavara: I do not like the tone of your voice, sire. You speak like one drunk with power.

King: You insult me.

Gautami, to Shakuntala: Come here, child—take off the veil. That may jog your husband's memory.

> *Shakuntala removes her veil.*
> *The King looks at her fixedly.*

King, aside: I can't remember a thing. Until I do I can neither take nor leave her, for she is very beautiful.

> *The King continues to stare at Shakuntala without speaking.*

Sarngavara: Why are you silent, sire?

King: I am sorry, but I remember nothing, certainly not the marriage you speak of. You must excuse me if I refuse to think of myself as an adulterer.

Shakuntala, aside: I am lost. He can't even remember what happened.

[Shakuntala tries to speak to the king.]

Shakuntala, aside: What can I possibly say that will change his mind? *She speaks aloud, hesitantly:* My husband … *She falters and speaks to herself:* But he says he never married me. *Again she summons her courage:* It is not right, O Puru, to reject so soon the girl you loved in the *ashrama* …

King, covering his ears: This is impossible! Why must you drag my ancestral name into it?

Shakuntala: If you think I am someone else's wife, this gift may remind you that I'm not.

King: Gift?

Shakuntala, touching her finger: Oh, no! Oh, no! The ring … it's gone!

> *Terrified, she looks at Gautami.*

Gautami: It must have slipped from your finger while you were bathing in the Ganges.

King, smiling: A fertile imagination—women are famous for it.

Shakuntala: Fate has intervened. But I can tell you some of the things we did. Then you will remember.

King: From rings to incidents!

Shakuntala: You remember the day you brought a lotus leaf filled with water …

King: Go on.

Shakuntala: And you offered it to Dhirgapangha, my adopted fawn, but he wouldn't drink it, for you were strange to the place; and when I gave him the water, he drank it immediately; and you said, "He trusts you, you both belong to the forest"?

King: Very pretty. That's the way painted girls trap a man.

Gautami: You're unfair, sire. You know she belongs to an *ashrama* and knows nothing of deceit.

King: I am not so sure, Mother. I find even the innocent birds very cunning. The cuckoo, for instance—she has her eggs hatched by others.

Shakuntala, in anger: Must you judge everyone by own small selfish heart? You are like a well that grass has grown over. Who will respect only a mask of virtue?

King, aside: Her anger seems genuine. Her eyes are red, and these are hard quick words. She looks straight into my eyes: her lip quivers and her eyebrows curve like bows.…

Shakuntala: So I am unchaste! You tricked me—you, a Puru!—honey-mouthed and poison-hearted! *She covers her face and weeps.*

Sarngavara: This is the inevitable result of rashness. Those who marry in secret should know each other well before doing so.… *To the King:* She is your wife, sire. Take her or leave her.… Lead the way, Gautami. *They start to leave.*

Shakuntala: And leave me behind? Rejected
  by him, and now by you? *She follows.*
Gautami, stopping: Let us take Shakuntala
  with us, Sarngavara. It's not her fault he
  won't accept her.
Sarngavara, turning in sudden anger: Never!
  Stay where you are! …
Shakuntala: If only the earth could open up
  and swallow me!

Questions for Reflection and Discussion

How does this scene emphasize the discrepancies between public and private sexuality?
How does it emphasize notions of men's and
women's honor? Why is the final comment
by Shakuntala—an allusion to the Ramayana
(excerpted in source 14)—significant?

36. HAREM LIFE FROM THE *KAMASUTRA*

Time: third century CE
Place: India
Author: Vatsyayana

The Kamasutra *("Book of Pleasure"), perhaps
the most famous historical source on sexuality, is mostly a manual for men: how to seduce
virgins or other men's wives, how to marry properly, and even how to enlarge one's own penis,
as well as sex techniques (all clearly aimed at
male readers). In a few sections, however, the*
Kamasutra *provides glimpses into a world seldom discussed in ancient literature: the world
of the harem, the enclosed space for the many
wives of high-status men in ancient India and in
other ancient societies. How common the experiences of these women were for other women
in polygamous marriages is hard to say. The
places mentioned in this excerpt are the different regions of India.*

The women of the harem cannot meet men,
because they are carefully guarded; and since
they have only one husband shared by many
women in common, they are not satisfied.
Therefore they give pleasure to one another
with the following techniques. They dress up
a foster-sister or girlfriend or servant girl like
a man and relieve their desire with dildoes or
with bulbs, roots, or fruits that have that form.
They lie on statues of men that have distinct
sexual characteristics…. The women of the
harem generally get their women servants to
bring in men-about-town dressed as women.
Their foster-sisters, too, if they are intimate
with the women on the inside, may make an
effort to accost these men, showing them what
a future there is in it. They describe how easy
it is to enter, the place where they can get out,
the spaciousness of the building, the careless-
ness of the guards, and the irregularities of the
entourage…. Among the people of the far West,
women who have business in the royal court
are the ones who bring likely looking men into
the harem, because they are not well guarded.
The Abhira women get what they want from
the guards of the harem themselves, the ones
who call themselves Warriors. The Vatsagulma
women bring in, together with errand girls, the
sons of men-about-town dressed in the girls'
clothing. The Vidarbha women use their own
sons, who move freely in and out of the harem,
each excepting the son she gave birth to. The
women who rule their own country use their
own kinsmen and relatives, who enter the harem
in the same way, but no other men. The women
of Gauda use Brahmins, friends, servants, attendants, and houseboys. The women of Sindh use
doormen, artisans, and any other men of that
sort who are not prevented from entering the
harem. The men of the Himalayas boldly bribe
the guard with money and enter *en masse.* In
Vanga, Anga, and Kalinga, the Brahmins of the
city, under the pretext of bringing flowers, go to

the harem with the king's full knowledge. They chat with the women from behind a curtain. Once they have met like that, they get together. In the East, nine or ten women *en masse* conceal one young man at a time…. That is the life of the women of the harem.

Questions for Reflection and Discussion

How seriously is such an exposé of the harem to be taken? How much are such speculations either male fantasies or male anxieties? Why bring the different regions of India into such an account?

37. MOCHE DRINKING CUP

Time: some time in the millennium before
  the eighth century CE
Place: what is modern Peru
Artist: unknown

The display of sexual acts in art is one way of challenging the boundaries between public and private sexuality. One ancient people, the Moche of early Peru, were known for their erotic art. These sculptures may have had a religious purpose, connected to some fertility cult, since the figures engage in various sex acts—masturbation, fellatio, oral and anal intercourse—except vaginal intercourse, which is never depicted. But there may have been an element of humor involved in the making of sculpted objects like the drinking cup on the right, since to drink out of it, one must take the liquid out of the end of the penis and simulate fellatio (if one tried to drink out of the top of the cup, the liquid would spill out of the holes in the headdress).

Questions for Reflection and Discussion

How does erotic art confront the boundaries between public and private sexuality?

What might be a ritual or religious purpose to such a drinking cup? How might its meaning change if we knew that the man seated was a god or a king?

38. *THE TALE OF GENJI*

Time: tenth century CE
Place: Japan
Author: Murasaki Shikibu

Although not an ancient source, this excerpt from one of the most famous stories of early Japan fits neatly into this discussion of private and public sexuality. Murasaki Shikibu was an educated Japanese noblewoman who lived and wrote during the Heian era. In this excerpt from the first part of her famous novel, a young man named Genji listens to advice from the older and more experienced To no Chujo and Uma no Kami on the discrepancies between ideals and realities in romance.

… said To no Chujo, and he continued: "I have at last discovered that there exists no woman of whom one can say 'Here is perfection. This is indeed she.' There are many who have the superficial art of writing a good running hand, or if occasion requires of making a quick repartee. But there are few who will stand the ordeal of any further test. Usually their minds are entirely occupied by admiration for their own accomplishments, and their abuse of all rivals creates a most unpleasant impression. Some again are adored by over-fond parents. These have been since childhood guarded behind lattice windows and no knowledge of them is allowed to reach the outer-world, save that of their excellence in some accomplishment or art; and this may indeed sometimes arouse our interest. She is pretty and graceful and has not yet mixed at all with the world. Such a girl by closely copying some model and applying herself with great industry will often succeed in really mastering one of the minor and ephemeral arts. Her friends are careful to say nothing of her defects and to exaggerate her accomplishments, and while we cannot altogether trust their praise we cannot believe that their judgment is entirely astray. But when we take steps to test their statements we are invariably disappointed."

He paused, seeming to be slightly ashamed of the cynical tone which he had adopted, and added "I know my experience is not large, but that is the conclusion I have come to so far." … The conversation went on. Many persons and things were discussed. Uma no Kami contended that perfection is equally difficult to find in other spheres. "The sovereign is hard put to it to choose his ministers. But he at least has an easier task than the husband, for he does not entrust the affairs of his kingdom to one, two or three persons alone, but sets up a whole system of superiors and subordinates. But when the mistress of a house is to be selected, a single individual must be found who will combine in her person many diverse qualities. It will not do to be too exacting. Let us be sure that the lady of our choice possesses certain tangible qualities which we admire; and if in other ways she falls short of our ideal, we must be patient and call to mind those qualities which first induced us to begin our courting.

"But even here we must beware; for there are some who in the selfishness of youth and flawless beauty are determined that not a dust-flick shall fall upon them. In their letters they choose the most harmless topics, but yet contrive to color the very texture of the written signs with a tenderness that vaguely disquiets us. But such a one, when we have at last secured a meeting, will speak so low that she can scarcely be heard, and the few sentences that she murmurs beneath her breath serve only to make her more mysterious than before. All this may seem to be the pretty shrinking of girlish modesty; but we may later find that what held her back was the very violence of her passions. Or again, where all seems plain sailing, the perfect companion will turn out to be too impressionable and will upon the most inappropriate occasions display her affections in so ludicrous a way that we begin to wish ourselves rid of her.

"Then there is the zealous housewife, who regardless of her appearance twists her hair behind her ears and devotes herself entirely to the details of our domestic welfare. The husband, in his comings and goings about the world, is certain to see and hear many things which he cannot discuss with strangers, but would gladly talk over with an intimate who could listen with sympathy and understanding, someone who could laugh with him or weep if need be. It often happens too that some political event will greatly perturb or amuse him, and he sits apart longing to tell someone about it. He suddenly laughs at some secret recollection or sighs audibly. But the wife only says lightly 'What is the matter?' and shows no interest...."

[To no Chujo replied,] "But when all is said and done, there can be no greater virtue in woman than this: that she should with gentleness and forbearance meet every wrong whatsoever that falls to her share." He thought as he said this of his own sister, Princess Aoi; but was disappointed and piqued to discover that Genji, whose comments he awaited, was fast asleep.

Questions for Reflection and Discussion

Is it possible to discern Murasaki Shikibu's attitude toward the sorts of men and women she described in her novel? Is she sympathetic to their dilemmas? What might be learned about the sexual customs of tenth-century Japan from this source and about contemporary attitudes toward the discrepancies between public and private sexuality?

39. THE DIARY OF LADY MURASAKI

Time: tenth century CE
Place: Japan
Author: Murasaki Shikibu

This excerpt comes from the same author as the previous source. In fact, her authorship of The Tale of Genji *brought fame to Murasaki Shikibu, to such an extent that she was invited to join the personal attendants of the Japanese empress and live at the imperial court. Her life there, however, proved less than exciting. She was one of countless attendants, many of whom came from far more prestigious families. In addition, as an attendant, she was expected to be present at—mostly to watch from a dis-tance—the endless rituals of court life. Finally, as a famous writer, she was also expected to be constantly charming and witty, and she found that tedious. In this excerpt from her diary, Murasaki describes her own attitude toward women's sexual behavior and the expectations of her society about that behavior.*

Her Majesty frowns on the slightest hint of seductive behavior as being the height of frivolity, so anyone who wants to be thought well of takes care never to seem too forward. Of course that is not to say we do not have women among us of quite a different persuasion, women who care nothing for being thought flirtatious and light-hearted and getting a bad name for themselves. The men strike up relationships with this kind of woman because they are such easy game.... Now it may seem that I pretend to know all there is to know about these women, but each one has her own personality and no one is particularly better or worse than anyone else. If they are good in one aspect, they are bad in another, it seems.... Her Majesty has gradually matured of late and now understands the ways of the world: that people have their good points and their bad, and that they sometimes go to excess and sometimes make mistakes.

Questions for Reflection and Discussion

To what does Murasaki attribute the different attitudes of individual women toward sex? How does the public appearance of these women relate to their private realities? Does this mark a change from the opinions that Murasaki wrote about in *The Tale of Genji*?

SOURCES AND FURTHER READING

I don't know any works that deal in a general manner with the discrepancies between public and private sexuality, although most discussions of sexuality in history incorporate insights on this point. On honor in traditional societies, among the best and most cited are works by anthropologists such as Julian Pitt-Rivers' *The Fate of Shechem, Or, The Politics of Sex: Essays in the Anthropology of the Mediterranean* (Cambridge: Cambridge University Press, 1977) on men's honor, or Lila Abu-Lughod's *Veiled Sentiments: Honor and Poetry in a Bedouin Society* (Berkeley, CA: University of California Press, 1986) on women's. On rape in ancient history, see the essays in *Rape in Antiquity*, Susan Deacy and Karen F. Pierce, eds. (London: Duckworth, 1997); or those in *Consent and Coercion to Sex and Marriage in Ancient and Medieval Societies*, Angeliki E. Laiou, ed. (Washington, DC: Dumbarton Oaks Research Library and Collection, 1993).

30. "Fragments of Sappho's Poems" are taken from *Sappho*, Willis Barnstone, trans. (Garden City, NY: Anchor Books, 1965), 25, 41, 43, 55, 83, 85.

Much has been written about Sappho, despite the virtually complete absence of any firm biographical details about her. The best efforts by modern scholars have typically analyzed the brief fragments of her poetry that do survive. See various essays in *Among Women: From the Homosocial to the Homoerotic in the Ancient World*, Nancy Sorkin Rabinowitz and Lisa Auanger, eds. (Austin, TX: University of Texas Press, 2002), which deal not only with the erotic in Sappho's poetry but the general parameters for same-sex eroticism among women in ancient Greece and Rome. Another good choice for historical context is *Making Silence Speak: Women's Voices in Greek Literature and Society*, Andre Lardinois and Laura McClure, eds. (Princeton, NJ: Princeton

University Press, 2001), which includes an essay on Sappho and several on other reconstructions of women's voices. More focused studies include Jane McIntosh Snyder's *Lesbian Desire in the Lyrics of Sappho* (New York: Columbia University Press, 1997) and Page DuBois's *Sappho is Burning* (Chicago: University of Chicago Press, 1995); another interesting study is Holt Parker's "Sappho Schoolmistress," *Transactions of the American Philological Association* 123 (1993): 309-51. Introductions to the many translations of Sappho's poems also discuss their significance.

31. "Augustine's Denunciations in *The City of God*" is taken from Augustine, *The City of God*, Henry Bettenson, trans. (Harmondsworth, UK: Penguin, 1972), 283-84, 286.

See note 18 for further readings on Augustine of Hippo, sources 26 and 27 on sacred prostitution and institutionalized castration, and source 66 for more on Augustine's views of sexuality. On *The City of God* itself, a good general commentary is Gerard O'Daly's, *Augustine's City of God: A Reader's Guide* (New York: Oxford University Press, 1999).

32. "The Rape of Lucretia" is taken from Livy, *The Early History of Rome*, Aubrey de Selincourt, trans. (London: Penguin, 1960), 97-99.

On Livy as historian, see Jane D. Chaplin's *Livy's Exemplary History* (New York: Oxford University Press, 2000); or Gary Forsythe's *Livy and Early Rome: A Study in Historical Method and Judgment* (Stuttgart: Franz Steiner, 1999); or Gary B. Miles's *Livy: Reconstructing Early Rome* (Ithaca, NY: Cornell University Press, 1995). On the significance of the rape episode, see Susanna Morton Braund's "Role Models for Roman

Women and Men in Livy" in *Latin Literature* (New York: Routledge, 2002), or Mary Beard's "The Erotics of Rape: Livy, Ovid and the Sabine Women" in *Female Networks and the Public Sphere in Roman Society*, Paivi Setala and Lusa Savunen, eds. (Rome: Institutum Romanum Finlandiae, 1999). On the afterlife of the episode in literature, see Ian Donaldson's *The Rapes of Lucretia: A Myth and Its Transformations* (Oxford: Clarendon Press, 1982); or Melissa M. Matthes's *The Rape of Lucretia and the Founding of Republics: Readings in Livy, Machiavelli, and Rousseau* (University Park, PA: Pennsylvania State University Press, 2000). For further readings on Roman women, see Judith Hallett's "Women in the Ancient Roman World," in *Women's Roles in Ancient Civilizations: A Reference Guide*, Bella Vivante, ed. (Westport, CT: Greenwood, 1999). Women figure so infrequently in Roman histories, like those of Livy and Tacitus (as well as those of Cassius Dio and Plutarch, who wrote in Greek but mostly about Romans), that their appearance in the text is usually significant and serves a larger moral purpose, and so is worth examining in these writers. For epic elegance, nothing surpasses Book 4 of Vergil's *Aeneid* that recounts the tragic love between Aeneas and Dido, a story that also revolves around the differences between duty and honor in men and women and that would be well worth reading in a history of sexuality.

33. "Suetonius on Augustus and Caligula" is taken from *Suetonius*, J.C. Rolfe, trans. (Cambridge, MA: Harvard University Press, 1951; orig. pub. 1913), 1: 177, 179, 217, 219, 221, 223, 441, 443, 461, with slight changes.

Further information on Suetonius may be found in Andrew Wallace-Hadrill's *Suetonius, the Scholar and his Caesars* (London: Duckworth, 1983). Further information on the life of Octavian, known as Caesar Augustus, may be found in Pat Southern's *Augustus* (New York: Routledge, 1999), the most recent of several biographies. On the era of Augustus, see Werner Eck's *The Age of Augustus*, Deborah Lucas Schneider, trans. (Malden, MA: Blackwell, 2003), again, one of a few similar works. Further readings on Augustus's attempts at marital reforms include P. Csillag's *The Augustan Laws on Family Relations* (Budapest: Akademiai Kiado, 1976); David Cohen's "The Augustan Law on Adultery: The Social and Cultural Context" in *The Family in Italy from Antiquity to the Present*, David I. Kertzer and Richard P. Saller, eds. (New Haven, CT: Yale University Press, 1991); Thomas McGinn's "Concubinage and the *Lex Iulia* on Adultery," *Transactions of the American Philological Association* 121 (1991): 335-75; or Leo Raditsa's "Augustus' Legislation Concerning Marriage, Procreation, Love Affairs and Adultery," *Aufstieg und Niedergang der Romischen Welt* 2:13 (1980): 278-339. For more background on Roman marriage, see Susan Treggiari's *Roman Marriage: Iusti Coniuges from the Time of Cicero to the Time of Ulpian* (Oxford: Clarendon Press, 1991). On Caligula, see Arther Ferrill's *Caligula: Emperor of Rome* (London: Thames and Hudson, 1991); or Anthony Barrett's *Caligula: The Corruption of Power* (New Haven, CT: Yale University Press, 1990). More details about and an analysis of Caligula's sexual excesses may be found in Stephen Barber and Jeremy Reed's *Caligula: Divine Carnage—Atrocities of the Roman Emperors* (London: Creation, 2000). See also Donna W. Hurley's *An Historical and Historiographical Commentary on Suetonius' Life of C. Caligula* (Atlanta, GA: Scholars Press, 1993). Other imperial biographers are fascinating to read, and most include similar details about the sex lives of the men who ruled Rome, especially the *Historia Augusta*, written in the late fourth or early fifth century CE and published in part as *Lives of the Later Caesars*, Anthony Birley, trans. (Harmondsworth, UK: Penguin, 1976). See also note 34 for more on Roman sexuality.

34. "Martial's Epigrams" is taken from Martial, *The Epigrams*, James Michie, trans. (Harmondsworth, UK: Penguin, 1972), 33, 47, 125, 171, 173.

On Martial's epigrams, see John Patrick Sullivan's *Martial, the Unexpected Classic: A Literary and Historical Study* (Cambridge: Cambridge University Press, 1991). An excellent study of Roman sexual humor generally is Amy Richlin's *The Garden of Priapus: Sexuality and Aggression in Roman Humor* (New Haven, CT: Yale University Press, 1983). More generally on Roman sexuality, see the various essays in *Roman Sexualities*, Judith P. Hallett and Marilyn B. Skinner, eds. (Princeton, NJ: Princeton University Press, 1997), which cover a broad range of topics and refer to other studies. On Roman customs of prostitution and pederasty, see Thomas A. McGinn's *Prostitution, Sexuality, and the Law in Ancient Rome* (New York: Oxford University Press, 1998) and Craig Williams's *Roman Homosexuality: Ideologies of Masculinity in Classical Antiquity* (New York: Oxford University Press, 1999), respectively. A number of Roman works deal frankly with various aspects of sexuality, including Juvenal's *Satires*, Ovid's *Art of Love*, and Catullus's poems, all available in several translations.

35. "Shakuntala" is taken from *Great Sanskrit Plays in Modern Translation*, P. Lal, trans. (Norfolk, CT: New Directions, 1957), 48-53.

See notes 4, 5 and 14 on women and sexual customs in ancient India. Some of the other plays translated in Lal's collection focus on obstacles to love, including Bhasa's "The Dream of Vasavadatta," Bhavabhuti's "The Later Story of Rama," and Harsha's "Ratnavali." Other works by Kalidasa have been translated into English and might be useful to study in a history of sexuality. These include *The Meghaduta* or *Transport of Love*, Leonard Nathan, trans. (Berkeley, CA: University of California Press, 1976), and *The Ritu-Samhara* or *Circle of the Seasons*, E. Powys Mathers, trans. (Berkshire, UK: Golden Cockerel, 1929). For a biography, see K. Krishnamoorthy's *Kalidasa* (New York: Twayne, 1972); and on the genre, see S.C. Bhatt's *Drama in Ancient India* (New Delhi: Amrit, 1961). *The Mahavamsa: The Great Chronicle of Sri Lanka*, Douglas Bullis, trans. (Fremont, CA: Asian Humanities, 1999) provides some interesting stories from the same period, if from the opposite end of India.

36. "Harem Life from the *Kamasutra*" is taken from Vatsyayana, *Kamasutra*, Wendy Doniger and Sudhir Kakar, trans. (Oxford: Oxford University Press, 2002), 125-29.

See notes 4, 5, and 14 on women and sexuality in ancient India. On the *Kamasutra*, see Haran Chandra Chakladar's *Social Life in Ancient India: Studies in Vatsyayana's Kamasutra* (Calcutta: Greater India Society, 1929), now somewhat out of date. In their introduction, Doniger and Kakar criticize the inaccuracies of older translations of the text, especially the most common Burton translation. The *Kamasutra* was only one of a number of erotic manuals circulating in ancient and medieval India; a later similar one is the *Kokashastra*, Alex Comfort, trans. (New York: Simon & Schuster, 1997).

37. "Moche Drinking Cup" is taken from Elizabeth Benson, *The Mochica: A Culture of Peru* (New York: Praeger, 1972), 145.

Only general works exist on the Moche, given the limited knowledge we have of their culture (even their name is a modern designation); what we have survives only as artwork and other material artifacts, since the Moche had no writing system. On Moche art, see Joanne Pillsbury's *Moche Art and Archeology in Ancient Peru* (Washington, DC: National Gallery of Art, 2001). The erotic art of the Moche has provided source material for a few more general studies, such as Federico Kauffmann Doig's *Sexual Behavior in Ancient Peru* (Lima: Kompaktos, 1979). Apart from the ancient Athenians, also known for their erotic art, especially in ceramic decorations (see note 20), the ancient Romans left numerous examples of erotic art, especially from Pompeii; see Antonio Varone's *Eroticism in Pompeii*, Maureen Fant, trans. (Los Angeles: J. Paul Getty Museum, 2001); or Michael Grant's *Eros in Pompeii* (New York: Stewart, Tabori & Chang, 1997).

38. "The Tale of Genji" is taken from Lady Murasaki, *The Tale of Genji*, Arthur Waley, trans. (New York: Modern Library, 1993), 24-30.

On Murasaki Shikibu, see Felice Fischer's "Murasaki Shikibu: The Court Lady" in *Heroic with Grace: Legendary Women of Japan*, Chieko Irie Mulhern, ed. (Armouk, NY: M.E. Sharpe, 1991); or the entry in *Herstory: Women who Changed the World*, Ruth Ashby and Deborah Gore Ohrn, eds. (New York: Viking, 1995). For more on the era, see Ivan Morris's *The World of the Shining Prince: Court Life in Ancient Japan* (London: Penguin, 1979). More of *The Tale of Genji*, although very lengthy, could be read in part in a history of sexuality; see *Approaches to Teaching Murasaki Shikibu's The Tale of Genji*, Edward Kamens, ed. (New York: Modern Language Association of America, 1993); or William J. Puette's *The Tale of Genji by Murasaki Shikibu: A Reader's Guide* (Rutland, VT: Charles E. Tuttle, 1992). There are also numerous studies of a literary nature, examining themes within the text, such as the various essays in *Ukifune: Love in The Tale of Genji*, Andrew Pekarik, ed. (New York: Columbia University Press, 1982). See also Peter Nickerson's "The Meaning of Matrilocality: Kinship, Property, and Politics in Mid-Heian," *Monumenta Nipponica* 48 (1993): 429-67, for a historical study; and Hitomi Tonomura's "Black Hair and Red Trousers: Gendering the Flesh in Medieval Japan," *The American Historical Review* 99 (1994): 129-54, who, although she discusses a twelfth-century text, includes a detailed and sophisticated background discussion.

39. "The Diary of Lady Murasaki" is taken from *The Diary of Lady Murasaki*, Richard Bowring, trans. (London: Penguin, 1996), 50-51.

See note 38 for further readings on Murasaki Shikibu and her era. She is only one of several women of her day who have left us a written record of their thoughts and feelings. Another well-known writer, and one who seems to have enjoyed court life much more than Murasaki Shikibu, was Sei Shonagon, whose *Pillow Book* exists in a few English translations. Yet another was Michitsuna no Haha, whose diary has been translated as *The Gossamer Years: The Diary of a Noblewoman of Heian Japan*, Edward Seidensticker, trans. (Rutland, VT: Charles E. Tuttle, 1964). See also selections from a few writers in *Diaries of Court Ladies of Old Japan*, Annie Shepley Omori and Kochi Doi, trans. (New York: AMS Press, 1970). Any of these might be studied as part of a history of sexuality.

PART II

Sexuality as Ideology

CHAPTER 5

SEX AND HUMAN EXISTENCE

Sex has always played an important role in human existence. From the earliest random human mating to the elaboration of complex rules and rituals for marriage and the detailed prohibitions of a host of illicit activities, human beings have tried to understand the place of sexuality and its relationship to larger aspects of human culture. That is what the following chapters in this part seek to describe.

Although sexuality follows social customs, as illustrated earlier, those customs and values do not arise haphazardly but are arranged deliberately and according to human wishes. Rules about sex, what to do and what not to do, come about through a complicated process of interaction: the abstract interaction of authoritative ideas with less compelling ones, and of all ideas with a social environment. Through time they become translated into social values and gradually cemented as social custom.

The term "ideology," as developed by Louis Althusser and other Marxist philosophers, is useful in helping to elaborate this concept. As opposed to the simple term "idea," from which it is derived, an ideology represents a network of connected ideas, values, and attitudes, as well as the behaviors that stem from them. We saw this concept at work earlier in this book. A patriarchal ideology not only deems women to be innately inferior to men, but also sets up marital customs that encourage women to see themselves as worthwhile only for child-bearing, and political customs that allow only men a public voice in the community's future. Proponents of a patriarchal ideology may also establish coordinating institutions of castration, to guard women's sexual exclusiveness, as well as pederasty, to provide men with a sexual companionship deemed more suitable to them, and they may encourage a medical science that sees females as undeveloped or incomplete males. Patriarchy is much more than a simple idea, then: it is an ideology.

Sexual ideologies, like other ideologies, are often connected to larger patterns of ideas, values, and attitudes. So the practice of polygamy will be related to ideas about the social order and class structure in a historical society, but also about the relative worth of men and women, the amount of expected interaction between husband and wife, the proper rules for inheritance of wealth and status, and the upbringing of children. Such ideas, values, and attitudes will be different in societies practicing monogamy. Although all societies obviously will have unique ideologies, their ideas may converge on certain points.

Ideologies are powerful social and intellectual forces, and their origins may often be obscure, in part deliberately. When they are perceived as normal or natural, ideologies gain greater influence. It is not, therefore, in the interest of an ideology's proponents to include much speculation about its origins, because that will only lead people to think about what came before and what might come after it. It is much better if an ideology is assumed as being simply the way things are and have always been.

The authority behind an ideology is key to its strength: The more powerful that is, the greater the ideology's influence. For this reason, even saying that a set of ideas, values, and attitudes is "the way things are" is sometimes not enough, because inevitably someone will ask why. So an ideology that is able to assert itself because of an authority behind it is in a much better position to maintain power.

What would that authority be? It might be Nature. Even writing it with a capital *N*, as is sometimes done, points out its authority. Nature is certainly often used to defend beliefs

or attitudes about sexuality. But Nature—or rather, nature—is a slippery slope, especially when used to describe sexual behavior. Is what is natural what is found in nature? If so, a whole range of sexual behaviors, from the asexual reproduction of some plants and animals to the incest and interspecies sex practiced among some animals might all be defended as natural. Does it mean "human nature" as opposed to "animal nature," that is, what separates us from other animals? If so, we would have to eliminate from human nature just about every sexual act, from the monogamy that imitates the pair-bonding of some animals to the promiscuity that imitates the sexual patterns of other animals. Nature, in the end, is not a reliable authority.

A much better authority than nature in most historical societies was the supernatural. The support from a deity, group of deities, or even the abstract forces of the cosmos for an ideology certainly provided an authority that was not easily challenged. Religious beliefs have often been called upon in history to bolster certain ideas or practices. A religious ideology, then, might combine ideas about divinity and the nature of the universe with values and attitudes toward sexuality. Human behavior could be justified as reflecting a divine reality or dismissed as counter to it. Myths and legends, passed from generation to generation in oral tradition before ever being written, provided details about the role of sex in a cosmic perspective and might help to educate about such a divine reality. Certain sexual acts, in addition, could be praised as being according to the dictates of a god or condemned as being against them. Here the sacred texts, often claimed to be the word of God, might precisely delineate these acts. Combining religious and sexual ideologies meant that challenges to the power of social custom around sex necessarily had also to challenge the power of religion.

Even without a deity as authority, philosophical traditions appealed to the supernatural. Philosophies insisted that they provided the answers to the questions that we all ask: How can I be happy? What is a well-ordered life? It is not difficult to see how philosophers might suggest that they have the answers, and that to be happy or to live rightly involved doing this or not doing that. There was no god or gods to bolster their authority, but they might use others' belief in their wisdom or enlightenment to strengthen their claims.

This chapter's readings deal with the role of sex in human existence. All come from a religious or philosophical tradition and are parts of texts considered authoritative, either as written forms of oral traditions long held sacred or as writings believed to be sacred, given by a divinity or legendary sage for the guidance of humanity.

40. JAPANESE CREATION MYTH FROM THE *KOJIKI*

Time: eighth century CE, from earlier oral
   traditions
Place: Japan
Author: unknown, traditionally ascribed to
   Opo no Yasumaro

The Kojiki, the oldest known writing from Japan, contains numerous legends and myths, such as the one that follows, that detail how the Japanese gods and the Japanese islands were created through great cosmic acts of sex between deities. The myths of many past societies shared similar beliefs about the origin of the world.

At the time of the beginning of heaven and earth, there came into existence in Takama-no-para a deity named Ame-no-minaka-nusi-no-kami; next Taka-mi-musubi-no-kami; next, Kami-musubi-no-kami. These three dei-

ties all came into existence as single deities, and their forms were not visible. Next, when the land was young, resembling floating oil and drifting like a jellyfish, there sprouted forth something like reed-shoots. From these came into existence the deity Umasi-asi-kami-piko-di-no-kami; next, Ame-no-toko-tati-no-kami. These two deities also came into existence as single deities, and their forms were not visible....

Next there came into existence the deity named U-pidi-ni-no-kami; next, his spouse Su-pidi-ni-no-kami. Next, Tuno-gupi-no-kami; next, his spouse Iku-gupi-no-kami. Next, Opo-to-no-di-no-kami; next, his spouse Opo-to-no-be-no-kami. Next, Omo-daru-no-kami; next, his spouse Aya-kasiko-ne-no-kami. Next, Izanagi-no-kami; next, his spouse Izanami-no-kami....

At this time the heavenly deities, all with one command, said to the two deities Izanagi-no-mikoto and Izanami-no-mikoto: "Complete and solidify this drifting land!" Giving them the Heavenly Jeweled Spear, they entrusted the mission to them. Thereupon, the two deities stood on the Heavenly Floating Bridge and, lowering the jeweled spear, stirred with it. They stirred the brine with a churning-churning sound; and when they lifted up the spear again, the brine dripping down from the tip of the spear piled up and became an island. This was the island Onogoro.

Descending from the heavens to this island, they erected a heavenly pillar and a spacious palace. At this time Izanagi-no-mikoto asked his spouse Izanami-no-mikoto, saying: "How is your body formed?" She replied, saying: "My body, formed though it be formed, has one place which is formed insufficiently." Then Izanagi-no-mikoto said: "My body, formed though it be formed, has one place which is formed to excess. Therefore, I would like to take that place in my body which is formed to excess and insert it into that place in your body which is formed insufficiently, and thus give birth to the land. How would this be?" Izanami-no-mikoto replied, saying: "That will be good." Then Izanagi-no-mikoto said: "Then let us, you and me, walk in a circle around this heavenly pillar and meet and have conjugal intercourse." … After having agreed to this, they circled around; then Izanami-no-mikoto said first: "Ana-ni-yasi, how good a lad!" Afterwards, Izanagi-no-mikoto said: "Ana-ni-yasi, how good a maiden!" After each had finished speaking, Izanagi-no-mikoto said to his spouse: "It is not proper that the woman speak first." Nevertheless, they commenced procreation and gave birth to a leech-child. They placed this child into a boat made of reeds and floated it away. Next, they gave birth to the island of Apa. This also is not reckoned as one of their children.

Then the two deities consulted together and said: "The child which we have just borne is not good. It is best to report this matter before the heavenly deities." Then they ascended together and sought the will of the heavenly deities. The heavenly deities thereupon performed a grand divination and said: "Because the woman spoke first, the child was not good. Descend once more and say it again." Then they descended again and walked once more in a circle around the heavenly pillar as they had done before. Then Izanagi-no-mikoto said first: "Ana-ni-yasi, how good a maiden!" Afterwards, his spouse Izanami-no-mikoto said: "Ana-ni-yasi, how good a lad!"

After they finished saying this, they were united and bore as a child the island Apadi-no-po-no-sa-wake-no-sima. Next they bore the double island of Iyo … [and] the triple island of Oki, also named Ame-no-osi-koro-wake. Next they bore the island of Tukusi…. Next they bore the island of Iki, also named Ame-pitotu-basira. Next they bore the island of Tu-sima, also named Ame-no-sade-yori-pime. Next they bore the island of Sado. Next they bore the island of Opo-yamato-toyo-aki-tu-sima, also named Ama-tu-mi-sora-Toyo-aki-tu-ne-wake. Thus, because the eight islands were born first, they are called Great Eight Island Land [Japan]….

After they had finished bearing the land, they went on to bear deities….

[In bearing the fire god, Izanami-no-mikoto is seriously injured and dies. Her husband, Izanagi-no-mikoto, travels to the underworld to try to retrieve her, but he disobeys her command not to look at her, and sees her decomposing body. She is ashamed, and chases him back to the land of the living in order to divorce him.]

They stood facing each other, one on each side of the boulder, and broke their troth [of marriage]. At this time Izanami-no-mikoto said: "O my beloved husband, if you do this, I will each day strangle to death one thousand of the populace of your country." To this Izanagi-no-mikoto said: "O my beloved spouse, if you do thus, I will each day build one thousand five hundred parturition huts [in which women give birth]." This is the reason why one thousand people inevitably die and one thousand five hundred people are inevitably born every day.

Questions for Reflection and Discussion

How is the discovery of sex linked to the creation of the world? How might the conventions of Japanese society have been woven into this myth? What sort of ideology about marriage, for example, can be determined from reading between the lines of this myth?

41. PERUVIAN MYTH

Time: sixteenth century CE, from earlier oral
    traditions
Place: what is modern Peru
Author: unknown

*This legend is one of many surrounding the figure
of Cuni Raya, also known as Vira Cocha, a god
of water, irrigation, and thus of fecundity. The
legends brought together various myths belonging to the peoples who were united within the
empire of the Incas, by associating their deities—
here called* huacas *(ancestor beings) and* villcas
*(demigods), but also spirits representing sacred
rocks and springs—with Vira Cocha. These
myths were preserved as part of the* Huarochiri
Manuscript, *and while it is the most important
of the rare historical sources that describe pre-
Spanish religious beliefs, it is possible that the
Christian priest who wrote down the legends
altered or misunderstood them.*

A long, long time ago, Cuni Raya Vira Cocha
used to go around posing as a miserably poor
and friendless man, with his cloak and tunic
all ripped and tattered. Some people who didn't
recognize him for who he was yelled, "You poor
lousy wretch!" Yet it was this man who fashioned all the villages. Just by speaking he made
the fields, and finished the terraces with walls
of fine masonry. As for the irrigation canals, he
channeled them out from their sources just by
tossing down the flower of a reed called pupuna.
After that, he went around performing all kinds
of wonders, putting some of the local *huacas* to
shame with his cleverness.

Once there was a female *huaca* named Caui
Llaca. Caui Llaca had always remained a virgin. Since she was very beautiful, every one
of the *huacas* and *villcas* longed for her. "I've
got to sleep with her!" they thought. But she
never consented.

Once this woman, who had never allowed
any male to fondle her, was weaving beneath
a lucuma tree. Cuni Raya, in his cleverness,
turned himself into a bird and climbed into
the lucuma. He put his semen into a fruit
that had ripened there and dropped it next to
the woman. The woman swallowed it down
delightedly. Thus she got pregnant even though
she remained untouched by man. In her ninth
month, virgin though she was, she gave birth
just as other women give birth. And so, too,
for one year she nursed her child at her breast,
wondering, "Whose child could this be?"

In the fullness of the year, when the young-
ster was crawling around on all fours, she
summoned all the *huacas* and *villcas* to find
out who was the child's father. When the *huacas* heard the message, they were overjoyed,
and they all came dressed in their best clothes,
each saying to himself, "It's me! It's me she'll
love!" The gathering took place at Anchi Cocha,
where this woman lived. When all the *huacas*
and *villcas* had taken their seats there, that
woman addressed them: "Behold, gentlemen
and lords. Acknowledge this child. Which of
you made me pregnant?" One by one she asked
each of them: "Was it you?" "Was it you?" But
nobody answered, "The child is mine."

The one called Cuni Raya Vira Cocha had
taken his seat at the edge of the gathering.
Since he looked like a friendless beggar sitting
there, and since so many handsome men were
present, she spurned him and didn't question
him. She thought, "How could my baby possibly be the child of that beggar?" Since no one
had said, "The child is mine," she first warned
the *huacas*, "If the baby is yours, it'll crawl up
to you," and then addressed the child: "Go,
identify your father yourself!" The child began
at one end of the group and crawled along on
all fours without climbing up on anyone, until
reaching the other end, where its father sat. On
reaching him, the baby instantly brightened

up and climbed onto his father's knee. When its mother saw this, she got all indignant: "*Atatay*, what a disgrace! How could I have given birth to the child of a beggar like that?" she said. And taking along only her child, she headed straight for the ocean. And then, while all the local *huacas* stood in awe, Cuni Raya Vira Cocha put on his golden garment. He started to chase her at once, thinking to himself, "She'll be overcome by sudden desire for me. Sister Caui Llaca!" he called after her. "Here, look at me! Now I'm really beautiful!" he said, and he stood there making his garment glitter. Caui Llaca didn't even turn her face back to him. "Because I've given birth to the child of such a ruffian, such a mangy beggar, I'll just disappear into the ocean," she said. She headed straight out into the deep sea near Pacha Camac, out there where even now two stones that clearly look like people stand. And when she arrived at what is today her dwelling, she turned to stone.

Questions for Reflection and Discussion

What do we learn about gender roles and sexuality from this legend? Can we assume that real men and women did or did not act as they do in this legend? How might the social order have been reinforced or undermined by the authority of such a legend?

42. THE SONG OF SONGS

Time: some time before the third century BCE,
    from earlier oral traditions
Place: Israel
Author: unknown

The Song of Songs or Canticle of Canticles, as it is also known, is one of the most mysterious books of the Bible. On its surface it is an extended love poem between a bride, the beloved, and her groom, the lover. Traditionally, the groom is said to be King Solomon, but that is hardly grounds for inclusion in a collection of sacred texts. A longstanding Jewish interpretation of the book has it that the groom symbolizes God, and the bride, the people of Israel. Christians adapted this metaphorical interpretation to have the groom represent Christ, and the bride, sometimes the Christian Church and sometimes the individual soul. More recently, scholars have suggested other possible reasons for its inclusion in the Bible. Among the more radical of them, that it is the text of an ancient Israelite sacred prostitution ritual.

Beloved
Let him kiss me with the kisses of his
mouth—
for your love is more delightful than wine.
Pleasing is the fragrance of your per-
fumes;
your name is like perfume poured out.
No wonder the maidens love you!
Take me away with you—let us hurry! …
My lover is to me a sachet of myrrh
resting between my breasts.
My lover is to me a cluster of henna blos-
soms
from the vineyards of En Gedi.
Lover
How beautiful you are, my darling!
Oh, how beautiful!
Your eyes are doves.
Beloved
How handsome you are, my lover!
Oh, how charming!
And our bed is verdant….
Lover
Like a lily among thorns
is my darling among the maidens.
Beloved
Like an apple tree among the trees of the
forest
is my lover among the young men.

I delight to sit in his shade,
and his fruit is sweet to my taste....
His left arm is under my head,
and his right arm embraces me....
My lover is like a gazelle or a young stag.
Look! There he stands behind our wall,
gazing through the windows,
peering through the lattice.
My lover spoke and said to me,
"Arise, my darling,
my beautiful one, and come with me.
See! The winter is past;
the rains are over and gone.
Flowers appear on the earth;
the season of singing has come,
the cooing of doves
is heard in our land.
The fig tree forms its early fruit;
the blossoming vines spread their fra-
grance.
Arise, come, my darling;
my beautiful one, come with me." ...
Lover
How beautiful you are, my darling!
Oh, how beautiful!
Your eyes behind your veil are doves.
Your hair is like a flock of goats
descending from Mount Gilead.
Your teeth are like a flock of sheep just
shorn,
coming up from the washing.
Each has its twin;
not one of them is alone.
Your lips are like a scarlet ribbon;
your mouth is lovely.
Your temples behind your veil
are like the halves of a pomegranate.
Your neck is like the tower of David,
built with elegance;
on it hang a thousand shields,
all of them shields of warriors.
Your two breasts are like two fawns,
like twin fawns of a gazelle

that browse among the lilies.
Until the day breaks
and the shadows flee,
I will go to the mountain of myrrh
and to the hill of incense.
All beautiful you are, my darling;
there is no flaw in you....
You have stolen my heart, my sister, my
bride;
you have stolen my heart
with one glance of your eyes,
with one jewel of your necklace.
How delightful is your love, my sister, my
bride!
How much more pleasing is your love
than wine,
and the fragrance of your perfume than
any spice!
Your lips drop sweetness as the honey-
comb, my bride;
milk and honey are under your tongue.
The fragrance of your garments is like
that of Lebanon.
You are a garden locked up, my sister, my
bride;
you are a spring enclosed, a sealed fountain.
Your plants are an orchard of pomegran-
ates
with choice fruits, with henna and nard,
nard and saffron, calamus and cinnamon,
with every kind of incense tree,
with myrrh and aloes and all the finest
spices.
You are a garden fountain,
a well of flowing water
streaming down from Lebanon.

Questions for Reflection and Discussion

How is the erotic bond described in this poem?
What effect do all of the references to plants and
animals give to the poem? What might it mean

to represent one's God as a groom and humanity collectively or individually as a bride?

43. MARRIAGE HYMN FROM THE RIG VEDA

Time: fifth century BCE from earlier oral traditions
Place: north India
Author: unknown

The Rig Veda contains the oldest rituals and beliefs of the religion now known as Hinduism. It was clearly a collection of prayers for Brahmin priests for various occasions, written down from long-remembered and long-transmitted rites and myths. The following hymn is taken from a more extensive description of the marriage between the goddess Surya, daughter of the sun god, and the god Soma, identified here as the god of the moon. There is reason to believe that it was recited at Hindu weddings.

Let Pusan lead you from here, taking you by the hand; let the Asvins carry you in their chariot. Go home to be mistress of the house with the right to speak commands to the gathered people. May happiness be fated for you here through your progeny. Watch over this house as mistress of the house....

I take your hand for good fortune, so that with me as your husband you will attain a ripe old age. Bhaga, Aryaman, Savitr, Purandhi—the gods have given you to me to be mistress of the house. Pusan, rouse her to be most eager to please, the woman in whom men sow their seed, so that she will spread her thighs in her desire for us and we, in our desire, will plant our penis in her. To you first of all they led Surya, circling with the bridal procession. Give her back to her husband, Agni, now as a wife with progeny....

Have no evil eye; do not be a husband-killer. Be friendly to animals, good-tempered and glowing with beauty. Bringing forth strong sons, prosper as one beloved of the gods and eager to please. Be good luck for our two-legged creatures and good luck for our four-legged creatures. Generous Indra, give this woman fine sons and the good fortune of her husband's love. Place ten sons in her and make her husband the eleventh. Be an empress over your husband's father, an empress over your husband's mother; be an empress over your husband's sister and an empress over your husband's brothers. Let all the gods and the waters together anoint our two hearts together. Let Matarisvan together with the Creator and together with her who shows the way join the two of us together.

Glossary of Terms
Pusan: god who drives the chariot of the sun and guardian of journeys
The Asvins: twin gods who accompany the chariot of the sun and bring the dawn
Bhaga: god of marriage and of prosperity
Aryaman: god of family inheritance and of hospitality
Savitr: god of the sun
Purandhi: goddess of childbirth and of abundance
Agni: god of fire, also of the hearth and thus of the home
Indra: warrior god of thunder and storms
Matarisvan: messenger of the gods

Questions for Reflection and Discussion

What ideology of marriage is expressed through this hymn? How does the participation of various gods help to reinforce this ideology? The reference to the bride's making her husband the eleventh son is probably a reference to reincarnation. How does this belief add to the importance of marriage from a Hindu perspective?

44. KRISHNA AND
THE MILKMAIDS

Time: tenth century CE
Place: India
Author: unknown

Krishna, an incarnation of the Hindu god Vishnu, has long been a favorite among Indian heroes, mainly because of his playfulness and enthusiasm for pleasure. The legends associated with Krishna, who is usually depicted as having blue skin, often represent him as an adolescent male who enjoys the finer things of life. The following legend, where Krishna is called Govinda as well as the son of Nanda and Devaki, is one of the most popular, combining religious devotion and flirtatiousness.

In the first month of winter, the girls of Nanda's village performed a certain vow to the goddess Katyayani. They ate rice cooked with clarified butter; they bathed in the water of the Kalindi river at sunrise; they made an image of the goddess out of sand and worshipped it with fragrant perfumes and garlands, with offerings and incense and lamps, and with bouquets of flowers, fresh sprigs of leaves, fruits, and rice. And they prayed: "Goddess Katyayani, great mistress of yoga, empress of great deluding magic, make the son of the cow-herd Nanda my husband. I bow to you." Saying this prayer, the girls would worship her, and having set their hearts on Krishna, the girls performed this vow for a month; they worshipped Bhadrakali so that the son of Nanda would be their husband. Arising at dawn, calling one another by name, they would join hands and go to bathe in the Kalindi every day, singing loudly about Krishna as they went.

One day, when they had gone to the river and taken off their clothes on the bank as usual, they were playing joyfully in the water, singing about Krishna. The lord Krishna, lord of all masters of yoga, came there with his friends of the same age in order to grant them the object of their rites. He took their clothes and quickly climbed a Nipa tree, and laughing with the laughing boys he told what the joke was: "Girls, let each one of you come here and take her own clothes as she wishes. I promise you, this is no jest, for you have been exhausted by your vows. I have never before told an untruth, and these boys know this. Slender-waisted ones, come one by one or all together and take your clothes." When the cow-herd girls saw what his game was, they were overwhelmed with love, but they looked at one another in shame, and they smiled, but they did not come out. Flustered and embarrassed by Govinda's words and by his jest, they sank down up to their necks in the icy water, and, shivering, they said to him, "You should not have played such a wicked trick. We know you as our beloved, son of the cow-herd Nanda, the pride of the village. Give us our clothes, for we are trembling. O darkly handsome one, we are your slaves and will do as you command, but you know dharma: give us our clothes or we will tell your father, the chieftain."

The lord said to them, "If you are my slaves and will do as I command, then come here and take back your clothes, O brightly smiling ones." Then all the girls, shivering and smarting with cold, came out of the water, covering their crotches with their hands. The lord was pleased and gratified by their chaste actions, and he looked at them and placed their clothes on his shoulder and smiled and said, "Since you swam in the water without clothes while you were under a vow, this was an insult to the divinity. Therefore you must fold your hands and place them on your heads and bow low in expiation of your sin, and then you may take your clothes." When the village girls heard what the infallible one said, they thought that bathing naked had been a violation of their vows, and they bowed down to Krishna, the very embodiment of all their rituals, who had thus fulfilled their desires and wiped out their disgrace and sin. Then the lord, the son of Devaki, gave their clothes to them, for he felt pity when he saw them bowed down in this way and he was satisfied with them.

Though they were greatly deceived and robbed of their modesty, though they were mocked and treated like toys and stripped of their clothes, yet they held no grudge against him, for they were happy to be together with their beloved. Rejoicing in the closeness of their lover, they put on their clothes; their bashful glances, in the thrall of their hearts, did not move from him. Knowing that the girls had taken a vow because they desired to touch his feet, the lord with a rope around his waist said to the girls, "Good ladies, I know that your desire is to worship me. I rejoice in this vow, which deserves to be fulfilled. The desire of those whose hearts have been placed in me does not give rise to further desire, just as seed corn that has been boiled or fried does not give rise to seed. You have achieved your aim. Now, girls, go back to the village and you will enjoy your nights with me, for it was for this that you fine ladies undertook your vow and worship." When the girls heard this from Krishna, they had obtained what they desired; and, meditating upon his lotus feet, they forced themselves to go away from him to the village.

Glossary of Terms
Katyayani: another name for the goddess
    Parvati, divine consort of Vishnu
Bhadrakali: another name for the goddess
    Kali, goddess of death and blood
Dharma: the Hindu concept of "duty" in the
    sense of one's responsibilities in life

Questions for Reflection and Discussion

To what extent is the girls' love for Krishna religious and to what extent is it erotic? How does Krishna view the girls' sexual appeal in relationship to his divinity? What ideas about sex are being expressed and promoted through this legend?

45. VISHNU AS MOHINI

Time: tenth century CE
Place: India
Author: unknown

Vishnu's enthusiasm for sexual activity, as evidenced in the exploits of Krishna, is also expressed in female incarnations, as in this example, where he turns into the woman known as Mohini in order to seduce a group of male demons who have stolen the nectar of immortality. Because Shiva did not witness this transformation, he asks Vishnu to repeat it, in the episode that follows, in the presence of the goddess who is his wife, here called Uma and Bhavani. In fact, there are many Hindu legends of men being turned into women and women being turned into men, often for sexual purposes or with sexual results.

Shiva waited there with Uma, looking in all directions. Then, in a garden with many-colored flowers and trees with red leaves, he saw a beautiful woman. She was playing with a ball. She wore a girdle, and a beautiful cloth covered her lower parts. It seemed as if her waist would collapse with the weight of her heavy breasts which trembled as she rose and bent with the ball, as well as with the weight of her necklaces and hips, as her tender leaflike feet went from place to place. The pupils of her large eyes anxiously followed the movements of the ball in various directions. Her face, framed with her dark flowing hair, looked beautiful, while her cheeks shone with the radiance of her earrings. She was tying her fine cloth, which had come loose, and tidying her disheveled hair with her beautiful left hand while hitting the ball with her other hand. She enchanted the whole world with her powers of illusion.

On seeing her playing with the ball, smiling shyly, glancing at him, the god, gazing at the woman and being looked at in return by her, forgot himself as well as Uma and his attendants. The ball slipped from her hand and rolled away. She followed it while a gust of wind blew off her cloth and girdle. The lord Shiva stood staring. Seeing that beautiful charming woman who tried to attract him with her eyes, Shiva fixed his heart on her. Being deprived of his wisdom by her, completely oblivious of discernment, overwhelmed with passion, and quite shameless, he approached her even as Bhavani looked on. Undressed as she was, she seemed to be very shy as he came to her. Laughing, she went behind a tree but did not stay still. The lord, his senses out of control, overpowered by desire, followed her as a lordly elephant would a she-elephant. Chasing her, he caught the unwilling woman, pulled her by the hair, and held her in his arms. The lord held her in a close embrace, just as an elephant holds a she-elephant. She struggled in his grasp, and her hair was disheveled.

Freeing herself from the arms of the bull-like god, she, the illusion created by the god, ran swiftly, her heavy hips swaying. Completely vanquished by the enemy, passion, the famed Shiva followed the footsteps of the woman who had been created by

Vishnu of miraculous exploits. While pursuing her, his semen, of unfailing power, fell, just as that of a prize bull chasing a fertile cow, or a lordly elephant a fertile she-elephant. O king, wherever the semen of the great one fell to the earth, there were fields of silver and gold. Hara [Shiva] pursued her over rivers, lakes, mountains, forests, gardens, and the abodes of sages. When his semen was completely drained, O best of kings, he realized that he was exhausted by the illusion of the god, and he recovered. It is said that, realizing the greatness of his own soul and of the universal soul, he was not surprised at what had been done by the lord of unknowable power. Vishnu was very pleased to see that he was neither remorseful nor embarrassed. He resumed his own masculine body.

Questions for Reflection and Discussion

How is Vishnu's beauty described, and what assumptions can we make from it about the ideals of women's beauty in medieval Indian society? Likewise, how are Shiva's sexual urges described, and what assumptions can we make about beliefs concerning men's sexuality in the same society? Does this passage celebrate homoeroticism?

46. EROTIC TEMPLE SCULPTURE

Time: eleventh century CE
Place: India
Artist: unknown

These images are from a group of almost a thousand erotic sculptures that adorns a series of Hindu temples in Khajuraho, India. This sample, from the Kandariya temple dedicated to Shiva (known here as Mahadeva), shows a vast array of couplings in just as extensive a

series of postures. The reason for such a profusion of erotic sculpture is not entirely clear, but Tantrism—the medieval Hindu movement that promoted sexual pleasure and energy as a means of approaching the divine—may play a role. Inside the temple is a stylized representation of Shiva's penis, called a linga *or* lingam, *worshipped throughout India.*

Questions for Reflection and Discussion

What do these images tell us about the religious and sexual ideologies of this time and place? What are the advantages of visual rather than literary expressions of those ideologies? How might such images, connecting the sexual and the divine, have influenced the ideas and lives of those who lived around this temple and saw them?

47. MENCIUS

Time: fourth century BCE
Place: China
Author: Mengzi

Mengzi (known also as Meng-tzu and by his Westernized name of Mencius) was a philosopher and a government official of one of the kingdoms of China before its ancient unification. A follower of Confucius who became a revered sage in his own right, Mencius believed that goodness would prevail in human relations at all levels, from those between a king and his subjects to those between family members, since human beings were good at their core. This fact also made human beings educable in good conduct by appealing to their goodness. Mencius told brief moral stories to make this point again and again, as this example demonstrates.

"I have a weakness," said the King. "I am fond of women." "In antiquity, Tai Wang was fond of women, and loved his concubines. The Book of Odes says,

> Gu Gung Dan Fu
> Early in the morning galloped on his horse
> Along the banks of the river in the West
> Till he came to the foot of Mount Chi.
> He brought with him the Lady Zhiang,
> Looking for a suitable abode.

At that time, there were neither girls pining for a husband nor men without a wife. You may be fond of women, but so long as you share this fondness with the people, how can it interfere with your becoming a true king?"

Questions for Reflection and Discussion

In Mencius's opinion, is sexual desire a weakness? What does the king's natural goodness require him to do? What does Mencius's natural goodness require him to do?

48. THE QUR'AN ON WOMEN

Time: seventh century CE
Place: Arabia
Author: Muhammad

Muhammad's recitations—for that is what the word "Qur'an" means—were believed to have come directly from God and so were written down by his followers and collected after his death. In this passage, part of a much longer section relating to women, marriage, and family life, Muhammad sets out God's decrees on a whole range of sexual matters. Unlike those religious and philosophical traditions where myths and other stories made points about sexual ideology indirectly, the Qur'an offers direct divine commandments.

In the Name of Allah, the Compassionate, the Merciful.

O people, fear your Lord who created you from a single soul, and from it He created its mate, and from both He scattered abroad many men and women; and fear Allah in whose name you appeal to one another, and invoke family relationships. Surely Allah is a watcher over you.

Render unto the orphans their property and do not exchange worthless things for good ones, and do not devour their property together with your property. That indeed is a great sin!

If you fear that you cannot deal justly with the orphans, then marry such of the women as appeal to you, two, three or four; but if you fear that you cannot be equitable, then only one, or captives of war or slave-girls. That is more likely to enable you to avoid unfairness.

And give women their dowries as a free gift, but if they choose to give you anything of it, then consume it with enjoyment and pleasure....

Allah commands you, with respect to your children, that the male shall inherit the equivalent of the share of two females. If there be more than two females, then they should receive two-thirds of what he leaves; but if there is only one female, she is entitled to one-half. To each of his parents, one-sixth of what he leaves, if he has any children; but if he has no children, then his parents will inherit him, the mother receiving one-third. But if he has any brothers, then his mother receives one-sixth, after any will he had made or any debt he had incurred is taken care of....

These are the ordinances of Allah, and whoever obeys Allah and His Apostle, He will admit him into gardens beneath which rivers flow, abiding therein forever. That is the great victory! But whoever disobeys Allah and His Apostle and transgresses His bounds, He will admit him into the Fire, wherein he shall abide forever, and his will be a demeaning punishment! As for those of your women who commit lewdness, call four witnesses from your own against them; and if they testify, then detain them in the houses till death overtakes them or Allah opens another way for them. If two men of you commit it, punish them both. If they repent and mend their ways, then leave them alone. Allah is truly All-Forgiving, Merciful....

O believers, it is not lawful for you to inherit the women of deceased kinsmen against their will; nor restrain them in order to take away part of what you had given them, unless they commit flagrant adultery. Associate with them kindly; and if you feel aversion towards them, it may well be that you will be averse to something, from which Allah brings out a lot of good. If you wish to have one wife in the place of another and you have given either of them a heap of gold, do not take any of it back. Would you take it by recourse to injustice and manifest sin? For how can you take it back, when you have been intimate one with the other, and they had taken from you a solemn pledge?

And do not marry women that your fathers had married, unless it has already happened. Surely it is indecent and hateful, and it is an evil course! Unlawful to you are your mothers, your daughters, your sisters, your paternal and maternal aunts, your brother's daughters and sister's daughters, your foster-mothers who gave you suck, your foster-sisters, your wives' mothers, your step-daughters who are in your custody, born to your wives whom you have lain with. But if you have not lain with them, then you are not at fault. It is also not lawful to marry the wives of your sons who are of your own loins, or to take in two sisters together, unless this has already happened. Allah is truly All-Forgiving and Merciful! Or married women, except the captives of war and slave-girls. This is Allah's decree for you. Beyond these it is lawful for you to seek, by means of your wealth, any women, to marry and not to debauch. Those of them you have enjoyed, you should give them their dowries as a matter of obligation; but you are not liable to reproach for whatever you mutually agree upon, apart from the obligatory payment. Allah is indeed All-Knowing, Wise!

Whoever of you cannot afford to marry a free, believing woman, let him choose from whatever your right hands possess of believing girls. Allah knows best your faith; you come one from the other. So marry them with their parents' leave and give them their dowry honorably, as chaste women, neither committing adultery nor taking lovers. If they are legally married and commit adultery, their punishment shall be half that of a free woman. Such is the law for those of you who fear committing sin; but to abstain is better for you. Allah is All-Forgiving and Merciful! ...

Men are in charge of women, because Allah has made some of them excel the others, and because they spend some of their wealth. Hence righteous women are obedient, guarding the unseen which Allah has guarded. And those of them that you fear might rebel, admonish them and abandon them in their beds and beat them. Should they obey you, do not seek a way of harming them; for Allah is Sublime and Great!

And if you fear a breach between the two, then send forth an arbiter from his relatives and another arbiter from her relatives. If they both desire reconciliation, Allah will bring them together. Allah is indeed All-Knowing, Well-informed.

Questions for Reflection and Discussion

Who are the believers to whom Muhammad is speaking? What can be learned about sexual and marital customs at the time of Muhammad? Which existing customs did he recommend and which did he condemn? What incentives does Muhammad offer for following his ideas, and what disincentives for refusing to follow them?

49. THE QUR'AN ON
THE AFTERLIFE

Time: seventh century CE
Place: Arabia
Author: Muhammad

Muhammad's descriptions of the afterlife in the Qur'an are among the most sensuous in all of the world's religions. Here, both the pleasures of paradise and the tortures of hell are depicted in vivid detail, and the former include sexual enjoyment with special virgin women, known as houris.

When the Happening comes to pass. Of its occurrence there is no denial; abasing some, exalting others. When the earth shall be shaken violently, and the mountains shall be reduced to rubble, so that they become scattered dust. And you shall be three categories: The Companions of the Right—behold the Companions of the Right? The Companions of the Left—behold the Companions of the Left?

And the outstrippers, the outstrippers; those are the favored ones, in the Gardens of Bliss; a throng of the ancients, and a small band of the latecomers. Upon beds interwoven with gold; reclining upon them, facing each other. While immortal youths go round them, with goblets, pitchers and a cup of limpid drink. Their heads do not ache from it and they do not become intoxicated. And with such fruits as they care to choose; and such flesh of fowl as they desire; and wide-eyed *houris*, like hidden pearls; as a reward for what they used to do. They do not hear therein idle talk or vilification; only the greeting: "Peace, peace!"

As for the Companions of the Right; and behold the Companions of the Right? They are in the midst of thornless Lotus Trees, and braided acacias, and extended shade, and over-flowing water; and abundant fruit, neither withheld nor forbidden, and uplifted mattresses. We have formed them originally; and made them pure virgins, tender and unaging, for the Companions of the Right; a throng of the ancients, and a throng of the latecomers.

As for the Companions of the Left; and what are the Companions of the Left? Amid searing wind and boiling water; and a shadow of thick smoke, which is neither cool nor bounteous. They lived before that in luxury; and they used to insist upon the Great Blasphemy. They used to say: "What? When we are dead and turn into dust and bones, shall we be raised from the dead? And our forefathers, too?" Say: "The first and the last, shall be gathered upon an appointed, pre-assigned day. Then you, erring ones and denouncers, shall eat from the Tree of Bitterness, filling your bellies therefrom, and drinking on top of it boiling water, lapping it like thirsty camels."

Questions for Reflection and Discussion

What kind of beings might the *houris* be? How do the pleasures of paradise replicate the Muslim ideology of the present life? Does the description of these pleasures imply that only men go to paradise, or that only they will enjoy sex in the afterlife?

For Louis Althusser on ideology, see especially his *Essays on Ideology* (London: Verso, 1984). For comparative studies on sexuality in religious traditions, see the essays in a number of recent collections: *Good Sex: Feminist Perspectives from the World's Religions*, Patricia Beattie Jung et al., eds. (New Brunswick, NJ: Rutgers University Press, 2001); *Love, Sex, and Gender in the World Religions*, Joseph Runzo and Nancy M. Martin, eds. (Boston: Oneworld, 2000); *Religion and Sexuality*, Michael A. Hayes et al., eds. (Sheffield: Sheffield Academic, 1998); and *Sexuality and the World's Religions*, David Machacek and Melissa M. Wilcox, eds. (Santa Barbara, CA: ABC-CLIO, 2003). Further information can be found in M. Christian Green and Paul D. Numrich's *Religious Perspectives on Sexuality: A Resource Guide* (Chicago: Park Ridge Center, 2001). Very readable is Edward Parrinder's *Sex in the World's Religions* (London: Sheldon, 1980) and his *Sexual Morality in the World's Religions* (Rockport, MA: Oneworld, 1996); readable but speculative is Riane Eisler's *Sacred Pleasure: Sex, Myth, and the Politics of the Body* (San Francisco: HarperSanFrancisco, 1995). More on sexuality in specific religious traditions is to be found in the notes below and in the next three chapters.

40. "Japanese Creation Myth from the *Kojiki*" is taken from *Kojiki*, Donald Philippi, trans. (Princeton, NJ: Princeton University Press, 1969), 47-55, 65-66, with slight changes.

The *Kojiki* has been little studied in English. See, however, Fuminobu Murakami's "Incest and Rebirth in *Kojiki*," *Monumenta Nipponica* 43 (1988): 455-63. On early Japanese mythology generally, including the *Kojiki*, see Juliet Piggott's *Japanese Mythology* (Feltham, NY:

Hamlyn, 1969; revised 1982); or Michiko Aoki's *Ancient Myths and Early History of Japan: A Cultural Foundation* (New York: Exposition Press, 1974). The other early account of Japanese history is the *Nihonji*, parts of which are also of interest for a history of sexuality, and exists in an English translation by William Aston (London: Allen & Unwin, 1956; revised 1972).

41. "Peruvian Myth" is taken from *The Huarochiri Manuscript*, Frank Salomon and George Urioste, trans. (Austin, TX: University of Texas Press, 1991), 46-48.

For more information on the early legends, see several of the essays in *From Oral to Written Expression: Native Andean Chronicles of the Early Colonial Period*, Roleno Adorno, ed. (Syracuse, NY: Syracuse University Press, 1982); or Frank Solomon's *Nightmare Victory: The Meanings of Conversion among Peruvian Indians* (College Park, MD: University of Maryland at College Park, 1990). For more on traditions of sexuality, insofar as they can be reconstructed, see Federico Kauffmann Doig's *Sexual Behaviour in Ancient Peru* (Lima: Kompaktos, 1979); or Constance Classen's *Inca Cosmology and the Human Body* (Salt Lake City, UT: University of Utah Press, 1993). On Vira Cocha, see Arthur Demarest's *Viracocha: The Nature and Antiquity of the Andean High God* (Cambridge, MA: Peabody Museum of Archeology and Harvard University, 1981). Other records of pre-Columbian religion can be found in Bernabe Cobo's *History of the Inca Empire*, Roland Hamilton, trans. (Austin, TX: University of Texas Press, 1979). The other American peoples for whom a historical record survives include the Maya and the Aztecs of Mesoamerica. See Rosemary Joyce's *Gender and Power in Prehispanic Mesoamerica* (Austin, TX: University of Texas Press, 2000); or the various essays in *Gender in Pre-Hispanic*

America, Cecilia Klein, ed. (Washington, DC: Dumbarton Oaks Research Library, 2001); or in *Ancient Maya Gender Identity and Relations*, Lowell Gustafson and Amelia Trevelyan, eds. (Westport, CT: Bergin & Garvey, 2002). See also the visual evidence of a Mayan marriage in Joyce Marcus's *The Inscriptions of Calakmul: Royal Marriage at a Maya City in Campeche, Mexico* (Ann Arbor, MI: University of Michigan Museum of Anthropology, 1987).

42. "The Song of Songs" is taken from *The Holy Bible: New International Version* (Grand Rapids, MI: Zondervan Bible, 1978), 726-30 (Song of Songs 1: 2-4a, 13-16, 2: 2-3, 6, 9-13, 4: 1-7, 9-15, 5: 10-16).

There are many general commentaries on the Song of Songs, also known as the Canticle of Canticles and as the Song of Solomon, as with all other books of the Bible, and since the eroticism of the poem is central, all deal with it, and especially with the metaphor that it is usually supposed to be between God and Israel, Christ and the Church, or God and the soul. Commentaries range from the traditional to the radical. Among recent ones: Athalya Brenner's *A Feminist Companion to the Song of Songs* (Sheffield: Sheffield Academic Press, 1993); Jacob Neusner's *Israel's Love Affair with God* (Valley Forge, PA: Trinity Press International, 1993); Howard Eilberg-Schwartz's *God's Phallus: And Other Problems for Men and Monotheism* (Boston: Beacon, 1994); Carey Walsh's *Exquisite Desire: Religion, the Erotic, and the Song of Songs* (Minneapolis, MI: Fortress, 2000). On the historical context for the poem, see Loren Fisher's *An Enthronement Ritual at Ugarit* (Claremont, CA: Institute for Antiquity and Christianity, 1971); John B. White's *A Study of the Language of Love in the Song of Songs and in Egyptian Poetry* (Missoula, MT: Scholars,

1978); or Michael V. Fox's *The Song of Songs and the Ancient Egyptian Love Songs* (Madison, WI: University of Wisconsin Press, 1985). On the Biblical book's influence in theology, art, and literature, see, for example, E. Ann Matter's *The Voice of My Beloved: The Song of Songs in Western Christianity* (Philadelphia, PA: University of Pennsylvania Press, 1990); or Marilyn Aronberg Lavin's *The Liturgy of Love: Images from the Song of Songs in the Art of Cimabue, Michelangelo, and Rembrandt* (Lawrence, KS: Spenser Museum of Art, University of Kansas, 2001); or Noam Flinker's *The Song of Songs in English Renaissance Literature: Kisses of Their Mouths* (Cambridge: D.S. Brewer, 2000).

43. "Marriage Hymn from the Rig Veda" is taken from *The Rig Veda: An Anthology*, Wendy Doniger O'Flaherty, ed. and trans. (London: Penguin, 1981), 267-71.

There is very little in English that would help to shed light on this hymn. Works on broader related topics include: Mildreth Worth Pinkham's *Women in the Sacred Scriptures of Hinduism* (New York: AMS Press, 1967); or Lynn E. Gatwood's *Devi and the Spouse Goddess: Women, Sexuality, and Marriage in India* (New Delhi: Manohar, 1985). On the Rig Veda itself, see *Textual Sources for the Study of Hinduism*, Wendy Doniger O'Flaherty, ed. and trans. (Manchester: Manchester University Press, 1988). See also notes 4, 5, and 14 for more on gender and sexuality in ancient India.

44. "Krishna and the Milkmaids" is taken from the *Bhagavata Purana in Hindu Myths: A Sourcebook Translated from the Sanskrit*, Wendy Doniger O'Flaherty, ed. and trans. (London: Penguin, 1975), 229-31.

A modern composite version of the legends of Krishna can be found in the essay "Krishna" in Purushottam Lal Bhargava's *Founders of India's Civilization: Lives of Ten Pre-Buddha Great Men of India* (Berkeley, CA: Asian Humanities Press, 1992). The importance of devotion to Krishna can be seen in Friedhelm Hardy's *Viraha-bhakti: The Early History of Krsna Devotion in South India* (Delhi: Oxford University Press, 1983). Aspects of Krishna's popularity and playfulness—while focusing on a different but equally prominent legend—may be found in John Stratton Hawley's *Krishna: The Butter Thief* (Princeton, NJ: Princeton University Press, 1983). Finally, some of the influence of the legends of Krishna may be seen in W.G. Archer's *The Loves of Krishna in Indian Painting and Poetry* (London: Allen and Unwin, 1957).

45. "Vishnu as Mohini" is taken from *Same-Sex Love in India*, Ruth Vanita and Saleem Kidwai, eds. (New York: St. Martin's, 2000), 69-71.

The history of devotion to Vishnu and his divine attributes can be found in J. Gonda's *Aspects of Early Visnuism* (Utrecht: A. Oosthoek, 1954); Shakti Gupta's *Vishnu and His Incarnations* (Bombay: Somaiya, 1974); or B.B. Bidyabinod's *Varieties of the Vishnu Image* (New Delhi: Indological Book, 1977). None of these books, however, mentions the particular legend in which Vishnu took on a feminine form. On this topic, see Robert Goldman's "Transsexualism, Gender, and Anxiety in Traditional India," *Journal of the American Oriental Society* 113 (1993): 374-401. Other interesting legends focus on Vishnu's penis (called the *linga* or *lingam* in Sanskrit and usually left untranslated); see, for example, the excerpt from the *Brahmanda Purana* on "The Origin of the *Lingam*," or from the *Vamana Purana* on "The Origin of the Shrine of the *Lingam*," both in *Textual Sources for the Study of Hinduism*, Wendy Doniger O'Flaherty, ed. and trans. (Manchester: Manchester University Press, 1988), 85-91.

46. "Erotic Temple Sculpture" is taken from photographs supplied to the author by Jude Polsky.

For more on the erotic sculpture of India, there is much from which to choose. See Francis Leeson's *Kama Shilpa: A Study of Indian Sculptures Depicting Love in Action* (Bombay: D.B. Taraporevala, 1962); or Mulk Raj Anand's *Kama Kala: Some Notes on the Philosophical Basis of Hindu Erotic Sculpture* (Geneva: Nagel, 1962); or Kanwar Lal's *The Cult of Desire* (New Hyde Park, NY: University Books, 1967); or Devangana Desai's *Erotic Sculpture of India: A Socio-Cultural Study* (New Delhi: Tata McGraw-Hill, 1975); or Richard Lannoy's *The Eye of Love: In the Temple Sculpture of India* (London: Rider, 1976). *The Great Liberation (Mahanirvana Tantra)*, John Woodroffe, trans. (Madras: Ganesh & Co., 1971), includes several Hindu tantric rituals from a text dating about 1500 CE, but the text is difficult for nonspecialists to follow.

47. "Mencius" is taken from *Mencius*, trans. D.C. Lau (London: Penguin, 1970), 66.

Not much in English describes Mencius's treatment of sexuality, and not surprisingly: His own comments on the subject were very brief. See the various essays in *Mencius: Contexts and Interpretations*, Alan K.L. Chan, ed. (Honolulu: University of Hawai'i Press, 2002), which discuss Mencius's general approach to human nature. A recent general study of Mencius's ideas can be found in Kwong-loi Shun's *Mencius and Early Chinese*

Thought (Stanford, CA: Stanford University Press, 1997). See note 6 for more on early Confucian views on women.

48. "The Qur'an on Women" is taken from *The Qur'an: A Modern English Translation*, Majid Fakhry and Mahmud Zayid, trans. (Reading, UK: Garnet, 1997), 51-54, with slight changes.

For more information on the Qur'an on women, see Amina Wadud's *Qur'an and Woman: Rereading the Sacred Text from a Woman's Perspective*, 2nd ed. (New York: Oxford University Press, 1999); or Barbara Freyer Stowasser's *Women in the Qur'an: Traditions and Interpretation* (New York: Oxford University Press, 1994); or Anwar Hekmat's *Women and the Koran: The Status of Women in Islam* (Amherst, NY: Prometheus Books, 1987). See also notes 64 and 65 for gender and sexuality in historical Islam. Interesting biographies of Muhammad include Uri Rubin's *The Eye of the Beholder: The Life of Muhammad as Viewed by the Early Muslims: A Textual Analysis* (Princeton, NJ: Darwin Press, 1995); or Clinton Bennet's *In Search of Muhammad* (London: Cassell, 1998); or Yahiya Emerick's *The Life and Work of Muhammad* (Indianapolis, IN.: Alpha Press, 2002); very readable is Karen Armstrong's *Muhammad: A Biography of the Prophet* (San Francisco: HarperSanFrancisco, 1992).

49. "The Qur'an on the Afterlife" is taken from *The Qur'an: A Modern English Translation*, trans. Majid Fakhry and Mahmud Zayid (Reading, UK: Garnet, 1997), 349-50.

See notes 48, 64, and 65 for further readings on Islam and women, and on Muhammad's ideas. An interesting treatment, comparing Jewish, Christian, and Islamic views of the afterlife, is Alan Segal's *Life After Death: A History of the Afterlife in Western Religion* (New York: Doubleday, 2004).

sexual renunciation

If sex is such an important part of human existence, what or who could inspire or oblige a person to renounce it? Throughout history, there have been individuals who have tried to persuade others that sex is *not* among the most important things in life, indeed, that it may well distract one from what is truly important. How these individuals persuaded others is the theme of this chapter.

Sexual renunciation—usually but not always joined with the renunciation of marriage and family life—formed a key part of several religious and philosophical ideologies in Late Antiquity and the Middle Ages and of course, remains a part of some ideologies even today. Some suggested that there were practical advantages to giving up sex: Individuals who did not marry could devote themselves to intellectual pursuits. They avoided the many "woes of marriage," as they were sometimes called, including incompatibility with spouses usually chosen by their parents. For men, giving up sex also meant reducing their medical risk, since many past cultures believed that ejaculation lessened vitality. For women, giving up sex meant avoiding the danger of death in childbirth, which was commonplace, especially given the young age of marriage for many women. Others suggested that there were spiritual advantages to sexual renunciation: weakening the hold of the mortal body over the immortal soul, purifying the mind of passing earthly distractions in order to concentrate on enlightenment, or modeling oneself after a religious founder or a divinity, who had also renounced sex. Often practical and spiritual reasons were combined in formulating an ideology of sexual renunciation.

So far I have been talking about ideologies as formulated and as promoted without mentioning *who* was doing the formulating and the promoting. Keeping the persons behind the ideas firmly in mind is essential for understanding how ideologies work. After all, ideas are not born into a vacuum, and they do not get passed around by osmosis. There is always *someone* there, writing their ideas down or speaking in public to persuade others to believe certain things. That was one of the insights of sociologist Max Weber in the early twentieth century who observed how individuals are disguised within authoritative structures. Most of us use convenient shorthand to speak or write that "their society believes" or "my religion teaches" or "our government feels" or "the law prohibits." The truth, however, is that all institutions and communities are composed of individuals, and that it is individuals who believe or teach or feel or prohibit something. Within societies or religions or governments or legislatures, individuals with influence or authority use their power to promote their ideas and values. That is not to say that these individuals are self-serving or cynical, although they may be; some are without a doubt genuinely convinced of the truth of their ideologies and see their power as an opportunity for the betterment of humanity by getting their message out. (I suspect that most of us tend to assume purer motives in those who promote an ideology similar to our own, and more sullied motives in those who promote a different ideology.)

Seeing the individuals behind the ideology is particularly important when thinking about how ideologies become successful: when the ideas and values voiced by a few are adopted by the many as their own. How exactly does that happen? In some cases, ideologies are spread by persuasion. Writers and speakers who hold certain beliefs and values express them to others who find them attractive. Perhaps the new ideology is attractive because it brings together in a coherent way various attitudes and opinions already held by the one who adopts it. The new ideology possibly challenges the individual to see him- or herself in a new way, reach for a new and attractive goal, or transform his or her life for the better. Philosophical ideologies often hold out the promise of a happier or more fulfilled life, social ideologies bring with them acceptance by the community, but religious ideologies can offer eternal happiness in the afterlife for those who adopt them. The power of persuasion can use negative disincentives as well as positive incentives. Those who refuse to believe in the new ideology can be threatened with unhappiness or a life consumed by unfulfilled desires, or social ostracism, or even eternal damnation.

Those in power can use coercion as well as persuasion to promote ideologies. Legislators, using the force of government, can write the law to reward behaviors that fit their ideology and to punish behaviors that don't. Religious leaders, using the power of belief, can elevate in status those who follow their ideology and shun those who won't. Or worse. Medieval Europe is known for the attempts by Christian leaders to work in conjunction with governments to compel belief in their ideology, through the institution known as the Inquisition. But many powers, both civil and religious, have used the threat of death or imprisonment to force acceptance of an ideology.

Even when no formal power exists to enforce an ideology, or the powers that be are not interested in doing so, the informal powers of social pressures can do the same job of enforcement. Parents try to instill their values and beliefs into their children as they raise them. Friends and relatives offer their own opinions. Neighbors watch and gossip about the good and bad behavior they see around them, especially in smaller communities where "everybody knows everybody." These informal mechanisms for the enforcement of an ideology can work just as well as more formal ones in getting the individual to tow the ideological line.

One sees all of these features of ideology at work in attempts to promote sexual renunciation. The following readings, most of which come from authoritative texts deemed sacred writings or at least ones that enjoyed great influence, demonstrate a variety of persuasive and coercive methods, incentives and disincentives, and formal and informal mechanisms of enforcement to convince others that they should give up sex.

50. THE EARLY LIFE OF THE BUDDHA

Time: first century CE, from earlier oral traditions
Place: Tibet
Author: unknown

Among the earliest and best-known writings from early Buddhism is the story of the Buddha's life. He was born as the Prince Siddhartha Gautama, son of the king of the Shakyas in northern India. He became the enlightened one—for that is what "Buddha" means—by abandoning the pleasures of earthly existence in order to minimize its pains, including old age, sickness, death. Indeed, the detachment from earthly things—including marriage and sex— is at the heart of Buddhism.

His childhood passed without serious illness, and in due course he reached maturity. In a few days he acquired the knowledge appropriate to his station in life, which normally it takes years to learn. Since the king of the Shakyas had, however, heard from Asita, the great seer, that the supreme beatitude would be the prince's future goal, he tried to tie him down by sensual pleasures, so that he might not go away into the forest [and become a religious hermit]. He selected for him from a family of long-standing unblemished reputation a maiden, Yashodhara by name, chaste and outstanding for her beauty, modesty, and good breeding, a true Goddess of Fortune in the shape of a woman. And the prince, wondrous in his flashing beauty, took his delight with the bride chosen for him by his father....

The monarch, however, decided that his son must never see anything that could perturb his mind, and he arranged for him to live in the upper storeys of the palace, without access to the ground. Thus he passed his time in the upper part of the palace, which was as brilliantly white as rain clouds in autumn, and which looked like a mansion of the Gods shifted to the earth. It contained rooms suited to each season, and the melodious music of the female attendants could be heard in them. This palace was as brilliant as that of Shiva on Mount Kailasa. Soft music came from the gold-edged tambourines which the women tapped with their fingertips, and they danced as beautifully as the choicest heavenly nymphs. They entertained him with soft words, tremulous calls, wanton swayings, sweet laughter, butterfly kisses, and seductive glances. Thus he became a captive of these women who were well versed in the subject of sensuous enjoyment and indefatigable in sexual pleasure. And it did not occur to him to come down from the palace to the ground, just as people who in reward for their virtues live in a palace in heaven are content to remain there, and have no desire to descend to the earth.

In the course of time the fair-bosomed Yashodhara bore to [Siddhartha] the son of Shuddhodana a son, who was named Rahula. It must be remembered that all the *Bodhisattvas,* those beings of quite incomparable spirit, must first of all know the taste of the pleasures which the senses can give. Only then, after a son has been born to them, do they depart to the forest. Through the accumulated effects of his past deeds the *Bodhisattva* possessed in himself the root cause of enlightenment, but he could reach it only after first enjoying the pleasures of the senses. In the course of time the women told him how much they loved the groves near the city, and how delightful they were. So, feeling like an elephant locked up inside a house, he set his heart on making a journey outside the palace. The king heard of the plans of his dearly beloved son, and arranged a pleasure excursion which would be worthy of his own affection and royal dignity, as well as of his son's youth. But he gave orders that all the common folk with any kind of affliction should be kept away from the royal road, because he feared that they might agitate the prince's sensitive mind. Very gently all cripples were driven away, and all those who were crazy, aged, ailing, and the like, and also all wretched beggars. So the royal highway became supremely magnificent. The citizens jubilantly acclaimed the prince.

But the Gods of the Pure Abode, when they saw that everyone was happy as if in Paradise, conjured up the illusion of an old man, so as to induce the king's son to leave his home. The prince's charioteer explained to him the meaning of old age. The prince reacted to this news like a bull when a lightning-flash crashes down near him. For his understanding was purified by the noble intentions he had formed in his past lives and by the good deeds he had accumulated over countless eons. In consequence his lofty soul was shocked to hear of old age. He sighed deeply, shook his head, fixed his gaze on the old man, surveyed the festive multitude, and, deeply perturbed, said to the charioteer: "So that is how old age destroys indiscriminately the memory, beauty, and strength of all!

And yet with such a sight before it the world goes on quite unperturbed. This being so, my son, turn round the horses, and travel back quickly to our palace. How can I delight to walk about in parks when my heart is full of fear of aging?" So at the bidding of his master's son the charioteer reversed the chariot. And the prince went back into his palace, which now seemed empty to him, as a result of his anxious reflections.

On a second pleasure excursion the same gods created a man with a diseased body. When this fact was explained to him, the son of Shuddhodana was dismayed, trembled like the reflection of the moon on rippling water, and in his compassion he uttered these words in a low voice: "This then is the calamity of disease, which afflicts people! The world sees it, and yet does not lose its confident ways. Greatly lacking in insight it remains cheerful under the constant threat of disease. We will not continue this excursion, but go straight back to the palace. Since I have learnt of the danger of illness, my heart is repelled by pleasures and seems to shrink into itself."

On a third excursion the same gods displayed a corpse, which only the prince and his charioteer could see being borne along the road. The charioteer again explained the meaning of this sight to the prince. Courageous though he was, the king's son, on hearing of death, was suddenly filled with dismay. Leaning his shoulder against the top of the chariot rail, he spoke these words in a forceful voice: "This is the end which has been fixed for all, and yet the world forgets its fears and takes no heed! The hearts of men are surely hardened to fears, for they feel quite at ease even while traveling along the road to the next life. Turn back the chariot! This is no time or place for pleasure excursions. How could an intelligent person pay no heed at a time of disaster, when he knows of his impending destruction?"

From then onwards the prince withdrew from contact with the women in the palace, and in answer to the reproaches of Udayin, the king's counselor, he explained his new attitude in the following words: "It is not that I despise the objects of sense, and I know full well that they make up what we call the 'world.' But when I consider the impermanence of everything in this world, then I can find no delight in it. Yes, if this triad of old age, illness, and death did not exist, then all this loveliness would surely give me great pleasure. If only this beauty of women were imperishable, then my mind would certainly indulge in the passions, though, of course, they have their faults. But since even women attach no more value to their bodies after old age has drunk them up, to delight in them would clearly be a sign of delusion. If people, doomed to undergo old age, illness, and death, are carefree in their enjoyment with others who are in the same position, they behave like birds and beasts. And when you say that our holy books tell us of gods, sages, and heroes who, though highminded, were addicted to sensuous passions, then that by itself should give rise to agitation, since they also are now extinct. Successful highmindedness seems to me incompatible with both extinction and attachment to sensory concerns, and appears to require that one is in full control of oneself. This being so, you will not prevail upon me to devote myself to ignoble sense pleasures, for I am afflicted by ill and it is my lot to become old and to die. How strong and powerful must be your own mind, that in the fleeting pleasures of the senses you find substance! You cling to sense-objects among the most frightful dangers, even while you cannot help seeing all creation on the way to death. By contrast I become frightened and greatly alarmed when I reflect on the dangers of old age, death, and disease. I find neither peace nor contentment, and enjoyment is quite out of the question, for the world looks to me as if ablaze with an all-consuming fire. If a man has once grasped that death is quite inevitable, and if nevertheless greed arises in his heart, then he must surely have an iron will not to weep in this great danger, but to enjoy it." This discourse indicated that the prince had come to a final decision and had combated the very foundations of sensuous passion. And it was the time of sunset.

Questions for Reflection and Discussion

How does the life of the Buddha offer a model for human life? How does the importance of sexuality compare to the other realities of life—old age, sickness, and death—and what insights might be involved in this comparison?

51. THE DHAMMAPADA

Time: some time before the fifth century CE, from earlier oral traditions
Place: Tibet
Author: unknown

The Dhammapada, or "Way of Duty," is another central text of early Buddhism. It offers brief and easily remembered sayings about the pursuit of enlightenment, including the renunciation of sex, said to have been the answers of the Buddha to questions posed to him. It may have been intended for study by Buddhist monks, although scholars dispute much about its origins.

The sensuous pleasures of men flow everywhere.
Bound for pleasures and seeking pleasures men suffer life and old age.
Men who are pursued by lust run around like a hunted hare.
Held in fetters and in bonds they suffer and suffer again.

Men who are pursued by lust run round like a hunted hare.

For a monk to conquer lust he must first conquer desires.

The man who free from desires finds joy in solitude,

but when free he then returns to his life of old desires,

people can say of that man: "He was free and he ran back to his prison!"

The wise do not call a strong fetter that which is made of iron, of wood or of rope; much stronger is the fetter of passion for gold and for jewels, for sons or for wives.

This is indeed a strong fetter, say the wise. It seems soft but it drags a man down, and it is hard to undo.

Therefore some men cut their fetters, renounce the life of the world and start to walk on the path, leaving pleasures behind.

Those who are slaves of desires run into the stream of desires,

even as a spider runs into the web that it made.

Therefore some men cut their fetters and start to walk on the path, leaving sorrows behind.

Leave the past behind; leave the future behind; leave the present behind.

Thou art then ready to go to the other shore.

Never more shalt thou return to a life that ends in death.

Questions for Reflection and Discussion

What metaphors are used to describe the lives of those who have sex, and what metaphors are used for those who renounce it? What might those metaphors reveal about the incentives and disincentives offered in support of sexual renunciation in the Buddhist tradition?

52. BUDDHA AND TARA

Time: fifteenth century CE
Place: Tibet
Artist: unknown

This image represents a movement in medieval Buddhism, influenced by Tantric Hinduism. According to the precepts of Tantric Buddhism, practiced mostly in Tibet, the detached contemplation of sexual activity could help one toward enlightenment. The image represents the Buddha in a sexual embrace with Tara, who is the female embodiment of wisdom (and was likely a goddess absorbed from Hinduism). According to some schools of Tantric Buddhism, even the detached participation in sexual activity could also help one toward enlightenment.

Questions for Reflection and Discussion

How can such an image of the Buddha be reconciled with the Buddhist tradition of sexual renunciation? Does the distinction between heavenly and earthly sex matter? Is the creation of a feminine personification of the Buddhist search for enlightenment significant?

53. THE CHARIOT OF MIND AND BODY

Time: fifth century BCE
Place: Greece
Author: Plato

In one of the most famous metaphors ever used to talk about love and lust, Plato compares the two feelings to two horses yoked together at a chariot. The image comes from the Phaedrus, *a treatise that is about the use of rhetoric, but includes Socrates making the impassioned speech excerpted below to the young man, Phaedrus. The speech shows how the adult male (the lover) and the boy (the beloved) in a peder-astic relationship should act toward each other. The speech, however, is also about the power of rhetoric; is Socrates merely saying what the boy wants to hear so that he can make him fall in love with him?*

Let us … compare the soul to a winged char-ioteer and his team acting together. Now all the horses and charioteers of the gods are good and come of good stock, but in other beings there is a mixture of good and bad. First of all we must make it plain that the rul-ing power in us men drives a pair of horses, and next that one of these horses is fine and good and of noble stock, and the other the opposite in every way. So in our case the task of the charioteer is necessarily a difficult and unpleasant business….

The horse that is harnessed on the senior side is upright and clean-limbed; he holds his neck high and has a somewhat hooked nose; his color is white, with black eyes; his thirst for honor is tempered by restraint and modesty; he is a friend to genuine renown and needs no whip, but is driven simply by the word of command. The other horse is crooked, lumbering, ill-made; stiff-necked, short-throated, snub-nosed; his coat is black and his eyes a bloodshot grey; wantonness and boastfulness are his companions, and he is hairy-eared and deaf, hardly controllable even with whip and goad.

Now when the charioteer sees the vision of the loved one, so that a sensation of warmth spreads from him over the whole soul and he begins to feel an itching and the stings of desire, the obedient horse, constrained now as always by a sense of shame, holds himself back from springing upon the beloved; but the other, utterly heedless now of the driver's whip and goad, rushes forward prancing, and to the great discomfiture of his yoke-fellow and the charioteer drives them to approach the lad and make mention of the sweetness of physical love. At first the two indignantly resist the idea of being forced into such mon-strous wrongdoing, but finally, when they can get no peace, they yield to the importunity of the bad horse and agree to do what he bids and advance.

So they draw near, and the vision of the beloved dazzles their eyes. When the driver beholds it the sight awakens in him the mem-ory of absolute beauty; he sees her again enthroned in her holy place attended by chas-tity. At the thought he falls upon his back in fear and awe, and in so doing inevitably tugs the reins so violently that he brings both horses down upon their haunches; the good horse gives way willingly and does not strug-gle, but the lustful horse resists with all his strength. When they have withdrawn a little distance the good horse in shame and dread makes the whole soul break into a sweat, but the other no sooner recovers from the pain of the bit and of his fall than he bursts into angry abuse, reproaching the driver and his fellow horse for their cowardice and lack of spirit in running away and breaking their word. After one more attempt to force his unwilling partners to advance he grudgingly assents to their entreaty that the attempt should be deferred to another time. When that time comes they pretend to forget, but he reminds them; forcing them forward, neighing and tugging, he compels them to approach the beloved once more with the same suggestion. And when they come near he takes the bit between his teeth and pulls shamelessly, with head down and tail stretched out.

The driver, however, experiences even more intensely what he experienced before; he falls back like a racing charioteer at the barrier, and with a still more violent backward pull jerks the bit from between the teeth of the lustful horse, drenches his abusive tongue and jaws with blood, and forcing his legs and haunches against the ground reduces him to torment. Finally, after several repetitions of this treatment, the wicked horse abandons his lustful ways; meekly now he executes the wishes of his driver, and when he catches sight of the loved one is ready to die of fear. So at last it comes about that the soul of the lover waits upon his beloved in reverence and awe.

Thus the beloved finds himself being treated like a god and receiving all manner of service from a lover whose love is true love and no pretence, and his own nature disposes him to feel kindly towards his admirer. He may repulse him at first because in the past he has imbibed from schoolfellows and others the mistaken idea that it is disgraceful to have dealings with a lover, but as time goes on his increasing maturity and the decree of destiny bring him to admit his lover to his society; after all it is not ordained that bad men should be friends with one another, nor yet that good men should not. When he has made him welcome and begun to enjoy his conversation and society, the constant kindness that he meets with in close companionship with his lover strikes the beloved with amazement; he realizes clearly that all his other friends and relations together cannot offer him anything to compare with the affection that he receives from this friend whom a god has inspired. When their intimacy is established and the loved one has grown used to being near his friend and touching him in the gymnasium and elsewhere … in its turn the soul of the beloved is filled with love.

So now the beloved is in love, but with what he cannot tell. He does not know and cannot explain what has happened to him; he is like a man who has an eye infection from another and cannot account for it, he does not realize that he is seeing himself in his lover as in a glass. In his lover's presence he feels a relief from pain like his; when he is away he longs for him even as he himself is longed for. He is experiencing a counter-love which is the reflection of the love he inspires, but he speaks of it and thinks of it as friendship, not as love. Like his lover, though less strongly, he feels a desire to see, to touch, to kiss him, and to share his bed. And naturally it is not long before these desires are fulfilled in action. When they are in bed together, the lover's unruly horse has a word to say to his driver, and claims to be allowed a little enjoyment in return for all that he has suffered. But his counterpart in the beloved has nothing to say; but swelling with a desire of whose nature he is ignorant he embraces and kisses his lover as a demonstration of affection to so kind a friend, and when they are in each other's arms he is in a mood to refuse no favor that the lover may ask; yet his yoke-fellow in his turn joins with the charioteer in opposing to this impulse the moderating influence of modesty and reason.

So, if the higher elements in their minds prevail, and guide them into a way of life which is strictly devoted to the pursuit of wisdom, they will pass their time on earth in happiness and harmony; by subduing the part of the soul that contained the seeds of vice and setting free that in which virtue had its birth they will become masters of themselves and their souls will be at peace. Finally, when this life is ended, their wings will carry them aloft; they will have won the first of the three bouts in the real Olympian Games, the greatest blessing that either human virtue or divine madness can confer on man.

But if they practice a less exalted way of life and devote themselves to the pursuit of honor rather than of wisdom, it may come about that in their cups or at some other unguarded moment their two unruly beasts will catch them unaware, and joining forces constrain them to snatch at what the world regards as the height of felicity and to consummate their desire. Once they have enjoyed this pleasure they will enjoy it again thereafter, but sparingly, because what they do does not carry with it the consent of their whole mind. Though their friendship is upon a lower plane, such a pair too will remain friends, not only while their passion lasts but after it has abated; they will regard themselves as having exchanged mutual pledges so sacred that they can never without great guilt break them and become enemies. In the end they emerge from the body without wings, it is true, but having made a strong effort to achieve them; this is no mean prize, and it comes to them from the madness of love … and together, when the time comes, they receive their wings, because of their love.

Questions for Reflection and Discussion

What associations does the metaphor of the charioteer bring to the feelings of love and lust? How dangerous is it to give into lust? Why is it better to restrain lust and hold out for nonsexual (what became known as Platonic) love?

54. ORIBASIUS ON THE DANGERS OF SEX

Time: fourth century CE
Place: The Roman Empire
Author: Oribasius

In this excerpt from his Medical Collection, *Oribasius, who was court physician to the Roman Emperor Julian, describes the dangers that can come from too much sex. His views both follow from but go much further than those of earlier Greek medical writers, but his ideas may reflect a contemporary consensus; in any case, his ideas became influential for later generations.*

The testicles are even more important than the heart, since, besides the heat and strength they give to animals, they are responsible for the continuance of the species, for they impart to the whole body a power similar to the sensory and motor power which the brain communicates to the nerves, and to the pulsatory power that the heart communicates to the arteries, and this power causes the male's vigor and virility.…

When, as a result of continual sexual excess, all the sperm has been lost, the testicles draw seminal liquid from the veins immediately above them. These veins contain only a small quantity of this condensed liquid; so when they are suddenly deprived of it by the testicles, which are stronger than they are, they in turn drain the veins above them and so on. This draining process does not stop until it has involved every part of the body, so if it is constantly repeated and if all the vessels and all the parts of the body are forced to give up their supplies until the strongest part is finally satisfied, the result will be that all the parts of the animal or the living creature are drained not just of seminal fluid but also of their vital spirit for this is taken from the arteries along with the seminal fluid. It is hardly surprising, therefore, that those who lead a debauched life become weak, since the purest part of both substances is removed from their body. As well as this, pleasure itself can dissolve vital tension to such an extent that people have died from an excess of pleasure. We should therefore not be surprised if those who indulge moderately in the pleasures of love become weak….

Those who engage in sexual relations, and particularly those who do so without restraint, must take greater care of themselves than others, so that by ensuring that their bodies are in the best possible condition they may suffer less from the harmful effects of sexual activity; to this end they must go for walks, have gentle massage and hot baths if that is their custom, and take pure food which is nourishing and yet light, and an ample supply of suitably diluted drinks; they must have sufficient sleep and avoid the tiredness that comes from anger, pain, joy, excessively weakening activities, steam baths, sweating, vomiting, drunkenness, heavy work, becoming too hot or too cold.

Questions for Reflection and Discussion

According to such beliefs, what constitutes a healthy lifestyle? What sort of an individual does Oribasius have in mind for his advice? What authority backs up his advice?

55. THE BOOK OF WISDOM ON SEX

Time: second century BCE
Place: Israel
Author: Jesus, son of Sirach

This is a passage from the Biblical book of Wisdom (part of the body of sacred writings preserved by the ancient Israelites, but a book not recognized as part of the Bible by modern Jews and by some Christians). Here, sex and marriage are downplayed as being much less important than other religious obligations. The comments about barren women and eunuchs contradict passages in the Torah or Law of Moses, so it is written expressly as a revision of the ancient Jewish law.

Blessed the barren woman is she be blameless,
she who has known no guilty bed;
her fruitfulness will be seen at the scrutiny of souls.
Blessed, too, the eunuch whose hand has committed no crime,
who has contemplated no wrong against the Lord;
for his loyalty special favor will be granted him,
a most desirable portion in the temple of the Lord.
For the fruit of honest labors is glorious,
and the root of understanding does not decay.
But children of adulterers, these shall have no future,
the offspring of an unlawful bed must vanish.
Even if they live long, they will count for nothing,
their old age will go unhonored at the last;
while if they die early, they have neither hope
nor comfort on the day of doom.
Yes, harsh is the fate of a race of evildoers.
Better to have no children yet to have virtue.

Questions for Reflection and Discussion

Does this passage discourage marriage and family life altogether? Why would the author of this passage be kinder to barren women and eunuchs than to the children of adulterers?

56. JESUS ON SEX AND MARRIAGE

Time: first century CE
Place: Israel
Author: unknown, traditionally ascribed to
  Matthew

This passage from the Christian Bible or New Testament gives us glimpses into Jesus' views on sex. It comes from the Gospel of Matthew, ascribed to a close follower of Jesus and perhaps written by one of his followers. It was almost certainly intended for a Jewish audience, so aspects of Jewish culture and religion are left unexplained, such as the contemporary debate between Pharisees and Saducees over the nature of the afterlife, or the references to the Torah or the Law of Moses and to the legend of Adam and Eve. The two passages come from different parts of the Gospel.

"You have heard that it was said, 'Do not commit adultery.' But I tell you that anyone who looks at a woman lustfully has already committed adultery with her in his heart. If your right eye causes you to sin, gouge it out and throw it away. It is better for you to lose one part of your body than for your whole body to be thrown into hell. And if your right hand causes you to sin, cut it off and throw it away. It is better for you to lose one part of your body than for your whole body to go into hell. It has been said, 'Anyone who divorces his wife must give her a certificate of divorce.' But I tell you that anyone who divorces his wife, except for marital unfaithfulness, causes her to commit adultery, and anyone who marries a woman so divorced commits adultery."

When Jesus had finished saying these things, he left Galilee and came into the region of Judea to the other side of the Jordan. Large crowds followed him, and he healed them there. Some Pharisees came to him to test him. They asked, "Is it lawful for a man to divorce his wife for any and every reason?" "Haven't you read," he replied, "that at the beginning the Creator 'made them male and female,' and said, 'For this reason a man will leave his father and mother and be united to his wife, and the two will become one flesh'? So they are no longer two, but one. Therefore what God has joined together, let man not separate." "Why then," they asked, "did Moses command that a man give his wife a certificate of divorce and send her away?" Jesus replied, "Moses permitted you to divorce your wives because your hearts were hard. But it was not this way from the beginning. I tell you that anyone who divorces his wife, except for marital unfaithfulness, and marries another woman commits adultery." The disciples said to him, "If this is the situation between a husband and wife, it is better not to marry." Jesus replied, "Not everyone can accept this teaching, but only those to whom it has been given. For some are eunuchs because they were born that way; others were made that way by men; and others have made themselves eunuchs because of the kingdom of heaven. The one who can accept this should accept it."

Questions for Reflection and Discussion

What advantages does Jesus recommend for renouncing sex? How does Jesus understand himself as relating to the Law of Moses on matters of sex, according to Matthew? Are there any clues that tell us whether the recommendations to amputate parts of the body or to castrate oneself should be understood literally or metaphorically?

57. PAUL ON SEX AND MARRIAGE

Time: first century CE
Place: Greece
Author: Paul

Paul's First Letter to the Corinthians, also from the Christian Bible, is one of the earliest of Christian writings. Paul himself did not know Jesus but was converted to his message and saw it as one of human freedom and as an escape from obligation to the Jewish Law. Here, in this letter to his fellow Christians among the Jewish community living at Corinth in Greece, Paul seems concerned that some had taken that message of freedom too far, especially sexually. So he attempted to explain to them what he thought the Christian message entailed in sexual matters.

Do you not know that the wicked will not inherit the kingdom of God? Do not be deceived: Neither the sexually immoral nor idolaters nor adulterers nor male prostitutes nor homosexual offenders nor thieves nor the greedy nor drunkards nor slanderers nor swindlers will inherit the kingdom of God. And that is what some of you were. But you were washed, you were sanctified, you were justified in the name of the Lord Jesus Christ and by the Spirit of our God. "Everything is permissible for me"—but not everything is beneficial. "Everything is permissible for me"—but I will not be mastered by anything. "Food for the stomach and the stomach for food"—but God will destroy them both. The body is not meant for sexual immorality, but for the Lord, and the Lord for the body. By his power God raised the Lord from the dead, and he will raise us also. Do you not know that your bodies are members of Christ himself? Shall I then take the members of Christ and unite them with a prostitute? Never! Do you not know that he who unites himself with a prostitute is one with her in body? For it is said, "The two will become one flesh." But he who unites himself with the Lord is one with him in spirit. Flee from sexual immorality. All other sins a man commits are outside his body, but he who sins sexually sins against his own body. Do you not know that your body is a temple of the Holy Spirit, who is in you, whom you have received from God? You are not your own; you were bought at a price. Therefore honor God with your body.

Now for the matters you wrote about: It is good for a man not to marry. But since there is so much immorality, each man should have his own wife, and each woman her own husband. The husband should fulfill his marital duty to his wife, and likewise the wife to her husband. The wife's body does not belong to her alone but also to her husband. In the same way, the husband's body does not belong to him alone but also to his wife. Do not deprive each other except by mutual consent and for a time, so that you may devote yourselves to prayer. Then come together again so that Satan will not tempt you because of your lack of self-control. I say this as a concession, not as a command. I wish that all men were as I am. But each man has his own gift from God; one has this gift, another has that.

Now to the unmarried and the widows I say: It is good for them to stay unmarried, as I am. But if they cannot control themselves, they should marry, for it is better to marry than to burn with passion. To the married I give this command (not I, but the Lord): A wife must not separate from her husband. But if she does, she must remain unmarried or else be reconciled to her husband. And a husband must not divorce his wife. To the rest I say this (I, not the Lord): If any brother has a wife who is not a believer and she is willing to live with him, he must not divorce her. And if a woman has a husband who is not a believer and he is willing to live with her, she must not divorce him. For the unbelieving husband has been sanctified through his wife, and the unbelieving wife has been sanctified through her believing husband. Otherwise your children would be unclean, but as it is, they are holy. But if the unbeliever leaves, let him do so. A believing man or woman is not bound in such circumstances; God has called us to live in peace. How do you know, wife, whether you will save your husband? Or, how do you know, husband, whether you will save your wife? Nevertheless, each one should retain the place in life that the Lord assigned to him and to which God has called him. This is the rule I lay down in all the churches....

Now about virgins: I have no command from the Lord, but I give a judgment as one who by the Lord's mercy is trustworthy. Because of the present crisis, I think that it is good for you to remain as you are. Are you married? Do not seek a divorce. Are you unmarried? Do not look for a wife. But if you do marry, you have not sinned; and if a virgin marries, she has not sinned. But those who marry will face many troubles in this life, and I want to spare you this. What I mean, brothers, is that the time is short. From now on those who have wives should live as if they had none; those who mourn, as if they did not; those who are happy, as if they were not; those who buy something, as if it were not theirs to keep; those who use the things of the world, as if not engrossed in them. For this world in its present form is passing away.

I would like you to be free from concern. An unmarried man is concerned about the Lord's affairs—how he can please the Lord. But a married man is concerned about the affairs of this world—how he can please his wife—and his interests are divided. An unmarried woman or virgin is concerned about the Lord's affairs: Her aim is to be devoted to the Lord in both body and spirit. But a married woman is concerned about the affairs of this world—how she can please her husband. I am saying this for your own good, not to restrict you, but that you may live in a right way in undivided devotion to the Lord.

If anyone thinks he is acting improperly toward the virgin he is engaged to, and if she is getting along in years and he feels he ought to marry, he should do as he wants. He is not sinning. They should get married. But the man who has settled the matter in his own mind, who is under no compulsion but has control over his own will, and who has made up his mind not to marry the virgin—this man also does the right thing. So then, he who marries the virgin does right, but he who does not marry her does even better. A woman is bound to her husband as long as he lives. But if her husband dies, she is free to marry anyone she wishes, but he must belong to the Lord. In my judgment, she is happier if she stays as she is—and I think that I too have the Spirit of God.

Questions for Reflection and Discussion

What kinds of sexual behaviour does Paul recommend and what does he only tolerate? What might some of the Christians at Corinth have been doing that Paul condemned, and what might their arguments have been to justify their actions?

58. PAUL ON SEX AND MARRIAGE, AGAIN

Time: possibly second century CE
Place: Greece
Author: unknown, traditionally attributed
   to Paul

The sentiments expressed in this passage seem so unlike those expressed in the previous passage

Wives, submit to your own husbands as to the
Lord. For the husband is the head of the wife
as Christ is the head of the church, his body,
of which he is the Savior. Now as the church
submits to Christ, so also wives should submit
to their husbands in everything. Husbands,
love your wives, just as Christ also loved the
church and gave himself up for her, to make her
holy, cleansing her by the washing with water
through the word, and to present her to himself
as a radiant church, without stain or wrinkle
or any other blemish, but holy and blameless.
In this same way, husbands ought to love their
wives as their own bodies. He who loves his wife
loves himself. After all, no one ever hated his
own body, but he feeds and cares for it, just as
Christ does the church—for we are members of
his body. "For this reason a man will leave his
father and mother and be united to his wife, and
the two will become one flesh." This is a profound mystery—but I am talking about Christ
and the church. However, each one of you also
must love his wife as he loves himself, and the
wife must respect her husband.

Questions for Reflection and Discussion

How is the relationship between husbands and
wives described, and what significance does
this metaphor have for the marital relationship? Is it possible to reconcile this passage
with the previous passage by Paul as a consistent philosophy on marriage?

59. JESUS ON SEX AND MARRIAGE, AGAIN

Time: third century CE
Place: Egypt in the Roman Empire
Author: unknown

*The Gospel of Philip, intended to be part of the
Christian Bible and believed by some early
Christians to be the authentic words of Jesus,
was ultimately rejected by the leaders of the
churches in the Roman Empire as inauthentic
and so was excluded from the Bible. It was discovered among a group of similar writings at
Nag Hammadi in Egypt in 1945, buried there
by believers in its message who did not want
to see the writings destroyed after they were
condemned. It offers more support for the renunciation of sex and marriage by early Christians,
in a series of sayings attributed to Jesus. It also
contains the suggestion that Jesus loved Mary
Magdalene in a special way, as a spiritual wife,
and (included below) the first appearance of the
legend of incubi and succubi, demons who have
sex with human beings.*

As for the unclean spirits, there are males
among them and there are females. The
males are they which unite with the souls
which inhabit a female form, but the females
are they which are mingled with those in a
male form, through one who was disobedi-
ent. And none shall be able to escape them,
since they detain him if he does not receive
a male power or a female power—the bridegroom and the bride—one receives them from
the mirrored bridal chamber. When the wanton women see a male sitting alone, they leap
down on him and play with him and defile
him. So also the lecherous men, when they see
a beautiful woman sitting alone, they persuade
her and compel her, wishing to defile her. But
if they see the man and his wife sitting beside

one another, the female cannot come into the man, nor can the male come into the woman. So if the image and the angel are united with one another, neither can any venture to go into the man or the woman.

If the woman had not separated from the man, she should not die with the man. His separation became the beginning of death. Because of this, Christ came to repair the separation, which was from the beginning, and again unite the two, and to give life to those who died as a result of the separation, and unite them. But the woman is united to her husband in the bridal chamber. Indeed, those who have united in the bridal chamber will no longer be separated. Thus Eve separated from Adam because she was never united with him in the bridal chamber.

The children a woman bears resemble the man who loves her. If her husband loves her, then they resemble her husband. If it is an adulterer, then they resemble the adulterer. Frequently, if a woman sleeps with her husband out of necessity, while her heart is with the adulterer with whom she usually has intercourse, the child she will bear is born resembling the adulterer. Now you who live together with the Son of God, love not the world, but love the Lord, in order that those you will bring forth may not resemble the world, but may resemble the Lord.

No one will be able to know when the husband and the wife have intercourse with one another, except the two of them. Indeed, marriage in the world is a mystery for those who have taken a wife. If there is a hidden quality to the marriage of defilement, how much more is the undefiled marriage a true mystery! It is not fleshly, but pure. It belongs not to desire, but to the will. It belongs not to the darkness or the night, but to the day and the light. If a marriage is open to the public, it has become prostitution, and the bride plays the harlot not only when she is impregnated by another man, but even if she slips out of her bedroom and is seen. Let her show herself only to her father and her mother, and to the friend of the bridegroom and the sons of the bridegroom. These are permitted to enter every day into the bridal chamber. But let the others yearn just to listen to her voice and to enjoy her ointment, and let them feed from the crumbs that fall from the table, like the dogs. Bridegrooms and brides belong to the bridal chamber. No one shall be able to see the bridegroom with the bride unless he become one.

Questions for Reflection and Discussion

How do earthly and heavenly marriage differ? Why might this writing have been rejected as heretical? Is it possible to reconcile the teachings of Jesus here with those from the Gospel of Matthew (source 56)?

60. POEMS OF MIRABAI

Time: sixteenth century CE
Place: India
Author: Mirabai

Mirabai (also known as Mira) was a mystic, that is, a person who claims to have had a direct and often emotional connection with a divinity. Mysticism forms a part of most religious traditions, and because many mystics have been women, modern scholars often consider it to be a form of devotion that provides women with a voice even in religions where they are not permitted to take positions of leadership. Mirabai's connection was with the Hindu god Krishna, whom she calls Giridhara and the Lord of Braj and Hari. Her devotion to her god meant that she eventually abandoned her marriage to a local prince for a life of prayer and the composition of love songs to Krishna, a few examples of which follow.

Let me go to the house of Giridhara.
Giridhara is my true lover:
On beholding His beauty, I long for Him
much.
As night falls I set out to see Him
And at break of day I return.
Day and night I sport in His company,
I please Him in any way I can.
Whatever He clothes me in, that I wear.
Whatever He offers, that I eat.
My love for Him
Is ancient and longstanding.
Without Him I could not live.
Wherever He places me, there I remain.
If He sold me into slavery,
I would acquiesce.
Mira's Lord is the courtly Giridhara,
She offers herself in sacrifice again and
again.

Sister, the Lord of the Poor
Came to wed me in a dream.
Five hundred and sixty million deities
formed the bridal procession
And the bridegroom was the Lord of Braj.
In my dream,
I saw the wedding arch constructed
And the Lord took my hand.
In my dream,
I underwent a wedding ceremony
And entered the married state.
Giridhara has revealed Himself to Mira:
Her fortunes stem
From good deeds in past births.

Come to my pavilion, O my king.
I have spread a bed
Made of delicately selected buds and
blossoms,
And have arrayed myself in bridal garb
From head to toe.
I have been Thy slave during many births,
Thou art the be-all of my existence.

Mira's Lord is Hari, the Indestructible.
Come, grant me Thy sight at once.

Questions for Reflection and Discussion

Is Krishna a substitute husband for Mirabai?
Why can't this spiritual eroticism co-exist
with earthly marriage? How might sexual
renunciation be understood as another form
of eroticism?

SOURCES AND FURTHER READING

On sexual renunciation in history, a very
good general work is Elizabeth Abbot's *The
History of Celibacy* (New York: Scribner,
2000), despite an anti-Catholic tone in its
final chapters. See also the essays in *Celibacy,
Culture, and Society: The Anthropology of
Sexual Abstinence*, Eliza Sobo and Sandra Bell,
eds. (Madison, WI: University of Wisconsin
Press, 2001) that contains both historical and
contemporary studies. Most comparative
studies focus on Christian traditions of sexual renunciation. Three American examples
are studied in Sally Kitch's *Chaste Liberation:
Celibacy and Female Cultural Status* (Urbana,
IL: University of Illinois Press, 1989). One
of these three is the Shakers, founded in
England, who advocated sexual renunciation for all the sect's members, about which
much has been written, and from whom
much survives in historical writings. A good
introduction is the chapter on the Shakers
in Lawrence Foster's *Religion and Sexuality:
Three American Communal Experiments
of the Nineteenth Century* (Oxford: Oxford
University Press, 1981). More recent new religious movements, such as Father Divine's
International Peace Mission (early twentieth-century US), or Marshall Applewhite's
Heaven's Gate (late twentieth-century US),
also advocated celibacy for all members and

would be worth studying. For more on sexual renunciation in specific religious traditions, see the notes below.

50. "The Early Life of the Buddha" was taken from *The Acts of the Buddha*, Edward Conze, trans. (Harmondsworth, UK: Penguin, 1959), 37-41, with slight changes.

For an introduction to the history of Buddhism, see N. Ross Reat's *Buddhism: A History* (Berkeley, CA: Asian Humanities, 1994); or Edward Conze's *Buddhism: A Short History* (Oxford and Boston: Oneworld, 2000). For works on early Buddhism in particular, see Govind Chandra Pande's *Studies in the Origins of Buddhism* (Allahabad, India: University of Allahabad, 1957); or Vishwanath Prasad Varma's *Early Buddhism and Its Origins* (New Delhi: Munshiram Manoharlal, 1971); or Kogen Mizuno's *The Beginnings of Buddhism*, Richard Gage, trans. (Tokyo: Kosei, 1980); or Uma Chakravarti's *The Social Dimensions of Early Buddhism* (New York: Oxford University Press, 1987). Recent good biographies of the Buddha include Karen Armstrong's *Buddha* (New York: Viking, 2001); Michael Carrithers's *The Buddha: A Very Short Introduction* (Oxford: Oxford University Press, 2001); and Patricia Eichenbaum Karetzky's *The Life of Buddha: Ancient Scriptural and Pictoral Traditions* (Lanham, MD: University Press of America, 1992). See note 51 for more on Buddhism and sexuality, and note 52 for more on women in Buddhism.

51. "The Dhammapada" was taken from *The Dhammapada*, Juan Mascaro, trans. (Harmondsworth, UK: Penguin, 1973), 83-84.

For more information on Buddhism and sexuality, see Bernard Faure's *The Red Thread: Buddhist Approaches to Sexuality* (Princeton, NJ: Princeton University Press, 1998) or his *The Power of Denial: Buddhism, Purity, and Gender* (Princeton, NJ: Princeton University Press, 2003); or the essays in *Buddhism, Sexuality, and Gender*, José Ignacio Cabezón, ed. (Albany, NY: State University of New York Press, 1992); less historical in focus is John Stevens's *Lust for Enlightenment: Buddhism and Sex* (Boston: Shambala, 1990). Many other early Buddhist sources have been translated in recent years, but few provide any details about sexuality. An exception is the *Vinaya Pitaka* or *Book of the Discipline*, which was intended as instructions for Buddhist monks, including avoidance of sex in a extremely detailed variety of ways; see *The Book of the Discipline*, I.B. Horner, trans., especially vol. 4 (Oxford: Pali Text Society, 2000; orig. pub. 1951).

52. "Buddha and Tara" was taken from Serenity Young, *Courtesans and Tantric Consorts: Sexualities in Buddhist Narrative, Iconography, and Ritual* (New York: Routledge, 2004).

Young's book, from which the image was taken, provides an excellent discussion of women and sexuality and early Buddhism. For more information on women in Buddhism, see also Rita M. Gross's *Buddhism After Patriarchy: A Feminist History, Analysis, and Reconstruction of Buddhism* (Albany, NY: State University of New York, 1993); or Masatoshi Ueki's *Gender Equality in Buddhism* (New York: Peter Lang, 2001); or Gill Farrer-Halls's *The Feminine Face of Buddhism* (Wheaton, IL: Quest, 2002). For more on Buddhist tantrism, see Teja Narayana Misra's *Buddhist Tantra and Buddhist Art* (New Delhi: D.K. Printworld, 2000); or Hugh B. Urban's *Tantra: Sex, Secrecy, Politics, and Power in the Study of Religion* (Berkeley, CA: University of California Press, 2003); Gudrun Buhnemann's "The Goddess Mahacinakrama-Tara (Ugra-Tara) in Buddhist and Hindu Tantrism," *Bulletin of Oriental and*

African Studies 59 (1996): 472-93; or the essays in *Tantra in Practice*, David Gordon White, ed. (Princeton, NJ: Princeton University Press, 2000). A good introduction on Buddhist art is Meher McArthur's *Reading Buddhist Art: An Illustrated Guide to Buddhist Signs and Symbols* (New York: Thames & Hudson, 2002).

53. "The Chariot of Mind and Body" is taken from Plato, *Phaedrus and Letters VII and VIII*, Walter Hamilton, trans. (Harmondsworth, UK: Penguin, 1973), 50-51, 61-65.

There are a few commentaries on Plato's *Phaedrus*, which is as much about rhetoric as about love, although the first part (including Phaedrus's speech and Socrates' two speeches) might be read with profit in a history of sexuality. See Graeme Nicholson's *Plato's Phaedrus: The Philosophy of Love* (West Lafayette, IN: Purdue University Press, 1999). See also Alfred Geier's *Plato's Erotic Thought: The Tree of the Unknown* (Rochester, NY: University of Rochester Press, 2002) for a broader study of Plato's ideas on love, including his *Symposium* (an excerpt of which is found in source 19). It is difficult to find specific works that trace broadly the influence of this metaphor, but two examples from the Italian Renaissance can stand for them: Giovanni Pico della Mirandola's *Commentary on a Poem of Platonic Love*, Douglas Carmichael, trans. (Lanham, MD: University Press of America, 1986); or *Marsilio Ficino and the Phaedran Charioteer: Introduction, Texts, Translations*, Michael J.B. Allen, ed. (Berkeley, CA: University of California Press, 1981).

54. "Oribasius on the Dangers of Sex" is taken from Aline Rousselle, *Porneia: On Desire and the Body in Antiquity*, Felicia Pheasant, trans. (Oxford: Blackwell, 1988), 14-15, 18.

See note 29 on ancient medical ideas. Only parts of Oribasius's writings have been translated into English: see *Dieting for an Emperor*, Mark Grant, ed. (Leiden, NLD: Brill, 1997), which, as the modern title suggests, is primarily about food rather than sex. Rousselle's book, from which the excerpt is taken, is best for further information. See also Mathew Kuefler's *The Manly Eunuch: Masculinity, Gender Ambiguity, and Christian Ideology in Late Antiquity* (Chicago: University of Chicago Press, 2001), chap. 3, on late ancient fears of sex.

55. "The Book of Wisdom on Sex" is taken from *The Jerusalem Bible* (New York: Doubleday, 1966), 878-79 (Wisdom 3: 13-19, 4: 1a).

The Book of Wisdom, also known as the Wisdom of Solomon, is found in Catholic and Orthodox Bibles, but not in Jewish or Protestant ones; on this point, see Otto Kaiser's *The Old Testament Apocrypha: An Introduction* (Peabody, MA: Hendrickson, 2004). On the book itself and its historical context, see John J. Collins's *Jewish Wisdom in the Hellenistic Age* (Louisville, KY: Westminster John Knox, 1997). Jewish experiments with sexual renunciation in the Late Second Temple period can be seen among the Therapeutae in Egypt or the Essenes in Israel; the latter probably included the Qumran Community where the Dead Sea Scrolls were found. For the first group, see the first-century account in Philo of Alexandria's *About the Contemplative Life*, F.C. Conybeare, trans. (New York: Garland, 1987); and modern scholarly analysis in Joan Taylor's *Jewish Women Philosophers of First-Century Alexandria: Philo's 'Therapeutae' Reconsidered* (Oxford: Oxford University Press, 2003). For the second, see Alex Deasley's *The Shape of Qumran Theology* (Carlisle, UK: Paternoster, 2000), among many general works.

56. "Jesus on Sex and Marriage" is taken from *The Holy Bible: New International Version* (Grand Rapids, MI: Zondervan Bible, 1978), 1039-40, 1057 (Matthew 5: 27-32, 19: 1-12).

The list of modern works on sexuality and marriage in the Christian Bible is almost limitless. Most take a broad approach, examining a variety of episodes from the legend of Adam and Eve on from which to draw their lessons, and specific works on Jesus' teachings on sex and marriage are usually included as part of these larger works. A few exceptions are Raymond Collins's *Sexual Ethics and the New Testament* (New York: Crossroad, 2000) or his *Divorce in the New Testament* (Collegeville, MN: Liturgical Press, 1992); or L. William Countryman's *Dirt, Greed, and Sex: Sexual Ethics in the New Testament and their Implications for Today* (Philadelphia: Fortress, 1988). As evidenced in the four gospel accounts of his life and teachings, however, Jesus seems to have spoken rarely about such matters. Different episodes, however, are recorded in the other accounts of Jesus' teachings, Gospels of Mark, Luke, and John. References for these texts may be found in the modern scholarly works.

57. "Paul on Sex and Marriage" is taken from *The Holy Bible: New International Version* (Grand Rapids, MI: Zondervan Bible, 1978), 1226-28 (1 Corinthians 6: 9-20, 7: 1-17, 25-40).

Paul, the other early founder of Christianity, was far more outspoken than Jesus on sexual matters. See also the extended comments from his letters in Romans 1, or 1 Corinthians 13. On Paul's attitudes toward sex, marriage, and women, there has been much written. Of recent works, see Francis Watson's *Agape, Eros, Gender: Towards a Pauline Sexual Ethic* (Cambridge: Cambridge University Press, 2000); or the essays in *A Feminist Companion to Paul*, Amy-Jill Levine, ed. (London: T & T International, 2004); or Craig Keener's *Paul, Women, and Wives: Marriage and Women's Ministry in the Letters of Paul* (Peabody, MA: Hendrickson, 1992). More specific to this passage is Will Deming's *Paul on Marriage and Celibacy* (Cambridge: Cambridge University Press, 1995); J. Duncan Derrett's "The Disposal of Virgins," *Man* 9 (1974): 23-30; or Dale Martin's "Paul without Passion: On Paul's Rejection of Desire in Sex and Marriage," in *Constructing Early Christian Families: Family as Social Reality and Metaphor*, Halvor Moxnes, ed. (New York: Routledge, 1997). Generally on the letter that Paul wrote to the Corinthians, see Kevin Quast's *Reading the Corinthian Correspondence: An Introduction* (New York: Paulist, 1994).

58. "Paul on Sex and Marriage, Again" is taken from *The Holy Bible: New International Version* (Grand Rapids, MI: Zondervan Bible, 1978), 1257 (Ephesians 5: 22-33).

The authenticity of Paul's Letter to the Ephesians is questioned because of the difficulty of reconciling the opinions expressed in it with his other writings; also, while Paul mentions his other letters in his writings, he never mentions a letter written to the Ephesians. For more on the debate, see A. van Roon's *The Authenticity of Ephesians* (Leiden, NLD: Brill, 1975). See Carolyn Osiek's *Families in the New Testament World: Households and House Churches* (Louisville, KY: Westminster John Knox, 1997). On the Greek word *mysterion* applied to marriage, which in this version is translated as "mystery" but into Latin as *sacramentum*, and from which originated the notion of marriage as a sacrament, see Chrys Caragounis's *The Ephesian Mysterion: Meaning and Content* (Lund: LiberLäromedel/Gleerup, 1977). See note 57 for more on Paul's attitude toward sex, marriage, and gender.

59. "Jesus on Sex and Marriage, Again" is taken from *The Gospel of Philip*, Wesley Isenberg, trans., in *The Nag Hammadi Library*, James Robinson, ed. (San Francisco: Harper & Row, 1978), 139, 142, 147, 149.

A good and readable introduction to Gnosticism and its texts, including the Gospel of Philip, is Elaine Pagels's *The Gnostic Gospels* (New York: Random House, 1979; revised 1989). It should be noted, however, that more recent scholars have questioned the lumping together of a variety of beliefs and movements as a single entity called Gnosticism; on this point, see Karen L. King's *What is Gnosticism?* (Cambridge, MA: Belknap Press of Harvard University Press, 2003). On Gnostic beliefs about sexuality, see Risto Uro's and Ingvild Saelid Gilhus's essays in *Constructing Early Christian Families: Family as Social Reality and Metaphor*, Halvor Moxnes, ed. (New York: Routledge, 1997). On Gnostic beliefs about gender, see Dennis MacDonald's *There is No Male or Female: The Fate of a Dominical Saying in Paul and Gnosticism* (Philadelphia: Fortress, 1987).

60. "Poems of Mirabai" is taken from *Poems of Mirabai*, A.J. Alston, trans. (Delhi: Motilal Banarsidass, 1998), 41, 44-45, 96, with slight changes.

There are several English translations of the poetry of Mirabai (sometimes referred to as Mira or Meera), and there are also sound recordings of her songs. For more on the *bhakti* movement of emotional devotion of which Mirabai is part, see John Stratton Hawley's *Three Bhakti Voices: Mirabai, Surdas, and Kabir in Their Time and Ours* (Delhi: Oxford University Press, 2005). On women's devotion to Krishna, see the essays in *Vaisnavi: Women and the Worship of Krishna*, Steven J. Rosen, ed. (Delhi: Motilal Banarsidass,

1996). See note 44 for more on devotion to Krishna. The literature on mystical religious experience, or mysticism, is vast but complicated, often relying on psychoanalytic models and vocabulary, so it is difficult to recommend much to students or nonspecialists. Readable exceptions, also demonstrating that much of the work done by scholars has focused on medieval and early modern Christian women, include Frances Beer's *Women and Mystical Experience in the Middle Ages* (Rochester, NY: Boydell, 1992); Elizabeth Petroff's *Body and Soul: Essays on Medieval Women and Mysticism* (Oxford: Oxford University Press, 1994); Carol Flinders's *Enduring Grace: Living Portraits of Seven Women Mystics* (San Francisco: HarperSanFrancisco, 1993); and Bernard McGinn's *The Presence of God: A History of Western Christian Mysticism*, 3 vols. (New York: Crossword, 1991-98). Further studies on specific individuals are abundant, and many writings of medieval women mystics have been translated, but the language of sex is often discreet and interwoven among other theological themes that make them less accessible. Hildegard of Bingen's discussions of Mother Church or Catharine of Siena's mystical marriage to Jesus might be worth investigating in a history of sexuality, though, and Margery Kempe's autobiography contains numerous references to her earthly marriage as well as to her erotic bond to Jesus; on these sources, see Barbara Newman's *Sister of Wisdom: St. Hildegard's Theology of the Feminine* (Berkeley: University of California Press, 1987); *The Letters of St. Catharine of Siena*, Suzanne Noffke, ed. and trans. (Binghampton, NY: Medieval & Renaissance Texts & Studies, 1988); or *The Book of Margery Kempe*, B.A. Windeatt, trans. (Harmondsworth, UK: Penguin, 1985). Margaret Smith's *Muslim Woman Mystics* (Oxford: Oneworld, 2001) is a rare study on women's mystical experience in Islam.

the eLaboration of tradition

While sacred texts, religious myths, and prophetic utterances provided a foundation for the sexual ideologies of the world's religious and philosophical traditions, these writings and words were seldom systematic in their approaches or always practical in their recommendations. The gap between inspired words and everyday advice was filled by interpretation and elaboration, with intellectual speculation and with commentaries that provided a comprehensive ideology as well as useful guidelines for life. The elaboration of traditions about sexuality is, therefore, the subject of this chapter.

Individuals elaborate upon ideologies, sometimes intentionally. As ideas pass from one person to another, slight alterations in ideologies happen if individuals consciously emphasize different aspects of their traditions or see connections in new ways. Reformers sometimes make changes even while arguing that they are returning things to the way they used to be. Even interpretations made by relying on one part may force a reappraisal of another part of the same ideology. For example, medieval Christian leaders wanted marriage to be both indissoluble and exogamous. Which principle would triumph when already married couples were discovered to be too closely related?

Elaboration is essential to any religious or philosophical tradition. After all, no ideology remains stagnant; it if did, it would not survive for long. Ideologies have to change to meet changing circumstances, even if the basic core stays unchanged. Technological developments are merely the clearest example of changing modern circumstances that can affect sexual ideologies, which must respond to such things as in vitro fertilization or abortifacient pills.

Sometimes changes in ideology are unintentional and even unnoticed. As time passes, individuals understand their environments differently. Individuals of diverse backgrounds—ethnicities, genders, statuses, or ages—sometimes understand ideologies in new ways. They may not be able to recreate the context in which their ideologies were first formulated, even when they have sacred texts at their disposal. Errors can occur in translation, in reproduction of the texts—for much of history, all writing was recopied by hand—or in misinterpretation.

Over time, these changes can be considerable. Religious and philosophical traditions have all had to reappraise aspects of their sexual ideologies as varied and as substantial as gender equality, the nature of marriage (including monogamy versus polygamy and endogamy versus exogamy), the permissibility of divorce and remarriage, and the tolerance of homosexuality. Indeed, beliefs about sexual customs often exhibit the greatest changes in religious ideologies, since they are usually considered as secondary rather than primary beliefs, as would beliefs about the divinity or the afterlife. Again, proponents of ideologies often try to disguise these changes, consciously or not, arguing that "things have always been this way," either because they believe it themselves or because it is an effective argument. Part of the value of studying history generally is in uncovering these changes to ideology and in learning the truth about the way things have been.

Justifications for these elaborations of ideology are often necessary. Sometimes they are said to be "logical," a reasonable extension or explanation of an idea or practice, and by calling them that, it is implied that any rational person would agree. An elaboration may be justified by the personal authority of whoever is doing the elaboration. Here historians and other scholars usually distinguish between different types of authority fig-

ures, following the scheme proposed by Max Weber. One type is "traditional," that is, their authority rests on their status within a tradition, a status that is usually formal. The Catholic pope and the Muslim caliph are two extreme examples of such an institutional authority (extreme because of the weight of the authority that each has claimed, as "vicar of Christ" or as "successor to Muhammad," that is, as heirs to the spiritual authority wielded by the founders of their religions). In each case, the individuals claim that their status within the institution allows them to add to or clarify beliefs or practices. The other type of authority is often described as "charismatic," that is, it relies on the personal charisma of the individual who elaborates a tradition, an individual who may not have any institutionalized or formal authority. Mystics, prophets, saints, shamans, and seers are all examples of charismatic authority. In such cases, the charismatic leader claims a special and extraordinary status that allows for the embellishment of an ideology.

For the historian, these different kinds of elaborations provide a wealth of written documents. Because each generation has had to reinterpret its ideology so that it will continue to be a useful and practical guide for believers, what we find in the historical record are layer upon layer of these elaborations. It is an excellent opportunity to track changes to ideology as well as to better understand the historical context of all ideologies. The following readings demonstrate the range of elaborations to religious and philosophical traditions on sexuality. These readings are certainly worth comparing to the excerpts from sacred texts and legends presented in the previous two chapters to see what has changed and what has remained the same.

61. THE TALMUD ON RAPE, SEDUCTION, AND SLANDER

Time: seventh or eighth century CE, from
    earlier oral traditions
Place: Israel
Author: unknown

*An excellent source within which to observe
the process of elaboration at work is the Jewish
Talmud. It is a collection of opinions about
how to follow the Torah or Law of Moses in
particular circumstances not described in the
Bible. Its argumentation is often difficult for
nonspecialists to follow, and it sometimes contains contradictory opinions as different Jewish
rabbis or teachers tried to understand the Law
and the ways to extend it into new situations.
In this example, rabbis debate the differences
between rape, seduction, and slander, a series
of actions that revolve around a woman's sexual honor, whether lost by word or deed, and
whether with her consent or not. The Talmud,
in this excerpt and throughout, also includes
passages taken from an earlier and similar
compilation of interpretations, known as the
Mishnah, but all of the words in italics in what
follows are from the Torah, and one can see how
it is used to justify the arguments.*

The one who seduces a girl pays on three
counts, and the one who rapes a girl pays on
four: the one who seduces a girl pays for the
shame, the damage, and a fine, and the one who
rapes a girl adds to these, for he in addition pays
for the pain which he has inflicted…. Now this
rule that there is compensation for the pain does
not conform to the view of Rabbi Simeon. For
Rabbi Simeon exempts the rapist from obligation to compensate for pain…. They said to him
[Rabbi Simeon], "There is no similarity between
the girl who is raped and the girl who has sexual
relations willingly, nor is the girl who is laid in
the garbage heap to be compared to the one who
has sexual relations under the marriage canopy.
How does Rabbi Simeon interpret, "*because he
has violated her*"? …

Rabbi Ishmael taught, "*If a man seduces a virgin who is not betrothed, and lies with her, he shall
give the marriage present for her, and make her his
wife.*" This teaches that he treats what is owing as
a bridal present, and a bridal present can only be
a marriage settlement. This is in line with what
Scripture has said, "*Ask of me ever so much as a
marriage present and gift, and I will give according as you say to me; only give me the maiden to
be my wife.*" Rabbi Eleazar asked, "In the view of
the party who holds that a woman who is married under these circumstances does not receive
a marriage settlement, as to the daughters of a
woman who has been raped and thereby married, what is the law about their enjoying the
stipulations of the normal marriage contract
which provides for their upkeep? …

If a matter of unchastity turned out to per-
tain to her, or if she is not appropriate to enter
into the Israelite congregation, he is not permitted to confirm her as his wife but, if he
has married her, he must divorce her, since it
is said, "*And she will be a wife to him*"—a wife
appropriate for him….

Rabbi Zeira, Ulla in the name of Rabbi
Ishmael in the name of Rabbi Eleazar,
"Scripture should not say, '*And she will be a
wife to him.*' For this refers to one who spreads
a bad story about his wife. Now it is hardly
necessary to state that she shall be his wife,
for she already is in his domain by definition.
Why does Scripture say, '*And she will be a wife
to him*'? It is so that you may derive from that
usage an argument by analogy. You will then
provide the following exegesis: '*And she shall
be a wife to him.*' Why does Scripture state, '*She
will be a wife to him*'? For further on it indicates that if he should divorce her, the court
instructs him to bring her back to his house-

hold. Also, '*She will be a wife to him*' stated here means that if he should divorce her, the court instructs him to bring her back.

Questions for Reflection and Discussion

What authority do the rabbis give for their advice? What kind of reasoning do they use? How easy is it to follow the relationship between the Torah and the rabbis' logic?

62. MAIMONIDES ON MARRIAGE

Time: twelfth century CE
Place: Egypt
Author: Moses ben Maimon

Moses ben Maimon, better known as Maimonides, was a highly educated Jew who began his life in Spain and ended it in Egypt. Among his writings was his Mishneh Torah *("Repetition of the Law"), an attempt to take the Jewish law and authoritative interpretations of it, such as the Talmud, and organize them into a comprehensive legal code. In doing so, he hoped to provide a clear and authoritative guide to a range of social and religious issues. The examples below discuss the marriage payment, conjugal rights to sex within marriage, and the public behavior of women.*

The bridegroom must write a *ketubbah* [marriage contract] before he inducts his bride into the bridal chamber, and only then is he permitted to approach her. It is also he who must pay the scribe's fee. And what is the amount of her *ketubbah*? If she is a virgin, not less than two hundred *denar*; if she is a nonvirgin, not less than a hundred *denar*. This is what is called "the statutory *ketubbah*." If he wishes to add to this, even up to a gold *talent*, he may do so.

What constitutes the charge of nonvirginity? When a man marries a woman presumed to be a virgin, and thereupon prefers charges against her, saying, "I did not find her to be a virgin." There are two tokens of virginity: the first is the blood that flows from her at the conclusion of the first intercourse, and the second is the tightness that is found in her at the first intercourse during coition....

If he charges her, saying, "I did not find her a virgin," while she says, "He did not yet have any intercourse with me, and I am still a virgin," she must be examined, or he must be made to have intercourse with her once more before witnesses. If she says, "He did have intercourse with me, and did find me a virgin like all virgins, and his charge is false," he should be asked, "What did happen that made you say she was not a virgin?" If he replies, "Because I did not find her bleeding," inquiry should be made of her family, perchance they do not bleed at all, neither menstrual blood nor the blood of virginity. If they are all found to bleed normally, she must be examined, perchance she suffers from a grave illness which has dried up the juices of her bodily members, or perchance she has been starving herself. If that is so, she should be bathed and plied with food and drink until she is restored to health, and then made to have intercourse once more, so that it might be seen whether she bleeds or not. If there is neither illness nor starvation, nor anything like it, the charge of nonvirginity stands valid. Even if the husband experiences tightness during intercourse, there is no virginity so long as there is no bleeding. For all virgins, whether minor or adult, whether a maiden or one who has come of age, do bleed unless they suffer from illness, as we have just explained. If he says, "Because I did not feel any tightness, but on the contrary found an open door," she should be questioned as to her age, perchance she has already come of age, because most women who are of age do not exhibit any appreciable tightness, for having grown up, her bodily members may have become loose and the tokens of virginity may have disappeared. If she has not yet come of age, he should be told, "Perchance you had turned aside or gone in gently, and therefore did not feel any tightness." If he replies, "Nay, on the contrary, it was definitely an open door," this constitutes a valid charge of nonvirginity against any virgin who has not yet come of age, whether a minor or a maiden, whether well or ill. For in the case of every virgin her door is shut, and therefore, even if there was bleeding, once he found the door open, there is no virginity.

The conjugal rights mentioned in the Torah are obligatory upon each man according to his physical powers and his occupation. How so? For men who are healthy and live in comfortable and pleasurable circumstances, without having to perform work that would weaken their strength, and do nothing but eat and drink and sit idly in their houses, the conjugal schedule is every night. For laborers, such as tailors, weavers, masons, and the like, their conjugal schedule is twice a week if their work is in the same city, and once a week if their work is in another city. For ass-drivers, the schedule is once a week; for camel-drivers, once in thirty days; for sailors, once in six months; for disciples of the wise, once a week, because the study of Torah weakens their strength. It is the practice of the disciples of the wise to have conjugal relations each Friday night. A wife may restrict her husband in his business journeys to nearby places only, so that he would not otherwise deprive her of her conjugal rights. Hence he may not set out without her permission. Similarly, she may prevent him from exchanging an occupation involving a frequent conjugal schedule, for one involving an infrequent schedule, as for example, if an ass-driver seeks to become a camel-driver, or if a camel-driver seeks to become a sailor. Disciples of the wise, however, may absent themselves for the purpose of studying Torah without their wives' permission for as long as two or three years. Similarly, if a man leading a comfortable and pleasurable life decides to become a disciple of the wise, his wife may not hinder him.

A man may marry several women, even a hundred of them, either at the same time or one after another, and his wife may not hinder him therein, provided that he is able to supply each one of them with the food, clothing, and conjugal rights due her. He may not, however, compel them to reside in the same courtyard, but must let each one reside by herself.

What then are their conjugal rights? It depends on their number. How so? In the case of a laborer who has two wives, each one's schedule is once a week. If he has four wives, each one's schedule comes to once every two weeks. Similarly, if a sailor has four wives, each one's schedule is once in two years. The Sages have therefore ordained that a man should not marry more than four wives, even if he has a great deal of money, in order that each wife's schedule should be at least once a month....

If a man subjects his wife to a vow that he will have no intercourse with her, he is given a week's grace; beyond that he must divorce her and pay her her *ketubbah*, or else effect a release from his vow. This applies even to a sailor, whose schedule is once in six months, because once he makes the vow he has caused her suffering and despair.

A man may not withhold from his wife her conjugal rights. If he transgresses and does so withhold in order to torment her, he has violated a negative commandment of the Torah, for it is said, "her food, her clothing, and her conjugal rights shall he not diminish." If he has become ill or enfeebled, so that he is unable to have sexual intercourse, he may wait six months, which is the least frequent schedule—perchance he will recover. After that, he must either obtain her consent or divorce her and pay her her *ketubbah*.

The wife who prevents her husband from having intercourse with her is called "a rebellious wife," and should be questioned as to the reason for her rebelliousness. If she says, "I have come to loathe him, and I cannot willingly submit to his intercourse," he must be compelled to divorce her immediately, for she is not like a captive woman who must submit to a man that is hateful to her. She must, however, leave with forfeiture of all of her *ketubbah*, but may take her worn-out clothes that are still on hand.... She may take nothing that belongs to her husband. Even the shoes on her feet, and the kerchief upon her head, which he had bought for her, she must remove and return to him. Everything he had given her as a gift she must likewise return to him, because he had not given all these to her on the understanding that she would take them and leave him.

And what constitutes Jewish practice? It is the custom of modesty as observed by the daughters of Israel, and the following acts, if indulged in by a woman, render her guilty of transgressing Jewish practice: going out into the street or into an open alley with head uncovered and without the veil worn by all women, even if her hair is covered with a kerchief; spinning in the street, with a rose or a similar ornament in front of her face, on her forehead, or on her cheeks, in the manner of brazen heathen women; spinning in the street, with her arms exposed to the public; frolicking with young men; demanding intercourse from her husband in a voice so loud that her neighbors can hear her discussing sexual matters; cursing her father-in-law in her husband's presence.

How does Maimonides justify his elaboration of the Jewish Law? How much flexibility in interpretation of the Law does he allow? Does the specificity of these regulations suggest that each of these situations had happened at one time or another?

63. JEWISH MARRIAGE CONTRACTS

Time: eleventh and twelfth centuries CE
Place: Egypt
Author: various, unknown

Legal and religious codes are intended to be authoritative. It is important to compare them, when possible, to the actual practices to which they refer. This comparison is possible for the medieval Jewish community of Cairo, Egypt, because the arid climate has preserved a fascinating range of documents from the geniza of the Jewish synagogue there, when most others have long dissolved. Among them are several parts of marriage contracts, two examples of which are included here. According to the modern editor of the sources, the first may belong to the Karaite tradition of Judaism (which rejected the interpretations of the rabbis), and the second may only be a draft.

I, Hezekiah, the bridegroom, will provide her with clothing, cover, and food, supply all her needs and wishes according to my ability and to the extent I can afford. I will conduct myself toward her with truthfulness and sincerity, with love and affection, I will not grieve nor oppress her and will let her have food, clothing and marital relations to the extent habitual among Jewish men.... Sarwa ["Cypress," the bride] heard the words of Hezekiah and agreed to marry him and to be his wife and companion in purity, holiness, and fear of God, to listen to his words, to honor and to hold him dear, to be his helper and to do in his house what a virtuous Jewish woman is expected to do, to conduct herself toward him with love and consideration, to be under his rule, and her desire will be toward him.

1. Should separation occur, the document freeing Sitt al-Dalal ["Lady Bold," the bride] will be produced by her husband without delay. 2. She is trustworthy in her statements concerning everything and no oath of any kind may be imposed on her. 3. He will not marry another wife nor keep a slave girl disliked by her. 4. He will not beat her. 5. He will not leave Fustat [in Egypt] and travel anywhere except with her consent. 6. Before setting out on a journey he will write her a conditional bill of divorce, and deposit the delayed installment of her marriage gift as well as the sums needed for her maintenance during his absence. 7. The young couple will live in her parents' house. The husband owes a yearly rent of 6 *dinars* and will never be late in paying it. 8. He will not separate her from her parents, as long as the latter are alive and cannot force her to live anywhere else. 9. A fine of 50 *dinars* is imposed on him in case he fails to fulfill any of the preceding conditions.

Questions for Reflection and Discussion

What is the implied justification for the decisions made in these documents? How do relations between Jewish husbands and wives compare in these documents to those implied in the previous two sources? Which type of document provides a better glimpse of life in the past? How might these different types of documents be used together for a fuller picture of the past?

64. EARLY ISLAMIC *HADITH*

Time: eighth century CE
Place: Arabia (modern Saudi Arabia) in the
  Abbasid Empire
Author: Malik ibn Anas

Malik ibn Anas, originator of the Maliki branch of Islamic legal interpretation, lived as a scholar at Medina, one of the holy cities of Islam, in the late eighth century, about a century and a half after Muhammad. His book, called Muwatta *or "Trodden Path," is said to contain the sayings of Muhammad that were never written down, but which were nonetheless the beliefs and practices of Muhammad, who is called "the Messenger of Allah." By Malik's day such oral traditions were considered an important means by which to extend the precepts of Islam when the Qur'an did not provide clear direction. These collections of oral tradition, of which Malik's is the earliest, are known generally as* hadith, *and an important aspect of them is the tracing of the oral tradition by naming the early followers of Muhammad from which the information was derived. A few examples are provided below; the text deals with a wide range of human activity.*

'Abd Allah ibn Abu Bakr b. Muhammad ibn 'Amr ibn Hazm reported that he heard from 'Urwah ibn Zubair who said that he had gone to Marwan ibn al-Hakam and spoke of things that necessitate ablution. Marwan said: Touching the organ makes ablution necessary. 'Urwah said: I have no knowledge of it. Marwan ibn al-Hakam said: I was told by Busrah, daughter of Safwan, who heard it from the Messenger of Allah (may peace be upon him) that if any one of you should touch his sexual organ, he should perform ablution. Mus'ab ibn Sa'd ibn Abi Waqqas reported: I used to hold the Holy Book and Sa'd ibn Abi Waqqas used to recite. One day I scratched myself. Sa'd said: Perhaps you have touched your organ. I said: Yes. Sa'd then said: Get up and perform your ablution. I rose, performed my ablution and returned. Nafi' reported that 'Abd Allah ibn 'Umar used to say that if anyone amongst you should touch his organ, ablution becomes obligatory for him. 'Urwah ibn Zubair reported: Ablution becomes obligatory for him who touches his sexual organ. Salim ibn 'Abd Allah reported: I saw my father 'Abd Allah ibn 'Umar performing ablution after having taken his bath. I asked: Father, does not a bath suffice for ablution? He replied: Yes, but sometimes I touch my organ and therefore perform ablution. Salim ibn 'Abd Allah reported: I was with 'Abd Allah ibn 'Umar on a journey. I saw that he performed his ablution after sunrise and said his prayer. I said to him: You have said a prayer which you were not wont to say. He answered: After performing my ablution for the morning prayer I had touched my organ and forgot to renew the ablution and said my prayer. It was, therefore, that I performed my ablution anew and repeated my prayer.

Ibn 'Umar used to say that kissing one's wife and fondling her with hand is close touch, and whoever kisses his wife and presses her close to him invites ablution upon himself. Malik learnt from 'Abd Allah ibn Mas'ud who used to say that ablution becomes obligatory for a man who kisses his wife. Ibn Shihab used to say that a man's kissing his wife made ablution obligatory for him.

'Abd Allah ibn 'Abbas and 'Abd Allah ibn 'Umar were asked whether a man who holds in marriage a free woman could marry a slave girl. Both of them considered it to be repugnant. Sa'id ibn al-Musayyab said that while having a free woman as wife, a slave girl should not be taken into marriage, but if the free woman consents, the man should spend two days with her and one with the slave girl.

'Abd Allah ibn Umayyah reported that a woman's husband died and she observed 'iddah [mourning] for four months and ten days and then married another. She was hardly four and half month with him she was delivered of a fully developed child. The husband came and reported the matter to 'Umar ibn al-Khattab, who sent for an old woman from amongst the women of the pagan times and enquired regarding the matter. One of the women said: I shall inform about this woman. When her husband died, she was pregnant. The menstrual fluid went on falling on the child and it dried up in her womb. When she married again, the man's semen reached it and it began to move again and grew. 'Umar ibn al-Khattab testified to it and annulled the marriage and said to the woman: It is well that no evil report reached me about you and the descent of the boy by the first husband has been proved.

Sulaiman ibn Yasar reported: If a man after acceptance of Islam claimed parentage of any child of the pagan times, 'Umar ibn al Khattab used to give the child after satisfaction over to him. On one occasion two persons came to him both claiming parentage of a boy. 'Umar ibn al-Khattab sent for a physiognomist [who studies physical features] to find out who the real father was. The man, after studying the boy, said that both the claimants seemed to be his fathers. 'Umar struck him and then sent for the mother of the boy and asked her to explain her position. She signed towards one of the two men and said: When I used to be amongst the camels of my people he used to come and embrace me until he and I suspected pregnancy. He then went away but I had my menses. The second man then came over and had connections with me. I do not know which of them is the father of the boy. The pleasure of the physiognomist, when he heard this, knew no bounds. 'Umar then spoke to the boy and said: You may choose whichever of the two you like as your father.

Questions for Reflection and Discussion

How was the authority of oral tradition verified in these examples? How might it have been challenged? How might such stories serve as models for the handling of future problems?

65. LATER ISLAMIC *HADITH*

Time: thirteenth century CE
Place: Syria
Author: Nawawi

Nawawi lived as a legal scholar in tumultuous times, witnessing Crusader and Mongol attacks against the Arab world, and the overthrow of Arab governments by Turkish slave soldiers known as Mamluks. In such times, religious traditions might provide stability to a society that desperately wanted something solid. Nawawi compiled 42 of what he considered to be the most important themes of the hadith *or oral traditions attributed to Muhammad, out of thousands available to him, and arranged them in a convenient book he called* Gardens of the Righteous. *Its brevity contrasted with most other* hadith *collections and helped to ensure its popularity among Muslims after Nawawi.*

Allah, the Exalted, has said [in the Qur'an]: "Consort with them in kindness." "You cannot keep perfect balance emotionally between your wives, however much you might desire it, but incline not wholly toward one leaving the other in suspense. If you will maintain accord and are mindful of your duty to Allah, surely Allah is Most Forgiving, Ever Merciful."

Abu Hurairah relates that the Holy Prophet said: Treat women kindly. Woman has been created from a rib and the most crooked part of the rib is the uppermost. If you try to straighten it you will break it and if you leave it alone it will remain crooked. So treat women kindly. Another version is: A woman is like a rib; if you try to straighten it you will break it and if you wish to draw benefit from it you can do so despite her crookedness....

Abu Hurairah relates that the Holy Prophet said: Let no Muslim man entertain any rancor against a Muslim woman. Should he dislike one quality in her, he would find another which is pleasing.

Amr ibn Ahwas Jashmi relates that he heard the Holy Prophet say in his address on the occasion of the Farewell Pilgrimage, after he had praised Allah and glorified Him and admonished people: Treat women kindly, they are like prisoners in your hands. You are not owed anything more by them. Should they be guilty of open indecency you may leave them alone in their beds and inflict slight chastisement. They if they obey you do not have recourse to anything else against them. You have your rights concerning your wives and they have their rights concerning you. Your right is that they shall not permit anyone you dislike to enter your home, and their right is that you should treat them well in the manner of food and clothing.

Mu'awiah ibn Haidah relates: I asked the Holy Prophet: What is the right of a wife against her husband? He said: Feed her when you feed yourself; clothe her when you clothe yourself, do not strike her on her face, do not revile her and do not separate yourself from her except inside the house.

Abu Hurairah relates that the Holy Prophet said: The most perfect of believers in the matter of faith is he whose behavior is best; and the best of you are those who behave best towards their wives.

Iyas ibn Abdullah relates that the Holy Prophet admonished: Do not strike the handmaidens of Allah. Some time later Umar came to him and said: Women have become very daring vis-à-vis their husbands. So he permitted their chastisement. Thereafter a large number of women came to the wives of the Holy Prophet and complained against their husbands. The Holy Prophet announced: Many women have come to my wives complaining against their husbands. These men are not well behaved.

Abdullah ibn Amr ibn 'As relates that the Holy Prophet said: The world is but a provision and the best provision of the world is a good woman.

Allah, the Exalted, has said [in the Qur'an]: "Men are appointed guardians over women, because of that in respect of which Allah has made some of them excel others, and because men spend their wealth. So virtuous women are obedient and safeguard, with Allah's help, matters the knowledge of which is shared by them with their husbands."

Abu Hurairah relates that the Holy Prophet said: When the husband calls his wife to his bed and she does not come and he spends the night offended with her, the angels keep cursing her through the night.... Another version runs: The Holy Prophet said: By Him in Whose hands is my life, when a husband calls his wife to his bed and she refuses him, He Who is in heaven is offended with her till her husband is pleased with her....

Ibn Umar relates that the Holy Prophet said: Every one of you is a steward and is accountable for that which is committed to his charge. The ruler is a steward and is accountable for his charge, a man is a steward in respect of his household, a woman is a steward in respect of her husband's house and his children. Thus every one of you is a steward and is accountable for that which is committed to his charge.

Abu Ali Talq ibn Ali relates that the Holy Prophet said: When a man calls for his wife for his need, she should go to him even if she is occupied in baking bread....

Umm Salamah relates that the Holy Prophet said: If a woman dies and her husband is pleased with her she will enter Paradise.

Mu'az ibn Jabal relates that the Holy Prophet said: Whenever a woman distresses her husband, his mate from among the *houris* of Paradise says to her: Allah ruin thee, do not cause him distress for he is only thy guest and will soon part from thee to come to us.

Ibn Abbas relates that the Holy Prophet cursed effeminate men and masculine women. Another version is: The Holy Prophet cursed men who ape women and cursed women who ape men. Abu Hurairah relates that the Holy Prophet cursed men who dress like women and cursed women who dress like men.

Questions for Reflection and Discussion

How does Nawawi authorize his statements? How do his concerns compare to those of Malik, the early compiler of *hadith*, as exemplified in the previous source? How do the different versions of the same oral tradition affect the reliability of that authority?

66. AUGUSTINE ON THE ORIGINS OF LUST

Time: fifth century CE
Place: North Africa (modern Algeria) in the Roman Empire
Author: Augustine of Hippo

We have already met the Christian bishop, Augustine, who described his informal marriage and the marriage of his parents (source 18) and denounced the religious customs of his day that involved sex (source 31). In this excerpt from The City of God, Augustine outlines the origins of lust, part of what he first called original sin.

What of the first human being? Or rather, what of the first human beings, since there was a married couple? We have every reason to ask whether they experienced these emotions in their animal bodies before they sinned—the kind of emotions which we shall not feel in our spiritual bodies, when all sin has been washed away and ended…. The pair lived in a partnership of unalloyed felicity; their love for God and each other was undisturbed…. How fortunate, then, were the first human beings! They were not distressed by any agitations of the mind, nor pained by any disorders of the body. And equally fortunate would be the whole united fellowship of mankind if our first parents had not committed an evil deed whose effect was to be passed on to their posterity….

[Now, however,] lust assumes power not only over the whole body, and not only from the outside, but also internally; it disturbs the whole man, when the mental emotion combines and mingles with the physical craving, resulting in a pleasure surpassing all physical delights. So intense is the pleasure that when it reaches its climax there is an almost total extinction of mental alertness; the intellectual sentries, as it were, are overwhelmed. Now surely any friend of wisdom and holy joys who lives a married life … would prefer, if possible, to beget children without lust of this kind. For then the parts created for this task would be the servants of the mind, even in their function of procreation, just as the other members are its servants in the various tasks to which they are assigned. They would begin their activity at the bidding of the will, instead of being stirred up by the ferment of lust.

In fact, not even the lovers of this kind of pleasure are moved, either to conjugal intercourse or to the impure indulgences of vice, just when they have so willed. Sometimes the impulse is an unwanted intruder, sometimes it abandons the eager lover, and desire cools off in the body while it is at boiling heat in the mind. Thus strangely does lust refuse to be a servant not only to the will to beget but even to the lust for lascivious indulgence; and although on the whole it is totally opposed to the mind's control, it is quite often divided against itself. It arouses the mind, but does not follow its own lead by arousing the body. It is right, therefore, to be ashamed of this lust, and it is right that the members which it moves or fails to move by its own right, so to speak, and not in complete conformity to our decision, should be called *pudenda* ("parts of shame"), which they were not called before man's sin; for, as Scripture tells us, "they were naked, and yet they felt no embarrassment." This was not because they had not noticed their nakedness, but because nakedness was not yet disgraceful, because lust did not yet arouse those members independently of their decision. The flesh did not yet, in a fashion, give proof of man's disobedience by a disobedience of its own.

Questions for Reflection and Discussion

How does Augustine use the legend of Adam and Eve for his larger purpose? How does he argue that his god let the punishment fit the crime? What other kind of authority does he use? How might his own experiences have shaped his views of human sexuality?

67. JEROME'S LETTER TO EUSTOCHIUM

Time: fourth century CE
Place: Israel, in the Roman Empire
Author: Jerome

Jerome, roughly a contemporary of Augustine, lived a monastic existence in Bethlehem. He was well educated and had given up a promising career in Rome, but he wrote often to individuals among the Roman aristocracy, attempting to show that the kind of life he had chosen, especially the giving up of sex and marriage, was imperative for all true Christians. One of his letters was written to an adolescent girl, Eustochium. He quotes frequently from the Bible in it and asks Eustochium to think of herself as marrying Jesus Christ when she rejects earthly marriage, following the Song of Songs (source 42).

"Hearken, O daughter, and see, and incline thy ear, and forget thy people and thy father's house; and the king shall greatly desire thy beauty." In Psalm 44, God is speaking to the human soul…. But it is not enough for you to go out from your native country, unless you forget your people and your father's house and, despising the flesh, are united in your bridegroom's embraces…. I write this to you, my lady Eustochium—I must call you lady, as the bride of my Lord—for this reason, that from the very beginning of my dissertation you may learn that I am not now about to speak the praises of virginity (which you have so excellently demonstrated by adopting it), nor to enumerate the disadvantages of wives: pregnancy, a wailing infant, the torment of a husband's unfaithfulness, household cares, and how death at last cuts off all fancied blessings…. I do not wish pride to come upon you by reason of your decision, but fear. If you walk laden with gold, you must beware of a robber…. Take care, I pray, lest sometime God may say of you: "The virgin of Israel has fallen; there is none to raise her up." I speak audaciously: although God can do all things, He cannot raise up a virgin after she has fallen….

Someone may say: "And do you dare disparage marriage, which was blessed by the Lord? It is not disparaging marriage when virginity is preferred to it. No one compares evil to good. Let married women glory too, since they come second to virgins. "Increase," He says, "and multiply, and fill the earth." Let him who is to fill the earth increase and multiply. Your company is in heaven…. I praise marriage, I praise wedlock, but I do so because they produce virgins for me. I gather roses from the thorns, gold from the earth, the pearl from the shell….

"Concerning virgins," says the Apostle, "I have no commandment of the Lord." And why? Because he too was a virgin—not by compulsion but of his own free will. Nor should we pay any attention to those who pretend that Paul had a wife. When he discusses continence and recommends perpetual chastity, he says: "For I would that all men were even as myself"; and later: "But I say to the unmarried and to the widows: It is good for them if they so continue, even as I." … Why, therefore, does he not have a commandment of the Lord concerning virginity? Because that has more value which is not taken by force but is voluntary. Because if virginity had been commanded, marriage would seem to have been forbidden. And it would have been very hard to impose what is against nature and to require of mankind the life of angels, and in a certain manner to condemn the plan of creation….

Let the secret retreat of your bedchamber ever guard you. Ever let the Bridegroom hold converse with you within. When you pray, you are speaking with your Spouse. When you read, He is talking to you, and when sleep comes upon you, He will come behind the wall and He "will put His hand through the opening and will touch your body." You will arise, trembling, and will say: "I languish with love." And again you will hear His reply: "My sister, my spouse, is a garden enclosed; a garden enclosed, a fountain sealed up." …

What shall that day be like when Mary, the mother of the Lord, shall come to meet you, accompanied by bands of virgins? … Then, too, shall your Spouse Himself come to meet you and shall say: "Arise, come, my love, my beautiful one, my dove, for winter is now past, the rain is over and gone." Then the angels shall marvel and shall say: "Who is she that looks forth as the morning rising, fair as the moon, excellent as the sun?" The daughters shall see you and shall praise you; the queens and concubines shall proclaim you.

Questions for Reflection and Discussion

How well do Jerome's frequent references to the Bible help to reinforce his points? What is the value in using a sexual or marital metaphor—here, the idea of the Bride of Christ—for describing sexual renunciation? What is Jerome most concerned about in his letter?

68. LIST OF CHRISTIAN SEXUAL SINS

Time: seventh or eighth century CE
Place: England
Author: unknown, attributed to Theodore, first Christian archbishop of Canterbury

The medieval Christian handbooks of penance, or Penitentials, survive in various forms. They seem to have been lists of sins and appropriate punishments used by priests (here called "presbyters") when hearing individual confessions. What methods were used to enforce the penalties is unknown; it is possible that enforcement relied solely on the consciences of individuals. They provide an interesting example of how the Christian message on sex and marriage might have been disseminated to believers. The Basil mentioned below was an early Christian bishop and writer.

1. If anyone commits fornication with a virgin he shall do penance for one year. If with a married woman, for four years, two of these entire, and in the other two during the three forty-day periods and three days a week.

2. He judged that he who often commits fornication with a man or with a beast should do penance for ten years.

3. Another judgment is that he who is joined to beasts shall do penance for fifteen years.

4. He who after his twentieth year defiles himself with a male shall do penance for fifteen years.

5. A male who commits fornication with a male shall do penance for ten years.

6. Sodomites shall do penance for seven years, and the effeminate man as an adulteress.

7. Likewise he who commits this sexual offense once shall do penance for four years. If he has been in the habit of it, as Basil says, fifteen years; but if not, one year less as a woman. If he is a boy, two years for the first offense; if he repeats it, four years.

8. If he does this between the thighs, one year, or the three forty-day periods.

9. If he defiles himself, forty days.

10. He who desires to commit fornication, but is not able, shall do penance for forty or twenty days.

11. As for boys who mutually engage in vice, he judged that they should be whipped.

12. If a woman practices vice with a woman, she shall do penance for three years.

13. If she practices solitary vice, she shall do penance for the same period.

14. The penance of a widow and of a girl is the same. She who has a husband deserves a greater penalty if she commits fornication.

15. He who ejaculates into the mouth of another shall do penance for seven years; this is the worst of evils. Elsewhere it was his judgment that both participants in this offense shall do penance to the end of life; or twelve years, or as above seven.

16. If one commits fornication with his mother, he shall do penance for fifteen years and never change except on Sundays. But this so impious incest is likewise spoken of by him in another way—that he shall do penance for seven years, with perpetual pilgrimage.

17. He who commits fornication with his sister shall do penance for fifteen years in the way which it is stated above of his mother. But this penalty he also elsewhere established in a canon as twelve years. Whence it is not unreasonable that the fifteen years that are written apply to the mother.

21. He who amuses himself with libidinous imagination shall do penance until the imagination is overcome.

OF THE PENANCE FOR SPECIAL
IRREGULARITIES IN MARRIAGE

1. In a first marriage the presbyter ought to perform Mass and bless them both, and afterwards they shall absent themselves from church for thirty days. Having done this, they shall do penance for forty days, and absent themselves from the prayer; and afterwards they shall communicate with the oblation.

2. One who is twice married shall do penance for a year; on Wednesdays and Fridays and during the three forty-day periods he shall abstain from flesh; however, he shall not put away his wife.

3. He that is married three times, or more, that is a fourth or fifth marriage, or beyond that number, for seven years on Wednesdays and Fridays and during the three forty-day periods they shall abstain from flesh; yet they shall not be separated. Basil so determined, but in the canon four years are indicated.

4. If anyone finds his wife to be an adulteress and does not wish to put her away but has had her in the matrimonial relation to that time, he shall do penance for two years on two days in the week and shall perform the fasts of religion; or as long as she herself does penance he shall avoid the matrimonial relation with her, because she has committed adultery.

5. If any man or woman who has taken the vow of virginity is joined in marriage, he shall not set aside the marriage but shall do penance for three years.

8. He who puts away his wife and marries another shall do penance with tribulation for seven years or a lighter penance for fifteen years.

9. He who defiles his neighbor's wife, deprived of his own wife, shall fast for three years two days a week and in the three forty-day periods.

10. If the woman is a virgin, he shall do penance for one year without meat and wine and mead.

11. If he defiles a vowed virgin, he shall do penance for three years, as we said above, whether a child is born of her or not.

12. If she is his slave, he shall set her free and fast for six months.

13. If the wife of anyone deserts him and returns to him undishonored, she shall do penance for one year; otherwise for three years. If he takes another wife he shall do penance for one year.

14. An adulterous woman shall do penance for seven years. And this matter is stated in the same way in the canon.

15. A woman who commits adultery shall do penance for three years as a fornicator. So also shall she do penance who makes an unclean mixture of food for the increase of love.

OF MATTERS RELATING TO MARRIAGE

1. Those who are married shall abstain from intercourse for three nights before they communicate.

2. A man shall abstain from his wife for forty days before Easter, until the week of Easter. On this account the Apostle says: "That ye may give yourselves to prayer."

3. When she has conceived a woman ought to abstain from her husband for three months before the birth, and afterward in the time of purgation, that is, for forty days and nights, whether she has borne a male or a female child.

4. It is also fully permitted to a woman to communicate before she is to bear a child.

5. If the wife of anyone commits fornication, he may put her away and take another; that is, if a man puts away his wife on account of fornication, if she was his first, he is permitted to take another; but if she wishes to do penance for her sins, she may take another husband after five years.

6. A woman may not put away her husband, even if he is a fornicator, unless, perchance, for the purpose of his entering a monastery. Basil so decided.

7. A legal marriage may not be broken without the consent of both parties.

30. A husband who sleeps with his wife shall wash himself before he goes into a church.

31. A husband ought not to see his wife nude.

32. If anyone has illicit connection or illicit marriage, it is nevertheless permissible to eat the food which they have, for the prophet has said: "The earth is the Lord's and the fullness thereof."

33. If a man and a woman have united in marriage, and afterward the woman says of the man that he is impotent, if anyone can prove that this is true, she may take another husband.

34. Parents may not give a betrothed girl to another man unless she flatly refuses to marry the original suitor; but she may go to a monastery if she wishes.

35. But if she who is betrothed refuses to live with the man to whom she is betrothed, the

GAVTIER LE CHAVBE FIT L'ABRE

money which he gave for her shall be paid back to him, and a third part shall be added; if, however, it is he that refuses, he shall lose the money which he gave for her.

36. But a girl of seventeen years has power over her own body.

37. Until he is fifteen years old a boy shall be in the power of his father, then he can make himself a monk; but a girl of sixteen or seventeen years who was before in the power of her parents can become a nun. After that age a father may not bestow his daughter in marriage against her will.

Questions for Reflection and Discussion

What might the origins be of these prohibitions? Is it possible to determine whether such a list reflects widespread contemporary ideas or practices?

69. A PERSONIFIED CONSANGUINITY TABLE

Time: thirteenth century CE
Place: France
Artist: unknown

Among the chief concerns of Christian leaders in the Middle Ages regarding marriage was the problem of consanguinity, or marriage between persons too closely related. In the early Middle Ages it was forbidden to marry someone who shared even one common ancestor within seven generations. This prohibition proved so unworkable that in 1215 it was modified so that one could not marry anyone related back through three generations; that is, no first cousins or closer relatives could marry. Keeping track of one's relatives before marriage was essential, then, and family trees like this one were often drawn up in marriage negotiations in case of challenges to the legality of a marriage.

Questions for Reflection and Discussion

How do the medieval Christian prohibitions on consanguineous marriages relate to Biblical prohibitions of incest (source 24)? What might some of the reasons be for the extension of such prohibitions? What might some of the reasons be for later limiting such prohibitions?

70. EARLY BUDDHIST LEGENDS

Time: seventh century CE
Place: China
Author: Xuanzang

In the seventh century, Xuanzang (also spelled Hsüan-tsang) traveled from China to India to learn more about Buddhism. During the era in which he lived, Buddhism was supported by the Tang Dynasty emperors and gained both influence and followers. He collected numerous legends, and when he returned to China he wrote them down in the book he called Records of the Western World. *Among these stories are a number that encourage sexual renunciation, stories that Xuanzang's book help to popularize.*

The old records say: "A former king of this country worshipped the three precious ones. Wishing to pay homage to the sacred relics of the outer world, he entrusted the affairs of the empire to his younger brother on the mother's side. The younger brother having received such orders, mutilated himself in order to prevent any evil risings of passion. He enclosed the mutilated parts in a golden casket, and laid it before the king. "What is this?" inquired the king. In reply he said, "On the day of your majesty's return home, I pray you open it and see." The king gave it to the manager of his affairs, who entrusted the casket to a portion of the king's bodyguard to keep.

And now, in the end, there were certain mischief-making people who said, "The king's deputy, in his absence, has been debauching himself in the inner rooms of the women." The king, hearing this, was very angry, and would have subjected his brother to cruel punishment. The brother said, "I dare not flee from punishment, but I pray you open the golden casket." The king accordingly opened it, and saw that it contained a mutilated member. Seeing it, he said, "What strange thing is this, and what does it signify?" Replying, the brother said, "Formerly, when the king proposed to go abroad, he ordered me to undertake the affairs of the government. Fearing the slanderous reports that might arise, I mutilated myself. You now have the proof of my foresight. Let the king look benignantly on me." The king was filled with the deepest reverence and strangely moved with affection; in consequence, he permitted him free ingress and egress throughout his palace.

After this it happened that the younger brother, going abroad, met by the way a herdsman who was arranging to geld five hundred oxen. On seeing this he gave himself to reflection, and taking himself as an example of what they were to suffer, he was moved with increased compassion, and said, "Are not my present sufferings the consequence of my conduct in some former condition of life?" He forthwith desired with money and precious jewels to redeem this herd of oxen. In consequence of this act of love, he recovered by degrees from mutilation, and on this account he ceased to enter the apartments of the women.

Buddha was preaching, for the sake of gods and men, the excellent doctrines of the law, when a female follower of the heretics, seeing from afar the Lord of the World surrounded by a great congregation who venerated and reverenced him, thought thus with herself, "I will this very day destroy the good name of this Gautama, in order that my teacher may alone enjoy a wide reputation." Then tying a piece of wood next her person, she went to the garden of Anathapindada, and in the midst of the great congregation she cried with a loud voice and said, "This preacher of yours has had private intercourse with me, and I bear his child in my womb, the offspring of the Sakya tribe." The heretics all believed it, but the prudent knew it was a slander. At this time, Sakra, the king of the gods, wishing to dissipate all doubt about the matter, took the form of a white rat, and nibbled through the bandage that fastened the wooden pillow to her person. Having done so, it fell down to the ground with a great noise, which startled the assembly. Then the people, witnessing this event, were filled with increased joy; and one in the crowd picking up the wooden bolster, held it up and showed it to the woman, saying, "Is this your child, thou bad one?" Then the earth opened of itself, and she went down whole into the lowest hell of Avichi, and received her due punishment.

Questions for Reflection and Discussion

How do the moral themes in these stories extend the benefits of sexual renunciation for Buddhists? How do they reinforce the dangers of sexual expression? Why might such stories have had greater impact within past societies than theological treatises?

71. THE LEVELS OF THE BUDDHIST HEAVEN

Time: eighth century CE or earlier
Place: China
Author: Paramiti

This text, called the Surangama Sutra, *was also translated into Chinese during the Tang Dynasty, according to legend, by an otherwise unknown Indian scholar named Paramiti, with the help of a government minister. The text emphasizes the importance of meditation alongside learning the teachings of the Buddha. Some scholars have questioned the text's Indian origins, suggesting instead that it is a Chinese forgery of the eighth century because of the use of Daoist words and ideas throughout, but Chinese writers often had to resort to Daoist terminology for difficult to translate Buddhist concepts. The work became well known, and there are many commentaries on it from later writers.*

There are men who do not seek the permanent because they cannot relinquish their love for their wives. They, however, do not commit adultery, and so their minds are clear and bright. After their death, they will be reborn in the regions near the sun and the moon, called the four heavens of the four god-kings.

There are men who, though living with their wives, are lukewarm about love and sexual desire. Their chastity is, therefore, not perfect and so, after their death, they will be reborn in the regions above the sun and the moon and on the top of the world, called the Trayastrimsa heavens.

Those whose sexual indulgence is only incidental and is then always forgotten, and who prefer tranquility to disturbance, will, after their death, be reborn in space where they will dwell in brightness which eclipses the light of the sun and moon because of their luminous bodies. This is the Suyama heaven.

Those who live in tranquility at all times but are still not yet immune to disturbance, will after their death, be reborn in the subtle region which is beyond the reach of men and lower gods and which remains unaffected by the three calamities of fire, water and wind during the eon of world-destruction. This is the Tusita heaven.

Those who have relinquished all sexual desires but are prepared to satisfy those of their wives and who feel as if they chew tasteless wax during the intercourse, will, after their death, be reborn in the region attainable by leaps and bounds directly from the realm of human beings. This is the Nirmanarati heaven.

Those who have cut off their worldly minds and are thus free from earthly prejudices when dealing with worldlings will, after their death, be reborn in the region beyond those where joy is attainable and unattainable at will. This is the Paranirmitavasavartin heaven.

Questions for Reflection and Discussion

How does this text rework the traditional Buddhist emphasis on sexual renunciation? Is it a concession to human sexual desire?

72. LIST OF BUDDHIST SEXUAL SINS

Time: fourteenth century CE
Place: China
Author: unknown, attributed to Lu Dongbin

Although this list of sexual sins was compiled in fourteenth-century China, it was attributed to Lu Dongbin, who lived in the ninth century. Lu Dongbin (also spelled Lu Tong-pin) was a Tang government official, but after his death, was remembered as one of the Daoist Eight Immortals, so the attribution of the text to him lends it much more authority. The list, based on the Buddhist "ten precepts" used for monks, is clearly intended for wealthy men with families. It also demonstrates Daoist and Confucian influences on Buddhism. The points are the demerits given for each improper action; individuals were expected to keep track of them through the year as a means for examining their moral state.

Keeping an excessively large number of wives and concubines—50
Showing preference for one of one's women—10
> If this includes encouraging the preferred person to be rude to the others—20

Comparing the charms of one's womenfolk—1
Gloating over the charms of one's womenfolk—1
Exciting lustful thoughts in oneself—10
Showing one's nakedness when easing nature in the night—1
Lewd dreams, every time—1
> If such a dream occasions a lewd action—5

Singing frivolous songs—2
Studying such songs—20
Reading novels and other light literature—5
Using frivolous language—2
> If no women are present—1
> If done with the intent to excite lust in women—10

Keeping on one's shelves erotic pictures, for every one—10
Careless behavior—5
> If no women are present—1
> If done with the intent to excite lust in women—20

Touching the hands of one's womenfolk while handing things to them—1
> If with lustful intent—10
> Exception: if done to assist them in case of emergency—none
> But if then such touching excites lust—10

Not yielding the way to a woman in the street—1

If at the same time one looks at the woman—2
If one looks longingly after her—5
If one conceives lewd thoughts about her—10
Carrying on one's person aphrodisiac incense—1
> Burning the same—1

Entering one's women's quarters without warning—1
Associating with friends addicted to whoring and gambling—50
Going to bed early and rising late (so as to devote much time to sexual dalliance)—1
Encouraging one's women to devote much time to their make-up—1
Watching frivolous theatrical plays, every time—1
> Taking part in same—50

Talking frivolously to one's women, without lewd intent—1
> If with the intent to excite lust—20

If one's women engage in frivolous talk, not to restrain them—1
> If one allows himself to become excited thereby—10

Praising the virtue of one's women—none
Praising their talent and ability—1
Praising their skill in embroidery, sewing, etc.—2
Praising their wisdom and generous nature—5
Telling one's women about some love affair—10
> If done with the intent to excite lustful thoughts in them—20

Telling smutty stories in order to excite them—20
> Exception: if one tells such stories in order to develop the women's sense of shame—none

Reading love poetry in front of one's women—5

If done in order to excite their lust—20
Reading poetry that extols profound passion, every time—10

If done to educate one's women—none
Talking to one's women about their make-up, hairdress, personal adornment, etc.—1
Showing them exaggerated politeness—1

Questions for Reflection and Discussion

What kind of home life is imagined by such a list? How much accommodation is there in this list to the realities of sex and marriage, and how much adherence to the Buddhist ideal of sexual renunciation?

SOURCES AND FURTHER READING

Scholarly discussions of the elaboration of religious traditions on sexual matters are usually specific to a topic and tradition but may often be found in studies addressing changes to a particular aspect through time. For example, works like Marjorie Wall Bingham and Susan Hill Gross's *Women in Islam: The Ancient Middle East to Modern Times* (Hudson, WI: G.E. McCuen, 1980), or *Marriage, Sex, and Family in Judaism*, Michael J. Broyde and Michael Ausubel, eds. (Lanham, MD: Rowman and Littlefield, 2005), clearly deal with the development of religious traditions. Collections of essays are often the best place to look for a comparative approach to this issue. See, for example, *Family, Religion, and Social Change in Diverse Societies*, Sharon Houseknecht and Jerry Pankhurst, eds. (Oxford: Oxford University Press, 2000), which focuses on modern history. Some scholars tackle the issue of elaboration through related questions such as how authority is exercised in a religious tradition, without specific reference to ideas about sexuality. See, for

example, Bruce Chilton and Jacob Neusner's *Types of Authority in Formative Christianity and Judaism* (New York: Routledge, 1999); or Wael Hallaq's *Authority, Continuity, and Change in Islamic Law* (Cambridge: Cambridge University Press, 2001). Elaine Huber's *Women and the Authority of Inspiration* (Lanham, MD: University Press of America, 1985) does look at gender issues in two Christian movements, one ancient and one modern. As with this last book, many works by scholars look at the ways in which charismatic authority through visions or mystical experience provide an alternative type of authority for religious change. See, for example, the comparative essays in *Mysticism and Sacred Scripture*, Steven T. Katz, ed. (Oxford: Oxford University Press, 2000); see also note 60. There are many more works on all of these questions.

61. "The Talmud on Rape, Seduction, and Slander" is taken from *The Talmud of the Land of Israel*, Jacob Neusner, trans. (Chicago: University of Chicago Press, 1985), 22: 108-11.

Vol. 22 (*Ketubot*) of the Talmud deals with marital matters, but its form is quite difficult for nonspecialists to follow. The Mishnah, which is included within the Talmud, is a bit easier to approach. A good translation and commentary on relevant sections of the Mishnah can be found in Jacob Neusner's *A History of the Mishnaic Law of Women* (Leiden, NLD: Brill, 1980); or, for the whole source, see his *The Mishnah: A New Translation* (New Haven, CT: Yale University Press, 1988). For studies on sexuality in the Talmud, see Reuven Bulka's *Sex in the Talmud: Reflections on Human Relations* (Mount Vernon, NY: Peter Pauper, 1979). Judith Hauptmann's *Rereading the Rabbis: A Woman's Voice* (Boulder, CO: Westview, 1998) includes a chapter on rape and seduction in

Jewish legal tradition. More generally on sexuality in the Jewish rabbinic tradition, including the Talmud, is Daniel Boyarin's *Carnal Israel: Reading Sex in Talmudic Culture* (Berkeley, CA: University of California Press, 1993); Howard Eilberg-Schwartz's *People of the Body: Jews and Judaism from an Embodied Perspective* (Albany, NY: State University of New York Press, 1992); Gershon Winkler's *Sacred Secrets: The Sanctity of Sex in Jewish Law and Lore* (Northvale, NJ: Jason Aronson, 1998); Michael Satlow's *Tasting the Dish: Rabbinic Rhetorics of Sexuality* (Atlanta, GA: Scholars, 1995); Judith Romney Wegner's *Chattel or Person? The Status of Women in the Mishnah* (Oxford: Oxford University Press, 1988); Leila Bronner's *From Eve to Esther: Rabbinic Reconstructions of Biblical Women* (Louisville, KY: Westminster John Knox, 1994); Judith Baskin's *Midrashic Women: Formations of the Feminine in Rabbinic Literature* (Hannover, VT: University Press of New England, 2002); or Lawrence Hoffman's *Covenant of Blood: Circumcision and Gender in Rabbinic Judaism* (Chicago: University of Chicago Press, 1996).

62. "Maimonides on Marriage" is taken from *The Code of Maimonides*, Isaac Klein, trans. (New Haven, CT: Yale University Press, 1972), 63, 70-72, 86-89, 154.

The whole of book 4 of *The Code of Maimonides* deals with matters pertaining to women, including marriage and sexuality. See also Isadore Twersky's *Introduction to the Code of Maimonides* (New Haven, CT: Yale University Press, 1980), for more background on the text. For more information on Maimonides himself (who wrote philosophical, medical, and theological treatises as well as legal ones, and who is also referred to as Rambam, which stands for Rabbi Moses ben Maimon), a readable choice is Abraham Heschel's *Maimonides: A Biography*,

Joachim Neugroschel, trans. (New York: Image, 1991). On the context of Maimonides' life, see Eliyahu Ashtor's *The Jews of Moslem Spain*, Aaron Klein and Jenny Machlowitz Klein, trans. (Philadelphia: Jewish Publication Society of America, 1984; revised 1992; orig. pub. 1973). On Maimonides and sexuality, see Fred Rosner's *Sex Ethics in the Writings of Moses Maimonides* (New York: Bloch, 1974). See note 61 for more general works on the Jewish rabbinic tradition about sexuality.

63. "Jewish Marriage Contracts" is taken from S.D. Goitein's *A Mediterranean Society: The Jewish Communities of the Arab World as Portrayed in the Documents of the Cairo Geniza*, vol. 3, *The Family* (Berkeley, CA: University of California Press, 1978), 50, 144.

Goitein's volume 3 is the best place to begin to learn more about the Cairo *geniza* and its texts on marriage and the family. More on the Karaite Jews can be found in Nathan Schur's *History of the Karaites* (Frankfurt am Main: Peter Lang, 1992). More on the Jews of medieval Egypt can be found in Jacob Mann's *The Jews in Egypt and in Palestine under the Fatimid Caliphs* (New York: Ktav, 1970; orig. pub. 1920-22; with supplement by Goitein); or in Elinoar Bareket's *Fustat on the Nile: The Jewish Elite in Medieval Egypt* (Leiden, NLD: Brill, 1999). Other studies have been done on the Cairo *geniza*, including Yedida Stillman's "The Importance of the Cairo Geniza Manuscripts for the History of Medieval Female Attire," *International Journal of Middle East Studies* 7 (1976): 579-89. For more examples of individual stories from medieval Judaism, the *responsa* are rabbis' answers to specific questions of interpretation of the Jewish Law, including on marital and sexual matters, many of which became established as legal precedent and have thus been preserved. See

The Responsa Anthology, Avraham Finkel, ed. and trans. (Northvale, NJ: Aaronson, 1990); or more specific collections, including Irving Agus's *Rabbi Meir of Rothenburg: His Life and His Works as Sources for the Religious, Legal, and Social History of the Jews of Germany in the Thirteenth Century* (New York: Ktav, 1970; orig. pub. 1947); or Isidore Epstein's *The Responsa of Rabbi Solomon ben Adreth of Barcelona, 1235-1310, as a Source of … the History of the Jews of Spain as Reflected in the Responsa, and the Responsa of Rabbi Simon b. Zemah Duran, as a Source of the History of the Jews in North Africa* (New York: Ktav, 1968; orig. pub. 1925 and 1930); or Aryeh Shmuelevitz's *The Jews of the Ottoman Empire in the Late Fifteenth and the Sixteenth Centuries: Administrative, Economic, Legal, and Social Relations as Reflected in the Responsa* (Leiden, NLD: E.J. Brill, 1984); or Nisson Shulman's *Authority and Community: Polish Jewry in the Sixteenth Century* (New York: Ktav, 1986). See also note 61 for more modern scholarship on the history of Judaism and sexuality.

64. "Early Islamic *Hadith*" is taken from *Muwatta' Imam Malik*, Muhammad Ashraf, trans. (Lahore, PAK: Kashmiri Bazar, 1980), 19-20, 237-38, 319-20.

On the development of *hadith* and the figure of Malik ibn Anas, see John Burton's *An Introduction to the Hadith* (Edinburgh: Edinburgh University Press, 1994); or Herbert Berg's *The Development of Exegesis in Early Islam* (Richmond, UK: Curzon, 2000). Norman Calder's *Studies in Early Muslim Jurisprudence* (Oxford: Clarendon, 1993) has a chapter on the *Muwatta* of Malik. On women in *hadith*, including marital matters, see Fatima Mernissi's *The Veil and the Male Elite: A Feminist Interpretation of Women's Rights in Islam* (Reading, MA: Addison-

Wesley, 1991); or Syed Mohammed Ali's *The Position of Women in Islam: A Progressive View* (Albany, NY: State University of New York Press, 2004). Another influential early legal writer in Islam was the early ninth-century Ibn Hanbal, and his writings on marriage have been translated; see his *Chapters on Marriage and Divorce: Responses of Ibn Hanbal and Ibn Rahwayh*, Susan Spectorsky, trans. (Austin, TX: University of Texas Press, 1993). The largest collection of *hadith* is that based on Bukhari, published in English translation as *Al-Hadis: Mishkat-ul-Masabih*, Al-Haj Maulana Fazlul Karim, ed. and trans. (Lahore, PAK: The Book House, n.d.), organized topically with sections on marriage, etc.

65. "Later Islamic *Hadith*" is taken from Nawawi, *Gardens of the Righteous*, Muhammad Zafrulla Khan, trans. (London: Curzon, 1975), 67-69, 277-78.

See note 64 for more on *hadith* in Islamic tradition. On women in Islamic tradition, including information on marriage and other aspects of sexuality, see Fatima Mernissi's *Women and Islam: An Historical and Theological Inquiry*, Mary Jo Lakeland, trans. (Oxford: Basil Blackwell, 1991); or Naila Minai's *Women in Islam: Tradition and Transition in the Middle East* (New York: Seaview, 1981); or the essays in *Women, the Family, and Divorce Laws in Islamic History*, Amira El Azhary Sonbol, ed. (Syracuse, NY: Syracuse University Press, 1996); or in *Women in the Medieval Islamic World: Power, Patronage, and Piety*, Gavin Hambly, ed. (New York: St. Martin's, 1998); or in *Writing the Feminine: Women in Arab Sources*, Manuela Marin and Randi Deguilhem, eds. (London: I.B. Tauris, 2002). Few other medieval Islamic commentaries on marriage have been translated into English; the only one of which I am aware is Madelain Farah's *Marriage and Sexuality in Islam: A Translation of al-Ghazzali's Book on the Etiquette of Marriage* (Salt Lake City, UT: University of Utah Press, 1984) on that late eleventh- and early twelfth-century theologian.

66. "Augustine on the Origins of Lust" is taken from Augustine, *The City of God*, Henry Bettenson, trans. (London: Penguin, 1972), 566-67, 577-78.

See also note 18 on Augustine and note 31 on his *The City of God*. One of the best sources for early Christian writings on sexuality is Peter Brown's *The Body and Society: Men, Women, and Sexual Renunciation in Early Christianity* (New York: Columbia University Press, 1988) that provides information on other scholars' writings as well as on the many sources from the period. Elaine Pagels's *Adam, Eve, and the Serpent* (New York: Random House, 1988) deals specifically with early Christian understandings of the Genesis legend. On Christian marriage, see Philip Reynolds's *Marriage in the Western Church: The Christianization of Marriage during the Patristic and Early Medieval Periods* (Leiden, NLD: E.J. Brill, 1994). On women in early Christian writings, Jo Ann McNamara's *A New Song: Celibate Women in the First Three Christian Centuries* (New York: Harrington Park, 1985) is one of the best overviews; on men, see Mathew Kuefler's *The Manly Eunuch: Masculinity, Gender Ambiguity, and Christian Ideology in Late Antiquity* (Chicago: University of Chicago Press, 2001). Augustine's views figure prominently in all of these works. Joyce Salisbury's *Church Fathers, Independent Virgins* (London: Verso, 1991) contrasts men's writings with early Christian legends about women; on these legends, see also Virginia Burrus's *Chastity as Autonomy: Women in the Stories of the Apocryphal Acts* (Lewiston, ME:

E. Mellon, 1987). See note 67 for more on other early Christian primary sources.

67. "Jerome's Letter to Eustochium" is taken from *The Letters of St. Jerome*, Charles Mierow, trans. (London: Longman's, Green, 1963), 134-36, 150, 152-53, 158, 178.

A recent biography of Jerome is Stefan Rebenich's *Jerome* (New York: Routledge, 2002); the classic work is J.N.D. Kelly's *Jerome: His Life, Writings, and Controversies* (London: Duckworth, 1975). Most of Jerome's letters discuss sexuality, and many have been translated into English. In general, most early Christian writers' works are available in English translation, most recently through the Ancient Christian Writers (ACW) series; earlier, through the Fathers of the Church: A New Translation (FC) series; and earliest but most completely, through the Ante-Nicene Christian Fathers (ANCF) and Nicene and Post-Nicene Christian Fathers (NPNF) twin series. Treatises relating to sexuality to look for among Latin writers include Tertullian's *To His Wife, An Exhortation to Chastity,* and *On Monogamy* (ACW, vol. 13) or his *The Apparel of Women* (FC, vol. 40); Ambrose of Milan's *On Widows* and *On Virgins* (NPNF, vol. 10); Augustine of Hippo's *The Good of Marriage, Adulterous Marriage,* and *Holy Virginity* (FC, vol. 27) or his *The Excellence of Widowhood* (FC, vol. 16). Among Greek writers one might read with profit Gregory of Nyssa's *On Virginity* (FC, vol. 58), or Basil of Caesarea's *On Virginity* (FC, vol. 9), just to skim the surface of what is available. See note 66 for works by modern scholars.

68. "List of Christian Sexual Sins" is taken from *Medieval Handbooks of Penance*, John McNeill and Helena Gamer, trans. (New York: Octagon, 1978), 184-86, 195-96, 208-11, with slight changes.

McNeill and Gamer's book is a good place to start; see also Pierre Payer's *Sex and the Penitentials: The Development of a Sexual Code, 550-1150* (Toronto, ON: University of Toronto Press, 1984) for a detailed analysis. On other aspects of sexuality in medieval Christianity, the literature is too vast to outline here, but a good reference to further readings on a range of relevant topics is the *Handbook of Medieval Sexuality*, Vern Bullough and James Brundage, eds. (New York: Garland, 1996); even works published since then are numerous. An excellent new overview of medieval sexuality, with a bibliographical essay as an appendix, is Ruth Mazo Karras's *Sexuality in Medieval Europe: Doing Unto Others* (New York: Routledge, 2005).

69. "A Personified Consanguinity Table" is taken from Frances and Joseph Gies, *Marriage and Family in the Middle Ages* (New York: Harper & Row, 1987), 85.

See note 68 for references to further readings on medieval sexuality. For more on the consanguinity prohibitions, a good resource is Georges Duby's *The Knight, the Lady, and the Priest: The Making of Modern Marriage in Medieval France*, Barbara Bray, trans. (New York: Pantheon, 1983); see also his *Medieval Marriage: Two Models from Twelfth-century France*, Elborg Forster, trans. (Baltimore: Johns Hopkins University Press, 1978; rev. 1991). Very readable is Frances and Joseph Gies's *Marriage and Family in the Middle Ages* (New York: Harper & Row, 1987). More sophisticated is Constance Bouchard's *"Those of My Blood": Constructing Noble Families in Medieval Francia* (Philadelphia: University of Pennsylvania Press, 2001).

70. "Early Buddhist Legends" is taken from *Buddhist Records of the Western World*, Samuel Beal, trans. (London: Kegan Paul, Trench, Trubner, 1906), 1: 22-23, 2: 9-10, with slight changes.

See note 51 for Buddhism and sexuality and note 52 and Buddhism and gender; see also note 23 on castration in Chinese history. On Xuangzang, see Sally Hovey Wriggins's *The Silk Road Journey with Xuanzang* (Boulder, CO: Westview, 2004; orig. pub. in 1996 as *Xuanzang: A Buddhist Pilgrim on the Silk Road*).

71. "The Levels of the Buddhist Heaven" is taken from *The Surangama Sutra (Leng Yen Ching)*, Upasaka Lu K'uan Yu, trans. (London: Rider, 1966), 190-91, with slight changes.

See note 51 for Buddhism and sexuality. On the afterlife in Buddhism, see Carl Becker's *Breaking the Circle: Death and the Afterlife in Buddhism* (Carbondale, IL: Southern Illinois University Press, 1993).

72. "List of Buddhist Sexual Sins" is taken from R.H. Van Gulik, *Sexual Life in Ancient China* (Leiden, NLD: E.J. Brill, 1961), 248-49.

See note 51 for Buddhism and sexuality. On the supposed author, Lu Dongbin, see Paul R. Katz's *Images of the Immortal: The Cult of Lü Dongbin at the Palace of Eternal Joy* (Honolulu: University of Hawai'i Press, 1999).

CHAPTER 8

DISSENTING VOICES

While religious and philosophical traditions provided the backbone of medieval—and much of modern—understandings of sexuality, the ideologies formulated and elaborated were never absolutely followed. Interpretations of religious ideologies about sex might just as easily be met with rejection as acceptance, or parts of ideologies might be reformulated in new and even competing ways. The mixed response to ideology is the theme for this chapter.

The last chapter discussed the continued need for the elaboration of ideology because of changes both intentional and unintentional. One serious consequence of such changes over time is that individuals can begin to hold varied ideas, elaborated in diverse circumstances, all the while claiming to be staying true to the ideology. And the range of individuals who might claim the institutional or charismatic authority to expand upon an ideology might also lead to differences in opinions about how precisely an ideology should fit into the context of the times. The disputes among modern religious groups over various beliefs, including those about sexual behavior, are all too familiar to need any examples, and they are plentiful in the historical record.

Once the outlines of these ideological debates were delineated, though, it was up to those who supported the ideology to throw their weight behind one of the interpretations. We don't hear much in history about this group, the ones who didn't write down their ideas or beliefs but accepted or rejected the interpretations of those who wrote. Even if they were silent, though, we know that they were there. What exactly they believed or how they interpreted their religious or philosophical tradition is difficult to say with any certainty. They must at least have acquiesced in the interpretations of those whose ideas took hold. That is, this silent majority decided which individual to support in any ideological debate, who triumphed because of their support. In turn, the opposing side was comprised of those who lost the debate in the court of public opinion, and whose alternative ideas were rejected.

In traditional religious terminology, the winners in these debates are known as the "orthodox" (from the Greek for "right belief") and the losers are known as "heretics" (from the Greek for "choice," possibly because they had made the wrong choice, but a word already used in antiquity for the competing philosophical schools). These terms provide a clear sense of who was right and who was wrong. Some scholars prefer different terms that are not so laden with judgment, such as "mainstream" or "dominant" for ideas that win the support of the larger group, and "minority" or "dissenting" for ideas that don't. Antonio Gramsci, the early twentieth-century political theorist, used the word "hegemonic" to describe dominant ideas. He argued that any of the powers-that-be require some intellectual consent to sustain and legitimate themselves, and they must achieve at least a limited acceptance that their ideas are the right ones, a dominance he called "hegemony."

Does this mean that this larger group fully supported the values and attitudes of the dominant group? Probably not. Just as those who wrote down their ideas had their own relationship to their ideological traditions, conscious or not, depending on their background and education, so we can presume that these silent listeners had made their own individualized responses to what they heard or read. They might have agreed with the "orthodox" or "hegemonic" thinkers wholeheartedly, but there might have been many other reasons why they supported them. Maybe the dominant writers held political or religious power,

for example, and prevented dissenting voices from being heard; that is what Gramsci suggested often happened.

Historians can speculate about what some of these ideas might have been, or why the majority supported one side of an ideological debate, but cannot do much more than that. In the historical record, there are sometimes only subtle hints of any challenges to a dominant ideology. For example, a writer might mention a widespread lack of support for a particular idea or the difficulties met in eliminating a criticized type of behavior, and that sometimes gives us indirect evidence of opposition to an ideology. The dissent may be more clearly shown. Writers who seem somewhat "heretical" often contain just enough "orthodox" ideas in their writings to have permitted them to be published and preserved in the historical record. Other dissenters are recorded as bad examples for others not to follow. Often dissent is most clearly registered in fictional accounts, since writers of fiction had a bit more leeway in recording opposing ideas in what were, after all, invented people and imaginary situations, which partly muted the dissent.

Sometimes the dissent from an established ideology makes itself known, however, and even reaches such a point that it might be referred to as a counterideology (borrowing from Gramsci's idea that hegemonic ideas could be overthrown only if a concerted intellectual opposition to them developed, what he called "counterhegemony"). I would define a counterideology as an ideology that arises in opposition to an existing one rather than having an independent origin. Unlike individualized dissent, a counterideology is formed when enough individuals have similar or the same complaints with the dominant ideology that they become aware of themselves as a group and begin to define common points of belief or values that separate them from the mainstream. In other words, counterideology depends on individual dissent becoming a "movement." The American hippie movement of the sixties is a great example of a counterideology, since it consciously rejected the emphasis on conservative family life and capitalist values that were dominant in the fifties and replaced them with experiments in communal living and sexual freedom. Counterideological movements have existed throughout history, and if they do not have sufficient strength to defeat the existing ideology, at least they are usually strong enough to leave evidence of their presence in the documents of the past.

Occasionally, counterideologies collect enough support that they become the dominant ideology and supplant the previous one, or promoters of the hegemonic ideology adopt certain features of the counterideology in a conscious or unconscious attempt to remain in power, leaving us with a kind of hybrid ideology. So, for example, the hippies' attitude of sexual freedom became a part of the dominant American ideology in the seventies, even while the hippies' opposition to capitalism did not. This give-and-take between ideologies—what is called a dialectic—is a fascinating part of the history of sexuality, as it is in other areas of history.

These different types of dissent to religious and philosophical ideologies, whether implicit or explicit, direct or indirect, individual or collective, are the subject of the following sources.

73. POEM OF MOSES IBN EZRA

Time: eleventh century CE
Place: Spain
Author: Moses ibn Ezra

Moses, son of Ezra, was born in the late eleventh century in a predominantly Muslim Spain, and died in the early twelfth century in an increasingly Christian Spain. He was perhaps a government official, but also a philosopher and poet, best remembered for his secular poetry. Some have seen Islamic influences in the content of these secular poems; they were certainly composed in the style of Arabic poetry.

Caress a lovely woman's breast by night,
And kiss some beauty's lips by morning light.
Silence those who criticize you, those
Officious talkers. Take advice from me:
With beauty's children only can we live.
Kidnapped were they from Paradise to gall
The living; living men are lovers all.
Immerse your heart in pleasure and in joy,
And by the bank a bottle drink of wine,
Enjoy the swallow's chirp and viol's whine.
Laugh, dance, and stamp your feet upon the floor!
Get drunk, and knock at dawn on some girl's door.
This is the joy of life, so take your due.
You too deserve a portion of the Ram
Of Consecration, like your people's chiefs.
To suck the juice of lips do not be shy,
But take what's rightly yours—the breast and thigh!

Questions for Reflection and Discussion

Who were the "officious talkers" condemned by Moses ibn Ezra? The reference to the breast and thigh of the ram of consecration is from the Torah or Jewish Law: there they belonged to the priests of Israel. How is the Biblical reference being used?

74. A MARRIAGE DISPUTE

Time: eleventh or twelfth century CE
Place: Egypt
Author: unknown

The geniza of the Jewish synagogue at Cairo provides not only examples of marriage contracts, as source 63 showed, but also a range of other documents relating to marriage and family life. This example documents the resolution of some sort of dispute between a husband, Abraham or Ibrahim, and his wife, Salma. If his accusations were true, they would indicate considerable dissent on her part from the norms established for wives.

She came before us and said: "I have sinned, make peace between us." She wept, she and her son, in the presence of the community. Everyone prodded her husband Abraham, saying: "Why do you not take her back?" Said he: "She treats me with contempt, me and my family, my brother, my sister, and their sons, and all my relatives." We investigated this statement and found that it was true. Consequently, we had her make the symbolic purchase [required for making a commitment binding], by which Salma, the daughter of Nathan, took upon herself the following obligations toward her husband, Abraham ibn Salam: She will stand up in his presence whenever he enters or leaves a room. She will serve and treat him with respect, be neat, and not refuse to do any work usually done in a house. When she sees him sorrowful, she will not argue with him, nor will she ask him to buy her expensive clothing, which he is not able to provide. She will not scorn him with contemptuous and derisive words, but be submissive toward him and his relatives. When mentioning his name or that of his relatives, she will add the honorific epithets due them such as "may God enhance his honored position." She will not improperly disobey him, in word or deed, and leave the house only with his permission. She will not demand that they move to the capital or any other place, unless he himself wishes to do so. In general, she should honor and serve him with respect, and never sit idle in the house, but either occupy herself with work on flax and wool, or the household, such as baking and cooking. Salma, the daughter of Nathan, undertook all these obligations unconditionally. Whenever she fails in any one of these, her husband is free to divorce her with no court refusing him the permission to do so. Abraham ibn Salam, on his side, promised to be with her with all his heart, with undivided attention, and, like virtuous Jewish men, to honor her and treat her with respect, also, to buy her clothing, as far as his means permit.

Questions for Reflection and Discussion

Do you think the accusations made against Salma by Abraham were realistic? If she acted in such a way, why might she be promising to end such behavior? Why might dissent such as Salma's seldom make it into the historical record?

75. ABU NUWAS ON SEXUAL CHOICE

Time: late eighth or early ninth century CE
Place: Mesopotamia (modern Iraq) in the
  Abbasid Empire
Author: Abu Nuwas

Abu Nuwas is regarded as one of the great poets of early Arabic literature, famous for his celebration of the finer things of life: wine, women, and song—and also boys. Even his name is playful: Abu Nuwas, a nickname, translates as something like "Curly" and is a reference, presumably, to his hair. In this poem, he uses a variety of methods to defend the practice of pederasty, methods involving both logic and the teachings of the Qur'an.

A woman criticized me
because of the love I feel
for a boy who struts around
like a wild young bull.
But why should I sail the sea, when I
can live so well on land?
Why look for fish, when I can find
gazelles, free, on every hand?
Let me be, and don't blame me
because I chose a path
in life that you've rejected
—and I'll follow it to my death!
Don't you know that the Holy Book
speaks the decisive word:
"Before the daughters
the sons shall be preferred"?

Questions for Reflection and Discussion

How did Abu Nuwas's metaphors challenge notions of "natural" and "unnatural"? The quotation Abu Nuwas used from the Qur'an refers to inheritance; how would you consider Abu Nuwas' reading of this passage: as playful? Critical? Heretical?

76. A TALE FROM *THE THOUSAND AND ONE NIGHTS*

Time: eighteenth century CE, from earlier
    oral traditions
Place: unknown
Author: unknown

The Thousand and One Nights, *an exhaustive set of tales circulating in the Islamic world, known from the tenth century* CE, *includes some tales from earlier Indian and Persian antecedents. In a legend that begins and ends the compilation, the stories are said to have been told by Sheherazade, who was married to a king, hostile to women, who killed his brides each morning after their wedding night. Desperate to preserve her life, Sheherazade tells the king a tale each night and promises him another the next night, managing to think up stories to tell him for a thousand and one nights, after which he has fallen in love with her. Many of the stories poke fun at the social conventions of traditional Islamic societies.*

Once upon a time, in a certain city, there lived a rich and beautiful young woman whose husband was a great traveler. It so chanced that he once journeyed to a distant land and was absent so long that at last his wife succumbed to the temptations of the flesh and fell in love with a handsome youth who himself loved her tenderly.

One day the youth was engaged in a savage brawl and a complaint was lodged against him with the Governor of that city, who had him thrown into prison. The young woman was deeply grieved at the news of her lover's arrest. Without losing a moment she put on her finest robes and hurried to the Governor's house. She greeted the Governor and handed him a petition which read: "My noble master, the young man So-and-so, whom you have arrested and thrown into prison, is my brother and my sole support. He is the victim of a villainous plot, for those who testified against him were false witnesses. I hereby beseech you to consider the justice of my cause and to order his release."

When he had read the petition the Governor lifted his eyes to the young woman and was so smitten with her seductive looks that he fell in love with her on sight. "Wait in the harem of my house," he said, "whilst I write out an order for your brother's release. I will join you there presently." The young woman, who lacked neither cunning nor knowledge of the ways of men, at once perceived the Governor's intent and answered: "You will be welcome, sir, at my own house, but custom forbids me to enter a stranger's dwelling." "And where is your house?" asked the old man, transported with joy. "At such-and-such a place," she replied. "I will expect you there this evening."

[The women next visits the Qadi or local judge of Islamic law, then the Vizier or governor of the district, then the King himself, trying to get her lover released, but with the same result: each man becomes infatuated with her. She invites each one of them to her home that evening.]

[Then] the young woman … went to look for a carpenter's shop. When she had found one she said to the carpenter: "Make me a large cupboard with four compartments, one above the other. To each compartment let there be a separate door fitted with a stout lock, and have it delivered at my house, at such-and-such a place, early this evening. What will be your charge?" "Four dinars," answered the carpenter. "But if you will consent, sweet lady, to step into the backroom of my shop, I will ask no payment at all." "In that case," said the young woman, "you will be welcome at my own house this evening. But I have just remembered that I require five compartments in that cupboard and not four." "I hear and obey," replied the carpenter, beaming with joy.

He set to work at once whilst the young woman waited in his shop. In a few hours a large cupboard with five compartments was completed, and his fair customer hired a porter and had it carried to her house…. At sunset she arrayed herself in splendid robes, putting on her richest jewels and sweetest perfumes, and sat waiting for her distinguished guests.

The first to arrive was the Qadi. She bowed low before him and, taking him by the hand, led him to a couch. No sooner had they seated themselves than the Qadi began to dally with her, and it was not long before he was roused to a frenzy of passion. But when he was about to throw himself upon her … a knocking was heard at the door. "Who may that be?" asked the Qadi, wincing with impatience. "By Allah, that must be my husband!" she exclaimed in great agitation. "What is to be done? Where shall I go?" cried the Qadi. "Have no fear," she replied. "I will hide you in this cupboard." The young woman took the Qadi by the hand, and, after he had crouched low she pushed him into the lowest compartment of the cupboard, and locked the door upon him.

[Again, as one man follows another, each is locked in the different compartments of the cupboard. The Governor brings with him a letter ordering her lover's release. The last man to arrive was the carpenter.]

Then she went to let the carpenter in. "Pray, what kind of cupboard is this you have made me?" snapped the young woman at the carpenter as he stepped into the reception hall. "Why, the top compartment is so small that it is quite useless." "It is a very large compartment," protested the fat carpenter. "It could hold me and three others of my size." "Try then," she said. And when the carpenter had climbed up into the fifth compartment of the cupboard, the door was locked upon him.

The young woman took the Governor's order to the superintendent of the prison, and rejoiced to see her lover free at last. She told him all that had happened, adding: "We must now leave this city and go to live in a distant land." Then they hurried back to the house, packed up all their valuables, and set out for another kingdom.

Not daring to utter a sound, the five men stayed in the cupboard without food or drink for three days; and for three days they resolutely held their water. The carpenter, however, was the first to give in; and his piss fell on the King below him. Then the King pissed on the Vizier; and the Vizier pissed on the Governor; and the Governor pissed on the Qadi. "Filth! Filth!" shouted the Qadi. "Has not our punishment been cruel enough? Must we be made to suffer in this vile fashion also?" The Governor and the Vizier were the next to speak, and the three recognized each other's voice. "Allah's curse be upon this woman," exclaimed the Vizier. "She has locked all the senior officers of the kingdom in this cupboard. Thank Allah the King has been spared!" "Hold your tongue!" muttered the King. "I am here too. And if I am not mistaken, I must have been the first to fall into the snares of this impudent whore." "And to think that I made her this cupboard with my own hands!" groaned the carpenter from the top compartment.

It was not long, however, before the neighbors, seeing no one enter or leave the house, began to suspect foul play. They all crowded around the door debating what action they should take. "Let us break down the door," urged one, "and find out if there is anyone at home." "We must investigate the matter," said another, "lest the Governor or the King himself should learn of it and have us thrown into prison for failing to do our duty." The neighbors forced open the door, and on entering the hall what should they find but a large wooden cupboard echoing with the groans of famished men! "There must be a *jinnee* in this cupboard!" exclaimed one of the neighbors. "Let us set fire to it!" cried another. "Good people," howled the Qadi from within, "in Allah's name do not burn us alive!" But they gave no heed to his cries and said to each other: "The *jinn* have been known to assume human shape and speak with men's voices."

Seeing that they were still in doubt, the Qadi intoned aloud some verses from the Qur'an and entreated them to draw closer. They came near, and in a few words he related to them all that had happened. The neighbors promptly called in a carpenter, who forced the locks, and delivered from the cupboard five men.

Questions for Reflection and Discussion

How does the story blend political, social, and religious satire? How does it subvert the traditional roles of men and women? How seriously does it challenge traditional Islamic religious and sexual ideologies?

77. PERSIAN MINIATURE

Time: sixteenth century CE
Place: Persia (modern Iran)
Artist: unknown

Erotic painting was not a traditional feature of Islamic art. In fact, early Islamic leaders forbid any representation of the human form, and women were supposed to remain veiled before all men but those in their families, so this painting was doubly transgressive. The cultural contacts between eastern Islamic peoples and the peoples of India, who had a long tradition of erotic art, inspired this and other artists to blend Persian and other Islamic art forms with those of India.

Questions for Reflection and Discussion

What aspects of the woman's beauty are highlighted in this painting? What does the array of her clothing signify? Why is she wearing clothing at all? What might the surrounding

objects signify? And what might the purpose be in collecting such art?

78. A HINDU WRITER ON BUDDHIST SEXUAL RENUNCIATION

Time: eleventh century CE
Place: India
Author: Somadeva Bhatta

Somadeva's stories, called the Kathasaritsagara, *are brief and interesting but woven together in highly complicated ways. Somadeva was Hindu but lived in north India at a time when Buddhists, Hindus, and Muslims all inhabited the region. In this grouping of stories, a local king, disappointed by the birth of a daughter, wanders into a Buddhist temple and hears a priest preaching about sexual renunciation, tell-*

ing a story about seven women who themselves tell a story about a wandering hermit.

He told the following story to illustrate his point. "Thus, long ago, a certain king named Krita had seven beautiful daughters born one after another. While they were still very young, they grew disinterested in life and left their father's house and went to the cremation grounds. When they were asked why they had done that, they said to their retainers, 'This world is meaningless. In it, the body, union with lovers and other such joys are like a dream. The only thing that gives meaning to the world is working for the benefit of others. We have decided to use our bodies for the good of other beings and will fling our living bodies to those creatures that live on flesh. What use are these lovely bodies to us? Listen to this tale.

'In the same way, long ago, there was a prince who, even though he was young and handsome, grew disinterested in the world and became a mendicant. One day, he went to the house of a certain merchant. The merchant's young wife was deeply attracted to the young man's eyes which were as long as lotus petals and she said to him, "How is it that someone as handsome as yourself has undertaken such a difficult vow? I envy the woman whom your eyes gaze upon!" The mendicant pulled out his eye and holding it in his hand, he said, "Mother, look at this eye for what it is! It is a revolting mess of flesh and blood. Take it if it pleases you! My other eye is also just like this. Tell me, what is so pleasant about them?" The merchant's wife was full of sorrow when she saw the eye and she said, "Alas! I have done a terrible thing! I have caused you to pull out your eye!" The young mendicant said, "Mother, don't be sad, for you have done me a favor: … you have aided my ascetic practices by causing me to pull out my eye," said the young hermit to the merchant's wife. She bowed to him with respect. The young hermit neglected his beautiful body and soon attained perfection.

'Therefore, though we are young and beautiful, what reason is there for holding on to our bodies? The wise know that the only good is to act for the benefit of others. We will give up our bodies for the benefit of the living beings in the cremation grounds which are the true home of happiness,' said the seven princesses and they attained perfection.

"Thus, the wise have little interest even in their own bodies, let alone such trivial things as a wife, a son and retainers," said the mendicant as the king listened to his discourse in the temple. He spent the day there and then returned to his palace where he was once again overcome with sorrow at the birth of a daughter.

Questions for Reflection and Discussion

Is there a criticism in Somadeva's exaggerated stories about Buddhist rejection of the body? Why is the preaching ultimately unsatisfying to the king's depression? Might this kind of story tell us something about why most Indians eventually rejected Buddhism?

79. DRUKPA KUNLEY'S ATTEMPT AT INCEST

Time: fifteenth century CE
Place: Tibet
Author: unknown

Drukpa Kunley, also known as Kunga Legpa, was one of many wandering Buddhist hermits who lived in Tibet. He is unique among Buddhist saints, however, in being remembered as having used sex to teach moral lessons—and not simply the threat of sex, as in the story below. Since this cut against the grain of traditional Buddhist teachings, he is known as the Divine Madman, yet he is still revered by Tibetan Buddhists.

The Master of Truth, Kunga Legpa was extremely precocious. With full memory of his previous life, he imitated *Naljorpas* [itinerant mystics] in meditation, he practiced breathing exercises, and yoga was his full preoccupation. These signs produced great faith in his family and devotees. By his third year, he could read with ease. When he was older, his father was assassinated in a family feud, and disillusioned with the world, he decided to enter upon the religious life. Leaving his home, patrimony, family, and friends, as though they were so much dust under his feet, he took the precepts of layman and novice from Lama Nenying Choje. Later, he received ordination as a monk from Jekhyen Rabpa of Zhalu…. By the age of twenty-five, Kunga Legpa had gained mastery of both mundane and spiritual arts. He was accomplished in the arts of prescience, shape-shifting, magical display, and the psychic power of flying.

Returning home to visit his mother in Ralung, she failed to recognize his achievement and judged him merely by his outward behavior. "You must decide exactly who you are," she complained. "If you decide to devote yourself to the religious life, you must work constantly for the good of others. If you are going to be a lay householder, you should take a wife who can help your old mother in the house." … Knowing that the time was ripe to demonstrate his crazy yet compassionate wisdom, he replied immediately, "If you want a daughter-in-law, I'll go and find one." He went straight to the market place, where he found a hundred-year-old hag with white hair and blue eyes, who was bent at the waist and had not so much as a single tooth in her head. "Old lady," he said, today you must be my bride. Come with me!" The old woman was unable to rise, but Kunley put her on his back, and carried her home to his mother. "O Ama! Ama!" he called to her. "You wanted me to take a wife, so I've just brought one home." "If that's the best that you can do, forget it," moaned his mother. "Take her back where she came from or you'll find yourself looking after her. I could do her work better than she." "All right," said Kunley with studied resignation. "If you can do her work for her, I'll take her back." And he returned her to the market place….

That night Kunley went to his mother's bed carrying his blanket. "What do you want?" asked his mother. "This morning you said you'd perform a wife's duties, didn't you?" he replied. "You shameless creature!" responded his mother. "I said I'd do her housework. Now don't be so stupid. Go back to your own bed." "You should have said what you meant this morning," the Lama told her, lying down. "It's too late now. We are going to sleep together." "Shut up and go away, you miserable man!" she swore at him. "My knee has gone bad and I can't get up. You'd better resign yourself to it," he persisted. "Even if you've no shame," she said, "what will other people think? Just imagine the gossip!" "If you're afraid of gossip, we can keep it a secret," he promised. Finally, unable to find words to rebuff him, she said, "You don't have to listen to me, just don't tell anyone else…. So do it if you're going to!" Her words fell into his ears like water into boiling *ghee*, and he sprang up and left her alone.

Early next morning he went down to the market place and shouted aloud, "Hey listen, you people! If you persist, you can seduce even your own mother!" When the whole crowd was aghast, he left. But by exposing the hidden foibles of his mother, her faults were eradicated, her sins expiated, and her troubles and afflictions removed. She went on to live to the ripe old age of one hundred and thirty years. Soon after this incident, he told his mother that he was going to Lhasa, and that in the future he would live the life of a *Naljorpa*.

Questions for Reflection and Discussion

How might Drukpa Kunley's practices be reconciled with Buddhist beliefs and practices? How does incest with one's mother function as the epitome of the kind of shock that the author is provoking? What purpose does this shock serve?

80. MARRIAGE AMONG THE FRANKS

Time: sixth century CE
Place: Gaul (modern France)
Author: Gregory of Tours

Good King Guntram at first took to bed as a concubine Veneranda, a slave of one of his followers; by her he had a son Gundobad. Afterwards he married Marcatrude, daughter of Magnachar. He sent his son Gundobad to Orleans. After Marcatrude had a son, she jealously set out to bring about Gundobad's death, poisoning him with a doctored drink, so they say. Following his death, by the judgment of God, she lost the son she had and incurred the hatred of the king. Sent away by him, she died not long after. After her Guntram took Austrechild, also named Bobilla. By her he again had two sons; the older of them was called Chlothar and the younger Chlodomer.

Next King Charibert married Ingoberga, by whom he had a daughter, who afterwards was taken to Kent to be married. Ingoberga had in her service at the time two girls, the daughters of a poor man. The first of them was called Marcovefa, who wore the religious habit, and the other was Merofled. The king was very much in love with them. They were, as I said, the daughters of a wool worker. Jealous that they were loved by the king, Ingoberga privately made sure that the father was put to work, supposing that when the king saw this he would take a dislike to the daughters.

While the father was working, she called the king, who expected to see something special, but only saw this man at a distance sorting the royal wool. The sight made him angry, so he left Ingoberga and married Merofled. He also had another girl named Theudogild, the daughter of a shepherd. By her he is said to have had a son, who, as soon as he came forth from the womb, was carried to the grave....

Afterward Charibert married Marcovefa, Merofled's sister. For this reason, they were both excommunicated by the holy bishop Germanus [of Paris]. But since the king would not leave her, she was struck by God's judgment and died. In no time at all the king himself followed her to the grave. After his death, Theudogild, one of his queens, took it upon herself to send messengers to King Guntram, offering to marry him. The king gave them this response, "Let her have no worry about coming to me with her treasure. For I will marry her and make her a great woman in everyone's eyes. Rest assured she will have greater honor with me than with my brother who has just died." Very pleased, she gathered up everything and went to him. When the king saw what she brought, he said, "It's better for this treasure to be in my hands than under the control of this woman who was unworthy to lie in my brother's bed."

Then, having taken away much and left little, he sent her to a monastery at Arles. Theudogild took it ill to be put to fasts and vigils and so she contacted a Goth by secret messengers, promising that she would leave the monastery with her treasure and follow him willingly if he would take her to Spain and marry her. He agreed without hesitation. But when she had gathered her things and bundled them up and was ready to leave the convent, the enterprise of the abbess frustrated her desires. The abbess detected the deceit and had her severely beaten and put her under guard. There she remained to the end of her life in this world, worn down by no slight suffering.

Next, when King Sigibert saw that his brothers were marrying unworthy wives, and were themselves so worthless as to even marry slaves, he sent an embassy to Spain with many gifts to ask for Brunhild, daughter of King Athanagild. She was a well-mannered, good-looking girl, decent and well behaved, with good judgment and a persuasive manner. Her father did not reject the request for her hand and sent her to Sigibert with great treasure. The king assembled his leading followers, prepared a feast, and took her as his wife with immense rejoicing and celebration. She had been a follower of the Arian [Christian] creed but was converted by the preaching of the bishops and the admonition of the king himself.... She continues to be a Catholic....

When Chilperic saw this, he asked for Brunhild's sister Galswinth, although he already had several wives, promising through his envoys that he would abandon the others, if only he could win a bride worthy of himself and the offspring of a king. With these assurances, her father sent his daughter, as he had the first, along with a great deal of wealth. Galswinth was older than Brunhild. When she came to King Chilperic, she was received with great honor and made his wife. Moreover his love for her was considerable, for she had brought great treasure. But because of his love for Fredegund, whom he had before, a disgraceful conflict arose to divide them. Galswinth had already been converted to the Catholic faith and received the chrism [anointing at baptism]. She complained to the king of the wrongs she constantly had to endure and told him that he had no respect for her. Finally she asked him to give her freedom to return to her native land if she left the treasures that she had brought with her. But he made up various excuses and mol-lified her with sweet words. In the end, he had her strangled by a slave, and he himself found the corpse on the bed.... The king wept over the body and then, after a few days, took Fredegund back again as his wife.

Questions for Reflection and Discussion

How does Gregory juxtapose the Franks' sexual customs and their religious beliefs? How might the Franks themselves have reconciled the two? Was it important to them to reconcile the two?

81. POEM OF MARBOD OF RENNES

Time: twelfth century CE
Place: France
Author: Marbod, bishop of Rennes

Marbod, the Christian bishop of Rennes in France, wrote many poems. How he reconciled the sentiments of this poem, about what we now call a "love triangle," with his Christian ideology is unknown, as is the public reaction to the poem. It echoes the Song of Songs (see source 42), but it is also a deliberate imitation of ancient Roman poetry. Nonetheless, it was an unusual choice of theme for a Christian bishop, even as a literary exercise.

A rare face, perfectly hued,
Whiter than snow, pinker than blushing
roses in spring,
A heavenly glance, a smile promising
sweetness,
Flame red offerings of full lips,
Shining white teeth in perfect array,
Limbs with strength, charming manners
without pretense—
All these the girl possesses who yearns to
unite herself to me;
And that spectacular youth, whose beauty

is my fire,
Loves her, catches her, does everything to
please her.
But she spurns him and wants me; she
orders me to love her,
Entreats me, and all but dies when I
refuse.

Questions for Reflection and Discussion

What purpose does the lengthy physical description of the girl serve? Even if Marbod chose classical models for his poetry, why might he have chosen such a theme? Is it possible to reconcile these ideas with a traditional Christian sexual ideology?

82. SONG OF A FEMALE TROUBADOUR

Time: twelfth century CE
Place: France
Author: La Comtessa de Dia ("The Countess of Die")

We know little about the Countess of Die except her title. She represents part of what can only be considered a counterideology to medieval Christianity, called the Courtly Love movement by modern scholars. Courtly Love—that is, the style of love talked about in the royal and noble courts of western Europe—emphasized romantic love as the highest human aspiration. Among the Courtly Love writers, troubadours set love poetry to melodies, and hundreds of their songs survive. Female troubadours—called trobaritz *in the Provençal language of southern France— were probably less common, and only about a dozen of their songs have been preserved. This example, as well as the previous and the next source, demonstrates that Courtly Love gave some medieval women a rare occasion to voice their views on love.*

I've lately been in great distress
over a knight who once was mine,
and I want it known for all eternity
how I loved him to excess.
Now I see I've been betrayed
because I wouldn't sleep with him;
night and day my mind won't rest
to think of the mistake I made.
How I wish just once I could caress
that knight with my bare arms,
for he would be in ecstasy
if I'd just let him lean his head against my
breast....
My heart and love I offer him,
my mind, my eyes, my life.
Handsome friend, charming and kind,
when shall I have you in my power?
If only I could lie beside you for an hour
and embrace you lovingly—
know this, that I'd give almost anything
to have you in my husband's place,
but only under the condition
that you swear to do my bidding.

Questions for Reflection and Discussion

What was the precise nature of the relationship between the woman who sings and the knight who loved her? What went wrong in their relationship? Why might she have been reluctant to love him in return?

83. ANOTHER SONG OF A FEMALE TROUBADOUR

Time: twelfth or thirteenth century CE
Place: France
Author: Bietris de Roman

Again, all we know of Bietris is her name. Hers is the only song of a trobaritz *that celebrates the love of one woman for another, a rarity in medieval literature altogether. Does it describe a lesbian relationship, as some scholars see it, or a familial relationship? Since the name of the woman being praised is Maria, is it a secular hymn to the Virgin Mary? In other words, does this song reflect the dominant Christian ideology or the Courtly Love counterideology?*

Lady Maria, in you merit and distinction,
joy, intelligence and perfect beauty,
hospitality and honor and distinction,
your noble speech and merry disposition,
the sweet look and the loving expression
that exist in you without pretension
cause me to turn toward you with a pure heart.
Thus I pray you, if it please you that true love
and celebration and sweet humility
should bring me such relief with you,
if it please you, lovely woman, then give me
that which most hope and joy promises
for in you lie my desire and my heart
and from you stems all my happiness,
and because of you I'm often sighing.
And because merit and beauty raise you high
above all others (for none surpasses you),
I pray you, please, by this which does you honor,
don't grant your love to a deceitful suitor.
Lovely woman, whom joy and noble speech uplift,
and merit, to you my stanzas go,
for in you are gaiety and happiness,
and all good things one could ask of a woman.

Questions for Reflection and Discussion

Which explanation for this song seems likeliest: sexual, emotional, devotional? Can any possibilities be excluded? Is a combination of feelings possible? What sort of audience might have enjoyed this song?

84. THE WIFE OF BATH

Time: fourteenth century CE
Place: England
Author: Geoffrey Chaucer

Chaucer's Canterbury Tales, *told as stories within a story, are among the best known of medieval European literature. In this case, pilgrims traveling to a Christian shrine in Canterbury pass the time by telling each other stories, each one appropriate to the teller. Few of the pilgrims are as memorable as the married woman from the town of Bath, who recounts her opposition to the traditional Christian ideology on sex and marriage. Some scholars see in her words the beginnings of the later Protestant rejection of the medieval Christian emphasis on virginity and celibacy.*

Experience, though no authority
Were in this world, were good enough for me,
To speak of woe that is in all marriage;
For, masters, since I was twelve years of age,
Thanks be to God who is for aye alive,
Of husbands at church door I had five;
For men so many times have wedded me;
And all were worthy men in their degree.
But someone told me not so long ago
That since Our Lord, save once, would never go
To wedding (that at Cana in Galilee),
Thus, by this same example, showed He me
I never should have married more than once.
Lo and behold! What sharp words, for the nonce,

Beside a well Lord Jesus, God and man,
Spoke in reproving the Samaritan:
"For thou hast had five husbands," thus
said He,
"And he whom thou hast now to be with
thee
Is not thine husband." Thus He said that
day,
But what He meant thereby I cannot say;
And I would ask now why that same fifth
man
Was not husband to the Samaritan?
How many might she have, then, in
marriage?
For I have never heard, in all my age,
Clear exposition of this number shown,
Though men may guess and argue up and
down.
But well I know and say, and do not lie,
God bade us to increase and multiply;
That worthy text can I well understand.
And well I know He said, too, my
husband
Should father leave, and mother, and
cleave to me;
But no specific number mentioned He,
Whether of bigamy or octogamy;
Why should men speak of it
reproachfully?
Lo, there's the wise old king Lord
Solomon;
I understand he had more wives than one;
And now would God it were permitted
me
To be refreshed one half as oft as he!
Which gift of God he had for all his wives!
No man has such that in this world now
lives.
God knows, this noble king, it strikes my
wit,
The first night he had many a merry fit
With each of them, so much he was alive!
Praise be to God that I have wedded five!

Welcome the sixth whenever come he
shall.
Forsooth, I'll not keep chaste for good
and all;
When my good husband from the world
is gone,
Some Christian man shall marry me
anon;
For then, the apostle says that I am free
To wed, in God's name, where it pleases
me.
He says that to be wedded is no sin;
Better to marry than to burn within.
What care I though folk speak
reproachfully
Of wicked Lamech and his bigamy?
I know well Abraham was holy man,
And Jacob, too, as far as know I can;
And each of them had spouses more than
two;
And many another holy man also.
Or can you say that you have ever heard
That God has ever by His express word
Marriage forbidden? Pray you, now, tell
me;
Or where commanded He virginity?
I read as well as you no doubt have read
The apostle when he speaks of
maidenhead;
He said, commandment of the Lord he'd
none.
Men may advise a woman to be one,
But such advice is not commandment, no;
He left the thing to our own judgment so.
For had Lord God commanded
maidenhood,
He'd have condemned all marriage as not
good;
And certainly, if there were no seed sown,
Virginity—where then should it be
grown?
Paul dared not to forbid us, at the least,
A thing whereof his Master'd no behest.

The dart is set up for virginity;
Catch it who can; who runs best let us see.
But this word is not meant for every
wight,
But where God wills to give it, of His
might....
This is the sum: he held virginity
Nearer perfection than marriage for
frailty.
And frailty's all, I say, save he and she
Would lead their lives throughout in
chastity.
I grant this well, I have no great envy
Though maidenhead's preferred to
bigamy;
Let those who will be clean, body and
ghost,
Of my condition I will make no boast.
For well I know, a lord in his household,
He has not every vessel all of gold;
Some are wood and serve well all their
days.
God calls folk unto Him in sundry ways,
And each one has from God a proper gift,
Some this, some that, as pleases Him to
shift....
Tell me also, to what purpose or end
The genitals were made, that I defend,
And for what benefit was man first
wrought?
Trust you right well, they were not made
for naught.
Explain who will and argue up and down
That they were made for passing out, as
known,
Of urine, and our two belongings small
Were just to tell a female from a male,
And for no other cause—ah, say you no?
Experience knows well it is not so....
I bear no malice to virginity;
Let such be bread of purest white wheat
seed,

And let us wives be called but barley
bread;
And yet with barley bread (if Mark you
scan)
Jesus Our Lord refreshed full many a
man.

Questions for Reflection and Discussion

How does the Wife of Bath see her position as Christian despite its contravention of the traditional Christian ideology on sex and marriage? How realistic does this portrayal of a medieval married woman seem? Does it still reflect the stereotypes of a male author?

SOURCES AND FURTHER READING

On religious dissent, there are many scholarly works on all aspects: specific to a time and place, comparative, and theoretical. A sampling of good examples of these works includes: Stephen J. Stein's *Communities of Dissent: A History of Alternative Religions in America* (Oxford: Oxford University Press, 2003); Steven Ozment's *Mysticism and Dissent: Religious Ideology and Social Protest in the Sixteenth Century* (New Haven, CT: Yale University Press, 1973); or, for the Middle Ages, R.I. Moore's *The Origins of European Dissent* (New York: St. Martin's, 1977; reprinted Toronto, ON: University of Toronto Press, 1994). Most of these works look at Judaism, Christianity, and Islam, since issues of dissent have mostly been handled differently in Hinduism and Buddhism, where there was often greater tolerance of religious difference. See, however, *Orthodoxy, Heterodoxy, and Dissent in India*, S.N. Eisenstadt, et al., eds. (Berlin: Mouton, 1984); or *Heterodoxy in Late Imperial China*, Kwang-Ching Liu and Richard Shek, eds. (Honolulu: University of Hawai'i Press, 2004). On dissent in sexual matters, the literature is more limited but still considerable. See, for example, Lyndal Roper's *Œdipus and the Devil: Witchcraft, Sexuality, and Religion in Early Modern Europe* (New York: Routledge, 1994); or Sarah Caldwell's *Oh Terrifying Mother: Sexuality, Violence, and Worship of the Goddess Kali* (Oxford: Oxford University Press, 1999) on a Hindu cult; or Richard DeMaria's *Communal Love at Oneida: A Perfectionist Vision of Authority, Property, and Sexual Order* (New York: E. Mellon, 1978) on a nineteenth-century American movement. There are also many works addressing contemporary religious controversies, such as Dawne Moon's *God, Sex, and Politics: Homosexuality and Everyday Theology* (Chicago: University of Chicago Press, 2004) on religious differences over homosexuality; or *Contraception: Authority and Dissent*, Charles Curran, ed. (New York: Herder and Herder, 1969) on contraception and modern Catholicism. For the ideas of Antonio Gramsci, see the various editions of his translated *Prison Letters*, or selections from his writings, although analyses of his ideas, such as Robert Bocock's *Hegemony* (London: Tavistock, 1986), are more accessible.

73. "Poem of Moses ibn Ezra" is taken from Raymond Scheindlin, *Wine, Women, and Death: Medieval Hebrew Poems on the Good Life* (Philadelphia: Jewish Publication Society, 1986), 91.

Scheindlin's book contains many other similar poems and good commentary. There is an extensive scholarly literature on medieval Jewish poetry. For more specifically on medieval Jewish and Muslim poetry from Spain, see Ross Brann, *The Compunctious Poet: Cultural Ambiguity and Hebrew Poetry in Medieval Spain* (Baltimore, MD: Johns Hopkins University Press, 1991); or the essays in *Wine, Women, and Song: Medieval Hebrew and Arabic Literature of Medieval Iberia*, Michelle M. Hamilton et al., eds. (Newark, DE: Juan de la Cuesta, 2004). For more on Moses ibn Ezra, see *Selected Poems of Moses ibn Ezra*, Solomon Solis-Cohen, trans., and Heinrich Brody, ed. (Philadelphia: Jewish Publication Society of America, 1934). Moses ibn Ezra's life overlapped only slightly with that of Maimonides, but since their social circumstances were similar, see the further readings on Jews in Muslim Spain from note 62. On Jews in Christian Spain, see Yitzhak Baer's *A History of the Jews in Christian Spain*, Louis Schoffman, trans. (Philadelphia: Jewish Publication Society, 1992); or Jane Gerber's *The Jews of Spain: A History of the Sephardic Experience* (New York: Free Press, 1992); or Paloma Díaz Más's *Sephardim: The Jews from Spain*, George Zucker, trans. (Chicago: University of Chicago Press, 1992).

74. "A Marriage Dispute" is taken from S.D. Gotein's *A Mediterranean Society: The Jewish Communities of the Arab World as Portrayed in the Documents of the Cairo Geniza*, vol. 3, *The Family* (Berkeley, CA: University of California Press, 1978), 215.

See note 63 for more on this type of source, as well as background and further readings.

75. "Abu Nuwas on Sexual Choice" is taken from Ahmad al-Tifashi, *The Delight of Hearts, Or What You Will Not Find in Any Book*, Edward Lacey, trans. (San Francisco: Gay Sunshine, 1988), 61.

On Abu Nuwas and his poetry, see Philip Kennedy's *The Wine Song in Classical Arabic Poetry: Abu Nuwas and the Literary Tradition* (Oxford: Clarendon, 1997). On homoeroticism in Muslim societies, see *Homoeroticism in Classical Arabic Literature*, J.W. Wright, Jr., and Everett Rowson, eds. (New York: Columbia University Press, 1997) which includes an essay on Abu Nuwas; or for comparisons between medieval and recent history, *Islamic Homosexualities: Culture, History, and Literature*, Stephen Murray and Will Roscoe, eds. (New York: New York University Press, 1997); or *Sexuality and Eroticism among Males in Moslem Societies*, Arno Schmitt and Jehoeda Sofer, eds. (Binghampton, NY: Harrington Park, 1992). See also Arno Schmitt's *Bio-Bibliography of Male-Male Sexuality and Eroticism in Muslim Societies* (Berlin: Rosa Winkel, 1995). The collection by al-Tifashi from which this excerpt is taken is also a candid source for homoeroticism in medieval Muslim societies, although it is marred by a faulty translation from Arabic into French and then into English.

76. "A Tale from *The Thousand and One Nights*" is taken from *Tales from the Thousand and One Nights*, N.J. Dawood, ed. and trans. (London: Penguin, 1954), 106-12, with slight changes.

Some interesting recent scholarship on *The Thousand and One Nights*, also known as the *Arabian Nights*, includes Daniel Beaumont's *Slave of Desire: Sex, Love, and Death in the 1001 Nights* (Madison, NJ: Farleigh Dickinson University Press, 2002); or Fedwa Malti-Douglas's *Woman's Body, Woman's Word: Gender and Discourse in Arabo-Islamic Writing* (Princeton, NJ: Princeton University Press, 1991) that includes a chapter on the Sheherezade frame for the tales. A good discussion of the work itself, including the problems of multiple versions of the text, can be found in Muhsin Mahdi's *The Thousand and One Nights* (Leiden, NLD: Brill, 1995). There are many English editions of selections from the *Thousand and One Nights*, mostly using Richard Burton's late nineteenth-century translation, which not only is in

purposely archaic language but has been criticized for inaccuracies. Still, many of the tales available in English describe sexual situations, usually with a humorous twist, and could be read with benefit in a history of sexuality.

77. "Persian Miniature" is taken from Philip Rawson's *Erotic Art of the East* (New York: G.P. Putnam's Sons, 1968), 198.

On Persian art from this, the Safavid period, see Sheila Canby's *The Golden Age of Persian Art, 1501-1722* (New York: Abrams, 1999). For more on the common genre of miniatures, see Oleg Grabar's *Mostly Miniatures: An Introduction to Persian Painting* (Princeton, N.J: Princeton University Press, 2000). On women in Islamic art, see Wiebke Walther's *Women in Islam* (Princeton, NJ: Wiener, 1993). On women, clothing, and eroticism in Islamic societies, see Faegheh Shirazi's *The Veil Unveiled: The Hijab in Modern Culture* (Gainesville, FL: University of Florida Press, 2001).

78. "A Hindu Writer on Buddhist Sexual Renunciation" is taken from Somadeva, *Tales from the Kathasaritsagara*, Arshia Sattar, ed. and trans. (London: Penguin, 1994), 70-72.

The introduction to this translation is the best place for information on Somadeva Bhatta and the *Kathasaritsagara*. On the rich tradition of folk tales and legends in the Indian traditions, see Roy Amore and Larry Shinn's *Lustful Maidens and Ascetic Kings: Buddhist and Hindu Stories of Life* (Oxford: Oxford University Press, 1981). Other examples may be found in *Folktales from India: A Selection of Oral Tales from Twenty-Two Languages*, A.K. Ramanujan, ed. (New York: Pantheon Books, 1991); or *Folktales of India*, Brenda Beck, ed. (Chicago: University of

Chicago Press, 1999). As with all folk tales, it is difficult to determine their precise origins, but they reflect traditional societies. For more historical precision, there are collections such as *Kama Katha: Tales of Love, Womanly Wiles, and Devotion from the Ancient Indian Classics*, Paul Thomas, ed. (Bombay: D.B. Taraporevala Sons, 1969).

79. "Drukpa Kunley's Attempt at Incest" is taken from *The Divine Madman: The Sublime Life and Songs of Drukpa Kunley*, Keith Dowman and Sonam Paljor, trans. (London: Rider, 1980), 24-28.

Recent works on Tibetan Buddhism include Tulku Thondup Rinpoche's *Buddhist Civilization in Tibet* (New York: Routledge & Kegan Paul, 1987); John Powers's *Introduction to Tibetan Buddhism* (Ithaca, NY: Snow Lion, 1995); or Matthew Kapstein's *The Tibetan Assimilation of Buddhism: Conversion, Contestation, and Memory* (Oxford: Oxford University Press, 2000). While there are quite a few studies of incest in other literatures, I know of nothing on incest as a theme in Buddhist literature. The rest of this source, however, is just as shocking in its depiction of sexual improprieties committed by Drukpa Kunley. See also note 52 on Tantric Buddhism.

80. "Marriage among the Franks" is taken from Gregory of Tours, *The Merovingians*, Alexander Callander Murray, trans. (Peterborough, ON: Broadview, 2006), 56-61.

The best analysis of marriage customs and gender relations is Suzanne Fonay Wemple's *Women in Frankish Society: Marriage and the Cloister, 500 to 900* (Philadelphia: University of Pennsylvania Press, 1981). Good introductions to Merovingian France include Katharine Scherman's *The Birth of France* (New York:

Random House, 1987); or Patrick Geary's *Before France and Germany* (Oxford: Oxford University Press, 1988). There are many other primary sources for the period. The laws of the early Franks, though brief, including laws dealing with marriage, etc., have been translated as *Laws of the Salian and Ripuarian Franks*, Theodore Rivers, trans. (New York: AMS, 1986), and as *The Laws of the Salian Franks*, Katherine Fischer Drew, trans. (Philadelphia: University of Pennsylvania Press, 1991). Other contemporary sources that demonstrate more commitment to Christian teachings on sex may be found in *Sainted Women of the Dark Ages*, Jo Ann McNamara and John Halborg, eds. and trans. (Durham, NC: Duke University Press, 1992); or in *Soldiers of Christ: Saints and Saints' Lives from Late Antiquity and the Early Middle Ages*, Thomas Noble and Thomas Head, eds. (University Park, PA: Pennsylvania State University Press, 1995). Interesting comparisons may also be made with Scandinavian societies, recently Christian, as reflected in the many Icelandic sagas (also known as Norse sagas) that have survived from the Middle Ages, too numerous to mention; most would be worth investigating in a history of sexuality.

81. "Poem of Marbod of Rennes" is taken from John Boswell, *Christianity, Social Tolerance, and Homosexuality: Gay People in Western Europe from the Beginning of the Christian Era to the Fourteenth Century* (Chicago: University of Chicago Press, 1980), 370.

The classic text on homosexuality in the Middle Ages is Boswell's book; its appendix contains this excerpt. See, however, the revisions of Boswell in Mark Jordan's *The Invention of Sodomy in Christian Theology* (Chicago: University of Chicago Press, 1997); or Mathew Kuefler's "Male Friendship and the Suspicion of Sodomy in Twelfth-Century

France," in *Gender and Difference in the Middle Ages*, Sharon Farmer and Carol Braun Pasternack, eds. (Minneapolis, MN: University of Minnesota Press, 2003), reprinted in *The Boswell Thesis: Essays on Christianity, Social Tolerance, and Homosexuality*, Mathew Kuefler, ed. (Chicago: University of Chicago Press, 2006). On male homoeroticism in the later Middle Ages, Michael Goodich's *The Unmentionable Vice* (New York: Dorset, 1979); or Richard Zeikowitz's *Homoeroticism and Chivalry: Discourses of Male Same-Sex Desire in the Fourteenth Century* (New York: Palgrave Macmillan, 2003). *The Penguin Book of Homosexual Verse*, Stephen Coote, ed. (London: Penguin, 1983), and *Gay and Lesbian Poetry: An Anthology from Sappho to Michaelangelo* (New York: Garland, 1995), both include many other medieval poems expressing homoerotic desire.

82. "Song of a Female Troubadour" is taken from Meg Bogin, *The Women Troubadours* (New York: W.W. Norton, 1976), 89, with slight changes.

Bogin's book is a good introduction to the *trobaritz* or female troubadours and their music; see also *The Voice of the Trobairitz: Perspectives on the Female Troubadours*, William Paden, ed. (Philadelphia: University of Pennsylvania Press, 1989); or *Unsung Women: The Anonymous Female Voice in Troubadour Poetry*, Carol Nappholz, ed. (New York: P. Lang, 1994). On male singers, called troubadours or *trouveres*, see *The Troubadours: An Introduction*, Simon Gaunt and Sarah Kay, eds. (Cambridge: Cambridge University Press, 1999). Many of these songs have been translated; see *Anthology of the Provençal Troubadours*, Raymond Hill and T.G. Bergin, eds. (New Haven, CT: Yale University Press, 1973; orig. pub. 1941); *Lyrics of the Troubadours and Trouveres: An Anthology and a History*, Frederick Goldin, ed. and trans. (Gloucester, MA: Peter Smith, 1983); or *113 Galician-Portuguese Troubadour Poems*, Richard Zenith, trans. (Manchester: Carcanet, 1995). There are also now many sound recordings of troubadour music and, although fewer, also of the music of the *trobaritz*. Useful too are studies on the historical context, such as Linda Paterson's *The World of the Troubadours: Medieval Occitan Society, c. 1100-c. 1300* (Cambridge: Cambridge University Press, 1993); *The Cultural Milieu of the Troubadours and Trouveres*, Nancy van Deusen, ed. (Ottawa, ON: Institute of Mediaeval Music, 1994); or Frederick Cheyette's *Ermengard of Narbonne and the World of the Troubadours* (Ithaca, NY: Cornell University Press, 2001). On the troubadours and the theme of love, see L.T. Topsfield's *Troubadours and Love* (Cambridge: Cambridge University Press, 1975). Troubadour music is linked to what scholars call Courtly Love, a movement that praised romantic love. On this movement, which is difficult to define, the classic work is C.S. Lewis's *The Allegory of Love* (Oxford: Oxford University Press, 1938), which is really too out of date. See instead Bernard O'Donoghue's *The Courtly Love Tradition* (Manchester: Manchester University Press, 1982); or Joachim Bumke's *Courtly Culture: Literature and Society in the High Middle Ages*, Thomas Dunlap, trans. (Berkeley, CA: University of California Press, 1991), although most general works on medieval literature discuss Courtly Love. A well-known medieval source on Courtly Love is Andreas Capellanus's *On Love*, P.G. Walsh, trans. (London: Duckworth, 1982), also translated as *The Art of Courtly Love*, John Jay Parry, trans. (New York: Columbia University Press, 1990); but any of the Arthurian Romances, whether French (especially Chretien de Troyes or the *Roman de la Rose*), English (especially *Sir Gawain and the Green Knight* or Thomas

Malory's *Le Morte d'Arthur*), or German (especially Wolfram von Eschenbach or Hartmann von Aue), would be read to great benefit in a history of sexuality.

83. "Another Song of a Female Troubadour" is taken from Meg Bogin, *The Women Troubadours* (New York: W.W. Norton, 1976), 133.

See note 82 for more on the *trobaritz* or female troubadours, and on the Courtly Love movement. On female homoeroticism in the Middle Ages, see the essays in *Same Sex Love and Desire among Women in the Middle Ages*, Francesca Canadé Sautman and Pamela Sheingorn, eds. (New York: Palgrave, 2001). A good overview is Jacqueline Murray's "Twice Marginal and Twice Invisible: Lesbians in the Middle Ages," in *A Handbook of Medieval Sexuality*, Vern Bullough and James Brundage, eds. (New York: Garland, 1996), which refers to this song; on premodern female homoeroticism in general see Judith Bennett's "'Lesbian-Like' and the Social History of Lesbianisms," *Journal of the History of Sexuality* 9 (2000): 1-24.

84. "The Wife of Bath" is taken from Geoffrey Chaucer, *Canterbury Tales*, U. Nicolson, trans. (New York: Covici Friede, 1934), 311-15, with slight changes.

Much of *The Canterbury Tales* contains stories dealing with sexuality in various forms, from solemn romances like "The Knight's Tale" to bawdy jokes like "The Miller's Tale" to proto-feminist stories like "The Wife of Bath's Tale," and could be read in a history of sexual-ity. Another similar narrative of short stories is Giovanni Boccaccio's *Decameron*, available in several translations, that also contains numerous stories dealing with sex, more anti-clerical in tone than Chaucer, often accusing priests and nuns of sexual indiscretions (but also accusing married men and women of the same). The secondary literature on Geoffrey Chaucer and *The Canterbury Tales* is vast. Recent works include Carolyn Dinshaw's *Chaucer's Sexual Poetics* (Madison, WI: University of Wisconsin Press, 1989); or Glenn Burger's *Chaucer's Queer Nation* (Minneapolis, MN: University of Minnesota Press, 2003). Works on Chaucer and gender also make much of the Wife of Bath character; see Elaine Tuttle Hansen's *Chaucer and the Fictions of Gender* (Berkeley, CA: University of California Press, 1992); or Anne Laskaya's *Chaucer's Approach to Gender in the Canterbury Tales* (Cambridge: D.S. Brewer, 1995); or Susan Crane's *Gender and Romance in Chaucer's Canterbury Tales* (Princeton, NJ: Princeton University Press, 1994). On sexuality in the Later Middle Ages, good overviews are Pierre Payer's *The Bridling of Desire: Views of Sex in the Later Middle Ages* (Toronto, ON: University of Toronto Press, 1993); or John Baldwin's *The Language of Sex: Five Voices from Northern France around 1200* (Chicago: University of Chicago Press, 1994); see also the essays in *Sexual Practices and the Medieval Church*, Vern Bullough and James Brundage, eds. (Buffalo, NY: Prometheus Books, 1982), and recently, Ruth Mazo Karras's *Sexuality in Medieval Europe: Doing Unto Others* (New York: Routledge, 2005), which includes a final bibliographical essay on the scholarly literature.

part III
sexuaLIty as IDentIty

CHAPTER 9

Puritans and Libertines

The proliferation of dissenting opinions about sexuality and their coalescence into identifiable factions is certainly one of the most easily recognized features of the modern period. This is not to say that dissent did not occur in earlier periods; previous chapters have attempted to show that there was such dissent. Rather, it is to recognize that a variety of changes to society made it more difficult to suppress dissent, and easier for dissenters to discover common ground.

What were the changes that made such a difference? Certainly the growing interconnectedness of the world's cultures was one of them. Connections had always existed, even among the earliest human civilizations, but new ties were made in the modern era—the most famous between the Americas and the rest of the world—and established links were regularized. Such connections were as important for the history of sexuality as they were in other areas as individuals saw the variety of human sexual experiences, including the surprising fact that behaviors proscribed in one society might be promoted in another, and behaviors censured in one, lauded in another. Another factor was also clearly the growth of literacy and the invention of the printing press, which together allowed for dissenting opinions to be disseminated more widely—meaning between one society and another as well as within different segments of the same society.

Experiencing these changes, some felt that the changes happening to society were going too far and taking their society away from its traditions and established values. They longed for a return to bygone days, and whether they viewed the past accurately or not, they thought that there had been a greater social cohesion in the past and less conflict. Others felt that these changes were not going far enough. They wanted more change, more experimentation with social customs, and more questioning of traditional values. They believed firmly in progress, the notion that human society is constantly improving, but felt that advances happen only by abandoning the old and acquiring the new.

Within the history of sexuality, two specific groups became associated with these opposing reactions. The first were the Puritans who fled what they felt to be the impurity of European life and the lukewarm commitment of other Christians to found a new and pure society in the wilderness of New England, basing their social customs and laws on what they considered to be the true belief in the Bible and the proper practice of religion—cleansed of centuries of false additions and misinterpretations. The second were the Libertines, writers and intellectuals who formed the backbone of the European Enlightenment, the movement that called for an end to despotism and state-sponsored religion and for the rise of democratic government and individual freedoms. The first group existed mainly in North America, the second group in Europe, but the phenomenon was worldwide. I call attention to these two groups only because these names, "puritan" and "libertine," became shorthand in the English language for referring to both ends of this spectrum of response to change in matters sexual. It could be argued that these two types still struggle for supremacy around the modern globe.

Each group justified its position in radically different but equally problematic ways. Puritans claimed that their society and government were based on the principles of the Bible, but they did so only by refuting other Christian interpretations of it. Even they disagreed vehemently about putting the Bible into practice, to the extent that the splintering of the New England colonies into factions and the expulsions of individuals and groups became a perennial problem. The truth is that the Bible cannot be plainly translated into guidelines for a modern lifestyle, as the proliferation of modern Jewish and Christian groups divided in their practices demonstrates. Likewise, the Libertines claimed that individual freedom was the principle on which to base decisions about sexual morality, and they tried, for example, to decriminalize homosexuality and make divorce easier to obtain. If individual freedom, however, is constrained in any way, is it truly free? On what basis are actions, however reprehensible to another, denied to someone who wants to engage in them? How are individual freedoms reconciled with the freedoms of others? Scholars have been fascinated in recent years by the writings of the Marquis de Sade who took the libertine principle of individual freedom to extremes, arguing for a detachment not only from custom and law but from the constraints of emotional connection to others and from concern for another's well-being. The appeals to a strict moral code and to individual freedom, in other words, each raise possibly irresolvable issues of sexual ethics.

Labels of "puritan" and "libertine" were important, nonetheless, despite their drawbacks. Both allowed likeminded individuals who were dissatisfied with the social status quo to associate themselves with a group, according to the principles associated with what psychologists call Social Identity Theory. There they found a sense of social identity: they were able to move beyond a sense of themselves as individuals thinking and acting alone in their dissatisfaction toward a view of themselves as belonging to a larger group. A group identity provided them with an articulated position and definite ideas. By identifying themselves with a larger group, they were able to move beyond their dissatisfaction to social or political action, working in conjunction with other individuals to make change happen in the direction that they wanted.

Neither the puritan nor the libertine labels were absolute; both conservative and radical elements are found within the ideas or writings of any individual. Even in the extremist libertine imagination of the Marquis de Sade, for example, an obvious patriarchal attitude remains. Still, the labels help us to identify associations between writers and thinkers and, more importantly, allowed the writers and thinkers themselves to unite.

The readings in this chapter are intended to demonstrate the puritan and libertine perspectives, broadly conceived, in a sampling of societies, mostly from the early modern world.

85. MARTIN LUTHER ON SEX AND MARRIAGE

Time: sixteenth century CE
Place: Germany
Author: Martin Luther

Martin Luther, founder of Lutheran Christianity, is best remembered for sparking the Protestant Revolt against the Catholic Church in Europe. He argued that Catholic leaders had misinterpreted or distorted the original message of Christianity, and through his many writings, he tried to return Christians to what he felt were the earliest and truest beliefs and behaviors required of them. This treatise, Table Talk, *was intended for a broad audience. Luther's basic position on sexual matters has been followed by most Protestants who mostly reject the Catholic emphasis on sexual renunciation.*

715. A preacher of the gospel, being regularly called, ought, above all things, first, to purify himself before he teaches others. Is he able, with a good conscience, to remain unmarried? Let him so remain; but if he cannot abstain living chastely, then let him take a wife; God has made that plaster for that sore.

716. It is written in the first book of Moses, concerning matrimony: God created a man and a woman, and blessed them. Now, although this sentence was chiefly spoken of human creatures, yet we may apply it to all the creatures of the world: to the fowls of the air, the fish in the waters, and the beasts of the field, wherein we find a male and a female consorting together, engendering and increasing. In all these God has placed before our eyes the state of matrimony. We have its image, also, even in the trees and earth.

719. Maternity is a glorious thing, since all mankind have been conceived, born, and nourished of women. All human laws should encourage the multiplication of families.

725. Men have broad and large chests, and small narrow hips, and more understanding than the women, who have but small and narrow breasts, and broad hips, to the end they should remain at home, sit still, keep house, and bear and bring up children.

726. Marrying cannot be without women, nor can the world subsist without them. To marry is remedy against incontinence. A woman is, or at least should be, a friendly, courteous, and merry companion in life, whence they are named, by the Holy Ghost, house honors, the honor and ornament of the house, and inclined to tenderness, for thereunto are they chiefly created, to bear children, and be the pleasure, joy, and solace of their husbands.

729. There is no greater plague in this life than a morose and unchaste wife. Solomon says that to be married to a woman he dislikes is the worst of calamities.

732. It is a grand thing for a married pair to live in perfect union, but the devil rarely permits this. When they are apart, they cannot endure the separation, and when they are together, they cannot endure the always seeing one another. It is as the poet says: I cannot live with you, or without you. Married people must assiduously pray against these assaults of the devil. I have seen marriages where, at first, husband and wife seemed as though they would eat one another up: in six months they have separated in mutual disgust. It is the devil inspires this evanescent ardor, in order to divert the parties from prayer.

734. Both the Old and the New Testament attribute eminence and honor to the married state. Abraham had three wives; Jesus Christ was present at a marriage ceremony, and performed his first miracle there. St. Paul, himself a widower, enjoins bishops to marry, and predicts that the injunction of celibacy will cause much evil; St. Peter had a son-in-law, and consequently must have been himself married; St. James, our Savior's brother, and indeed all the apostles, except St. John, were married men; Spiridiron, bishop of Cyprus, was a married man, and so was bishop Hilary, of whom we have a letter, addressed to his daughter, telling her he knows a rich man, meaning Christ, who, if she remains pious and good, will give her a fine robe, adorned with gold.

742. The polygamy of the patriarchs, Gideon, David, Solomon, etc., was a matter of necessity, not of libertinism. The Jews were constrained to have several wives, from the necessity of the promise, and of consanguinity. Abraham, Isaac, and Jacob received from God the promise that he would multiply their seed as the stars of heaven, or the sands of the sea. The Jews, having their attention constantly directed to this promise, to

accomplish it used to take several wives each. The necessity of consanguinity was this, that when a man was elected judge or king, all his poor female relations crowded about him, and he had to take them as wives or concubines. Concubinage was lawful among the Jews, and was, indeed, a mode of aiding distressed relatives, widows and orphans, to whom it secured food and raiment. It was a burdensome imposition rather than an agreeable relaxation. Solomon's wives, most of them, were probably no more to him than my nieces, Magdalen and Elizabeth, are to me, who have remained under my roof virgins, as when they came here.

751. The hair is the finest ornament women have. Of old, virgins used to wear it loose, except when they were in mourning. I like women to let their hair fall down their back; it is a most agreeable sight.

752. The reproduction of mankind is a great marvel and mystery. Had God consulted me in the matter, I should have advised him to continue the generation of the species by fashioning them in clay, in the way Adam was fashioned; as I should have counseled him also, to let the sun remain always suspended over the earth, like a great lamp, maintaining perpetual light and heat.

753. The celibacy of spiritual persons began in the time of Cyprian, who lived two hundred and fifty years after the birth of Christ; so that this superstition has continued thirteen hundred years. St. Ambrose and others believed not that they were human creatures, like other people.

754. St. Ulrich, bishop of Augsburg, related a fearful thing that befell at Rome. Pope Gregory, who confirmed celibacy, ordered a

fishpond at Rome, hard by a convent of nuns, to be cleared out. The water being let off, there were found, at the bottom, more than six thousand skulls of children, that had been cast into the pond and drowned. Such were the fruits of forced celibacy. Hereupon Pope Gregory abolished celibacy, but the popes who succeeded him, reestablished it. In our own time, there was in Austria, at Nieuberg, a convent of nuns, who, by reason of their licentious doings, were removed from it, and placed elsewhere, and their convent filled with Franciscans. These monks, wishing to enlarge the building, foundations were dug, and in excavating there were found twelve great pots, in each of which was the carcass of an infant. How much better to let these people marry, than, by prohibition thereof, to cause the murder of so many innocent creatures.

Questions for Reflection and Discussion

How does Luther justify his viewpoints? How does he criticize opposing viewpoints? How is social custom and tradition mixed with divine commandment in his suggestions?

86. BERNARD MANDEVILLE'S DEFENSE OF PROSTITUTION

Time: eighteenth century CE
Place: England
Author: Bernard Mandeville

The eighteenth century was an age in which many of the traditions of European society were being called into question, sexual customs among them. This excerpt from a longer treatise by Mandeville, a Dutch-born physician living in London, sets out his case for legalized prostitution. The archaic language and spelling has been preserved, such as the term "stew" for "brothel," and "French Pox" for "syphilis." His ideas are typ-ical of the libertine rethinking of sexual customs; still, prostitution had only been criminalized in western Europe since the sixteenth century, a fact to which Mandeville makes allusion.

The Practice of Whoring has, of late Years, become so universal, and its Effects so prejudicial to Mankind, that several Attempts have been made to put a Stop to it; and a certain Society of Worthy Gentlemen have undertaken that Affair with a Zeal truly commendable, tho' the Success does put too plainly make it appear, that they were mistaken in their Measures, and had not rightly consider'd the Nature of this Evil, which we are all equally solicitous to prevent, however we may differ in our Opinions as to the Manner. And tho' the Method I intend to propose, of erecting Publick Stews for that purpose, may seem at first sight somewhat ludicrous, I shall, never-theless, make it appear to be the only Means we have now left for redressing this Grievance. As this Redress is the whole Scope and Design of this Treatise, I hope to be acquitted of my Design, when I have prov'd the following Proposition; That publick Whoring is nei-ther so criminal in itself, nor so detrimental to the Society, as private Whoring; and that the encouraging of publick Whoring, by erect-ing Stews, will not only prevent most of the ill Consequences of this Vice, but even lessen the Quantity of Whoring in general, and reduce it to the narrowest Bounds which it can possibly be contain'd in....

The greatest Evil that attends this Vice, or could well befall Mankind, is the Propagation of that infectious Disease, called the French Pox, which, in two Centuries, has made such incredible Havock all over Europe. In these Kingdoms it so seldom fails to attend Whoring, now-a-days mis-taken for Gallantry and Politeness, that a hale, robust Constitution is esteem'd a Mark of Ungentility; and a healthy young Fellow is look'd upon with the same View, as if he had spent his Life in a Cottage. Our Gentlemen of the Army, whose unsettled way of Life makes it inconvenient for them to marry, are hereby very much weaken'd and enervated, and render'd unfit to undergo such Hardships as are necessary for defending and supporting the Honour of their Country: And our Gentry in general seem to distinguish themselves by an ill State of Health, in all probability the Effect of this pernicious Distemper.... But what makes this Mischief the more intolerable, is, that the Innocent must suffer by it as well as the Guilty: Men give it to their Wives, Women to their Husbands, or perhaps their Children; they to their [Wet]Nurses [through breast feeding], and the Nurses again to other Children; so that no Age, Sex, or Condition can be intirely safe from the Infection....

There is one thing more we ought to consider in this Vice, and that is the Injury it does to particular Persons and Families, either by alienating the Affections of Wives from their Husbands, which often proves prejudicial to both, and sometimes fatal to whole Families; or else by debauching the Minds of Young Women, to their utter Ruin and Destruction: for the Reproach they must undergo, when a Slip of this nature is discover'd, prevents their marrying in any Degree suitable to their Fortune, and by degrees hardens them to all Sense of Shame; and when they have once overcome that, the present View of Interest as well as Pleasure, sways them to continue in the same Course, till at length they become common Prostitutes.

These are the several bad Effects of Whoring; and it is an unhappy Thing, that a Practice so universal as this is, and always will be, should be attended with such mischievous Consequences: But since few or none of them are the necessary Effects of Whoring, consider'd in itself, but only proceed from the Abuse and ill Management of it; our Business is certainly to regulate this Affair in such sort as may best prevent these Mischiefs. And I must here beg pardon of those worthy Gentlemen of the Society, if I can't conceive how the Discouragement they have given, or rather attempted to give, to publick Whoring, could possibly have the desired Effect. If this was a Vice acquired by Habit or Custom, or depended upon Education, as most other Vices, there might be some Hope of suppressing it; and then it would, no doubt, be commendable to attack it, without Distinction, in whatever Form or Disguise it should appear: But alas! this violent love for Women is born and bred with us; nay, it is absolutely necessary to our being born at all: And however some People may pretend, that unlawful Enjoyment is contrary to the Law of Nature; this is certain, that Nature never fails to furnish us largely with this Passion, tho' she is often sparing to bestow upon us such a Portion of Reason and Reflection as is necessary to curb it....

History affords us several Instances of this Truth; I shall mention but one, and that is of Pope Sixtus the Fifth, who was so strictly severe in the Execution of Justice, if such Severity may be call'd Justice, and particularly, against Offenders of this kind, that he condemned a young Man to the Galleys, only for snatching a Kiss of a Damsel in the Street: yet notwithstanding this his Holiness's Zeal, he never attempted once to extirpate Whoring intirely: But like a true Pastor separated the clean Sheep from the unclean, and confin'd all the Courtezans to one Quarter of the City. It is true, he did attempt to moderate this Vice, and banish'd as many Courtezans as he thought exceeded the necessary Number; but he was soon convinc'd of the Error of his Computation, for Sodomy, and a thousand other unnatural Vices sprung up, which forc'd him soon to recall them, and has left us a remarkable Instance of the Vanity of such Attempts.

Questions for Reflection and Discussion

How does Mandeville justify his viewpoints? How does he criticize opposing viewpoints? To what sort of audience might Mandeville be addressing his arguments?

87. THE MARQUIS DE SADE

Time: eighteenth century CE
Place: France
Author: Donatien-Alphonse-François de Sade

The Marquis de Sade was given a long prison sentence in the Bastille, France's most notorious prison, for what amounted to a long series of sexually related crimes. There, he wrote hundreds of stories, including his One Hundred and Twenty Days of Sodom, *in which four men kidnap a group of women and children, brutalize them sexually, mutilate, and eventually murder them. It was intended to shock, and shock it did, so much so that the stories were destroyed and only partly reconstituted at a later date. In this excerpt from that tale, the leader of the men—an imaginary French duke—explains his philosophy of life, which may have been much like de Sade's own.*

The Duke de Blangis, at eighteen the master of an already colossal fortune which his later speculations much increased, experienced all the difficulties which descend like a cloud of locusts upon a rich and influential young man who need not deny himself anything; it almost always happens in such cases that the extent of one's assets turns into that of one's vices, and one stints oneself that much less the more one has the means to procure oneself everything. Had the Duke received a few elementary qualities from Nature, they might possibly have counterbalanced the dangers which beset him in his position, but … Nature, I say, in destining Blangis for immense wealth, had meticulously endowed him with every impulse, every inspiration required for its abuse. Together with a tenebrous and very evil mind, she had accorded him a heart of flint and an utterly criminal soul, and these were accompanied by the disorders in tastes and irregularity of whim whence were born the dreadful libertinage to which the Duke was in no common measure addicted. Born treacherous, harsh, imperious, barbaric, selfish, as lavish in the pursuit of pleasure as miserly when it were a question of useful spending, a liar, a gourmand, a drunk, a dastard, a sodomite, fond of incest, given to murdering, to arson, to theft, no, not a single virtue compensated that host of vices. Why, what am I saying! Not only did he never so much as dream of a single virtue, he beheld them all with horror, and he was frequently heard to say that to be truly happy in this world a man ought not merely fling himself into every vice, but should never permit himself one virtue, and that it was not simply a matter of always doing evil, but also and above all of never doing good.

"Oh, there are plenty of people," the Duke used to observe, "who never misbehave save when passion spurs them to ill; later, the fire gone out of them, their now calm spirit peacefully returns to the path of virtue and, thus passing their life going from strife to error and from error to remorse, they end their days in such a way there is no telling just what roles they have enacted on earth. Such persons," he would continue, "must surely be miserable: forever drifting, continually undecided, their entire life is spent detesting in the morning what they did the evening before. Certain to repent of the pleasures they taste, they take their delight in quaking, in such sort they become at once virtuous in crime and criminal in virtue. However," our hero would add, "my more solid character is a stranger to these contradictions; I do my choosing without hesitation, and as I am always sure to find pleasure in the choice I make, never does regret arise to dull its charm. Firm in my principles because those I formed are sound and were formed very early, I always act in accordance with them; they have made me understand the emptiness and nullity of virtue; I hate virtue, and never will I be seen resorting to it. They have persuaded me that through vice alone is man capable of experiencing this moral and physical vibration which is the source of the most delicious voluptuousness; so I give myself over to vice.

"I was still very young when I learned to hold religion's fantasies in contempt, being perfectly convinced that the existence of a creator is a revolting absurdity in which not even children continue to believe. I have no need to thwart my inclinations in order to flatter some god; these instincts were given me by Nature, and it would be to irritate her were I to resist them; if she gave me bad ones, that is because they were necessary to her designs. I am in her hands but a machine which she runs as she likes, and not one of my crimes does not serve her: the more she urges me to commit them, the more of them she needs; I should be a fool to disobey her. Thus, nothing but the law stands in my way, but I defy the law, my gold and my prestige keep me well beyond reach of those vulgar instruments of repression which should be employed only upon the common sort."

Questions for Reflection and Discussion

How does the Duke de Blangis use Nature as a foil for God in his self-justification? Is atheism always a corollary of libertinism? Could one counter the Duke's opinion, also arguing from nature?

88. THE *CODE NAPOLÉON*

Time: nineteenth century CE
Place: France
Author: unknown

The Code Napoléon, *promulgated in 1803, translated many of the aims of the moderate libertines into legislation. In the aftermath of the French Revolution, lawmakers were anxious to find alternative justifications for social order than religious commandment and found what they were seeking in the Enlightenment philosophers' elevation of human freedom. The excerpts here demonstrate a mixture of liberal and traditional values. The* Code Napoléon *shaped the law codes of most modern European states.*

OF THE RESPECTIVE RIGHTS AND
DUTIES OF MARRIED PERSONS

212. Married persons owe each other fidelity, succor, assistance.

213. The husband owes protection to his wife, the wife obedience to her husband.

214. The wife is obliged to live with her husband, and to follow him to every place where he may judge it convenient to reside: the husband is obliged to receive her, and to furnish her with every thing necessary for the wants of life, according to his means and station.

215. The wife cannot plead in her own name, without the authority of the husband, even though she should be a public trader, or non-communicant, or separate in property.

216. The authority of the husband is not necessary when the wife is prosecuted in a criminal matter, or relating to police.

217. A wife, although non-communicant or separate in property, cannot give, alienate, pledge, or acquire by free or chargeable title, without the concurrence of her husband in the act, or his consent in writing.

218. If the husband refuse to authorize his wife to plead in her own name, the judge may give her authority.

220. The wife, if she is a public trader, may, without the authority of her husband, bind herself for that which concerns her trade; and in the said case she binds also her husband, if there be a community between them. She is not reputed a public trader, if she merely retail goods in her husband's trade, but only when she carries on a separate business.

222. If the husband is interdicted or absent, the judge, on cognizance of the cause, may authorize his wife either to plead in her own name or to contract.

226. The wife may make a will without the authority of her husband.

227. Marriage is dissolved, 1st. By the death of one of the parties; 2d. By divorce lawfully pronounced; 3d. By condemnation become final of one of the married parties to a punishment implying civil death.

228. A woman cannot contract a new marriage until ten months have elapsed from the dissolution of the preceding marriage.

229. The husband may demand a divorce on the ground of his wife's adultery.

230. The wife may demand divorce on the ground of adultery in her husband, when he shall have brought his concubine into their common residence.

231. The married parties may reciprocally demand divorce for outrageous conduct, ill-usage, or grievous injuries, exercised by one of them towards the other.

232. The condemnation of one of the parties to an infamous punishment, shall be to the other a ground of divorce.

233. The mutual and unwavering consent of the married parties, expressed in a manner prescribed by law, under the conditions, and after the proofs which it points out, shall prove sufficiently that their common life is insupportable to them; and that there exists, in reference to them, a peremptory cause of divorce.

Questions for Reflection and Discussion

What seems most traditional in the law, and what most radical? How does the law respond overall to what are clearly the changing realities of men's and women's lives: by trying to hold them back or move them forward?

89. NAFZAWI ON PHYSICAL ATTRACTIVENESS AND ABORTION

Time: sixteenth century CE
Place: north Africa (modern Tunisia) in the Ottoman Empire
Author: Umar ibn Muhammad al-Nafzawi

Nafzawi—called a sheikh, *that is, the leader of his clan—wrote an erotic treatise on the art of sexual love, which he called* The Perfumed Garden. *In many ways, it owed more to the Indian tradition of erotic writings like the* Kamasutra *and to longstanding medical practices than to Islamic tradition, although Nafzawi attempted to situate it within his own religious tradition. It is dedicated to the* vizir, *a local government official, a courtesy that may also have helped to win his support despite the frankness of the book's discussion of sexuality.*

Listen, O Vizir, God's blessing be upon you, that there are different sorts of men and women, that amongst these are those who are worthy of praise, and those who deserve reproach. When a meritorious man finds himself near to women, his member grows, gets strong, vigorous and hard; he is not quick to discharge, and after the trembling caused by the emission of the sperm, he is soon stiff again. Such a man is liked and appreciated by the women; this is because the woman loves the man only for the sake of the coition. His member should, therefore, be of ample dimensions and length. Such a man ought to be broad in the chest, and heavy in the stern; he should know how to regulate his emission, and ready as to erection; his member should reach to the end of the canal of the female, and completely fill the same in all its parts....

In order that a woman may be relished by men, she must have a perfect waist, and must be plump and lusty. Her hair will be black, her forehead wide, she will have eyebrows of Ethiopian blackness, large black eyes, with the white in them very limpid. With cheek of a perfect oval, she will have an elegant nose and a graceful mouth; lips and tongue vermilion, her breath will be of pleasant odor, her throat long, her neck strong, her bust and her belly large; her breasts must be full and firm, her belly in good proportion, and her navel well-developed and marked; the lower part of her belly is to be large, the vulva projecting and fleshy from the point where the hairs grow to the buttocks; the conduit must be narrow and not moist, soft to the touch, and emitting a strong heat and no bad smell; she must have the thighs and buttocks hard, the hips large and full, a waist of fine shape, hands and feet of striking elegance, plump arms and well-developed shoulders. If one looks at a woman with those qualities in front, one is fascinated; if from behind, one dies with pleasure. Looked at sitting, she is a rounded dome; lying, a soft bed; standing, the staff of a standard. When she is walking, her natural parts appear as set off under her clothing.

She speaks and laughs rarely, and never without a reason. She never leaves the house even to see neighbors of her acquaintance. She has no woman friends, gives her confidence to nobody, and her husband is her sole reliance. She takes nothing from anyone, excepting from her husband and her parents. If she sees relatives she does not meddle with their affairs. She is not treacherous, and has no faults to hide, nor bad reasons to proffer. She does not try to entice people. If her husband shows the intention to fulfill the conjugal rite, she is agreeable to his desires and occasionally even provokes them. She assists him always in his affairs, and is sparing in complaints and tears; she does not laugh or rejoice when she sees her husband moody or sorrowful, but shares his troubles, and wheedles him into good humor, till he is quite content again. She does not surrender herself to anybody but her husband, even if abstinence would kill her. She hides her secret parts, and does not allow them to be seen; she is always elegantly attired, of the utmost personal propriety, and takes care not to let her husband see what might be repugnant to him. She perfumes herself with scents, uses antimony for her toilet, and cleans her teeth with *souak*. Such a woman is cherished by all men.

Know, O Vizir (God be good to you!) that the medicines which will bring on abortion, and the ejection of the fetus, are innumerable. But I shall speak of those to you which I have proved, and therefore acknowledge as good, so that everybody may learn what may benefit and what may do harm. I shall in the first place speak of the madder root. A small quantity of this substance freshly gathered, or even dried, but in the latter case bruised and moistened at the time when it is to be used, vitiates the virile sperm or kills the fetus, bringing abortion on and provoking the menstruation when introduced in the woman's vagina. The same end may be obtained by means of a decoction of the same plant taken fasting by the woman, and used at the same time by an external application to moisten the vagina. Fumigations with the smoke of burnt cabbage seeds cause abortion, if the woman introduces the vapor into her vagina by means of a tube or reed. I now come to alum. This substance, powdered, and introduced into the vagina, or sprinkled on the verge before coition, prevents the woman from conceiving by obstructing the arrival of the sperm in the uterus; for it has the property of drying up and contracting the vagina. But the too frequent use of it will make the woman barren and annihilate all her capability of conception. The man who at the moment of copulation coats his member with tar, deprives his sperm of its generative faculty. This is the most powerful of all applications, and if a woman during her pregnancy introduces some of the substance repeatedly into her vagina, she will be sterile, and the child will be born dead. The woman who drinks the weight of a mitskal of laurel water, with a little pepper, will cause her courses to flow again, and clear her uterus from the clots of blood which sometimes lodge there. If she makes use of this medicine when she is already pregnant, the embryo will be expelled; and taken after confinement, this medicine has the property of causing the expulsion from the matrix of all deleterious matter and of the afterbirth. The woman who drinks an infusion of coarse cinnamon mixed with red myrrh, and then introduces into her vagina a plug of wool saturated with the mixture, kills the fetus and provokes its expulsion, with the will of God the Highest! If the fetus dies in the womb, a decoction of yellow wall-flowers in water will cause the expulsion of the same, with the will of God the Highest! All the above enumerated medicines are efficacious and their effect is certain.

Questions for Reflection and Discussion

How does Nafzawi bring his God into this erotic discussion? Is it merely an attempt to make a libertine treatise seem puritan? How easily might his ideas be reconciled with those of Islamic tradition? What is new and what is old in what Nafzawi said about men and women?

90. JADE SCENT AND HONEST QUAN

Time: seventeenth century CE
Place: China
Author: Li Yu

Li Yu, a famous writer in his own day, liked to challenge his readers' notions of sexual and social taboos. The hero of this story from The Carnal Prayer Mat, *Honest Quan, enjoys a series of sexual adventures. In this episode, Quan finds work in the household of a woman whose husband is frequently away on business; their romantic affair breaks both marital and class taboos. Li Yu's stories are typical of a whole genre of libertine writings from the late Ming and early Qing eras in Chinese history, despite—or perhaps because of—increasingly conservative government policies on sex.*

Well before he entered the household, Mistress Jade Scent had fallen prey to a secret melancholy, which our brush has been too busy to describe but which we shall now address. Just at the height of her sexual enjoyment, her husband had been driven away by her monster of a father, a development that left her feeling like a drunkard who has just sworn off wine or a gourmet who has just given up meat. She couldn't even get through the next few days, let alone survive for years as a grass widow. Deprived of real pleasures, she was reduced to placing the erotic album in front of herself and trying to quench her thirst by looking at plums and satisfy her hunger by drawing a cake. To her dismay, however, she found that looking at plums increases rather than quenches one's thirst and that drawing a cake sharpens rather than satisfies one's hunger. The longer she looked at the album, the worse she felt, until at length she put it aside and brought out

a few idle books instead, in the hope of relieving her distress and boredom....

Day after day she would get up and, neglecting her needlework, match herself against these idle books, trying to bring her sexual excitement to a fever pitch so that when her husband returned, they could relieve it together. But when time passed and no word came from him, she could not help feeling a certain resentment. I've noticed that there's not a single woman in any of these books who does not have several lovers, she thought. Evidently it is not at all unusual to take a lover....

Thus when she first set eyes on Honest Quan, she was like a ravenous eagle spotting a chicken or a hungry cat coming upon a mouse—rough or smooth, goodlooking or ugly, she wanted nothing better than to gobble him up. While he was still working his land, she could do nothing about her desires; firstly, because she had observed that he was a terribly prudish soul who would not even look at her as he passed by and would certainly not jump at an invitation; and secondly, because he came in the daytime and left at night, and even if he did accept, they would have had neither the time nor the place for sex. But when she heard he was selling himself as a bondservant, her heart leaped and she resolved that on his very first night in the house he would not escape her....

[Honest Quan, however, marries another servant of the household, Ruyi.]

Jade Scent watched with a pang of jealousy as the bridal couple took their vows and entered the bedroom together. Waiting until her father was asleep, she then stole out of her room to eavesdrop on their lovemaking. Honest Quan's penis was by no means insignificant, and Ruyi, although in her twenties, was still a virgin because her highly principled master had never molested her. How could a space scarcely big enough to hold a finger endure a laundry beater stuffed inside it? Naturally she screamed and wailed fit to shake the heavens, until the eavesdropper herself began to feel pain on her behalf…. Henceforth Jade Scent was obsessed with Quan. He, for his part, changed his tune the moment he entered the household, dropping his prudish ways completely. Whenever he met Jade Scent, he stole glance after glance at her. If she smiled, he smiled, too, and if she looked sad, he responded with a sad look of his own.

One day she was taking a bath in her room, when he passed by and happened to cough. She realized who it was and, hoping to arouse his desires by getting him to look at her, called out, "I'm taking a bath in here! Whoever that is outside, don't come in!" … Jade Scent saw there was someone outside the window and knew it must be Quan. Previously she had had her back to the window, but now she turned around until her breasts and vulva faced it directly, offering them for his inspection. Lest the most important part of all be half hidden underwater, she lay back and spread her legs, giving him a full frontal view. Then, after lying like that for a while, she sat up, cradled her vulva in both hands, looked at it, and heaved a deep sigh, as if to say she was longing for a chance to put it to use.

At this sight Quan's desires flared up until they could no longer be held in check. Moreover, he knew that her desire was at its height and that she felt bitterly frustrated. If he did not accept the invitation to her party, he would be blamed, and conversely, if he did accept it, he would never be turned away…. "Mistress, the only reason I sold myself was to get inside the household and be with you. I meant to declare my feelings when we were alone together and get your permission before I did anything rash. But today I happened to be passing by and saw how incredibly soft and del-

icate your precious person was, and I couldn't restrain myself any longer, but had to come in and inflict myself upon you. Spare my life, Mistress, I beg you! Jade Scent had a few more stock protestations ready, but she feared they might take too long to deliver and in the meantime someone might come upon them….

Their arrangements made, the pair separated. By this time it was evening. Jade Scent dried herself, but did not dress or eat dinner. She lay on her bed, intending to take a nap and build up her strength for the night's encounter, but she could not get to sleep and lay there impatiently until the beginning of the second watch, when she heard the door creak and knew it must be Quan. "Brother Suixin," she whispered. "Is that you?" "Yes, Mistress dearest, it's me," he whispered back. Worried that Suixin might not be able to find his way to her bed in the dark, Jade Scent scrambled out and guided him in. She was worried, too, that in his ignorance of her proportions he might be too wild, so she gave him instructions: "Dearest, I've noticed that that thing of yours is different from other men's. I won't be able to bear it at first, so please go slow." "I wouldn't dare offend your precious person. I know a very effective means of entry that will cause you no discomfort at all." "I would be ever so grateful," murmured Jade Scent….

Observing that he was an expert in sexual technique, Jade Scent felt even more loving. Clasping him tightly, she asked, "Dearest one, how is it you're so sophisticated when you've had no experience with women? My husband had affairs and went to brothels all the time, and yet he was never as gentle and considerate as you are. Oh, I could love you to death!" Receiving this accolade so soon after assuming his duties, Quan naturally redoubled his efforts. This was no time to rest on his laurels. He feared she would scorn him as weak if he thrust too slowly and as violent if he went too fast, so he proceeded neither too fiercely nor too gently, neither too slowly nor too fast, until she was totally, incapable of uttering a word of praise, let alone an accolade—at which point he stopped. Jade Scent had never in her life experienced such a thrill. From then on nothing would do but that he come to her every night.

At first they kept Ruyi in ignorance, but then it occurred to them that they could not go on doing so forever and that they might as well tell her now and act openly. Fearing she might be jealous, Jade Scent went to great lengths to make up to her. In name they were mistress and maid, but in fact they were more like wife and concubine. Sometimes one of them slept with him all night and at other times they shared him, changing places at midnight. And there were even a few festive occasions when they all slept together, and Quan, unsure who was the mistress and who the maid, would cry out darling indiscriminately on reaching his climax.

His original motive had been revenge. He had hoped to seduce Jade Scent, sleep with her for a few months, and then leave. He could not afford to become captivated and waste his powers so badly with constant sex that she would be the one taking revenge. But it is always hard to free ourselves from a predestined enemy. He had slept several years with Fragrance without having any children, but the very first time he slept with Jade Scent, she became pregnant. She did not realize it at first, but after two or three months she began to suffer morning sickness and knew well enough. They tried desperately to find a medicine that would induce a miscarriage, but without success. "My death will be on your head," sobbed Jade Scent. "You know the kind of man my father is. A word out of place, and he rants and raves. You surely don't imagine he'll let me get away with something as bad as this? When he finds out, I'll die anyway. Far better to die now and spare myself the agony." She tried to hang herself then and

there, while Quan pleaded with her to stop. "If you want me to go on living," she retorted, "you'll have to think of a plan to get me away from here to some distant place where we can escape all our troubles and live together as husband and wife.

Questions for Reflection and Discussion

What are the most radical aspects of Li Yu's story? What are its most conservative elements? How might Li Yu's popularity as an author, and the popularity of others like him, be evidence for a community of like-minded people in China in his day?

91. PAGE FROM A CHINESE EROTIC ALBUM

Time: seventeenth century CE
Place: China
Artist: unknown

In the previous source, Jade Scent is said to look at images in an erotic album, and such albums survive in large numbers from the era of Li Yu and The Carnal Prayer Mat. *The image below shows a scene from one of them. Note that, as in* The Carnal Prayer Mat, *a man has sex with two women. Note also his fascination with one of the women's bound foot. Foot binding was widespread in China by the early modern period and apparently inspired sexual desire in many men.*

Questions for Reflection and Discussion

Why would footbinding seem erotic to many men in early modern China? Does this image of a man having sex with two women seem realistic or merely an artist's fantasy? What does the market for such albums say about sexual mores in early modern China?

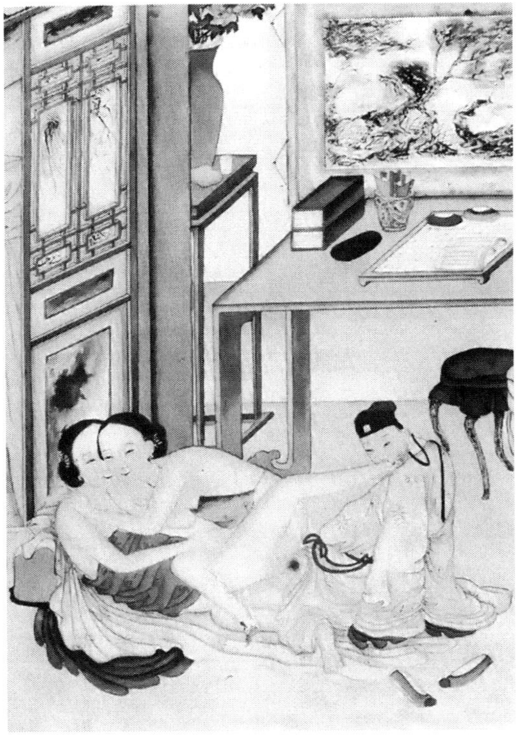

92. THE MYSTERIOUS WOMAN

Time: seventeenth century CE
Place: China
Author: Pu Songling

Pu Songling, another Chinese writer of the late Ming and early Qing eras, authored a collection of short stories called Strange Stories, *which often featured sexual situations, as in this example, and magical elements. His plain rather than scholarly style was intended to appeal to moderately educated people rather than solely to an intellectual elite.*

There was once a young man by the name of Ku, born of a poor family in Chinling [modern Nanjing]. He was talented and skilled in a variety of arts and crafts. However, since he could not bear to leave his aging mother, he made a simple living by selling calligraphy and paintings. He was single even at the age of twenty-five. Opposite to where he lived was an empty house. One day, an old woman and a young girl came by to rent the place, but since there was no man in their family, Ku did not feel that it was appropriate for him to make a courtesy call.

One day when he returned home he saw the young girl coming out of his mother's room. She was about eighteen or nineteen, and of rare beauty and gracefulness. She made no attempt to hide when she saw Ku. There was an air of awe-inspiring composure about her. Ku went inside and questioned his mother. Mrs. Ku said, "That is the girl across the street. She came to borrow my scissors and ruler. She told me that only her mother lived with her. She doesn't seem to come from a poor family. When I asked why she isn't married, she said that she has to take care of her aged mother. I shall pay her mother a visit tomorrow, and sound her out. If they don't ask for too much, perhaps you can take care of her mother for her."

The next day, she went over to the young girl's house. She found the mother hard of hearing, and when she looked around the house, there did not seem to be enough food there for the following day. She asked the old woman how they managed to get by, and the latter replied that they depended solely on the young girl's needlework. Finally, Mrs. Ku brought up the question of a possible marriage between the two families. The old woman seemed agreeable and turned around to seek the opinion of her daughter. Though the girl did not say anything, she was apparently not too happy about it. So Mrs. Ku returned home. Later, as she thought about the girl's reaction, she said to her son, "Do you think we've been turned down because we're too poor? What a strange girl! So quiet and so straight-faced. Just as the saying goes. 'As beautiful as the peach and pear blossoms, but cold as the frost and snow.'" Mother and son exchanged their views on the matter for a good while and then ended their discussion with a sigh.

One day ... when Ku went inside, his mother said, "The young girl just came over to borrow some rice. She said that they haven't eaten for one whole day. This girl is devoted to her mother; what a pity that she should be in such circumstances. We should try to help her." Ku agreed with what his mother said, and carried a peck of rice over to the girl's house, conveying his mother's goodwill. The girl accepted the rice but did not say a word of thanks to him. After that, she often went over to Ku's house, helping with his mother's sewing and other needlework. She took care of all the household chores like a housewife. So Ku held her in even higher esteem....

Once, when Ku's mother got an abscess on her private parts which caused her to cry out day and night in pain, the girl frequently stayed by her bedside, looking after her, washing the wound, and applying medicine to it three or four times a day. Mrs. Ku felt uneasy, but the girl did not seem to mind the task at all. Ku's mother sighed and said to her, "Ah, where can I find a daughter-in-law such as you to see me through the end of my days?" As she said that, her voice was choked with tears. "Your son is devoted to you," the girl comforted her, "so you're much better off than my mother, who has only a helpless girl to look after her." "But surely even a devoted son can't do bedside chores like these! Anyhow, I'm old and could die any day. What I'm worried about is an heir for the family." As she spoke, Ku came in. Mrs. Ku wept and said, "I'm grateful for all that this young lady has done for us. Don't you forget to repay her kindness." ... Ku's respect and love for her grew deeper; yet she remained just as cold and aloof to him as before.

One day, Ku had his gaze fixed on the girl as she walked out the door. Suddenly she turned and smiled bewitchingly at Ku. Ku was overjoyed and followed her to her house. When he flirted with her, she did not rebuke him, so they went to bed happily and made love. Afterward, she cautioned Ku, "I hope you understand that this is a one-time thing." Ku returned home without saying anything. The next day, he approached the girl again, but she flatly refused him and left. However, she went to Ku's place as frequently as before and met him quite often; but she did not give him the slightest encouragement. Any effort on his part to exchange pleasantries with her was met with unyielding sternness.... [Then] one night, when Ku was sitting alone at home, the girl came in unexpectedly and greeted him with a smile. "It seems that our love hasn't ended yet." Ku was overwhelmed with joy and held the girl tightly in his arms.... Ku then brought up the subject of marriage again, and in reply she said, "I sleep with you in the same bed, and I do all the housework here; what am I if not a wife to you? Since we live like husband and wife already, why talk about marriage?" "Is it because I'm poor?" "If you're poor, I'm not any better off. It's only because I feel for you in your poverty that I'm here with you tonight." Before she left, she reminded Ku again, "Meetings such as this can't be repeated too often. If I can come, I will; but if I cannot, it's no use forcing me." Afterward, whenever they ran into each other and Ku wanted to talk privately with her, she avoided him. Yet she kept doing all the housework and needlework in Ku's house, as before.

[The girl became pregnant, and she decided to give the baby to Ku and his mother.]

More than a month had passed, and when the girl failed to show up for several days in a row, Mrs. Ku became suspicious and went over to have a look. The door was tightly shut and all was quiet inside. She knocked for a long time before the girl came out, with her hair all disheveled and her face soiled. She opened the door for Ku's mother and closed it immediately. Inside her room, Mrs. Ku found a baby crying on the bed. The old woman was surprised and asked, "When was he born?" "Three days ago," she replied. Mrs. Ku unwrapped the baby and found it to be a chubby boy with a wide forehead. Overjoyed, she said, "You have given me a grandson, but what is a single girl like you going to do all alone in the world?" "This is my secret, and I'm afraid I can't explain it to you," the girl replied. "You can carry the baby home at night when there is no one around." The old lady returned and told her son, and both of them were puzzled. They went over and took the baby home at night.

Several nights later, the girl suddenly came over around midnight…. She smiled and said, "… It's time for me to say good-bye." Ku immediately pressed her for a reason, to which she answered, "I've always remembered your kindness in helping me to support my mother. I once told you that our bedding together was a one-time affair because one should not repay one's debt in bed. But since you're so poor and could not afford to get married, I tried to give you an heir. I was hoping to bear you a boy by taking you just once, but unfortunately my period came as usual afterward so I had to break my rules and do it again. Now that I have repaid your kindness, my wish is fulfilled and I have no regrets."

Questions for Reflection and Discussion

Would you consider this story a puritan or libertine one? How are traditional values upheld, and how are they challenged? How might that tension between conventional and new elements have helped to contribute to Pu Songling's popularity as a writer?

93. MARX AND ENGELS ON THE FAMILY

Time: nineteenth century CE
Place: England
Author: Karl Marx and Friedrich Engels

This excerpt from The Communist Manifesto *demonstrates how the radical ideas about sex and marriage found their way into Communist philosophy and, through the influence of that philosophy, to a worldwide audience. Both Marx and Engels were German expatriates living in England; there, they founded the International Workingmen's Association to work for social and political change. Before moving to England, Marx had promoted his ideas as the editor of a radical newspaper, the* Rheinische Zeitung, *which was eventually banned by the Prussian government.*

Abolition of the family! Even the most radical flare up at this infamous proposal of the Communists. On what foundation is the present family, the bourgeois family, based? On capital, on private gain. In its completely developed form this family exists only among the bourgeoisie. But this state of things finds its complement in the practical absence of the family among the proletarians, and in public prostitution. The bourgeois family will vanish as a matter of course when its complement vanishes, and both will vanish with the vanishing of capital.

Do you charge us with wanting to stop the exploitation of children by their parents? To this crime we plead guilty. But, you will say, we destroy the most hallowed of relations, when we replace home education by social. And your education! Is not that also social, and determined by the social conditions under which you educate, by the intervention of society, direct or indirect, by means of schools, etc.? The Communists have not invented the intervention of society in education; they do but seek to alter the character of that intervention, and to rescue education from the influence of the ruling class. The bourgeois claptrap about the family, and education, about the hallowed co-relation of parent and child, becomes all the more disgusting, the more, by the action of modern industry, all family ties among the proletarians are torn asunder, and their children transformed into simple articles of commerce and instruments of labor.

But you Communists would introduce common use of women, screams the whole bourgeoisie in chorus. The bourgeois sees in his wife a mere instrument of production. He hears that the instruments of production are to be exploited in common, and, naturally, can come to no other conclusion than that the lot of being common to all will likewise fall to the women. He has not even a suspicion that the real point aimed at is to do away with the status of women as mere instruments of production. For the rest, nothing is more ridiculous than the virtuous indignation of our bourgeois at the community of women which, they pretend, is to be openly and officially established by the Communists. The Communists have no need to introduce community of women; it has existed almost from time immemorial. Our bourgeois, not content with having the wives and daughters of their proletarians at their disposal, not to speak of common prostitutes, take the greatest pleasure in seducing each other's wives.

Bourgeois marriage is in reality a system of wives in common and thus, at the most, what the Communists might possibly be reproached with is that they desire to introduce in substitution for a hypocritically concealed, an openly legalized community of women. For the rest, it is self-evident that the abolition of the present system of production must bring with it the abolition of the community of women springing from that system, i.e., of prostitution both public and private.

Questions for Reflection and Discussion

How do Marx and Engels manage to appeal to both puritan and libertine ideals in this discussion of marriage and the family? How does their emphasis on economics as the determining factor in human history influence their ideas about sex? What connections exist between their ideas about economic development and sexual progress?

94. HAN YI'S *DESTROYING THE FAMILY*

Time: twentieth century CE
Place: China
Author: Han Yi, pseudonym

This treatise was written in 1907 by someone who referred to him- or herself only as "a member of the Chinese people," which is what "Han Yi" means. The anonymity was meant to protect the author from retribution for his or her radical ideas in imperial China, where new political and social ideas were forced to circulate underground. The excerpt, probably influenced by Marxist thought, shows how libertine ideas might be part of a larger call for social and political reform. In 1911, the Manchu-dominated Qing Dynasty in China was overthrown, and a Chinese Republic was proclaimed.

All of society's accomplishments depend on people to achieve, while the multiplication of the human race depends on men and women. Thus if we want to pursue a social revolution, we must start with a sexual revolution—just as if we want to reestablish the Chinese nation, expelling the Manchus is the first step to the accomplishment of other tasks.… Yet, whenever we speak of the sexual revolution, the masses doubt and obstruct us, which gives rise to problems. In bringing up this matter then we absolutely must make a plan that gets to the root of the problem. What is this plan? It is to destroy the family. The family is the origin of all evil. Because of the family, people become selfish. Because of the family, women are increasingly controlled by men. Because of the family, everything useless and harmful occurs (people now often say they are embroiled in family responsibilities while in fact they are all just making trouble for themselves, and so if there were no families, these trivial matters would instantly disappear). Because of the family, children—who belong to the world as a whole—are made the responsibility of a single woman (children should be raised publicly since they belong to the whole society, but with families the men always force the women to raise their children and use them to continue the ancestral sacrifices). These examples constitute irrefutable proof of the evils of the family.…

Moreover, from now on in a universal commonwealth, everyone will act freely, never again will they live and die without contact with one another as in olden times. The doctrine of human equality allows for neither forcing women to maintain the family nor having servants to maintain it. The difficulties of life are rooted in the family. When land belongs to everyone and the borders between here and there are eradicated, then there will be no doubt that the "family" itself definitely should be abolished. As long as the family exists, then debauched men will imprison women in cages and force them to become their concubines and service their lust, or they will take the sons of others to be their own successors. If we abolish the family now, then such men will disappear.

The destruction of the family will thus lead to the creation of public-minded people in place of selfish people, and men will have no way to oppress women. Therefore, to open the curtain on the social revolution, we must start with the destruction of the family.

Questions for Reflection and Discussion

How does Han Yi see changes to sexual customs as prerequisites for broader social change? How does Han Yi compare to his or her seventeenth-century Chinese predecessors (sources 90, 91, and 92)? Are Han Yi's ideas the natural extension of those earlier ideas?

95. FIDEL CASTRO'S ADDRESS TO THE WOMEN OF CUBA

Time: mid-twentieth century CE
Place: Cuba
Author: Fidel Castro

Fidel Castro, leader of the Communist revolt in Cuba in the 1950s, inherited the radical social ideas of Marxism about sexuality together with its radical political ideas. Castro's Cuba, as with Communist regimes in China, Russia, and elsewhere, viewed the restructuring of marriage, the family, and relations between men and women as part of eliminating oppressive traditions of inequality and individualism. This example is preserved from a conference address given in 1966 to a group of Cuban women.

This is one of the great lessons we spoke about before: one of the great lessons and perhaps one of the greatest victories over prejudices that have existed, not for decades or centuries but for thousands of years. We refer to the belief that all a woman could do was wash dishes, wash and iron clothes, cook, keep house, and bear children—age-old prejudices that placed women in an inferior position in society. In effect, she did not have a productive place in society. Such prejudices are thousands of years old and have survived through various social systems. If we consider capitalism, women—that is, lower-class women—were doubly exploited or doubly humiliated. A poor woman, part of the working class or of a working-class family, was exploited simply because she was poor, because she was a member of the working class. But in addition, although she was a woman of the working class, even her own class looked down on and underrated her. Not only was she underestimated, exploited, and looked down upon by the exploiting classes, but even within her own class she was the object of numerous prejudices. So all these events have been a great lesson to all of us, to every revolutionary. Naturally, a considerable amount of prejudice still persists. If women were to believe that they have totally fulfilled their role as revolutionaries in society, they would be making a mistake. It seems to us that women must still fight and exert great efforts to attain the place that they should really hold in society. If women in our country were doubly exploited, doubly humiliated in the past, then this simply means that women in a social revolution should be doubly revolutionary. And perhaps this is the explanation, or at least the social basis, for the resolute, enthusiastic, firm, and loyal support given by Cuban women to this revolution.

This revolution has really been two revolutions for women; it has meant a double liberation: as part of the exploited sector of the country, and second, as women, who were discriminated against not only as workers but also as women, in that society of exploitation. The attitude of Cuban women toward the revolution corresponds to this reality; it corresponds to what the revolution has meant to them. And the support of the popular masses for the revolution is directly proportional to what the revolution has meant to them in terms of their liberation.

There are two sectors in this country, two sectors of society which, aside from economic reasons, have had other motives for sympathizing and feeling enthusiasm for the revolution. These two sectors are the Black population of Cuba and the female population. I suppose you recall that in Cuba's old bourgeois constitution, there was an article which declared illegal any discrimination for reasons of race or sex. The constitution declared such discrimination illegal. But a constitution in a capitalist society, or such an article in a capitalist society, solves nothing, because discrimination for reasons of race and for reasons of sex existed in practice. And the basis for all of this was the existence of a class society which practiced exploitation.

In a class society, which is to say, a society of exploiters and exploited, there was no way of eliminating discrimination for reasons of race or sex. Now the problem of such discrimination has disappeared from our country, because the basis for these two types of discrimination which is, quite simply the exploitation of man by man, has disappeared. Much news reaches us from the United States, for example, about the civil rights struggle of Blacks. Nevertheless, racial discrimination in the United States will not disappear until capitalist society has disappeared. That is, discrimination will never be wiped out within the framework of capitalist society. Discrimination with respect to race and sex can only be wiped out through a socialist revolution, which eradicates the exploitation of man by man.

Now, does the disappearance of the exploitation of man by man mean that all the conditions are immediately created whereby woman may elevate her position in society? No. The conditions for the liberation of women, for the full development of women in society, for an authentic equality of rights, or for authentic equality of women with men in society, require a material base; they require the material foundations of economic and social development. I described before the opinion held by many men concerning the functions of women, and I said that among the functions considered to belong to women was—almost exclusively—that of having children. Naturally, reproduction is one of the most important of women's functions in human society, in any kind of human society. But it is precisely this function, relegated by nature to women, which has enslaved them to a series of chores within the home.

There is a sign here in front of us, for example, which says, "One million women working in production by 1970." Unfortunately, it will not be possible to have one million working in production by 1970. We feel that this goal may be reached, perhaps, within ten years but not within four. We could propose it as a goal to be reached by 1975. Why can't this goal be reached in four years? Because in order to have one million women working in production, we must have thousands of children's day nurseries, thousands of primary boarding schools, thousands of school dining halls, thousands of workers' dining halls; thousands of centers of social services of this type must be set up, because if not, who is going to cook for the second- or third-grade child when he comes home for lunch? Who is going to care for unweaned infants, or babies of two, three, and four years of age? Who is going to prepare dinner for the man when he comes home from work? Who is going to wash, clean, all of those things?

In other words, in order to reach the social goal of liberating women from all these activities that enslave her and impede her from full incorporation into work outside the home and all these activities she can engage in society, it is necessary to create the nec-essary material base, to attain the necessary social development. It is impossible to construct the required thousands of children's day nurseries, school dining halls, laundries, workers' dining halls, boarding schools, in four years. In fact, merely to meet present needs, great effort is necessary on all fronts. Everywhere women are working it has been necessary to make a special effort to establish day nurseries, set up boarding schools and all of the necessary institutions so that these women could be free to work.

Questions for Reflection and Discussion

How does Castro tie sexual inequality to racial inequality? To economic structures? What are the puritan elements within Castro's libertine speech?

96. THE NAZI FAMILY

Time: mid-twentieth century CE
Place: Germany
Artist: unknown

While libertines continued to push at the traditional definitions of marriage and family, puritans maintained the need to preserve them from such changes. As democracies expanded in the late nineteenth and early twentieth centuries—admitting adult women, for example, to the ranks of voters—politicians found that speaking out in favor of traditional marriage and family life could be a popular political stance. Some exploited those traditional values for political gain, as exemplified by the following Nazi art poster that reads: "The NSDAP [Nazi Party] protects the national community of citizens. If you need counsel and help turn to your local organization." The use of mass-produced posters guaranteed that the influence of such images would be widespread

and encourage voters to link the Nazis and the traditional—and happy—family.

Questions for Reflection and Discussion

How does the poster's text and image complement each other? What role does the eagle play in the image? How does the image reflect the Nazis' policies about German superiority and call for population growth?

97. LETTERS FROM RADEN ADJENG KARTINI

Time: late nineteenth and early twentieth century CE
Place: Java (in modern Indonesia)
Author: Raden Adjeng Kartini

The woman who wrote these letters, Kartini, was the daughter of a governor or "regent" at Japara on the island of Java. Her title, Raden Adjeng, *means "princess," but it was an honorific one since Java was then a Dutch colony. Still, her family was wealthy, and she studied at a Dutch school, where she made lifelong friends with whom she corresponded. She also wrote against colonialism, and her letters have become encouraged reading in Indonesian schools after its independence. Her thoughts, as expressed in these letters, show an individual torn between puritan and libertine impulses and demonstrate the interior, psychological dimension to the struggles between competing ideas.*

MAY 25, 1899

We girls, so far as education goes, fettered by our ancient traditions and conventions, have profited but little by these advantages. It was a great crime against the customs of our land that we should be taught at all, and especially that we should leave the house every day to go to school. For the custom of our country forbade girls in the strongest manner ever to go outside of the house. We were never allowed to go anywhere, however, save to the school, and the only place of instruction of which our city could boast, which was open to us, was a free grammar school for Europeans. When I reached the age of twelve, I was kept at home—I had to go into the "box." I was locked up, and cut off from all communication with the outside world, toward which I might never turn again save at the side of a bridegroom, a stranger, an unknown man whom my parents would choose for me, and to whom I should be betrothed without my own knowledge. European friends—this I heard later—had tried in every possible way to dissuade my parents from this cruel course toward me, a young and life-loving child; but they were able to do nothing. My parents were inexorable; I went into my prison. Four long years I spent between thick walls, without once seeing the outside world. How I passed through that time, I do not know. I only know that it was terrible. But there was one great happiness left me: the reading of Dutch books and correspondence with Dutch friends was not forbidden. This—the only gleam of light in that empty, somber time, was my all, without which, I should have fallen, perhaps, into a still more pitiable state. My life, my soul even, would have been starved. But then came my friend and my deliverer—the Spirit of the Age; his footsteps echoed everywhere. Proud, solid ancient structures tottered to their foundation at his approach. Strongly barricaded doors sprang open, some as of themselves, others only painfully half way, but nevertheless they opened, and let in the unwelcome guest. At last in my sixteenth year, I saw the outside world again. Thank God! Thank God! I could leave my prison as a free human being and not chained to an unwelcome bridegroom…. Our European friends rejoiced, and as for ourselves, no queen was so rich as we. But I am far from satisfied. I would go still further, always further. I do not desire to go out to feasts, and little frivolous amusements. That has never been the cause of my longing for freedom. I long to be free, to be able to stand alone, to study, not to be subject to any one, and, above all, never, never to be obliged to marry. But we must marry, must, must. Not to marry is the greatest sin which the Muslim woman can commit; it is the greatest disgrace which a native girl can bring to her family. And marriage among us—miserable is too feeble an expression for it. How can it be otherwise, when the laws have made everything for the man and nothing for the woman? When law and convention both are for the man; when everything is allowed to him? Love! what do we know here of love? How can we love a man whom we have never known? And how could he love us? That in itself would not be possible. Young girls and men must be kept rigidly apart, and are never allowed to meet.

NOVEMBER 6, 1899

I shall never, never fall in love. To love, there must first be respect, according to my thinking; and I can have no respect for the Javanese young man. How can I respect one who is married and a father, and who, when he has had enough of the mother of his children, brings another woman into his house, and is, according to the Muslim law, legally married to her? And who does not do this? And why not? It is no sin, and still less a scandal. The Muslim law allows a man to have four wives at the same time. And though it be a thousand times over no sin according to the Muslim law and doctrine, I shall forever call it a sin. I call all things sin which bring misery to a fellow creature. Sin is to cause pain to another, whether man or beast. And can you imagine what hell pain a woman must suffer when her husband comes home with another—a rival—whom she must recognize as his legal wife? He can torture her to death, mistreat her as he will; if he does not choose to give her back her freedom, then she can whistle to the moon for her rights. Everything for the man, and nothing for the woman, is our law and custom. Do you understand now the deep aversion I have for marriage? I would do the humblest work, thankfully and joyfully, if by it I could be independent. But I can do nothing, less than nothing, on account of Father's position among our people.

AUGUST 23, 1900

In thinking over Javanese and European conditions and comparing them with one another, one can easily see that it is hardly better there than here in so far as the morality of the men is concerned, and that women are unfortunate there as here, with this difference, however, that the great majority there, of their own free will follow the man in the marriage bond; while here the women have no say at all in the matter, but are simply married out of hand, according to the will of their parents, to whomsoever those powerful ones shall find good. In the Islamic world the approval, yes, even the presence of the woman is not necessary at a marriage. Father can come home any day at all and say to me, "You are married to so and so." I must then follow my husband. It is true I can refuse, but that gives the man the right to chain me to him for my whole life, without ever having come near. I am his wife although I will not follow him, and if he will not allow me to be divorced, then I am bound to him all my life, while he is free to do as he pleases. He may marry as many women as he chooses without being concerned in the least about me. If Father should marry me off in this manner then I should find a way out at the beginning, one way or another. But then Father would never do that. God has created woman as the companion of man and the calling of woman is marriage. Good! it is not to be denied, and I gladly acknowledge that the highest happiness for a woman is, and shall be centuries after us, a harmonious union with the man of her choice. But how can one speak of a harmonious union as our marriage laws are now? I have tried to picture them to you. Must I not for myself, hate the idea of marriage, scorn it, when by it the woman is so cruelly wronged? No, fortunately every Muslim has not four wives or more, but every married woman in our world knows that she is not the only one, and that any day the man's fancy can bring a companion home, who will have just as much

right to him as she. According to the Islamic law she is also his wife.

AUGUST 1, 1903

A few words to announce to you, as briefly as possible, a new turn in my life. I shall not go on with our great work as a woman alone! A noble man will be at my side to help me. He is ahead of me in work for our people; he has already won his spurs while I am just beginning. Oh, he is such a lovable, good man, he has a noble heart and a clever head as well. And he has been to Holland, where his bride would so gladly go, but must not for her people's sake. It is a great change; but if we work together, and support and help one another, we may be able to take a far shorter road to the realization of our hopes than could either alone. We meet at many, many points. You do not yet know the name of my betrothed; it is Raden Adipati Djojo Adiningrat, Regent of Rembang.

DECEMBER 11, 1903

You do not know with what affection this, my first letter from my new home, is written. A home where, praise God, there is peace and love everywhere, and we are all happy with and through one another. I regret so deeply that through the press of circumstances I have not been able to write to you before. Forgive me. The first days were so frightfully hard; then our children [of her husband, who was a widower] were ailing, and at last I felt the reaction from the wearisome days through which we had passed. I was far from well and was obliged to take care of myself. Now I am again fresh and happy. Once more it is the old irresponsible, hare-brained creature of other days, who can look forward to the future with smiling eyes. Do I have to express myself still more plainly, dearest? I bless the day on which

I laid my hand in that of him who was sent by God to be my comrade in the journey through this great and difficult life. Everything that was noble and beautiful in my eyes I find here realized before me. Some of the dreams that I still dream he has carried out years ago, or he dreams them now with me. We are so entirely one in thought and ideas that often I am frightened. You would both love him if you knew him. You would admire his clear brain and honor his good heart.

MARCH 6, 1904

I wish that I could throw my arms around your neck, I long from my soul to tell you of my great joy, to make you a sharer in our splendid secret. A great, sweet happiness awaits me. If God so wills it, toward the end of September, there will come one sent from heaven to make our beautiful life still more beautiful, to draw the bond closer and tighter that already binds us together. Mother, my mother, think of the little soul that will be born from our two souls to call me mother. Can you picture it? I a mother! … My husband is so glowingly happy because of this new life which I carry under my heart. That alone was wanting to our happiness.

JUNE 28, 1904

We do not go out often, and we entertain very little, yet my life is always full. Splendid! I divide my days between my dear husband, my housekeeping, and my children—both my own and the adopted ones. And these last take the largest share of my time and attention. When their father is at work, then the children work with me from nine until twelve o'clock. At half past twelve, father finds a troop of clean-faced but very hungry children. At half-past one the little ones are sent to bed, and if father is in bed, and

I am not too tired, I work with the young girls. At four o'clock I preside at the tea table. When the little ones have drunk their milk and have bathed, they can drive the fowls to the coops, or walk with us, or play in the garden. We amuse ourselves for a little, and prattle about everything or about nothing. When our little troop comes in, then we are done with play. Father sits down to read the paper, and they range themselves around mother. I sit in a rocking chair with the two smallest on my lap, a child on each arm of the chair and the two eldest at my knee. We tell stories; soon afterward suppertime comes around. We eat early with the little ones, the smallest of all sits next to mother. The little fellow has taken upon himself the task of lifting the glass cover for mother. No one must take that little work away from him, and if he is not allowed to do it, he knows it is because he has deserved a punishment. At eight o'clock the little treasures are sent to bed. And we parents sit up and talk to each other…. Sunday is a holiday for both of us. We begin it always with a walk; after that I teach my girls cooking, and then the mother and wife can do the things for which she has not had time during the week. It is not much that I can do, for my husband is happier when I sit by him. He charms me sometimes with beautiful *gamelan* music and songs. I think it is delightful in my husband to add the songs. For the *gamelan* music alone makes too great an impression upon me. It takes me back to times of which I must not think. It makes me weak and sad. So the days fly by, calm, quiet and peaceful as a little brook deep in the forest. If the child that I carry under my heart is a girl, what shall I wish for her? I shall wish that she may live a rich full life, and that she may complete the work that her mother has begun. She shall never be compelled to do anything abhorrent to her deepest feelings. What she does must be of her own free will. She shall have a mother who will watch over the welfare of her inmost being and a father who will never force her in anything. It will make no difference to him if his daughter remains unmarried her whole life long; what will count with him will be that she shall always keep her esteem and affection for us.

[On September 13, 1904, Kartini gave birth to a son, but died four days later of complications from the birth, at the age of twenty-five.]

Questions for Reflection and Discussion

Is there a contradiction between Kartini's earlier and later letters? What role did Europe as a mental image play in her letters? What role did Islam play? Is there any evidence in this chapter's other sources for the internal struggle that Kartini articulated in her letters?

SOURCES AND FURTHER READING

Works that take on the daunting task of examining the impact of global exchanges on sexuality are understandably few and usually address only one aspect of the topic or only contemporary exchanges. An exception is Peter Stearns's *Gender in World History* (New York: Routledge, 2000), which is brief yet truly comparative and deals with a number of topics related to the history of sexuality. For general studies on sex in the modern world, see Dennis Altman's *Global Sex* (Chicago: University of Chicago Press, 2001); or Spencer Rathus et al.'s *Human Sexuality in a World of Diversity* (Boston: Allyn and Bacon, 2000); or *Families in Multicultural Perspective*, Bron Ingoldsby and Suzanna Smith, eds. (New York: Guilford, 1995). More historical in focus, although dealing with more specific aspects of sexuality, are Göran Therborn's *Between Sex and Power: Family in the World, 1900-2000* (New York: Routledge, 2004); or Robert Aldrich's

Colonialism and Homosexuality (New York: Routledge, 2003); or Nils Ringdal's *Love for Sale: A World History of Prostitution*, Richard Daly, trans. (New York: Grove, 2004). On the historical realities of the Puritans' sex lives, see James Johnson's *A Society Ordained by God: English Puritan Marriage Doctrine in the First Half of the Seventeenth Century* (Nashville, TN: Abingdon, 1970); or Roger Thompson's *Sex in Middlesex: Popular Mores in a Massachusetts County, 1649-1699* (Amherst, MA: University of Massachusetts Press, 1986). On the Puritans as a historical memory of sexual repressiveness, see Edmund Leites's *The Puritan Conscience and Modern Sexuality* (New Haven, CT: Yale University Press, 1986); or *The Puritan Origins of American Sex: Religion, Sexuality, and National Identity in American Literature*, Tracy Fessenden et al., eds. (New York: Routledge, 2001). On the Libertines as a historical group, see *Libertine Enlightenment: Sex, Liberty, and License in the Eighteenth Century*, Peter Cryle and Lisa O'Connell, eds. (New York: Palgrave Macmillan, 2004); or James Turner's *Libertines and Radicals in Early Modern London: Sexuality, Politics, and Literary Culture, 1630-1685* (Cambridge: Cambridge University Press, 2002). On the influence of Libertinism in history, see *Libertinage and Modernity*, Catherine Cusset, ed. (New Haven, CT: Yale University Press, 1998). On Social Identity Theory, a good collection that can serve as an introduction to the field is *Social Identity: International Perspectives*, Stephen Worchel et al., eds. (Thousand Oaks, CA: Sage, 1998); other interesting essays showing its application are in *Social Theory and the Politics of Identity*, Craig Calhoun, ed. (Oxford: Blackwell, 1994); and in *Attitudes, Behavior, and Social Context: The Role of Norms and Group Membership*, Deborah Terry and Michael Hogg, eds. (Mahwah, NJ: Erlbaum Associates, 2000). More detailed studies include Craig Calhoun's

Critical Social Theory: Culture, History, and the Challenge of Difference (Oxford: Blackwell, 1995); or Harrison White's *Identity and Control: A Structural Theory of Social Action* (Princeton, NJ: Princeton University Press, 1992). A fascinating application of Social Identity Theory to the history of sexuality is Joane Nagel's *Race, Ethnicity, and Sexuality: Intimate Intersections, Forbidden Frontiers* (Oxford: Oxford University Press, 2003).

85. "Martin Luther on Sex and Marriage" is taken from Martin Luther, *Table Talk*, William Hazlitt, trans. (London: George Bell and Sons, 1895), 297-308, with slight changes.

Recent biographies of Luther include Martin Marty's *Martin Luther* (New York: Penguin, 2004); or Michael Mullett's *Martin Luther* (New York: Routledge, 2004). Luther wrote much on a variety of topics, including sex. See *Luther's Works*, vol. 45, for "A Sermon on the Estate of Marriage" (1519), "The Persons Related by Consanguinity and Affinity Who Are Forbidden to Marry According to the Scriptures, Leviticus 18" (1522), and "The Estate of Marriage" (1522). See also the collection entitled *Luther on Women: A Sourcebook*, Susan Karant-Nunn and Merry Wiesner-Hank, eds. and trans. (Cambridge: Cambridge University Press, 2003). The other early Protestant Reformers, such as John Calvin, did not seem nearly as interested in sexual matters, at least as evidenced by their writings. More recently, historians have sought to compare Protestant teachings and actual practice; see, for example, Scott Hendrix's "Masculinity and Patriarchy in Reformation Germany," *Journal of the History of Ideas* 56 (1995): 177-93; or Rosalind Mitchison and Leah Leneman's *Sexuality and Social Control: Scotland, 1660-1780* (Oxford: Blackwell, 1989). Later Protestant groups often differed immensely among them-

selves in attitudes toward sexuality; a good introduction to an interesting assortment of American Protestant sects is Lawrence Foster's *Religion and Sexuality: Three American Communal Experiments of the Nineteenth Century* (Oxford: Oxford University Press, 1981), on Shakers, the Oneida Community, and Mormons; there are many other studies on these groups individually.

86. "Bernard Mandeville's Defense of Prostitution" is taken from Bernard Mandeville, *A Modest Defence of Publick Stews* (Los Angeles: William Andrews Clark Memorial Library, University of California at Los Angeles, 1973), 1-8.

On Bernard Mandeville, who is best remembered for his *Fable of the Bees* on social cooperation, see D.H. Monro's *The Ambivalence of Bernard Mandeville* (Oxford: Clarendon, 1975); or Richard I. Cook's *Bernard Mandeville* (New York: Twayne, 1974); or M.M. Goldsmith's *Private Vices, Public Benefits: Bernard Mandeville's Social and Political Thought* (Cambridge: Cambridge University Press, 1985). On the era of the Restoration in England, and the Augustan era that followed it, when Mandeville lived and which were known for their erotic writings, see David Foxon's *Libertine Literature in England, 1660-1745* (London: The Book Collector, 1964), or more specialized studies, such as Tiffany Potter's *Honest Sins: Georgian Libertinism and the Plays and Novels of Henry Fielding* (Montreal, QC: McGill-Queen's University Press, 1999). For other examples of eighteenth-century British literature, see many of the *100 Great Monologues from the Neo-Classical Theater*, Jocelyn Beard, ed. (Lyme, NH: Smith and Kraus, 1994); or *When Flesh Becomes Word: An Anthology of Early Eighteenth-Century Libertine Literature*, Bradford Mudge, ed.

(Oxford: Oxford University Press, 2004), both of which also provide an entry into the sources for the period. The most famous of such writings is John Cleland's *Memoirs of a Woman of Pleasure*, also known as *Fanny Hill*, of which there are numerous editions (and for another contemporary novel about a prostitute, see Daniel Defoe's *Moll Flanders*).

87. "The Marquis de Sade" is taken from The Marquis de Sade, *The 120 Days of Sodom and Other Writings*, Austryn Wainhouse and Richard Seaver, trans. (New York: Grove, 1966), 197-99, with slight changes.

Recent biographies of the Marquis de Sade include Francine du Plessix Gray's *At Home with the Marquis de Sade: A Life* (New York: Simon & Schuster, 1998); Neil Shaeffer's *The Marquis de Sade: A Life* (New York: Knopf, 1999); and Laurence Bongie's *Sade: A Biographical Essay* (Chicago: University of Chicago Press, 1998). De Sade's writings are of great interest to a history of sexuality but often disturbing to read. Studies of de Sade include Timo Airaksinen's *Of Glamor, Sex, and De Sade* (Wakefield, NH: Longwood Academic, 1991); *Sade and the Narrative of Transgression*, David Allison et al., eds. (Cambridge: Cambridge University Press, 1995); and Lucienne Frappier-Mazur's *Writing the Orgy: Power and Parody in Sade*, Gillian Gill, trans. (Philadelphia: University of Pennsylvania Press, 1996). A good history of studies about de Sade is chapter 1 of Philippe Seminet's *Sade in His Own Name: An Analysis of Les Crimes de l'Amour* (New York: P. Lang, 2003). More about French Libertine writings may be found in Jean Marie Goulemot's *Forbidden Texts: Erotic Literature and Its Readers in Eighteenth-Century France*, James Simpson, trans. (Philadelphia: University of Pennsylvania Press, 1994); or in *The Libertine Reader: Eroticism and Enlightenment in Eighteenth-Century France*, Michel Feher, ed. (New York: Zone, 1997); for more on sexual attitudes in this period see Vernon Rosario's *The Erotic Imagination: French Histories of Perversity* (Oxford: Oxford University Press, 1997). For earlier traditions of Libertine writings, see James Turner's *Schooling Sex: Libertine Literature and Erotic Education in Italy, France, and England, 1534-1685* (Oxford: Oxford University Press, 2003). A libertine novel of the same era, Choderlos de Laclos's *Dangerous Liaisons*, published in 1782 and made popular by a 1988 American film of the same name, has recently been the inspiration for a Korean film, *Untold Scandal* (2003). An Italian libertine author of the same era was Giacomo Casanova, whose *Memoirs* describe his erotic encounters (translated many times into English) and whose name became synonymous with "libertine."

88. "The *Code Napoléon*" is taken from *Code Napoleon, or The French Civil Code*, trans. unknown (Baton Rouge, LA: Claitor's Book Store, 1960), 59-63.

An introduction to the period is Alistair Horne's *The Age of Napoleon* (New York: Modern Library, 2004); or Alexander Grab's *Napoleon and the Transformation of Europe* (New York: Palgrave Macmillan, 2003). I know of no studies of the *Code Napoléon* in English that demonstrate any specific interest in its approach to marriage or the family.

89. "Nafzawi on Physical Attractiveness and Abortion" is taken from *The Perfumed Garden of the Shaykh Nefzaoui*, Richard Burton, trans. (New York: Castle, 1964), 11, 21-22, 114, with slight changes.

Neither Nafzawi (spelled Nefzaoui by Burton) nor his *The Perfumed Garden* has been well studied. On the history of contraception and abortion in the Islamic world, however, see Abdel Omran's *Family Planning in the Legacy of Islam* (New York: Routledge, 1992); or Basim Musallam's *Sex and Society in Islam: Birth Control before the Nineteenth Century* (Cambridge: Cambridge University Press, 1983); or Marion Holmes Katz's "The Problem of Abortion in Classical Sunni *fiqh*," in *Islamic Ethics of Life: Abortion, War, and Euthanasia*, Jonathan Brockopp, ed. (Columbia, SC: University of South Carolina Press, 2003). A comparison with ancient and medieval Christian medical writers on sex is available in John Riddle's "Oral Contraceptives and Early-Term Abortifacients during Classical Antiquity and the Middle Ages," *Past and Present* 132 (1991): 3-32. On Nafzawi's English translator, Sir Richard Francis Burton, who first published many Arab and Indian erotic writings, see Glenn Burne's *Richard F. Burton* (Boston: Twayne, 1985); or James Casada's *Sir Richard F. Burton: A Biobibliographical Study* (London: Mansell, 1990). Burton's own essay, "The Sotadic Zone," published as an appendix to his translation of *The Thousand and One Nights*, relates his odd theories about pederasty and its relationship to world climate; see *The Sotadic Zone* (New York: Panurge, 1930).

90. "Jade Scent and Honest Quan" is taken from Li Yu, *The Carnal Prayer Mat*, Patrick Hanan, trans. (New York: Ballantine, 1990), 205-15.

The whole of *The Carnal Prayer Mat* is worth reading in a history of sexuality, but is mostly more of the same. More varied but still relevant is the same author's *Silent Operas*, Patrick Hanan, trans. (Hong Kong: Research Centre for Translation, Chinese University of Hong Kong, 1990), which is a collection of short stories; or his *A Tower for the Summer Heat*, Patrick Hanan, trans. (New York: Columbia University Press, 1998). All of these translations contain biographical information about the author in English in their introductions; their translator, Patrick Hanan, has also written *The Invention of Li Yu* (Cambridge, MA: Harvard University Press, 1988) on the author. More generally on the erotic literature of seventeenth-century China (the Ming Dynasty gave way to the Qing in 1644), see Keith McMahon's *Causality and Containment in Seventeenth-Century Chinese Fiction* (Leiden, NLD: E.J. Brill, 1988); or Martin Huang's *Desire and Fictional Narrative in Late Imperial China* (Cambridge, MA: Harvard University Press, 2001). Other studies include Matthew Sommer's *Sex, Law, and Society in Late Imperial China* (Stanford, CA: Stanford University Press, 2000); Cuncun Wu's *Homoerotic Sensibilities in Late Imperial China* (New York: RoutledgeCurzon, 2004); or some of the essays in *Chinese Femininities, Chinese Masculinities: A Reader*, Susan Brownell and Jeffrey Wasserstrom, eds. (Berkeley, CA: University of California Press, 2002).

91. "Page from a Chinese Erotic Album" is taken from Philip Rawson, *Erotic Art of the East* (New York: G.P. Putnam's and Sons, 1968), 260.

See note 90 for more on sexuality in seventeenth- and eighteenth-century China. On the Ming and Qing tradition of erotic art, see Robert van Gulik's *Erotic Colour Prints of the Ming Period*, vol. 1 (Leiden, NLD: Brill, 2004); or John Byron's *Portrait of a Chinese Paradise: Erotica and Sexual Customs of the Late Qing Period* (London: Quartet, 1987); or Ferdinand Bertholet's *Dreams of Spring: Erotic Art in China from the Bertholet Collection* (Amsterdam: Pepin, 1997); or Ferdinand Bertholet's *Gardens of Pleasure: Eroticism and Art in China, Works from the Bertholet Collection* (Munich: Prestel,

2003). On the tradition of footbinding, see Ping Wang's *Aching for Beauty: Footbinding in China* (Minneapolis, MI: University of Minnesota Press, 2000), which discusses its erotic appeal, and which now replaces Howard Levy's *Chinese Footbinding: The History of a Curious Erotic Custom* (New York: Bell, 1967); and Yong-pil Pang's "Footbinding in China," *Journal of Asian Culture* 3 (1979): 97-108.

92. "The Mysterious Woman" is taken from P'u Sung-ling, *Traditional Chinese Stories*, trans. W.J.F. Jenner, in *Rice Bowl Women*, Dorothy Blair Shimer, ed. (New York: New American Library, 1982), 77-83.

On Pu Songling, also spelled P'u Sung-ling, see Judith Zeitlin's *Historian of the Strange: Pu Songling and the Chinese Classical Tale* (Stanford, CA: Stanford University Press, 1993). His stories have been translated by Herbert Giles as *Strange Stories from a Chinese Studio*, available in several editions, although most do not focus on sexual aspects. Of greater note is Pu Songling's novel, *The Bonds of Matrimony*, Alison Nyren, trans. (Lewiston, NY: E. Mellen, 1995). *Under Confucian Eyes: Writings on Gender in Chinese History*, Susan Mann and Yu-Yin Cheng, eds. (Berkeley, CA: University of California Press, 2001) also contains several short writings about marriage from the Ming and Qing eras. See also notes 90 and 91 on sexuality in early modern China.

93. "Marx and Engels on the Family" is taken from Karl Marx and Friedrich Engels, *The Communist Manifesto*, trans. unknown (London: Penguin, 1967), 100-101, with slight changes.

For a relevant analysis of Marx and Engels's writings on women's status, marriage, and the family, studied more often as a whole than separately, see *Engels Revisited: New Feminist Essays*, Janet Sayers et al., eds. (London: Tavistock, 1987). For a few examples of Marxism's influence on the study of sexuality, see Alan Soble's *Pornography: Marxism, Feminism, and the Future of Sexuality* (New Haven, CT: Yale University Press, 1986); *Feminism and Socialism*, Linda Jenness, ed. (New York: Pathfinder, 1972); or *Marxism, Queer Theory, Gender*, Mas'ud Zavarzadeh et al., eds. (Syracuse, NY: Red Factory, 2001). For more excerpts from Marx and Engels's writings, see *Women and Communism: Selections from the Writings of Marx, Engels, Lenin, and Stalin* (Westport, CT: Greenwood, 1973).

94. "Han Yi's *Destroying the Family*" is taken from *Sources of Chinese Tradition*, W. Theodore de Bary and Richard Lufrano, eds. (New York: Columbia University Press, 2000), 2: 395.

Nothing is known about Han Yi, since the pseudonym was used to protect the author from identification. On other radical ideas about sexuality in the Republican period of Chinese history, however, see Frank Dikötter's *Sex, Culture, and Modernity in China: Medical Science and the Construction of Sexual Identities in the Early Republican Period* (Honolulu: University of Hawai'i Press, 1995).

95. "Fidel Castro's Address to the Women of Cuba" is taken from *Women and the Cuban Revolution*, Elizabeth Stone, ed. (New York: Pathfinder, 1981), 50-53.

An interesting comparison can be made with *Cuban Women: Changing Roles and Population Trends*, S. Catasús et al., eds. (Geneva: International Labour Office, 1988), which studied fertility rates, birth control use, etc.; see also *Working Women in Socialist Countries:*

The Fertility Connection, Valentina Bodrova and Richard Anker, eds. (Geneva: International Labour Office, 1985), with chapters on eastern European nations and Cuba. For scholars' assessments of Cuban women's changing roles and the changes to marriage and family patterns, see Lois Smith and Alfred Padula's *Sex and Revolution: Women in Socialist Cuba* (Oxford: Oxford University Press, 1996); or Marisela Fleites Lear's "Women, Family and the Cuban Revolution" in *Cuban Communism*, Irving Horowitz and Jaime Suchlicki, eds. (New Brunswick, NJ: Transaction, 2003); or Sheryl Lutjens's "Remaking the Public Sphere: Women and Revolution in Cuba," in *Women and Revolution in Africa, Asia, and the New World*, Mary Ann Tetreault, ed. (Columbia, SC: University of South Carolina Press, 1994); the other essays in the last collection provide an international comparative analysis. For the background to the changes of the late twentieth century, see K. Lynn Stoner's *From the House to the Streets: The Cuban Woman's Movement for Legal Reform, 1898-1940* (Durham, NC: Duke University Press, 1991). More general analyses of sexuality in modern Cuba and the Caribbean include Rosemarie Skaine's *The Cuban Family: Custom and Change in an Era of Hardship* (Jefferson, NC: McFarland, 2004); Marvin Leiner's *Sexual Politics in Cuba: Machismo, Homosexuality, and AIDS* (Boulder, CO: Westview, 1994); *The Culture of Gender and Sexuality in the Caribbean*, Linden Lewis, ed. (Gainesville, FL: University Press of Florida, 2003); and *Sun, Sex, and Gold: Tourism and Sex Work in the Caribbean*, Kamala Kempadoo, ed. (Lanham, MD: Rowman & Littlefield, 1999). Other interesting sources for a history of sexuality might be found in *Breaking the Silences: An Anthology of 20th-Century Poetry by Cuban Women*, Margaret Randall, ed. and trans. (Vancouver, BC: Pulp, 1982); or *Cubana: Contemporary Fiction by Cuban Women*, Mirta Yañez, ed., Dick Cluster and Cindy Schuster, trans. (Boston: Beacon, 1998).

96. "The Nazi Family" is taken from Peter Adam, *Art of the Third Reich* (New York: Harry N. Abrams, 1992), 16.

For the official attitudes of the Nazis to various aspects of sexuality, see Lisa Pine's *Nazi Family Policy, 1933-1945* (Oxford: Berg, 1997); or Geraldine Horan's *Mothers, Warriors, Guardians of the Soul: Female Discourse in National Socialism, 1924-1934* (Berlin: W. de Gruyter, 2003); see also the special issue of the *Journal of the History of Sexuality*, vol. 11, combined issues 1 and 2 (January and April 2002), on "Sexuality and German Fascism," several articles of which examine the discrepancies between official policy and social reality.

97. "Letters from Raden Adjeng Kartini" is taken from *Letters of a Javanese Princess*, Agnes Symmers, ed. and trans. (New York: W.W. Norton, 1964), 32-34, 41-42, 81-83, 224, 233, 237, 239-40.

Summaries of Kartini's life are available in the introduction to this translation and in Joost Cote, *Letters from Kartini: An Indonesian Feminist, 1900-1904* (Clayton, Australia: Monash Asia Institute, Monash University, 1992). On women's status in Indonesia in this period, see Elspeth Locher-Scholten's *Women and the Colonial State: Essays on Gender and Modernity in the Netherlands Indies, 1900-1941* (Amsterdam: Amsterdam University Press, 2000). For interesting modern comparisons, see Linda B. Williams's *Development, Demography, and Family Decision-Making: The Status of Women in Rural Java* (Boulder, CO: Westview, 1990); Saskia Wieringa's *Sexual Politics in Indonesia* (New York: Palgrave Macmillan, 2002); Tineke Hellwig's *In the*

Shadow of Change: Women in Indonesian Literature (Berkeley, CA: Centers for South and Southeast Asia Studies, University of California at Berkeley, 1994). See also the essays in *Kartini Centenary: Indonesian Women Then and Now*, Ailsa Thomson Zainu'ddin et al., eds. (Clayton, Australia: Monash University, 1980), the first essay being Zainu'ddin's "Kartini: Her Life, Work, and Influence." There are numerous nineteenth- and twentieth-century diaries and collections of personal letters now published in collections, and they provide fascinating glimpses into individuals' lives.

the other

Few other areas of our human personality seem so central to us as our sexuality. Shaped by our participation in groups, as outlined in the last chapter, it comes to represent who we are to others. In turn, differences of sexuality—among a host of other human differences—are used to distinguish us from each other. That very process of separation and distinction may be instrumental in determining who we ourselves are, and is the subject of this chapter.

Long ago, Freud suggested that we are shaped by observing others around us and understanding ourselves in relation to them. Psychologist Jacques Lacan was the first to suggest that we need others to complete ourselves. According to Lacan, we understand ourselves as incomplete and fragmented, because as soon as we realize that there are others out there, we recognize that we are not everything and that there are things outside of ourselves, missing in us, beyond our control. (Lacan used the term "phallus" to symbolize everything that we lacked, and in doing so, obviously understood sexual identity as an important part of this process.) So we observe others in order to learn how to make ourselves whole, using others as models for ourselves, either of what to be or what not to be.

The importance of the other—often capitalized as The Other, and contrasted with The Self—in studies of modern sexuality cannot be overstated. Some scholars have used it to explain the persistence of misogyny in human history, arguing that men, in identifying themselves as separate from women, have had to justify that distinction by creating a whole series of stereotypes about women. According to the principles of misogyny, women are emotional, stupid, sexually promiscuous, and fickle. Behind these stereotypes are men's attempts to define themselves positively, as reserved, intelligent, sexually restrained, and loyal. In other words, men in patriarchal societies associate themselves with all of the good qualities and women with all of the bad qualities that human beings can possess.

Other scholars have relied on the concept of The Other to understand a variety of differences in the history of sexuality: heterosexuality and homosexuality, white and person of color, colonizer and colonized, or native and immigrant. In each case, the same opposites or binarisms have been used to justify separation and distinction between the two groups. But in each case, these processes say as much about how the dominant group understands itself, or how it wants to see itself, as it says anything about real differences between the two.

Stereotypes about The Other help in this process of self-identification in a number of ways. First, comments made about the behavior of the subordinate group help to reinforce ideals about behavior within the dominant group. In other words, saying to someone: "*We* are not like them, because *they* do such-and-such, which *we* never do," also sends the clear message: "Do not do such-and-such, or risk being ostracized as one of *them*, rather than one of *us*." Thus one's own identity, both individually and collectively, is reinforced by identifying The Other. Second, stereotypes about the behavior of The Other have often been used to justify the subordination of minority groups. It was often said in the nineteenth-century debates about women's suffrage, for example, that women were led too much by their emotions to vote. But the same arguments have been used by other dominant groups against other subordinated groups. The colonizing European powers reasoned that the other peoples of the world were less intelligent, even childlike, and needed their political guidance; in many countries, native-born citizens have said much the same about immigrants.

In such stereotyping, sexuality often plays a vital role, probably because it is an aspect of life already heavily regulated and filled with taboos. The colonized peoples were not only politically backward, it was claimed, but they also had "bizarre" sexual customs that were portrayed as "brutish" by the colonizers, who often, while in power, tried diligently to eliminate such customs. Members of ethnic minorities in the countries that received them as immigrants not only resisted the government's attempt to impose any political order on them, it was argued, but they also resisted all attempts to impose any sexual order. Homosexuals were not only uninterested in traditional marriage and family life, it was alleged, but they were also sexually promiscuous and predatory.

It is essential that those who study the history of sexuality read between the lines of the historical documents about The Other and see in these claims and stereotypes important comments on The Self. Does the writer fear that everyone will act as the others do, if the condemnations are not made? Does the writer worry that those within the dominant group are already acting in such ways? Comments about "pollution" or "contagion" often disguise just such fears about the transference of values or behaviors from one group to another. In turn, statements about "purity" often express the hope that such contagion will be contained. But how realistic are these comments? How accurate are the statements about what is "polluted" and what is "pure"? These questions provide fertile ground for future historians of sexuality.

The sources that follow all deal in some way with this question of The Self and The Other.

98. MARCO POLO

Time: fourteenth century CE
Place: Italy
Author: Rustichello of Pisa

Marco Polo is one of the most famous of world travelers, mostly because he decided to write about his adventures as a merchant passing through the regions of the Mongol or Tartar Empire. Well, he almost wrote about his travels. He seems to have dictated them to Rustichello of Pisa, who wrote them down in French so that they might find a wider audience of readers. Which stories got changed in translation, which ones Rustichello added for dramatic effect, and which ones Polo himself invented is a subject of considerable debate among modern scholars. Nonetheless, the stories captured the European imagination. This first passage probably refers to the gait of Chinese or Cathayan women whose feet were bound; the second describes a great-great-granddaughter of Chingiz Khan.

Some of the Cathayan customs are worthy of further comment; the way of life is interesting and the young girls are especially well brought up. No girls are better mannered or more modest in their behavior than the Cathayans. They never indulge in immoderate mirth, they do not dance or aggravate others. Neither do they spend their time at windows watching passers-by and hoping to be admired; they never listen to immodest talk, nor do they go to festivals. When they do go out, they go to respectable places like the temples of their idols or to visit relatives. They are always accompanied by their mothers and they never look brazenly in people's faces, but wear elegant hats which oblige them to look at the ground, so they only look where they are putting their feet. They are quiet in the presence of their elders and never speak unnecessarily; in fact they only speak when they are spoken to. They spend much of their time working in their rooms and rarely see their fathers and brothers or the older people in the house. They do not entertain suitors. The young boys do not speak in front of their elders either unless they are spoken to. They are so modest, even among members of their own family, that two of them would never take a bath together.

When a marriage is arranged, either a girl's father offers her to another family, or the other family asks for her. The father has to guarantee that his daughter is a virgin; he signs an agreement with the bridegroom and if the bride is not a virgin, the marriage is not valid. When the agreement has been signed the girl's chastity is put to the test. She is taken to the baths where her mother, the bridegroom's mother, the relations of both families and certain matrons versed in these matters are waiting for her. These women test her virginity with a pigeon's egg. If this experiment does not satisfy the women of the bridegroom's family—who know that lost virginity can be disguised—then one of the matrons wraps a cloth around her finger and inserts it into the girl until it is stained with blood. This blood can never be washed clean, so if the stain disappears when the cloth is rinsed, the girl is not a virgin. If her virginity is proved, the marriage is valid. If not, the father has to pay compensation. In order to keep their virginity intact, the girls in these parts avoid all violent movement and walk with the tiniest possible steps. The Tartars in Cathay, however, are not concerned with such details and allow their wives and even their daughters to go riding with them, which could easily damage them. But the people in Manzi abide by the same customs as the Cathayans.

King Kaidu had a daughter called Aiyaruk which means "shining moon." This girl was so strong that no young man or boy could beat her in a trial of strength. Her father, the King, wished to find her a husband, but Aiyaruk did not want to marry and said that she would only accept a husband who was a nobleman and stronger than she. Her father agreed to her conditions. It should be explained that when a Tartar prince or nobleman marries, he does not insist on his wife being noble too; he will marry a beautiful and attractive woman even if she is not of his rank. No family takes the name of the woman, only of the man. No one is referred to as the son of Bertha or Maria, but as the son of Peter or Paul, so the social position of the mother is unimportant.

When the King's daughter received her father's permission to marry whom she chose, she was delighted and let it be known in many parts of the world that if there was a young nobleman who could overcome her by force, she would marry him. Young noblemen arrived from many different places ready to try their strength against Aiyaruk's. The contest took place in the following manner. The King, with a great suite of men and women, took his place in the largest room of the palace. Aiyaruk then arrived dressed in a richly ornamented leather tunic. Then came the suitor, also dressed in a leather tunic. It was agreed that if the young man managed to make Aiyaruk's shoulders touch the ground, he could marry her; if, however, she won, the young man would forfeit 100 horses. In this way she collected some 10,000 horses, which is hardly surprising as she was not only beautiful but magnificently built, as tall and strong as a giantess.

In 1280 the handsome and rich young son of a king came with a large suite and 1,000 magnificent horses to try his strength against the young princess. Kaidu was delighted because this was the husband he wanted for his daughter, and he told his daughter in secret to allow herself to be beaten. She replied that she would not dream of doing any such thing. The King and Queen, with a gathering of men and women, assembled in the largest room of the palace. Then came the King's daughter and the King's son, both of them so beautiful and attractive that they were a joy to behold. The young man was strong and robust; no one could equal him. When the two stood in the middle of the crowded room, the rules of the contest were read out. If the young man won, the girl would have to marry him; if he lost he would forfeit the 1,000 horses he had brought with him. The two then confronted each other. Everyone who was watching hoped the young man would win and marry Aiyaruk. The King and Queen hoped so too. The two young people began to fight, vigorously grappling with each other and pulling each other this way and that until finally the King's daughter floored the young man. So the prince was beaten. He lost his 1,000 horses and hurried back, humiliated, to his own country. Not one of those who witnessed the combat was glad.

After that Aiyaruk was often taken into battle by her father, and no cavalryman was ever more courageous than she. She often threw herself into the mêlée, captured one of the enemy by force and took him back to her army. This happened many times.

Questions for Reflection and Discussion

In what ways does Marco Polo define his own people—Christians, Europeans, Italians—in contrast to those peoples he observed during his travels? Which customs does he respect, and which not? Why might he be so interested in the warrior maiden?

99. *THE HAMMER OF WITCHES*

Time: fifteenth century CE
Place: Germany
Authors: Heinrich Kramer and James
    Sprenger

Question: Whether Witches may work some Prestidigitatory Illusion so that the Male Organ appears to be entirely removed and separate from the Body.

... There is no doubt that certain witches can do marvelous things with regard to male organs, for this agrees with what has been seen and heard by many, and with the general account of what has been known concerning that member through the senses of sight and touch. And as to how this thing is possible, it is to be said that it can be done in two ways, either actually and in fact, as the first arguments have said, or though some illusion…. It is no wonder that the devil can deceive the outer human senses, since, as has been treated of above, he can illude the inner senses, by bringing to actual perception ideas that are stored in the imagination. Moreover, he deceives men in their natural functions, causing that which is visible to be invisible to them, and that which is tangible to be intangible, and the audible inaudible, and so with the other senses. But such things are not true in actual fact, since they are caused through some defect introduced in the senses, such as the eyes or the ears, or the touch, by reason of which defect a man's judgment is deceived. And we can illustrate this from certain natural phenomena. For sweet wine appears bitter on the tongue of the fevered, his taste being deceived not by the actual fact, but through his disease. So also in the case under consideration, the deception is not due to fact, since the member is still actually in place; but it is an illusion of the senses with regard to it. Again, as has been said above concerning the generative powers, the devil can obstruct that action by imposing some other body of the same color and appearance, in such a way that some smoothly fashioned body in the color of flesh is interposed between the sight and touch, and between the true body of the sufferer, so that it seems to him that he can see and feel nothing but a smooth body with its surface interrupted by no genital organ….

In the town of Ratisbon a certain young man who had an intrigue with a girl, wishing to leave her, lost his member; that is to say, some illusion was cast over it so that he could see or touch nothing but his smooth body. In his worry over this he went to a tavern to drink wine; and after he had sat there for a while he got into a conversation with another woman who was there, and told her the cause of his sadness, explaining everything, and demonstrating in his body that it was so. The woman was astute, and asked whether he suspected anyone; and when he named such a one, unfolding the whole matter, she said: "If persuasion is not enough, you must use some violence, to induce her to restore to you your health." So in the evening the young man watched the way by which the witch was in the habit of going, and finding her, prayed her to restore to him the health of his body. And when she maintained that she was innocent and knew nothing about it, he fell upon her, and winding a towel tightly round her neck, choked her, saying: "Unless you give me back my health, you shall die at my hands." Then she, being unable to cry out, and growing black, said: "Let me go, and I will heal you." The young man then relaxed the pressure of the towel, and the witch touched him with her hand between the thighs, saying: "Now you have what you desire." And the young man, as he afterwards said, plainly felt, before he had verified it by looking or touching, that his member had been restored to him by the mere touch of the witch.

Questions for Reflection and Discussion

What concerns may have prompted the young man to believe that he had lost his penis? Or the authors' own belief in the occurrence, in repeating the story? How does the discussion switch from the devil's power to the witch's power? How did such beliefs rationalize violence against women?

100. THE SEXUAL CUSTOMS OF UTOPIA

Time: sixteenth century CE
Place: England
Author: Thomas More

Thomas More, who is much more famous for his later conflict with King Henry VIII over the separation of the Church of England from the Roman Catholic Church, was a writer before becoming the Speaker of the House of Commons and then Lord Chancellor of England. In his description of Utopia—a Greek word meaning "nowhere"—he imagined an ideal society and included details about sexual and marriage customs. In 1935, he was proclaimed a saint in the Roman Catholic Church.

Girls aren't allowed to marry until they're eighteen—boys have to wait four years longer. Any boy or girl convicted of premarital intercourse is severely punished, and permanently disqualified from marrying, unless this sentence is remitted by the Mayor. The man and woman in charge of the household in which it happens are also publicly disgraced, for not doing their jobs properly. The Utopians are particularly strict about that kind of thing, because they think very few people would want to get married—which means spending one's whole life with the same person, and putting up with all the inconveniences that this involves—if they weren't carefully prevented from having any sexual intercourse otherwise.

When they're thinking of getting married, they do something that seemed to us quite absurd, though they take it very seriously. The prospective bride, no matter whether she's a spinster or a widow, is exhibited stark naked to the prospective bridegroom by a respectable married woman, and a suitable male chaperon shows the bridegroom naked to the bride. When we implied by our laughter that we thought it a silly system, they promptly turned the joke against us.

"What we find so odd," they said, "is the silly way these things are arranged in other parts of the world. When you're buying a horse, and there's nothing at stake but a small sum of money, you take every possible precaution. The animal's practically naked already, but you firmly refuse to buy until you've whipped off the saddle and all the rest of the harness, to make sure there aren't any sores underneath. But when you're choosing a wife an article that for better or worse has got to last you a lifetime, you're unbelievably careless. You don't even bother to take it out of its wrappings. You judge the whole woman from a few square inches of face, which is all you can see of her, and then proceed to marry her—at the risk of finding her most disagreeable, when you see what she's really like. No doubt you needn't worry, if moral character is the only thing that interests you—but we're not all as wise as that, and even those who are sometimes find, when they get married, that a beautiful body can be quite a useful addition to a beautiful soul. Certainly those wrappings may easily conceal enough ugliness to destroy a husband's feelings for his wife, when it's too late for a physical separation. Of course, if she turns ugly after the wedding, he must just resign himself to his fate—but one does need some legal protection against marriage under false pretences!"

In their case, some such precautions are particularly necessary, since unlike all their neighbors they're strictly monogamous. Most married couples are parted only by death, except in the case of adultery or intolerably bad behavior, when the innocent party may get permission from the Council to marry someone else—the guilty party is disgraced, and condemned to celibacy for life. But in no circumstances can a man divorce his wife simply because, through no fault of her own, she has deteriorated physically. Quite apart from the cruelty of deserting a person at the very time when she most needs sympathy, they think that, if this sort of thing were allowed, there'd be no security whatever for old age, which not only brings many diseases with it, but is really a disease in itself.

Occasionally, though, divorce by mutual consent is allowed on grounds of incompatibility, when both husband and wife have found alternative partners that seem likely to make them happier. But this requires special permission, which can only be got after a thorough investigation by the Bencheaters [community elders] and their wives. Even then they're rather reluctant to give it, for they think there's nothing less calculated to strengthen the marriage tie than the prospect of easy divorce.

Adulterers are sentenced to penal servitude of the most unpleasant type. If both offenders are married, their injured partners may, if they like, obtain a divorce and marry one another, or anyone else they choose. But if they continue to love their undeserving mates, they're allowed to stay married to them, provided they're willing to share their working conditions. In such cases the Mayor is sometimes so touched by the guilty party's remorse and the innocent party's loyalty that he lets them both go free. But a second conviction means capital punishment.

Otherwise there are no fixed penalties prescribed by law—the Council decides in each case what sentence is appropriate. Husbands are responsible for punishing their wives, and parents for punishing their children, unless the offence is so serious that it has to be dealt with by the authorities, in the interests of public morality. The normal penalty for any major crime is slavery. They say it's just as unpleasant for the criminals as capital punishment, and more useful to society than getting rid of them right away, since live workers are more valuable than dead ones, and have a more prolonged deterrent effect. However, if convicts prove recalcitrant under this treatment, and don't respond to any sort of prison discipline, they're just slaughtered like wild beasts. But the prospects of those who accept the situation aren't absolutely hopeless. If, after being tamed by years of hardship, they show signs of feeling really sorry, not merely for themselves, but for what they've done, their sentence is either reduced or cancelled altogether, sometimes at the discretion of the Mayor, and sometimes by a general plebiscite.

Attempted seduction is punished no less severely than actual seduction. The same applies to every other type of offence—anyone who deliberately tries to commit a crime is legally assumed to have committed it. It's no fault of his, they argue, that he didn't bring it off, so why give him credit for his failure?

Questions for Reflection and Discussion

How does describing this imaginary society allow More to express his ideals about sex and marriage? Are they puritan or libertine ideals? How seriously should such opinions be taken, given that they were ascribed to "Nowhere"?

101. A LETTER FROM AMERIGO VESPUCCI

Time: sixteenth century CE
Place: somewhere along the east coast of
   South America
Author: Amerigo Vespucci

An Italian in the service of Spain and then of Portugal, Vespucci—like Christopher Columbus—also attempted to sail west to reach Asia. Instead he reached the Caribbean, in the first of several voyages, and also sailed along the coast of South America, which was eventually named after him. He left a detailed account of his voyages; unfortunately, his later statements put some of these details in dispute, and according to some scholars, much of what he wrote must therefore be considered unreliable. Unlike Columbus, Vespucci discussed the sexual customs of the peoples he encountered in his account of his travels.

What we knew of their life and customs was that they all go naked, as well the men as the women, without covering anything, no otherwise than as they come out of their mothers' wombs. They are of medium stature, and very well proportioned. The color of their skins inclines to red, like the skin of a lion, and I believe that, if they were properly clothed, they would be white like ourselves. They have no hair whatever on their bodies, but they have very long black hair, especially the women, which beautifies them. They have not very beautiful faces, because they have long eyelids, which make them look like Tartars [Mongols]. They do not allow any hairs to grow on their eyebrows, nor eyelashes, nor in any other part except on the head, where it is rough and disheveled....

They have neither king nor lord, nor do they obey anyone, but live in freedom.... They do not bring men to justice, nor punish a criminal. Neither the mother nor the father chastise their children, and it is wonderful that we never saw a quarrel among them. They show themselves simple in their talk, and are very sharp and cunning in securing their ends.... Their mode of life is very barbarous, for they have no regular time for their meals, but they eat at any time that they have the wish, as often at night as in the day—indeed, they eat at all hours. They take their food on the ground, without napkin or any other cloth.... They are a people of cleanly habits as regards their bodies, and are constantly washing themselves. When they empty the stomach they do everything so as not to be seen, and in this they are clean and decent; but in making water they are dirty and without shame, for while talking with us they do such things without turning round, and without any shame.

They do not practice matrimony among them, each man taking as many women as he likes, and when he is tired of a woman he repudiates her without either injury to himself or shame to the woman, for in this matter the woman has the same liberty as the man. They are not very jealous, but lascivious beyond measure, the women much more so than the men. I do not further refer to their contrivances for satisfying their inordinate desires, so that I may not offend against modesty. They are very prolific in bearing children ... [but] if they are angry with their husbands they easily cause abortion with certain poisonous herbs or roots, and destroy the child. Many infants perish in this way. They are gifted with very handsome and well-proportioned bodies, and no part or member is to be seen that is not well formed. Although they go naked, yet that which should be concealed is kept between the thighs so that it cannot be seen. Yet there no one cares, for the same impression is made on them at seeing anything indecent as is made on us at seeing a nose or mouth....

They have none of the riches which are looked upon as such in our Europe and in other parts, such as gold, pearls, or precious stones: and even if they have them in their country, they do not work to get them. They are liberal in their giving, for it is wonderful if they refuse anything, and also liberal in asking, as soon as they make friends. Their greatest sign of friendship is to give their wives or daughters, and a father and mother considered themselves highly honored when they brought us a daughter, especially if she was a virgin, that we should sleep with her, and in doing this they use terms of warm friendship.

Questions for Reflection and Discussion

What is the tone of Vespucci's comments: condescending, curious, impressed, or something else? How do his comments reveal his own society's concerns about sexuality and other matters?

102. BERNAL DIAZ DEL CASTILLO'S *TRUE HISTORY*

Time: sixteenth century CE
Place: modern Central America
Author: Bernal Diaz del Castillo

Bernal Diaz del Castillo called his work The True History of New Spain, *emphasizing its truthfulness in his very title because he was concerned that readers would not believe his account. A common soldier from Spain, he participated in several of the Spanish conquests of the Aztec Empire and was eventually made governor of a district in what is modern Guatemala.*

In addition to this nearly all of them were sodomites, especially those who live on the coast and hot country, to such an extent that boys go about clothed in the dress of women to gain a livelihood in that diabolical and abominable employment. Then they ate human flesh, just as we bring beef from the butchers, and they have in all the *pueblos* prisons of stout beams, made like houses, as cages, and in them they place and fatten many Indian men and women and boys, and when they are fat they sacrifice and eat them. In addition to this, in the wars which some provinces and *pueblos* wage against others, those who are captured and taken prisoners are sacrificed and eaten. Then sons have carnal connection with mothers, and brothers with sisters, and uncles with nieces; many are found who indulge in this iniquitous vice. About drunkards I do not know what to say, so many obscenities take place among them; I wish to note only one here which we found in the province of Panuco; they make an injection by the anus with some hollow canes and distend the intestines with wine, and this is done among them in the same way as among us an enema is applied. Then they have as many women as they wish, and they have many other vices and iniquities. From all these things which I have enumerated it pleased our Lord Jesus Christ that, with his holy aid, we, the true *Conquistadores*, who have escaped from the wars, battles, and dangers of death, already recorded by me, have freed them, and led them into cleanly ways and taught them holy doctrine.

Questions for Reflection and Discussion

What is the tone of Diaz del Castillo's comments? How might his role in the conquest of the Aztec Empire have shaped his memory of the peoples he conquered? How does his emphasis on the truthfulness of his account affect the reading of such a passage?

103. JOHN FRYER ON THE ZOROASTRIANS

Time: seventeenth century CE
Place: Persia (modern Iran)
Author: John Fryer

John Fryer was one of many early English travelers who attempted to establish economic and political links for the English across the globe. The letters he sent back to England, later published as an account of his voyages, described the peoples he met, including the religious sect called Zoroastrians, whom he calls Gabers. His description of the orgies is suspiciously similar to those associated with early modern witches and with medieval heretics before them. Archaic spellings and punctuation have been preserved.

The Gabers, or Gaures, are the true Persian Race, the undoubted Heirs both of their Gentilism and Succession, attributing Divine Honour to the Fire, maintaining it always alive in their Delubriums, or Places set apart for their Worship … from the first time the Sun, their Chief Deity, was pleased to enlighten it with Sparks from its own Rays.…

These are Instances how momentary the Grandeur of this World is: These, once the Lords of all the Earth that the Ocean washes on this Side, and the Hellespont shuts in on the other, forgetful of the Everlasting Name of the Grand Cyrus, who first subjugated the Medes and Assyrians under the Persian Yoak, and established the Seat of the Empire among their Renowned Ancestry: These, unhappy for their Sloth and Cowardise, are the reproachful Relicks, nay, Dregs rather of the former Glory of their Name and Nation, which once gave her Laws, as Unalterable Decrees to all People, Nations, and Languages: These thus dwindled and degenerated, are the miserable Posterity of the Persians; who for so many Ages have with a tame Patience submitted by a sordid Servitude to those whom their Forefathers would have scorn'd to have admitted to be their Slaves; only that they might idely enjoy their Country Gods, Adore the Eternal Fire, and the Influence of the Sun upon their Altars, now Beastly and Impious more than ever, because they have contaminated them with the Impure Rites and Diabolical Customs of the worst of Pagans. For there are some of them Couple together in their Sacred Feasts (as they term them) promiscuously, when they meet in their Delubriums, where they spread a clean Table-cloth on the Floor, on which they place their Banquets to inflame their Lascivious Heat, which must be acknowledged to be set on Fire by Hell, whatever the Extract that they Worship as a Spark of the Sun, may be defended to be. When they take away, they strew the foul Cloth with Meal-Flower, and the better to perpetrate, their Incestuous Lusts, they put out the Lights, and shifting themselves stark naked, both Men and Women, the Men cast their Breeches on an heap in a Corner of the Room: Which being done, the Women run in the dark to catch as catch can; and whatever Lot they light on, the Lamps being again lighted, they firmly embrace for their Lover, if it be Father or Brother, or any other Relation: And which is still worse, the Night being spent in Bestiality, the nasty Flower (which by their Filthiness either of Vomit or Excrement in which they wallowed like Brutes) is kneaded into a Paste, and eaten as a Sacrament to repeat the same ungodly Festival Annually, as if it were a Sacrifice well-pleasing to their Deities. But Propagation after this kind is as odious to Mankind, as offering Children to Moloch, or making them run through the Fire is execrable and abhorrent to Nature: Which made an Ancient Heathen, in detestation of such horrid Crimes offered as grateful Services to the Gods, burst out into this Exclamation: Every one indeed ought to have a Sense of Religion, and a Profound Veneration for their Country-Gods transmitted by Tradition; but that the Immortal Gods should be appeased or pleased with such Wickedness, is the highest Frenzy to believe.

Questions for Reflection and Discussion

England was embroiled in civil wars fought over religion through much of the sixteenth and seventeenth centuries. Might this background have influenced how Fryer viewed the other peoples of the world? How might the disparaging of such peoples be related to his larger purpose as a promoter of English trade?

104. GEORGE ROBERTSON ON THE PEOPLE OF TAHITI

Time: eighteenth century CE
Place: Tahiti
Author: George Robertson

Tahiti, one of the Polynesian islands in the South Pacific Ocean, seemed a paradise to the British sailors of the late eighteenth century, George Robertson among them, who first visited the island in 1767. They enjoyed not only its climate but also the sexual customs of its inhabitants. Robertson, the ship's master, recorded the crew's daily activities in his log that was later published. The original spelling has been kept.

But our Young men seeing several very handsome Young girls, they could not help feasting their Eyes with so agreeable a sight this was observed by some of the Elderly men, and several of the Young Girls was drawen out, some a light coper colour oythers a mullato and some almost White. The old men made them stand in Rank, and made signs for our people to take which they lyked best, and as many as they lyked and for fear our men hade been Ignorant and not known how to use the poor young Girls, the old men made signs how we should behave to the Young women, this all the boats crew seemd to understand perfectly well, and begd the Officer would receive a few of the Young Women onboard, at same time they made signs to the Young Girls, that they were no so Ignorant as the old men supposed them, this seemd to please the Old men Greatly when they saw our people merry, but the poor young Girls seemd a little afraid, but soon after turnd better aquanted. The Officer in the boat having no orders to bring off any of the natives, would not receive the Young Girls but made signs that he would see them afterwards, and Orderd all our men on bd the Boats, and returnd onbd the Ship, when our boats returnd to the ship all the sailors swore they neaver saw handsomer made women in their lives, and declard they would all to a man, live on two thirds allowance, rather nor lose so Ane an opportunity of geting a Girl apiece—this piece of news made all our men madly fond of the shore, even the sick which hade been on the Doctors list for some weeks before, now declard they would be happy if they were permited to go ashore, at same time said a Young Girl would make an Excelent Nurse, and they were Certain of recovering faster under a Young Girls care nor all the Doctor would do for them, we past this Night very merry supposing all hostilitys was now over and to our great joy it so happend.

Questions for Reflection and Discussion

How surprised does Robertson seem about the type of welcome extended to the British sailors? What is the girls' reaction to this welcome? Does the reference to the end of hostilities in the final sentence indicate a hidden purpose behind such a welcome? What can be said about the Tahitians' view of sexuality on the basis of such evidence?

105. A MISSIONARY IN TAHITI

Time: nineteenth century CE
Place: Tahiti
Author: unknown

After the sailors came Christian missionaries who attempted to change the beliefs and sexual practices of the Tahitians. In this excerpt, a missionary who lived in Tahiti only a few decades after Robertson's crew first arrived there described the island's inhabitants from a different perspective.

Tahiti is a vortex of iniquity, the Sodom of the Pacific and gazing stock to the world, a thorn in the eyes of the just. All contradiction, licentiousness and obsequiousness. Even now we dare not suffer our children to assemble with the native tribes. Virtue is not in Tahiti; chastity is unknown save in the presence of some only of the Missionaries. If a female be taken into the parlour for conversation those outside say, "Oh, she is a whore, to the Missionary, and therefore soon taken into the church." If our children, by the turgency of their breasts, shew signs of puberty, it is immediately asked who was her man, or was it the father. For it is maintained that no one can menstruate till she has been ruptured by coition. By 7 or 9 years of age all are ruptured. They say, "Oh let them alone, they are only children, and will grow the faster for it." Be not shocked, the half has not been told you. The moral character of the Tahitian Mission is hateful. Would to God that the Missionaries were free from blame, but let a man be ever so wicked, if he gets the chiefs and the King on his side, it is impossible, however guilty, to find him out.

Questions for Reflection and Discussion

How does the contrast between this description of the Tahitians and that of the previous source reveal something about the writers rather than the Tahitians themselves? What does this writer's final comment mean, that the missionaries are not entirely free from blame? What other fears of "contagion" of sexual values does the writer express?

106. GEORGE ANGAS ON THE ABORIGINES OF AUSTRALIA

Time: nineteenth century CE
Place: Australia
Author: George Angas

George Angas, chairman of the South Australian Company, promoted the colonization of the continent in the 1830s and 40s. He was committed to bringing upstanding Protestant Christians to Australia to counter its heritage as a former penal colony, and he worked hard to establish schools among the settlements. His descriptions of the Aborigines, including the passage below from an account published in 1847, were intended in part to familiarize potential settlers with the native people inhabiting the land.

The population of the native tribes inhabiting South Australia is not considerable. Constant wars and quarrels between the tribes, polygamy, and infanticide are amongst the causes of this. Their mode of life, too—not cultivating the ground, but seeking a scanty and precarious subsistence by wandering over large tracts of country in search of food, when the soil naturally produces but little comparatively for the support of the human race—necessarily causes their numbers to be limited….

Families are usually small; three or four children by the same parents may be considered as an average proportion. When the boys arrive at a certain age they undergo initiatory rites, which vary amongst tribes. Some practice circumcision; others knock out the front tooth, as is the custom with the natives of New South Wales. Tattooing is performed amongst all the tribes. They do not mark the face like the New Zealanders, but raise large protuberances upon the back and shoulders, and cut deep incisions longitudinally across the chest, which they fill with clay, rendering them hard and horny, resembling tubes of gristle.

There does not appear to be any distinct ceremony of marriage amongst them. In battle the successful warriors endeavor to possess themselves of the young women of the opposite party; and it generally happens that the old and experienced men obtain the youngest and most comely women, whilst the old and haggard females are left for the more youthful portion of the opposite sex.

One of the surest marks of the low position of the Australian savage in the scale of the human species, is the treatment of their women. The men walk along with a proud and majestic air; behind them, crouching like slaves, and bearing heavy burdens on their backs, with their little ones astride on their shoulders, come the despised and degraded women. They are the drudges in all heavy work; and after their lords have finished the repast which the women have prepared for them, these despised creatures contentedly sit at a distance, and gather up the bones and fragments, which the men throw to them across their shoulders, just as we should throw meat to a dog….

Infanticide is commonly practiced immediately after birth; girls being the most frequent victims to this horrible custom….

Questions for Reflection and Discussion

What aspects of the Aborigines' lifestyle does Angas point out as revealing their true nature? How does this differ from earlier judgments about what made peoples seem "savage" to Europeans? What does this difference say about changing European beliefs regarding sexuality, to which Angas is appealing?

107. MARY KINGSLEY IN WEST AFRICA

Time: nineteenth century CE
Place: West Africa (modern Gabon)
Author: Mary Kingsley

Mary Kingsley visited Africa on several occasions in the 1890s in order to complete the book that her father, a noted traveler, had begun on the peoples of west Africa. After publishing it in 1897 as Travels in West Africa, *she became something of a media sensation. Journalists loved to reprint her outspoken opinions on women's suffrage (she was against it), polygamy (she thought it should be permitted in the British colonies), and prohibition (she refused to condemn the use of alcohol). Toward the end of her life, she denounced the damage that colonialism was inflicting on Africa generally. In this passage, Kingsley pauses from her description of the Fan people to reflect on the Irish. In her day, Ireland was part of the British Empire, and its people, lacking educational and economic opportunities at home, often took menial jobs in England.*

It is totally impossible for one woman to do the whole work of a house—look after the children, prepare and cook the food, prepare the rubber, carry the same to the markets, fetch the daily supply of water from the stream, cultivate the plantation, etc., etc. Perhaps I should say it is impossible for the dilatory African woman, for I once had an Irish charwoman, who drank, who would have done the whole week's work of an African village in an afternoon, and then been quite fresh enough to knock some of the nonsense out of her husband's head with that of the broom, and throw a kettle of boiling water or a paraffin lamp at him, if she suspected him of flirting with other ladies. That woman, who deserves fame in the annals of her country, was named Harragan. She has attained immortality some years since, by falling down stairs one Saturday night from excitement arising from "the Image's" (Mr. Harragan) conduct; but we have no Mrs. Harragan in Africa.

The African lady does not care a traveling whitesmith's execration if her husband does flirt, so long as he does not go and give to other women the cloth, etc., that she should have. The more wives the less work, says the African lady; and I have known men who would rather have had one wife and spent the rest of the money on themselves, in a civilized way, driven into polygamy by the women; and of course this state of affairs is most common in non-slaveholding tribes like the Fan. But then there is that custom which, as far as I know, is common to all African tribes, and I suspect to Asiatic, which is well known to ethnologists, and which once caused a missionary to say to me: "A blow must be struck at polygamy, and that blow must be dealt with a feeding-bottle [to replace breast-feeding, during which sexual relations were prohibited between husband and wife]." …

Now polygamy is, like most other subjects, a difficult thing to form an opinion on, if, before forming that opinion, you go and make a study of the facts and bearings of the case. It is therefore advisable to follow the usual method employed by the majority of people. Just take a prejudice of your own, and fix it up with the so-called opinions of people who go in for that sort of prejudice too. This method is absolutely essential to the forming of an opinion on the subject of polygamy among African tribes, that will be acceptable in enlightened circles. Polygamy is the institution which above all others governs the daily life of the native; and it is therefore the one which the missionaries who enter into this daily life, and not merely into the mercantile and legal, as do the trader and the government official, are constantly confronted with and hindered by. All the missionaries have set their faces against it and deny Church membership to those men who practice it; whereby it falls out that many men are excluded from the fold who would make quite as good Christians as those within it. They hesitate about turning off from their homes women who have lived and worked for them for years, and not only for them, but often for their fathers before them.

One case in the Rivers I know of is almost tragic if you put yourself in his place. An old chief, who had three wives, profoundly and vividly believed that exclusion from the Holy Communion meant an eternal damnation. The missionary had instructed him in the details of this damnation thoroughly, and the chief did not like the prospect at all; but on the other hand he did not like to turn off the three wives he had lived with for years. He found the matter was not even to be compromised, by turning off two and going to church to be married with accompanying hymns and orange-blossoms with number three, for the ladies held together; not one of them would marry him and let the other two go, so the poor old chief worried himself to a shammock and anybody else he could get to listen to him. His white trader friends told him not to be such an infernal ass. Some of his black fellow chiefs said the missionary was quite right, and the best thing for him to do would be to hand over to them the three old wives and go and marry a young girl from the mission school. Personally they were not yet afflicted with scruples on the subject of polygamy, and of course (being "missionary man" now) he would not think of taking anything for his wives, so they would do their best, as friends, to help him out of the difficulty. Others of his black fellow chiefs, less advanced in culture just said: "What sort of fool palaver you make;" and spat profusely. The poor old man smelt hell fire, and cried "Yo yo, yo," and beat his hands upon the ground. It was a moral mess of the first water all round.

Still do not imagine the mission-field is full of yo yo-ing old chiefs; for although the African is undecided, he is also very ingenious, particularly in dodging inconvenient moral principles. Many a keen old chief turns on his pastor and asks driving questions regarding the patriarchs, until I have heard a sorely tried pastor question the wisdom of introducing the Old Testament to the heathen.

Questions for Reflection and Discussion

How does the shift from one ethnic Other to another demonstrate their relative significance in Kingsley's opinion? What are the humorous anecdotes about Mrs. Harragan and the unnamed chief supposed to tell her readers about their peoples?

108. CHINA AND THE UNITED STATES COMPARED

Time: nineteenth century CE
Place: United States
Author: Kate Bushnell

Kate Bushnell, an American physician, was a leader in the Women's Christian Temperance Union's Department of Social Purity. This tract, published in the WCTU's Voice Extra *in 1886, demonstrates how complicated the relationship between The Self and The Other might be. In this case, Bushnell warned Americans not to become complacent, lest they become the same as The Other. Indeed, she suggests, they are already as "savage" as the "heathens." The hidden dangers of immigrants in the United States and the problem of infanticide in China are the themes of this tract (although there is apparently no other evidence for the "baby tower" custom she mentions). Still, as Bushnell reminds her readers, there is immorality everywhere, in the United States as in China.*

"I saw a most shocking thing tonight!" exclaimed a fellow missionary to the writer, one evening several years ago, as she entered our home in far away China. "I was going down the street that leads to the south city gate, and came upon the dead body of a girl by the roadside! It was a ghastly encounter, blackened and bloated as the body was, and liable, in its exposed condition, to be devoured by a jackal or some other animal during the night. I judged they were the remains of some poor creature who had been struck by lightning during this afternoon's heavy storm."

"You know, I suppose," she continued, "the Chinese superstition? Every murderer is in danger of being killed by lightning as a judgment from Heaven, and none but murderers ever die in that shocking manner."

[Bushnell continues by suggesting that the murder of female children and even wives is tolerated by the Chinese, and the fact that their murderers are seldom struck by lightning offered as evidence that it is not a serious crime. Then she addresses her readers.]

You smile at its obtuse impracticability. You characterize it as heathenish, barbarous. But may we not find here a remarkable analogy to the common method of civilized nations in dealing with sexual crime? I emphatically think we do; for while in Christian countries the severest penalties that society can inflict are visited upon disgraced girls, this sin, *per se*, is neither dealt with by forceful laws nor high moral sentiment. Houses of prostitution are permitted to exist everywhere, and men are allowed, without fear of molestation from the officers of the law, to visit them and boast openly of their exploits as libertines in houses of ill-fame or as seducers in the homes of Christian families. Think of it! Such liberty is not allowed to any other criminal. And of how serious a nature is the crime they commit! The vast majority of our murders and suicides have their provocation in illicit love, and thousands of times every year young innocent girls are brutally outraged—a crime by the side of which murder pales into meanest insignificance.

Worse than all, this crime of all crimes has to do with the ushering into existence of thousands of children yearly, of basest inherent tendencies—a vast horde, who crowd our pauper institutions and blacken our criminal records. This evil is so common that every sixth child in one county in Scotland is officially recorded as illegitimate. If thus common there—and only cases are recorded as illegitimate where parents do not try to hide their shame by falsehood— what may it not be in our country? According to Noeggerath, of New York, and Ricord, of France, eight tenths of all men are diseased from one form only of disease resulting from early indiscretions, and their wives are almost universally infected also.

Shall we speak of the crime of murder in connection with such iniquity? It belongs in decenter company. Supposing I tell you that in heathen China, across the sea, the walls of some of the large cities are reinforced by hollow pillars, the object of which is to find a place for the deposition of living female babies! And mothers and fathers come to these "baby-towers," as they are called, and drop their living children down into the pit on the squirming mass of corruption below. It is said that the stench of the lower stratum of the dead is sickening, while the moans of the upper living stratum are horrible.

Why, that is nothing to shudder over! It merely expresses the light estimate that heathens put on female life. Let me rather turn your attention to the light estimate modern civilization puts on female virtue. Let us go to the city of Chicago and see the houses of ill-fame, the veritable "maiden-towers," for the destruction of young womanhood's chastity that have been erected all over that city. And innocent girls are dropped into these pits almost daily. Our papers have recently described how girls are being allured from their homes in Canada to be incarcerated in these "maiden-towers." Within a month or six weeks the Women's Reading Room of Chicago helped to fish out five girls who had been deposited there. On Dearborn Street you will see the upper stratum of these victims, and their cries for escape, if not deadened by padded walls, would rend your heart with horror. On Pacific Avenue you can see the lower stratum of this writhing, dying mass. The stench of their vileness is horrible. Most of them are past struggling any longer—they are hopelessly waiting to rot....

I have heard heathen women relate with considerable gusto the circumstances of their murder of female offspring. But there is greater wrong on the earth than this. And men are standing on our street corners, sitting on our judicial benches, even kneeling among the worshippers in the house of God, who, when alone with men, find no richer theme of discussion than the stealing of the forbidden fruit of lust, and the memory of its flavor causes their vile mouths to water….

What does the law of our boasted civilization do to stamp out of existence this nameless crime? Does it hush the libertine's boast? No. Does it punish his crime? No. Does it seek information upon which to punish the adulterer's infamy? Rather, it shields his secrets by the perversion of the blackmail law. Does it tear down the houses of ill-fame? No; it rather struggles to license the "maiden-tower" as a necessary evil, and disinfect it by Contagious Diseases Acts….

Half-civilized China furnishes an example of how heathen superstition may confuse the moral perception of a people in regard to even such glaring crimes as murder. Natives sometimes recite on the street details of their destruction of female infants; "baby-towers" exist in some places for the convenience of the child slayer, and parents of girls and husbands of women, too cowardly to openly slay, very commonly harass daughters and wives by hunger and hardship to the suicide's death, just as libertines in America worry the unprotected working-girl to moral death. All this evil is wrought under the impression that female life is not so valuable as male, and with the thought that as these kinds of crime have never yet been avenged by thunderbolts from Heaven, therefore they are trivial in nature.

Let China sink lower in moral degradation as to the crime of murder, while at the same time she catches a reflection of the polish of western civilization. Then she will say, "These 'baby-towers' are a necessity of our advanced civilization. Let us disinfect their corrupting contents by the enforcement of Contagious Diseases Acts. Let us also reap some benefit from them as a nation as well as individuals. We will license them." Then shall have dawned a day for China when moral teacher and philosopher alike will be saying, "It is natural and not necessarily sinful for man to have murderous impulses toward wife, and parents toward female children." And murderous men with garments all spattered with the blood of wives will enter the best of native homes, to be fawned over and flattered by the sisters of their victims. And when this day of blood shall have dawned upon China, America and England will be furnished with a parallel to their present day of lust—a parallel fainter indeed in outline by so much as a profligate waste of female life is less horrible than a profligate waste of female virtue….

One more important link is the heathen superstition, from which modern civilization can scarcely rid itself—that the sinner upon whom misfortune falls is the worst sinner of all. Fallen woman is the "lightning struck" sinner. She is an exposed criminal; she cannot keep her crime hid as man can. It tells too painfully on her health; it lies too weightily on her conscience; or the offspring of lust enters the world through her bedchamber. So that in some way or other, either by haggard look or confession or enforced motherhood, the lightning shaft of God's seeming judgment descends, and she becomes a castaway.

A young girl of hitherto unblemished reputation comes to disgrace. Immediately all society is stunned by the horrible revelation. But men had sat around street corners week in and week out, entertaining each other with full details of their sensual exploits, and none thought of horror then. Chinese mothers confess to killing their female babies, and it does not horrify the native listeners. But how they are shocked over the crimes of one struck by lightning! What is the difference between the one kind of sexual sin and the other? The one kind of Chinese murder and the other? Both the sexual sin and the murder in their two forms are measured by the same heathen-ish rule, and the verdict is that the girl's sin and the lightning victim's sin, in that they are attended by a seeming judgment from Heaven, are worse in nature than the libertine's and the infanticide's. Therefore the woman's sin, which brings open disgrace, is regarded by society as worse than the man's, which can be hidden at pleasure.

Questions for Reflection and Discussion

How apt is the complicated parallel that Bushnell draws between infanticide in China and prostitution in the United States? What is the purpose of such a comparison? Where does its rhetorical strength lie? What does Bushnell *not* talk about that also links these activities?

109. AN ANTI-IMMIGRANT POSTER

Time: nineteenth century CE
Place: United States
Artist: unknown

This cartoon image, published in the American Harper's Weekly *magazine in 1869, depicts a Chinese immigrant and a woman of European descent walking arm in arm. Innocuous to us, it would have been shocking at the time in its portrayal of a mixed ethnic couple. The year the image was published was also the year that the Pacific Railroad was completed, and many Americans wondered what would happen to the Chinese immigrants—mostly men—who had been brought to the US to work on the railroad. Fears worsened, and in the Chinese Exclusion Act of 1882, Chinese immigration to the US was halted for a decade, a ban later extended for another 10 years, in large part because of worries like those depicted in this cartoon.*

Questions for Reflection and Discussion

On what is the fear of mixed ethnic marriages based? Is it fear of the unknown customs or moral values of The Other? Is it the fear of assimilation of The Other? Is it fear of the attractiveness of the exotic?

110. JOHN GUNTHER ON AUSTRALIA AND NEW GUINEA

Time: late twentieth century CE
Place: Australia
Author: John Gunther

John Gunther, an American journalist and novelist, published a series of world travel guides beginning in the 1930s. His Inside Australia, published two years after his death in 1970, included a description of the modern Aborigines that reveals something of the persistence of sexual stereotypes of The Other even recently.

The basic concept of profane and sacred life … requires elaborate manhood initiation ceremonies, including circumcision. A particular horror in these rites among many Aborigines has been the practice of subincision: some time after circumcision, a young man, perhaps out hunting, is suddenly pinioned by his elders and thrown to the ground, and the underside of his penis slit from end to end through the urethra. The purpose of this mutilation, which in Australian slang is called "whistlecock," is as vague as the purpose of ritual circumcision. The operation does not affect the man's sexual powers. A much repeated story about the Aborigines is that they do not connect copulation with conception, and apparently in the past they did not, but nowadays they are mostly a bit wiser than that. They seem to think that intercourse is necessary for conception, some holding that it takes five or six ejaculations on successive days, but sex is less a prerequisite to procreation than the entry into the fetus of its spirit. Women associate awareness of pregnancy with an animal, rock, tree, whirlwind, or whatever. This spirit, entering the mother through foot, flank, navel, or mouth (but never vagina), becomes the totem of the child…. Aborigines always marry spouses who bear some degree of consanguinity. Among some tribes, a man must marry a woman who is his mother's brother's daughter; among others, the prescribed relationship is mother's mother's brother's daughter's daughter.

[Gunther's book also includes sections on Papua New Guinea, which was then an Australian protectorate.]

One inscrutable cult in New Guinea goes by the unlikely name of the Hahalis Welfare Society. Its field of operations is the small island of Buka, just across a narrow passage from the northern tip of Bougainville. The founder of "The Welfare," as it is commonly called, is a burly, handsome man named John Teosin, now thirty-three, the product of a good education by American Roman Catholic priests in Buka, and later in government schools in Rabaul. This training won him a position of leadership in Hahalis, a village twenty-three miles up the Buka coast from the straits, when he was only sixteen. The Welfare's first goal was to force the government to build a road to the straits over which to truck out the village's main product, *copra*. Teosin achieved this goal, by a perfectly flabbergasting method. Hahalis, it seems, had a sex problem: the old men, by reason of seniority, got all the young girls, and the young men had to wait. Hahalis also had a motivation problem—no one could see any really good reason to work.

Teosin's solution, in 1961, was to start what soon became famous throughout New Guinea as the Hahalis Baby Garden. The town built a two-story house big enough to contain two hundred tiny cubicles, and stocked it with a corresponding number of toothsome young local girls, aged twelve and up. In return for productive work for the Welfare, young men were authorized to disport themselves among these lovelies, and the more of them they made pregnant, the better. The children became the property of the Welfare. White blood was prized—half-breed children were "easy to educate," said Teosin— and quite a few white men helped to fertilize the Baby Garden. The Welfare quickly became such a dominant institution that Teosin decided his people could dispense with the official local government, which seemed chiefly interested in collecting taxes. Hahalis men clashed bloodily with government patrol officers. Teosin was jailed for a while. But the Australian Administrator in Port Moresby perceived that "European civilization and the government" had been deficient in developing Hahalis, and proceeded to build the road that Hahalis wanted. Soon the Welfare's *copra* trucks were churning down to market. The Baby Garden was reorganized, and opened with an exhibition of sex acts for the benefit of invited guests, the members of the local government council. In fact, Teosin has several times used sex orgies performed in public (or the threat of doing so) to bludgeon the government. But he himself, married in a Catholic mission church years ago, stays strictly away from the Baby Garden. Such is politics in Buka.

Questions for Reflection and Discussion

How are the myths about sexual behavior "updated"; that is, how do the activities emphasized in these passages correspond to modern concerns about sexuality? What is Gunther's tone toward the Aborigines and inhabitants of Buka Island? How do sexual stereotypes combine with other stereotypes?

111. IMAGE OF AN AFRICAN WOMAN

Time: mid-twentieth century CE
Place: central Africa (modern Congo)
Artist: Boris de Rachewiltz

This image of a Bira woman comes from Black Eros: Sexual Customs of Africa from Prehistory to the Present Day, *a book by Boris de Rachewiltz, who also took the photograph. He was a professor of Egyptian culture and history at the University of Rome, and part of the book's thesis was that many modern African sexual customs could be traced to ancient Egypt. It also showed his particular interest in aspects of appearance—hair and dress, body painting and scarification—especially those linked to sexuality. This image presents a woman whose upper lip has been split and stretched to accommodate a large plate.*

Questions for Reflection and Discussion

What questions arise as to the origins and purpose of such a custom? How might such a custom be linked to sexuality? How does such an image reinforce the image of traditional Africans as "other" to many viewers?

112. COMMUNIST SEX

Time: mid-twentieth century CE
Place: United States
Author: Peter Stafford

Although it was not possible to locate information on the author of this book, Sexual Behavior *in the Communist World, published in 1967, it provides another modern twist to the depiction of The Other. Here, it is not ethnic difference but political difference that is highlighted by calling attention to the supposed distinctions in sexuality.*

Totalitarianism provides an unparalleled opportunity for sexual deviation, especially for sadism. Torture on the largest possible scale has been a weapon used by secret police all over the world; but nowhere with such ingenuity, persistence and enjoyment as in the Communist countries. This is no wild generalization; there have been thousands of survivors' eyewitness accounts; men and women are living among us whose bodies bear the scars of the refined torments that sadistic inventiveness could produce. I have several personal friends among them. In Eastern and Central Europe it has been an appalling but well documented fact that many of these torture experts first served the Gestapo or its local branch and then, without much ado, continued their special services for their Communist masters.

Sadism for sexual satisfaction has a certain justification, however abhorrent it might be to so-called "normal" people. At least it serves an attainable end: once orgasm has occurred, the sadist stops inflicting pain. But the sadists who sublimate their sexual detumescence by purely mental and intellectual fulfillment, by triumphing over the flesh of their helpless victims and destroying human dignity and the integrity of the human spirit, are a thousand times worse. And yet they have flourished and are still flourishing in every Communist country.

Naturally, along with sadism, masochism, necrophilia, zoophily and other deviations from normal sexual practices have also been encouraged by the peculiar social and economic circumstances in these countries. Rape, for instance, has been the normal approach of male to female during and after the Second World War. When the Germans invaded Eastern Europe, they treated all Slavs as an inferior race and their women as chattels. In turn, when the Russian armies flooded over Eastern and Central Europe, they claimed the sexual spoils of the victor. In most countries they "liberated," abortion was automatically legalized, as there were hundreds of thousands of matrons and girls in their early teens who became pregnant, some of whom had to endure the sexual assault of a whole platoon of Cossacks or a squad of Siberian sharpshooters. There were innumerable tragedies, and the subsequent brutalization of sex life in these countries might well be due to this apocalyptic rampage of the conquering male. As a matter of fact, it wasn't the male alone, for there are well documented cases of Russian girl soldiers, the *barishnyas*, forcing men into sexual intercourse when they took a fancy to them.

The irony is that, in addition to its economic and political aims, the avowed purpose of Communism has been the creation of a "new man," the complete transformation of humanity. Lenin spoke of the "engineers of the human spirit"; Pavlov's behaviorism sought techniques by which conditioned reflexes could dominate and guide human actions and emotions. The Soviet Man, the Communist Adam, the partisan—these are only some of the ideals which have been set as attainable goals. Building Communism—for the Communist countries maintain they have only achieved an intermediate, Socialist stage—includes the attainment of a society in which "from each according to his ability, to each according to his needs" would apply just as much to sex life and marriage as to collective fanning and industrialization.

After fifty years of Soviet Communism and almost two decades of Communist regimes in China and Eastern Europe, it is now possible to draw a cautious balance sheet as to the success or failure of this program. The answer is fairly simple, even if one is bound to be extra careful about hasty and sweeping generalizations. Whatever progress has been made in abolishing illiteracy, building factories, launching sputniks, improving agriculture—human nature has stubbornly resisted the various attempts to change it in its fundamentals. Adam and Eve, man and woman, are still the same as they were twenty or fifty years ago. The Pavlovian methods have proved totally inadequate to cope with anything as primeval and basic as the sex urge and human emotions.

Questions for Reflection and Discussion

Stafford mentions personal friends as eyewitnesses: does this make him more or less reliable as an authority on the subject? How are the "perversions" of sexuality among Communists related to other aspects of the economic and political system?

113. HOMOSEXUALS AS THE OTHER

Time: late twentieth century CE
Place: United States
Author: Anita Bryant

Anita Bryant, a former Miss Oklahoma and gospel singer, made news headlines in 1977 when she launched a successful campaign to repeal a Miami, Florida, law extending protection from discrimination in hiring and housing to gay men and lesbians, forming a group called Save Our Children. She followed her local success by traveling across North America, urging the repeal of similar laws. After her divorce in 1980, which alienated many of her conservative supporters, she mostly retired from the public spotlight. The following excerpt is part of a full-page advertisement by Save Our Children in the Miami newspapers before the repeal.

Homosexuality is nothing new. Cultures throughout history, moreover, have dealt with homosexuals almost universally with disdain, abhorrence, disgust—even death. While times certainly have changed, and American society largely has developed an attitude of tolerance, that tolerance toward homosexuality is based on the understanding that homosexuals will keep their deviate activity to themselves, will not flaunt their lifestyles, will not be allowed to preach their sexual standards to, or otherwise influence, impressionable young people. That attitude of tolerance, most unfortunately, recently was destroyed in this community by the Metropolitan Dade County Commission, which voted, in effect, to legitimize homosexuals' presence in our society—by forcing our private and religious schools to accept them as teachers, by forcing property owners and employers to open their doors to homosexuals no matter how blatant their perverted lives may be.

Civil Wrong vs. Civil Rights. Homosexual acts are illegal under Florida law and the laws of most states. The Metro Commission, nevertheless, chose to ignore the spirit of our laws and caved in to a small, vocal group of "gays." (Interestingly, Webster's third definition of "gay" is "licentious," which further is defined as "lacking legal or moral restraints; disregarding sexual restraints; marked by disregard of rules.") Despite the obvious fact that homosexual acts *are* illegal—and, in the eyes of most people, immoral—some *non*-homosexual supporters of the homosexuals' point of view contend that the issue is one of "civil rights." Metro's blundering "gay" ordinance is no more a civil rights issue than is the arrest of a drunk for disturbing the peace.... In fact the leaders of the homosexuals in testifying before the Metro Commission repeatedly bragged that they "already are here"—in jobs, in schools, in every conceivable niche. They further stated that they had not suffered discrimination. Why no discrimination? Because, until *now*, they kept their sexual deviation private, and, thus, no one except their own kind knew or cared about their "affectional preference."

Invitation to Recruit our Children. That has all been changed by Metro. Unless repealed, the ordinance will allow homosexuals, as one leader has promised, to provide "role models" for the impressionable—that is, the right to tell all society, especially our youth, that homosexuality isn't wrong, just "different"—and, of course, "gay." This recruitment of our children is absolutely necessary for the survival and growth of homosexuality—for since homosexuals cannot reproduce, they *must* recruit, *must* freshen their ranks. And who qualifies as a likely recruit: a 35-year-old father or mother of two—or a teenage boy or girl who is surging with sexual awareness? (The Los Angeles Police Department recently reported that 25,000 boys 17 years old or younger in that city alone have been recruited into a homosexual ring to provide sex for adult male customers. One boy, just 12 years old, was described as a $1,000-a-day prostitute.) …

The Price of Saving our Children. This message, prepared for the people of Dade County, is expensive to publish in our daily Miami newspapers—but no cost is too great to save our children, and we are grateful to the many hundreds of concerned parents who have contributed to this cause…. Your children are precious assets to you and our nation. Please help us protect them, with your prayers, your active participation—and your financial contribution today.

    Anita Bryant, President
    Save Our Children, Inc.

Questions for Reflection and Discussion

What characteristics typify the homosexual, according to Bryant, and how might she characterize herself in opposite ways? What kind of "tolerance" does Bryant recommend toward homosexuals? Why do children figure so prominently in her discussion, even in the name of her organization?

SOURCES AND FURTHER READING

On Lacan's theory of the Other, see the essays in *Interpreting Lacan*, Joseph H. Smith and William Kerrigan, eds. (New Haven, CT: Yale University Press, 1983); a more extended study, comparing Lacan to other modern French philosophers, can be found in Franco Rella's *The Myth of the Other: Lacan, Deleuze, Foucault, Bataille*, trans. Nelson Moe (Washington, DC: Maisonneuve, 1994). A useful global application of the theory is the collection entitled *Who, Exactly, is "The Other"? Western and Transcultural Perspectives*, Steven Shankman and Massimo Lollini, eds. (Eugene, OR: University of Oregon Books/University of Oregon Humanities Center, 2002). In sociological language, such depictions of the other are known as stereotypes; studies of sexual stereotypes include Sander Gilman's *Difference and Pathology: Stereotypes of Sexuality, Race, and Madness* (Ithaca, NY: Cornell University Press, 1985); or the essays in *Stereotypes and Prejudice: Essential Readings*, Charles Stangor, ed. (Philadelphia: Psychology, 2000). For applications of stereotypes in contemporary societies, most work has been done on ethnic and gender stereotypes; on the latter, see Tricia Szirom's *Teaching Gender? Sex Education and Sexual Stereotypes* (Boston: Allen & Unwin, 1988), focusing on Australia; or John E. Williams and Deborah Best's *Measuring Sex Stereotypes: A Thirty-Nation Study* (Beverly Hills, CA:

Sage, 1982); revised in 1990 as *Measuring Sex Stereotypes: A Multination Study*. Many works on sexual stereotypes look at representations in mass media, such as Richard Dyer's *The Matter of Images: Essays on Representations* (New York: Routledge, 2002) on homosexuality; or the essays in *Images that Injure: Pictorial Stereotypes in the Media*, Paul Martin Lester, ed. (Westport, CT: Praeger, 1996); or in *Mediated Women: Representations in Popular Media*, Marian Meyers, ed. (Cresskill, NY: Hampton, 1999). Anthropologists have also been working with categories of separation in a variety of different terms. See Claude Levi-Strauss's *The Raw and the Cooked*, trans. John Weightman and Doreen Weightman (New York: Harper & Row, 1969); or Mary Douglas's *Purity and Danger: An Analysis of Concepts of Pollution and Taboo* (New York: Praeger, 1966; revised most recently in 2000).

98. "Marco Polo" is taken from Marco Polo, *The Travels of Marco Polo*, trans. Teresa Waugh (London: Sidgwick & Jackson, 1984), 115-16, 186-87.

A recent biography is John Larner's *Marco Polo and the Discovery of the World* (New Haven, CT: Yale University Press, 1999). Of several medieval accounts of long travels, including that of the North African Muslim Ibn Battuta and others by European Christians, Marco Polo is uniquely frank about sexual matters. More on China in the era when Polo visited, the Yuan Dynasty (but studies are best for its recent predecessor, the Song Dynasty), can be found in Priscilla Ching's *Palace Women in the Northern Sung, 960-1126* (Leiden, NLD: Brill, 1981); or Patricia Buckley Ebrey's *The Inner Quarters: Marriage and the Lives of Chinese Women in the Sung Period* (Berkeley, CA: University of California Press, 1993); or Bettine Birge's *Women, Property,*

and Confucian Reaction in Sung and Yüan China (960–1368) (Cambridge: Cambridge University Press, 2001). See also note 91 on footbinding. An interesting relevant primary source can be found in *Family and Property in Sung China: Yuan Ts'ai's Precepts for Social Life*, Patricia Buckley Ebrey, ed. and trans. (Princeton, NJ: Princeton University Press, 1984). A brief history of the Mongol Empire during the era of Polo can be found in David Morgan's *The Mongols* (Oxford: B. Blackwell, 1986). On Mongol women, see Morris Rossabi's "Khubilai Khan and the Women in his Family," in *Studia Sino-Mongolica*, Wolfgang Bauer, ed. (Wiesbaden: Steiner, 1979). See also Jeannine Davis-Kimball's *Warrior Women* (New York: Warner, 2002) on general central Asian traditions of such women.

99. "*The Hammer of Witches*" is taken from Heinrich Kramer and Jacob Sprenger, *Malleus Maleficarum*, trans. Montague Summers (London: John Rodker, 1928), 58–59, 119, with slight changes.

The secondary literature on witchcraft is vast and impossible to summarize here. On sex and witchcraft, see Lauran Paine's *Sex in Witchcraft* (New York: Taplinger, 1972); or Lyndal Roper's *Œdipus and the Devil: Witchcraft, Sexuality, and Religion in Early Modern Europe* (New York: Routledge, 1994). On witchcraft accusation as misogyny, see Anne Llewellyn Barstow's *Witchcraze: A New History of the European Witch Hunts* (San Francisco: Pandora, 1994); or Marianne Hester's *Lewd Women and Wicked Witches: A Study of the Dynamics of Male Domination* (New York: Routledge, 1992). Most historical societies have understood some form of witchcraft, so it is a topic with real possibilities for global comparisons. The treatise *Hammer of Witches* includes much more information on sexuality and witchcraft.

100. "The Sexual Customs of Utopia" is taken from Thomas More, *Utopia*, Paul Turner, trans. (Harmondsworth, UK: Penguin, 1965), 102–05.

Commentaries on this text include George Logan's *The Meaning of More's Utopia* (Princeton, NJ: Princeton University Press, 1983); Alistair Fox's *Utopia: An Elusive Vision* (New York: Twayne 1993); and Dominic Baker-Smith's *More's Utopia* (Toronto, ON: University of Toronto Press, 2000). See also Patricia Huckle's "Women in Utopias," in *The Utopian Vision*, E.D.S. Sullivan, ed. (San Diego, CA: San Diego State University Press, 1983). For studies of the context of the text, see David Weil Baker's *Divulging Utopia: Radical Humanism in Sixteenth-Century England* (Amherst, MA: University of Massachusetts Press, 1999). For other utopian literature, see *Ideal Commonwealths*, Henry Morely, ed. (London: George Routledge and Son, 1889).

101. "A Letter from Amerigo Vespucci" is taken from *The Letters of Amerigo Vespucci*, Clements Markham, trans. (London: Hakluyt Society, 1894), 6–10.

The standard biography of Vespucci is still that written by German Arciniegas and published in 1952 and recently translated into English as *Why America? 500 Years of a Name: The Life and Times of Amerigo Vespucci* (Bogota, Colombia: Villegas, 2002). It is the most detailed account of sexual customs of all of the sixteenth-century European explorers in the Americas, including those by Christopher Columbus, Juan Cabrillo, Alvar Nuñez Cabeza de Vaca, Francisco Vazquez de Coronado, and others. The peoples of the South American interior approximate the native coastal South Americans of Vespucci's day most closely; studies on their sexual customs include the

essays in *Cultures of Multiple Fathers: The Theory and Practice of Partible Paternity in Lowland South America*, Stephen Beckerman and Paul Valentine, eds. (Gainesville, FL: University of Florida Press, 2002); or João Silvério Trevisan's "Tivira, The Man with the Broken Butt: Same-Sex Practices among Brazilian Indians," in *Lusosex: Gender and Sexuality in the Portuguese-speaking World*, Susan Canty Quinlan and Fernando Arenas, eds. (Minneapolis, MI: University of Minnesota Press, 2002). See also note 102 for sexual customs of past societies of the Americas.

102. "Bernal Diaz del Castillo's *True History*" is taken from Bernal Diaz del Castillo, *The True History of the Conquest of New Spain*, Alfred Percival Maudslay, trans. (London: Hakluyt Society, 1916), 263–64.

On the homoerotic traditions of the Americas, see Richard Trexler's *Sex and Conquest: Gendered Violence, Political Order, and the European Conquest of the Americas* (Ithaca, NY: Cornell University Press, 1995); or the first essays in *Infamous Desire: Male Homosexuality in Colonial Latin America*, Pete Sigal, ed. (Chicago: University of Chicago Press, 2003). See also the literature on the *berdache*, especially Will Roscoe's *Changing Ones: Third and Fourth Genders in Native North America* (New York: St. Martin's, 1998); or Charles Callender and Lee Kochems's "The North American Berdache," *Current Anthropology* 24 (1983): 443–70. Generally on the sexual customs of the past societies of the Americas, see *Gender in Pre-Hispanic America*, Cecelia Klein, ed. (Washington, DC: Dumbarton Oaks Research Library and Collection, 2001).

103. "John Freyer on the Zoroastrians" is taken from John Fryer, *East India and Persia* (London: Hakluyt Society, 1912), 2: 253–56.

See Mary Boyce's *Zoroastrians: Their Religious Beliefs and Practices* (London: Routledge & Kegan Paul, 1979; revised 1984), for accurate information about the religion. Similar accusations had been made against the early Christians, against heretics and Jews in the Middle Ages, against witches in early modern Europe, and against modern Satanists. I know of no serious studies on the history of the orgy or the orgy accusation. Another early Indian Ocean travel account, with more believable descriptions of sexual customs, is the Dutch explorer, Francois Valentijn's *Description of Ceylon*, Sinnappah Arasaratnam, trans. (London: The Hakluyt Society, 1978), from his travels in the 1720s.

104. "George Robertson on the People of Tahiti" is taken from George Robertson, *The Discovery of Tahiti* (London: Hakluyt Society, 1948), 166–67.

On traditional Tahiti, see Douglas Oliver's *Ancient Tahitian Society* (Honolulu, HI: University of Hawai'i Press, 1974); and on its later history, see David Howarth's *Tahiti: A Paradise Lost* (New York: Viking, 1983); or C.W. Newbury's *Tahiti Nui: Change and Survival in French Polynesia, 1767–1945* (Honolulu: University of Hawai'i Press, 1980). On Tahitian sexual customs, usually studied as part of Pacific Island or Polynesian traditions, and mix historical and contemporary research, see Robert Suggs's *Marquesan Sexual Behavior* (New York: Harcourt, Brace & World, 1966); the more recent essays in *Bitter Sweet: Indigenous Women in the Pacific*, Alison Jones et al., eds. (Dunedin, NZ: University of Otago Press, 2000); or *Sites of Desire, Economies of Pleasure: Sexualities in Asia and the Pacific*, Lenore Manderson and Margaret Jolly, eds. (Chicago: University of Chicago Press, 1997).

105. "A Missionary in Tahiti" is taken from *The History of the Tahitian Mission, 1799–1830* (London: Hakluyt Society, 1959), 358.

See note 104 on Tahiti's history and sexual customs.

106. "George Angas on the Aborigines of Australia" is taken from George French Angas, *Savage Life and Scenes in Australia and New Zealand* (London: Smith, Elder, 1847), 81–83, 113.

George Angas also wrote about the native inhabitants of the South Pacific in *Polynesia: Popular Description, etc.* (Christchurch, NZ: Kiwi, 2000; orig. publ. 1866). On relations between early European explorers and settlers and Aboriginal Australians, see Derek Mulvaney's *Encounters in Place: Outsiders and Aboriginal Australians, 1606–1985* (St. Lucia, Australia: University of Queensland Press, 1989); or Richard Broome's *Aboriginal Australians: Black Response to White Dominance, 1788–1980* (Sydney: Allen & Unwin, 1982). Older studies of sexual customs, which tend to mix historical and contemporary realities, include John Hopkins's *The Family Chain Marriage and Relationships of Native Australian Tribes, etc.* (London: Watts, 1914); or Ashley Montagu's *Coming into Being among the Australian Aborigines: A Study of the Procreative Beliefs of the Native Tribes of Australia* (New York: E.P. Dutton, 1938). Modern correctives and new studies include Aslaug Falkenberg and Johannes Falkenberg's *The Affinal Relationship System: A New Approach to Kinship and Marriage among the Australian Aborigines at Port Keats* (Oslo: Universitatsforlaget, 1981); and the Australian Law Reform Commission's Aboriginal Customary Law Research Papers: 1. "Promised Marriage in Aboriginal Society"; 2. "The Recognition of Aboriginal Customary or Tribal Marriage"; 3. "The Recognition of Aboriginal Tribal Marriage: Areas of Functional Recognition"; and 4. "Aboriginal Customary Law: Child Custody, Fostering, and Adoption"; all printed in Sydney in 1982; see also Sarah Colley's "Sisters Are Doing It for Themselves? Gender, Feminism, and Australian (Aboriginal) Archeology," in *Gender and Material Culture in Archeological Perspective*, Moira Donald and Linda Hurcombe, eds. (New York: St. Martin's, 2000). Other nineteenth-century travel accounts also provide interesting details; see James Backhouse's *A Narrative of a Visit to the Australian Colonies* (London: Hamilton, Adams, 1843) of his travels in the 1830s; or *The Letters of F.W. Ludwig Leichhardt*, M. Aurosseau, trans. (London: The Hakluyt Society, 1968) of his travels in the 1840s.

107. "Mary Kingsley in West Africa" is taken from Mary Kingsley, *Travels in West Africa* (London: Frank Cass, 1965), 211–13.

Recent biographies of Mary Kingsley include Katherine Frank's *A Voyager Out: The Life of Mary Kingsley* (Boston: Houghton Mifflin, 1986); Valerie Grosvenor Myer's *A Victorian Lady in Africa: The Story of Mary Kingsley* (Southampton, UK: Ashford, 1989); R.D. Pearce's *Mary Kingsley: Light at the Heart of Darkness* (Oxford: Kensal, 1990); and Alison Blunt's *Travel, Gender, and Imperialism: Mary Kingsley and West Africa* (New York: Guilford, 1994). She may be compared to many others, as described in Catherine Barnes Stevenson's *Victorian Women Travel Writers in Africa* (Boston: Twayne, 1982); or Lila Marx Harper's *Solitary Travelers: Nineteenth-Century Women's Travel Narratives and the Scientific Vocation* (Madison, NJ: Farleigh Dickinson University Press, 2001). Polygamy remained a contentious issue among African converts to Christianity; discussions of the issue, from different periods, include: H.C. Trowell's *The Passing of Polygamy: A Discussion of Marriage and of Sex for African Christians* (London: H. Milford, 1940); Thomas Price's *African Marriage* (London: SCM, 1954); Lucy Mair's *African Marriage and Social Change* (London: Cass, 1969); and Benezeri Kisembo's *African Christian Marriage* (London: Chapman, 1977). There are many other accounts of nineteenth-century travelers to Africa, with details of the sexual customs they observed; such as *King Kazembe and the Marave, Cheva, Bisa, Bemba, Lunda, and Other Peoples of Southern Africa, Being the Diary of the Portuguese Expedition to that Potentate in the Years 1831 and 1832*, Ian Cunnison, trans. (Lisbon: Junta de Investigações do Ultramar, 1960); Paul du Chaillu's *Explorations and Adventures in Equatorial Africa* (London: John Murray, 1861); Henry Stanley's *How I Found Livingstone: Travels, Adventures and Discoveries in Central Africa* (New York: Scribner, Armstrong, 1872); or Georg Schweinfurth's *The Heart of Africa: Three Years' Travels and Adventures in the Unexplored Regions of Central Africa from 1868 to 1871*, Ellen Frewer, trans. (New York: Harper & Row, 1874).

108. "China and the United States Compared" is taken from Kate Bushnell, *The Woman Condemned* (New York: Funk & Wagnalls, 1886), 3, 6–11.

On the realities of suicide and infanticide in late nineteenth-century China, see the essays in *Passionate Women: Female Suicide in Late Imperial China*, Paul Ropp et al. eds. (Leiden, NLD: Brill, 2001); Margery Wolf's "Women and Suicide in China," in *Women in Chinese Society*, Margery Wolf and Roxane Witke, eds. (Stanford, CA: Stanford University Press, 1975); or James Z. Lee's *One Quarter of Humanity: Malthusian Mythology and Chinese Realities, 1700–2000* (Cambridge, MA: Harvard University Press,

1999), the latter on birth control and infanticide. See notes 132 and 143 on prostitution in the nineteenth-century United States.

109. "An Anti-Immigrant Poster" is taken from *Truth*, 21 May 1892.

On Chinese immigration to the United States, see Madeline Yuan-yin Hsu's *Dreaming of Gold, Dreaming of Home: Transnationalism and Migration between the United States and South China, 1882–1943* (Stanford, CA: Stanford University Press, 2000); or Erika Lee's *At America's Gates: Chinese Immigration during the Exclusion Era, 1882–1943* (Chapel Hill, NC: University of North Carolina Press, 2003). On global Chinese migration, see Lynn Pan's *Sons of the Yellow Emperor: A History of the Chinese Diaspora* (Boston: Little, Brown, 1990); or the essays in *Globalizing Chinese Migration: Trends in Europe and Asia*, Pál Nyíri and Igor Savelev, eds. (Aldershot, UK: Ashgate, 2002). On anti-Chinese sentiment and government policy in the United States, see Andrew Gyory's *Closing the Gate: Race, Politics, and the Chinese Exclusion Act* (Chapel Hill, NC: University of North Carolina Press, 1998); or *Entry Denied: Exclusion and the Chinese Community in America, 1882–1943*, Sucheng Chan, ed. (Philadelphia: Temple University Press, 1991). On mixed marriages, see Betty Lee Sung's *Chinese American Intermarriage* (New York: Center for Migration Studies, 1990). There is more literature on the history of intermarriage between European- and African-Americans; see, for example, Rachel Moran's *Interracial Intimacy: The Regulation of Race and Romance* (Chicago: University of Chicago Press, 2001); or Peter Wallenstein's *Tell the Court I Love My Wife: Race, Marriage, and Law: An American History* (New York: Palgrave Macmillan, 2002).

110. "John Gunther on Australia and New Guinea" is taken from John Gunther, *Inside Australia* (San Francisco: Harper & Row, 1972), 68–69, 257–58.

John Gunther also published *Inside Europe* (London: Hamilton, 1936), *Inside Asia* (New York: Harper, 1939), *Inside Latin America* (New York: Harper, 1941), and *Inside Africa* (New York: Harper, 1955), as well as updated versions with slightly different titles, that provide fascinating glimpses of this man's impressions of world societies. See note 106 for studies on sexual customs among Aboriginal Australians. On the sexual customs of the peoples of Papua New Guinea, see the essays in *Sexual Antagonism, Gender and Social Change in Papua New Guinea*, Fitz John Poole and Gilbert Herdt, eds. (Adelaide, Australia: Department of Anthropology, University of Adelaide, 1982). Of course, there are so many distinct societies in New Guinea that it is difficult for general studies to be accurate.

111. "Image of an African Woman" is taken from Boris de Rachewiltz, *Black Eros: Sexual Customs of Africa from Prehistory to the Present Day*, trans. Peter Whigham (London: George Allen & Unwin, 1964), 163.

Black Eros includes many of the author's photographs of women from many different societies. For comparative studies of feminine beauty, see the essays in *Many Mirrors: Body Image and Social Relations*, Nicole Sault, ed. (New Brunswick, NJ: Rutgers University Press, 1994); in *Dress and Ethnicity: Change across Space and Time*, Joanne Eicher, ed. (Oxford: Berg, 1995); or in *Clothing and Difference: Embodied Identities in Colonial and Post-Colonial Africa*, Hildi Hendrickson, ed. (Durham, NC: Duke University Press, 1996). Shorter studies include Jeannette Mageo's

"Hairdos and Don'ts: Hair Symbolism and Sexual History in Samoa," *Man* 29 (1994): 407–32.

112. "Communist Sex" is taken from Peter Stafford, *Sexual Behavior in the Communist World* (New York: Julian, 1967), 3–4.

On Cold War mentalities, see Michael Barson and Steven Heller's *Red Scared! The Commie Menace in Propaganda and Popular Culture* (San Francisco: Chronicle, 2001); or Cynthia Hendershot's *Anti-Communism and Popular Culture in Mid-Century America* (Jefferson, NC: McFarland, 2003). On connections between politics and issues of gender and sexuality, see Robert Dean's *Imperial Brotherhood: Gender and the Making of Cold War Foreign Policy* (Amherst, MA: University of Massachusetts Press, 2001); Cynthia Enloe's *The Morning After: Sexual Politics at the End of the Cold War* (Berkeley, CA: University of California Press, 1993); J. Ann Tickner's *Gendering World Politics: Issues and Approaches in the Post-Cold War Era* (New York: Columbia University Press, 2001); Joanne Meyerowitz's "Sex, Gender, and the Cold War Language of Reform," in *Rethinking Cold War Culture*, Peter Kuznick and James Gilbert, eds. (Washington, DC: Smithsonian Institute Press, 2001); or John D'Emilio's "The Homosexual Menace: The Politics of Sexuality in Cold War America," in his *Making Trouble: Essays on Gay History, Politics, and the University* (New York: Routledge, 1992).

113. "Homosexuals as the Other" is taken from Anita Bryant, *The Anita Bryant Story: The Survival of Our Nation's Families and the Threat of Militant Homosexuality* (Old Tappan, NJ: Fleming H. Revell, 1977), 145–46, 148.

On the history of the gay rights movement, see John D'Emilio's *Sexual Politics, Sexual Communities: The Making of a Homosexual Minority in the United States, 1940–1970* (Chicago: University of Chicago Press, 1983); Barry Adam's *The Rise of a Gay and Lesbian Movement* (Boston: Twayne, 1987); or Eric Marcus's *Making History: The Struggle for Gay and Lesbian Equal Rights, 1945–1990: An Oral History* (New York: HarperCollins, 1992). On the anti-homosexual movement, see John Gallagher and Chris Bull's *Perfect Enemies: The Religious Right, the Gay Movement, and the Politics of the 1990s* (New York: Crown, 1996): or Didi Herman's *The Antigay Agenda: Orthodox Vision and the Christian Right* (Chicago: University of Chicago Press, 1997).

science and sexuality

One of the most notable shifts in the modern history of sexuality has been the emphasis on science as a paramount authority for understanding human sexual behavior. Whether that science is medicine, psychology, anthropology, genetics, or statistics, the belief that human nature can be demonstrated as reflecting patterns suitable for observation and extrapolation is a dominant force in the world today. That belief is the subject of this chapter.

Scientific ideas about sexuality are not all entirely new. From the earliest literate societies we have evidence of individuals who studied human behavior according to some knowledge based on observation. Ancient medical writers sought to understand the patterns of human behavior based on the physiology of the body. Although less credible to modern scientific notions, ancient astrologists also did the same, basing their observations about human behavior on the position of the stars and planets at crucial moments in the lives of their subjects. Physiognomy, another ancient science now discredited, taught that human behavior could be predictable based on the shape of an individual's physical features: heads, torsos, and limbs, even genitals.

Scientific beliefs about sexuality, though, were mostly confined to a small minority of literate persons. For most others, religious or philosophical beliefs provided a greater authority for understanding. What is new about the modern world is that more people are influenced by scientific ideas and fewer by religious ones than ever before. That is not to say that religion does not still play a major role in shaping social perspectives on sex, and it is especially true in more traditional societies and in more conservative segments of most societies. Many of the conflicts over sexual values, indeed, stem from competing understandings of religion and science. Think, for example, about homosexuality or adultery. In conservative religious traditions, they are understood as sin, and placed within a context of breach of sacred laws or commandments, of the necessity of avoiding temptation, and of repentance and self-reform. Scientists think about homosexuality and adultery in very different contexts: Geneticists have speculated about the genes that determine sexual orientation, psychologists have interrogated individuals' personal histories for clues in upbringing or key events that have shaped their sexual selves, and anthropologists compare human to primate behavior or cross-culturally to see whether sexual pairing is instinctive or culturally defined. More liberal religious traditions try to reconcile the two methods of understanding sexuality, even while conservative religious traditions ignore the challenge of science. Nonetheless, such a contest would not have taken place more than a few centuries ago. That itself is evidence of the new strength of science in the competition.

Where did the strength of science come from? In European history, at least, the proliferation of divergent religious ideas in the early modern period weakened religious attempts at providing answers to the questions about human nature, since competing interpretations undermined any single answer as absolute. The European voyages of discovery and conquest also made individuals aware of just how many variations there were in human sexual traditions. The Enlightenment's emphasis on the individual provided a new standard for sexual behavior, arguing that sexual expression was a human right. The institutions of higher education, especially universities, also contributed to the strength of science. Most European universities had been founded in the Middle Ages as religious institutions, even if philos-

ophy and natural science had always formed part of the curriculum. But in the early modern period, religious organizations mostly left the university system for separate educational institutions, and that left philosophers and natural scientists to train future intellectuals.

By the nineteenth century in Europe, the strength of science was clear. Political revolutions had overthrown traditional regimes, regimes that were often associated with religious authorities, and brought the university-educated intellectuals into government as elected officials and bureaucrats. Even if these educated individuals held religious beliefs, they also had great respect for scientific methods. The formation of professional organizations added to the authority of scientists, since they could act as a collective body to disseminate ideas among their members and to the wider public. As universal education for children was imposed in the nineteenth century, scientific ideas formed the basis for the curriculum in schools.

This combination of factors may help to explain why Europeans dominated the early discussions of science and sexuality. In some parts of the world, such as the Americas, the process was similar to that of Europe and greatly influenced by what was happening there. Where religious traditions were still strong and where the political and social disruptions were not as sweeping as in Europe, science did not gain the same authority, except as part of Western alternatives to local customs. The political revolutions that have swept through much of the world in the twentieth century have, however, brought in scientific ideas as part of a modernization process.

The claims of science were also popularized not only through educational systems but also in literature. The novels of the nineteenth and twentieth centuries, available to a growing readership thanks to increases in literacy rates, meant that educated individuals who were writers could shape the ways that their readers made sense of their experiences. Treatises on sexual matters also circulated more widely than ever before—even if they also faced obstacles in censorship through obscenity laws (one common practice used to avoid censorship problems was to translate the most explicit words into Latin so that only the well educated could read them). When films first appeared, at the end of the nineteenth century, their popularity ensured that filmmakers could influence viewers with their ideas about sex, as about other matters.

All of this is not to say that science speaks about sexuality with a united voice. Just as religious traditions disagreed about interpretation on specific issues and relied on different types of sacred authority to bolster their claims, so too do scientists rely on very different standards to assert their positions, some arguing for the pre-eminence of genetics in human behavior, others for childhood development, others for instinct, and so on. The separation of academic disciplines in the universities, also a development of the nineteenth century, allowed each science to reinforce its authority with its own vocabulary and training, and important writings in each of these disciplines were sometimes elevated to the status of semi-sacred texts. Think back to the primacy of the ideas of Darwin, Marx, and Freud mentioned in the introduction to this book.

Science claims to be objective—indeed, that is one of the standards of the scientific method, to observe reality rather than to impose one's perspective on it—but modern scholars are also critical of the objectivity of some of the claims made by previous generations of scientists. These critiques often look at the historical context in which scientists developed their ideas and attempt to find unexamined assumptions in their writings. The intro-duction mentioned some recent criticisms of Darwin, Marx, and Freud. Some modern scholars are skeptical about *any* claims by science to objectivity. This skepticism is strong among feminist scholars who see a patriarchal bias in many assumptions of the scientific method, given that so much of the literature was written by men and that the universities and academic disciplines have long been dominated by men without proper insight into or concern about the lives of women. Skepticism about science's claims has also been expressed worldwide in the postcolonial era by scholars who see Western dominance and assumptions in much of the scientific literature. Of course, the rejection of older scientific ideas is often accompanied by new but equally scientific ones.

Psychologists have often reflected on the importance of belief systems in human lives, and the processes by which individuals commit themselves to a belief system, and their insights can help historians to understand the strength of modern science. From Freud on, psychologists have studied how religious belief systems attract and retain adherence. In some ways, though, a commitment to scientific explanations is not unlike a commitment to religious explanations: Both require acceptance of a certain set of assumptions explained by a leadership whose authority overall must be beyond reproach. According to Alfred Adler, an associate of Freud, individuals seek a set of beliefs that will go furthest toward overcoming the inconsistencies and difficulties in their lives; their adherence depends both on their willingness to overlook the assumptions they must make to believe and on the credibility of the system demanding their loyalty.

The selections in this chapter are intended to give a sense of the range of scientific thought on sexuality in the modern era.

114. THE PROBLEM WITH MASTURBATION

Time: eighteenth century CE
Place: Switzerland
Author: Simon Tissot

*Tissot, a Swiss physician, wrote a famous trea-
tise on the dangers of masturbation, called*
Onanism, *published in 1760. (This synonym
for masturbation was derived from "Onan," the
name of a Biblical figure who "spilled his seed
on the ground.") In this passage, Tissot summed
up the "observed" effects of masturbation in a
group of patients, clearly all male. His was not
the only pamphlet circulating in the eighteenth
century warning of the dangerous side effects
of the practice, but his medical training lent it
a particular authority.*

1. All of the intellectual faculties weaken, they
lose their memory, their thought becomes confused, they even sometimes fall into a state of
slight dementia; they are constantly harassed by
a kind of internal anxiety, a continual anguish,
by pangs of conscience so strong that they are
often brought to tears. They are prone to dizzy
spells; all their senses, but especially sight and
hearing, weaken; their sleep, if they are able to
sleep at all, is disturbed by troubling dreams.

2. The body loses all of its strength; the growth
of those who indulge in these abominable
practices before they reach their full height is
significantly stunted. Some do not sleep at all,
others are almost continually drowsy. Almost
all become hypochondriacs or hysterics, and
are afflicted by all the troubles that accompany
these unfortunate diseases: sadness, sighs, tears,
palpitations, choking fits, fainting spells. Some
have been seen to spit up calcareous matter. For
others, coughing fits, slow fevers, consumption
are the wages of their sin.

3. Patients also complain of sharp pains; some
of headaches, others of chest, stomach or
intestinal pain, external rheumatic pain, and
sometimes of a painful numbness throughout
the body resulting from the application of even
the slightest pressure.

4. We see not only pimples, one of the most common symptoms, but true suppurating pustules
on the face, the nose, the chest, the thighs....

5. The organs of generation are also subject to
their share of miseries, of which they are the
primary cause. Some patients become incapable
of erection; for others, the seminal liquid pours
out at the slightest pruritis and the weakest
erection, or in their attempts to move their bowels. A great number are afflicted with chronic
gonorrhea, which saps all of their strength,
and which produces a discharge that resembles a fetid pus or a dirty mucus. Others are
tormented by painful priapisms. Dysuria, stran-
gury, burning upon urination, the weakening of
the stream cause some patients to suffer cruelly.
Some have very painful tumors on the testicles, the penis, the bladder or the sperm ducts.
Finally, either the impossibility of coitus or the
degeneration of the seminal liquid, rendering
sterile nearly all those who have indulged in
this crime for a long time.

6. The functioning of the intestines is sometimes completely disrupted, and some patients
complain of persistent constipation, others of
hemorrhoids or a flow of fetid matter from the
fundament.

Questions for Reflection and Discussion

What does the proliferation of problems supposedly brought on by masturbation tell us
about its perceived danger? What does Tissot's
reference to it as a sin and a crime as well as a

disease almost interchangeably tell us about his own view of it?

115. CURING MASTURBATION

Time: nineteenth century CE
Place: France
Authors: various

Physicians debated about the best way to prevent masturbation in children; it was believed to be particularly harmful to their physical and mental development. This series of writings by various physicians of the Surgical Society in Paris from 1864 discussed their different methods that give some idea of the procedures used, including chastity belts, infibulation (placing a clamp around the penis that prevented erection), and amputation of the clitoris.

DR. BROCA

My patient was a little five year-old girl, quite intelligent before her deplorable habit began; she had been masturbating repeatedly for some time and thwarted all attempts to curb her habit. Neither the constant surveillance of her mother, nor the use of a chastity belt fabricated by Dr. Charrière had the slightest effect. We know, in any event, that this device is much more effective in the case of little boys, by imprisoning their penis in a metal case, than it is for girls. Our little girl, thin, wasted and extremely flexible, managed to insert her toe between the belt's metal plate and her soft parts, and thus succeeded in masturbating. Her memory, her intellect were weakening; momentary mental blanks were becoming increasingly frequent. My colleague Dr. Moreau, of the Salpêtrière hospital, had been consulted and had considered amputation of the clitoris. Questioned in turn, I indicated that I found the section of the clitoral nerves, a procedure employed by some

surgeons, to be of doubtful efficacy, leaving the door open to recidivism; that the amputation of the clitoris was the destruction, the irreparable ruin of the organ of pleasure and an excessive thing in the case of a young girl whom one is seeking to cure, and I thus came to the idea which I then put into practice. I operated on the child on December 31.... I joined the top two superior or anterior thirds of the major labia at their thickest point with the aid of a metal suture, leaving in the inferior section an orifice barely large enough to accommodate the small finger, to permit the flow of urine and later, of menstrual blood. Today the union is perfect, and the clitoris is placed out of all reach underneath a thick cushion of soft parts. I propose to continue the use of all the other mechanisms; active surveillance, chastity belt, etc., considering infibulation only as an important secondary method.

DR. DEGUISE

I must admit that I share the concerns of Dr. Morel. In one way or another, the child will continue her vicious behavior.... At such an advanced stage, the vice is incurable. I did, however, once succeed in curing a young boy of masturbation and I ask Dr. Broca why he did not try the method which I successfully used, cauterization. For an entire year, with a persistency that was almost cruel, and despite the pleas of the young patient, I maintained a constant irritation in the urethra by means of repeated cauterizations, that irritation being sufficiently painful to render any touch impossible. Today the young boy is a man who thanks me for my tenacity.

DR. RICHET

It seems to be generally believed that it is in the external genitalia and more precisely in the clitoris that the masturbatory impulse is located. Along with Dr. Stolz and other observers, I believe that these excitations can be produced along the entire length of the genital organs. A fact which I observed in my practice appears to confirm this opinion. A 27-year-old girl from a good family came to the Saint-Louis hospital in order to be delivered, by operation, of the irresistible impulse to masturbate repeatedly. Her general health had been severely compromised and the patient was extremely thin. I performed a total amputation of the clitoris…. For several months, it seemed that a full cure had been effected…. The patient left the hospital and returned home. A year later, she asked to be admitted to my unit at the Pitié hospital. What had arisen were … very frequent excitations (that is the word the patient used) of the vagina and the neck of the womb, excitations which led her to fondle the neck of the uterus. During eight months, … all possible treatments of these excitations which, in the absence of the clitoris were now produced in the deep parts of the genital organs, failed. This failure seems to support the opinion that I expressed earlier.

Questions for Reflection and Discussion

What kinds of assumptions do these physicians make about their patients? How confident do they seem about their knowledge or the effectiveness of their treatments?

116. ANTI-HYSTERIA DEVICE

Time: nineteenth century CE
Place: France
Artist: unknown

At the same time that physicians were overly anxious to prevent masturbation, they were involved in the development and use of electric and mechanical devices that served the same functions as modern personal vibrators. These devices were claimed to help in the cure of hysteria, a neurological disease believed to affect women (the term is derived from the Greek word for "womb") and that was supposed to result in a variety of symptoms from sleeplessness to lethargy and from frigidity to frequent sexual fantasy. Women treated with these devices, or who used them at home, applying them to their genitals, experienced a "hysterical spasm" that was deemed beneficial. This particular device, pictured in a medical book on women's diseases published in 1883, produced brief electrical pulses.

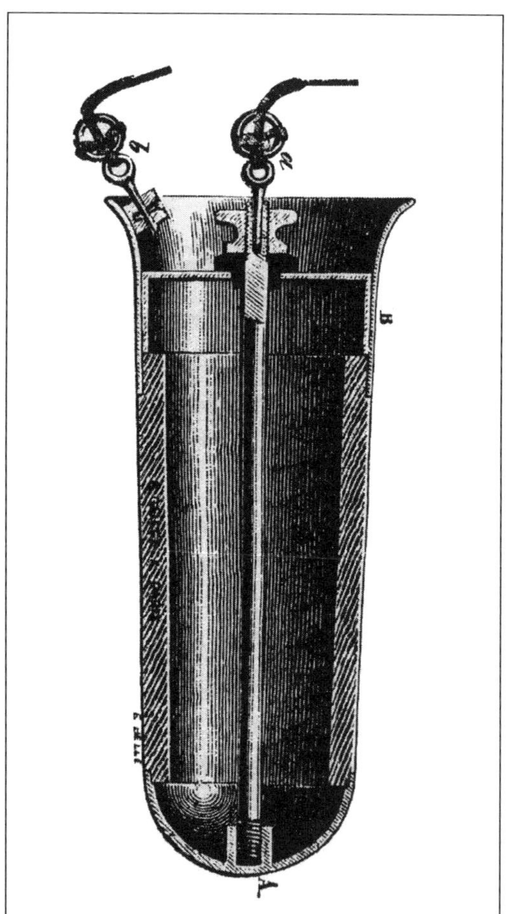

How can such a device be reconciled with the anti-masturbation campaigns of physicians in the same era? Does it seem likely that the physicians knew the effect that a device such as this one had on women? Does it seem likely that the women themselves knew what the effects were?

117. FREUD ON HYSTERIA

Time: late nineteenth century CE
Place: Austria
Author: Sigmund Freud

Many of Freud's writings involve case studies of patients who had inspired his theories. He drew inferences from his discussions with them, often based on their dreams. Gradually, he developed elaborate theories of the conscious and subconscious mind. This example of "Dora" (a pseudonym for a woman named Ida Bauer), one of Freud's most famous cases of hysteria, is typical of his approach.

In Dora's case, thanks to her father's shrewdness, which I have remarked upon more than once already, there was no need for me to look about for the points of contact between the circumstances of the patient's life and her illness, at all events in its most recent form. Her father told me that he and his family while they were at B—— had formed an intimate friendship with a married couple who had been settled there for several years. Frau K. had nursed him during his long illness, and had in that way, he said, earned a title to his undying gratitude. Herr K. had always been most kind to Dora. He had gone on walks with her when he was there, and had made her small presents; but no one had thought any harm of that. Dora had taken the greatest care of the K.'s two little children, and been almost a mother to them.

When Dora and her father had come to see me two years before in the summer, they had been just on their way to stop with Herr and Frau K., who were spending the summer on one of our lakes in the Alps. Dora was to have spent several weeks at the K.'s, while her father had intended to return after a few days. During that time Herr K. had been living there as well. As her father was preparing for his departure the girl had suddenly declared with the greatest determination that she was going with him, and she had in fact put her decision into effect. It was not until some days later that she had thrown any light upon her strange behavior. She had then told her mother—intending that what she said should be passed on to her father—that Herr K. had had the audacity to make her a proposal while they were on a walk after a trip upon the lake.

Herr K. had been called to account by her father and uncle on the next occasion of their meeting, but he had denied in the most emphatic terms having on his side made any advances which could have been open to such a construction. He had then proceeded to throw suspicion upon the girl, saying that he had heard from Frau K. that she took no interest in anything but sexual matters, and that she used to read Mantegazza's *Physiology of Love* and books of that sort in their house on the lake. It was most likely, he had added, that she had been overexcited by such reading and had merely "fancied" the whole scene she had described.

"I have no doubt," continued her father, "that this incident is responsible for Dora's depression and irritability and suicidal ideas. She keeps pressing me to break off relations with Herr K. and more particularly with Frau K., whom she used positively to worship formerly. But that I cannot do. For, to begin with, I myself believe that Dora's tale of the man's immoral suggestions is a fantasy that has forced its way into her mind; and besides, I am bound to Frau K. by ties of honorable friendship and I do not wish to cause her pain. The poor woman is most unhappy with her husband, of whom, by the by, I have no very high opinion. She herself has suffered a great deal with her nerves, and I am her only support. With my state of health I need scarcely assure you that there is nothing wrong with our relations. We are just two poor wretches who give one another what comfort we can by an exchange of friendly sympathy. You know already that I get nothing out of my own wife. But Dora, who inherits my obstinacy, cannot be moved from her hatred of the K.'s. She had her last attack after a conversation in which she had again pressed me to break with them. Please try and bring her to reason."

Her father's words did not always quite tally with this pronouncement, for on other occasions he tried to put the chief blame for Dora's impossible behavior upon her mother—whose peculiarities made the house unbearable for every one. But I had resolved from the first to suspend my judgment of the true state of affairs till I had heard the other side as well.

The experience with Herr K.—his making love to her and the insult to her honor which was involved—seems to provide in Dora's case the psychic trauma which Breuer and I declared long ago to be the indispensable prerequisite for the production of a hysterical disorder…. Dora told me of an earlier episode with Herr K., which was even better calculated to act as a sexual trauma. She was fourteen years old at the time. Herr K. had made an arrangement with her and his wife that they should meet him one afternoon at his place of business in the principal square of B—— so as to have a view of a church festival. He persuaded his wife, however, to stay at home, and

sent away his clerks, so that he was alone when the girl arrived. When the time for the procession approached, he asked to girl to wait for him at the door which opened upon the staircase leading to the upper story, while he pulled down the outside shutters. He then came back, and, instead of going out by the open door, suddenly clasped the girl to him and pressed a kiss upon her lips.

This was surely just the situation to call up a distant feeling of sexual excitement in a girl of fourteen who had never before been approached. But Dora had at that moment a violent feeling of disgust, tore herself free from the man, and hurried past him to the staircase and from there to the street door. She nevertheless continued to meet Herr K. Neither of them ever mentioned the little scene; and according to her account Dora kept it a secret till her confession during the treatment. For some time afterwards, however, she avoided being alone with Herr K. The K.'s had just made plans for an expedition which was to last for some days and on which Dora was to have accompanied them. After the scene of the kiss she refused to join the party, without giving any reason.

In this scene—second in order of mention, but first in order of time—the behavior of this child of fourteen was already entirely and completely hysterical. I should without question consider a person hysterical in whom an occasion for sexual excitement elicited feelings that were preponderantly or exclusively unpleasurable…. Instead of the genital sensation which would certainly have been felt by a healthy girl in such circumstances, Dora was overcome by the unpleasurable feeling which is proper to the mucous membrane at the entrance to the alimentary canal—that is, by disgust….

In accordance with certain rules of symptom-formation which I have come to know, and at the same time taking into account other of the patient's peculiarities, which were otherwise inexplicable—such as her unwillingness to walk past any man whom she saw engaged in eager or affectionate conversation with a lady—I have formed in my own mind the following reconstruction of the scene. I believe that during the man's passionate embrace she felt not merely his kiss upon her lips but also the pressure of his erect member against her body. This perception was revolting to her; it was dismissed from her memory, repressed, and replaced by the innocent sensation of pressure upon her thorax, which in turn derived an excessive intensity from its repressed source. Once more, therefore, we find a displacement from the lower part of the body to the upper.... The pressure of the erect member probably led to an analogous change in the corresponding female organ, the clitoris.... Her avoidance of men who might possibly be in a state of sexual excitement follows the mechanism of a phobia, its purpose being to safeguard her against any revival of the repressed perception.

Questions for Reflection and Discussion

How does Freud understand the buried secrets in the young woman's past? How much is based on his assumptions that there was a psychological cause for her behavior? How might this example help to explain "hysterical" behavior in women of that time?

118. SEXUAL EXCITABILITY AND EUGENICS

Time: early twentieth century CE
Place: United States
Author: Anna Galbraith

Anna Galbraith was a New York physician concerned with the physical health of women. She was part of a mostly American movement of the late nineteenth and early twentieth century known as Social Hygiene, a belief promoted especially by physicians who argued that government and social leaders needed to promote good public health. Social hygienists often repeated conservative arguments on sexuality, but they reconceptualized them as the elimination of disease rather than of vice. The popularity of Galbraith's The Four Epochs of Woman's Life: A Study in Hygiene, *first published in 1901, was such that it was revised and reprinted several times in the decade that followed.*

Sexual Instinct in Women.—After careful observation of the sexes in the married state, it is found that the sexual appetite is less in women than it is in men. Much of this difference in sexual appetite is doubtless due to the chastity of their lives, coupled with and resulting from the difference of education. The girl is taught repression, and the boy expression; that girls must be chaste; that chastity for boys is impossible.

According to the intensity of the sexual instinct women have been divided into three classes: A larger number than is supposed have little or no sexual feeling. Second, those who are subject to strong passion; this class is larger than the first, but small as compared with the whole of their sex. Third, those in whom the sexual appetite is moderate; this class comprises the vast majority of women.

And, even granting to women more pleasure in sexual indulgence than usually comes to her by largest allowance, it is safe to say that in nine cases out of ten maternity, with its early pains and later cares, greatly lessens her power of enjoyment; and that for the larger part of her married life she is either positively distressed by the apparently necessary demands of her husband upon her, and irresponsive to them, or kept to a cheerful response by a self-abnegation and regard for his comfort, not to say fear of his moral aberration, which is a positive drain upon her health and strength.

Excessive Coitus.—Those who are most frequently found to suffer from venereal excesses are the newly married; especially if they have weak constitutions and excitable temperaments. A great deal of mischief is done by two persons of unequal constitutions being matched together; the husband may exhaust the wife or vice versa, the weaker party being constantly tempted to exceed his strength. In all sexual matters there must be a consideration for others. It is not so much from selfishness as from ignorance that such a mistake is made. The ignorance comes from a lamentable morbid delicacy which prevails on all sexual matters, and which prevents all open and rational conversation on them, even between those who have the most intimate knowledge of each other.

When the conjugal act is repeated too often, the man will become gradually conscious of diminished strength, diminished nerve force, and diminished mental powers. Excess weakens a man's energies, and enervates and effeminates him. Moreover, it renders him liable to an infinity of diseases and a readier victim to death.

Not only is the strength of the constitution lowered by the excessive expenditure of force and matter requisite for the perpetuation of the species, but this lowered standard of vitality is transmitted to children. There can be but little doubt that this is one of the reasons why so many healthy parents beget sickly children, who die early. They have exhausted themselves of the material from which a new life is created, and so it is not properly started at the beginning and never reaches its highest development. To the truth of this statement attests the mental imbecility, the pallid and attenuated forms, of the children who are the earlier products of marriage. The effect of excessive coitus in women is seen by the confirmed ill health of so many women after marriage and repeated child-bearing. A large number of these cases are dependent upon alteration and diseases of the genitalia; but a considerable number are unconnected with local disease, and in many other cases the health is never regained after all local phenomena have disappeared.

Sexual excitement in the woman causes certain congestion of the genital organs; and at the time of the orgasm there is a reflex movement which corresponds to erection, and which consists of a peristaltic movement of the tubes and uterus; to the uterus also is ascribed an act of suction by which the spermatozoa are drawn up into its interior. Even when pregnancy does not follow, the too frequent excitation and activity of the uterus in weak constitutions causes illness, first of the genital organs and then of the nervous system....

Causes of Sexual Excitability.—Too frequent genital irritation, onanism, too frequent intercourse, alcohol, too rich and too highly seasoned foods, lack of exercise.

Treatment of Sexual Excitability.—Avoid alcohol and precocious puberty. Strictest attention must be paid to the diet; everything is to be avoided which is difficult of digestion or which retards it. The following articles of diet must all be avoided: cheese, foods seasoned with pepper and curry, highly salted and acid foods, and all rich foods; and meat must be eaten only in moderate quantities. Constipation irritates the genitalia directly and increases the inflammation....

As heavy gymnastics as the strength of the individual will admit, and plenty of exercise out-of-doors must be taken. There must also be constant mental and physical employment. In women sexual excitability is often caused by local diseases, and passes off with their cure; if not, she must use her will-power, and take the various forms of cold baths. Sexual intercourse not oftener than once in two or three weeks, and avoid all intimate approaches; if this is not sufficient, she will have to leave her husband for a few months.

Eugenics is a branch of genetics which refers particularly to the human race; it is the science of producing better human beings by applying the established laws of genetics and heredity. On the positive side it means selecting desirable people as parents; and negatively, preventing propagation by undesirables. It proposes a better race of men through selective mating…. It is to spare both man and woman from the unhappiness that must occur from uncongenial, vicious, or otherwise unfit companionship; and from the burden and the humiliation of unworthy or even degenerate progeny. Viewed from the standpoint of society or of the nation, the problem is to mitigate the burden of inefficiency, vice or degeneracy, and crime that today occasions the chief expense of governments and the chief menace to the progress of the human race. Reproduction is not an individual right…. No child should be born into the world save from good stock. By "good stock" the eugenist means one relatively free from undesirable unit characters; and the most important of these are alcoholism, feeble-mindedness, epilepsy, insanity, pauperism, and criminality. All of these classes should be excluded from the list of those to whom is granted the high privilege of exercising the highest, holiest, and most important function of the race—parenthood….

Eugenic Medical Examinations…. The state should require certificates not only of complete freedom from venereal diseases and degenerative defects from all applicants for marriage, but also a certain grade of physical efficiency…. These papers would be filed and become the property of the state…. These eugenic records, placed on file, would in time come to have very great value, because they would cover the history of successive genera-

tions and would materially add to the family pride not only in keeping the stock pure, but in improving it. And in case of contemplated marriage they could be referred to just as in investigating the title to property.

Questions for Reflection and Discussion

How are Galbraith's views on sexual excitability related to her views on eugenics? What is the individual's role in encouraging greater health, and what is the government's role? How effective would her "cures for sexual excitability" or her "eugenic" program have been?

119. THE NEW SCIENCE OF SEXOLOGY

Time: nineteenth century CE
Place: Germany
Author: Richard von Krafft-Ebing

Richard von Krafft-Ebing, a German physician, became keenly interested in sexuality. In fact, it could be said that he founded the research into sex that would become known as sexology. In 1886 his Psychopathia Sexualis, *meaning "Psychosexual Disorders," first published in German, described his experiences as a physician and his thoughts on the patterns of human sexual behavior that he observed. He coined several new terms, to avoid using existing derogatory ones: "sadism," for example, after the Marquis de Sade, and "urning" for "homosexual," although it did not achieve popularity. Presented here are two case studies; the italicized words were in Latin when his book was first published.*

CASE 125

I am an official, and, as far as I know, come from an untainted family. My father died of an acute disease; my mother, still living, is very nervous. A sister has been very intensely religious for some years. I myself am tall, and, in speech, gait and manners, give a perfectly masculine impression. Measles is the only disease I have had; but since my thirteenth year I have suffered with so-called nervous headaches. My sexual life began in my thirteenth year, when I became acquainted with a boy somewhat older than myself, *with whom I used to delight in touching each other's genitals.* I had the first ejaculation in my fourteenth year. Seduced to onanism by two older schoolmates, I practiced it partly with others and partly alone; in the latter case, however, always with the thought of persons of the female sex. My *sexual lust* was very great, as it is today. Later, I tried to win a pretty, stout servant girl who had very large *breasts; I only was able to get her to bare the upper part of her body in my presence and allow me to kiss her mouth and breasts, then she took my vigorously erect penis in her hand and rubbed it. As much as I enthusiastically begged for intercourse, she only allowed that I might touch her genitals.*

After going to the university, I visited a brothel and succeeded without special effort.

Then an event occurred which brought about a change in me. One evening I accompanied a friend home, and in a mild state of intoxication I grasped him *by the genitals.* He made but slight opposition. I then went up to his room with him, and we practiced mutual masturbation. From that time we indulged in it quite frequently; in fact, it came to *insertion of the penis in the mouth*, with resultant ejaculations. But it is strange that I was not at all in love with this person, but passionately in love with another friend, near whom I never felt the slightest sexual excitement, and whom I never connected with sexual matters, even in thought. My visits to brothels, where I was gladly received, became more infrequent; in

my friend I found a substitute, and did not desire sexual intercourse with women. We never practiced pederasty [anal intercourse?]. That word was not even known between us. From the beginning of this relation with my friend, I again masturbated more frequently, and naturally the thought of females receded more and more into the background, and I thought more and more about young, handsome, strong men with the largest possible genitals. I preferred young fellows, from sixteen to twenty-five years old, without beards, but they had to be handsome and clean. Young laborers dressed in trousers of Manchester cloth or English leather, particularly masons, especially excited me. Persons in my own position had hardly any effect on me; but, at the sight of one of those strapping fellows of the lower class, I experienced marked sexual excitement. It seems to me that the touch of such trousers, the opening of them and the grasping of the penis, as well as kissing the fellow, would be the greatest delight.

My sensibility to female charms is somewhat dulled; yet in sexual intercourse with a woman, particularly when she has well developed *breasts*, I am always potent without the help of imagination. I have never attempted to make use of a young laborer, or the like, for the satisfaction of my evil desires, and never shall; but I often feel a longing to do it. I often impress on myself the mental image of such a man, and then masturbate at home. I am absolutely devoid of taste for female work. I rather like to move in female society, but dancing is repugnant to me. I have a lively interest in the fine arts. That my sexual sense is partly reversed is, I believe, in part due to greater convenience, which keeps me from entering into a relation with a girl; as the latter is a matter of too much trouble. To be constantly visiting houses of prostitution is, for aesthetic reasons, repugnant to me; and thus I am returning to solitary onanism, which is very difficult for me to avoid.

Hundreds of times I have said to myself that, in order to have a normal sexual sense, it would be necessary for me, first of all, to overcome my irresistible passion for onanism,—a practice so repugnant to my aesthetic feeling. Again and again I have resolved with all my might to fight this passion; but I am still unsuccessful. When I felt the sexual impulse gaining strength, instead of seeking satisfaction in the natural manner, I preferred to masturbate, because I felt that I would thus have more enjoyment. And yet experience has taught me that I am always potent with girls, and that, too, without trouble and without the vision of masculine genitals. In one case, however, I did not attain ejaculation because the woman—it was in a brothel—was devoid of every charm. I cannot avoid the thought and severe self-accusation that, to a certain extent, my inverted sexuality is the result of excessive onanism; and this especially depresses me, because I am compelled to acknowledge that I scarcely feel strong enough to overcome this vice by the force of my own will.

CASE 126

Ilma S., aged twenty-nine, single, merchant's daughter; of a family having bad nervous taint. Father was a drinker and died by suicide, as also did the patient's brother and sister. A sister suffered with convulsive hysteria. Mother's father shot himself while insane. Mother was sickly, and paralyzed after apoplexy. The patient never had any severe illness. She was bright, enthusiastic and dreamy. Menses at the age of eighteen without difficulty; but thereafter they were very irregular. At fourteen, chlorosis and catalepsy from fright. Later, serious hysteria and an attack of hysterical insanity. At eighteen, relations with a young

man which were not platonic. This man's love was passionately returned. From statements of the patient, it seemed that she was very sensual, and after separation from her lover practiced masturbation.

After this she led a romantic life. In order to earn a living, she put on male clothing, and became a tutor; but she gave up her place because her mistress, not knowing her sex, fell in love with her and courted her. Then she became a railway employee. In the company of her companions, in order to conceal her sex, she was compelled to visit brothels with them, and hear the most vulgar stories. This became so distasteful to her that she gave up her place, resumed the garments of a female, and again sought to earn her living. She was arrested for theft, and on account of severe hystero-epilepsy was sent to the hospital. There inclination and impulse toward the same sex were discovered. The patient became troublesome on account of passionate love for female nurses and patients. Her sexual inversion was considered congenital. With regard to this, the patient made some interesting statements:

I am judged incorrectly, if it is thought that I feel myself a man toward the female sex. In my whole thought and feeling I am much more a woman. Did I not love my cousin as only a woman can love a man? The change of my feelings originated in this, that, in Pesth, dressed as a man, I had an opportunity to observe my cousin. I saw that I was wholly deceived in him. That gave me terrible heart-pangs. I knew that I could never love another man; that I belonged to those who love but once. Of similar effect was the fact that, in the society of my companions at the railway, I was compelled to hear the most offensive language and visit the most disreputable houses. As a result of the insight into men's motives gained in this way, I took an unconquerable dislike to them. However, since I am of a very passionate nature and need to have some loving person on whom to depend, and to whom I can wholly surrender myself, I felt myself more and more powerfully drawn toward intelligent women and girls who were in sympathy with me.

The antipathic sexual instinct of this patient, which was clearly acquired, expressed itself in a stormy and decidedly sensual way, and was further augmented by masturbation; because constant control in hospitals made sexual satisfaction with the same sex impossible. Character and occupation remained feminine. There were no manifestations of viraginity. According to information lately received by the author, this patient, after two years of treatment in an asylum, was entirely freed from her neurosis and sexual inversion, and discharged cured.

Questions for Reflection and Discussion

How do these individuals understand their sexual problems? What do they consider to be the cause of their same-sex attractions? What does Dr. Krafft-Ebing consider to be the cause?

120. THE CORSET

Time: nineteenth century CE
Place: United States
Artist: unknown

This 1882 advertisement for corsets, racy enough in its depiction of a partially undressed woman, also demonstrates their effect on women's bodies. The corset's popularity rose in the late nineteenth century as that of the hoopskirt declined, since an "hourglass figure" or "wasp

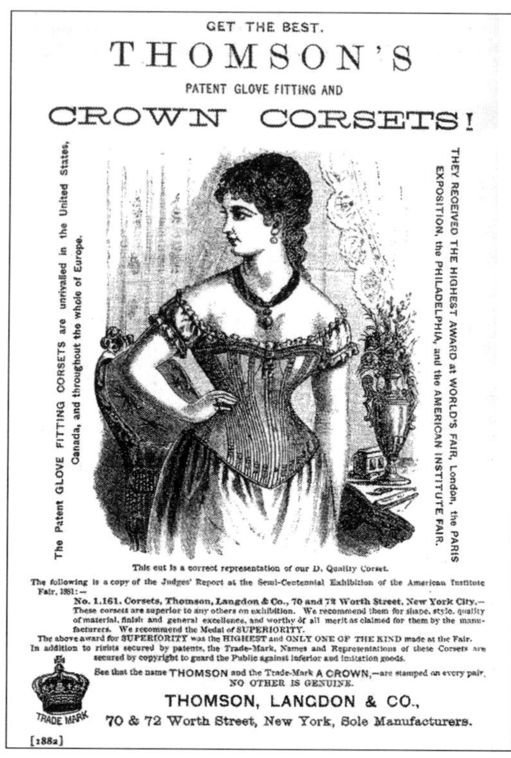

waist" (to use two contemporary metaphors) could no longer be obtained by enlarging the appearance of the hips. Any freedom of movement gained for women by the abandonment of the hoopskirt, with its bone or metal supports, was mostly lost by the corset's constriction on the diaphragm. Indeed, both fainting couches and smelling salts were made necessary by the resulting inhibition of women's breathing. Physicians condemned its use with only gradual success, suggesting that it made childbearing more difficult. The corset made a brief popular comeback in the 1950s but is worn today mostly as a fetish item.

Questions for Reflection and Discussion

Is it difficult to believe that many women would participate in a fashion that was dangerous to their health? What does this fashion say about women's participation in late nine-teenth-century society? What does it mean that physicians' advice on the subject was so often ignored?

121. THE KINSEY REPORT

Time: mid-twentieth century CE
Place: United States
Author: Alfred Kinsey and others

Few scientific reports caused such a stir as Kinsey's Sexual Behavior in the Human Male, *published in 1948 and followed by* Sexual Behavior in the Human *Female in 1953. Physicians had conducted earlier sexual studies, but Kinsey, a professor of biology at Indiana University, collected a team of assistants who interviewed about 20,000 individuals face-to-face across the US to arrive at these reports. The numbers of them involved in what were considered to be morally reprehensible and isolated behaviors were most shocking: Almost two-thirds of women and almost all men engaged in masturbation; about a quarter of married women and half of married men had engaged in extramarital sex; and about a quarter of all women and half of all men had engaged in homosexual sex at least once. After that it was much harder to claim that these behaviors were rare; in the case of masturbation, it abruptly ended medical discussion that it was dangerous to one's health. See table on page 280.*

Questions for Reflection and Discussion

How does the use of statistics change the nature of the discussion about sexuality? What might be the ways that these studies could be called into question for their accuracy? Can it be assumed that what was true about how Americans behaved in the 1940s and 50s would still be true today? Why or why not?

122. FRIGIDITY

Time: late twentieth century CE
Place: United States
Author: Fritz Kant

Fritz Kant, a psychiatrist and neurologist at the University of Alabama, published Frigidity: Dynamics and Treatment *in 1969. Frigidity was a difficult diagnosis: To some it meant a woman's unwillingness to engage in sexual relations, or her physical discomfort during sex; to others it meant her inability to achieve orgasm. Kant's opinion, and that of many twentieth-century psychologists, was that it was related to marital and social problems.*

It is not possible to understand the problem of frigidity in women by comparing it with impotence in men. In the usual cases of frigidity, the dynamics are conscious or unconscious resistance to giving herself completely to the male partner. The causes that have led to this attitude vary with the individual case. Organic causes are rare.... The feminine woman's response is closely related to love. The potency of the man is not. The woman can usually respond to the male partner only when she is in love. We have ample case material showing this convincingly. It is common knowledge that men can be potent in sexual relations with women to whom they are not emotionally attached in any way, for example, prostitutes.

Certain women have the capacity to identify completely with their men and are happy in their role as encouraging and contributing companions. They inspire and rejoice in their men's success as their own. They may be the most intelligent and lovely women, but they are unaggressive and not competitive. They have, in addition, other interests of a charitable, artistic, or political nature. Even if they are successful in a profession or any

MASTURBATION	IN FEMALES	IN MALES
Learning to Masturbate		
Self-discovery	57%	28%
Verbal and printed sources	43%	75%
Petting	12%	—
Observation	11%	40%
Homosexual contact	3%	9%
Relation to Age and Marital Status		
Accumulative incidence		
Total: experience	62%	93%
Total: with orgasm	58%	92%
By age 12	12%	21%
By age 15	20%	82%
By age 20	33%	92%
Frequency (active median) to orgasm	UNIFORM TO MID-FIFTIES	STEADY DECREASE
Average, unmarried groups	0.3-0.4 per wk	0.4-1.8 per wk
Average, married groups	0.2 per wk	0.1-0.2 per wk
Techniques of Masturbation		
Genital manipulation	84%	95%
Thigh pressures	10%	RARE
Muscular tensions	5%	RARE
Vaginal insertions, ever	20%	—
Fantasy alone	2%	EXTREMELY RARE

EXTRA-MARITAL COITUS	IN FEMALES	IN MALES
Relation to Age		
Accumulative incidence, experience		
By age 20	6%	
By age 30	16%	
By age 40	26%	±50%
Nature and Conditions of Extra-Marital Coitus		
Partners		
One	41%	
Two to five	40%	
Number of years involved		
Depends on length of marriage	Yes	Yes
One year or less	42%	
Over ten years	10%	

HOMOSEXUAL RESPONSES AND CONTACTS	IN FEMALES	IN MALES
Relation to Age and Marital Status		
Accumulative incidence		
Homosexual response, by age 45	28%	±50%
Homosexual experience, by age 45	20%	
Single	26%	±50%
Married	3%	±10%
Previously married	10%	
Homo. exper., to orgasm, by age 45	13%	±37%
Number of partners		
1-2	71%	51%
Over 10	4%	22%

other kind of gainful employment, they retain a concern encompassing their entire being in the stature and success of their men and their children. The home and the raising of their children remain an important domain. They derive satisfaction from this role which gives them awareness of success and leaves no room for envy. These women are not frigid, but only after long courting do they allow any intimacies.

In contrast to the woman described, from whom emanates the extraordinary beauty of femininity, we find the woman with the masculinity complex, characterized by aggressive tendencies and envy of the male. This attitude frequently originates from frustrating experiences in her role as a woman. Even after marriage and the birth of several children, she must find satisfaction in a job or profession to overcome her unconscious feeling of inferiority towards the male sex. However it is often marked by feelings of guilt with regard to her duties towards her family. The woman who has given birth to children is, of course, handicapped in the competition with the male. During her childbearing period in the twenties and beginning thirties, the male acquires the education and preparation for his position in life. To start at a later period in life is much harder for women. Because of their rebellion towards what they interpret as superiority of the male, they unconsciously and, in some instances, consciously resist a response to the lovemaking of the male. They are either frigid or they respond rarely.

For some men, it appears to be traumatic if they are not able to bring the partner to the point of response by normal intercourse alone. Also, some women think there must be something essentially wrong if they are not able to achieve an orgasm in this way. Although some manual stimulation of the clitoris in the precoital period of foreplay is common, it may be distressing for both parties if the fixation is so strong that a response can be produced only by manipulation of the clitoris.

To overcome this difficulty, the couple will need advice. Both partners have to cooperate and should be told that the period of adjustment will require perseverance and time. After genital union has taken place, the male partner will stimulate the clitoris at the same time that cohabitation progresses. At the first signs of an approaching orgasm, manipulation of the clitoris should cease while coital movements continue. Gradually the period of clitoral stimulation will be shortened until, in many cases, it can be abandoned completely. In others some initial manual stimulation will still be required, however this will not be of significance. In a small group, nothing was achieved because the program was not carried out consistently. The male partner was not concerned and wanted a rapid female response. Producing the female response before or after sexual union should be avoided. It is essential for marital harmony and complete fulfillment that the response occurs in the closeness of the embrace during sexual union.

Questions for Reflection and Discussion

Does Kant's use of "common knowledge" undermine or bolster his scientific claims? How many of his opinions seem based on "common knowledge" of his day rather than scientific method? How might the concerns of his day have influenced his scientific method? What sexual ideal does he have in mind?

123. SOCIOBIOLOGY

Time: late twentieth century CE
Place: United States
Author: Edward O. Wilson

Wilson, a Harvard professor of biology, pioneered the science he called sociobiology, an attempt to understand the laws of human interaction with the help of physiology, genetics, primate studies, and other aspects of biology. This excerpt from Sociobiology: The New Synthesis, *published in 1975, is one of the earliest of Wilson's many books that explain his theories. A year after its publication, Wilson won the National Medal of Science.*

Perhaps the earliest form of barter in early human societies was the exchange of meat captured by the males for plant food gathered by the females. If living hunter-gatherer societies reflect the primitive state, this exchange formed an important element in a distinctive kind of sexual bond....

[Some scholars have] argued from ethnographic evidence that a key early step in human social evolution was the use of women in barter. As males acquired status through the control of females, they used them as objects of exchange to cement alliances and bolster kinship networks. Preliterate societies are characterized by complex rules of marriage that can often be interpreted directly as power brokerage. This is particularly the case where the elementary negative marriage rules, proscribing certain types of unions, are supplemented by positive rules that direct which exchanges must be made. Within individual Australian aboriginal societies two moieties exist between which marriages are permitted. The men of each moiety trade nieces, or more specifically their sisters' daughters. Power accumulates with age, because a man can control the descendants of nieces as remote as the daughter of his sister's daughter. Combined with polygyny, the system insures both political and genetic advantage to the old men of the tribe. For all its intricacy, the formalization of marital exchanges between tribes has the same approximate genetic effect as the haphazard wandering of male monkeys from one troop to another or the exchange of young mature females between chimpanzee populations. Approximately 7.5 percent of marriages contracted among Australian aborigines prior to European influence were intertribal, and similar rates have been reported in Brazilian Indians and other preliterate societies. It will be recalled that gene flow of the order of 10 percent per generation is more than enough to counteract fairly intensive natural pressures that tend to differentiate populations. Thus intertribal marital exchanges are a major factor in creating the observed high degree of genetic similarity among populations. The ultimate adaptive basis of exogamy is not gene flow per se but rather the avoidance of inbreeding. Again, a 10 percent gene flow is adequate for the purpose. The microstructure of human social organization is based on sophisticated mutual assessments that lead to the making of contracts....

The building block of nearly all human societies is the nuclear family. The populace of an American industrial city, no less than a band of hunter-gatherers in the Australian desert, is organized around this unit. In both cases the family moves between regional communities, maintaining complex ties with primary kin by means of visits (or telephone calls and letters) and the exchange of gifts. During the day the women and children remain in the residential area while the men forage for game or its symbolic equivalent in the form of barter and money. The males cooperate in bands to hunt or deal with neighboring groups. If not actually blood relations, they tend at least to act as "bands of brothers." Sexual bonds are carefully contracted in observance with tribal customs and are intended to be permanent. Polygamy, either covert or explicitly sanctioned by custom, is practiced predominantly by the males. Sexual behavior is nearly continuous through the menstrual cycle and marked by extended foreplay....

[One scholar], drawing on the data of … others, has enumerated the unique features of human sexuality that he considers to be associated with the loss of body hair: the rounded and protuberant breasts of the young woman, the flushing of areas of skin during coition, the vaso-dilation and increased erogenous sensitivity of the lips, soft portions of the nose, ear, nipples, areolae, and genitals, and the large size of the male penis, especially during erection. As Darwin himself noted in 1871, even the naked skin of the woman is used as a sexual releaser. All of these alterations serve to cement the permanent bonds which are unrelated in time to the moment of ovulation. Estrus has been reduced to a vestige, to the consternation of those who attempt to practice birth control by the rhythm method. Sexual behavior has been largely dissociated from the act of fertilization. It is ironic that religionists who forbid sexual activity except for purposes of procreation should do so on the basis of "natural law." Theirs is a misguided effort in comparative ethology, based on the incorrect assumption that in reproduction man is essentially like other animals.

The extent and formalization of kinship prevailing in almost all human societies are also unique features of the biology of our species. Kinship systems provide at least three distinct advantages. First they bind alliances between tribes and subtribal units and provide a conduit for the conflict-free emigration of young members. Second they are an important part of the bartering system by which certain males achieve dominance and leadership. Finally, they serve as a homeostatic device for seeing groups through hard times. When food grows scarce, tribal units can call on their allies for altruistic assistance in a way unknown in other social primates. The Athapaskan Dogrib Indians, a hunter-gatherer people of the northwestern Canadian arctic, provide one example. The Athapaskans are organized loosely by the bilateral primary linkage principle. Local bands wander through a common territory, making intermittent contacts and exchanging members by intermarriage. When famine strikes, the endangered bands can coalesce with those temporarily better off. A second example is the Yanomamo of South America, who rely on kin when their crops are destroyed by enemies.

As societies evolved from bands through tribes into chiefdoms and states, some of the modes of bonding were extended beyond kinship networks to include other kinds of alliances and economic agreements. Because the networks were then larger, the lines of communication longer, and the interactions more diverse, the total systems became vastly more complex. But the moralistic rules underlying these arrangements appear not to have been altered a great deal. The average individual still operates under a formalized code no more elaborate than that governing the members of hunter-gatherer societies.

Questions for Reflection and Discussion

Which scientific and academic disciplines does Wilson use for his sociobiology? How compelling is the biological imperative at work in human relationships, according to Wilson? How conscious are human beings of these biological factors?

124. SCIENTIFIC MATCHMAKING

Time: mid-twentieth century CE
Place: United States
Author: Karl Miles Wallace

Wallace, a sociologist by profession and a Mormon by belief, founded the Personal Acquaintance Service in 1947. Love Is More Than Luck, his autobiography from which this excerpt is taken, described how he wanted to

*create something to help dating couples coun-
teract the greater anonymity of modern urban
life. So he developed a questionnaire based on
five personality traits that he considered important to romantic compatibility: 1) temperament,
2) sociability, 3) conformity to social standards, 4)
attitude toward sex, and 5) religious orthodoxy.
Then he matched couples based on their similar
responses and claimed an overwhelming success
rate. Here are some of the questions he asked.*

CONFORMITY TO SOCIAL STANDARDS

Should sex education be taught in our public
  elementary schools?
Should women have as much right to propose
  dates to men, as men to women?
Are shows with scantily dressed performers a
  bad influence on most people?
Is it all right for a married man to take
  another woman to lunch?
Should our divorce laws be more strict?
Should women enter the profession of law?
Do you think trial by jury is the most effec-
  tive way of securing justice?
Should a school teacher be allowed to smoke
  and drink in night clubs?
Is stealing sometimes justifiable?
Would a respectable unmarried couple take a
  trip together without a chaperone?

ATTITUDE TOWARD SEX

Do you enjoy the company of the opposite sex
  more than that of your own?
Do you like to be kissed and caressed?
Are you often disgusted with sexual things?
Do you have an affectionate and passionately
  warm nature?
Can happiness in marriage be achieved with-
  out good sexual compatibility?
Do you think romantic love is important to
  successful marriage?
Are you strongly attracted to members of the
  opposite sex?

Do kissing and petting among young men
  and women today disgust you?
Do you think the importance of sex is greatly
  overemphasized today?
Could you be happy in marriage with a mate
  who was not very affectionate?

Questions for Reflection and Discussion

Do Wallace's questions get at the heart of romantic compatibility? If not, what sorts of questions
would? Does scientific matchmaking have a better chance at success than random acquaintance
or marriages arranged by families?

125. EVELYN HOOKER'S RESEARCH ON HOMOSEXUALITY

Time: mid-twentieth century CE
Place: United States
Author: Evelyn Hooker

*One aspect of sexuality on which scientists were
greatly divided in the twentieth century was
homosexuality. Older scientific approaches condemned it as deviant sexuality and associated
it with mental illness; some scientists challenged those assumptions. One of the earliest
of the latter group was psychologist Dr. Evelyn
Hooker, who presented a paper at the 1956
American Psychological Association meeting,
after conducting standard psychological exams
that showed no noticeable difference between
results for heterosexual and homosexual men.
She later described her struggles with preserving objectivity.*

The research began with a relatively simple
design—to compare a group of adult, male,
overt homosexuals who were not seeking therapy for homosexuality or other problems and
who were able to manage a viable way of life
with a group of heterosexual males who met

the same criteria in order to determine whether particular patterns of personality organization characterized a particular psychosexual object choice. In the course of the interviews with the homosexual men, it became clear that the essential features of personality organization could not be understood apart from the social setting in which they were functioning, so that the scope of the research was extended to the total homosexual community. Perhaps a more accurate way of describing the sequence is to say that the social patterns of the research subjects, about which I had been asking questions from the beginning, inevitably led me to an interest in the homosexual community, or "world," as a form of social organization and to the important theoretical question of the relation between personality and social organization.

The first problems were finding research subjects and securing their cooperation.... Having made a pilot study of an informal group of friends at their invitation shortly before beginning the research project, I had a working knowledge of the special language, the general "round of life," and the areas of concern and concealment. Perhaps most important, I had found that direct, genuine ways of establishing relationships with persons whose patterns of behavior differ from one's own were as effective in producing cooperation in this group as in any other. Although my original access to a group of research subjects had been by chance and had, in part, made it easier to establish a research contact with homosexual organizations, there is every reason to believe that today any qualified research worker could secure the initial cooperation of potential research subjects from any one or all of the three sources.

In asserting that locating potential sources of subjects and securing their cooperation does not involve unusual difficulties I am making some assumptions about the qualifications of the investigator which should be made explicit.

In addition to the usual prerequisites of training in the social sciences and experience in field work which involves working with persons whose social patterns differ markedly from his own, he must have developed the capacity to view the behavior of homosexuals and to listen to whatever he hears as simply matters of interest. He must be able to look *with* them at their world. The researcher is not an agent of change; his task is to see "how things are," to understand the phenomenon which he is investigating. Research on preventive or therapeutic aspects of homosexuality might, of course, alter the role of the investigator so that he does become an agent of change.

Objectivity, as the prime qualification for any scientific undertaking, is never more needed than in the relationship established with homosexuals and the world in which they live. If the investigator cannot detach himself from the evaluative attitudes of the larger society, on the one hand, or of the homosexual world, on the other, and take a dispassionate, objective view, he cannot succeed in obtaining either the cooperation of research subjects or reliable information about their world. That this is extraordinarily difficult to do, in view of the intensity with which homosexuality is condemned in some sectors of our society, on the one hand, and of the intensity with which some homosexuals view that condemnation, on the other, will be so apparent as to require no documentation. That the objective view is not achieved all at once or that, even having been achieved, it is not constantly maintained, will also be apparent. The struggle is continuous.

Questions for Reflection and Discussion

How does Hooker describe the obstacles to the scientist achieving objectivity? Does the scientific study of sexuality present particular obstacles?

126. NEITHER MEN NOR WOMEN

Time: early twentieth century CE
Place: India
Author: Hakim Muhammad Yusuf Hasan

While most of the scientific ideas about sexuality came out of a Western context, educated individuals throughout the world had access to these ideas and adapted them in different ways. One example is a scientific treatise by Hakim Muhammad Yusuf Hasan, called The Virgin (Do Shiza), *and written in Urdu, the dominant language of the Muslims of North India, at a time when India was part of the British Empire. Due to the book's popularity, it was reprinted three times before 1935. It demonstrated how scientific ideas might be used to reinterpret older customs, in this case, the* hijras *or self-castrating priests of a Hindu goddess.*

I have informed the readers of the necessary details about men and women, boys and girls. Therefore it is necessary to discuss those beings who are neither men nor women. Eunuchs exist not only in India and in the East but also in Europe and America.

In India the eunuchs are formally organized. There is complete agreement and unity among them and they are constantly intent on expanding their community. You can well ask what sort of wretched person would want to join the community of these *hijras.* You might not know but there are countless such men who are counted as men but whose emotions are exactly the same as those of women. Some of these men are married and have children but in them is an inherent emotion which makes them love only other men. They might be with women for sexual needs or to fulfill the needs of being man and wife. However, they are not completely satisfied with this. Their desires are not fulfilled and they are not happy. In their

hearts they wish that they were with an attractive man, one with large dark eyes, a rosy and glowing complexion, red lips and a beautiful mustache, one who would take them in his arms, hold them tight and make love to them. They are constantly in search of such a man. Sometimes they are successful in finding such a match. European doctors have mentioned such cases in their medical books. In India too, after some search, such men can be found. The moment they get the opportunity, men with such feelings join the community of *hijras.*

Since there are men who prefer to love men and who find satisfaction in it, there is no reason why there should not be women who dislike men and prefer other women. Therefore there are women who to all intents and purposes are free from the qualities of women and have manly qualities. Such women are well built and slightly fair with a muddy complexion. Desire and lust drips from their eyes. They laugh often and prefer masculine manners. They stride along with their heads held high and they try to make friends with beautiful women. Gradually they entrap them in their magic and get closer to them. Simple, respectable women, trusting them as other women, accept their love and friendliness as affection. Slowly they start kissing and petting. Finally they seduce them towards illicit relations. If by chance or in the course of joking and playing, a woman falls into their hands, we should take this as the end of that poor creature. These illicit relations develop so fast that in a couple of months the poor woman starts looking as if she suffers from tuberculosis. The simple one turns into the unbought slave of the manly, shameless one. She constantly waits for the moment when her husband leaves the house. She sacrifices her wealth, honor and health to the shameless one. She begins to hate her husband and wants to spend all her time with this shameless one. If, by chance, the husband finds out, then such lewd acts are stopped. Otherwise, the woman loses her health and finds a place in the grave. The shameless one then starts to entrap some other woman.

Even if such events are rare and unusual, it is necessary to mention them so that men can protect their homes from the poisonous atmosphere that can be created by those women who pay visits in order to get familiar with the wife while the husband is away. I have treated one such woman. This woman admitted to her crimes in detail but I cannot describe them here because they are obscene. Physicians and the intelligent will recognize the necessary symptoms.

Questions for Reflection and Discussion

How does medical science and popular imagination combine in this excerpt? Why might sex between men be treated as a psychological issue, but sex between women be treated as a medical threat?

127. *THE HITE REPORT*

Time: late twentieth century CE
Place: United States
Author: Shere Hite

The Hite Report: A Nationwide Study on Female Sexuality *was first published in 1976. As Hite expressed in her preface, she had asked women about sex and then published the results under headings that included masturbation, orgasm, clitoral stimulation, lesbianism, the sexual revolution, and other areas that covered a range of women's sexual lives not often discussed even in scientific literature. Most of the study consists of the women's answers, but Hite also added her own commentary in the introduction to each section. In this excerpt, she laments women's "sexual slavery" to men, her thoughts that begin a chapter with that title.*

"I have wanted to have orgasms with a man for years—about twelve. Seems like the impossible dream. I can be a loving eunuch with him, but only a full sexual person by myself."

Why does this woman say this? Why, if she can be "a full sexual person" by herself, can she be only "a loving eunuch" with a man? This woman's comment points up a dilemma that has become clearer and clearer throughout this book. We have seen that heterosexual sex usually involves the pattern of foreplay, penetration, and intercourse ending with male ejaculation—and that all too often the woman does not orgasm. But women *know* very well how to orgasm during masturbation, whenever they want. If they know how to have orgasms whenever they want, why don't they feel free to use this knowledge during sex with men? Why do women habitually satisfy men's needs during sex and ignore their own?

The fact is that the role of women in sex, as in every other aspect of life, has been to serve the needs of others—men and children. And just as women did not recognize their oppression in a general sense until recently, just so sexual slavery has been an almost unconscious way of life for most women—based on what was said to be an eternally unchanging biological impulse. We have seen, however (in the intercourse chapter), that our model of sex and physical relations is culturally (not biologically) defined, and can be redefined—or undefined. We need not continue to have only one model of physical relations—foreplay, penetration, intercourse, and ejaculation.

Women are sexual slaves insofar as they are (justifiably) afraid to "come out" with their own sexuality, and forced to satisfy others' needs and ignore their own. As one woman put it, "Sex can be political in the sense that it can involve a power structure where the woman is unwilling or unable to get what she really needs for her fullest amount of pleasure, but the man is getting what he wants, and the woman, like an unquestioning and unsuspecting lackey, is gratefully supplying it." The truth is that almost everything in our society pushes women toward defining their sexuality only as intercourse with men, and toward not defining themselves as full persons in sex with men. Lack of sexual satisfaction is another sign of the oppression of women. This, of course, is not to say that women don't like sex, or that they don't enjoy intercourse in many ways. When asked if they enjoyed sex, almost all woman said yes, they did. Furthermore, there was no correlation with frequency of orgasm: women who did not orgasm with their partners were just as likely to say they enjoyed sex as women who did. And women who never orgasmed during intercourse were just as likely to say they enjoyed intercourse as women who did. However, the important question is: What is it that women enjoy about sex/intercourse, and what do women mean when they say they like them?

Questions for Reflection and Discussion

How does Hite's philosophy of asking women about sex and then reporting their answers shift the role of expert opinion in scientific method? How are this shift and her conclusions related to her feminist ideals?

128. NANCY CHODOROW ON CHILDREN'S SEXUAL DEVELOPMENT

Time: late twentieth century CE
Place: United States
Author: Nancy Chodorow

Nancy Chodorow was one of a number of psychoanalytically trained feminists who attempted to revise and correct Freud and other early psychologists on gender and sexual dynamics. In this excerpt, from The Reproduction of Mothering *published in 1978, Chodorow attempted to improve Freud's œdipal complex, his theory to explain the development of heterosexuality, by re-examining the relationships between children and their parents.*

According to psychoanalytic theory, heterosexual erotic orientation is a primary outcome of the œdipus complex for both sexes. Boys and girls differ in this, however. Boys retain one primary love object throughout their boyhood. For this reason, the development of masculine heterosexual object choice is relatively continuous…. In theory, a boy resolves his œdipus complex by repressing his attachment to his mother. He is therefore ready in adulthood to find a primary relationship with someone *like* his mother…. Things are not so simple for girls…. Because her first love object is a woman, a girl, in order to attain her proper heterosexual orientation, must transfer her primary object choice to her father and men. This creates asymmetry in the feminine and masculine œdipus complex, and difficulties in the development of female sexuality, given heterosexuality as a developmental goal.

For girls, just as for boys, mothers are primary love objects. As a result, the structural inner object setting of female heterosexuality differs from that of males. When a girl's father does become an important primary person, it is in the context of a bisexual relational triangle. A girl's reaction to him is emotionally in reaction to, interwoven and competing for primacy with, her relation to her mother. A girl usually turns to her father as an object of primary interest from the exclusivity of the relationship to her mother, but this libidinal turning to her father does not substitute for her attachment to her mother. Instead, a girl retains her preœdipal tie to her mother (an intense tie involved with issues of primary identification, primary love, dependence, and separation) and builds œdipal attachments to both her mother and her father upon it. These attachments are characterized by eroticized demands for exclusivity, feelings of competition, and jealousy. She retains the internalized early relationship, including its implications for the nature of her definition of self, and internalizes these other relationships in addition to and not as replacements for it.

For girls, then, there is no absolute change of object, nor exclusive attachment to their fathers. Moreover, a father's behavior and family role, and a girl's relationship to him, are crucial to the development of heterosexual orientation in her. But fathers are comparatively unavailable physically and emotionally. They are not present as much and are not primary caretakers, and their own training for masculinity may have led them to deny emotionality. Because of the father's lack of availability to his daughter, and because of the intensity of the mother-daughter relationship in which she participates, girls tend not to make a total transfer of affection to their fathers but to remain also involved with their mothers, and to oscillate emotionally between mother and father....

Freud speaks to the way that women seek to recapture their relationship with their mother in heterosexual relationships. He suggests that as women "change object" from mother to father, the mother remains their primary internal object, so that they often impose on their relation to their father, and later to men, the issues which preoccupy them in their internal relation to their mother. They look in relations to men for gratifications that they want from a woman. Freud points to the common clinical discovery of a woman who has apparently taken her father as a model for her choice of husband, but whose marriage in fact repeats the conflicts and feelings of her relationship with her mother....

But children seek to escape from their mother as well as return to her. Fathers serve in part to break a daughter's primary unity with and dependence on her mother. For this and a number of other reasons, fathers and men are idealized. A girl's father provides a last ditch escape from maternal omnipotence, so a girl cannot risk driving him away.... Thus a daughter looks to her father for a sense of separateness and for the same confirmation of her specialness that her brother receives from her mother. She (and the woman she becomes) is willing to deny her father's limitations (and those of her lover or husband) as long as she feels loved.... Because her sense of self is firmer, and because œdipal love for her father is not so threatening, a girl does not "resolve" her œdipus complex to the same extent as a boy. This means that she grows up more concerned with both internalized and external object-relationships, while men tend to repress their œdipal needs for love and relationship. At the same time, men often become intolerant and disparaging of those who can express needs for love, as they attempt to deny their own needs.

Men defend themselves against the threat posed by love, but needs for love do not disappear through repression. Their training for masculinity and repression of affective relational needs, and their primarily nonemotional and impersonal relationships in the public world make deep primary relationships with other men hard to come by. Given this, it is not surprising that men tend to find themselves in heterosexual relationships.... Women have not repressed affective needs. They still want love and narcissistic confirmation and may be willing to put up with limitations in their masculine lover or husband in exchange for evidence of caring and love....

Men both look for and fear exclusivity. Throughout their development, they have tended to repress their affective relational needs, and to develop ties based more on categorical and abstract role expectations, particularly with other males. They are likely to participate in an intimate heterosexual relationship with the ambivalence created by an intensity which one both wants and fears—demanding from women what men are at the same time afraid of receiving.

Questions for Reflection and Discussion

How convincingly does Chodorow describe the emotional development of girls and boys? How much does her analysis rest only on certain types of family dynamics? Why does she avoid the issue of homosexual desire in her analysis?

SOURCES AND FURTHER READING

There is a vast literature on the competition and connection between religion and science, most of which, in English at any rate, assumes that Christianity and/or Judaism is the religion in question, and much of which aims at a reconciliation of these viewpoints. Works with a historical focus are less likely to attempt to resolve the disputes and simply outline them. Recent among these are James Arieti and Patrick A. Wilson's *The Scientific and the Divine: Conflict and Reconciliation from Ancient Greece to the Present* (Lanham, MD: Rowman & Littlefield, 2003); Harold Nebelsick's *The Renaissance, the Reformation, and the Rise of Science* (Edinburgh: T & T Clark, 1992); *Evangelicals and Science in Historical Perspective*, David N. Livingstone et al., eds. (Oxford: Oxford University Press, 1999); John Hedley Brooke's *Science and Religion: Some Historical Perspectives* (Cambridge: Cambridge

University Press, 1991); Ian Barbour's *Religion and Science: Historical and Contemporary Issues* (San Francisco: HarperSanFrancisco, 1997; orig. pub. 1990). These works, however, show little interest in competing ideas about sexuality; one must go to studies of contemporary issues for that, such as the essays in *Integrating Faith and Science through Natural Family Planning*, Richard Fehring and Theresa Notare, eds. (Milwaukee, WI: Marquette University Press, 2004), for example, emphasizing similarities between the two approaches; or in *Same Sex: Debating the Ethics, Science, and Culture of Homosexuality*, ed. John Corvino (Lanham, MD: Rowman & Littlefield, 1997), emphasizing dissimilarities.

114. "The Problem with Masturbation" is taken from Jean Stengers and Anne Van Heck, *Masturbation: The History of a Great Terror*, Kathryn Hoffman, trans. (New York: Palgrave, 2001), 49–50.

Stengers and Van Heck's book is the best place to begin to learn more about the anxieties about masturbation. See also Thomas Laqueur's *Solitary Sex: A Cultural History of Masturbation* (New York: Zone, 2003); or *Solitary Pleasures: The Historical, Literary, and Artistic Discourses of Autoeroticism*, Paula Bennett and Vernon Rosario, eds. (New York: Routledge, 1995). Numerous treatises warned their readers about the dangers of masturbation; ones that I have located include Cornelius Eldridge's *Self-Enervation: Its Consequences and Treatment* (Chicago: C.S. Halsey, 1869); or Wilhelm Stekel's *Auto-Erotism: A Psychiatric Study of Onanism and Neurosis*, James Van Teslaar, trans. (New York: Liveright, 1950; orig. pub. 1921), but numerous writers of health advice manuals discreetly mentioned the subject.

115. "Curing Masturbation" is taken from Jean Stengers and Anne Van Heck, *Masturbation: The History of a Great Terror*, Kathryn Hoffman, trans. (New York: Palgrave, 2001), 111-13, with slight changes.

See note 114.

116. "Anti-Hysteria Device" is taken from Rachel Maines, *The Technology of Orgasm* (Baltimore, MD: Johns Hopkins University Press, 1999), 86.

Maines's book is the best source for more information on these devices. For more on the history of hysteria as a medical concept, see Ilza Veith's *Hysteria: The History of a Disease* (Chicago: University of Chicago Press, 1965); Monique David-Menard's *Hysteria from Freud to Lacan*, Catherine Porter, trans. (Ithaca, NY: Cornell University Press, 1989); Mark Micale's *Approaching Hysteria: Disease and Its Interpretations* (Princeton, NJ: Princeton University Press, 1995); or *Hysteria Beyond Freud*, Sander Gilman et al., eds. (Berkeley, CA: University of California Press, 1993). Again, there are numerous medical and psychological writings on hysteria from the nineteenth and early twentieth centuries; I located several from different eras: Frederic Skey's *Hysteria: Six Lectures* (New York: Moorhead, Simpson & Bond, 1868); S.W. Mitchell's *Lectures on Diseases of the Nervous System, Especially in Women* (Philadelphia: Lea Brothers, 1885); Charles D. Fox's *Psychopathology of Hysteria* (Boston: R.G. Badger, 1913); and D. Wilfrid Abse's *The Diagnosis of Hysteria* (Baltimore, MD: Williams and Wilkins, 1950).

117. "Freud on Hysteria" is taken from Sigmund Freud, *Freud on War, Sex, and Neurosis*, trans. unknown (New York: Arts & Science, 1947), 47–54.

See note 116 for historical studies on hysteria. Since Freud believed that sexual drives lay at the heart of human motivation, most of his writings deal with sexuality in some form and would be suitable in a history of sexuality. The classic English translation of Freud's writings is that by James Strachey, begun in 1953, in 24 volumes. *The Concordance to the Standard Edition of Complete Psychological Works of Sigmund Freud*, Samuel Guttman et al., eds. (Boston: G.K. Hall, 1980) can provide precise locations on any specific topic. There are also excerpts published in collections, like *Freud on Women: A Reader*, Elisabeth Young-Bruehl, ed. (New York: W.W. Norton, 1990). Scholarly analyses of Freud are even more plentiful. For a history of the context in which Freud developed his theories, Peter Gay's many writings are often considered the best; see his five-volume *The Bourgeois Experience: Victoria to Freud* (Oxford: Oxford University Press, 1994–98). Gay's biography of Freud, *Freud: A Life for Our Time* (New York: Norton, 1988) is both readable and profound.

118. "Sexual Excitability and Eugenics" is taken from Anna Galbraith, *The Four Epochs of a Woman's Life* (Philadelphia: W.B. Saunders, 1920), 138–43, 26–28, 40–41, with slight changes.

The whole of Galbraith's book is worth reading, as are her other books, *Hygiene and Physical Culture for Women* (New York: Dodd, Mead & Co, 1895), *Personal Hygiene and Physical Training for Women* (Philadelphia: W.B. Saunders, 1911); or *The Family and the New Democracy: A Study in Social Hygiene* (Philadelphia: W.B. Saunders, 1920). For more on Social Hygiene and related movements, see Martha Verbrugge's *Able-Bodied Womanhood: Personal Health and Social Change in Nineteenth-Century Boston* (Oxford:

Oxford University Press, 1988); or Marjorie Levine-Clark's *Beyond the Reproductive Body: The Politics of Women's Health and Work in Early Victorian England* (Columbus, OH: Ohio State University Press, 2004). Social Hygiene's most famous proponent was probably Havelock Ellis, who wrote *The Task of Social Hygiene* (Boston: Houghton Mifflin, 1914). And probably the most famous proponent of the dangers of sexual excitability was John Harvey Kellogg (inventor of "Kellogg's Corn Flakes"); his writings on the subject include *Man, the Masterpiece: Or, Plain Truths Plainly Told about Boyhood, Youth, and Manhood* (Battle Creek, MI: Health, 1890); *Plain Facts for Old and Young: Embracing the Natural History and Hygiene of Organic Life* (Burlington, IA: I.F. Segner, 1982; orig. publ. 1890); and *Ladies' Guide in Health and Disease: Girlhood, Maidenhood, Wifehood, and Motherhood* (Battle Creek, MI: Modern Medicine, 1901). A biography of Kellogg exists in Richard Schwartz's *John Harvey Kellogg, M.D.* (Nashville, TN: Southern, 1970); as does a semi-fictionalized film about his work, *The Road to Wellville* (U.S.A., Columbia Pictures, 1994). On eugenics, see G.R. Searle's *Eugenics and Politics in Britain, 1900–1914* (Leyden: Noordhoff, 1976); or D.J. Galton's *In Our Own Image: Eugenics and the Genetic Modification of People* (London: Little, Brown, 2001). Other writings on eugenics are numerous; opposition to eugenics may be found in G.K. Chesterton's *Eugenics and Other Evils* (London: Cassell, 1922). Another earlier text warning of the dangers of overindulgence in sex, even between married couples, is Henry Wright's *Unwelcome Child; or, The Crime of an Undesigned and Undesired Maternity* (Boston: Bela Marsh, 1858).

119. "The New Science of Sexology" is taken from Richard von Krafft-Ebing, *Psychopathia Sexualis*, trans. unknown (New York: Pioneer, 1950), 290–96, with slight changes.

Works on the history of sexology as a science include Vern Bullough's *Science in the Bedroom: A History of Sex Research* (New York: Basic, 1994); Roy Porter and Lesley Hall's *The Facts of Life: The Creation of Sexual Knowledge in Britain, 1650–1950* (New Haven, CT: Yale University Press, 1995); Julia Ericksen and Sally Steffen's *Kiss and Tell: Surveying Sex in the Twentieth Century* (Cambridge, MA: Harvard University Press, 1999); and Paul A. Robinson's *The Modernization of Sex: Havelock Ellis, Alfred Kinsey, William Masters, and Virginia Johnson* (Ithaca, NY: Cornell University Press, 1989; orig. pub. 1976). On homosexuality in this era, see Nicholas Edsall's *Toward Stonewall: Homosexuality and Society in the Modern Western World* (Charlottesville, VA: University of Virginia Press, 2003); Jeffrey Weeks's *Coming Out: Homosexual Politics in Britain from the Nineteenth Century to the Present* (London: Quartet, 1977); Graham Robb's *Strangers: Homosexual Love in the Nineteenth Century* (London: Picador, 2003); Jennifer Terry's *An American Obsession: Science, Medicine, and Homosexuality in Modern Society* (Chicago: University of Chicago Press, 1999); or Jay Hatheway's *The Gilded Age Construction of Modern American Homophobia* (New York: Palgrave Macmillan, 2003). On female homo-eroticism and sexology, see George Chauncey's "From Sexual Inversion to Homosexuality: Medicine and the Changing Conceptualization of Female Deviance," *Salmagundi* 58–59 (1982–83): 114–46. On the other figures in the early history of sexology, see Charlotte Wolff's *Magnus Hirschfeld: A Portrait of a Pioneer in Sexology* (London: Quartet, 1986); or Phyllis Grosskurth's *Havelock Ellis: A Biography* (New York: New York University Press, 1980).

120. "The Corset" is taken from Juliann Sivulka, *Soap, Sex, and Cigarettes: A Cultural History of American Advertising* (Belmont, CA: Wadsworth, 1998), 54.

On the corset in the history of fashion, some more specific to the particular article of clothing, others more generally on unusual fashions, see Valerie Steele's *The Corset: A Cultural History* (New Haven, CT: Yale University Press, 2001) or her *Fetish: Fashion, Sex and Power* (Oxford: Oxford University Press, 1996); Leigh Summers' *Bound to Please: A History of the Victorian Corset* (Oxford: Berg, 2001); David Kunzle's *Fashion and Fetishism: A Social History of the Corset, Tight-Lacing, and Other Forms of Body-Sculpture in the West* (Totowa, NJ: Rowman and Littlefield, 1982); or Leslie Miller's "The Many Figures of Eve: Styles of Womanhood Embodied in a Late-Nineteenth-Century Corset," in *American Artifacts: Essays in Material Culture*, Jules Prown and Kenneth Haltman, eds. (East Lansing, MI: Michigan State University Press, 2000).

121. "The Kinsey Report" is taken from Alfred Kinsey et al., *Sexual Behavior in the Human Female* (Philadelphia: W.B. Saunders, 1953), 173–75, 436–38, 487–89.

There are several biographies of Kinsey, including James H. Jones's *Alfred C. Kinsey: A Public/Private Life* (New York: W.W. Norton, 1997); and Jonathan Gathorne-Hardy's *Sex the Measure of All Things: A Life of Alfred C. Kinsey* (Bloomington, IN: Indiana University Press, 2000). There also exist numerous reflections on the Kinsey Reports, mostly published in the 1950s, and decades of publications from what became the Kinsey Institute for Sex Research, but most are fairly dry statistics, as are Kinsey's own reports. On the history of the Institute, see Wardell Baxter Pomeroy's *Dr. Kinsey and the Institute for Sex Research* (New Haven, CT: Yale University Press, 1972). Kinsey was not the only individual developing statistics about people's sex lives, even if he was the most famous. Earlier studies had been done by Clelia Mosher (although not published in her lifetime) and Katharine Bement Davis; see *The Mosher Survey: Sexual Attitudes of 45 Victorian Women*, James Mahood and Kristine Wenburg, eds. (New York: Arno, 1980); or Davis's *Factors in the Sex Life of Twenty-Two Hundred Women* (New York: Harper & Brothers, 1929); later surveys included William Masters and Virginia Johnson's *Human Sexual Response* (Boston: Little, Brown, 1966); Shere Hite's *The Hite Report* (New York: Collier Macmillan, 1976); see also note 127 on this last one. For a history of such surveys in Britain, see Liz Stanley's *Sex Surveyed, 1949–1994* (London: Taylor & Francis, 1995).

122. "Frigidity" is taken from Fritz Kant, *Frigidity: Dynamics and Treatment* (Springfield, IL: Charles C. Thomas, 1969), 8–9, 29, 48–49.

Kant's is one of a number of mid-twentieth century writings on frigidity, the clinical definition for which was as problematic as that for hysteria, which it often replaced; see note 116. For studies from different eras, see also Wilhelm Stekel's *Frigidity in Women in Relation to her Love Life*, trans. James van Teslaar (New York: Boni and Liveright, 1926); Eduard Hitschmann and Edmund Bergler's *Frigidity in Women: Its Characteristics and Treatment*, trans. Polly Leeds Weil (Washington, DC: Nervous and Mental Disease Publishing, 1936); Edmund Bergler's *Neurotic Counterfeit Sex: Impotence, Frigidity, "Mechanical" and Pseudosexuality, Homosexuality* (New York: Grune & Stratton, 1951); Marie Nyswander Robinson's *The Power of Sexual Surrender* (London: W.H. Allen, 1959); Donald Hastings' *Impotence and Frigidity* (Boston: Little, Brown, 1963); or Edwin Hirsch's *Impotence and Frigidity* (New York: Citadel, 1966). I know of no studies that have examined the cultural assumptions of those who wrote about frigidity.

123. "Sociobiology" is taken from Edward O. Wilson, *Sociobiology: The New Synthesis* (Cambridge, MA: Belknap, 1975), 553–54.

Other writings on sociobiology and sexuality include Glenn D. Wilson's *The Coolidge Effect: An Evolutionary Account of Human Sexuality* (New York: Morrow, 1981), revised as *Love and Instinct* (New York: Quill, 1983); Timothy Perper's *Sex Signals: The Biology of Love* (Philadelphia: ISI, 1985); Jerome Barkow's *Darwin, Sex, and Status: Biological Approaches to Mind and Culture* (Toronto: University of Toronto Press, 1989); Sam Kachigan's *The Sexual Matrix: Boy Meets Girl on the Evolutionary Scale* (New York: Radius, 1990); Harmon Holcomb's *Sociobiology, Sex, and Science* (Albany, NY: State University of New York Press, 1993); Niles Eldridge's *Why We Do It: Rethinking Sex and the Selfish Gene* (New York: Norton, 2004); *The Sociobiology of Sexual and Reproductive Strategies*, Anne Rasa et al., eds. (London: Chapman and Hall, 1989); and *Evolution, Gender, and Rape*, Cheryl Brown Travis, ed. (Cambridge, MA: Massachusetts Institute of Technology Press, 2003).

124. "Scientific Matchmaking" is taken from Karl Miles Wallace, *Love is More than Luck: An Experiment in Scientific Matchmaking* (New York: Wilfred Funk, 1957), 43–44.

Wallace's is one of few books on the subject; see also Louis Harris' *None But the Lonely Heart* (New York: Readers, 1943). Recent studies include Bob Mullan's *The Mating Trade* (London: Routledge & Kegan Paul, 1984).

For other scientific theories about how individuals choose marriage partners, mostly relying on psychology and sociobiology, see David Klimek's *Beneath Male Selection and Marriage: The Unconscious Motives in Human Pairing* (New York: Van Nostrand Reinhold, 1979); Glenn D. Wilson's *Love's Mysteries: The Psychology of Sexual Attraction* (London: Open, 1976); James L. Gould's *Sexual Selection: Mate Choice and Courtship in Nature* (New York: Scientific American Library, 1989; revised 1997); or Bernard Murstein's *Who Will Marry Whom? Theories and Research in Marital Choice* (New York: Springer, 1976).

125. "Evelyn Hooker's Research on Homosexuality" is taken from *Taboo Topics*, Norman L. Farberow, ed. (New York: Atherton, 1963), 45–47.

Hooker's famous study was published as "The Adjustment of the Male Overt Homosexual," *Journal of Projective Techniques* 21 (1957): 18–31. Biographical information about Hooker can be found in A.M. Boxer and J.M. Carrier's "Evelyn Hooker: A Life Remembered," *Journal of Homosexuality* 36 (1998): 1–17; there is also a documentary film about her life, entitled *Changing our Minds* (U.S.A., Frameline, 1992). While there are numerous studies of homosexuality from a psychological perspective, few deal with historical aspects of the removal of homosexuality as a category of mental illness; see Charles Silverstein's "Psychotherapy and Psychotherapists: A History," in *Gays, Lesbians, and their Therapists: Studies in Psychotherapy*, Charles Silverstein, ed. (New York: Norton, 1991). In his *Cures: A Gay Man's Odyssey* (New York: Plume, 1992), Martin Duberman reflects on the meaning of such a change in his own life.

126. "Neither Men Nor Women" is taken from Hakim Muhammad Yusuf Hasan, *Do Shiza,*

trans. Saleem Kidwai, in *Same-Sex Love in India*, Ruth Vanika and Saleem Kidwai, eds. (New York: St. Martin's, 2000), 260–61.

On the *hijras*, see Serena Nanda's *Neither Man Nor Woman: The Hijras of India* (Belmont, CA: Wadsworth, 1990); Gayatri Reddy's *With Respect to Sex: Negotiating Hijra Identity in South India* (Chicago: University of Chicago Press, 2005); or any of Nanda's essays in *Deviance: Anthropological Perspectives*, Morris Freilich et al., eds. (New York: Bergin & Garvey, 1991); *Third Sex, Third Gender: Beyond Sexual Dimorphism in Culture and History*, Gilbert Herdt, ed. (New York: Zone, 1994); or *Religion and Sexuality in Cross-Cultural Perspective*, Stephen Ellingson and M. Christian Green, eds. (New York: Routledge, 2002). On the influence of European and American scientific theories on societies of the world, including India, see the essays in *Deviant Bodies: Critical Perspectives on Difference in Science and Popular Culture*, Jennifer Terry and Jacqueline Urla, eds. (Bloomington, IN: Indiana University Press, 1995); in *Gender, Sexuality, and Colonial Modernities*, Antoinette Burton, ed. (New York: Routledge, 1999); or in the special issue of *Gender and History* 11:3 (1999).

127. "*The Hite Report*" is taken from Shere Hite, *The Hite Report* (New York: Macmillan, 1976), 281–82.

The Hite Report, which is fascinating to read in its entirety, was only one of a number of works published in the 1960s and 70s, some more radical than others, but all attempting to educate scientists and others on their ignorance of women's bodies and sex lives. Other famous works include Betty Friedan's *The Feminine Mystique* (New York: Norton, 1963); Dana Densmore's *Sex Roles and Female Oppression* (Boston: New England Free Press, 1969); Shulamith Firestone's *The Dialectic of Sex: A Case for Feminist Revolution* (New York: Morrow, 1970); Kate Millett's *Sexual Politics* (Garden City, NY: Doubleday, 1970); Germaine Greer's *The Female Eunuch* (New York: McGraw-Hill, 1971); and the Boston Women's Health Book Collective's *Our Bodies, Ourselves* (New York: Simon and Schuster, 1973). On these writings, see Jane Gerhard's *Desiring Revolution: Second-Wave Feminism and the Rewriting of American Sexual Thought, 1920 to 1982* (New York: Columbia University Press, 2001). On the problems of ignorance about women's bodies in scientific research, see Evelyn Reed's *Sexism and Science* (New York: Pathfinder, 1978); Michael Ruse's *Is Science Sexist? And Other Problems in the Biomedical Sciences* (Boston: Kluwer, 1981); Ruth Bleier's *Science and Gender: A Critique of Biology and Its Theories on Women* (New York: Pergamon, 1984); Sandra Harding's *The Science Question in Feminism* (Ithaca, NY: Cornell University Press, 1986); or the essays in *Feminism and Science*, Nancy Tuana, ed. (Bloomington, IN: Indiana University Press, 1989). Comparisons might be made between the results in *The Hite Report* and those of Linda Wolfe's *The Cosmo Report* (New York: Arbor House, 1981), conducted among readers of *Cosmopolitan* magazine in 1980. See also note 121 for other sex surveys.

128. "Nancy Chodorow on Children's Sexual Development" is taken from Nancy Chodorow, *The Reproduction of Mothering: Psychoanalysis and the Sociology of Gender* (Berkeley, CA: University of California Press, 1978), 192–99.

Chodorow's other writings are equally fascinating but also difficult for nonspecialists; see her *Feminism and Psychoanalytic Theory* (New Haven, CT: Yale University Press, 1989); or her

Feminities, Masculinities, Sexualities: Freud and Beyond (Lexington, KY: University Press of Kentucky, 1994). Other influential early feminist psychologists were Karen Horney and Clara Thompson; see Horney's *Feminine Psychology* (New York: W.W. Norton, 1967); or *The Unknown Karen Horney: Essays on Gender, Culture, and Psychoanalysis* (New Haven, CT: Yale University Press, 2000); and Thompson's *On Women* (New York: New American Library, 1971). The psychological literature on gender is now immense; some idea of the issues now addressed is given by the essays in *Charting a New Course for Feminist Psychology*, Lynn Collins et al., eds. (Westport, CT: Praeger, 2002). Relatively recent, too, is an emphasis on understanding masculinity by using psycho-analytical tools; on this point, see *Constructing Masculinity*, Maurice Berger et al., eds. (New York: Routledge, 1995). The dismissal of sex-ual orientation from earlier psychoanalytical studies is now being addressed; see *Lesbians and Psychoanalysis: Revolutions in Theory and Practice*, Judith Glassgold and Suzanne Iasenza, eds. (New York: Free Press, 1995); and *Gay Masculinities*, Peter Nardi, ed. (Thousand Oaks, CA: Sage, 2000).

CHAPTER 12
Social factors

Sexuality is not solely driven by conscious decisions—political choices, or examining the self in relation to others, or even altering the authorities one trusts to interpret how sexuality works— but is also influenced by a variety of social factors individuals may not even be aware of. These factors, which are the subject of this chapter, provide an environment that restricts the range of choices or understandings available to individuals and thus limits the ability to make free decisions about one's sexuality.

The growth of capitalism in modern life is certainly one of the most significant social factors shaping modern sexuality. The steady development of a global economy has made a whole range of products—foods, other raw materials, manufactured goods—available to an ever larger market of consumers. The agricultural basis of many of the world's cultures, where wealth was measured in land and farming provided the basis for many livelihoods, has given way to a mercantile economy, where wages provide income and most jobs exist in the creation, transportation, or sale of consumer goods. The impact on sexual customs has been tremendous. Wage labor meant less reliance on family support for both men and women, and with it, more independence from family control, with effects on the choice of marriage partner; the age of marriage, especially for men (often delayed in agricultural societies because of the necessity of waiting for an inheritance); and the use of contraception (large families are an asset to farm labor but a detriment to wage earners). Many scholars have recently delineated the multifaceted impact of capitalism on sexuality.

Urbanization, which is itself a side effect of capitalism, also has impacted sexual lifestyles. Urban living allowed for greater freedom from social control, since cities provided an "anonymity" of sorts that was usually not possible in smaller centers. Individuals who left farms or small towns for the big city enjoyed a freedom to experiment sexually with fewer fears about permanent repercussions, such as a degraded reputation. Urbanization also provided a greater opportunity for sexual encounters, since cities brought large numbers of individuals together on a regular basis. Again, while individuals who remained on farms or in small towns had a limited pool of persons from which to choose marriage or sexual partners, city dwellers had vast numbers, increasing the importance of individual choice and of opportunities for sexual experimentation. These new realities not only changed dating and marriage patterns, but also opened up new opportunities for same-sex encounters. Men who wanted to have sex with other men or women who wanted to have sex with other women took advantage of such opportunities and even began forming subcultures of like-minded individuals.

Capitalists were not slow to appreciate the moneymaking opportunities afforded by individuals who were sexually freer, and consumerism has created more and more of a sexually liberal environment. Advertisers realized early on that "sex sells," that is, it gets the attention of potential consumers better than most other advertising. Capitalists also marketed sexual opportunities for more direct gain. From the amusement parks and movie houses of the late nineteenth century to the drive-in theaters and dance halls of the twentieth, capitalists have repeatedly invented ways for individuals to enjoy each other's company while also spending money. Dating patterns show the clearest changes related to this consumer mentality. Nineteenth-century adolescents might have talked quietly in their families' homes while courting or met at large public gatherings; twentieth-century teenag-

ers generally left their homes on unsupervised dates, at least in industrialized regions, especially after the widespread introduction of the automobile.

Other social factors that have influenced the course of modern sexuality are not difficult to find. The mass migrations of the modern world meant that peoples with different customs and traditions were thrown together side by side and had to come to terms with each other. The melting pot of the United States is perhaps the most familiar but certainly not the only place to have received large numbers of immigrants, and few nations in the modern world have a culturally homogeneous population. The integration of newcomers, including through intermarriage, meant further changes to sexual patterns. A common nineteenth-century pattern saw single men immigrating earlier than women, finding work and earning enough money to marry or to send for wives and children, who lived with their parents in the interim. For single men, increased numbers of prostitutes provided sexual services. (While prostitution seems to have always existed, the greater use of wage labor was generally responsible for its increase in modern centuries.) The sad reality of war, including two world wars and numerous smaller conflicts in the twentieth century, often disrupted the social order that kept sexual patterns in check. Wartime accounts often describe a loosening of sexual morals, as individuals tried to make the most of the short time they feared was left to them. Rape has also remained a common aspect of modern war.

New technologies have also had substantial impact on modern sexuality. While methods of contraception have always been known to human societies, improvements in these methods—guaranteed by capitalism's constant search for the "new and improved" to market to customers—meant greater effectiveness of, and increased reliance on, artificial methods of family planning. The invention of the contraceptive pill in itself was a turning point in sexual customs, since its use became so widespread. More refined methods of abortion made the procedure safer. While its impact is still not completely known, the creation of the Internet has made sexual images available for discreet viewing and allowed for the possibility of sexual encounters in ways never before imagined.

The impact of disease is a final social factor worth considering. Again, there have always been sexually transmitted diseases, as described by medical writers throughout history. Globalization has made the impact of these diseases felt in far-reaching ways. A syphilis epidemic in the sixteenth century, widely reported in the literature of the day, was probably responsible for the criminalization of prostitution across Europe and the closing of previously state-sponsored brothels. (The fact that syphilis is first mentioned in the sixteenth century has led some historians to see it as a disease of the Americas, brought back to Europe by sailors, but there are problems with this hypothesis.) The recent impact of AIDS, of course, has also changed sexual customs worldwide and is probably as responsible as anything else for increased public discussions of homosexuality in recent decades.

Moralists have taken advantage of the unintended consequences of social changes to promote their messages of reform. In the nineteenth century, they condemned prostitution and unchaperoned dating; in the next century, they denounced the drinking of alcohol, dancing, and men and women's swimming together as all leading to unwelcome sex. Already in this century, moralists have criticized Internet pornography and the distribution of condoms in schools. Moralists often point to rising social problems caused by the activities they condemn, but it is sometimes hard for historians to see whether such increases are real or imagined for rhetorical purposes. Looking back at these denunciations, however, can sometimes give historians the best clues as to how aware individuals were of the social factors associated with changes in sexual customs, and perhaps also how uncomfortable they were with those changes.

All of these factors are felt by individuals living in the environments produced by them, some consciously and some not. For example, everyone who came of age after the early eighties will never know what it was like to live in a world without AIDS; those who came of age after the early nineties will never know what it was like to live in a world without the Internet. What impact those social factors will have on future sexual customs is difficult or even impossible to say.

Psychologist Erik Erikson was the first to point out that human psychological development did not end with childhood, about which Freud had said so much, but continued throughout adulthood, as we continually adapt ourselves to our changing environment. Our identities have been permanently shaped by such social factors, as those living in past centuries had been, and even if we are not aware precisely how, we live our lives differently because of them.

This chapter's readings all demonstrate the impact of a range of social forces on sexual identity.

129. A WOMAN OF QUALITY

Time: seventeenth century CE
Place: Japan
Author: Ihara Saikaku

The prominence of prostitution is one of the most noted changes of the modern world. An early writer to draw attention to the subject was the Japanese novelist Ihara Saikaku, famous for his "books of the floating world" (ukiyo-zoshi). Ukiyo or "the floating world" referred specifically to the world of prostitution and generally to the world of physical pleasures and to the Buddhist notion that earthly existence was but an illusion. Prostitution seems to have flourished in seventeenth- and eighteenth-century Japan. The economic strength of the stable shogun-ruled government rose, and the urban centers at Kyoto and Edo (modern Tokyo) swelled with a growing population, including large numbers of unmarried samurai. The Life of an Amorous Man, the source of this excerpt, recounts a single man's sexual adventures within the "floating world."

Yoshino had indeed earned the reputation of being an admirable woman because she was gentle and courteous and big of heart. No one could point the finger of scorn at her or complain that she was wanting in conduct or behavior. She was a good woman, liked by all who knew her. Yonosuke had heard of her—her goodness, her refinement. And then one day he saw her on the street with his own eyes, and he felt great torment. This wasn't a case of casual infatuation with a common harlot or a woman of easy virtue. She was a first-class hostess, a woman of quality presiding in giddily high circles. It saddened Yonosuke to think that with all his newly acquired wealth she was inaccessible to him. He fell actually in love for the first time in his life. Frustration begets humility, and Yonosuke started to earn money with his own hands—just fifty-three *me*, the price of admission to her presence for one brief hour of glorious entertainment. It was to be an expression of sincerity, unadulterated by any sordid urge. Daily he worked at the anvil of a smithy in Lord Kintsuna's studio. Every day he forged one small knife blade, earning one *me* for his labor. In fifty-three days he had amassed the needed fifty-three *me*.

And every day thereafter he waited for a chance to be admitted to Yoshino's table. But the keeper of the teahouse in the Shimabara district would not let him see her. She was barred to anyone unknown to the keeper as a man of wealth, position, and probity. Yonosuke refused to reveal his true identity, and those who had heard of his past misdeeds shunned him. His sincerity proved to be of no avail. So then one night when the festival of the forge came around, he went secretly to the same establishment to pour out his woes to a woman attendant. "I'm mortified," he told her. "I can well understand it," the woman said sympathetically. "I shall let Yoshino-sama know secretly anyhow that you are here." When Yoshino heard about Yonosuke's plight and lament, she said without hesitation: "Of course he can see me if he wants to. Bring him into my room, please." Unable to believe his ears, Yonosuke crept through the dark hallway into her dazzling presence. He felt humble and ashamed. "But at least I am sincere," he said pensively. "I have come to you with love in my heart, knowing you will reject me." Yoshino was greatly surprised and excited. No one had ever spoken to her of sincere love. "Tell me all about it," she invited. Yonosuke made a clean breast of everything. "That is all," he concluded. "I must thank you for letting me come here to see you. Now I am satisfied. I shall always carry the thought of your generosity in my heart." He rose to go. "Wait!" Yoshino cried, seizing his sleeve. "Don't go yet."

But the secret could not be kept. When the keeper of the establishment on the following morning heard what Yoshino had done on her own initiative, he complained sternly and bitterly. Yoshino protested: "But I have not done anything that would ruin the reputation of this house or anyone else here. I have nothing to hide. You may not know the man who came to see me because he came as a poor and humble man, without displaying the privilege of wealth. He is Yonosuke-sama. He impressed me greatly with his simple, unadorned sincerity." Nevertheless it seemed as if Yoshino had committed an indiscretion that could not be excused. "It is against the rules of the house," the master insisted. While her career thus hung in the balance, Yonosuke himself dropped in, now through the front door. When the master told him pointblank that he would not tolerate such clandestine defiance of rules and that in any event Yoshino's future was as good as ruined thereby, Yonosuke said: "Very well, I shall hold myself responsible for her conduct. She has done no more than what a generous-hearted courtesan would do. I will never let her suffer for it. In fact, I will pay ransom to secure her release from your contract. As of today she shall be a free woman." And with Yoshino's glad consent he paid the ransom and took her home as his wife.

Pride and prejudice hurt the establishment, and sincerity was richly rewarded. For Yoshino proved herself to be a model wife. Wise and gentle in her ways and speech, she quickly familiarized herself with the affairs of her new environment and adapted herself to its manners and peculiarities without a trace of condescension. She joined the Buddhist church to prepare herself for the future world, the same as Yonosuke. She gave up smoking her long-stemmed pipe when Yonosuke confessed aversion for the ill-smelling weed. Yonosuke was pleased in every respect. But his family and clan of relatives came forth to voice objections. Whatever she might be now, Yoshino was once a courtesan, a dishonorable profession in their eyes. She could not be entered in the family registry. "Get rid of her," they demanded of Yonosuke. Yoshino was heartbroken. Yonosuke stood resolutely by her, but

the clan council refused to budge too. Relations became strained all around.

Finally, after discussing the matter sorrowfully with Yonosuke, Yoshino asked for separation. "I shall be content to be your mistress," she said. "Please let me stay in a separate house for servants, and you can come to see me whenever you like." "That won't do at all," Yonosuke replied. "I will not consent to any such arrangement." "Then I shall make a final appeal to your clan council. I shall try to persuade your relatives to change their attitude toward us." "How can you convince them when even Buddhist and Shinto priests have tried in vain to intercede for us?" "Well then," Yoshino was persistent, "I have a scheme. Please write an invitation to all of your relatives. Tell them you are sending me away tomorrow, so please come to renew the former pleasant relationship. It is to be a feast of reconciliation, between yourself and them. The cherries in the garden are just about to bloom. Tell them to bring along their servants too and enjoy the day together here—the whole clan. And leave the rest to me." "Whatever you wish," Yonosuke agreed pleasantly enough, and the letters were duly dispatched by messenger.

The clan members came, all of them—children, servants and all—in palanquin after palanquin, for they bore no ill will toward Yonosuke. There was feasting and drinking in the great family hall overlooking the garden and in the pavilions overlooking hillocks, ponds, and flower beds. At the height of the festivities Yoshino went before the revelers and bowed low with both hands on the mat. She wore a pale blue robe, a red apron denoting the status of a servant, and a kerchief on her head. She addressed the older members of the clan: "My name is Yoshino, and I was once a courtesan on Misuji-machi. I feel I am unworthy to appear before this family gathering. Today, however, I am to be sent away from this household as an unwanted wife. I should like, if you will let me, to serve and entertain you as my last act here." Thereupon she began to sing a song of olden times. Next she entertained the guests by playing a haunting musical piece on the *koto*. Then she brewed ceremonial tea, serving it to the guests in a charming, well-bred way. And she recited poems. She arranged flowers in trays to brighten up the hall. She did all these things serenely in a way that suggested they were not something merely to be enjoyed by men at first-class teahouses. She showed that they were accomplishments that any wife, in any home, might freely and profitably exercise for the enjoyment of her family. After that she mixed easily with the guests as a hostess should, looking after the children's disheveled hair, making up a twosome for the game of *go*, going back and forth from the kitchen for more drinks and delicacies. She looked after the guests' every need, far into the night.

And the guests unconsciously accepted her as the hostess herself. They forgot that the time to leave was long past due. In the small hours of the morning the many clan members finally left for their homes. The womenfolk said: "We must never let Yonosuke get rid of such a fine wife. Even we women have never felt so pleasant as in her company. No one need feel ashamed with a bride so gentle and wise and capable." Then they told the menfolk: "Please forgive her for her past and let her become Yonosuke's legitimate wife." The menfolk nodded their heads vigorously in affirmation. "She is a fine and lovable woman," they agreed emphatically. "Who said they must part?"

Questions for Reflection and Discussion

What do we learn about prostitution in seventeenth-century Japan? What is the tone toward the prostitute and prostitution in this story? How are the questions of honor and reputa-tion resolved? How easily does Yoshino create a new identity for herself?

130. BOY ACTRESSES

Time: seventeenth century CE
Place: Japan
Author: Ihara Saikaku

Urban life is often credited with creating the first homosexual communities in the modern world. In seventeenth- and eighteenth-century Japan, for example, the "floating world" of the cities also included boys who not only dressed as women and performed female roles in Kabuki plays, but also supplemented their income by serving as prostitutes to men. Ihara Saikaku, who loved to depict the "floating world," described the practice in his collection of stories entitled The Great Mirror of Male Love.

After the prohibition of Grand Kabuki, Murayama Matabei opened a mime and dance show for which he gathered together a large troupe of handsome young actors. Until that time it was uncommon even in the capital for men to take pleasure with boy actors. Each went for the same sum, one *bu* of gold, and took on customers much the way street boys do nowadays. At some point, it became the custom to celebrate a boy's promotion as a full-fledged actor of female roles by inviting the entire cast to Higashiyama for a tremendous feast. After that, his fee increased to five *ryo* of silver. In those days, having fun was easy. For two *momme* of small cash to the sandal carrier and a payment of two *ryo* of silver to the teahouse, you could have a boy of your own to play with from the final curtain call until daybreak the following morning. Boys in those days were real boys. Though you might visit them night after night for love, they never demanded spending money. A toy doll, a colorfully dyed towel, or some tooth powder, none of which cost more than four or five *fun* of silver, would delight them.

Then one year wealthy priests assembled in the capital from all over the country to commemorate the 350th anniversary of the death of Zen Master Kanzan, first rector of Myoshin-ji. After the religious services were over, they went sight-seeing at the pleasure quarter on the dry riverbed. They fell in love with the handsome youths there, the likes of which they had never seen in the countryside, and began buying them up indiscriminately without a thought for their priestly duties. Any boy with forelocks who had eyes and a nose on his face was guaranteed to be busy all day. Since that time, boy actors have continued to sell themselves in two shifts, daytime and nighttime. The fee for a boy who was appearing onstage rose to one piece of silver. The priests did not care about the cost, since they had only a short time to amuse themselves in the capital. But their extravagance continues to cause untold hardship for the pleasure-seekers of our day.

How is seventeenth-century Japanese sexual culture glimpsed in this passage? How is it mocked? How dependent were such practices on a money-oriented and urban society?

131. AN IMAGE OF THE FLOATING WORLD

Time: eighteenth century CE
Place: Japan
Artist: Masanobu

This erotic image, one of many that have survived from seventeenth- and eighteenth-century Japan, is entitled "Initiation of a Young Girl into the Class of Courtesan." The girl's unwillingness seems clearly highlighted. The image may reflect a darker side to prostitution than the previous two sources admit. The man's hairstyle reveals him to be a samurai. Typical of Japanese erotic art, the mixture of naked flesh and luxurious

clothing may have held more erotic appeal than nakedness alone, since nudity was commonplace in public bathing. The large penis is also typical of Japanese erotic art, but here lends additional trauma to the moment.

Questions for Reflection and Discussion

How does the violence of the action in the image counter the romantic image of prostitution in early modern Japan provided by source 129? What do you imagine the role of the older woman to be? What kind of audience might have been expected for such drawings?

132. ADDRESS TO THE MAGDALEN SOCIETY OF NEW YORK

Time: nineteenth century CE
Place: United States
Author: unknown

The following excerpt, from the 1831 address to a society dedicated to helping women out of lives of prostitution, shows that many individuals were well aware of the social causes that led women to become prostitutes. Its members were mostly middle- and upper-class Christian women who used their time to advocate for social reform. They had time because they were excluded from most professional occupations, but many had employed women of the lower classes as domestic servants, women who—as the author admits—were often as much at risk from sexual advances there as elsewhere.

In preparing for an address for a meeting like this, for the purpose of forming an association to endeavor to rescue a portion of our female community from a life of shame and misery, we are impressed with the great responsibilities of the undertaking, and our minds would naturally shrink from engaging in it were it not

that we remember they are our sisters.… Does it not lead us into our investigations, and cause us to trace the evil to its source? To fathom the deep mysteries that have shrouded so large a portion of our population in unutterable, indescribable misery? We are told there are six thousand women in our city, who are leading lives of shame and crime; and yet we have been sleeping calmly and quietly, in the midst of these scenes of horror; or, when the knowledge of some of these circumstances have been forced upon us, we have shrunk from them with disgust.…

We know that the majority of those who are thus living in violation of the laws of God and man, are of what are considered the lower classes of society, those whom too many of us are in the constant habit of oppressing. At this charge do we not instinctively feel the glow of indignation? And is not the denial ready to spring from our lips? But let us examine into this matter! We are aware of the small reward female labor receives, under usual circumstances, and the temptations subsequent upon this, into which many women are thrown; while too many of them have neither moral nor religious training, to imbue them with a principle to withstand the inducements of a life of greater apparent ease, and more enlarged pecuniary acquisitions. With this knowledge, which we have received in various ways, can we bring forward any efforts, any attempts on our part, to remedy this evil? Have we labored in the families of this class, to implant a proper principle, in the minds of either parents or children? Have we sought to give to Women's labor the true compensation? Or, are we, and ours, enjoying what ought to have been the meed of their honest industries. These are important questions; and, as we can answer them, will be the reward of our consciences.

There is another point on which we ought to reflect, with deep earnestness. Young girls have been placed [as servants] in our families. Have we endeavored to give them the same moral and religious training as our own daughters? … Or, have we, by our coldness and haughtiness, endeavored to impress them with the idea, that there was a marked line between us; and by our conduct, wounded spirits, perhaps as proud as our own, and urged them to abandon our firesides, for the greater equality in a home of vice? And, when our sister (owing perhaps to our treatment,) seeks to escape from what she feels to be the tyranny of wealth, and yields to temptation, what have been our efforts to reclaim her? Have we gone to her wretched habitation, and sought to win her back to virtue? Have we offered her a happier home, and told her we had wronged her, and perhaps prompted her to err? Have we opened to her the avenues by which she might regain a degree of respectability, and consulted her taste, and feelings, in the occupation we offered her? Have we compared her fate with ours, and owned, that under the circumstances in which she had been placed, we too might have fallen?

Questions for Reflection and Discussion

What does the author of the address think was responsible for women turning to prostitution? How does the author hope to limit the practice? What factors might the author be ignoring?

133. DATING IN NINETEENTH-CENTURY CUBA

Time: nineteenth century CE
Place: Cuba
Author: Joseph Dimock

Joseph Dimock, a merchant from Virginia, traveled to Cuba in 1859 on business. The diary of his visit recorded a fascinating glimpse into a range of customs, albeit from an outsider's point of view and with his own strong racial prejudices and preconceptions. (The United States was, after all, on the brink of the Civil War, fought in part over the existence of African-American slaves.) His comments about dating customs, reprinted here, described what was probably typical of urban centers.

While in Havana, I noticed many things of which I haven't had time to speak. Some of the every day habits and customs of the people are so different from what we are accustomed to seeing at the North, that it naturally attracts the attention of a stranger.

The fashionable hour for making calls in the cities is just after dark…. The ladies generally kiss each other, and shake hands with their gentlemen acquaintances and then chat about the opera, dancing, riding on the *paseo* etc., but there is less said about "what she wore" and that sort of thing, than we generally hear at the North. The Cuban ladies show their weakness in jewelry, which is worn in great profusion, and their taste is generally for high colors in dress, but as their clothing is necessarily thin, they do not indulge in expensive silk, shawls, etc., and I presume there is less complaint of nothing to wear. Bonnets are not worn at all, so that luxury is dispensed with, but the magnificent lace veils worn in their place must cost quite or nearly as much. Every lady carries a fan, some of very elaborate workmanship, and they handle them in a style hardly to be imitated, for in fact a great portion of the flirting here is done with a fan. The gentlemen present during the call smoke if they feel so disposed, as the ladies find no fault with it, for a great many of them smoke *cigarros* at home, and I have seen some who were dressed as ladies riding in a *volante*, and puffing away at their cigars. (In the country 'tis a common occurrence to see the women among the ordinary people smoking long and strong plantation cigars.) When the ladies signify they are willing to end the visit, some one of the gentlemen present must offer his arm to the eldest and escort them to the *volante*, where he receives in return some complimentary expression for his polite attention and *adios*, accompanied with a quiet little flirt of the fan.

The ladies here always ride about the streets of Havana, and though American ladies will disregard the custom, they do it at the risk of being insulted not only by the odorous filthy negroes (the very worst class of which are the free negroes in Havana) but also by the Spaniards, who wear the clothing of, and profess to be gentlemen. They think they have a right to address a lady whom they have never seen before, and to say to her, "How handsome you are" or "I am greatly in love with you," etc., etc. This is a Spanish custom, and in the cities of old Spain, a lady considers herself slighted, if in passing a crowd of men she does not receive from them some flattering or endearing expression, and these Catalans bring this custom to Havana, where I regret to say the Cuban ladies do not receive them with the contempt and indignation they deserve. Occasionally an American lady who understands the language resents these liberties, and the case has been known where her cavalier has taught the Spaniard a lesson with his cane. There is one peculiar custom here not found elsewhere, I think. It is courting at the window. Where the suitor is not admitted to the house on account of not having had an introduction, or where the girls' parents disapprove the acquaintance, she finds means for an interview. Young ladies are not allowed to go out, except in company with a *duenna* and so they have no opportunity of communicating in public with their lovers, so the admirer posts himself at the window which is nearly on a level with the street, and projecting from the house, and here he makes love through the bars. If he is likely to be interrupted, she gives him notice and he retires to the next house or the adjoining corner till she gives him the signal to come forward to the window. Their communications are most generally verbal, for I regret to say a large portion of the Cuban ladies have a very limited education, and especially are they said to be deficient in writing, perhaps this is wisely forbidden by *los viejos* (the old folks), consequently their amatory epistles are very few and far between. I have from a seat on the Alameda d'Paula, watched some of these outdoor courtships with a good deal of interest, and been much amused by the skill the young lady exhibits to prevent discovery.

Questions for Reflection and Discussion

What is the role of the family in contacts between individuals? How do individuals make their romantic preferences known? How much are such practices dependent on an urban setting?

134. SUSAN B. ANTHONY ON WOMEN

Time: nineteenth century CE
Place: United States
Author: Susan B. Anthony

Changes in sexuality are part of much larger social shifts, including in the status of women. Susan B. Anthony, one of the best-known American figures in the early struggle for women's equality, joined the women's movement in 1852. For decades after that, she continued to publish and speak publicly on the issue, as well as advocating for the abolition of slavery, for improved education and working conditions, and against alcohol. This excerpt from an article in The Arena *magazine in 1897, when Anthony was 77, looked back on the changes in women's rights that she had witnessed. It was not until 1920, however, that the United States government gave women the right to vote.*

Fifty years ago woman in the United States was without a recognized individuality in any department of life. No provision was made in public or private schools for her education in anything beyond the rudimentary branches. An educated woman was a rarity and was gazed upon with something akin to awe…. Such was the helpless, dependent, fettered condition of woman when the first Woman's Rights Convention was called just forty-nine years ago, at Seneca Falls, N.Y., by Elizabeth Cady Stanton and Lucretia Mott…. Now, at the end of half a century, we find that, with few exceptions, all of the demands formulated at this convention have been granted. The great exception is the yielding of political rights, and toward this one point are directed now all the batteries of scorn, of ridicule, of denunciation that formerly poured their fire all along the line. Although not one of the predicted calamities occurred upon the granting of the other demands, the world is asked to believe that all of them will happen if this last stronghold is surrendered.

There is not space to follow the history of the last fifty years and study the methods by which these victories have been gained, but there is not one foot of advanced ground upon which women stand today that has not been obtained through the hard-fought battles of other women. The close of this 19th century finds every trade, vocation, and profession open to women, and every opportunity at their command for preparing themselves to follow these occupations. The girls as well as the boys of a family now fit themselves for such careers as their tastes and abilities permit. A vast amount of the household drudgery that once monopolized the whole time and strength of the mother and daughters has been taken outside and turned over to machinery in vast establishments. A money value is placed upon the labor of women. The ban of social ostracism has been largely removed from the woman wage earner. She who can make for herself a place of distinction in any line of work receives commendation instead of condemnation. Woman is no longer compelled to marry for support, but may herself make her own home and earn her own financial independence.

With but few exceptions, the highest institutions of learning in the land are as freely opened to girls as to boys, and they may receive their degrees at legal, medical, and theological colleges, and practice their professions without hindrance. In the world of literature and art, women divide the honors with men; and our civil service rules have secured for them many thousands of remunerative positions under the government. It is especially worthy of note that along with this general advancement of women has come a marked improvement in household methods. Woman's increased intelligence manifests itself in this department as conspicuously as in any other. Education, culture, mental discipline, business training develop far more capable mothers and housewives than were possible under the old regime. Men of the present generation give especial thought to comradeship in the selection of a wife, and she is no less desirable in their eyes because she is a college graduate or has learned the value and the management of money through having earned it.

There has been a radical revolution in the legal status of women. In most states the old common law has been annulled by legislative enactment, through which partial justice, at least, has been done to married women. In nearly every state they may retain and control property owned at marriage and all they may receive by gift or inheritance thereafter, and also their earnings outside the home. They may sue and be sued, testify in the courts, and carry on business in their own name, but in no state have wives any ownership in the joint earnings. In six or seven states, mothers have equal guardianship of the children. While in most states the divorce laws are the same for men and women, they never can bear equally upon both while all the property earning during marriage belongs wholly to the husband. There has been such a modification in public sentiment, however, that, in most cases, courts and juries show a marked leniency toward women.

The department of politics has been slowest to give admission to women. Suffrage is the pivotal right, and if it could have been secured at the beginning, women would not have been half a century in gaining the privileges enumerated above, for privileges they must be called so long as others may either give or take them away. If women could make the laws or elect those who make them, they would be in the position of sovereigns instead of subjects. Were they the political peers of man, they could command instead of having to beg, petition, and pray. Can it be possible it is for this reason that men have been so determined in their opposition to grant to women political power? But even this stronghold is beginning to yield to the long and steady pressure. In twenty-five states women possess suffrage in school matters, in four states they have a limited suffrage in local affairs; in one state they have municipal suffrage; in four states they have full suffrage, local, state, and national…. These radical changes have been effected without any social upheaval or domestic earthquakes, family relations have suffered no disastrous changes, and the men of the states where women vote furnish the strongest testimony in favor of women's suffrage.

There is no more striking illustration of the progress that has been made by woman than that afforded by her changed position in the church. Under the old regime the Quakers were the only sect who recognized the equality of women. Other denominations enforced the command of St. Paul, that women should keep silence in the churches. A few allowed the women to lift up their voices in class and prayer meetings, but they had no vote in matters of church government. Even the missionary and charity work was in the hands of men. Now the Unitarians, Universalists, Congregationalists, Wesleyan and Protestant Methodists, Christians, Free-Will Baptists, and possibly a few others, ordain women as ministers, and many parishes, in all parts of the country, are presided over by women preachers. The charitable and missionary work of the churches is practically turned over to women, who raise and disburse immense sums of money. While many of the great denominations still refuse to ordain women, to allow them a seat in their councils, or a vote in matters of church government, yet women themselves are, in a large measure, responsible for this state of affairs….

By far the larger part of the progressive movements just enumerated have taken place during the last twenty-five years, and the progress has been most rapid during the last half of this quarter of a century. With the advantages already obtained, with the great liberalizing of public sentiment, and with the actual proof that the results of enlarged opportunities for women have been for the betterment of society, the next decade ought to see the completion of the struggle for the equality of the sexes…. Who can measure the advantages that would result if the magnificent abilities of these women could be devoted to the needs of government, society, home, instead of being consumed in the struggle to obtain their birthright of individual freedom? Until this be gained we can never know, we cannot even prophesy, the capacity and power of woman for the uplifting of humanity. It may be delayed longer than we think; it may be here sooner than we expect; but the day will come when man will recognize woman as his peer, not only at the fireside but in the councils of the nation. Then, and not until then, will there be the perfect comradeship, the ideal union between the sexes that shall result in the highest development of the [human] race. What this shall be we may not attempt to define, but this we know, that only good can come to the individual or to the nation through the rendering of exact justice.

Questions for Reflection and Discussion

Why does Anthony suggest that political changes have lagged behind social, economic, and religious changes for women? Why does she begin with economic changes? What role do technological advances play in women's changing status?

135. A DENUNCIATION OF URBAN LIFE

Time: early twentieth century CE
Place: United States
Author: Jane Addams

In 1931 Jane Addams became the first American woman to receive a Nobel Peace Prize. She was honored for her efforts to improve working conditions for the poor and in a number of civil rights organizations, including as a founding member of the National Association for the Advancement of Colored People, the American Civil Liberties Union, and the International Congress of Women. Her writings on urban conditions, including this one published in 1912, derived from those experiences. Addams mentioned the prohibition of alcohol in this book; between 1920 and 1933, all sale of alcohol in the United States was banned; a decision that seemed only to add to rather than solve social problems. At the time she wrote, Chicago had a population slightly over two million; at the beginning of the twenty-first century there were more than 150 cities worldwide as large or larger.

The social relationships in a modern city are so hastily made and often so superficial, that the old human restraints of public opinion, long sustained in smaller communities, have also broken down. Thousands of young men and women in every great city have received none of the lessons in self-control which even savage tribes imparted to their children when they taught them to master their appetites as well as their emotions. These young people are perhaps further from all community restraint and genuine social control than the youth of the community have ever been in the long history of civilization. Certainly only the modern city has offered at one and the same time every possible stimulation for the lower nature and every opportunity for secret vice. Educators apparently forgot that this unrestrained stimulation of young people, so characteristic of our cities, although developing very rapidly, is of recent origin, and that we have not yet seen the outcome. The present education of the average young man has given him only the most unreal protection against the temptations of the city. Schoolboys are subjected to many lures from without just at the moment when they are filled with an inner tumult which utterly bewilders them and concerning which no one has instructed them save in terms of empty precept and unintelligible warning.

We are authoritatively told that the physical difficulties are enormously increased by uncontrolled or perverted imaginations, and all sound advice to young men in regard to this subject emphasizes a clean mind, exhorts an imagination kept free from sensuality and insists upon days filled with wholesome athletic interests. We allow this regime to be exactly reversed for thousands of young people living in the most crowded and most unwholesome parts of the city. Not only does the stage in its advertisements exhibit all the allurements of sex to such an extent that a play without a "love interest" is considered foredoomed to failure, but the novels which form the sole reading of thousands of young men and girls deal only with the course of true or simulated love, resulting in a rose-colored marriage, or in variegated misfortunes.

Often the only recreation possible for young men and young women together is dancing, in which it is always easy to transgress the proprieties. In many public dance halls, however, improprieties are deliberately fostered. The waltzes and two-steps are purposely slow, the couples leaning heavily on each other barely move across the floor, all the jollity and bracing exercise of the peasant dance is eliminated, as is all the careful decorum of the formal dance. The efforts to obtain pleasure or to feed the imagination are thus converged upon the senses which it is already difficult for young people to understand and to control. It is therefore not remarkable that in certain parts of the city groups of idle young men are found whose evil imaginations have actually inhibited their power for normal living. On the streets or in the poolrooms where they congregate their conversation, their tales of adventure, their remarks upon women who pass by, all reveal that they have been caught in the toils of an instinct so powerful and primal that when left without direction it can easily overwhelm its possessor and swamp his faculties. These young men, who do no regular work, who expect to be supported by their mothers and sisters and to get money for the shows and theatres by any sort of disreputable undertaking, are in excellent training for the life of the procurer, and it is from such groups that they are recruited. There is almost a system of apprenticeship, for boys when very small act as "look outs" and are later utilized to make acquaintances with girls in order to introduce them to professionals. From this they gradually learn the method of procuring girls and at last do an independent business....

The girls with a desire for adventure seem confined to this one dubious outlet even more than the boys, although there are only one-eighth as many delinquent girls as boys brought into the juvenile court in Chicago, the charge against the girls in almost every instance involves a loss of chastity.... The little girls brought into the juvenile court are usually daughters of those poorest immigrant families living in the worst type of city tenements, who are frequently forced to take boarders in order to pay the rent. A surprising number of little girls have first become involved in wrongdoing through the men of their own households....

One is also inclined to reproach educators for neglecting to give children instruction in play when one sees the unregulated amusement parks which are apparently so dangerous to little girls twelve or fourteen years old. Because they are childishly eager to pay for a ride on the scenic railway or for a ticket to an entertainment, these disappointed children easily accept many favors from the young men who are standing near the entrances for the express purpose of ruining them. The hideous reward which is demanded from them later in the evening, after they have enjoyed the many "treats" which the amusement park offers, apparently seems of little moment. Their childish minds are filled with the memory of the lurid pleasures to the oblivion of the later experience, and they eagerly tell their companions of this possibility "of getting in to all the shows." These poor little girls pass unnoticed amidst a crowd of honest people seeking recreation after a long day's work, groups of older girls walking and talking gaily with young men of their acquaintance, and happy children holding their parents' hands. This cruel exploitation of the childish eagerness for pleasure is, of course, possible only among a certain type of forlorn city children who are totally without standards and into whose colorless lives a visit to the amusement park brings the acme of delirious excitement. It is possible that these children are the inevitable product of city life….

Many children are also found who have been decoyed into their first wrongdoing through the temptation of the saloon…. Yet many mothers, hard pressed by poverty, are obliged to rent houses next to vicious neighborhoods and their children very early become familiar with all the outer aspects of vice. Among them are the children of widows who make friends with their dubious neighbors during the long days while their mothers are at work…. Who cannot recall at least one of these desperate mothers, overworked and harried through a long day, prolonged by the family washing and cooking into the evening, followed by a night of foreboding and misgiving because the very children for whom her life is sacrificed are slowly slipping away from her control and affection? … Nevertheless, such a woman whose wages are fixed on the basis of individual subsistence, who is quite unable to earn a family wage, is still held by a legal obligation to support her children with the desperate penalty of forfeiture if she fail….

We may soberly hope that some of the experiments made by governmental and municipal authorities to control and regulate the sale of liquor will at last meet with such a measure of success that the existence of public prostitution, deprived of its artificial stimulus of alcohol, will in the end be imperiled. The Chicago Vice Commission has made a series of valuable suggestions for the regulation of saloons and for the separation of the sale of liquor from dance halls and from all other places known as recruiting grounds for the white slave traffic. There is still need for a much wider and more thorough education of the public in regard to the historic connection between commercialized vice and alcoholism, of the close relation between politics and the liquor interests, behind which the social evil so often entrenches itself.

Questions for Reflection and Discussion

What does Addams see as the key to the problems of urbanization? What does she see as the key to their solution? Are there contradictions in her assessment of the problems?

136. CHANGING MARITAL PATTERNS AMONG THE KGATLA

Time: mid-twentieth century CE
Place: southern Africa (modern Botswana)
Author: Isaac Schapero

Isaac Schapero, a professor of social anthropology at the University of Cape Town, South Africa, studied the peoples of southern Africa, including the Tsana people of Botswana (then Bechuanaland, a South African Protectorate). Published in 1941, Married Life in an African Tribe, *his study on the Kgatla branch of the Tsana people, included many comments about the transformation of marriage and family life.*

The old Kgatla family, in its typical form, was a polygamous unit in which each wife had a separate rank and establishment. The majority of families were actually monogamous, but certain matrimonial customs and laws of property, succession, and inheritance, were all based upon the conception of polygamy. A man's first wife was sought for him by his parents preferably from among his close relatives. His other wives, if any, he usually chose himself. After the betrothal had been confirmed, he cohabited with the woman for some time at her parents' home before bringing her to live among his own people. His marriage to her was not regarded as legally valid, nor could he claim as his own the children she bore him, until the cattle known as *bogadi* had been given for her. These cattle were contributed jointly by his father and other relatives, and were divided among the wife's people, especially her father and maternal uncle. Like the discussions preceding the choice of a wife or the approval of a suitor, *bogadi* showed that a marriage involved not only the two spouses themselves but also their kinsmen.

Marriage served, among other purposes, to regulate sexual relations. Premarital chastity was an ideal the attainment of which was attempted by segregating the older boys and girls, and by condemning childbearing by an unmarried woman. Extramarital relations, again, were punished as unlawful except when practiced to raise up seed to an impotent or dead husband. Sexual intercourse was normally considered proper only if the couple were married to each other. Even then its pattern was culturally determined, in that it was prohibited on certain occasions and prescribed on others. But the main object of marriage was the production of legitimate offspring. Only married women were entitled to bear children, and if an unmarried girl did so both she and her lover were punished severely, while their child had no legal claim upon us father.

Large families were the ideal, and it was partly for this reason that polygamy was practiced. Children of both sexes were desired to ensure adequate help in all the household task. Daughters were a source of wealth through the *bogadi* received for them, but sons were preferred, for they would perpetuate the father's line and inherit his property and rank. Various special customs were therefore practiced if a woman was barren or produced daughters only. These included magical rites to make her fruitful, the adoption of a child from some near relative, the provision of a "substitute wife" by her family, and the employment of an authorized lover "to enter her hut" and raise up seed to her husband. The last two customs were practiced also when either wife or husband had died. They indicated once more that marriage was in part a contract between two families, each of which had to ensure the fulfillment of the associated obligations if its original representative was unable to do so himself....

Some reference should here be made to the general status of women. They were regarded as socially inferior to men, and in Kgatla law were always treated as minors. Before marriage a woman was under the authority of her father or guardian, while after it she came under the control of her husband, and, on his death, of some other male member of his family. She could never sue independently at court, she could own property but might not dispose of it without her guardian's consent, and she could not inherit cattle or other livestock from her father or husband. Women took no part in the government of the tribe; they did not attend the tribal assemblies, and all the political offices were kept exclusively in the hands of men. Even in family life preference was given to males, and a woman bearing daughters only was held to have failed in one of her most important duties to her husband. Certain activities, too, were assigned to men only, others to women, and neither sex would readily undertake work normally performed by the other. The ritual impurity associated with menstruation imposed upon women various taboos and other observances peculiar to their sex. They were also excluded from taking a leading part in sacrifice and other active phases of ancestor-worship. At feasts and on other public occasions when both sexes met, men and women always sat in separate groups, while in ordinary social life they had little in common.

The modern Kgatla family does not perform all the functions noted above. Some have been taken over, either wholly or in part, by specialized agencies that formerly did not exist in the tribe. The change has been most marked in religion. With the evolution of Christianity, the Churches have become the dominant religious units, and people who are not professing Christians have no organized system of worship. The family has therefore lost its ancient role of serving as the social basis for the tribal religion….

In economic life, the family has lost much of its traditional self-sufficiency. Although in the main it still produces its own food and builds its own home, it has become increasingly dependent upon outside markets like the trading stores for most of its clothes, utensils, and other manufactured goods. The consequent decay of local industries has deprived both men and women of tasks in which they formerly engaged. On the other hand, the desire for imported goods, and the necessity of paying taxes, levies, and other cash dues, have forced people to seek new sources of income, the most important of which is wage labor for money. The result has been a change in the traditional division of labor between the members of the household. Most of the younger men, whether married or not, spend a good deal of their time working in European industrial or farming areas, and through the money they earn contribute more than before to the support of their families. A few other men have taken up specialized occupations at home. But they all still rely upon farming for the great bulk of their food supply. Their absence abroad, however, or their preoccupation with other tasks at home, means that they cannot as a rule participate very greatly in agriculture and other domestic work.

The attendance of children at school has also to some extent deprived the family of labor resources it could formerly command. As a result, many women have been burdened with more work than before, and where, as occasionally happens, a husband while away fails to provide for his wife, she may be almost entirely responsible for maintaining herself and her children. A few women have engaged locally in such new occupations as teaching, nursing, or domestic service for European residents, and others go to work abroad, but the great majority are still concerned primarily with running their homes and cultivating their fields.

The production and rearing of children are still among the main tasks of the family. But it has become less exclusively the reproductive unit. In contrast with the trend of development in European societies, the proportion of unmarried mothers has increased very considerably. Their children are still considered illegitimate, but the woman herself and her lover are no longer punished as severely as before. Some of the customs traditionally associated with childbearing in marriage have also decayed. The taking of a substitute wife, or the entering of a woman's hut, are both less commonly practiced. Polygamy, again, has declined so considerably that very few men can nowadays have as many lawful children as in the old days. The later age of marriage, and the lengthy absences of men working abroad, may also have contributed to reduce the size of the family. Statistical evidence is not available, but the Kgatla themselves maintain that women nowadays bear fewer children than formerly. The spread of venereal diseases, another innovation, makes it probable that their contention is not unfounded.

Marriage continues to regulate sexual relations, which are still considered improper except between husband and wife. But premarital affairs are now treated much more tolerantly, and have become the rule instead of the exception. Married men, again, unable or unwilling for religious or economic reasons to have more than one wife, take concubines instead, while married women, during the absence at work of their husbands, seldom remain faithful for long. It is therefore no longer so exclusively within marriage itself that people find sexual satisfaction. On the other hand, the greater role played nowadays by personal attraction in the choice of a mate probably serves to enhance the pleasure husband and wife get from sleeping together. There is, nevertheless, a good deal of maladjustment. This may have existed in the old days also, but the frequent separations of the spouses, and the infidelity of one or both, are contributory factors that have been greatly intensified more recently.

In tribal law, the head of a family is still the guardian of his wife, and of his children as long as they live with him; he controls their movements and property, and is responsible for their debts and civil offences. In marriages contracted under European civil law, a wife was at first theoretically entitled to new property rights and other privileges. These, however, were never accepted inside the tribe, and since 1926 have in effect also been excluded from the provisions of the law. But women married under civil law are entitled to divorce their husbands for adultery, a right that does not extend to others; they can also resort independently to the European courts, and are

trying to enforce the same right for the tribal courts, although hitherto with little success. In other respects, too the status of women has changed. Daughters are now entitled to share in their father's estate, and failing sons they are the main heirs in preference to a paternal uncle. The great majority of Church members are women, while four times as many girls as boys go to school. Women are therefore on the whole the more "educated" section of the tribe. Some, as teachers, dressmakers, nurses, or domestic servants, have also attained a measure of economic freedom. The result of all this is that they have become more independent in their attitude, and less submissive to the men. Nevertheless, they are still obliged to live either among their own people or among their husbands', and are perpetually subject to the authority of a male guardian. It is therefore as yet impossible for them, while still inside the Reserve, ever to feel completely emancipated. This applies as much to widows and divorcees as to wives or unmarried daughters. Adult sons, again, are in European law individually liable for the payment of tax. This implicit recognition of their independent status, however, is not acknowledged in tribal law. But they are notoriously tending to act with more freedom than before, and no longer look always to their father for advice and approval. Many, for instance, now choose their own wives instead of relying upon their parents to do so for them; occasionally a man may even go to reside permanently among his wife's people, an innovation often regarded with disgust, but illustrating the decay of parental control. Daughters, too, have much greater say nowadays in the choice of their husbands. In practice, therefore, the head of a family is less powerful than he used to be, although in tribal law the traditional ideal persists of a husband's dominance and his wife's subservience, and of unquestioning obedience to parents by children.

There have been other changes in marriage itself. The traditional wedding ceremonies have been supplemented by the corresponding Christian rites, which, although practiced by a minority of the people, are now considered more respectable. Polygamy, the inheritance of widows, and the taking of a substitute wife, are forbidden by the Church to its members, but even among the heathens they are no longer so extensively practiced. Child betrothals have virtually disappeared. Marriages with relatives or neighbors are still common, but wives are now more frequently taken from strange families. Finally, people seem to marry somewhat later in life than they formerly did, a fact partly responsible for the changed attitude towards premarital unchastity. But betrothal negotiations are still conducted along the same lines as before, and *bogadi*, at one time prohibited, is now again an essential part of marriage. The two features traditionally considered necessary to validate a marriage are therefore still retained, even where the couple are married in church and so under European civil law.

The family remains the only unit providing people with a home. But more than ever, it is mainly the women and the younger children who participate habitually in the domestic community of life. The traditional separation of the sexes in everyday social intercourse has largely broken down but most men, especially if they go to work abroad, spend a good deal of their time away from their wives. The older boys still live mainly at the cattle-posts, or also go out to work abroad, and the children attending school stay alone in the villages for part of the year while other people are at the fields. The members of the family tend therefore to be more scattered than formerly, and as a result it is seldom that relations between them are very intimate. The older men, who no longer go to work abroad, see more of their families than do the rest, but even they are so often away at their cattle-posts and elsewhere that there can be little companionship between them and their wives....

Questions for Reflection and Discussion

What factors have contributed to the transformation of Kgatla sexual life? How are these factors interrelated? How much do individuals consciously participate in making such changes, and what changes are unconscious ones?

137. WOMEN'S EDUCATION AND MARRIAGE IN JAPAN

Time: mid-twentieth century CE
Place: Japan
Author: Sumie Seo Mishima

Sumie Seo Mishima grew up in early twentieth-century Japan but traveled to the United States to attend Wellesley College near Boston. Returning to Japan, she had difficulty adjusting to what she considered to be the more traditional lifestyle and duties expected of her. Her experience was common—most female college graduates at that time never married—reflecting that of the countless individuals who had to balance old and new values and customs. Japan itself was undergoing rapid social change in the era when Mishima was raised. Its Meiji government (since 1861 under the democratic rule of the emperor after the overthrow of the Tokugawa shogun) vigorously followed a policy of westernization and modernization.

One Christmas I was invited by Mr. and Mrs. Edward Easton of Albany for the whole vacation. At the coming out dance of Kate Easton, their daughter, who was then a junior at Wellesley, I danced with boys for the first time in my life. I was completely flustered and was very grateful to these courteous and handsome Albany boys who so kindly led me in spite of my clumsy following in cumbrous *kimono* and heavy silk and felt sandals. What a lovely thing, I thought, that boys and girls came to know each other this way, instead of as in Japan men and women stealthily looking at each other and girls being taught that it was the most unwomanly and irredeemable crime to fall in love with a man. I was charmed by the courtesy of American boys and particularly by their beautiful table manners.

[Eventually, Mishima returned home to Japan to teach.]

I wanted to become a college teacher and enjoy economic and intellectual independence and refined social life, like Wellesley professors. But here in Japan I found that intellectual living was a strictly masculine privilege. The mass of women were required to bury themselves completely in domestic cares, hardly reading a book and never claiming a social life of their own, while men monopolized intellectual society among themselves. If ever they came in contact with feminine company outside their homes, it was that of professional entertainers. In this scheme of life an unmarried woman without family and social life had no place....

"Why don't you marry?" said some of my old schoolmates tenderly. "You must marry. It is the duty of every woman," said some elderly ladies rebukingly. But my relatives said nothing. It had cost them too much to send me to America, and now I was earning a good income from the Japanese point of view. They feared that marriage would ruin all my past efforts and career. And how could I marry? I thought I knew all about men; they were selfish and intellectual and therefore interesting and profitable as friends, but impossible as husbands!

But marriage came to me suddenly, and when it came I had no power to resist. When I was attending the evening lectures at the university, I came to be on friendly terms with some of the professors there. One of them lived not very far from where I did.... Some time later the professor called on me in a very depressed mood and told me that his wife had left him for good. I knew that she had been living apart from him and that his mother had been keeping house for him and taking care of his four little children. A few days later his mother came with a pair of beautiful silk sandals as a present for me. She was extremely engaging and asked me to marry her son; and then she spoke in a bitter tone of her daughter-in-law, who had deserted her. I felt completely repulsed at first, but had not determination enough to refuse her at once. I asked her and the professor to wait, as I wanted to think the matter over before I gave them a definite answer.... I could not imagine myself becoming the stepmother of four lively little children, feeding them and washing and mending for them from morning till night, putting aside my books and expensive American college education. But the mother said that she would take care of the children so that I could continue studying, teaching, and tutoring, and keep what I had earned for my own use; and that, if I would only supervise the children's education, she would feel most grateful. Moreover, the family was intending to move into a bigger house and hire another maid since one servant was not enough for looking after so many children. I began to consider her proposition seriously.

I could not tell whether I loved the professor or not. Certainly I felt no romantic sort of love. I could not possibly take at once into my mental and emotional scope the professor, the engaging mother, and the four pretty but rather delicate children—two boys and two girls—and the family debts bequeathed from the late father. But at the same time I could not say a definite no. I had been too aware of the emotional and intellectual starvation I had been suffering, while desperately trying to make headway in my true career. Then I knew that if I married at all, I must choose a poor man who could not afford to shut up his wife in the home, but had to have her go out and work to earn money….

But there were four children. But I knew that a Japanese woman after twenty-five could seldom marry a man without children. Four were not very many, considering the fact of Japanese men marrying young in the prosperous days of the early 1900s and having children in close succession. I knew of girls younger than I marrying into families with five, seven, or even eight children. Moreover, it was clear that the professor and his children could not live without someone to serve as wife and mother to them; and perhaps very few women could play the part as fitly as I could, making them happy by offering spiritual and material contributions to their life….

Then I had to obtain consent from my numerous relatives, all of whom were furiously opposed to my marrying this poor professor with four children. They said that, with my education and "accomplishments," I could marry, if I married at all, a family far richer and of greater social standing. Even a short time before, some great family was inquiring about me through a mutual credit bureau. My aunts were particularly angry, because I had refused all the candidates they had looked up for me, only to choose in the end such a man. But I was not to be moved. And they all yielded, though very unwillingly, because by that time they had known that when I was once determined I did not move. "Go on, then; and may you be happily married!" they all said at last, and gave me handsome presents….

[Once married, however, Mishima finds her life not as she expected it. In particular, she finds out disturbing things about the married life of her husband's parents.]

Evidently the husband loved the wife most passionately, and so he was bitterly jealous when she was too much occupied with the care of her father-in-law and the labor of the complicated household management. As many Japanese husbands do when they are dissatisfied with their family life, he tried to find comfort in the company of *geisha* women, who flattered and spoiled him as long as he showered money on them, as it was their occupation, and who eventually made him impossible for his wife to please. He was gay and generous with *geisha* women, but usually sullen toward his wife…. It seems that our *geisha* institution flourished under the patronage of the adventurous leaders of the Meiji era. The daring patriots in the turbulent days of the downfall of the Tokugawa feudal regime obtained truly valuable cooperation, social, spiritual, and even political, from the courtesans of the time, when other classes of Japanese women were too limited in imagination and activity…. Thus came about the flowering of our *geisha* society, until the ladies of that circle came practically to represent the women of Japan to the world. But it meant to Japanese wives a new and painful burden, the like of which was unknown to the women of the Tokugawa days, whose husbands had concubines in some cases, but seldom such grand and extravagant female friends.

Another factor which influenced Japanese home life was the economic result of the speedy Westernization of the country. Men trained under the feudal regime now turned to business and the management of capital. Many ex-*samurai*, utterly lacking commercial training, lost whatever little had been bequeathed them by their fathers and went heavily into

debt. In the days of such social and economic upheavals, only the exceptionally wise and sensible got along well enough to bring happiness to their family life. And my husband's father was one of the many who did not succeed.

Questions for Reflection and Discussion

To what forces does Mishima attribute the changes in family life? How does she reconcile the old and new ways in her own life? What role did education play in the choices that Mishima made and the opportunities available to her?

138. SEX IN ADVERTISING

Time: early twentieth century CE
Place: United States
Artist: unknown

This American produce label from around 1930 needs little commentary: It is clear what is being compared. The use of sex in advertising attracted customers' attention, one of the chief goals of consumerism. Such blatant use of sexual imagery—note that the strap of the young woman's blouse has slipped partly down, to further allude to the comparison—might offend as many people as it appeals to, but the image also projects an innocence that somewhat masks its overtness. Yet even her innocence has a sexual side: The "farmer's daughter" jokes, about young women too naïve to recognize their seduction at the hands of an urban sophisticate, has long been a staple of the American West.

Questions for Reflection and Discussion

How much has sex in advertising changed since this label was drawn? How might this image, and the "farmer's daughter" jokes, play on the contrasts between the sexualities of rural and urban dwellers?

139. PROSTITUTION IN BOMBAY

Time: mid-twentieth century CE
Place: India
Authors: S.D. Punekar and Kamala Rao

Modern writers on prostitution are often just as interested in determining its causes as earlier writers were but have different methodological tools at their disposal. S.D. Punekar, a founding member of the Indian Society of Labour Economics, published a study with Kamala Rao on prostitutes in Bombay (modern Mumbai) in

Though the *devadasi* system is an anachronism in modern civilization, one-third of the common prostitutes interviewed for this study were found to be *devadasis*, most of whom were dedicated to the goddess Yellamma. It was observed that dedication of girls was still prevalent among the backward communities, predominantly the Harijans, in the rural areas. We may draw the attention of the law enforcing authorities to the fact that in spite of the law prohibiting the dedication of girls as *devadasis*, many are being dedicated and virtually forced into prostitution. It is also noted that prostitution has been so much the accepted way of life with the *devadasis* that they not only enter it irrespective of other background factors, but also claim that they have a right to prostitute. Thus, it may be said that the *devadasis* system conspicuously augments the problem of prostitution….

The country being predominantly populated by the Hindus, it is not surprising that 86 per cent of the prostitutes are Hindus. However, it is worth noting that nearly half of the Hindu prostitutes are Harijans, which calls for an intensive program of social uplift among these communities in particular.

About 10 per cent of the respondents were found to be literate, and a vast majority of the women interviewed were graded as mentally average. They should, therefore, make a strong case for compulsory education for girls, not with a view to make them merely literate but to educate them for a responsible adult life.

A large majority of the prostitutes in the City brothels are from the rural areas and belong to poor peasant families which are mostly single families. We may safely infer that the common prostitutes, considered to be the lowest class of prostitutes, are largely constituted of women from the lowest social and economic cadre…. Our data, however, do not fully support the general presumption that the most important cause of prostitution is poverty.

The case histories generally indicated that a large majority of the respondents were indifferently brought up as girls, and gave no evidence of any binding attachment having existed between the family members—at least between the respondents and their family members…. In most cases, both the parents, or the guardians, worked from dawn to dusk and had no time for the children who, with no one to guide them and with no schooling or healthy occupation to keep them busy, were left to themselves to grow up anyhow. They were open to the hazards of evil influences, and free to indulge their uncontrolled, often misguided, adolescent fancies and temptations…. Nearly two-thirds of the girls had lost both or either of their parents before they entered prostitution and in the majority of the cases, they were less than ten years of age when the death of their parents occurred. Most of these respondents grew up as unwanted children, grudgingly brought up by their relatives who did not care for them…. In the case of the grown up girls also, destitution rendered them helpless since they lacked the strength and confidence to face life alone, as they were ill-equipped for it due to lack of education, enlightenment, vocational training, etc., which help an individual to become self-reliant.

About two-thirds of the non-*devadasis* are married women of whom girls widowed at an early age and runaway wives form a large majority. Most of the married respondents were unhappily married—ill-treatment, drunkenness and unfaithfulness of the husband being the major causes of their marital discord. It was seen that unequal marriages were responsible to a considerable extent for such marital disharmony....

Over half of our interviewees left their homes between the age of 11 and 20 years, the model age group being 15-17 years for the non-*devadasis* and 13-14 years for the *devadasis*. All the *devadasis* and nearly half of the non-*devadasis* left their homes for the purpose of prostitution. About one-third of the non-*devadasis* seem to have left their homes and entered the brothels under conditions which may be broadly termed as "involuntary," that is, due to deception, kidnapping or being forced into the profession with no choice whatsoever. What is more significant however is that the other two-thirds seem to have left their homes and taken to prostitution of their own volition, inasmuch as they did not resist becoming prostitutes even if they did not actively volunteer to be so. How many of them were actually aware of the full implications of the life they had chosen to enter, we cannot exactly say....

Their life in the profession is by no means satisfying to most prostitutes. The living conditions are indeed unhealthy and the majority of the women earn only a meager income.... About 36 per cent of the respondents said that they were suffering from venereal diseases. (The actual number suffering from them might be much more.) In spite of these and other distressing conditions of their life, less than 10 per cent of the respondents were willing to give up their profession for a respectable job.... Many of them even said, "We like this free life." ... Another factor that probably accounts for their unwillingness to get out of the profession is that in many instances the relations between the brothel-keepers and the prostitutes are friendly and cordial.... This too indicates that above all human beings need the security of being wanted and cared for.

Questions for Reflection and Discussion

How reliable does this study appear to be? Do the authors of the study seem surprised at their results? Do they have assumptions that might have manipulated its results?

140. DATING IN MODERN TAIWAN

Time: late twentieth century CE
Place: Taiwan, China
Authors: Lou Tsu-k'uang and Wolfram
  Eberhard

It is not difficult to get information on modern dating. This example, from a study published in Taiwan in 1974, described some patterns that the authors observed among high-school and college students at the time. Their comments, contrasting those patterns with older Chinese customs, make this worth reprinting here.

In Taiwan as well as Taipei, dating is not a simple matter. Although younger or more liberal participants do not necessarily feel it must lead directly to marriage, one still cannot "play the field," date on an entirely casual basis, as the reputation of both parties is thereby put in jeopardy. Therefore, a certain amount of care must be taken, first by the male in deciding he wants to go out with a girl, and then by the girl herself in deciding whether or not to accept.... If he has been involved with a mixed group and wants to focus his attention on a group member, he will have little problem, because the two will have gotten to know each other under proper circumstances, i.e., they can trace their acquaintanceship to ties that are recognized as upright by Chinese society (e.g., a friend of one's sister or brother, a classmate, or an introduction through a close friend or relative). If the boy has no such source of potential dating partners, his task will be more difficult. Hopefully he can find a mutual acquaintance who will be able to introduce him to a girl, or at least tell him her name. If not, he must resort to other means. A common one is to find out where the girl lives and her schedule—what time she goes and comes to school, work, etc., and which route or bus she takes. Then he will "happen" to be on that bus, or perhaps will be content to wait at a corner and watch her as she walks by. With one exception, unless he knows the girl, Chinese custom precludes his talking to her directly....

After finding out her name and address, the boy can begin to send her letters. These are not love letters, although he will probably express his admiration (but by no means his love) for the girl. He will begin very apologetically, excusing himself for "bothering" her, begging her indulgence, and hoping she will read on. He will proceed to tell the girl, without being too personal, what he likes about her, and then tells her about himself, his interests and his thoughts. If he feels he has the skill, he will include a poem, something which shows the depth of his thinking. He will probably give his name, although he may send several letters before doing so. The next move is up to the girl. She is not expected to respond immediately, but if after several months she still has not done so, the boy will probably give up. If the girl begins to reply to his letters, however, the relationship can continue....

The Chinese have been very proud of their writing system and their literature for centuries. A good pen was the mark of an educated, distinguished man. The way a boy writes a letter to a girl can greatly influence her decision whether to accept or reject him. Whereas young American girls are impressed with a boy's appearance, automobile, or athletic prowess, a Chinese girl is more impressed with his skill at letters. Thus, in writing a letter, a Chinese boy can show off to a girl. More important, writing letters allows all concerned to save face. Traditionally, nothing was done in China in a direct manner. There was always something or someone intervening between the two parties, softening any rebuff. Today, a letter has the same advantages....

When a boy does ask a girl out, he must be prepared to be turned down. The way this is done gives him a hint of how the girl feels about him. If she gives a valid excuse and turns him down without damaging his pride, he knows he should ask again. If not, he will probably try again, but if he receives similar treatment, he will give up on that girl. I had a Chinese roommate from Taiwan several years ago who told me the reason for this. He said that if one wished to date a Chinese girl, he must be prepared to be turned down a half dozen times or so. "This is because she is testing you," he said. "She wants to make sure you are sincere in your desire to take her out." ...

Dating, as was pointed out earlier, is considered quite serious. Affection is even more so.... Most young people would consider kissing a person only if there was a fairly strong feeling between them.... Besides the seriousness with which kissing is seen, there are other factors which can inhibit young people in physically expressing affection toward one another. In public—on the streets, in theaters and in other such places—the only permissible physical displays are holding hands or having one's arm around the shoulder or waist of one's partner, and even these are frowned upon. The problem is that there are few other places for a couple who wants to neck or pet to go. It has already been mentioned that most boys do not escort their girl friends all the way home. Even if they did, it is doubtful that they would find a place sufficiently private to put the girl's mind at rest so that she could be affectionate to her boy friend. Moreover, very few families have private automobiles to take young people away from the crowded neighborhoods to the more deserted outskirts of the city where they can neck. There are a few parks, but these are dangerous places for young couples; gangs of toughs roam there in the evening to collect *ai-ch'ing shui*, "love tax," from them.

Questions for Reflection and Discussion

How do social realities set the parameters for modern dating in Taiwan? How are older traditions reshaped in modern times?

141. EGYPTIAN WOMEN AND WORK

Time: late twentieth century CE
Place: Egypt
Author: Nawal El Saadawi

Nawal El Saadawi, a physician and novelist, has written numerous books on the conditions of women in modern Egypt, including The Hidden Face of Eve, *published in 1977 and the source for this excerpt. In 1980, and largely because of the Egyptian government's reaction to her writings, El Saadawi was imprisoned for two years for "crimes against the state." She continues to publish on Arab women's lives, although she no longer lives in Egypt.*

Egyptian and Arab society still considers that women have been created to play the role of mothers and wives, whose function in life is to serve at home and bring up the children. Women have only been permitted to seek jobs outside the home as a response to economic necessities in society or within the family. A woman is permitted to leave her home every day and go to an office, a school, a hospital or a factory on condition that she returns after her day of work to shoulder the responsibilities related to her husband and children, which are considered more important than anything else she may have done. Although some Arab countries such as Egypt, Algeria, Syria, Sudan, South Yemen, Somalia and Iraq have, to different degrees, followed policies which they consider as socialist, in none of these countries have any real steps been taken to solve the problems of working women, and above all to provide facilities that could reduce the burdens of cooking, cleaning, serving in the home, and bringing up the children. The provision of appropriate institutions or facilities does not seem to be a matter of importance to the rulers of these countries. The working women in these Arab countries have not yet become a sufficiently strong and organized force that could exert pressure on the State and ruling classes, and so ensure a more rapid and radical response to their needs. Women's organizations are still either groups of women from the upper classes seeking an outlet for their charitable or social inclinations, or sections of the socialist political parties or federations that have no independent existence or initiative of their own and function as passive bureaucratic appendages only marginally concerned with the real problems of women in general, or of working women in particular.

Undoubtedly, the employment of women outside the home has helped them to attain a greater degree of freedom and independence from the husband or father. This is particularly so since Islam has clearly given women the right to control their own possessions and money, without any form of tutelage by the men. Nevertheless, work and a job can be a new form of exploitation if it is within the context and social circumstances of a class society which is governed by unequal relations between people of different social strata or sexes, or of a patriarchal family where the man dominates the woman, body and mind, in accordance with law, customs and religious legislation. For if a woman's body and mind are enslaved, how can she be free to dispose of her money? Is it possible for a woman who is afraid that her husband might divorce her at any moment, to oppose him when he interferes with the way she handles her own earnings? The law can force a woman to return to her husband, and send her back under police escort, so how can she be free to dispose of her money, when she is not even free to dispose of her life? That is why jobs and work for women outside the home have not yet led, in general, to the liberation of the Arab woman, and in most cases have only burdened her with new anxieties, problems and responsibilities....

Despite the ever growing number of employed and educated women in the Arab countries, the great majority of them still do not know even how to read or write. The educational system so far has played almost no role in ridding society of the outmoded conventions and customs and conservative ideas that still hold sway over the minds of both men and women. Even educated people are still dominated by backward concepts, superstitions and fantasies that have been handed down to them by their mothers and fathers, and that are often taken up and repeated by Arab rulers, politicians and thinkers. Thus people continue to be misled and exploited....

For most Arab men, to even think of a wife working outside the home is nothing more or less than a direct reflection on his position and prestige as a male, and an affront to him as a man. The maleness of a man or his manliness is still considered to reside mainly in his capacity to rule over his wife, to dominate her, to cater to her needs financially, and not to allow her to mix with other men in offices, on the streets, or in a public transport. This is especially so if he is a real "he man," a man with a capital "M." Cultured Arab intellectuals, on the whole, have been able to overcome these complexes, but most other men are still captive to such ideas. An Arab man might be obliged to allow his wife to work outside the home for economic reasons, but deep down within himself he will always feel his inability to provide for his family alone as a weakness or something to be ashamed of. The working wife herself might even share his reactions and feel some contempt for him because he is obliged to make her work. A wife who does not work may, in turn, take pride in the fact that her man is sufficiently well off to take care of her needs. All these distorted ideas and feelings are due to the fact that woman's work outside the home does not of itself lead to the true liberation of the woman as long as it continues to operate within the framework of a class society and under the patriarchal system.

Questions for Reflection and Discussion

How does El Saadawi link women's equality to changing social factors? Why does she insist that both men and women must change in order for true equality to happen? Is any of her argument specific to Arab or Islamic society?

SOURCES AND FURTHER READING

Most histories of sexuality take social factors into consideration, so finding books and articles that separate them out for study is somewhat artificial. Still, there are some useful readings that address a range of social influences. On capitalism and its relationship to sexuality, for example, there are detailed studies such as Wally Seccombe's *A Millennium of Family Change: Feudalism to Capitalism in Northwestern Europe* (London: Verso, 1992); and David T. Evans's *Sexual Citizenship: The Material Construction of Sexualities* (New York: Routledge, 1993); a few examples of interesting related articles include John D'Emilio's "Capitalism and Gay Identity," in *Making Trouble: Essays on Gay History, Politics, and the University* (New York: Routledge, 1992); Zine Magubane's "Capitalism, Female Embodiment, and the Transformation of Commodification into Sexuality," in *Bringing the Empire Home: Race, Class, and Gender in Britain and Colonial South Africa* (Chicago: University of Chicago Press, 2004); and Marjolein van der Veen's "Beyond Slavery and Capitalism: Producing Class Difference in the Sex Industry," in *Class and Its Others*, J. K. Gibson-Graham et al., eds. (Minneapolis, MN: University of Minnesota Press, 2000).

Some of the work on urbanization and sexuality includes the essays in *Cities of Difference*, Ruth Fincher and Jane M. Jacobs, eds. (New York: Guilford, 1998); a sampling of the many more specialized studies would include Jane Rendell's "Gendered Identities and the Early Nineteenth-Century Street," in *Images of the Street: Planning, Identity, and Control in Public Space*, Nicholas Fyfe, ed. (New York: Routledge, 1998); Ayse Öncü's "Global Consumerism, Sexuality as Public Spectacle, and the Cultural Remapping of Istanbul in the 1990s," in *Fragments of Culture: The Everyday of Modern Turkey*, Deniz Kandiyoti and Ayse Saktanber, eds. (New Brunswick, NJ: Rutgers University Press, 2002); Peter A. Jackson's "Gay Capitals in Global Gay History: Cities, Local Markets, and the Origins of Bangkok's Same-Sex Cultures," in *Postcolonial Urbanism: Southeast Asian Cities and Global Processes*, Ryan Bishop et al., eds. (New York: Routledge, 2003); Leena Abraham's "Redrawing the Lakshman Rekha: Gender Differences and Cultural Constructions in Youth Sexuality in Urban India," in *Sexual Sites, Seminal Attitudes: Sexualities, Masculinities, and Culture in South Asia*, Sanjay Srivastava, ed. (Thousand Oaks, CA: Sage, 2004); and the essays in *The Margins of the City: Gay Men's Urban Lives*, ed. Stephen Whittle (Brookfield, VT: Ashgate, 1994).

Further readings on consumerism and sexuality might well begin with the essays in *Feminism and Cultural Studies*, Morag Shiach, ed. (Oxford: Oxford University Press, 1999); more specialized studies, often mixing historical and contemporary realities, include Lori Loeb's *Consuming Angels: Advertising and Victorian Women* (Oxford: Oxford University Press, 1994); Noliwe Rooks's *Ladies' Pages: African American Women's Magazines and the Culture that Made Them* (New Brunswick, NJ: Rutgers University Press, 2004); Ellen Gruber Garvey's *The Adman in the Parlor: Magazines and the Gendering of Consumer Culture, 1880s to 1910s* (Oxford: Oxford University Press, 1996); Daniel Hill's *Advertising to the American Woman, 1900–1999* (Columbus, OH: Ohio State University Press, 2002); Rachel Bowlby's *Carried Away: The Invention of Modern Shopping* (New York: Columbia University Press, 2001); Jennifer Scanlon's *Inarticulate Longings: The Ladies' Home Journal, Gender, and the Promises of Consumer Culture* (New

York: Routledge, 1995); *Gays, Lesbians, and Consumer Behavior*, Daniel Wardlow, ed. (New York: Haworth, 1996); and *Consuming Motherhood*, Janelle Taylor et al., eds. (New Brunswick, NJ: Rutgers University Press, 2004).

On technology's impact on sexuality, see Bernice Hausman's *Changing Sex: Transsexualism, Technology, and the Idea of Gender* (Durham, NC: Duke University Press, 1995); Adele Clarke's *Disciplining Reproduction: Modernity, American Life Sciences, and "The Problems of Sex"* (Berkeley, CA: University of California Press, 1998); Dena Davis's *Genetic Dilemmas: Reproductive Technology, Parental Choices, and Children's Futures* (New York: Routledge, 2001); Ellen Lupton's *Mechanical Brides: Women and Machines from Home to Office* (New York: Cooper-Hewitt, National Museum of Design, Smithsonian Institution, Princeton Architectural Press, 1993); Laurence O'Toole's *Pornocopia: Porn, Sex, Technology and Desire* (London: Serpent's Tail, 1998); Robin Baker's *Sex in the Future: The Reproductive Revolution and How It Will Change Us* (New York: Arcade, 2000), just to list a few of the studies that exist.

129. "A Woman of Quality" is taken from Ihara Saikaku, *The Life of an Amorous Man*, trans. Kenji Hamada (Rutland, VT: Tuttle, 1963), 125–30.

The rest of this or any other of Ihara Saikaku's writings would fit neatly into a history of sexuality. Works that have been translated include *The Life of an Amorous Woman*, trans. Ivan Morris (Norfolk, CT: New Directions, 1963); *Five Women who Loved Love*, trans. W. Theodore de Bary (Rutland, VT: CE Tuttle, 1959); and *The Great Mirror of Male Love*, trans. Paul Schalow (Stanford, CA: Stanford University

Press, 1990). On sexuality in Tokugawa-era Japan, the literature in English is limited, but see several of the essays in *Women and Class in Japanese History*, Hitomi Tonomura et al., eds. (Ann Arbor, MI: Center for Japanese Studies, University of Michigan, 1999). On *ukiyo* or the "floating world" of Edo (modern Tokyo), see Timon Screech's *Sex and the Floating World: Erotic Images in Japan, 1700–1820* (Honolulu: University of Hawai'i Press, 1999). On homo-eroticism in Japanese history, see note 130. On erotic art, see note 131.

130. "Boy Actresses" is taken from Ihara Saikaku, *The Great Mirror of Male Love*, trans. Paul Schalow (Stanford, CA: Stanford University Press, 1990), 189–90.

See note 129 on sexuality in early modern Japan and note 131 on erotic art. On homo-eroticism in this period, see Gary Leupp's *Male Colors: The Construction of Homosexuality in Tokugawa Japan* (Berkeley, CA: University of California Press, 1995); which is preferable to Tsuneo Watanabe and Jun'ichi Iwata's *The Love of the Samurai: A Thousand Years of Japanese Homosexuality*, trans. D.R. Roberts (London: Gay Men's Press, 1989); or the first chapter in Mark McLelland's *Male Homosexuality in Modern Japan: Cultural Myths and Social Realities* (Richmond, UK: Curzon, 2000). On the history of Kabuki theater, see Margaret Young's *Kabuki: Japanese Drama* (Bloomington, IN: Eastern, 1985); and the essays in *A Kabuki Reader: History and Performance*, Samuel Leiter, ed. (Armonk, NY: M.E. Sharpe, 2002), especially the editor's essay, "From Gay to *Gei*: The *Onnagata* and the Creation of Kabuki's Female Characters," on *onnagata* or men playing female roles. See also Jennifer Robertson's "The Politics of Androgyny in Japan: Sexuality and Subversion in the Theater and Beyond," *American*

Ethnologist 19 (1992): 419–42, on comparisons between contemporary and historical Japan. Men impersonating women on stage has been part of several historical societies; see Anthony Slide's *Great Pretenders: A History of Female and Male Impersonation in the Performing Arts* (Lombard, IL: Wallace-Homestead, 1986); Laurence Senelick's *The Changing Room: Sex, Drag, and Theatre* (New York: Routledge, 2000); or Roger Baker et al.'s *Drag: A History of Female Impersonation in the Performing Arts* (New York: New York University Press, 1994).

131. "An Image of the Floating World" is taken from Philip Rawson, *Erotic Art of the East* (New York: G.P. Putnam's Sons, 1968), 325.

See notes 129 and 130 on sexuality in early modern Japan. On the art of the "floating world," see *The Dawn of the Floating World, 1650–1765: Early Ukiyoe Treasures from the Museum of Fine Arts, Boston*, Timothy Clark et al., eds. (New York: H.N. Abrams, 2001); *The Floating World of Ukiyo-e: Shadows, Dreams, and Substance* (New York: H.N. Abrams, 2001); or *The Women of the Pleasure Quarter: Japanese Paintings and Prints of the Floating World*, Elizabeth de Sabato, ed. (New York: Hudson Hills, 1995). More generally on Japanese erotic art, see Richard Illing's *Japanese Erotic Art and the Life of the Courtesan* (New York: St. Martin's, 1978); Gabriele Mandel's *Shunga: Erotic Figures in Japanese Art* (New York: Crescent, 1983); or Tom and Mary Anne Evans's *Shunga: The Art of Love in Japan* (New York: Paddington, 1975).

132. "Address to the Magdalen Society of New York" is taken from *Remarks on the Report of the Executive Committee of the New York Magdalen Society* (New York: privately printed, 1831), 2–4.

On the history of groups like the Magdalen Society designed to end prostitution, see Larry Whiteaker's *Seduction, Prostitution, and Moral Reform in New York, 1830–1860* (New York: Garland, 1997); or Daniel Pivar's *Purity Crusade: Sexual Morality and Social Control, 1868–1900* (Westport, CT: Greenwood, 1973). An excellent biographical study of just the sort of woman described in this address is Patricia Cline Cohen's *The Murder of Helen Jewett: The Life and Death of a Prostitute in Nineteenth-Century New York* (New York: Alfred A. Knopf, 1998), which discusses much background information on the historical context. See also Marilynn Wood Hill's *Their Sisters' Keepers: Prostitution in New York City, 1830–1870* (Berkeley, CA: University of California Press, 1993); or Timothy Gilfoyle's *City of Eros: New York City, Prostitution, and the Commercialization of Sex, 1790–1920* (New York: W.W. Norton, 1992).

133. "Dating in Nineteenth-century Cuba" is taken from Joseph Dimock, *Impressions of Cuba in the Nineteenth Century*, Louis Perez, ed. (Wilmington, DE: Scholarly Resources/SR Books, 1998), 65–68.

On sexual customs in traditional Latin America, see Patricia Seed's *To Love, Honor, and Obey in Colonial Mexico: Conflicts over Marriage Choice, 1574–1821* (Stanford, CA: Stanford University Press, 1988); Ann Twinam's *Public Lives, Private Secrets: Gender, Honor, Sexuality, and Illegitimacy in Colonial Latin America* (Stanford, CA: Stanford University Press, 1999); *Sexuality and Marriage in Colonial Latin America*, Asunción Lavrin, ed. (Lincoln, NE: University of Nebraska Press, 1989); or *The Women of Colonial Latin America*, Susan Migden Socolow, ed. (Cambridge: Cambridge University Press, 2000). See also note 95 for studies of Cuba in the twentieth century.

134. "Susan B. Anthony on Women" is taken from *The Annals of America* (Chicago: Encyclopedia Britannica, 1968), 12: 144–46, 148.

A recent biography of Anthony is Kathleen Barry's *Susan B. Anthony: A Biography of a Singular Feminist* (New York: New York University Press, 1988); most of her writings have been published in a variety of collections; and a documentary film, directed by Ken Burns and Paul Barnes, entitled *Not For Ourselves Alone* (1999) also depicts her life. On the history of women's political enfranchisement in the United States, see Sylvia Hoffert's *When Hens Crow: The Woman's Rights Movement in Antebellum America* (Bloomington, IN: Indiana University Press, 1995); Nancy Isenberg's *Sex and Citizenship in Antebellum America* (Chapel Hill, NC: University of North Carolina Press, 1998); Ellen Carol DuBois's *Feminism and Suffrage: The Emergence of an Independent Women's Movement in America, 1848-1869* (Ithaca, NY: Cornell University Press, 1978; revised 1999) or her *Woman Suffrage and Women's Rights* (New York: New York University Press, 1998); Israel Kugler's *From Ladies to Women: The Organized Struggle for Woman's Rights in the Reconstruction Era* (New York: Greenwood, 1987); and Jean Matthews's *Women's Struggle for Equality: The First Phase, 1828-1876* (Chicago: Ivan R. Dee, 1997), or her *The Rise of the New Woman: The Women's Movement in America, 1875-1930* (Chicago: Ivan R. Dee, 2003); see also Thomas Jablonksy's *The Home, Heaven, and Mother Party: Female Anti-Suffragists in the United States, 1868–1920* (Brooklyn, NY: Carlson, 1994).

135. "A Denunciation of Urban Life" is taken from Jane Addams, *A New Conscience and an Ancient Evil* (New York: Macmillan, 1912), 104–15, 190–91.

Several biographies of Jane Addams exist, including Allen Freeman Davis's *American Heroine: The Life and Legend of Jane Addams* (Oxford: Oxford University Press, 1973; revised 2000); Jean Bethke Elshtain's *Jane Addams and the Dream of American Democracy: A Life* (New York: Basic, 2002); and Victoria Brown's *The Education of Jane Addams* (Philadelphia: University of Pennsylvania Press, 2004). Addams's own writings have been edited and published. For more on sexuality and the history of urban life for recent immigrants and the poor, see Randy McBee's *Dance Hall Days: Intimacy and Leisure Among Working-Class Immigrants in the United States* (New York: New York University Press, 2000). For more on alcohol and the Prohibition era, see Thomas Pegram's *Battling Demon Rum: The Struggle for a Dry America, 1800-1933* (Chicago: Ivan R. Dee, 1998); or Perry Duis's *The Saloon: Public Drinking in Chicago and Boston, 1880–1920* (Urbana, IL: University of Illinois Press, 1983). Canadian comparisons may be found in some of the essays in *Gender Conflicts: New Essays in Women's History*, Franca Iacovetta and Mariana Valverde, eds. (Toronto, ON: University of Toronto Press, 1992); and in *Drink in Canada: Historical Essays*, Cheryl Krasnick Warsh, ed. (Montreal, PQ: McGill-Queens University Press, 1993).

136. "Changing Marital Patterns among the Kgatla" is taken from I. Schapero, *Married Life in an African Tribe* (New York: Sheridan House, 1941), 333–41.

Schapero published several ethnographical studies on the peoples of southern Africa, but no others focused on sexual customs. Other accounts of the Tsana peoples provide interesting historical comparisons: an earlier one, John Brown's *Among the Bantu Nomads: A Record of Forty Years Spent among the Bechuana*

(London: Seeley, Service, 1926), and a later one, David Suggs's *A Bagful of Locusts and the Baboon Woman: Constructions of Gender, Change, and Continuity in Botswana* (Fort Worth, TX: Harcourt College, 2002). More generally on changing sex roles and marriage customs in different regions of Africa, see Kenneth L. Little's *African Women in Towns: An Aspect of Africa's Social Revolution* (Cambridge: Cambridge University Press, 1973); Philip Kilbride's *Changing Family Life in East Africa: Women and Children at Risk* (University Park, PA: Pennsylvania State University Press, 1990); and the essays in *Gendered Colonialisms in African History*, Nancy Rose Hunt et al., eds. (Oxford: Blackwell, 1997); or in *Women in African Colonial Histories*, Jean Allman et al., eds. (Bloomington, IN: Indiana University Press, 2002); and *African Families and the Crisis of Social Change*, Thomas Weisner et al., eds. (Westport, CT: Bergin & Garvey, 1997). Older texts, such as Arthur Phillips's *Survey of African Marriage and Family Life* (Oxford: Oxford University Press, 1953), now provide glimpses of past realities. See also note 107 for more on African polygamy and conversion to Christianity. The writings of early twentieth-century anthropologists often provide fascinating glimpses into the recent past, if the assumptions that they made about the peoples they studied are taken into account. See, for example, Bronislaw Malinowski's *Sex and Repression in Savage Society* (London: Routledge & Kegan Paul, 1927).

137. "Women's Education and Marriage in Japan" is taken from Sumie Seo Mishima, *My Narrow Isle: The Story of a Modern Woman in Japan* (Westport, CT: Hyperion, 1941), 128–29, 165–69, 190–92.

On changes to sex roles, marriage, and family life in twentieth-century Japan, see Joanna Liddle's *Rising Suns, Rising Daughters: Gender, Class, and Power in Japan* (London: Zed, 2000); Emiko Ochiai's *The Japanese Family System in Transition: A Sociological Analysis of Family Change in Postwar Japan* (Tokyo: LTCB International Library Foundation, 1997); Sumiko Iwao's *The Japanese Woman: Traditional Image and Changing Reality* (New York: Free Press, 1993); Nicholas Bornoff's *Pink Samurai: The Pursuit and Politics of Sex in Japan* (London: Grafton, 1991); and *Women and Women's Issues in Post World War II Japan*, Edward Beauchamp, ed. (New York: Garland, 1998). Most of these studies, however, focus on post- rather than pre-World War II Japan. An exception is Barbara Hamill Sato's *The New Japanese Woman: Modernity, Media, and Women in Interwar Japan* (Durham, NC: Duke University Press, 2003). For more on the *geishas* and prostitutes of twentieth-century Japan, see Sara Harris's *House of the 10,000 Pleasures: A Modern Study of the Geisha and of the Streetwalker of Japan* (New York: Dutton, 1962); or Sheldon Garon's "The World's Oldest Debate? Prostitution and the State in Imperial Japan, 1900–1950," *The American Historical Review* 98 (1993): 710–32; fascinating is the account of an anthropologist who lived as a *geisha* in 1970s Japan: Liza Crihfield Dalby's *Geisha* (Berkeley, CA: University of California Press, 1983; revised 1998).

138. "Sex in Advertising" is taken from James Peterson, *The Century of Sex: Playboy's History of the Sexual Revolution, 1900–1999* (New York: Grove, 1999).

On sex in advertising, most of the literature is focused on the American experience: see Tom Reichert's *The Erotic History of Advertising* (Amherst, NY: Prometheus, 2003); or Rodger Streitmatter's *Sex Sells! The Media's Journey from Repression to Obsession* (Cambridge, MA:

Westview, 2004); on the family in advertising, see Bruce W. Brown's *Images of Family Life in Magazine Advertising, 1920–1978* (New York: Praeger, 1981); and on gender in advertising, see Anne Cronin's *Advertising and Consumer Citizenship: Gender, Images, and Rights* (New York: Routledge, 2000); Diane Barthel's *Putting on Appearances: Gender and Advertising* (Philadelphia: Temple University Press, 1988); or Jacques Boyreau's *The Male Mystique: Men's Magazine Ads of the 1960s and 70s* (San Francisco: Chronicle, 2004); see also *Sex in Advertising: Perspectives on the Erotic Appeal* (Mahwah, NJ: Lawrence Erlbaum Associates, 2003).

139. "Prostitution in Bombay" is taken from S.D. Punekar and Kamala Rao, *A Study of Prostitutes in Bombay* (Bombay: Lalvani, 1962), 178–84.

On prostitution in twentieth-century India, see Biswanath Joardar's *Prostitution in Historical and Modern Perspectives* (New Delhi: Inter-India, 1983) and his *Prostitution in Nineteenth- and Early Twentieth-Century Calcutta* (New Delhi: Inter-India, 1985). Earlier studies include Sumanta Banerjee's *Dangerous Outcast: The Prostitute in Nineteenth-Century Bengal* (Calcutta: Seagull, 1998), also published as *Under the Raj: Prostitution in Colonial Bengal* (New York: Monthly Review, 1998). Other recent studies that are now historical documents of a sort include Promilla Kapur's *The Life and World of Call-Girls in India: A Socio-Psychological Study of the Aristocratic Prostitute* (New Delhi: Vikas, 1978); Mary Ellen Mark's *Falkland Road: Prostitutes of Bombay* (New York: Knopf, 1981). On the *devadasis*, see Kay Jordan's *From Sacred Servant to Profane Prostitute: A History of the Changing Legal Status of the Devadasis in India, 1857–1947* (New Delhi: Manohar, 2003); or Nagendra Singh's

Divine Prostitution (New Delhi: A.P.H., 1997); regional studies include Frédérique Marglin's *Wives of the God-King: The Rituals of the Devadasis of Puri* (Oxford: Oxford University Press, 1985); and Saskia Kersenboom-Story's *Nityasumangali: Devadasi Tradition in South India* (Delhi: Motilal Banarsidass, 1987).

140. "Dating in Modern Taiwan" is taken from Lou Tsu-k'uang, *Asian Folklore and Social Life Monographs* (Taipei, Taiwan: Orient Cultural Service, 1974), 15: 150–55, 179–82.

I know of no works in English on dating customs in modern China. For a history of changing dating customs in the United States, however, see Beth L. Bailey's *From Front Porch to Back Seat: Courtship in Twentieth-Century America* (Baltimore, MD: Johns Hopkins University Press, 1988); and for Britain, Ernest Sackville Turner's *A History of Courting* (London: M. Joseph, 1954). The history of dating may be traced by examining writings giving advice on the subject, from different eras, such as *The Art of Courtship, or, The School of Delight* (London: I.M. Back, 1686); *The Lover's Instructor, or, The Whole Art of Courtship Rendered Plain and Easy* (Norwich, CT: John Trumbull, 1796); Albert Ellis's *The Intelligent Woman's Guide to Man-Hunting* (New York: L. Stuart, 1963); or Margaret Leroy's *Some Girls Do: Why Women Do and Don't Ask Men Out* (London: HarperCollins, 1997).

141. "Egyptian Women and Work" is taken from Nawal El Saadawi, *The Hidden Face of Eve: Women in the Arab World*, trans. Sherif Hetata (London: Zed, 1980), 188–89, 192.

On changes to sex roles and marriage and family customs in modern Arab nations, see Mona Mikhail's *Seen and Heard: A Century of Arab Women in Literature and Culture*

(Northampton, MA: Olive Branch, 2004) or her *Images of Arab Women: Fact and Fiction: Essays* (Washington, DC: Three Continents, 1979); Edwin Prothro's *Changing Family Patterns in the Arab East* (Beirut: American University of Beirut, 1974); and *Women and the Family in the Middle East: New Voices of Change*, Elizabeth Warnock Fernea, ed. (Austin, TX: University of Texas Press, 1985); and in *The New Arab Family*, Nicholas Hopkins, ed. (Cairo: American University in Cairo Press, 2003). Specifically on Arab women and work, see Nadia Hijab's *Womanpower: The Arab Debate on Women at Work* (Cambridge: Cambridge University Press, 1988). Specifically on Egypt, see Valerie Hoffman-Ladd's "Polemics on the Modesty and Segregation of Women in Contemporary Egypt," *International Journal of Middle East Studies* 19 (1987): 23–50.

speaking sex

It cannot be denied that some topics in sexuality generate more public interest than others and that topics seem to wax and wane in popular discussion. If all words say as much about the speaker as the listener, and perhaps more, then investigating these topics and how they have changed from generation to generation can provide insight into the values of those who lived in the past and how they understood themselves. That is the theme for this chapter.

Many scholars, in psychology and disciplines like philosophy and literary studies, have emphasized the importance of words. Taking a cue from the famous "Freudian slip," the word or phrase meant not consciously but subconsciously to be said, philosopher Jacques Derrida suggested that language—whether verbal or written—is full of deeper meanings, some known to the speaker and some unknown. Reading carefully between the lines—or deconstructing the text, as Derrida phrased it—one can determine hidden assumptions and implied ideals. So our language reflects in a profound way who we are and what we hold to be true, whether we are aware of it or not.

Other scholars have tried to see historical documents as texts to be deconstructed. This process can be particularly useful for historians of sexuality, as you can imagine, since our ideas and values about sexuality are often complicated and even contradictory. One of the best ways of seeing this process at work is to look at those topics that generate a lot of public discussions. Historian Michel Foucault, for example, looked at Victorian writings about sex and found that three types of individuals were mentioned repeatedly: the perverted man, the hysterical woman, and the masturbating child. Each discussion drew on popular stereotypes of the day—the oversexed man, the overemotional woman, and the misbehaving child—taking them to an extreme sexual form, suggesting that everyone—man, woman, and child—was capable of falling into the depths of sexual vice if not rescued by a social order that was imposed from without, in the unwritten rules of society, and should be equally self-imposed, by learning and appreciating those rules for oneself. Discussions about sex, then, revealed profound values about society.

The topics have changed through the years, but their importance has not. At the end of the nineteenth century, for example, prostitution was a common topic for social reformers in the United States. Interestingly, while writers from many different segments of the population all talked about it, they did so in diverse ways that let slip their deeper thoughts. Former abolitionists, fresh from successfully ending slavery in the South, argued that the "white slavery" of prostitution should be eliminated next. Anglo-Saxon politicians, still dominant in the American government, referred to the dangers of prostitution among immigrant groups, highlighting their fears of changing ethnic demographics. Clergymen denounced prostitution for revealing the falling away from Christian values by an increasingly secular society. The female suffragists complained that prostitution perpetuated men's mistreatment of women and constituted further proof that women needed to have a say in public life. Physicians associated prostitutes with the spread of diseases that they claimed they could otherwise control. Each group "used" the discussion of prostitution, it might be said, as an opportunity to talk about their most important issues.

One might take any topic of sexuality in public discussion and "deconstruct" the statements made about it: censorship, birth control, homosexuality, and so on. For exam-ple, recent debates on abortion, which are so central to American politics, reveal similar disparate concerns. Abortion can be used to talk about a host of other topics, from women's liberation to belief in the Bible, to the impact of technology on family life. Sexuality is an ideal arena for such essential dialogue, because it affects everyone in one way or another.

Understanding the power of rhetoric is also essential when thinking about speech and sex. The best public speakers and writers are those who can appeal to the same anxieties and fears that their listeners and readers share. Often, the best among these are those who only *allude* to such concerns. After all, if a public speaker made a remark openly that could be contradicted by evidence or another's experience, that speaker would fail to be persuasive. If a remark can be made subtly and indirectly, however, the speaker can always deny its full impact, even while planting a seed of concern in the listeners' minds. It is important, therefore, to pay attention to the metaphors used in speaking or writing about controversial topics: They can provide useful clues as to the worries they hint at.

Even more important questions are raised when speaking about sex. What precisely is the nature of human liberation? What are the limits of human rights and freedoms? What should or should not be discussed? How is adherence to the Bible or other religious codes reconciled with life in a pluralistic society? How are moral decisions made about the use of technology in reproduction or in other aspects of human existence? Does society have a stake in what kinds of sexual relationship human beings form? Must society protect some of its individuals from harm by others? Is society required to bear the social and financial burden of unwanted children? These controversies in sexuality, in fact, can approach some of the deepest values about human life and human freedom.

The following sources represent some issues that have been hotly debated in the last century or so, as well as those around which there has been silence and silencing. It is, therefore, equally important to hear what is not said.

142. ABORTION AND THE FLOATING WORLD IN JAPAN

Time: seventeenth century CE
Place: Japan
Author: unknown

This story, about a minor civic official in what was called the "floating world district" of Edo (modern Tokyo; see also sources 129, 130, and 131), reflects a more dismal view of urban life in seventeenth-century Japan. Given the strong Buddhist moral to the tale, it was probably performed as a type of public preaching, a common and traditional method of speaking about sex. The core of the sermon is the uncovering of what is hidden. A commentary attached to the story says that it happened in 1685.

Takano Shinuemon was the Neighborhood Chief of Nakabashi in Edo. He had an affair with a maidservant named Yoshi, and she became pregnant. Shinuemon's wife was jealous when it became known publicly, so, using an excuse of illness, Shinuemon sent Yoshi back to her family and had her drink an abortifacient. Instead of its intended effect, however, the drug poisoned Yoshi, and she died in agony. Her parents were griefstricken, but there was nothing they could do, so they held her funeral at the Jisho-in Temple in Asakusa.

Later on, Shinuemon's daughter Miyo married, but she was soon divorced and returned home. She became ill and gradually began to waste away. She looked as if she were termi-nally ill. One night, she collapsed in agony. Rising after a while, she confronted her father asking, "Who do you think I am? I am Yoshi, who used to work in this house, the one you callously took to your bed, in whom, without love, you planted your seed. Then you made me drink an evil medicine, and both mother and child lost their lives. Even without this, women's sins are deep, but you had no pity for me in my condition. You did not even have Buddhist rites performed for me, so I was forced to wander from darkness to darkness, confused and grieving." She screamed and cried in resentment.

Shinuemon was terrified and consulted many spiritualists…. Shinuemon's temple was Zojoji, so he prevailed upon its priest, and Saint Yuten accepted the case. He came and prayed for Miyo. Addressing the spirit within her, he said, "There is ample reason for you to hate Shinuemon, but why attack Miyo?" The spirit answered. "I do not hate her, but, without attacking Miyo I had no way to make my pain known, so I had to use her as a medium." Yuten replied, "Whatever pain you now endure is the bitter fruit of your own actions." Hearing this interchange, the people listening felt every hair on their bodies bristle up in terror. But the saint spoke with infinite pity, tears rolling down his cheeks: "You must not be resentful. Even though Shinuemon seduced you, had you refused, you would not have become pregnant. Even though he gave you medicine, if you had not drunk it, you would not have lost your life. All this is your own doing."

The spirit was unconvinced. "Even seeing my fate in this light, with my unbearable pain, I cannot help hating Shinuemon." Yuten said, "No matter how much you hate him, even if you kill his whole family you will only succeed in accumulating more sin-ful *karma* and your own suffering will find no relief. Instead of that, open your heart and repent of your sin. Rely on Amida [Buddha]'s original vow and seek rebirth in the Pure Land…." The spirit relented. "I will follow your instructions, but there are many other spirits who hate Shinuemon. Please save those resentful spirits also. Yuten inquired. "Who are these other spirits of the dead who hate Shinuemon?" The spirit replied, "There are fifteen others besides myself. All of them are children whom Shinuemon caused to be aborted." She then provided the names and present whereabouts of all the women whom Shinuemon had made pregnant with these children, all precisely and without error, as if looking into a bright mirror.

Hearing all this, Shinuemon was terrified. In his complete and utter loss of face, his chagrin knew no bounds. He just sat there, silently repentant. Yuten instructed Shinuemon as follows: "Repent for your sins, and recite the *nenbutsu* prayer for the sixteen who have died. Grant each one a posthumous name." Returning to the temple, Yuten recited the *nenbutsu* for seventeen days, repeatedly giving sermons and religious instruction for these spirits of the dead. Nevertheless, Miyo continued to worsen. After a three-day fever, she turned at last to Shinuemon and said, "It was my *karma* to become the medium for those children. Relying on Saint Yuten's instructions and his merit transfer for me, the cloud of illusion has dissipated, and I will now go to the Pure Land." Thanking him again and again, she appeared to lie down to sleep, but her sickness only worsened, and she died.

Questions for Reflection and Discussion

What is the lesson in this story? What does it say about early modern Japanese attitudes toward abortion? How does the author of the tale shift the blame for abortion?

143. THE REGULATION OF PROSTITUTION

Time: nineteenth century CE
Place: United States
Author: William Barret

William Barret was a health officer for the city of St. Louis, Missouri. In May of 1873, he submitted a report, part of which is reprinted below, describing the success of its efforts to regulate prostitution, starting in July 1870. It was the first American city to attempt this sort of regulation although public pressure eventually forced it to end this social experiment. In the report through which he justifies the experiment, Barret compared the city before and after the regulation of prostitution. Ideas like his and the fervent opposition to them made prostitution a hot topic in the late nineteenth century.

TO THE HONORABLE BOARD OF HEALTH—

Gentlemen: The "Social Evil," a plant of mature growth wide spread, deep rooted, existing from the time of the patriarchs and prophets, attracts at this time unusual interest, deserves and should receive the sober consideration of every Christian man and woman in the land. To protect the innocent from disease is a sacred duty; to put the vicious under restraint is the province of law. Whether that unhappy being whose very name it is a shame to speak, who counterfeits with a cold heart the transports of affection, who "fills her maw from a filthy vice," who lives by the evil she causes to be done, who is the symbol of degradation, should be prohibited from plying her vocation, should prosecute it unmolested, or should be controlled, and how? is the question agitating our community. Certain it is, "she remains while creeds and civilizations rise and fall." This being the indisputable state of the case, the regulation system would seem to be the course clearly indicated....

We come now to the plain question: is the regulation system as established in St Louis calculated to lessen prostitution and diminish disease? In our effort to solve this problem, we shall compare the prevalence of disease during the past two years, in which prostitution was regulated, with the prevalence of disease during the two preceding years....

The population of the city when the law went into operation was 312,968

The number of prostitutes when the law went into operation was 718

The proportion of prostitutes to the population was one is 435 plus

The population of the city in 1873 (Gould's Directory) was 428,126

The number of prostitutes registered March 31, 1873, was 653

The proportion of prostitutes to the population was one in 655 plus

The total number of cases treated at City and Quarantine Hospitals in 1869 and 1870 was 9,330

The total number of venereal cases was 1,124

The proportion of venereal cases treated to the population was one in 278

The proportion of venereal cases treated to the whole number of cases treated was one in 8.3 plus

The total number of cases treated at City and Quarantine Hospitals in 1871 and 1872 was 10,076

The total number of venereal cases treated was 925

The proportion of venereal cases treated to the population was one in 462 plus

The proportion of venereal cases treated to the whole number of cases treated was one in 10.8 plus

The proportion of prostitutes found diseased when the law went into operation in 1870 was 58 in 718, or one in 12.37

The average number of prostitutes treated at the Social Evil Hospital during the past six months was 34 plus in 653, or one diseased in 19.06 plus

The number of deaths from venereal disease during 1869 and 1870 was 36

The number of deaths from venereal disease during 1871 and 1872 was 18

The total number of bawdy houses when the law went into operation (1870) was 119

The total number of bawdy houses March 31, 1873 was 133

The total number of bawds living in private apartments when the law went into operation was 205

The total number of bawds living in private apartments, March 31, 1873, was 7

The average number of bawds in each house when the law went into operation was 6.03 plus

The average number of bawds March 31, 1873 was 4.98 plus....

We confess to inexperience in the management of the vice of prostitution. Since ours is the first attempt in the United States to control it, the novelty of the undertaking precluded any other possibility, nor could very many useful lessons as to detail, or any definite predictions of results be drawn from European experience. We live in another land, our habits, sentiments, laws, and necessities are radically different, and our own experience must be our guide.... But we do contend that our experience, so far as it goes, and more extensive experience in foreign countries, demonstrates with unmistakable clearness the correctness of the principles on which regulation and license systems are predicated. Our experience to the present time proves the enforcement of regulation to be economical and humane, that it is efficient in the promotion of morals and prevention of disease. This is all its most sanguine advocates claimed or expected. It is an ample vindication of the experiment made, and an unanswerable reason why the experiment should be continued until the ultimate result is fully and conclusively settled.

To determine that result with any degree of certainty will require an experience of at least ten years. Legislators are being asked to surrender, without sufficient trial of the present system, the hopeful promise of future good so beneficently foreshadowed by past experience, and to sacrifice lives, health, morals and money on the altar of prejudice. Have the opponents of the system any substitute to propose in lieu of registration? Would compliance with their request be consonant with the mighty interests legislators are chosen to cherish and protect? Would it be a fulfillment of the sacred obligation under which they rest? It is, indeed, within our power to choose between good and evil, to act with wisdom and prudence, or to be guided only by illiberal bias not tempered with discretion, and, as time unfolds the scheme of the future, let us hope the choice may be for good.

Very respectfully,
Wm. L. Barret, M. D.
Health Officer

Questions for Reflection and Discussion

What is Barret's main argument regarding the regulation of prostitution? How effective is his use of statistics in support of his argument? What are the "sacred obligations" of legislators to which he alludes, in relation to this topic?

144. A MUCKRAKER ON PROSTITUTION

Time: nineteenth century CE
Place: United States
Author: Benjamin Orange Flower

B.O. Flower, founding editor of The Arena, *published in Boston between 1889 and 1909, wrote on the moral issues of his day. Indeed, he was known as a radical thinker and published opinion pieces on topics that few "respectable" journals would discuss, including poverty, labor unions, and socialism. One of many like-minded journalists who became known as the "muckrakers," Flower was happy to use his magazine to speak out about social problems. In 1895 he presented an address to the first National Purity Congress, held in Baltimore, Maryland, a meeting aimed at countering the attempts to legalize prostitution, from which this excerpt is taken.*

I have no sympathy with the threadbare, and, in my opinion, thoroughly vicious plea, which urges that prostitution always has existed, always will exist and therefore the best thing is to license and place it under the supervision of medical officials. This cry that an evil has ever existed and must, therefore, always prevail, has been the slogan of the children of night in every battle for the abolition of giant evils which man has waged in the history of civilization. The overthrow of chattel slavery, and, indeed, every victory for humanity, has been won in face of this plea of a soul deadening materialism, which ignores the very principles of human progress, and seems to find in man nothing beyond the animal.

I know the claims which are advanced. We are assured that by licensing this evil it can be confined within certain bounds, and that wives and children will stand a better chance of escaping the most loathsome of diseases frequently contracted by married men who patronize houses of ill fame. The premises on which these assumptions are based are false, and the conclusions deducted are no less erroneous, which will be seen by a careful survey of the subject. We are assured that by licensing prostitution we can restrict the evil to certain locations, and better restrain it. Let us see. We will suppose a certain colony of moral lepers is districted off in one of our large cities. No one is allowed to live there and ply her trade unless she has a clean bill of health from the examining officer. Here is special security granted by government to the adulterous among the married men or the licentiously disposed among the unmarried, but there is no protection afforded the prostitutes which might shield them against those whose blood is poisoned with the virus of the most loathsome diseases. Hence, with each recurring week, numbers of those unfortunates would be refused a certificate, provided the officers observed their oath, and consequently, be legally prohibited from plying their trade. These unfortunates would rapidly multiply, as they have multiplied in Paris and other cities, where the cause of sound morality has been surrendered to sensual supremacy and a short-sighted expediency, and in time they would necessarily find lodgment within the poorer and more wretched parts of the city. Having no other possible means of earning a livelihood, with society constituted as it is at the present time, they would be driven to plying their loathsome trade in a clandestine manner, and thus the virus of disease would rapidly be disseminated among the working classes and the exiles of society, while the licensed colony would be weekly recruited from above so as to fill the quota required to gratify the rapidly increasing traffic in vice.

Any law which would license prostitution might well be entitled a law for encouraging adultery and licentiousness. And just here let me point out another fact which must be borne in mind. There is unquestionably a large number of unmarried men who are restrained from patronizing houses of prostitution from fear of one of two things: (1) that the houses maybe raided by the police and they dragged before the court, and thus be disgraced, if not ruined in their social standing; (2) they are restrained from fear of contracting disease; but once license these houses and you relieve both these restrictive influences, with the result that prostitution would not only be increased and the demand for healthy girls be greatly augmented, but also it would inevitably increase the percentage of sexual maniacs among the generations of tomorrow; for fathers thus polluted from continual carnivals of lust and the accompanying dissipation would necessarily, according to the inexorable law of heredity, transmit, in a large number of cases, an almost insatiable passion to their children.

Moreover, the evil effects upon the young men would be immeasurable. There are thousands upon thousands of boys and youths who are thoughtless, and, to a degree, reckless. They cannot be said to have "come to themselves" as yet, but they have a wholesome dread of contracting a disease as terrible and loathsome as leprosy, and this fear unquestionably oftentimes restrains them until they come to that time in life when moral responsibilities appeal to them. Now, had the sensual gained supremacy before this maturity of soul life, they would have been weakened in body, brain and spirit—too weak in many instances to heed the warning voice of conscience.

Moreover, we must remember the futility which has attended the iniquitous attempts at licensing prostitution. Dr. Arthur K. Stone, in a thoughtful address recently delivered before the Boston Society for Medical Improvement, gave some admirable facts collated from recent authorities along this line. He called attention to the fact that "the Prefect of Police in Paris admitted to Dr. Lassar, of Berlin, who had been sent by the German government to investigate the methods of control in Paris, that there were fully one hundred thousand prostitutes in Paris, although this estimate simply included women who had no regular means of support except their ill famed profession. Some very significant facts in relation to the claim that licensing prostitution would be in the interest of health are also given. The eminent German physician, Dr. Blaschko, of Berlin, stated, in the course of a very thoughtful paper, that from the standpoint of public hygiene no benefit was received whatever from the control as then practiced. In Paris Dr. Vidal, of the Hospital St. Louis, which is the centre of skin diseases of all Paris and France, states that the number of syphilitic patients is daily increasing…. Dr. Passavant, of Paris, is quoted as saying that out of every hundred inscribed women thirty-five to fifty per cent have venereal disease. Dr. Fiaux shows that in Belgium in 1881-1889, one half of the inmates of the licensed houses had to be sent to the hospitals for treatment with venereal disease, of whom about fifty per cent were syphilitic." These facts are exceedingly important, going far toward confuting the strongest and most plausible claims which have been advanced in favor of licensing prostitution….

Had I space I should like to notice this question from the humanitarian point of view, pointing out its essential inhumanity, and showing how intimately it is connected with the old idea that women's rights and interests are thoroughly secondary to man's; but I deem it far more important at the present time to point out some facts which may prove helpful in the pending conflict which I believe to be inevitable. The voice which calls for the licensing of prostitution issues from the black cave of sensual materialism, and insults every divine impulse in man.

Questions for Reflection and Discussion

How do Flower's arguments counter the arguments Barret made in the previous source? How does Flower use authorities to bolster the weight of his arguments? What are the hidden issues in Flower's denunciation?

145. ANTHONY COMSTOCK AND CENSORSHIP

Time: nineteenth century CE
Place: United States
Artist: F.M. Howarth

THAT · FERTILE IMAGINATION.

A-n-y C-m-st-k: Hold! I arrest you for painting indecent pictures!
Artist: Indecent! Why the head is the only portion visible.
A-n-y C-m-st-k: That makes no difference. Don't you suppose I can imagine what is under the water?

This cartoon from a Life *magazine in 1888 reflected one artist's view of the censorship debates of the late nineteenth and early twentieth century. In the United States, Anthony Comstock figured prominently in these debates. A New York clerk, he spearheaded a campaign to prohibit all literature and images with a sexual theme, including information about contraception. He provided public support for a series of laws prohibiting the distribution of any "obscene" materials through the US post. These laws remained in effect until the 1960s, when a series of court challenges using the principle of "free speech" and pointing out the difficulty in defining "obscenity" undermined them.*

Questions for Reflection and Discussion

What is the artist suggesting motivates Comstock's enthusiasm for censorship? Is it possible to target some forms of art and literature as obscene and allow others that have "artistic merit"?

146. THE HAYS CODE

Time: early twentieth century CE
Place: United States
Author: unknown

The Production Code of the Motion Pictures Producers and Distributors Association, published in 1930, is usually called the Hays Code after Will Hays, the association's leader at that time. It imposed a self-censorship on film producers, an agreement among themselves on what themes they would avoid in films, and a concession to the US government that was threatening legal action against obscenity in films. The Code remained in effect into the 1950s and 60s, when changing social values and the commercial threat of television induced filmmakers to push at the limits of the Code. Only

the portions relating to sex and nudity have been included below, but its other topics included the depiction of religion, the glorification of violence, and the use of profanity.

Motion picture producers recognize the high trust and confidence which have been placed in them by the people of the world and which have made motion pictures a universal form of entertainment. They recognize their responsibility to the public because of this trust and because entertainment and art are important influences in the life of a nation. Hence, though regarding motion pictures primarily as entertainment without any explicit purpose of teaching or propaganda, they know that the motion picture within its own field of entertainment may be directly responsible for spiritual or moral progress, for higher types of social life, and for much correct thinking. During the rapid transition from silent to talking pictures they have realized the necessity and the opportunity of subscribing to a Code to govern the production of talking pictures and of reacknowledging this responsibility. On their part, they ask from the public and from public leaders a sympathetic understanding of their purposes and problems and a spirit of cooperation that will allow them the freedom and opportunity necessary to bring the motion picture to a still higher level of wholesome entertainment for all the people.

II. SEX
The sanctity of the institution of marriage and the home shall be upheld. Pictures shall not infer that low forms of sex relationship are the accepted or common thing.

1. Adultery, sometimes necessary plot material, must not be explicitly treated, or justified, or presented attractively.
2. Scenes of Passion

a. They should not be introduced when not essential to the plot.
  b. Excessive and lustful kissing, lustful embraces, suggestive postures and gestures, are not to be shown.
  c. In general passion should so be treated that these scenes do not stimulate the lower and baser element.
3. Seduction or Rape
  a. They should never be more than suggested, and only when essential for the plot, and even then never shown by explicit method.
  b. They are never the proper subject for comedy.
4. Sex perversion or any inference to it is forbidden.
5. White slavery shall not be treated.
6. Miscegenation (sex relationships between the white and black races) is forbidden.
7. Sex hygiene and venereal diseases are not subjects for motion pictures.
8. Scenes of actual child birth, in fact or in silhouette, are never to be presented.
9. Children's sex organs are never to be exposed.

VI. COSTUME
1. Complete nudity is never permitted. This includes nudity in fact or in silhouette, or any lecherous or licentious notice thereof by other characters in the picture.
2. Undressing scenes should be avoided, and never used save where essential to the plot.
3. Indecent or undue exposure is forbidden.
4. Dancing or costumes intended to permit undue exposure or indecent movements in the dance are forbidden.

VII. DANCES
1. Dances suggesting or representing sexual actions or indecent passions are forbidden.

2. Dances which emphasize indecent movements are to be regarded as obscene.

IX. LOCATIONS
The treatment of bedrooms must be governed by good taste and delicacy.

[In addition, some sections of the Code were given further justification.]

II. SEX
Out of a regard for the sanctity of marriage and the home, the triangle, that is, the love of a third party for one already married, needs careful handling. The treatment should not throw sympathy against marriage as an institution. Scenes of passion must be treated with an honest acknowledgement of human nature and its normal reactions. Many scenes cannot be presented without arousing dangerous emotions on the part of the immature, the young or the criminal classes. Even within the limits of pure love, certain facts have been universally regarded by lawmakers as outside the limits of safe presentation. In the case of impure love, the love which society has always regarded as wrong and which has been banned by divine law, the following are important:

1. Impure love must not be presented as attractive and beautiful.
2. It must not be the subject of comedy or farce, or treated as material for laughter.
3. It must not be presented in such a way to arouse passion or morbid curiosity on the part of the audience.
4. It must not be made to seem right and permissible.
5. In general, it must not be detailed in method and manner.

VI. COSTUME
General Principles:

1. The effect of nudity or semi-nudity upon the normal man or woman, and much more upon the young and upon immature persons, has been honestly recognized by all lawmakers and moralists.
2. Hence the fact that the nude or semi-nude body may be beautiful does not make its use in the films moral. For, in addition to its beauty, the effect of the nude or semi-nude body on the normal individual must be taken into consideration.
3. Nudity or semi-nudity used simply to put a "punch" into a picture comes under the head of immoral actions. It is immoral in its effect on the average audience.
4. Nudity can never be permitted as being necessary for the plot. Semi-nudity must not result in undue or indecent exposures.
5. Transparent or translucent materials and silhouette are frequently more suggestive than actual exposure.

VII. DANCES

Dancing in general is recognized as an art and as a beautiful form of expressing human emotions. But dances which suggest or represent sexual actions, whether performed solo or with two or more; dances intended to excite the emotional reaction of an audience; dances with movement of the breasts, excessive body movements while the feet are stationary, violate decency and are wrong.

IX. LOCATIONS

Certain places are so closely and thoroughly associated with sexual life or with sexual sin that their use must be carefully limited.

Questions for Reflection and Discussion

What might the filmmakers have gained in limiting their use of sexual topics and nudity? Are there loopholes in the Hays Code that might still have permitted the depiction of sexual situations in film?

147. LYNCHING AND SEX

Time: nineteenth century CE
Place: United States
Author: Ida B. Wells-Barnett

Sometimes speaking about sex involves uncovering secrets that others would rather remained hidden. That is the point of this passage condemning lynching, a chapter in a booklet entitled Southern Horrors *published by African-American journalist Ida Wells-Barnett in 1892. Wells-Barnett was attempting to interest northern social welfare advocates to take up the cause but had little success, since few believed her accusations. She also suffered from physical attacks on her home and business by those who wanted to silence her. Exposés like Wells-Barnett's reveal social practices that might not otherwise be found in historical documents.*

The *Cleveland Gazette* of January 16, 1892, publishes a case in point. Mrs. J.S. Underwood, the wife of a minister of Elyria, Ohio, accused an Afro-American of rape. She told her husband that during his absence in 1888, stumping the State for the Prohibition Party, the man came to the kitchen door, forced his way in the house and insulted her. She tried to drive him out with a heavy poker, but he overpowered and chloroformed her, and when she revived her clothing was torn and she was in a horrible condition. She did not know the man but could identify him. She pointed out William Offett, a married man, who was arrested and, being in Ohio, was granted a trial. The prisoner vehemently denied the charge of rape, but confessed he went to Mrs. Underwood's residence at her invitation and was criminally intimate with her at her request. This availed him nothing against the sworn testimony of a minister's wife, a lady of the highest respectability. He was found guilty, and entered the penitentiary, December 14, 1888, for fifteen years. Some time afterwards the woman's remorse led her to confess to her husband that the man was innocent.

These are her words: "I met Offett at the Post Office. It was raining. He was polite to me, and as I had several bundles in my arms he offered to carry them home for me, which he did. He had a strange fascination for me, and I invited him to call on me. He called, bringing chestnuts and candy for the children. By this means we got them to leave us alone in the room. Then I sat on his lap. He made a proposal to me and I readily consented. Why I did so, I do not know, but that I did is true. He visited me several times after that and each time I was indiscreet. I did not care after the first time. In fact I could not have resisted, and had no desire to resist." When asked by her husband why she told him she had been outraged, she said: "I had several reasons for telling you. One was the neighbors saw the fellow here, another was, I was afraid I had contracted a loathsome disease, and still another was that I feared I might give birth to a Negro baby. I hoped to save my reputation by telling you a deliberate lie." Her husband horrified by the confession had Offett, who had already served four years, released and secured a divorce.

There are thousands of such cases throughout the South, with the difference that the Southern white men in insatiate fury wreak their vengeance without intervention of law upon the Afro-Americans who consort with their women. A few instances to substantiate the assertion that some white women love the company of the Afro-American will not be out of place. Most of these cases were reported by the daily papers of the South.

In the winter of 1885-6 the wife of a practicing physician in Memphis, in good social standing whose name has escaped me, left home, husband and children, and ran away with her black coachman. She was with him a month before her husband found and brought her home. The coachman could not be found. The doctor moved his family away from Memphis, and is living in another city under an assumed name…. Sarah Clark of Memphis loved a black man and lived openly with him. When she was indicted last spring for miscegenation, she swore in court that she was not a white woman. This she did to escape the penitentiary and continued her illicit relation undisturbed. That she is of the lower class of whites, does not disturb the fact that she is a white woman. "The leading citizens" of Memphis are defending the "honor" of all white women….

What is true of Memphis is true of the entire South. The daily papers last year reported a farmer's wife in Alabama had given birth to a Negro child. When the Negro farm hand who was plowing in the field heard it he took the mule from the plow and fled. The dispatches also told of a woman in South Carolina who gave birth to a Negro child and charged three men with being its father, *every one of whom has since disappeared.* In Tuscumbia, Ala., the colored boy who was lynched there last year for assaulting a white girl told her before his accusers that he had met her there in the woods often before…. In Natchez, Miss., Mrs. Marshall, one of the *crème de la crème* of the city, created a tremendous sensation several years ago. She has a black coachman who was married, and had been in her employ several years. During this time she gave birth to a child whose color was remarked, but traced to some brunette ancestor, and one of the fashionable dames of the city was its godmother. Mrs. Marshall's social position was unquestioned, and wealth showered every dainty on this child which was idolized with its brothers and sisters by its white papa. In course of time another child appeared on the scene, but it was unmistakably dark. All were alarmed, and "rush of blood, strangulation" were the conjectures, but the doctor, when asked the cause, grimly told them it was a Negro child. There was a family conclave, the coachman heard of it and leaving his own family went West, and has never returned. As soon as Mrs. Marshall was able to travel she was sent away in deep disgrace. Her husband died within the year of a broken heart....

Hundreds of such cases might be cited, but enough have been given to prove the assertion that there are white women in the South who love the Afro-American's company even as there are white men notorious for their preference for Afro-American women. There is hardly a town in the South which has not an instance of the kind which is well known, and hence the assertion is reiterated that "nobody in the South believes the old thread bare lie that negro men rape white women." Hence there is a growing demand among Afro-Americans that the guilt or innocence of parties accused of rape be fully established. They know the men of the section of the country who refuse this are not so desirous of punishing rapists as they pretend. The utterances of the leading white men show that with them it is not the crime but the *class*.... But when the victim is a colored woman it is different.

Last winter in Baltimore, Md., three white ruffians assaulted a Miss Camphor, a young Afro-American girl, while out walking with a young man of her own race. They held her escort and outraged the girl. It was a deed dastardly enough to arouse Southern blood, which gives its horror of rape as excuse for lawlessness, but she was an Afro-American. The case went to the courts, an Afro-American lawyer defended the men and they were acquitted.

In Nashville, Tenn., there is a white man, Pat Hanifan, who outraged a little Afro-American girl, and, from the physical injuries received, she has been ruined for life. He was jailed for six months, discharged, and is now a detective in that city. In the same city, last May, a white man outraged an Afro-American girl in a drug store. He was arrested, and released on bail at the trial. It was rumored that five hundred Afro-Americans had organized to lynch him. Two hundred and fifty white citizens armed themselves with Winchesters and guarded him. A cannon was placed in front of his home, and the Buchanan Rifles (State Militia) ordered to the scene for his protection. The Afro-American mob did not materialize. Only two weeks before Eph. Grizzard, who had only been *charged* with rape upon a white woman, had been taken from the jail, with Governor Buchanan and the police and militia standing by, dragged through the streets in broad daylight, knives plunged into him at every step, and with every fiendish cruelty a frenzied mob could devise, he was at last swung out on the bridge with hands cut to pieces as he tried to climb up the stanchions....

At the very moment these civilized whites were announcing their determination "to protect their wives and daughters," by murdering Grizzard, a white man was in the same jail for raping eight year-old Maggie Reese, an Afro-American girl. He was not harmed. The "honor" of grown women who were glad enough to be supported by the Grizzard boys and Ed Coy, as long as the liaison was not known, needed protection; they were white. The outrage upon helpless childhood needed no avenging in this case; she was black. A white man in Guthrie, Oklahoma Territory, two months ago inflicted such injuries upon another Afro-American child that she died. He was not punished, but an attempt was made in the same town in the month of June to lynch an Afro-American who visited a white woman. In Memphis, Tenn., in the month of June, Ellerton L. Dorr, who is the husband of Russell Hancock's widow, was arrested for attempted rape on Mattie Cole, a neighbor's cook; he was only prevented from accomplishing his purpose, by the appearance of Mattie's employer. Dorr's friends say he was drunk and not responsible for his actions. The grand jury refused to indict him and he was discharged.

Questions for Reflection and Discussion

What speech about sex is permitted in the American South, according to Wells-Barnett, and what speech is not? What are the values that underlie these differences? What purpose does the proliferation of examples serve?

148. MARGARET SANGER AND MAHATMA GANDHI ON BIRTH CONTROL

Time: early twentieth century CE
Place: India
Author: Mahadev Desai

Gandhi, most famous for his support of non-violent struggle for independence in India, was a generally revered spiritual leader there. Margaret Sanger was a lifelong advocate of birth control, best remembered for her role in founding Planned Parenthood. During a visit to India, Sanger appealed to Gandhi to join her in advocating the use of contraception throughout India, and the two met in November 1935, but he declined to support her cause. In the following article, written by Gandhi's personal secretary, Gandhi and Sanger both laid out their points of view, even if he was clearly more sympathetic to the former's ideas. Public debates such as these provide an excellent opportunity for historians to see the differences in public opinion.

Since the time Mrs. Margaret Sanger, the famous leader of the birth-control movement, paid a visit to Wardha, I have seen several different aspects of her. First as she appeared to me there during those remarkable interviews with Gandhiji—interviews in which she appealed to Gandhiji as a great moral teacher "to advise something practical, something that can be applied to solve the problem of too frequent child-bearing," "to give some message for those who are not yet sure, but who are anxious to limit their families." She seemed, during those conversations into which Gandhiji poured his whole being, desperately anxious to find out some point of contact with Gandhiji....

He revealed himself inside out, giving Mrs. Sanger an intimate glimpse of his own private life. He also declared to her his own limitations, especially the stupendous limitation of his own philosophy of life—a philosophy that seeks self-realization through self-control, and said that from him there could be one solution and one alone. "I could not recommend the remedy of birth-control to a woman who wanted my approval. I should simply say to her: My remedy is of no use to you. You must go to others for advice." Mrs. Sanger cited some hard cases. "I agree," said Gandhiji, "there are hard cases. Else birth-control enthusiasts would have no case. But I would say, do devise remedies by all means, but the remedies should be other than the ones you advise. If you and I, as moral reformers, put our foot down on this remedy, and said: 'You must fall back on other remedies,' those would surely be found." Both seemed to be agreed that woman should be emancipated, that woman should be the arbiter of her destiny. But Mrs. Sanger would have Gandhiji work for woman's emancipation through her pet device, just as believers in violence want Gandhiji to win India's freedom through violence, since they seem to be sure that non-violence can never succeed....

Well, this is what he said: "… The remedy is in the hands of women themselves. The struggle is difficult for them, and I do not blame them. I blame the men. Men have legislated against them. Man has regarded woman as his tool. She has learned to be his tool, and in the end found it easy and pleasurable to be such, because when one drags another in his fall the descent is easy.… I have felt that during the years still left to me, if I can drive home to women's minds the truth that they are free, we will have no birth-control problem in India. If they will only learn to say 'no' to their husbands when they approach them carnally. I do not suppose all husbands are brutes, and if women only know how to resist them, all will be well. I have been able to teach women to resist their husbands. The real problem is that many do not want to resist them.… No resistance bordering upon bitterness will be necessary in 99 out of 100 cases. If a wife says to her husband: 'No, I do not want it' he will make no trouble. But she hasn't been taught. Her parents, in most cases, won't teach it to her. There are some cases, I know, in which parents have appealed to their daughters' husbands not to force motherhood on their daughters. And I have come across amenable husbands too. I want woman to learn the primary right of resistance. She thinks now that she has not got it." …

Mrs. Sanger raises the phantasmagoria of "irritations, disputes, and thwarted longings that Mr. Gandhi's advice would bring into the home," of the absence of "loving glances," and of "tender good-night kisses," and of "words of endearment," forgetting all the while that birth-control and all its tender or vulgar accompaniments have contributed in America to countless irritations and disputes, divorces and worse. But the America we know … would seem to be different from the America that Mrs. Sanger claims to know. She cited cases of great nervous and mental breakdowns, as a result of the practice of self-control. Gandhiji spoke from a knowledge of the numerous letters he receives every mail, when he said to her that, "the evidence is all based on examination of imbeciles. The conclusions are not drawn from the practice of healthy-minded people. The people they take for examples have not lived a life of even tolerable continence. These neurologists assume that people are expected to exercise self-restraint, while they continue to lead the same ill-regulated life. The consequence is that they do not exercise self-restraint but become lunatics. I carry on correspondence with many of these people, and they describe their own ailments to me. I simply say that if I were to present them with this method of birth-control, they would lead far worse lives." …

Mrs. Sanger mocks at what she calls Mr. Gandhi's "appalling fear of licentiousness and over-indulgence," following upon a life of unrestrained birth-control, and she pointedly asks: "Has he ever thought that the same frequency can occur during the nine months of a woman's pregnancy?" I must say that in advancing this argument, Mrs. Sanger is less than fair to her own sex. None but the most abnormally lewd or suppressed would submit to even legitimate sexual advances during pregnancy. What was to be done with couples who wanted to resist the impulse of sex, and yet could not do so? Mrs. Sanger was thus led on to her apotheosis of "sex love," which she said "is a relationship which makes for oneness, for completeness between husband and wife, and contributes to a finer understanding and a greater spiritual harmony." An obviously harmless proposition, but full of confusion when, in the same breath, one identifies love with lust and then tries to separate the one from the other. The distinction that Gandhiji drew between love and lust will be evident from the following excerpts from the conversation:

Gandhiji: When both want to satisfy animal passion, without having to suffer the consequences of their act, it is not love, it is lust. But if love is pure, it will transcend animal passion and will regulate itself. We have not had enough education of the passions. When a husband says: "Let us not have children, but let us have relations," what is that but animal passion? If they do not want to have more children, they should simply refuse to unite. Love becomes lust, the moment you make it a means for the satisfaction of animal needs. It is just the same with food. If food is taken only for pleasure, it is lust. You do not take chocolates for the sake of satisfying your hunger. You take them for pleasure and then ask the doctor for an antidote. Perhaps, you tell the doctor that whisky befogs your brain, and he gives you an antidote. Would it not be better not to take chocolates or whisky?

Mrs. Sanger: No, I do not accept the analogy.

Gandhiji: Of course, you will not accept the analogy because you think this sex-expression, without desire for children, is a need of the soul, a contention I do not endorse.

Mrs. Sanger: Yes, sex-expression is a spiritual need, and I claim that the quality of this expression is more important than the result, for the quality of the relationship is there regardless of results. We all know that the great majority of children are born as an accident, without the parents having any desire for conception. Seldom are two people drawn together in the sex act by their desire to have children…. Do you think it possible for two people who are in love, who are happy together, to regulate their sex act only once in two years, so that relationship would only take place when they wanted a child! Do you think it possible?

Gandhiji: I had the honor of doing that very thing, and I am not the only one.

Mrs. Sanger thought it was illogical to contend that sex-union for the purpose of having children would be love, and union for the satisfaction of the sexual appetite was lust, for the same act was involved in both. Gandhiji immediately capitulated, and said he was ready to describe all sexual union as partaking of the nature of lust. He made the whole thing abundantly clear by citing facts from his own life. "I know," he said, "from my own experience, that as long as I looked upon my wife carnally, we had no real understanding. Our love did not reach a high plane. There was affection between us always, but we came closer and closer the more we or rather I became restrained. There never was want of restraint on the part of my wife. Very often she would show restraint, but she rarely resisted me, although she showed disinclination very often. All the time I wanted carnal pleasure, I could not serve her. The moment I bade goodbye to a life of carnal pleasure, our whole relationship became spiritual. Lust died and love reigned instead."

But Mrs. Sanger, probably, regards every free embrace an act of love, and a married life without sexual relationship and its blandishments a dull lifeless affair. Gandhiji's own personal witness made no impression upon her. She dismissed it as that of an "idealist." … Mrs. Sanger forgets that all moral advancement has proceeded on the practice of a "small group of idealists," and that even the apparent progress of her own movement depends a lot on the clever way in which she idealizes her nostrum, and describes it as the upward path "demanding of us who inhabit this globe all that we possess in intelligence, knowledge, courage, vision and responsibility." The road that "leads to the fulfillment of human destiny on this planet."

Mrs. Sanger is so impatient to prove that Gandhiji is a visionary, that she forgets the practical ways and means that Gandhiji suggested to her. "Must the sexual union take place only three or four times in an entire lifetime?" she asked. "Why should people not be taught," replied Gandhiji, "that it is immoral to have more than three or four children, and that after they have had that number they should sleep separately? If they are taught this, it would harden into custom. And if social reformers cannot press this idea upon the people, why not a law? …" And yet, as Mrs. Sanger was so dreadfully in earnest, Gandhiji did mention a remedy which could, conceivably, appeal to him. That method was the avoidance of sexual union during unsafe periods, confining it to the "safe" period of about ten days during the month. That had at least an element of self-control, which had to be exercised during the unsafe period. Whether this appealed to Mrs. Sanger or not, I do not know…. Perhaps, if birth-controllers were to be satisfied with this simple method, the birth-control clinics and propagandists would find their trade gone.

Questions for Reflection and Discussion

Are arguments that appeal to ideals and realities of human behavior really opposing arguments? Which has the better argument: the appeal to ideals or to realities?

149. GANDHI ON *SATI* AND *PURDAH*

Time: mid-twentieth century CE
Place: India
Author: Mahatma Gandhi

Gandhi wrote regularly in newspapers and magazines, using his political stature to publicize his views on many subjects, and he did not shy away from controversial topics. Two examples follow, both still hotly debated issues. The first deals with sati, *meaning an "ideal wife," used most often in relation to the Hindu practice whereby widows throw themselves on the funeral fires after their husband's death. The second deals with* purdah, *referring to the Muslim practice of veiling women or otherwise secluding them in public spaces.*

A *sati* has been described by our ancients, and the description holds good today, as one who ever fixed in her love and devotion to her husband signalizes herself by her selfless service during her husband's lifetime as well as after, and remains absolutely chaste in thought, word and deed. Self-immolation at the death of the husband is not a sign of enlightenment, but of gross ignorance as to the nature of the soul. The soul is immortal, unchangeable and immanent. It does not perish with the physical body but journeys on from one mortal frame to another, till it completely emancipates itself from earthly bondage. The truth of it has been attested to by the experience of countless sages and seers, and can be realized by any one who may wish to even today. How can suicide be, then, justified in the light of these facts?

Again, true marriage means not merely union of bodies. It connotes the union of the souls too. If marriage meant no more than a physical relationship, the bereaved wife should be satisfied with a portrait or a waxen image of her husband. But self-destruction is worse than futile. It cannot help to restore the dead to life, on the contrary it only takes away one more from the world of the living. The ideal that marriage aims at is that of spiritual union through the physical. The human love that it incarnates is intended to serve as a stepping-stone to the divine or universal love….

It follows from this, that a *sati* would regard marriage not as a means of satisfying the animal appetite, but as a means of realizing the ideal of selfless and self-effacing service by completely merging her individuality in her husband's. She would prove her *sati*hood not by mounting the funeral pyre at her husband's death, but she would prove it with every breath that she breathes from the moment that she plighted her troth to him at the *saptapadi* ceremony, by her renunciation, sacrifice, self-abnegation and dedication to the service of her husband, his family and the country. She would shun creature comforts and delights of the senses. She would refuse to be enslaved by the narrow domestic cares and interests of the family, but would utilize every opportunity to add to her stock of knowledge and increase her capacity for service by more and more cultivating renunciation and self discipline, and by completely identifying herself with her husband learn to identify herself with the whole world. Such a *sati* would refuse to give way to wild grief at the death of her husband, but would ever strive to make her late husband's ideals and virtues live again in her actions, and, thereby win for him the crown of immortality. Knowing that the soul of him whom she married is not dead but still lives, she will never think of remarrying....

All that I have said about the wife applies equally to the husband. If the wife has to prove her loyalty and undivided devotion to her husband, so has the husband to prove his allegiance and devotion to his wife. You cannot have one set of weights and measures for the one, and a different one for the other. Yet, we have never heard of a husband mounting the funeral pyre of his deceased wife. It may, therefore be taken for granted that the practice of the widow immolating herself at the death of her husband had its origin in superstitious ignorance and the blind egotism of man. Even if it could be proved that at one time the practice had a meaning, it can only be regarded as barbarous in the present age. The wife is not the slave of the husband but his comrade, otherwise known as his better-half, his colleague and friend. She is a co-sharer with him of equal rights and of equal duties. Their obligations towards each other and towards the world must, therefore, be the same and reciprocal.

I, therefore, regard the alleged self-immolation of this sister as vain. It certainly cannot be set up as an example to be copied. Don't I appreciate at least her courage to die?—I may, perhaps, be asked. My reply is 'no,' in all conscience. Have we not seen evildoers display this sort of courage? Yet no one has ever thought of complimenting them on it. Why should I take upon me the sin of even unconsciously leading astray some ignorant sister by my injudicious praise of suicide? *Sati*hood is the acme of purity. This purity cannot be attained or realized by dying. It can be attained only through constant striving, constant immolation of the spirit from day to day.

Whenever I have gone to Bengal, Bihar or the United Provinces, I have observed the *purdah* system more strictly followed than in the other provinces. But when I addressed a meeting at Darbhanga late at night, and amid surroundings free from noise and bustle and unmanageable crowds, I found in front of me men, but behind me and behind the screen were women, of whose presence I knew nothing till my attention was drawn to it. The function was in connection with the laying of the foundation stone of an orphanage, but I was called upon to address the ladies behind the *purdah*. The sight of the screen behind which my audience, whose numbers I did not know, was seated made me sad. It pained and humiliated me deeply. I thought of the wrong being done by men to the women of India by clinging to a barbarous custom which, whatever use it might have had when it was first introduced, had now become totally useless and doing incalculable harm to the country. All the education that we have been receiving for the past 100 years seems to have produced but little impression upon us, for I note that the *purdah* is being retained even in educated households, not because the educated men believe in it themselves, but because they will not manfully resist the brutal custom and sweep it away at a stroke.

I have the privilege of addressing hundreds of meetings of women attended by thousands. The din and the noise created at these meetings make it impossible to speak with any effect to the women who attend them. Nothing better is to be expected so long as they are caged and confined in their houses and little courtyards. When, therefore, they find themselves congregated in a big room and are expected all of a sudden to listen to some one, they do not know what to do with themselves or with the speaker. And when silence is restored, it becomes difficult to interest them in many everyday topics, for they know nothing of them having been never allowed to breathe the fresh air of freedom. I know that this is a somewhat exaggerated picture. I am quite aware of the very high culture of these thousands of sisters whom I get the privilege of addressing. I know that they are capable of rising to the same height that men are capable of, and I know, too, that they do not have occasions to go out. But this is not to be put down to the credit of the educated classes. The question is, why have they not gone further? Why do not our women enjoy the same freedom that men do? Why should they not be able to walk out and have fresh air? Chastity is not a hot-house growth. It cannot be superimposed. It cannot be protected by the surrounding wall of the *purdah.* It must grow from within, and, to be worth

anything, it must be capable of withstanding every unsought temptation. It must be as defiant as Sita's. It must be a very poor thing that cannot stand the gaze of men. Men, to be men, must be able to trust their women-folk, even as the latter are compelled to trust them. Let us not live with one limb completely or partially paralyzed. Rama would be nowhere without Sita, free and independent, even as he was himself…. By seeking today to interfere with the free growth of the womanhood of India, we are interfering with the growth of free and independent spirited men. What we are doing to our women, and what we are doing to the untouchables, recoils upon our heads with force thousand times multiplied. It partly accounts for our weakness, indecision, narrowness and helplessness. Let us, then, tear down the *purdah* with one mighty effort.

Questions for Reflection and Discussion

How do Gandhi's arguments see the relationship between an individual's identity and role within the community? How might opposing arguments be framed?

150. SHE MAY LOOK CLEAN

Time: mid-twentieth century CE
Place: United States
Artist: unknown

This image was part of a campaign undertaken by the United States Armed Forces to reduce the spread of sexually transmitted diseases among the troops during World War II. The cost of medical treatment and the loss of manpower due to illness prompted the campaign, but military officials faced considerable pressure from politicians and civic leaders, who did not want publicized the numbers of military men who took advantage of wartime opportunities

for temporary sexual encounters. In the end, the concerns of public health overruled moral discretion.

Questions for Reflection and Discussion

How effective is the woman's image, given the message of the poster? In what ways does the poster appeal to military men? To what extent does the poster promote a message that women are agents of sexually transmitted disease, but men its victims?

151. MEN AND WOMEN AT THE BEACH

Time: early twentieth century CE
Place: Australia
Author: unknown

If many of the previous sources reveal ongoing issues of debate, two newspaper articles from August 1911 in the Sydney Sun *reflect a controversy that no longer seems to attract public discussion and even in its day possibly lacked support. The issue was whether to permit men and women to use the same beaches at the same time, given the revealing—at least to contemporaries—bathing suits of the era. The media carefully managed to find spokespersons for opposite positions, since, as they say, controversy sells newspapers. The "surfers" mentioned below are simply those who relax on the surf.*

"I think promiscuous surf-bathing is offensive in general to propriety, and a particular feature of that offensiveness is the attraction it has for idle onlookers," said Archbishop Kelly this morning when approached by a *Sun* representative on the subject of surf-bathing, to which His Grace had referred in a recent sermon. While thus expressing his objection to mixed surf-bathing as at present practiced along our beaches, his Grace was careful to make it plain that as far as surf-bathing itself was concerned it had in him a strong advocate. "I regard it as an invigorating and healthy pastime," he said, "so long as it is conducted with a proper respect for domestic modesty. What I strongly object to is the promiscuous commingling of the sexes, which is the chief feature of surf-bathing as at present indulged in."

"Would you suggest a reform in respect of surf-bathing?" "I think that the municipal authorities should take such steps in the regulation of surf-bathing as would eliminate its present objectionable features," replied his Grace. "There is no borderline between vice and virtue. Our worst passions are but the abuse of our good ones. And I believe that the promiscuous intermingling of sexes in surf-bathing makes for the deterioration of our standard of morality. If we wish to have happy homes, our women must be respected. Every time they appear under immodest circumstances in public there is a diminution of that respect. It is what I would call subversive of domestic respect. For a woman to be exposed to public view as she is under the circumstances of surf-bathing is utterly destructive of that modesty which is one of the pillars of our nationhood. I would that our municipal authorities had taken more mature counsel in this matter, so that arrangements could have been made for the sexes to bathe separately....

"I have known of this promiscuous bathing at the Channel ports in the north of France, and there it has become decidedly demoralizing. Compare what one sees at these Channel ports of France with the decorum observed at the English seaside resorts on the opposite side! On the English side of the Channel the most circumspect person can go and bathe with modesty. Cross over to the French side, and a self-respecting, modest person could not fail to have his sense of the proprieties shocked by even looking on.... Woe betide Australia if she is going to encourage immodesty in her women."

[On the following day, the Mayor of Randwick, a town outside of Sydney and near to the beaches, gave this reply to a *Sun* reporter.]

It is my belief that women who surf mix with the men more from a sense of safety than a desire to besport their figures in full view of admirers. And I also believe that the crowd who collect at the water's edge watching the parties diving under and riding on the crest of the breakers are animated by motives quite wholesome. To watch the crowd besporting in the breakers, to see the varied manners in which the waves are met, to see the bathers shooting the breakers and the general enjoyment which the water creates, is surely sufficient to justify the gathering of thousands of people. With the view of preserving the "modesty which is one of the pillars of our nationhood," numerous representatives of surf-bathing clubs armed with full authority as inspectors under the local governing bodies are always at hand to prevent any interference by one sex with the other....

It is just as well for a high ecclesiastical dignitary to sound a note of warning in the interests of womanly modesty, but the prevention of the "deterioration of our standard of morality" must at all times rest with the individuals themselves as against any set of rules, bylaws, or regulations. The beauty of the human form has at all times appealed to the world's greatest painters and sculptors, and surely we, living in an enlightened age, can be permitted to add our quota of admiration without shocking our modesty....

Questions for Reflection and Discussion

What are the different perspectives and assumptions from which the Archbishop and the Mayor present their arguments? How do they each appeal to potential supporters?

152. A DRAG BALL IN BERLIN

Time: nineteenth century CE
Place: Germany
Author: unknown

Meetings of homosexuals have often been held in secret so that those who took part would not suffer from the hostility of others. Drag balls, at which men dressed as women and women dressed as men, were part of this underground world, known in Europe from at least the eighteenth century. Occasionally, however, outsiders found out about the gatherings and reported them to the wider community. This report came from the 1884 edition of a Berlin newspaper. In Germany, the rise of the Nazis in the 1930s put an end to such a subculture as "decadence."

Almost every social element of Berlin has its social reunions—the fat, the bald-headed, the bachelors, the widowers—and why not the woman-haters? This species of men, so interesting psychologically and none too edifying, had a great ball a few days ago. "Grand Vienna Fancy Dress Ball" ran the notice. The sale of tickets is very rigorous; they wish to be very exclusive. Their rendezvous is a well-known dancing-hall. We enter the hall about midnight. The merry dancing is to the strains of a fine orchestra. Thick tobacco-smoke, veiling the gaslights, does not allow the details of the moving mass to become obvious; only during the pause between the dances can we obtain a closer view. The masks are by far in the majority; black dress-coats and ball-gowns are seen only now and then.

But what is that? The lady in rose-tarletan, that just now passed us, has a lighted cigar in the comer of her mouth, and puffs like a trooper; and she also wears a small, blonde beard, lightly painted out. And yet she is talking with a very *décolleté* "angel" in *tricots*, who stands there, with bare arms folded behind him, likewise smoking. The two voices are masculine, and the conversation is likewise very masculine; it is about the "d—— tobacco smoke, that permits no air." Two men in female attire! A conventional clown stands there, against a pillar, in soft conversation with a ballet-dancer, with his arm around her faultless waist. She has a blonde "Titus-head" sharp-cut profile, and apparently a voluptuous form. The brilliant earrings, the necklace with a medallion, the full, round shoulders and arms, do not permit a doubt of her "genuineness," until, with a sudden movement, she disengages herself from the embracing arm, and, yawning, moves away, saying, in a deep bass, "Emile, you are too tiresome today!" The ballet-dancer is also a male!

Suspicious now, we look about further. We almost suspect that here the world is topsy-turvy; for there goes or, rather, trips, a man—no, no man at all, even though he wears a carefully trained moustache. The well-curled hair; the powdered and painted face with the blackened eyebrows; the golden earrings; the bouquet of flowers reaching from the left shoulder to the breast, ornamenting the elegant black gown; the golden bracelets on the wrists; the elegant fan in the white-gloved hand—all these things are anything but masculine. And how he toys with the fan! How he dances and turns and trips and lisps! And yet kindly Nature made this doll a man. He is a salesman in a large sweet shop, and the ballet-dancer mentioned is his "colleague." …

On closer examination of the assembly, to my astonishment, I discover acquaintances on all hands: my shoemaker, whom I should have taken for anything but a woman-hater—he is a "troubadour," with sword and plume; and his "Leonora," in the costume of a bride, is accustomed to place my favorite brand of cigars before me in a certain cigar-store. "Leonora," who, during an intermission, removes her gloves, I recognize with certainty by her large, blue hands. Right! There is my haberdasher, also; he is the swain of a repugnantly bedecked Diana, who works as a waiter in a beer-restaurant. The real "ladies" of the ball cannot be described here. They associate only with one another, and avoid the woman-hating men; and the latter are exclusive, and amuse themselves, absolutely ignoring the charms of the women.

Questions for Reflection and Discussion

What tone about this event does the newspaper writer exhibit? Is he surprised to see so many individuals he knows? Did the men and women at the ball seem to think of themselves as the other sex, or were they simply having fun at the expense of gender conventions?

153. THE STONEWALL RIOTS

Time: late twentieth century CE
Place: United States
Author: Dick Leitsch

The Stonewall Riots, said to be the birth of the modern gay liberation movement, have been commemorated every year since with "pride marches" in many major cities worldwide. This description of the riots by a New York gay newsletter, an eyewitness to the events, was reprinted in a gay magazine, The Advocate. *Given the exclusion of certain topics from public discussion, reports such as these from "underground" sources provided information to interested parties where it might not otherwise be obtained.*

The first gay riots in history took place during the predawn hours of Saturday and Sunday, June 28-29, in New York's Greenwich Village. The demonstrations were touched off by a police raid on the popular Stonewall Inn, 53 Christopher St. This was the last to date in a series of harassments that plagued the Village area for the last several weeks. Plainclothes officers entered the club at about 2 a.m., armed with a warrant, and closed the place on grounds of illegal selling of alcohol. Employees were arrested and the customers told to leave. The patrons gathered on the street outside and were joined by other Village residents and visitors to the area…. Pennies were thrown at the cops by the crowd, then beer cans, rocks, and even parking meters. The cops retreated inside the bar, which was set afire by the crowd. A hose from the bar was employed by the trapped cops to douse the flames, and reinforcements were summoned. A melee ensued, with nearly a thousand persons participating, as well as several hundred cops….

[The next day, the riot resumed.]

Christopher Street from Greenwich to Seventh Avenue had become an almost solid mass of people—most of them gay. No traffic could pass, and even walking the few blocks on foot was next to impossible…. Squad cars from the fourth, fifth, sixth, and ninth precincts had brought in a hundred or so cops who had no hope of controlling the crowd of nearly 2,000 people in the streets…. They huddled with some of the top brass that had already arrived, and isolated beer cans, thrown by the crowd, hit their van and cars now and again. Suddenly, two cops darted into the crowd and dragged out a boy who had done absolutely nothing. As they carried him to a waiting van brought to take off prisoners, four more cops joined them and began pounding the boy in the face, belly, and groin with nightsticks. A high, shrill voice called out, "Save our sister!" and there was a general pause, during which the "butch"-looking "numbers" looked distracted. Momentarily, 50 or more homosexuals who would have to be described as "nelly" rushed the cops and took the boy back into the crowd. They then formed a solid front and refused to let the cops into the crowd to regain their prisoner, letting the cops hit them with their sticks, rather than let them through. (It was an interesting sidelight on the demonstrations that those usually put down as "sissies" or "swishes" showed the most courage and sense during the action. Their bravery and daring saved many people from being hurt, and their sense of humor and "camp" helped keep the crowds from getting nasty or too violent.)

The cops gave up on the idea of taking prisoners and concentrated on clearing the area…. They made full use of their nightsticks, brandishing them like swords. At one point a cop grabbed a wild Puerto Rican queen and lifted his arm to bring a club down on "her." In his best Maria Montez voice, the queen challenged, "How'd you like a big Spanish dick up your little Irish ass?" The cop was so shocked he hesitated in his swing, and the queen escaped. At another point, two lonely cops were chasing a hundred or more people down Waverly Place. Someone shouted out that the queens outnumbered the cops and suggested catching them, ripping off their clothes, and screwing them. The cops abandoned the chase and fled back to the main force for protection.

Questions for Reflection and Discussion

How reliable is this eyewitness? How does he subvert expectations of what is manly and unmanly in this account, and why? Why is this event still commemorated each year?

154. SILENCE = DEATH

Time: late twentieth century CE
Place: United States
Artists: unknown

AIDS has devastated communities worldwide, but among its first victims were gay men. In 1981 doctors began noticing among their gay patients previously healthy men who developed rare and life-threatening illnesses. By 1987, when the "Silence = Death" symbol first appeared, over 4,000 had died from the disease in the US, but those affected believed that anti-gay prejudice had prevented money and energy from being directed to fighting the disease. The image, created in New York by some graphic artists involved in ACT UP (AIDS Coalition To Unleash Power), a group using civil disobedience to force AIDS into public discussion, included a pink triangle, the symbol worn by homosexuals imprisoned in Nazi Germany. In the same year, a memorial quilt was begun in San Francisco, each large square representing a person lost to the disease, sewn by lovers, families, and friends. By the end of 2005, an estimated 25 million people worldwide had died of AIDS, and 40 million infected with the virus that causes it.

Questions for Reflection and Discussion

In what ways does the symbol "Silence = Death" move the message beyond the specifics of AIDS? In what ways is it a challenge to action? How does this symbol and the memorial quilt work in different ways to raise public awareness?

155. ABORTION ARGUMENTS

Time: late twentieth century CE
Place: United States
Authors: various

In January 1973, the United States Supreme Court ruled in Roe v. Wade that a Texas law outlawing abortions was unconstitutional and, by doing so, made abortions legal in the United States, but by no means ended the controversy over the mat-

ter. One week later, a member of the US House of Representatives introduced a proposal to amend the Constitution to prohibit abortion once again. The Senate Committee on the Judiciary, Subcommittee on Constitutional Amendments, held hearings later that year and considered arguments from a variety of individuals both for and against the proposed amendment. The amendment ultimately failed.

JAMES BUCKLEY, SENATOR FROM NEW YORK

About 4 months ago, the Supreme Court, in a pair of highly controversial, precedent-shattering decisions, Roe against Wade and Doe against Bolton, ruled that a pregnant woman has the constitutional right to destroy the life of her unborn child. In so doing, the Court not only contravened the express will of every State legislature in the country; it not only removed every vestige of legal protection hitherto enjoyed by the child in the mother's womb; but it reached its result through a curious and confusing chain of reasoning that, logically extended, could apply with equal force to the genetically deficient infant, the retarded child, or the insane or senile adult. After reviewing these decisions, I concluded that, given the gravity of the issues at stake and the way in which the Court had carefully closed off alternative means of redress, a constitutional amendment was the only way to remedy the damage wrought by the Court.

JOHN CARDINAL KROL, ROMAN CATHOLIC ARCHBISHOP OF PHILADELPHIA

We do not propose to advocate sectarian doctrine but to defend human rights, and specifically, the most fundamental of all rights, the right to life itself…. We reject any suggestion that we are attempting to impose "our" morality on others. First, it is not true. The right to life is not an invention of the Catholic Church or any other church. It is a basic human right which must undergird any civilized society. Second, either we all have the same right to speak out on public policy or no one does. We do not have to check our consciences at the door before we argue for what we think is best for society.

RABBI BALFOUR BRICKNER OF NEW YORK

Judaism does not believe that the word "person" connotes a full human being. It does not equate abortion with murder. To the contrary, in Judaism, a fetus is not considered a full human being and for this reason has no "juridical personality" of its own. Jewish law is quite clear in its statement that an embryo is not reckoned a viable living thing (in Hebrew, a *bar kayyama*) until 30 days after its birth.

DR. GERALD M. EDELMAN, PROFESSOR OF BIOLOGY, ROCKEFELLER UNIVERSITY

I speak as a scientist with some experience in cell biology and in molecular biology…. As I understand it, one of the main questions before this committee is whether we can tell when life, particularly human life, begins. I hope to show that, from the scientific point of view, this question is unanswerable, because it is not formulated in terms that can be dealt with operationally…. If one asserts that a fertilized egg contains a full complement of genes from the father and the mother, and is therefore privileged as "more alive," then counter examples can easily be brought to mind. Biologists have produced complete frogs from eggs alone without sperm and have even produced frogs from the nuclei of skin cells, which contain just as much genetic information as a fertilized egg. Such complete genetic information is, in fact, in every cell of the body except sperm and eggs, yet no one raises issues about the loss of skin cells or even brain cells for that matter.

PAT GOLTZ, FEMINISTS FOR LIFE

The only consistent philosophy a feminist can have about other instances of human life is one of granting dignity to all of them…. We who were once defined as less than human cannot, in claiming our rights, deny rights to others based on a subjective judgment that they are less than human…. The solution to the rape problem [and resulting pregnancy, as in Roe v. Wade], is not abortion, but the creation of a society in which rape is unknown. The immediate solution is to teach women to report their rapes immediately so that pregnancy can be prevented. Failure to do so is implied consent to provide life support to the unborn child who may result. The immediate solution also consists of forcing changes in attitude toward raped women so that they are not treated as common criminals if they report their rapes. In rape with pregnancy resulting there are actually two victims: the mother and her baby. It is not just, to kill one of the victims for the father's crime.

BELLA ABZUG, CONGRESSWOMAN
FROM NEW YORK

I appear before you as a Member of Congress, but also as a woman who is aware that in the consideration of this proposal, the fate of women is once again to be decided by men…. Man and woman are equal in the act of conception, but after that single act has occurred, it is the woman's body that carries and nurtures the embryo and the fetus. It is the woman who experiences the physical and psychological changes of pregnancy. It is the woman who has the discomforts and sometimes the medical complications that accompany pregnancy. It is the woman who feels the pain of childbirth. It is the woman who may have the *post partem* depression…. And in our society, it is still the woman who bears the major responsibility of caring for and raising the child and who often must leave school or her work to do so. Childbearing and childraising is a great experience for most women. For some it is not. For some it is sometimes. The point is that it is a totally individual experience, the most highly personal process in a woman's life. And yet the [proposed amendment] … might mobilize the full power and authority of the state and its legal apparatus to interfere in this private process, to dictate to the individual citizen who is a woman what she is to do with her body and with her life.

MARY HARTLE OF MINNEAPOLIS

When the move to legalize abortion started heavily a decade ago, the proponents originally argued that abortion should be legalized for women who had had German measles during pregnancy and for women and young girls who had been raped…. During the first trimester of pregnancy with me, my mother contracted German measles…. I was born in 1952 with a heart defect and cataracts in my eyes…. My first year of life was in a very precarious state. I underwent heart surgery in December 1952 and eye surgery in October 1952 and again in June 1953. After the operations my health improved immensely. My heart condition has been corrected such that my heart is now normal. My vision was improved to the point where I can see at 20/200 with correction. Thus, I can see objects clearly and read regular size print at a close distance. It is said that those who may be deformed should be aborted so they do not have to lead an unhappy life and so as to not cause a great hardship on their families. I wholeheartedly disagree with this argument…. It is thought by most people that a handicap incapacitates a person so completely that they are rendered unemployable persons who are dependent on their relatives and society at large. However, this is a falsehood.

KAY JACOBS OF WASHINGTON, DC

I am not here to speak about every facet of the abortion question, but to help develop an understanding of the need to preserve the right to abortion when a fetus is known to have Tay-Sachs disease or a comparable disorder. There are a great many people who wish to deny potential parents of infants with fatal genetic disorders the option to terminate affected pregnancies. However, once a doomed baby is born, these same people who insist on his birth disappear, leaving total responsibility to his parents. Besides the heartbreak, mental anguish, and, quite frankly, physical burden that the parents must endure, there is the problem of finding people willing or qualified to help in caring for such a child…. It all started for us 4 ½ years ago when we had our first baby. She was beautiful and, we were assured, healthy and normal. She grew and developed very normally for several months, or so we were told…. By 10 months of age, she had begun to grow weak and to lose some of the skills she had learned, and once again I pleaded with the pediatrician to tell me what was wrong…. We brought Joann home the day before her 1st birthday with the knowledge that she had Tay-Sachs disease, that the birthday cake placed in front of her the next day would be the only one she would ever see, and that she would no doubt be dead before her 4th birthday.

Questions for Reflection and Discussion

How do these arguments appeal in different ways to reason and to the emotions? Which sorts of argument are most compelling?

156. FEMALE CIRCUMCISION

Time: late twentieth century CE
Place: Egypt
Author: Nawal El Saadawi

Part of Nawal El Saadawi's The Hidden Face of Eve, *published in 1977 (see source 141), highlighted the controversy over female circumcision, also known as female genital mutilation. Practiced in different parts of the world, its precise nature varies but usually involves removing the clitoris and/or removing the labia or sewing them together. Its origins are unknown, although it is often claimed to date back to antiquity. In her book, El Saadawi also discussed her own circumcision at age six. Part of her work has been to initiate public discussions about the origins of the practice and its implications for women's self-esteem as well as for their health.*

The practice of circumcising girls is still a common procedure in a number of Arab countries such as Egypt, the Sudan, Yemen and some of the Gulf states. The importance given to virginity and an intact hymen in these societies is the reason why female circumcision still remains a very widespread practice despite a growing tendency, especially in urban Egypt, to do away with it as something outdated and harmful. Behind circumcision lies the belief that, by removing parts of girls' external genital organs, sexual desire is minimized. This permits a female who has reached the "dangerous age" of puberty and adolescence to protect her virginity, and therefore her honor, with greater ease. Chastity was imposed on male attendants in the female harem by castration which turned them into inoffensive eunuchs. Similarly female circumcision is meant to preserve the chastity of young girls by reducing their desire for sexual intercourse.

Circumcision is most often performed on female children at the age of seven or eight (before the girl begins to get menstrual periods). On the scene appears the *daya* or local midwife. Two women members of the family grasp the child's thighs on either side and pull them apart to expose the external genital organs and to prevent her from struggling—like trussing a chicken before it is slain. A sharp razor in the hand of the *daya* cuts off the clitoris. During my period of service as a rural physician, I was called upon many times to treat complications arising from this primitive operation, which very often jeopardized the life of young girls. The ignorant *daya* believed that effective circumcision necessitated a deep cut with the razor to ensure radical amputation of the clitoris, so that no part of the sexually sensitive organ would remain. Severe hemorrhage was therefore a common occurrence and sometimes led to loss of life. The *dayas* had not the slightest notion of asepsis, and inflammatory conditions as a result of the operation were common.

Above all, the lifelong psychological shock of this cruel procedure left its imprint on the personality of the child and accompanied her into adolescence, youth and maturity. Sexual frigidity is one of the aftereffects which is accentuated by other social and psychological factors that influence the personality and mental makeup of females in Arab societies. Girls are therefore exposed to a whole series of misfortunes as a result of outdated notions and values related to virginity, which still remains the fundamental criterion of a girl's honor. In recent years, however, educated families have begun to realize the harm that is done by the practice of female circumcision. Nevertheless a majority of families still impose on young female children the barbaric and cruel operation of circumcision. The research that I carried out on a sample of 160 Egyptian girls and women showed that 97.5 of uneducated families still insisted on maintaining the custom, but this percentage dropped to 66.2 among educated families.

When I discussed the matter with these girls and women it transpired that most of them had no idea of the harm done by circumcision, and some of them even thought that it was good for one's health and conducive to cleanliness and purity. (The operation in the common language of the people is in fact called the cleansing or purifying operation.) … The dialogue that occurred between these women and myself would run more or less as follows: "Have you undergone circumcision?" "Yes." "How old were you at the time?" "I was a child, about seven or eight years old." "Do you remember the details of the operation?" "Of course. How could I possibly forget?" "Were you afraid?" "Very afraid. I hid on top of the cupboard (in other cases she would say under the bed, or in the neighbor's house), but they caught hold of me, and I felt my body tremble in their hands."

"Did you feel any pain?" "Very much so. It was like a burning flame and I screamed. My mother held my head so that I could not move it, my aunt caught hold of my right arm and my grandmother took charge of my left. Two strange women whom I had not seen before tried to keep me from moving my thighs by pushing them as far apart as possible. The *daya* sat between these two women, holding a sharp razor in her hand which she used to cut off the clitoris. I was scared and suffered such great pain that I lost consciousness at the flame that seemed to sear me through and through." "What happened after the operation?" "I had severe bodily pains, and remained in bed for several days, unable to move. The pain in my external genital organs led to retention of urine. Every time I wanted to urinate the burning sensation was so unbearable that I could not bring myself to pass water. The wound continued to bleed for some time, and my mother used to change the dressing for me twice a day."

"What did you feel on discovering that a small organ in your body had been removed?" "I did not know anything about the operation at the time, except that it was very simple, and that it was done to all girls for purposes of cleanliness, purity and the preservation of a good reputation. It was said that a girl who did not undergo this operation was liable to be talked about by people, her behavior would become bad, and she would start running after men, with the result that no one would agree to marry her when the time for marriage came. My grandmother told me that the operation had only consisted in the removal of a very small piece of flesh from between my thighs, and that the continued existence of this small piece of flesh in its place would have made me unclean and impure, and would have caused the man whom I would marry to be repelled by me." "Did you believe what was said to you?" "Of course I did. I was happy the day I recovered from the effects of the operation, and felt as though I was rid of something which had to be removed, and so had become clean and pure." Those were more or less the answers that I obtained from all those interviewed, whether educated or uneducated....

In the face of all these strange and complicated procedures aimed at preventing sexual intercourse in women except if controlled by the husband, it is natural that we should ask ourselves why women, in particular, were subjected to such torture and cruel suppression. There seems to be no doubt that society, as represented by its dominant classes and male structure, realized at a very early stage that sexual desire in the female is very powerful, and that women, unless controlled and subjugated by all sorts of measures, will not submit themselves to the moral, social, legal and religious constraints with which they have been surrounded, and in particular the constraints related to monogamy. The patriarchal system, which came into being when society had reached a certain stage of development and which necessitated the imposition of one husband on the woman whereas a man was left free to have several wives, would never have been possible, or have been maintained to this day, without the whole range of cruel and ingenious devices that were used to keep her sexuality in check and limit her sexual relations to only one man, who had to be her husband.

This is the reason for the implacable enmity shown by society towards female sexuality, and the weapons used to resist and subjugate the turbulent force inherent in it. The slightest leniency manifested in facing this "potential danger" meant that woman would break out of the prison bars to which marriage had confined her, and step over the steely limits of a monogamous relationship to a forbidden intimacy with another man, which would inevitably lead to confusion in succession and inheritance, since there was no guarantee that a strange man's child would not step into the waiting line of descendants. Confusion between the children of the legitimate husband and the outsider lover would mean the unavoidable collapse of the patriarchal family built around the name of the father alone.

History shows us clearly that the father was keen on knowing who his real children were, solely for the purpose of handing down his landed property to them. The patriarchal family, therefore, came into existence mainly for economic reasons. It was necessary for society simultaneously to build up a system of moral and religious values, as well as a legal system capable of protecting and maintaining these economic interests. In the final analysis we can safely say that female circumcision, the chastity belt and other savage practices applied to women are basically the result of the economic interests that govern society. The continued existence of such practices in our society today signifies that these economic interests are still operative. The thousands of *dayas*, nurses, paramedical staff and doctors, who make money out of female circumcision, naturally resist any change in these values and practices which are a source of gain to them. In the Sudan there is a veritable army of *dayas* who earn a livelihood out of the series of operations performed on women, either to excise their external genital organs, or to alternately narrow and widen the outer aperture according to whether the woman is marrying, divorcing, remarrying, having a child or recovering from labor. Economic factors and, concomitantly, political factors are the basis upon which such customs as female circumcision have grown up.

It is important to understand the facts as they really are, and the reasons that lie behind them. Many are the people who are not able to distinguish between political and religious factors, or who conceal economic and political motives behind religious arguments in an attempt to hide the real forces that lie at the basis of what happens in society and in history. It has very often been proclaimed that Islam is at the root of female circumcision, and is also responsible for the underprivileged and backward situation of women in Egypt and the Arab world. Such a contention is not true…. The reasons for the lower status of women in our societies, and the lack of opportunities for progress afforded to them, are not due to Islam, but rather to certain economic and political forces, namely those of foreign imperialism operating mainly from the outside, and of the reactionary classes operating from the inside. These two forces cooperate closely and are making a concerted attempt to misinterpret religion and to utilize it as an instrument of fear, oppression and exploitation.

Religion, if authentic in the principles it stands for, aims at truth, equality, justice, love and a healthy wholesome life for all people, whether men or women. There can be no true religion that aims at disease, mutilation of the bodies of female children, and amputation of an essential part of their reproductive organs. If religion comes from God, how can it order man to cut off an organ created by Him as long as that organ is not diseased or deformed? God does not create the organs of the body haphazardly without a plan. It is not possible that He should have created the clitoris in woman's body only in order that it be cut off at an early stage in life. This is a contradiction into which neither true religion nor the Creator could possibly fall. If God has created the clitoris as a sexually sensitive organ, whose sole function seems to be the procurement of sexual pleasure for women, it follows that He also considers such pleasure for women as normal and legitimate, and therefore as an integral part of mental health. The psychic and mental health of women cannot be complete if they do not experience sexual pleasure.

Questions for Reflection and Discussion

How does El Saadawi counter the arguments raised in favor of female circumcision? Might the same arguments be made against male circumcision?

SOURCES AND FURTHER READING

There are numerous interesting studies on rhetoric and sexuality in ancient, medieval, and modern history, often by scholars focusing on texts about sexuality; see, for example, Nicolas Gross's *Amatory Persuasion in Antiquity* (Newark, DL: University of Delaware Press,

1985); Phyllis Trible's *God and the Rhetoric of Sexuality* (Philadelphia: Fortress, 1978) on ancient Israel; Lawrence Kritzman's *The Rhetoric of Sexuality and the Literature of the French Renaissance* (Cambridge: Cambridge University Press, 1991); Mahdavi Menon's *Wanton Words: Rhetoric and Sexuality in English Renaissance Drama* (Toronto, ON: University of Toronto Press, 2004); Sabine Sielke's *Reading Rape: The Rhetoric of Sexual Violence in American Literature and Culture, 1790-1990* (Princeton, NJ: Princeton University Press, 2002); or Shannon Bell's *Reading, Writing, and Rewriting the Prostitute Body* (Bloomington, IN: Indiana University Press, 1994). The list could go on and on, and most scholars are cognizant of the rhetorical purposes of the sources they use (after all, all writers had some reason for writing what they did, and writers about sexuality perhaps more explicitly than most). For more on deconstruction theory and history, where this analysis of the "source as text" is more sharply in focus, see Nicholas Royle's "Writing History: From New Historicism to Deconstruction," in his *After Derrida* (Manchester, UK: Manchester University Press, 1995); or Alan Munslow's *Deconstructing History* (New York: Routledge, 1997); or Tejaswini Niranjana's *Siting Translation: History, Post-Structuralism, and the Colonial Context* (Berkeley, CA: University of California Press, 1992).

142. "Abortion and the Floating World in Japan" is taken from Helen Hardacre, *Marketing the Menacing Fetus in Japan* (Berkeley, CA: University of California Press, 1997), 36–38.

See notes 129, 130, and 131 for more on the "floating world" in early modern Japan. On discussions of abortion in Japanese history, see Hardacre's book, from which this source is taken; see also William LaFleur's *Liquid Life:*

Abortion and Buddhism in Japan (Princeton, NJ: Princeton University Press, 1992); or Tiana Norgren's *Abortion before Birth Control: The Politics of Reproduction in Postwar Japan* (Princeton, NJ: Princeton University Press, 2001); or *Buddhism and Abortion*, Damien Keown, ed. (Honolulu: University of Hawai'i Press, 1999), which has essays on abortion in modern Japan, Korea, and Thailand, as well as historical essays.

143. "The Regulation of Prostitution" is taken from William Barret, *Prostitution in its Relation to the Public Health* (St. Louis, MO: privately printed, 1873), 3, 7–9, 13–14.

On prostitution in the late nineteenth- and early twentieth-century US, see Thomas Mackey's *Red Lights Out: A Legal History of Prostitution, Disorderly Houses, and Vice Districts, 1870–1917* (New York: Garland, 1987); Josie Washburn's *The Underworld Sewer: A Prostitute Reflects on Life in the Trade, 1871–1909* (Lincoln, NA: University of Nebraska Press, 1997); Barbara Meil Hobson's *Uneasy Virtue: The Politics of Prostitution and the American Reform Tradition* (New York: Basic, 1987; revised 1990); Frederick Grittner's *White Slavery: Myth, Ideology, and American Law* (New York: Garland, 1990); David Pivar's *Purity and Hygiene: Women, Prostitution, and the "American Plan," 1900–1930* (Westport, CT: Greenwood, 2001); Mark Connelly's *The Response to Prostitution in the Progressive Era* (Chapel Hill, NC: University of North Carolina Press, 1980); or David Langum's *Crossing Over the Line: Legislating Morality and the Mann Act* (Chicago: University of Chicago Press, 1994). See also note 132.

144. "A Muckraker on Prostitution" is taken from Aaron Powell, *The National Purity Congress, Its Papers, Addresses, Portraits*

(New York: American Purity Alliance, 1896), 308–11.

See notes 132 and 143 for more on prostitution in the late nineteenth- and early twentieth-century US. On the career of Benjamin Orange Flower, see Allen Matusow's "The Mind of B.O. Flower," *New England Quarterly* 1961 (34): 492–509. Flower's magazine, *Arena*, was published between 1889 and 1909, and addressed a range of "unmentionable" topics, and might be worth studying in a history of sexuality. A fascinating English equivalent was William T. Stead, editor of the *Pall Mall Gazette*; on his career, see Raymond Schults's *Crusader in Babylon: W.T. Stead and the Pall Mall Gazette* (Lincoln, NB: University of Nebraska Press, 1972).

145. "Anthony Comstock and Censorship" is taken from Robert Bremner, *Traps for the Young by Anthony Comstock* (Cambridge, MA: Belknap, 1967), no page indicated.

On Comstock's career, see Nicola Beisel's *Imperiled Innocents: Anthony Comstock and Family Reproduction in Victorian America* (Princeton, NJ: Princeton University Press, 1997). On censorship and definitions of obscenity in American history, see Felice Flanery Lewis's *Literature, Obscenity, and Law* (Carbondale, IL: Southern Illinois University Press, 1976); Paul Boyer's *Purity in Print: Book Censorship in America from the Gilded Age to the Computer Age* (Madison, WI: University of Wisconsin Press, 2002); Marjorie Heins's *Not in Front of the Children: "Indecency," Censorship, and the Innocence of Youth* (New York: Hill and Wang, 2001); Leigh Wheeler's *Against Obscenity: Reform and the Politics of Womanhood in America, 1873–1935* (Baltimore, MD: Johns Hopkins University Press, 2004); or Richard Hixson's *Pornography and the Justices: The Supreme Court and the Intractable*

Obscenity Problem (Carbondale, IL: Southern Illinois University Press, 1996).

146. "The Hays Code" is taken from Leonard Leff and Jerold Simmons, *The Dame in the Kimono: Hollywood, Censorship, and the Production Code* (Lexington, KY: University of Kentucky Press, 2001), 286–89, 298–300.

On censorship and film, Leff and Simmons's book is a great place to start; see also Mark Vieira's *Sin in Soft Focus: Pre-Code Hollywood* (New York: Harry N. Abrams, 1999); Thomas Doherty's *Pre-Code Hollywood: Sex, Immorality, and Insurrection in American Cinema, 1930–1934* (New York: Columbia University Press, 1999); or Lea Jacobs's *The Wages of Sin: Censorship and the Fallen Woman Film, 1928–1942* (Madison, WI: University of Wisconsin Press, 1991). On the history of the Catholic National Legion of Decency, a group that lobbied for film censorship, see Gregory D. Black's *Hollywood Censored: Morality Codes: Catholics, and the Movies* (Cambridge, MA: Cambridge University Press, 1994) or his *The Catholic Crusade against the Movies, 1945–1975* (Cambridge, MA: Cambridge University Press, 1997); or Frank Walsh's *Sin and Censorship: The Catholic Church and the Motion Picture Industry* (New Haven, CT: Yale University Press, 1996). Also on sex in film, see Janet Staiger's *Bad Women: Regulating Sexuality in Early American Cinema* (Minneapolis, MN: University of Minnesota Press, 1995); Bruce Babington and Peter Evans's *Affairs to Remember: The Hollywood Comedy of the Sexes* (Manchester, UK: Manchester University Press, 1989); Mark Rubinfield's *Bound to Bond: Gender, Genre, and the Hollywood Romantic Comedy* (Westport, CT: Praeger, 2001); David Shipman's *Caught in the Act: Sex and Eroticism in the Movies* (London: Elm Tree, 1985); David Hogan's *Dark Romance: Sexuality in the Horror Film* (Jefferson, NC: McFarland,

1986); Neil Fulwood's *One Hundred Sex Scenes that Changed Cinema* (London: Batsford, 2003); and many more.

147. "Lynching and Sex" is taken from Ida B. Wells-Barnett, *On Lynchings: Southern Horrors, A Red Record, Mob Rule in New Orleans* (New York: Arno/New York Times, 1969), 7–12.

For a biography, see Mildred Thompson's *Ida B. Wells-Barnett: An Exploratory Study of an American Black Woman, 1893–1930* (Brooklyn, NY: Carlson, 1990); or Patricia Schechter's *Ida B. Wells-Barnett and American Reform, 1880–1930* (Chapel Hill, NC: University of North Carolina Press, 2001); a briefer biography is included in Dorothy Sterling's *Black Foremothers: Three Lives* (Old Westbury, NY: Feminist, 1979; revised 1988). Other discussions of Wells-Barnett's career include Anthony Bogues's "The Radical Praxis of Ida B. Wells-Barnett: Telling the Truth Freely," in his *Black Heretics, Black Prophets: Radical Political Intellectuals* (New York: Routledge, 2003); Linda O. McMurry's "Ida Wells-Barnett and the African-American Anti-Lynching Campaign," in *Against the Tide: Women Reformers in American Society*, Paul Cimbala and Randall Miller, eds. (Westport, CT: Praeger, 1997); Gail Bederman's "Civilization, the Decline of Middle-Class Manliness, and Ida B. Wells's Anti-Lynching Campaign (1892–94)," in *Gender and American History since 1890*, Barbara Melosh, ed. (New York: Routledge, 1993); and Mary Jane Brown's *Eradicating this Evil: Women in the American Anti-Lynching Movement, 1892–1940* (New York: Garland, 2000). There is a vast literature on lynching and sexuality in American history.

148. "Margaret Sanger and Mahatma Gandhi on Birth Control" is taken from Mahatma Gandhi, *To the Women* (Karachi, Pakistan: Anand T. Hingorani/Allahabad, India: J.K. Sharma, 1941), 55–62.

Both Gandhi and Sanger wrote autobiographies that provide information about their views on sexual matters, which were of importance to both. See Gandhi's *An Autobiography, Or, The Story of My Experiments with Truth*, trans. Mahadev Desai (Ahmedabad: Navajivan, 1940); a recent biography is Stanley Wolpert's *Gandhi's Passion: The Life and Legacy of Mahatma Gandhi* (Oxford: Oxford University Press, 2001); but see also Arun Gandhi et al.'s *The Forgotten Woman: The Untold Story of Kastur Gandhi, Wife of Mahatma Gandhi* (Huntsville, AR: Ozark Mountain, 1998); Gandhi's other writings can be found in many translated editions; see especially his *The Law of Continence* (Bombay: Bharatiya Vidya Bhavan, 1964) on Hindu sexual renunciation or *brahmacharya*. See *Margaret Sanger: An Autobiography* (New York: Norton, 1938); a recent biography is Ellen Chesler's *Woman of Valor: Margaret Sanger and the Birth Control Movement in America* (New York: Simon & Schuster, 1992). Both Gandhi and Sanger have been the subject of several films, both documentaries and dramatized films; for the latter, see *Gandhi* (UK and India, dir. Richard Attenborough, 1982) and *Choices of the Heart: The Margaret Sanger Story* (USA, dir. Paul Shapiro, 1995). For more on birth control in Indian history, there are many modern studies, only some of which provide some information on historical patterns. For more on birth control in American history, see Linda Gordon's *The Moral Property of Women: A History of Birth Control Politics in America* (Urbana, IL: University of Illinois Press, 2002); Andrea Tone's *Devices and Desires: A History of Contraceptives in America* (New York: Hill and Wang, 2001); and Kathleen Tobin's *The*

American Religious Debate over Birth Control, 1907–1937 (Jefferson, NC: McFarland, 2001).

149. "Gandhi on *Sati* and *Purdah*" is taken from Mahatma Gandhi, *To the Women* (Karachi, Pakistan: Anand T. Hingorani/Allahabad, India: J. K. Sharma, 1941), 136–39, 213–15.

On *sati* in Hindu tradition, see V.N. Datta's *Sati: A Historical, Social and Philosophical Enquiry into the Hindu Rite of Widow Burning* (Riverdale, MD: Riverdale, 1988); Sakuntala Narasimhan's *Sati: Widow Burning in India* (New York: Doubleday, 1992); Lata Mani's *Contentious Traditions: The Debate on Sati in Colonial India* (Berkeley, CA: University of California Press, 1998); Pompa Banerjee's *Burning Women: Widows, Witches, and Early Modern European Travelers in India* (New York: Palgrave Macmillan, 2003); Mala Sen's *Death by Fire: Sati, Dowry Death, and Female Infanticide in Modern India* (London: Weidenfeld & Nicolson, 2001); and *Sati, the Blessing and the Curse: The Burning of Wives in India*, John Stratton Hawley, ed. (Oxford: Oxford University Press, 1994). On *purdah* in Indian Muslim tradition, and the larger question of the veiling and seclusion of modern Muslim women, see Shahida Lateef's *Muslim Women in India: Political and Private Realities, 1890s–1980s* (London: Zed, 1990); *Purdah: An Anthology*, Eunice de Souza, ed. (Oxford: Oxford University Press, 2004); or in *Indian Women, from Purdah to Modernity*, B.R. Nanda, ed. (New Delhi: Vikas, 1976); see also the different ethnic studies in Nilüfer Göle's *The Forbidden Modern: Civilization and Veiling* (Ann Arbor, MI: University of Michigan Press, 1996); Faegheh Shirazi's *The Veil Unveiled: The Hijab in Modern Culture* (Gainesville, FL: University of Florida Press, 2001); Fadwa El Guindi's *Veil: Modesty, Privacy and Resistance* (Oxford: Berg, 1999); or *The Muslim Veil in*

North America: Issues and Debates, Sajida Alvi et al., eds. (Toronto: Women's, 2003).

150. "She May Look Clean" is taken from James Peterson, *The Century of Sex: Playboy's History of the Sexual Revolution, 1900–1999* (New York: Grove, 1999), no page indicated.

On sexuality and military history, see Leisa Meyer's *Creating GI Jane: Sexuality and Power in the Women's Army Corps during World War II* (New York: Columbia University Press, 1996); and several of the essays in *Women and War in the Twentieth Century: Enlisted With or Without Consent*, Nicole Dombrowski, ed. (New York: Garland, 1999); and in *Medicine and Modern Warfare*, Roger Cooter et al., eds. (Amsterdam: Rodopi, 1999). See also Allan Bérubé's *Coming Out Under Fire: The History of Gay Men and Women in World War Two* (New York: Plume, 1990), on homosexuality and the American military. For more on sexually transmitted diseases in history, see Peter L. Allen's *The Wages of Sin: Sex and Disease, Past and Present* (Chicago: University of Chicago Press, 2000); or Allan Brandt's *No Magic Bullet: A Social History of Venereal Disease in the United States since 1880* (Oxford: Oxford University Press, 1985). An earlier study is Mary Spongberg's *Feminizing Venereal Disease: The Body of the Prostitute in Nineteenth-Century Medical Discourse* (New York: New York University Press, 1997). Studies of sexually transmitted diseases in other regions of the world, in the twentieth century and earlier, include Philippa Levine's *Prostitution, Race, and Politics: Policing Venereal Disease in the British Empire* (New York: Routledge, 2003); Johannes Fabricius's *Syphilis in Shakespeare's England* (London: Jessica Kingsley, 1994); Kevin Siena's *Venereal Disease, Hospitals, and the Urban Poor: London's "Foul Wards," 1600–1800* (Rochester, NY: University of Rochester

Press, 2004); *The Secret Malady: Venereal Disease in Eighteenth-Century Britain and France*, Linda Merians, ed. (Lexington, KY: University Press of Kentucky, 1996); Roger Davidson's *Dangerous Liaisons: A Social History of Venereal Disease in Twentieth-Century Scotland* (Amsterdam: Rodopi, 2000); Jay Cassel's *The Secret Plague: Venereal Disease in Canada, 1838–1939* (Toronto, ON: University of Toronto Press, 1987); Milton Lewis's *Thorns on the Rose: The History of Sexually Transmitted Diseases in Australia in International Perspective* (Canberra, Australia: Australian Government Public Service, 1998); and *Sex, Sin, and Suffering: Venereal Disease and European Society since 1870*, Roger Davidson and Lesley Hall, eds. (New York: Routledge, 2001). Some studies are more global and comparative in scope, such as *Sex, Disease, and Society: A Comparative History of Sexually Transmitted Diseases and HIV/AIDS in Asia and the Pacific*, Milton Lewis, et al., eds. (Westport, CT: Greenwood, 1997) or *Histories of Sexually Transmitted Diseases and HIV/AIDS in Sub-Saharan Africa*, Philip Setel et al., eds. (Westport, CT: Greenwood Press, 1999).

151. "Men and Women at the Beach" is taken from F.K. Crowley, *Modern Australia in Documents* (Melbourne, Australia: Wren, 1973), 177–79.

On the history of Australia's beaches, see Douglas Booth's *Australian Beach Cultures: A History of Sun, Sand, and Surf* (London: Frank Cass, 2001); or, for an earlier period, Caroline Ralston's *Grass Huts and Warehouses: Pacific Beach Communities of the Nineteenth Century* (Canberra: Australian National University Press, 1977). For related studies of beach culture and sexuality in different periods and places, see Jean-Didier Urbain's *At the Beach*, Catherine Porter, trans. (Minneapolis, MN:

University of Minnesota Press, 2003); Patrik Alac's *The Bikini: A Cultural History* (New York: Parkstone, 2002); Marla Matzer Rose's *Muscle Beach* (New York: St. Martin's Griffin, 2001); or some of the essays in *Water, Leisure, and Culture: European Historical Perspectives*, Susan C. Anderson and Bruce Tabb, eds. (Oxford: Berg, 2002).

152. "A Drag Ball in Berlin" is taken from Richard von Krafft-Ebing, *Psychopathia Sexualis*, trans. unknown (New York: Pioneer, 1950), 590–93.

For a history of homosexuality in Germany in this period, see James W. Jones's *"We of the Third Sex": Literary Representations of Homosexuality in Wilhelmine Germany* (New York: P. Lang, 1990); or James Steakley's *The Homosexual Emancipation Movement in Germany* (New York: Arno, 1975); for an earlier period, see Robert Tobin's *Warm Brothers: Queer Theory and the Age of Goethe* (Philadelphia: University of Pennsylvania Press, 2000); or Susan Gustafson's *Men Desiring Men: The Poetry of Same-Sex Identity and Desire in German Classicism* (Detroit, MI: Wayne State University Press, 2002); for an even earlier period, see Helmut Puff's *Sodomy in Reformation Germany and Switzerland, 1400–1600* (Chicago: University of Chicago Press, 2003); for a later period, see Jack Porter's *Sexual Politics in the Third Reich: The Persecution of the Homosexuals during the Holocaust* (Newton, MA: Spencer, 1995); Frank Rector's *The Nazi Extermination of Homosexuals* (New York: Stein and Day, 1981); Richard Plant's *The Pink Triangle: The Nazi War against Homosexuals* (New York: H. Holt, 1986); or Claudia Schoppmann's *Days of Masquerade: Life Stories of Lesbians during the Third Reich*, trans. Allison Brown (New York: Columbia University Press, 1996); *Hidden Holcaust? Gay and Lesbian Persecution in Germany, 1933–*

45, Gunter Grau, ed., Patrick Camiller, trans. (Chicago: Fitzroy Dearborn, 1995); and Gary Schmidt's *The Nazi Abduction of Ganymede: Representations of Homosexuality in Postwar German Literature* (Oxford: P. Lang, 2003). There have been a few films made about homosexuality in German history, especially during the Nazi era, including *Bent* (UK, dir. Sean Mathias, 1997); *Desire: Sexuality in Germany, 1910–1945* (US, Water Bearer Films, dir. Stuart Marshall, 1989); and *Paragraph 175* (US, New Yorker Films, dir. Rob Epstein and Jeffrey Friedman, 2002). See also note 96 for more on the Nazis and sexuality.

153. "The Stonewall Riots" is taken from *Witness to Revolution: The Advocate Reports on Gay and Lesbian Politics, 1967–1999*, ed. Chris Bull (Los Angeles: Alyson, 1999), 11–14.

On the Stonewall Riots and the modern gay rights movement, see note 113. On homosexuality in twentieth-century New York, see George Chauncey's *Gay New York: Gender, Urban Culture, and the Makings of the Gay Male World, 1890–1940* (New York: Basic, 1994); A.B. Christa Schwartz's *Gay Voices of the Harlem Renaissance* (Bloomington, IN: Indiana University Press, 2003); Mark W. Turner's *Backward Glances: Cruising the Queer Streets of New York and London* (London: Reaktion, 2003); or Charles Kaiser's *The Gay Metropolis, 1940–1996* (Boston: Houghton Mifflin, 1997). On homosexuality in the twentieth-century US, see Martin Duberman's *About Time: Exploring the Gay Past* (New York: Meridian, 1991; orig. publ. 1986); Leila Rupp's *A Desired Past: A Short History of Same-Sex Love in America* (Chicago: University of Chicago Press, 1999); Molly McGarry and Fred Wasserman's *Becoming Visible: An Illustrated History of Lesbian and Gay Life in Twentieth-Century America* (New York: Penguin Studio, 1998). See also the more specialized studies of Jennifer Terry's *An American Obsession: Science, Medicine, and Homosexuality in Modern Society* (Chicago: University of Chicago Press, 1999); or Henry Minton's *Departing from Deviance: A History of Homosexual Rights and Emancipatory Science in America* (Chicago: University of Chicago Press, 2002); as well as numerous regional and local (mostly urban) studies, and numerous studies of American literature. A reference guide now exists: *Encyclopedia of Lesbian, Gay, Bisexual, and Transgender History in America*, Marc Stein, ed. (New York: Charles Scribner's Sons/Thomson/Gale, 2004); and sourcebooks in *Gay American History: Lesbians and Gay Men in the U.S.A.: A Documentary History*, Jonathan Ned Katz, ed. (New York: Crowell, 1976; revised 1985 and 1992); and in *Gay and Lesbian Rights in the United States: A Documentary History*, Walter L. Williams and Yolanda Retter, eds. (Westport, CT: Greenwood, 2003); or see the collection from which this source was taken.

154. "Silence = Death" is taken from ACT UP, New York (www.actupny.org).

For histories of AIDS and the gay community in the US, see Andrew Holleran's *Ground Zero* (New York: Morrow, 1988); Lawrence Mass's *Dialogues of the Sexual Revolution* (New York: Haworth, 1990); G.W. Dowsett's *Practicing Desire: Homosexual Sex in the Era of AIDS* (Stanford, CA: Stanford University Press, 1996). On ACT-UP and AIDS activism, see Larry Kramer's *Reports from the Holocaust: The Making of an AIDS Activist* (New York: St. Martin's, 1989); Brett Stockdill's *Activism against AIDS: At the Intersection of Sexuality, Race, Gender, and Class* (Boulder, CO: Lynne Rienner, 2003). Studies also exist on the history of the AIDS epidemic in other countries and regions of the world; see note 173.

155. "Abortion Arguments" is taken from *The Abortion Controversy: A Documentary History*, Eva Rubin, ed. (Westport, CT: Greenwood, 1994), 156–57, 192, 195–97, 201–3, 209–11.

On Roe v. Wade, see N.E.H. Hull and Peter Hoffer's *Roe v. Wade: The Abortion Rights Controversy in American History* (Lawrence, KS: University Press of Kansas, 2001); or David Garrow's *Liberty and Sexuality: The Right to Privacy and the Making of Roe v. Wade* (New York: Macmillan, 1994). See Marvin Olasky's *Abortion Rites: A Social History of Abortion in America* (Wheaton, IL: Crossway, 1992); or *Abortion Wars: A Half Century of Struggle, 1950–2000*, Rickie Solinger, ed. (Berkeley, CA: University of California Press, 1998); or, for more recent consequences, Dallas Blanchard's *The Anti-Abortion Movement and the Rise of the Religious Right: From Polite to Fiery Protest* (New York: Twayne, 1994). For earlier histories, see James Mohr's *Abortion in America: The Origins and Evolution of National Policy, 1800–1900* (Oxford: Oxford University Press, 1978); Janet Farrell Brodie's *Contraception and Abortion in Nineteenth-Century America* (Ithaca, NY: Cornell University Press, 1994); Nathan Stormer's *Articulating Life's Memory: U.S. Medical Rhetoric about Abortion in the Nineteenth Century* (Lanham, MD: Lexington, 2002); Clifford Browder's *The Wickedest Woman in New York: Madame Restell, the Abortionist* (Hamden, CT: Archon, 1988); or Leslie Reagan's *When Abortion Was a Crime: Women, Medicine, and Law in the United States, 1867–1973* (Berkeley, CA: University of California Press, 1997). See also the sourcebook from which these excerpts are taken. For an international perspective, see Colin Francome's *Abortion Freedom: A Worldwide Movement* (London: Allen & Unwin, 1984); histories of abortion exist for many other countries and regions of the world.

156. "Female Circumcision" is taken from Nawal El Saadawi, *The Hidden Face of Eve: Women in the Arab World*, trans. Sherif Hetata (London: Zed, 1980), 33–35, 40–42.

On female circumcision, including contemporary and historical evidence for the practice, see the brief study by Leonard Kouba and Judith Muasher, "Female Circumcision in Africa: An Overview," *African Studies Review* 28 (1985): 95–110; more detailed studies include Anne Cloudsley's *Women of Omdurman: Life, Love and the Cult of Virginity* (London: Ethnographica, 1983); Fran Hosken's *The Hosken Report: Genital and Sexual Mutilation of Females* (Lexington, MA: Women's International Network News, 1993); Alice Walker and Pratibha Parmar's *Warrior Marks: Female Genital Mutilation and the Sexual Blinding of Women* (New York: Harcourt Brace, 1993); Efua Dorkenoo's *Cutting the Rose: Female Genital Mutilation, the Practice and its Prevention* (London: Minority Rights Group, 1994); and Nahid Toubia's *Female Genital Mutilation: A Call for Global Action* (New York: Women, Ink, 1995). On the modern practice, see also the World Health Organization's statement, *Female Genital Mutilation* (Geneva: World Health Organization, 1997). These studies might be compared with an early account of the practice, Felix Bryk's *Circumcision in Man and Woman: Its History, Psychology and Ethnology* (New York: American Ethnological Press, 1934). There are now several films about FGM, including *Warrior Marks* (US, Women Make Movies, dir. Pratibha Parmar, 1993); *Fire Eyes* (dir. Soraya Mire, 1994); and *Female Circumcision: Human Rites* (US, Journeyman Pictures/Princeton Films for the Humanities and Sciences, dir. 1998).

CHAPTER 14
sex and self-fulfillment

One of the characteristics of the modern world has been the promise that sex somehow holds the key to self-fulfillment. Whether it is the promise of true love in a romantic connection, or the liberation of the self from inhibition and guilt, or self-discovery through identification with sexuality, in various ways, sex has been seen as the means to happiness. That promise is the theme for this chapter.

Past generations wanted happiness as much as we do; they may not always have looked for it in sex. Although sexual desire has always been one of the strongest of human feelings, it does not necessarily follow that happiness can be found in pursuing one's feelings. In antiquity, many philosophies were based on subordinating such feelings and desires for one purpose or another, either for the maintenance of the social order, as in Confucianism, or in favor of reason, as in Platonism. Nor did medieval religious traditions promise that happiness was found in the pursuit of sexual pleasure. Some religions, such as Christianity, had strong traditions that the pursuit of sexual pleasure distracted one from finding true happiness. Even those religions that encouraged sexual pleasure, such as Tantric Hinduism, always saw it as part of a larger cycle of life or individual regimen, and thus as a means to an end rather than the end in itself. It was left to the modern age to correlate sex and self-fulfillment so closely.

This connection can be seen especially in changes to marriage. Past generations participated in marriage for a variety of reasons, including for opportunities to enjoy sex. But given the social arrangements surrounding marriage, such as the involvement of parents and other family members in the selection of a marriage partner; or the requirement of procreation for the sake of family continuity; or the variations on marriage in the past, such as concubinage or polygamy; or alternatives to marriage, such as prostitution and pederasty, the pursuit of sexual pleasure was probably not paramount among the concerns of those entering marriage. At the least, sexual pleasure may have been a welcome side effect rather than an expectation for married persons. Not so with modern marriage. The idea that marriage should provide one with a romantic companion for life came from the nineteenth century when social changes were undermining older notions of marriage, and has gained strength ever since. This notion of "companionate marriage," the term used by those who study the history of marriage, may not have matched the realities of many nineteenth-century lives. As an ideal, however, it promised the happiness of lifelong love through marriage.

The idea that self-fulfillment could be found in marriage was in turn undermined by the changes of the twentieth century when increasing numbers found that the customs surrounding marriage—cohabitation, lifelong partnership, and so on—often detracted from, rather than added to, individual happiness. In their place, individual self-fulfillment was promoted as the ideal, a self-fulfillment that could sometimes be found more readily in informal sexual liaisons rather than in the permanence of marriage. These changes, usually called "the sexual revolution," are often associated with the 1960s when, suddenly, every convention around sex seemed up for grabs. More women voiced their desire for real equality; gay men and lesbians (who preferred these terms to the older and more clinical "homosexuals") also struggled for equality. There were sexual experiments of all sorts, from communal sexual living to "fast-food" style sex clubs, and divorces were easier to obtain. The openness about such experiments often made them seem new, but most sexual behaviors had historical roots.

Where did this idea of sex as self-fulfillment come from? Some scholars attribute it to Freud and his followers because he had suggested that sexuality played a crucial role in human development. The popularization of Freudian ideas throughout the twentieth century, often by novels and other forms of literature, meant that they became increasingly taken for granted. Others link the change to the medicalization of sex, whereby physicians and other medical specialists attempted to position themselves as the experts on human life, including sexuality, in place of religious or other authorities. Still others note the central role of capitalism and especially consumerism in the notion of sex as self-fulfillment because advertisers were only too quick to exploit sex as a gimmick to catch people's attention and then to promise romantic benefits from their products.

Nowadays it is rare to find an individual who believes that romantic and sexual satisfaction is not a basic element in human happiness. Carl Jung, who studied with Freud but eventually developed his own theories on human personality, was convinced that love could bring transcendence, since through the erotic and emotional attraction to another, we bring another's characteristics into relationship with our own, especially those personality traits we have learned to downplay in ourselves, and that helps to complete us. Jung theorized in various ways the integration of opposites, but he described the result as syzygy (from the Greek for "yoked" or "paired," a word also used in astronomy for the conjunction of planets). Still, is it realistic to attempt to find self-fulfillment in sexual pleasure or even in romantic love that can be fleeting and fickle?

This chapter examines some of the historical ideas about sex and the promise of self-fulfillment, especially in the last century.

157. A POEM ABOUT MARRIAGE

Time: late nineteenth or early twentieth century CE
Place: India
Author: Lakshmibai Tilak

Lakshmibai Tilak, born in 1868 and married through her parents' arrangement at 11, wrote about her marriage at length in her autobiography, I Follow After, *published sometime in the mid-1930s. She also wrote poetry celebrating the joys of marriage, such as this example from an unknown date.*

As a river loses itself when it blends with the ocean, so the bride becomes one with the family of her husband.
This is no mere marriage; it is the blending by love of their lives in one. And how can our words describe such a union?
Drenched by the billows of joy and sorrow in the ocean of life, this bond of love emerges, rendered indissoluble for evermore.
Ever on the hearts of husband and wife nectar is sprinkled; and by it the bond of joy and sorrow grows firmer, more divine, more lovely.
The relationship of husband and wife is full of love, yea, it is all pure love. The fragrant, cool wind of love fills their whole world.
Those are called husband and wife who have one soul, though their bodies and feelings be divided.
They are like two wheels in the cart of life; and vainly will one try to draw it without the help of the other.
Where this is not so, life is but wearisome. Apart from his wife, a husband is lame; and so is she apart from him.
When oil and wick combine, the flame leaps up; so, in the experience of the world, union alone is potent.

Questions for Reflection and Discussion

How do the metaphors of separateness and union reinforce Tilak's thoughts on marriage and love? How does Tilak's own experience as a child bride in an arranged marriage alter our understanding of her views about married love?

158. AN UNHAPPY MARRIAGE

Time: early twentieth century CE
Place: Japan
Author: Baroness Shidzue Ishimoto

Shidzue Ishimoto, later Shidzue Kato, led a fascinating life. She was raised in a very traditional family, as recounted in her autobiography, East Way, West Way *(also translated as* Facing Two Ways*), published in 1935, the source of these extracts. She had been married to the Baron Keikechi Ishimoto, but in part because of her increasingly radical politics—as a keen supporter of birth control she is known as "the Margaret Sanger of Japan," and she opposed Japan's militarism and spent much of World War II in prison—she divorced him and remarried Kanju Kato. In 1946 she was elected as a Senator to the Japanese parliament.*

In spite of the tide of liberalism that had been breaking over Japan with the new social order, influencing literature, men's education and other aspects of culture, women's world remained true to the conception which survived from the feudal age. "A good wife" and "a wise mother"! How well these words sound! Indeed, there could seem to be no objection to them in any society or age. But when we peel off the skin from this perfect fruit of feudalism, we expose bondage to husbands and subjection to the tyranny of the family system as a whole. Consciously or unconsciously my mother taught her daughter to crush her desires and ambitions, and trained her to be ready to submerge her individuality in her husband's personality and his family's united temper. Girls were to study first of all how to please their husbands' parents with absolute obedience. Mother never thought it possible that I should become a good companion, discussing social problems or politics with my husband or reading books with him. She was not worried about the plight of women or the state of the nation but thought it of the greatest importance that she should educate me in such a way that I might not be criticized....

Marriage for the Japanese girl meant losing individual freedom. She was allowed a peep into the romantic side of marriage through classic stories such as *The Tale of Genji*. The few books selected for us to read treated of the romance of court life in ancient times. But what the teachers preached in the classroom about a woman's morals, and the repeated words from our mothers' lips, made us aware that a step out from the school gate was a step into the woman's destiny of subjection, where every girl's lot was inevitably cast. Three of my former classmates were already married, having left school when they were sixteen. One of them was already a mother. There were also a few who were engaged to be married very soon. Those marriages and engagements were arranged by their families regardless of the girls' individual interests....

[Soon, the young Shidzue found herself in a similar situation.]

On a bright day in my seventeenth year, I had finished my morning duties in the house and was sitting alone on the silk cushion by the balcony window, looking down on the fresh young leaves of the weeping willow in the garden, whose slim green branches were swaying to and fro in the soft breeze. At such times romantic sentiments without any reason occupy a young maiden's heart. Suddenly the back screen slipped open and a servant told me that I was called to my father's room. Cheerfully as usual I appeared in his presence; mother was also there. I bowed lightly to them and asked: "Is there anything you would like me to do, honorable father?" He replied, "I have something to tell you, Shidzue. Sit down, please." My father said this in an affectionate but solemn tone. I sat down on one of the big English chairs, feeling that something very important was at hand. "You have finished your schooling now," he continued. "So your mother and I are thinking about your future, wishing to make you happy by arranging a suitable marriage for you!" ... I sat with my head low and my eyes fixed on the edge of the Turkish carpet. Father went on to say that a marriage was proposed by Baron Keikichi Ishimoto, the son of Baron and Lieutenant General Shinroku Ishimoto whose services in the Mikado's army during the Russo-Japanese War had been rewarded with a title, many decorations and great honors.... Father closed his exposition of the suitor's merits by saying, "Think it over quietly, for your parents desire your happiness. But they are not forcing you against your will." I did not answer, but burst into tears and covered my face with the long sleeves of my wisteria *kimono*. "Do you hate to marry, Shidzue?" father inquired gently, patting my shaking shoulders. "No, father, I ... I just feel like crying." Father and mother did not seem quite to understand.

[Shidzue eventually accepted the husband who has been chosen for her, and met his mother, her future mother-in-law.]

She was a woman of strong character. She had helped her husband win glory and wealth, she had brought up her seven children with strict discipline and she had worked hard to keep her domestic affairs in order. She cooked well; she sewed swiftly. In later years when she felt that she had done all that she could do as a good wife and wise mother, she had begun to devote more time to her own pleasure such as writing thirty-one syllable poems and learning *utai* (the singing part of the No play). She liked to have parties at home, inviting her friends to see her azaleas or to hear the cuckoos in her garden. Often she went to see the No drama and to the Kabuki theater. Being a widow, complete mistress of her own home, and moreover, the practical head of the family, she was at liberty to live her life as she pleased. And her choice was the traditional Japanese way. She had very little sympathy with objects or ideas that came out of the West. Westerners were to her "red-haired barbarians." Her adherence to custom had prevented her son's visiting his fiancée freely, for she thought it beneath his dignity to visit a woman often. To talk over the telephone or to write to each other unnecessarily was in her mind a sort of promiscuous conduct in violation of her moral standard and not to be countenanced even after our engagement. She wanted to pound into her future daughter-in-law's brain the Confucian doctrine of female inferiority.

[From the day following her wedding, Shidzue found her married life less than she expected.]

I was awakened next morning. It was dark and cold. I had to dress before my mother-in-law left her bed, and she had a habit of retiring late and of waking up early. It was the duty of a bride to please first her mother-in-law and serve her husband next. My mother-in-law did not treat me like a young girl as my parents did. She looked on me as a full-grown woman. Perhaps this was natural since my husband was much older than I and I must correspond with his age. Besides, I had to behave with an elder sisterly dignity toward my brothers-in-law, some of whom were several years older than I. I took my first breakfast in the midst of the entire family. My mother-in-law and my husband sat on silk cushions, but I, with the rest of the family, sat directly on the mat without a cushion. I had three sets (one consisting of five pieces) of cushions for the guests and three pairs for my own use in my trousseau, yet I had to sit on the cold mat, shivering, to show my humble attitude toward my elders.

After the meal, my mother-in-law admitted that I was still too young to take on my shoulders the whole responsibility for the house, but she would show me the ways of the Ishimoto family and I must learn them as quickly as possible. She did not lay down any definite rules or principles. She wanted me to learn by observation. She did not fail to remark, however, that I had to serve my husband with respect as he was the head of the family since the death of his father. I must wait on him when he dressed and bow to him when he went out and again bow to him at the entrance hall when he returned. Of course the same formalities were to be observed toward my mother-in-law herself. Every act of mine must be approved beforehand by these two. When I wished to go out of the house I was to get their consent to leave. As for what I was to wear I had to bring two or three *kimonos* and *obis* to my mother-in-law's room, asking which *kimono* and *obi* it pleased her to have me don…. The task of being a mother-in-law is indeed never an easy one. She has to be a perfect example to her daughter-in-law. She cannot sit lazily in the presence of her son's wife. She has to refrain from spending too much time for her own pleasure because she admonishes the younger woman to think only of family interests. She must, in short, practice what she preaches.

Questions for Reflection and Discussion

How was Shidzue's unhappiness related to her expectations about romance and marriage? If she had not had those expectations, would she have been happier? How had Shidzue's mother-in-law found happiness?

159. AN ODE TO BREASTS

Time: nineteenth century CE
Place: United States
Author: Lyman Hodge

The ability to write poetry to express one's emotions has been valued in many places in the world at many times. In this example from an 1867 letter to his fiancée, Mary Granger, Hodge attempted to express his erotic feelings for her with a poem celebrating her breasts.

What will make man's heart beat quicker
Than ale or any other liquor?
Do you wish to know?
Two breasts as white as snow
Warming cold hands with their amorous glow
Twin roses pressing
Out from their laces,
Ripe for caressing,
Bed of the graces,
Love thoughts confessing,
Lover's hands blessing,
Warming embraces....
How they redden and tremble and swell
When a lover's warm lips
Are pressing their tips,
And the honey he sips
From each pearl tinted shell

But adds to the fire,
Till each rose fully bloom
Stands erect and alone....

[Then, he imagined her breasts responding to him.]

To us you belong;
Yield us thy love fearless and strong,
Kiss us, caress us,
Handle us, press us,
Toy with us, play with us, do as you will,
Bite us, unlace us,
Squeeze us, embrace us,
Drink from us, suck from us, drink up your fill.
Press us together till we touch each other,
Press us apart till the valley lies bare,
Bind us with ringlets from our common mother,
Part us with rivulets made from her hair.
How our mistress pants and sighs,
How the love lights her eyes!

Questions for Reflection and Discussion

What does this poem say about the enjoyment of sexual pleasure? Is it the man's desire alone that is being satisfied, or the woman's also? How important is it to note that this pleasure was expressed as part of a loving relationship but that the couple was not yet married?

160. *REKHTI* EROTIC POEM

Time: late seventeenth or early eighteenth century CE
Place: India
Author: Shaikh Qalandar Baksh

Traditions of erotic poetry stretch back further in some areas than others. In the poetry of the Urdu language (the official language of modern

Pakistan), a tradition of men writing as women, called rekhti, *existed from the late seventeenth century until it was discouraged as immoral in the early twentieth century. Included within this tradition are a number of poets; Shaikh Qalandar Baksh, who wrote under the name Jur'at ("Audacity") was the earliest. His poem about lesbian sexual desire is full of plays on words: the woman's name, Dogana, for example, comes from the root* do, *meaning "doubling."*

There's no love lost between women and
men these days—
New ways of being intimate are seen all
around.
Everyone knows about women who love
women—
At night these words are always to be
heard:
The way you rub me, ah! It drives my
heart wild—
Stroke me a little more, my sweet Dogana.

I'd sacrifice all men for your sake, my life,
I'd sacrifice a hundred lives for your
embraces
How delightful it is when two vulvas
meet—
This is the tale they tell each other all the
time:
The way you rub me, ah! …

When you join your lips to my lips,
It feels as if new life pours into my being,
When breast meets breast, the pleasure is
such
That from sheer joy the words rise to my
lips:
The way you rub me, ah! …

How can I be happy with a man—as soon
as he sits by me

He starts showing me a small thing like a
mongoose—
I'd much rather have a big dildo
And I know you know all that I know
The way you rub me, ah! …

When I take your tongue in my mouth
and suck on it—
With what tongue shall I describe the
state I am in?
Long are the hours I wait for you,
deprived of love—
Why then, my life, should I not lose
myself and say:
The way you rub me, ah! …

You are the best of all—to whom can I
compare you?
Whoever I tell about your skills, starts
desiring you.
Oh, oh, what kinds of pleasure your
strokes give me—
To tell the truth, there is no delight
greater than this:
The way you rub me, ah! …

I'd give up anything for that moment
when you come in,
Dressed pretty as a picture, and put your
arms around my neck!
For that pleasure when our nipples touch
and meet,
And when we caress each other any way
we please!
The way you rub me, ah! …

I'm taken with your manner, your style is
entrancing,
I from above, you from below, let's put in
more energy,
When our bodies come together, we will
lose ourselves—

Oh how much I enjoy this, why shouldn't
I tell you:
The way you rub me, ah! …

Who can find words for the pleasure of
this act?
For hours when we're together, I'm deaf to
other voices.
How to describe the taste of sweets eaten
in secret?
There's no pleasure in the world like
clinging to a woman.

Questions for Reflection and Discussion

Does this poem reflect lesbian sexual desire
or a man's image of it? In other words, does it
correspond to the feelings of real individuals?
Is the desire expressed only sexual?

161. ANOTHER KIND OF LOVE

Time: nineteenth century CE
Place: United States
Author: Walt Whitman

*Sometimes eroticism is easy to see; at other
times it is much more ambiguous, as in Walt
Whitman's poetry. In* Leaves of Grass, *his collection first published in 1855, a number of
poems allude to "manly attachment" and "the
need of comrades." Modern scholars generally interpret those sentiments as homosexual.
Whitman's diaries are sprinkled with recollec-
tions of his affections for young men—during
the American Civil War he nursed injured soldiers, for example, and wrote of his "undignified
pursuit" of one of them, Peter Doyle. Whitman
himself, who became aware of the writings of
homosexual Europeans, disavowed such a
sexual meaning to his poetry. Nonetheless, his
poetry asserted that inspiration is found only
in love.*

IN PATHS UNTRODDEN

In paths untrodden,
In the growth by margins of pond-waters,
Escaped from the life that exhibits itself,
From all the standards hitherto publish'd,
from the pleasures, profits, conformities,
Which too long I was offering to feed my
soul,
Clear to me now standards not yet
publish'd, clear to me that my soul,
That the soul of the man I speak for
rejoices in comrades,
Here by myself away from the clank of the
world,
Tallying and talk'd to here by tongues
aromatic,
No longer abash'd, (for in this secluded
spot I can respond as I would not dare
elsewhere,)
Strong upon me the life that does not
exhibit itself, yet contains all the rest,
Resolv'd to sing no song to-day but those
of manly attachment,
Projecting them along that substantial
life,
Bequeathing hence types of athletic love,
Afternoon this delicious Ninth-month in
my forty-first year,
I proceed for all who are or have been
young men,
To tell the secret of my nights and days,
To celebrate the need of comrades.

TO A STRANGER

Passing stranger! you do not know how
longingly I look upon you,
You must be he I was seeking, or she I was
seeking, (it comes to me as of a dream,)
I have somewhere surely lived a life of joy
with you,

All is recall'd as we flit by each other,
fluid, affectionate, chaste, matured,
You grew up with me, were a boy with me
or a girl with me,
I ate with you and slept with you, your
body has become not yours only nor left
my body mine only,
You give me the pleasure of your eyes,
face, flesh, as we pass, you take of my
beard, breast, hands, in return,
I am not to speak to you, I am to think
of you when I sit alone or wake at night
alone,
I am to wait, I do not doubt I am to meet
you again,
I am to see to it that I do not lose you.

Questions for Reflection and Discussion

Do these poems seem erotic or affectionate, or
both? What are the "standards" to which the
first poem alludes, or the "life that does not
exhibit itself"? What is to be made of the "he"
or "she" of the second poem? How does love
inspire Whitman?

162. JUNG ON LOVE

Time: early twentieth century CE
Place: Switzerland
Author: Carl Jung

*While poets and novelists were describing the
happiness that romantic love and sex made
possible, theorists were exploring its nature
in new ways. Carl Jung was first a protégé of
Freud's, then one of his chief rivals. Jung's
psychology emphasized the collective unconscious of humanity, as revealed in mythology
and cultural traditions but also in the common
patterns of art and dreams. In this passage from
an address to his students at Zurich in 1922,*

*Jung recommends the importance of exploring
romantic love as a means of self-development.*

Platonic relationships are very important during the student period. The form they most
commonly take is flirting. Flirting is the
expression of an experimental attitude which
is altogether appropriate at this age. It is a voluntary activity which, by tacit agreement, puts
neither side under an obligation. This is an
advantage and at the same time a disadvantage.
The experimental attitude enables both parties
to get to know each other without any immediately undesirable results. Both exercise their
judgment and skill in self-expression, adap-
tation, and defense. An enormous variety of
experiences which are uncommonly valuable
in later life can be picked up from flirting. On
the other hand, the absence of any obligation
can easily lead to one's becoming an habitual
flirt, shallow, frivolous, and heartless. The man
turns into a drawing-room hero and professional heart-breaker, never dreaming what a
boring figure he cuts; the girl a coquette, and
a serious man instinctively feels that she is not
to be taken seriously.

A phenomenon that is as rare as flirting is
common is the conscious cultivation of a serious love. We might call this simply the ideal,
without, however, identifying it with traditional romanticism. For the development of
personality, there can be no doubt that the
timely awakening and conscious cultivation
of deeply serious and responsible feelings are
of the utmost value. A relationship of this kind
can be the most effective shield against the
temptations that beset a young man, as well
as being a powerful incentive to hard work,
loyalty, and reliability. However, there is no
value so great that it does not have its unfavor-
able side. A relationship that is too ideal easily
becomes exclusive. Through his love the young
man is too much cut off from the acquaintance

of other women, and the girl does not learn the art of erotic conquest because she has got her man already. Women's instinct for possession is a dangerous thing, and it may easily happen that the man will regret all the experiences he never had with women before marriage and will make up for them afterwards.

Hence it must not be concluded that every relationship of this kind is ideal. There are cases where the exact opposite is true—when, for instance, a man or girl trails round with a school sweetheart for no intelligible reason, from mere force of habit. Whether from inertia, or lack of spirit, or helplessness they simply cannot get rid of each other. Perhaps the parents on both sides find the match suitable, and the affair, begun in a moment of thoughtlessness and prolonged by habit, is passively accepted as a *fait accompli*. Here the disadvantages pile up without a single advantage. For the development of personality, acquiescence and passivity are harmful because they are an obstacle to valuable experience and to the exercise of one's specific gifts and virtues. Moral qualities are won only in freedom and prove their worth only in morally dangerous situations. The thief who refrains from stealing merely because he is in prison is not a moral personality. Though the parents may gaze benignly on this touching marriage and add their children's respectability to the tale of their own virtues, it is all a sham and a delusion, lacking real strength, and sapped by moral inertia.

After this brief survey of the problems as we meet them in actual life, I will, in conclusion, turn to the land of heart's desire and Utopian possibilities. Nowadays we can hardly discuss the love problem without speaking of the Utopia of free love, including trial marriage. I regard this idea as a wishful fantasy and an attempt to make light of a problem which in actual life is invariably very difficult. It is no more possible to make life easy than it is to grow a herb of

immortality. The force of gravity can be overcome only by the requisite application of energy. Similarly, the solution of the love problem challenges all our resources. Anything else would be useless patchwork. Free love would be conceivable only if everyone were capable of the highest moral achievement. The idea of free love was not invented with this aim in view, but merely to make something difficult appear easy. Love requires depth and loyalty of feeling; without them it is not love but mere caprice. True love will always commit itself and engage in lasting ties; it needs freedom only to effect its choice, not for its accomplishment. Every true and deep love is a sacrifice. The lover sacrifices all other possibilities, or rather, the illusion that such possibilities exist. If this sacrifice is not made, his illusions prevent the growth of any deep and responsible feeling, so that the very possibility of experiencing real love is denied him.

Love has more than one thing in common with religious faith. It demands unconditional trust and expects absolute surrender. Just as nobody but the believer who surrenders himself wholly to God can partake of divine grace, so love reveals its highest mysteries and its wonder only to those who are capable of unqualified devotion and loyalty of feeling. And because this is so difficult, few mortals can boast of such an achievement. But, precisely because the truest and most devoted love is also the most beautiful, let no man seek to make it easy. He is a sorry knight who shrinks from the difficulty of loving his lady. Love is like God: both give themselves only to their bravest knights.

I would offer the same criticism of trial marriages. The very fact that a man enters into a marriage on trial means that he is making a reservation; he wants to be sure of not burning his fingers, to risk nothing. But that is the most effective way of forestalling any real experience. You do not experience the terrors of the Polar ice by perusing a travel-book, or climb the

Himalayas in a cinema. Love is not cheap—let us therefore beware of cheapening it! All our bad qualities, our egotism, our cowardice, our worldly wisdom, our cupidity—all these would persuade us not to take love seriously. But love will reward us only when we do. I must even regard it as a misfortune that nowadays the sexual question is spoken of as something distinct from love. The two questions should not be separated, for when there is a sexual problem it can be solved only by love. Any other solution would be a harmful substitute. Sexuality dished out as sexuality is brutish; but sexuality as an expression of love is hallowed. Therefore, never ask what a man does, but how he does it. If he does it from love or in the spirit of love, then he serves a god; and whatever he may do is not ours to judge, for it is ennobled.

Questions for Reflection and Discussion

How does love contribute to the development of the self? How does love challenge us to transcend our human limitations?

163. WILHELM REICH AND SEX-ECONOMY

Time: mid-twentieth century CE
Place: Austria
Author: Wilhelm Reich

Wilhelm Reich, a German psychologist who fled the rise of the Nazis to the United States, studied with but went much further than Freud or Jung or other early psychologists in understanding the importance of sexuality to human existence: so far, in fact, that many thought him insane or a fraud, and he ended his life in prison. For Reich, the power of the orgasm connected human beings to the very life force of the universe, and free sexual expression should be encouraged. Later he even believed that the power of sexual orgasms—what he called "orgone"—could be collected and contained in boxes and used for medical benefit. In the passages below from The Discovery of the Orgone, *published in 1942, he explains the science he called "sex-economy."*

The theory of sex-economy can be put in a few sentences. Psychic health depends on orgastic potency, that is, on the capacity for surrender in the acme of sexual excitation in the natural sexual act. Its basis is the un-neurotic character attitude of capacity for love. Mental illness is a result of a disturbance in the natural capacity for love. In the case of orgastic impotence, from which a vast majority of humans are suffering, biological energy is dammed up, thus becoming the source of all kinds of irrational behavior. The cure of psychic disturbances requires in the first place the establishment of the natural capacity for love. It depends as much upon social as upon psychic conditions. Psychic disturbances are the results of the sexual chaos brought about by the nature of our society. This chaos has, for thousands of years, served the function of making people submissive to existing conditions, in other words, of internalizing the external mechanization of life. It serves the purpose of bringing about the psychic anchoring of a mechanized and authoritarian civilization by way of making people lack self-confidence.

The vital energies, under natural conditions, regulate themselves spontaneously, without compulsive duty or compulsive morality. The latter are a sure indication of the existence of antisocial tendencies. Antisocial behavior springs from secondary drives which owe their existence to the suppression of natural sexuality. The individual brought up in an atmosphere which negates life and sex acquires a pleasure-anxiety (fear of pleasurable excitation) which is represented physiologically in chronic muscular spasms. This pleasure-anxiety is the soil on which the individual recreates the life-negating ideologies which are the basis of dictatorships. It is the foundation of the fear of a free, independent way of living. This becomes the most potent source of strength for any kind of reactionary political activity and for the domination of majorities of working people by individuals or groups of individuals. It is bio-physiological anxiety and constitutes the central problem of psychosomatic research. Up to now, it has been the greatest obstacle to the investigation of the involuntary life functions, which the neurotic person can experience only as something weird and frightening.

The character structure of man of today—who is perpetuating a patriarchal, authoritarian culture some four to six thousand years old—is characterized by an armoring against nature within himself and against social misery outside himself. This armoring of the character is the basis of loneliness, helplessness, craving for authority, fear of responsibility, mystical longing, sexual misery, of impotent rebelliousness as well as of resignation of an unnatural and pathological type. Human beings have taken a hostile attitude toward that in themselves which is living, and have alienated themselves from it. This alienation is not of biological, but of social and economic origin. It is not found in human history before the development of the patriarchal social order.

Since then, duty has taken the place of the natural enjoyment of work and activity. The average character structure of human beings has changed in the direction of impotence and fear of living, so that authoritarian dictatorships not only can establish themselves, but can even justify themselves by pointing to existing human attitudes, such as lack of responsibility and infantilism. The international catastrophe we are passing through is the ultimate consequence of this alienation from life. This

formation of character in the authoritarian mold has as its central point, not parental love, but the authoritarian family. Its chief instrument is the suppression of sexuality in the infant and the adolescent. Owing to the split in the human character structure of today, nature and culture, instinct and morality, sexuality and achievement, are considered incompatible. That unity of culture and nature, work and love, morality and sexuality for which mankind is forever longing, this unity will remain a dream as long as man does not permit the satisfaction of the biological demands of natural (orgastic) sexual gratification. Until then, true democracy and responsible freedom will remain an illusion, and helpless submission to existing social conditions will characterize human existence. Until then, the extinguishing of life will prevail, be it in compulsive education, in compulsive social institutions, or in wars.

[Reich also saw the orgasm pattern of tension-release-relaxation as a basic principle of the human person.]

Orgastic gratification is a bio-electrical discharge, followed by a mechanical relaxation (detumescence). The biological process of expansion, as exemplified in the erection of an organ or the putting out of pseudopodia in the ameba, is the outward manifestation of the movement of bio-electric energy from the center to the periphery of the organism. What is moving here is—in the psychic as well as the somatic sense—the bio-electrical charge itself. Since only vegetative pleasure sensations are accompanied by an increased charge of the body surface, pleasurable excitation must be considered the specifically productive process in the biological system. All other affects, such as pain, annoyance, anxiety, depression, as well as pressure are antithetical to it from the point of view of energy and consequently represent functions negative to life. Thus the process of sexual pleasure is the life process per se. This is not just a manner of speaking, but an experimentally proven fact. Anxiety, as the fundamental antithesis of sexuality, is concurrent with death. It is, however, not identical with death. For, in death the central source of energy becomes extinguished; in anxiety, however, the energy is withdrawn from the periphery and dammed up in the center, creating the subjective sensation of oppression (*angustiae*). These facts give the concept of sex-economy a concrete meaning in terms of natural science. It means the manner of regulation of bio-electric energy, or, what is the same thing, of the economy of the sexual energies of the individual.

[Eventually, Reich believed that this same pattern existed throughout the universe, in particles of orgone he called bions.]

The orgone energy can be demonstrated visually, thermically and electroscopically in the soil, the atmosphere and in plant and animal organisms. The flickering in the sky which many physicists ascribe to terrestrial magnetism, and the flickering of the stars, are the immediate expression of the motion of the atmospheric orgone. The "electrical storms" which disturb electrical apparatus at times of increased sun spot activity, are, as can be shown experimentally, an effect of the atmospheric orgone energy. Thus far, it is tangible only as a disturbance of electric currents.

The color of the orgone is blue or bluish gray. In our laboratory, the atmospheric orgone is accumulated by means of especially constructed apparatus. A special arrangement of materials allows to make it visible. The stoppage of the kinetic energy of the orgone expresses itself as a temperature rise. The concentration of the orgone energy is reflected in the varying speed of discharge in the static electroscope.

The orgone contains three different kinds of radiation: bluish gray fog-like formations; deep blue-violet expanding and contracting dots; and whitish, rapidly moving dots and lines. The color of the atmospheric orgone is apparent in the blue sky and the bluish haze which one sees in the distance, particularly on hot summer days. Similarly, the blue-gray Northern lights, the so-called St. Elmo's Fire and the bluish formations which astronomers recently observed during a period of increased sun spot activity, are manifestations of the orgone energy. Cloud formation and thunderstorms—phenomena which to date have remained unexplained—depend on changes in the concentration of atmospheric orgone.

[Reich, then, saw sexuality as integral to life itself.]

The investigation of living matter went beyond the confines of depth psychology and physiology; it entered biological territory as yet unexplored. The subject of "sexuality" became one with that of "the living." It opened a new avenue of approach to the problem of biogenesis. Psychology came to be biophysics and genuine, experimental natural science. Its center remains always the same: the enigma of love, to which we owe our being.

Questions for Reflection and Discussion

How does sexuality relate to other aspects of human culture, according to Reich? How does it relate to other aspects of the natural world? How are the two connected?

164. SIMONE DE BEAUVOIR

Time: mid-twentieth century CE
Place: France
Author: Simone de Beauvoir

While many male theorists were content to assume that men's and women's experience of sexuality was more or less the same, Simone de Beauvoir tried to show in The Second Sex, published in 1949, that women's sexuality, like other aspects of their lives, was distorted by gender inequality. Her book became a classic to those who became known as "second-wave feminists," the women of the sixties and seventies who tried to build on the gains of the "first wave" of the suffragists. In this excerpt, de Beauvoir warned of the bind facing women wanting independent lives and meaningful relationships with men, even within a context of sexual liberation, a theme that became central to second-wave feminism.

From a more or less unsatisfactory affair a man is almost sure of obtaining at least the benefit of sex pleasure; a woman can very well obtain no pleasure at all. Even when indifferent, she lends herself politely to the embrace at the decisive moment, sometimes only to find her lover impotent and herself compromised in a ridiculous mockery. If all goes well except that she fails to attain satisfaction, then she feels "used," "worked." If she finds full enjoyment, she will want to prolong the affair. She is rarely quite sincere when she claims to envisage no more than an isolated adventure undertaken merely for pleasure, because her pleasure, far from bringing deliverance, binds her to the man; separation wounds her even when supposedly a friendly parting. It is much more unusual to hear a woman speak amicably of a former lover than a man of his past mistresses.

The peculiar nature of her eroticism and the difficulties that beset a life of freedom urge a woman toward monogamy. Liaison or marriage, however, can be reconciled with a career much less easily for her than for man. Sometimes her lover or husband asks her to renounce it…. If she yields, she is once more a vassal; if she refuses, she condemns herself to a withering solitude. Today a man is usually willing to have his companion continue her work…. But for the most part it is still the woman who bears the cost of domestic harmony.

To a man it seems natural that it should be the wife who does the housework and assumes alone the care and bringing up of the children. The independent woman herself considers that in marrying she has assumed duties from which her personal life does not exempt her. She does not want to feel that her husband is deprived of advantages he would have obtained if he had married a "true woman"; she wants to be presentable, a good housekeeper, a devoted mother, such as wives traditionally are. This is a task that easily becomes overwhelming. She assumes it through regard for her partner and out of fidelity to herself also, for she intends, as we have already seen, to be in no way unfaithful to her destiny as woman. She will be a double for her husband and at the same time she will be herself; she will assume his cares and participate in his successes as much as she will be concerned with her own fate—and sometimes even more. Reared in an atmosphere of respect for male superiority, she may still feel that it is for man to occupy the first place; sometimes she feels that in claiming it she would ruin her home; between the desire to assert herself and the desire for self-effacement she is torn and divided….

Through twenty years of waiting, dreaming, hoping, the young girl has cherished the myth of the liberating savior-hero, and hence the independence she has won through work is not enough to abolish her desire for a glorious abdication. She would have had to be raised exactly like a boy to be able easily to overcome her adolescent narcissism; but as it is, she continues into adult life this cult of the ego toward which her whole youth has tended. She uses her professional successes as merits for the enrichment of her image; she feels the need for a witness from on high to reveal and consecrate her worth…. To be justified by a god is easier than to justify herself by her own efforts; the world encourages her to believe it possible for salvation to be *given*, and she prefers to believe it. Sometimes she gives up her independence entirely and becomes no more than an *amoureuse*; more often she essays a compromise; but idolatrous love, the love that means abdication, is devastating; it occupies every thought, every moment; it is obsessing, tyrannical. If she meets with professional disappointments, the woman passionately seeks refuge in her love; then her frustrations are expressed in scenes and demands at her lover's expense…. Here again, for woman to love as man does—that is to say, in liberty, without putting her very *being* in question—she must believe herself his equal and be so in concrete fact; she must engage in her enterprises with the same decisiveness. But this is still uncommon, as we shall see.

There is one feminine function that it is actually almost impossible to perform in complete liberty. It is maternity. In England and America and some other countries a woman can at least decline maternity at will, thanks to contraceptive techniques. We have seen that in France she is often driven to painful and costly abortion; or she frequently finds herself responsible for an unwanted child that can ruin her professional life. If this is a heavy charge, it is because, inversely, custom does not allow a woman to procreate when she pleases. The unwed mother is a scandal to the community, and illegitimate birth is a stain on the child; only rarely is it possible to become a mother without accepting the chains of marriage or losing caste….

Thus the independent woman of today is torn between her professional interests and the problems of her sexual life; it is difficult for her to strike a balance between the two; if she does, it is at the price of concessions, sacrifices, acrobatics, which require her to be in a constant state of tension.

Why does de Beauvoir concentrate on internal rather than outward signs of women's equality? What is required for women to achieve real sexual self-fulfillment?

165. PICASSO'S COUPLE

Time: mid-twentieth century CE
Place: Spain
Artist: Pablo Picasso

Pablo Picasso, one of the twentieth century's most celebrated artists, sketched this erotic image in 1964. It reflects Picasso's use of the multidimensional perspective, for which he became famous, displaying the couple's body parts as they engage in sex. Throughout history, artists

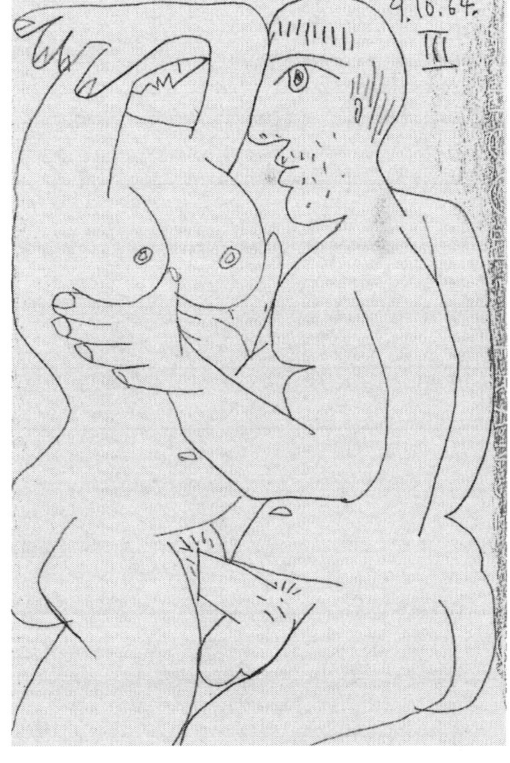

have attempted to represent the erotic in a number of ways: shockingly, arousingly, or discreetly, tenderly, passionately, or dispassionately.

Questions for Reflection and Discussion

Is this a sensual image of erotic pleasure or a crude display of sex? What actions and body parts are emphasized in the sketch, and which are minimized? Is there a deeper significance to the choice made about scale and position within the art?

166. JAGUA NANA

Time: mid-twentieth century CE
Place: Nigeria
Author: Cyprian Ekwensi

Modern novels often examine the role of sexual relationships in advancing or limiting one's deepest aspirations. Jagua Nana's title character is an aging prostitute who makes her living in Lagos, Nigeria. Ekwensi paints a bleak portrait of her: She is in love with a younger man, Freddie, whose ambition is to earn a law degree in England and thus get out of the poverty in which he and Jagua live. She, on the other hand, is caught in memories of her more glamorous youth, when she was nicknamed "Jagwa" (the local pronunciation of the Jaguar luxury automobile). The novel proved so successful that Ekwensi wrote a sequel, Jagua Nana's Daughter *(1986), that follows the loves and aspirations of another generation of Nigerians.*

She thought of the time when she was living in Eastern Nigeria, long before she went to Ghana, before she thought of coming to Lagos to live, before she met the late Freddie Namme. She was Jagwa then. In her early thirties. She was an only daughter. Her father doted on her. In his Godly way he wanted her to marry a serious man from the village. Poor Dad. He was only a catechist at the time, although he struggled hard and later became a pastor. The husband he approved of said he worked in the Coal City. He had come to Ogabu on leave and he noticed her and wanted to take her back with him as wife. Jagua was fond of changing her clothes often, and—in those early days of make-up—of painting her face. Every few hours she went down to the waterside and took off her clothes and swam in the clean cool water. The boys used to hide and peep at her breasts and hips. She knew it and always teased them. All the girls in her age-group had married and had children but she had resisted to the last, hoping ever, for some eminent man to come along to Ogabu to marry her. To the shock of the villagers she wore jeans and rode her bicycle through the narrow alleys of Ogabu and talked loudly and her laughter was throaty so that the men drew to her side and wanted her. She considered herself above the local boys, most of whom she had bedded and despised as poor experience.

The Coal City man pressed home his claim, and he paid the bride price of one hundred and twenty pounds; so the marriage was concluded and later on they went to the church and her father gave her away with his blessing to the Coal City man. God knows, she wanted to settle down and become the good wife. But she was bored. She was Jagwa, and the man was not Jagwa-ful. His main interest was his petrol-filling station and garage. He was up early and he went there to supervise the selling of his petrol and to make entries in his books. Often when she got there, she found him sleeping on the bare office table. He soon had a chain of filling stations all over the city and was able to buy a small car. But he never took her to parties, and would not dress well, for fear the money would leak away. In no way did his ideas of living attract her. She found that she had obeyed her parents but now they were not there to see her misery and they would never understand her longing, the hot thirst for adventure in her blood. She refused to adapt herself to his humdrum life and she wondered how she had been able to remain with him as she did for over three years. What grieved her most was that no child came. His mother and father and brothers and sisters came and made a fuss about it, and told him to take a younger wife as Jagua was too old. At first he did not listen to them, but after a time he began to weaken. Jagua knew that he took periodical leaves to his home town to look at some maiden who had been procured for him; she heard also that they brought him brides to the petrol-filling station. She took the blame for sterility, and it was becoming a thing between them.

One day when he went to his filling station, leaving the house to her, she dressed up and walked into the streets. She was passing by the Railway Station and on a sudden impulse she went in and asked for the time table. A young man smilingly told her when the next train would be leaving for L-A-G-O-S. Lagos! The magic name. She had heard of Lagos where the girls were glossy, worked in offices like the men, danced, smoked, wore high-heeled shoes and narrow slacks, and were "free" and "fast" with their favors. She heard that the people in Lagos did not have to go to bed at eight o'clock. Anyone who cared could go roaming the streets or wandering from one night spot to the other right up till morning. The night spots never shut, and they were open all night and every night; not like "here" where at 8 p.m. (latest) everywhere was shut down and the streets deserted, so that it looked odd to be wandering about.

When she came away from the railway counter, Jagua felt a sudden uneasiness. There was something sinful in her act, and from that moment on, she began to look at her man with a detached air. To her, he was good as dead. Dead and buried in her heart though he did not know it. She gave him her body, and thought instead of the slim young men in the dark bow-ties and elegantly cut lounge suits. She cooked for him, but longed for quiet restaurants where the lining was velvet and the music was soft and wine glasses clinked and men spoke in whispers to girls who burst suddenly into outraged laughter but were devils in nylon skins. She stopped taking treatment from the doctor who was giving her something to make her pregnant. Her husband found out and when they quarreled she was glad. She waited for him to leave for the filling station. They had not been on speaking terms for two whole days. She caught the train and it was too slow for her mood, taking three days to drop her into Lagos. She knew no one and was glad when a young bandleader picked her up and housed her for a time. His friends called him Hot Lips because of his manner of playing the trumpet and the scars on his lips. He had no money but he had style in all he did....

She remembered the morning when she was walking down the street, going from shop to shop. Being followed was something new for her then. She did not know why they did it in Lagos. As she turned the corner into William Street, they came quickly to her. "We live for Ikoyi," they said, after greeting her. "Our master—a white man, jus' come out from England. He let him wife for dem country. 'Es lookin' for some fine lady, special." They looked at her with approval. She was Jagwa: nothing exaggerated, the earrings, painted cheeks and lips, the cut of the Accra-style printed blouse and sarong-type wrapper, the smooth shoulders elastic and supple in the sun; the toes, waxed and peeping through high-heeled shoes. And when she walked, they whistled. "He will treat you fine, is a very kind man," said the second one. She observed that they were both dressed in white shirts and white trousers, starched and dazzling. She concluded that they must be servants of some highly-placed official. She weighed the situation. If she could break away from Hot Lips and live all by herself in a room of her own, she would be able to buy many of the fine things in the shops and make herself even more Jagwa.

"What time he want me?" she asked. "Is better for night time. If you tell me where you live—" "No, no! Ah live wit' some man. But I kin meet you somewhere, some place." Could it be true? Suppose there was some big practical joke in it somewhere? But Jagua believed in daring. If the worst happened, at least she could still find her way back to Tinubu Square. They later picked her up by the taxi park and sped to Ikoyi. When she stepped out of the taxi she glanced round her with breath suspended. She had never in her life dreamt of being in such dazzling surroundings. The deep soft carpets and well-padded chairs were things she saw in films. As she sat down the boys brought her something to drink and with trembling fingers she took the glass from the tray and sipped at the red liquid. Her head seemed to spin round. She lit a cigarette and the white man leaned over the enormous radiogram and put on a long-play record of some Nigerian music. His name was John Martell and he told her that his wife was in England. He had come out to work with a firm of builders. If she pleased him, he would treat her well.

She must have satisfied him for he took a room for her and furnished it, maintaining it till he went on leave. He told her he would be returning with his wife and two children. He would write to her. She never heard from him, nor did she ever see him again. With the allowance he gave her she traveled by Mammy Wagon to Accra. She had heard that the women of Accra were Jagwa-ful. They were the real black mermaids from the Guinea Gulf and their ideas came from Paris. When she got to Accra she was breathless with wonder. She returned to Lagos loaded with a pile of wax prints and *kente* cloth which she sold at a profit. She lowered the neckline of her sleeveless blouses and raised the heels of her shoes. She did her hair in the Jagua mop, wore earrings that really rang bells, as she walked with deliberately swinging hips. She was out-Jagwaring the real Jagwas. She found it thrilling to combine the retail of cloth with the dissemination of Accra fashion. In Lagos they called her Jagwa. This must have been her happiest time in the city. Going to Accra was always an adventure and she managed to keep her head high. She made and broke a number of lovers in Lagos and Accra. One whom she remembered well owned the old Lou-Lou Club in Accra and the money he made over to her and the contacts he made for her, helped her to establish a name in the wax-prints trade.

But things became different when she found a front room in a street in Lagos just off Skylark Avenue. In the same house there lived a young teacher named Freddie Namme. He lived on the ground floor and he was a bachelor and good looking. She saw him just once and decided it was time she settled down— with him. She would spare no effort to win him. Imperceptibly her interest in the cloth trade began to dwindle. She thought mainly of Freddie. She passed often by his door and greeted him loudly and clearly. Then she began cooking for him, home dishes that made him talk about his mother. She discovered that he was not engaged to anyone, but even so she found it difficult to reach his ears with her talk about love. She was afraid of the differences in their ages, but she made him talk of his ambition to become a lawyer. If he would give her the security she craved, if he would give her a child of her own, she would help him.

Questions for Reflection and Discussion

Does Jagua think of herself as a prostitute? How does she understand her life's path? How does the novelist show us life as a series of compromises between what we want and what we get?

167. HELEN GURLEY BROWN ON BEING SEXY

Time: mid-twentieth century CE
Place: United States
Author: Helen Gurley Brown

Helen Gurley Brown is often seen as the quintessential sexually liberated woman and spokeswoman for the sexual revolution. She first gained public attention with the 1962 publication of Sex and the Single Girl, *her advice book that included suggestions for women who were single and sexually active. Between 1965 and 1996 she was editor in chief of* Cosmopolitan *magazine and spearheaded its redesign as a forum for similar frank advice on sex to women throughout the sexual revolution.*

Have you got it? Can you get it? Are you sexy? Let's see.

What *is* a sexy woman?

Very simple. She is a woman who enjoys sex.

Being sexy means that you accept yourself as a woman—with all the functions of a woman. You like to make love, have babies, nurse them and mother them (or think you would). Being sexy means that you accept all the parts of your body as worthy and lovable—your reproductive organs, your breasts, your alimentary tract. You even welcome menstruation as the abiding proof of your fertility.

A woman who feels as this is sexy. She wears it like a perfume....

Outside of some mildly eccentric fellows who are sexually aroused only by girls who wear hobnail boots and paperclip necklaces ... or union suits plastered with chicken feathers, I think we can nearly all agree on what attitudes and accessories are sexy—and what aren't—in our time. Bear in mind you are sure to know a girl who does all the don'ts and none of the do's and has more *beaux* than a Greyhound bus can load, as well as those other girls who do the do's and don't the don'ts and whose loneliness is heart-rending!

Clean hair is sexy. Lots of hair is sexy, too. Skimpy little hair styles and hair under your arms, on your legs and around your nipples, isn't.

Lovely lingerie is sexy. And so is *not* wearing any! You can go for both looks on different occasions—or combine them at the same time! I never wear a bra at *all* but adore little half-slips because they're so pretty. A flowered, lace-trimmed mini-slip barely peek-a-booing from your miniest skirt when you sit down is quite delicious. Beige or bone pantyhose—without too many snags, please—are sexier than patterns.... Girdles are not sexy and thank God they are vanishing completely for girls who take care of their bodies.

Not sexy either are: food particles between your teeth, baggy stockings or pantyhose, bitten fingernails, borrowing money (very unsexy), flesh not secured firmly to the bone, and jitters (the dart-around, jerk-about kind that makes people feel *sandpapered!*).

Being able to sit very still is sexy.

Smiles are sexy....

Liking men is sexy. It is by and large just about the sexiest thing you can do. But I mean really liking, not just pretending. And there is quite a lot more to it than simply wagging your tail every time a man pats you on the head. You must wag your tail, of course—his collie dog does *that* much—but there are about five thousand more aggressive ways to demonstrate liking, none of which is dashing along to the nearest motel. You must spend time plotting how to make him happier.... Granted, it *is* harder to like men generously and selflessly when you're single. They are, after all, the enemy! One kindly smile from you, they think you're sweet on them. It's true, there has to be quite a lot of unrequited liking on your part for a while, but then men stop being suspicious and allow you to collect them as sons and lovers.

Questions for Reflection and Discussion

How much is "being sexy" an attitude about the self? How much is it a commodity, bought and sold? How is the "single girl" of Brown's book "liberated"?

168. ADVERTISING AND THE INVENTION OF HALITOSIS

Time: early twentieth century CE
Place: United States
Artist: unknown

Although it is not a recent one, the link between sex appeal and consumerism—suggesting that buying a certain product will improve one's love life—has been one of the most effective advertising strategies of the last century. This image, part of a marketing campaign by the Listerine Company in the 1920s, attempted to link the sale of their mouthwash with romantic success. In 1921, the company introduced the concept of "halitosis," a term they invented to describe bad breath, that sounded enough like a disease to imply that their product was its cure. The slogan from this 1925 advertisement was so popular that it became a well-known saying.

Questions for Reflection and Discussion

How does sex-appeal marketing work? How does this advertisement appeal to traditional notions of accomplishment? How does it link personal happiness to consumerism?

169. THE GAY LIBERATION FRONT'S *MANIFESTO*

Time: late twentieth century CE
Place: England
Author: unknown

The Gay Liberation Front, a group formed a few weeks after the Stonewall Riots (see source 153) and based on a Marxist model of revolution, spread quickly from New York to London and other cities. This Manifesto, privately published in London in 1971, laid out the basic issues facing gay liberationists in the seventies and suggested an agenda for ongoing reforms. Its purpose was to point the way to happiness and pride for gay men and lesbians.

*I*ntroduction. Throughout recorded history, oppressed groups have organized to claim their rights and obtain their needs. Homosexuals, who have been oppressed by physical violence and by ideological and psychological attacks at every level of social interaction, are at last becoming angry. To you, our gay sisters and brothers, we say that you are oppressed; we intend to show you examples of the hatred and fear with which straight society relegates us to the position and treatment of sub-humans, and to explain their basis. We will show you how we can use our righteous anger to uproot the present oppressive system with its decaying and constricting ideology, and how we, together with other oppressed groups, can start to form a new order, and a liberated lifestyle, from the alternatives which we offer.

[The author begins by pointing out ways in which gay men and lesbians are oppressed: within the family and the workplace, through education, religious and psychiatric institutions, media, and the law, and by means of physical violence.]

Self-Oppression. The ultimate success of all forms of oppression is our self-oppression. Self-oppression is achieved when the gay person has adopted and internalized straight people's definition of what is good and bad. Self-oppression is saying: "When you come down to it, we are abnormal." Or doing what you most need and want to do, but with a sense of shame and loathing, or in a state of disassociation, pretending it isn't happening; cruising or cottaging not because you enjoy it, but because you're afraid of anything less anonymous. Self-oppression is saying: "I accept what I am," and meaning: "I accept that what I am is second-best and rather pathetic." Self-oppression is any other kind of apology…. The ultimate in self-oppression is to avoid confronting straight society, and thereby provoking further hostility: Self-oppression is saying, and believing: "I am not oppressed."

We can do it. Yet although this struggle will be hard, and our victories not easily won, we are not in fact being idealistic to aim at abolishing the family and the cultural distinctions between men and women. True, these have been with us throughout history, yet humanity is at last in a position where we can progress beyond this. Only reactionaries and conservatives believe in the idea of "natural man." Just what is so different in human beings from the rest of the animal kingdom is their "unnaturalness." Civilization is in fact our evolution away from the limitations of the natural environment and towards its ever more complex control. It is not "natural" to travel in planes. It is not "natural" to take medicines and perform operations. Clothing and shoes do not grow on trees. Animals do not cook their food. This evolution is made possible by the development of technology—i.e. all those tools and skills which help us to control the natural environment.

We have now reached a stage at which the human body itself, and even the reproduction of the species, is being "unnaturally" interfered with (i.e. improved) by technology. Reproduction used to be left completely to the uncontrolled biological processes inherited from our animal ancestors, but modern science, by drastically lowering infant mortality, has made it unnecessary for women to have more than two or three babies, while contraceptives have made possible the conscious control of pregnancy and the freeing of sexuality from reproduction. Today, further advances are on the point of making it possible for women to be completely liberated from their biology by means of the development of artificial wombs. Women need no longer be burdened with the production of children as their main task in life, and need be still less in the future. The present gender-role system of "masculine" and "feminine" is based on the way that reproduction was originally organized. Men's freedom from the prolonged physical burden of bearing children gave them a privileged position which was then reinforced by an ideology of male superiority. But technology has now advanced to a stage at which the gender-role system is no longer necessary.

However, social evolution does not automatically take place with the steady advance of technology. The gender-role system and the family unit built around it will not disappear just because they have ceased to be necessary. The sexist culture gives straight men privileges which, like those of any privileged class, will not be surrendered without a struggle, so that all of us who are oppressed by this culture (women and gay people), must band together to fight it. The end of the sexist culture and of the family will benefit all women, and all gay people. We must work together with women, since their oppression is our oppression, and by working together we can advance the day of our common liberation….

Particularly oppressive aspects of gay society are the Youth Cult, Butch and Femme role-playing, and Compulsive Monogamy.

The Youth Cult. Straight women are the most exposed in our society to the commercially manipulated (because very profitable) cult of youth and "beauty"—i.e. the conformity to an ideal of "sexiness" and "femininity" imposed from without, not chosen by women themselves. Women are encouraged to look into the mirror and love themselves because an obsession with clothes and cosmetics dulls their appreciation of where they're really at—until it's too late. The sight of an old woman bedizened with layers of make-up, her hair tortured into artificial turrets, provokes ridicule on all sides. Yet this grotesque denial of physical aging is merely the logical conclusion to the life of a woman who has been taught that

her value lies primarily in her degree of sexual attractiveness. Gay women, like straight men, are rather less into the compulsive search for youth, perhaps because part of their rebellion has been the rejection of themselves as sex objects—like men they see themselves as people; as subjects rather than objects. But gay men are very apt to fall victim to the cult of youth—those sexual parades in the "glamorous" meat-rack bars of London and New York, those gay beaches of the South of France and Los Angeles haven't anything to do with liberation. Those are the hang-outs of the plastic gays who are obsessed with image and appearance. In love with their own bodies, these gay men dread the approach of age, because to be old is to be "ugly," and with their youth they lose also the right to love and be loved, and are valued only if they can pay. This obsession with youth is destructive. We must all get away from the false commercial standards of "beauty" imposed on us by movie moguls and advertising firms, because the youth/beauty hang-up sets us against one another in a frenzied competition for attention, and leads in the end to an obsession with self which is death to real affection or real sensual love….

Butch and Femme. Many gay men and women needlessly restrict their lives by compulsive role playing. They may restrict their own sexual behavior by feeling that they must always take either a butch or a femme role, and worse, these roles are transposed to make even more distorting patterns in general social relationships. We gay men and women are outside the gender-role system anyway, and therefore it isn't surprising if some of us—of either sex—are more "masculine" and others more "feminine." There is nothing wrong with this. What is bad is when gay people try to impose on themselves and on one another the masculine and feminine stereotypes of straight society, the butch seeking to expand his ego by dominating his/

her partner's life and freedom, and the femme seeking protection by submitting to the butch. Butch really is bad—the oppression of others is an essential part of the masculine gender role. We must make gay men and women who lay claim to the privileges of straight males understand what they are doing; and those gay men and women who are caught up in the femme role must realize, as straight women increasingly do, that any security this brings is more than offset by their loss of freedom.

Compulsive Monogamy. We do not deny that it is as possible for gay couples as for some straight couples to live happily and constructively together. We question however as an ideal, the finding and settling down eternally with one "right" partner. This is the blueprint of the straight world which gay people have taken over. It is inevitably a parody, since they haven't even the justification of straight couples—the need to provide a stable environment for their children (though in any case we believe that the suffocating small family unit is by no means the best atmosphere for bringing up children). Monogamy is usually based on ownership—the woman sells her services to the man in return for security for herself and her children—and is entirely bound up in the man's idea of property; furthermore in our society the monogamous couple, with or without children, is an isolated, shut-in, up-tight unit, suspicious of and hostile to outsiders. And though we don't lay down rules or tell gay people how they should behave in bed or in their relationships, we do want them to question society's blueprint for the couple. The blueprint says "we two against the world," and that can be protective and comforting. But it can also be suffocating, leading to neurotic dependence and underlying hostility, the emotional dishonesty of staying in the comfy safety of the home and garden, the security and narrowness of the life built for two, with the secret guilt of fancying someone else while remaining in

thrall to the idea that true love lasts a lifetime—as though there were a ration of relationships, and to want more than one were greedy. Not that sexual fidelity is necessarily wrong; what is wrong is the inturned emotional exclusiveness of the couple which stunts the partners so they can no longer operate at all as independent beings in society. People need a variety of relationships in order to develop and grow, and to learn about other human beings....

Free our heads. The starting point of our liberation must be to rid ourselves of the oppression which lies in the head of every one of us. This means freeing our heads from self-oppression and male chauvinism, and no longer organizing our lives according to the patterns with which we are indoctrinated by straight society. It means that we must root out the idea that homosexuality is bad, sick or immoral, and develop a gay pride. In order to survive, most of us have either knuckled under or pretended that no oppression exists, and the result of this has been further to distort our heads. Within gay liberation, a number of consciousness-raising groups have already developed, in which we try to understand our oppression and learn new ways of thinking and behaving. The aim is to step outside the experience permitted by straight society, and to learn to love and trust one another. This is the precondition for acting and struggling together. By freeing our heads we get the confidence to come out publicly and proudly as gay people, and to win over our gay brothers and sisters to the ideas of gay liberation.

Questions for Reflection and Discussion

How does the author of this *Manifesto* link the oppression of gay men and lesbians to others' oppression? Are the obstacles to pride and happiness addressed specific to the gay and lesbian communities, or more general?

170. S/M SEX

Time: late twentieth century CE
Place: United States
Author: unknown

These two letters, anonymously reprinted from the 1985 issue of an S/M magazine, DungeonMaster, *demonstrate how participants in sadomasochism understand their desires. The first letter comes from a bottom or submissive partner, the other from a Top or dominant partner. The terms "sadist," "masochist," and "sadomasochism" are usually avoided by participants in S/M behaviors as too clinical and because they do not distinguish between voluntary and involuntary participation in S/M, which is for practitioners a more significant divide than the heterosexual/homosexual divide, since S/M encompasses both.*

Here I am inside, bound, helpless, vulnerable. The man who bound me can keep me here for as long as it pleases him. He can display me to others or just leave me alone. There is time now to dwell upon my condition, consider my limits, concentrate my will and stamina to stay the course. I want to prove myself to myself as well as to him. I *must* endure this bondage. I am forced to live with it—in it. I abandon myself to a fate totally beyond my control. And the deeper the restraint infuses my spirit, the more it liberates, and—yes, gives freedom! And all the time there is a stirring warmth, a sense of unutterable joy in my loins, and even orgasm, though eventually desirable, is now unimportant. The whole trip is an orgasm. I occasionally drift away from the consciousness of my surroundings; my senses do turn off from time to time, and I'm left with only the struggle of my mind to come to terms with isolation and discomfort; to transcend, and be released from pain by the sheer force of my will. I'm proud to be here. It turns me on to know that the person suffering, struggling, exhilarated and satisfied—is me. *The more I'm bound, the freer I feel.* I'm glad to have others know this. Bondage means different things to different people. To some, it's the means to an end; to others, an end in itself. It's as awesomely beautiful to behold as it is to experience. It's aesthetic as well as erotic; mental as well as physical. True bondage is inescapable bondage; it is when my Top puts me into restraints from which I cannot free myself. The man who binds me, binds me to himself as the instigator and perpetrator of whatever agony and ecstasy is to follow. I start by indulging in fantasy, then grow inward, and finally retreat from superficial reality into true reality. If we understand each other, if we have a rapport, he may then take me deeper, and as I approach my endurance limit, he will help me to steel myself against the Panic. The ultimate, and the most rewarding, aspect of bondage is that moment when I feel that I cannot endure another second of the restraint, and I cry out for release. But he, my Top, is there to guide me through the barriers of my limits. I would not want to fail him, much less myself. He knows that I always try not to use a release code—that despite my pleas and whimperings, his is the judgment, his the decision. Then my "Thank You" for the trip from Heaven to Hell and back is heartfelt and sincere. Thank You, Sir.

There you are, inside the little cocoon that I have made for you. I have put you there, and for my purposes and enjoyment, you shall stay. You have given up all rights: the right to see, the right to hear, the right to move about as you please, the right to sensation and feeling. You have not thrown them cautiously to the wind but have placed them firmly in my hands, knowing full well that they will be returned to you. You may think it took a long time to put you in this position; in truth, it took years. Sometimes it truly blows me away how much of yourself you give to me in this moment, and how much responsibility that involves when I accept it from you. The trust that you imply, simply by being in the position that you find yourself, is overwhelming. Do you realize, little one, that in my own sadistic way, I can take away your right to breathe? Why do I do this to you? What do I get out of it? I am an artist; I have used you to create something of great aesthetic beauty. I am an exhibitionist; I get off on the sighs and whispers from any onlookers; the admiration of fellow Tops; the desire of other bottoms. I am a sadist. I enjoy the look of you, the knowledge that with each passing moment, you are in torment, and I need not lift a finger. I am also your biggest fan. I silently root for you, supporting you in going the distance I have set, cheering you on, and proud of you when you win. Thank *you*!

Questions for Reflection and Discussion

What does the Top and the Bottom each derive from the experience? What does each give to the other? How does each understand his experience as self-fulfillment?

171. A POEM ABOUT BISEXUALITY

Time: late twentieth century CE
Place: India
Author: Vikram Seth

A novelist and poet who lives in New Delhi and London, Vikram Seth published this short poem in a collection first published in 1981. It succinctly addressed the question of bisexuality, often ignored in public discussions of homosexuality and heterosexuality. The poet reminds us with remarkable succinctness of the infinite human capacity for sexual self-realization.

Some men like Jack
and some like Jill;
I'm glad I like
them both, but still
I wonder if
this freewheeling
really is an
enlightened thing—
or is its greater
scope a sign
of deviance from
some party line?
In the strict ranks
of Gay and Straight
what is my status?
Stray? or Great?

Questions for Reflection and Discussion

How does the poet poke fun at the assumptions of sexual orientation? What is the challenge of bisexuality to the dual identities of homosexuality and heterosexuality? How does the existence of bisexuals challenge notions of the origins and development of sexual desire, whether genetic or environmental or otherwise?

SOURCES AND FURTHER READING

The self-help guides to finding contentment in sex, or love in marriage, or self-fulfillment in some sexual matter are legion. Some interesting discussions of the relationship between the physical and the emotional—whether defined as love, happiness, self-fulfillment, or something else—from a historical perspective, however, exist, most treating it for nonspecialists in a general way. They include Gail Hawkes's *Sex and Pleasure in Western Culture* (Cambridge, MA: Polity, 2004); Marcus Collins's *Modern Love: An Intimate History of Men and Women in Twentieth-Century Britain* (London: Atlantic, 2003); Morton Hunt's *The*

Natural History of Love (New York: Anchor, 1994); Helen Fisher's *Anatomy of Love: The Natural History of Monogamy, Adultery, and Divorce* (New York: Norton, 1992); Steven Seidman's *Romantic Longings: Love in America, 1830–1980* (New York: Routledge, 1991); Paul Abramson et al.'s *Sexual Rights in America: The Ninth Amendment and the Pursuit of Happiness* (New York: New York University Press, 2003); or Barbara Foster et al.'s *Three in Love: Ménages à Trois from Ancient to Modern Times* (San Francisco: HarperSanFrancisco, 1997). On the modern "sexual revolution," see David Allyn's *Make Love, Not War: The Sexual Revolution, an Unfettered History* (Boston: Little, Brown, 2000). While most writings in English deal with English-speaking nations, see also Scot Barme's *Woman, Man, Bangkok: Love, Sex, and Popular Culture in Thailand* (Lanham, MD: Rowman & Littlefield, 2002). Likewise, while modern historians have been fascinated by the relationship between the emotional and the physical, premodern historians have also contributed to our understanding of this relationship in past societies. See, for example, Eric Fuchs's *Sexual Desire and Love: Origins and History of the Christian Ethic of Sexuality and Marriage*, trans. Marsha Daigle (Cambridge, UK: J. Clarke, 1983); Guido Ruggiero's *Binding Passions: Tales of Magic, Marriage, and Power at the End of the Renaissance* (Oxford: Oxford University Press, 1993); Alan Macfarlane's *Marriage and Love in England: Modes of Reproduction, 1300–1840* (Oxford: B. Blackwell, 1986); or Carmen Martin Gaite's *Love Customs in Eighteenth-Century Spain*, trans. Maria Tomsich (Berkeley, CA: University of California Press, 1991).

157. "A Poem about Marriage" is taken from *Poems by Indian Women*, ed. Margaret Macnicol (Oxford: Oxford University Press, 1923), 95–96.

Tilak's autobiography is available in English as *I Follow After: An Autobiography*, trans. E. Josephine Inkster (Oxford: Oxford University Press, 1998). On marriage in colonial India, see Mary Prodica's "All in the Family: Marriage, Gender, and the Family Business of Imperialism in British India," in *Colonialism and the Modern World: Selected Studies*, Gregory Blue et al., eds. (Armonk, NY: M.E. Sharpe, 2002); and several of the essays in *Community, Gender and Violence*, Partha Chatterjee and Pradeep Jaganathan, eds. (London: Hurst, 2000); in *Everyday Life in South Asia*, Diane Mines and Sarah Lamb, eds. (Bloomington, IN: Indiana University Press, 2002); and in *A Question of Silence: The Sexual Economies of Modern India*, Janaki Nair and Mary E. John, eds. (London: Zed, 1998). On love in modern India, see Rachel Dwyer's *All You Want Is Money, All You Need Is Love: Sexuality and Romance in Modern India* (London: Cassell, 2000). The film *The Jewel in the Crown* (UK, Granada Television, dir. Christopher Morahan and Jim O'Brien, 1984) set in 1942, also focuses on issues of love and sexuality in colonial India.

158. "An Unhappy Marriage" is taken from Shidzue Ishimoto, *East Way, West Way: A Modern Japanese Girlhood* (New York: Farrar & Rinehart, 1935), 106–9, 140–42, 155–56, 183–85.

See note 137 on women and marriage in twentieth-century Japan. Two related biographies of Shidzue exist: Helen Hopper's *A New Woman of Japan: A Political Biography of Kato Shidzue* (Boulder, CO: Westview, 1996), and her *Kato Shidzue: A Japanese Feminist* (New York: Pearson Longman, 2004).

159. "An Ode to Breasts" is taken from Karen Lystra, *Searching the Heart: Women, Men,*

and Romantic Love in Nineteenth-Century America (Oxford: Oxford University Press, 1989), 85–86.

On sexuality in Victorian America from a variety of perspectives, see Lystra's book, from which the excerpt is taken; see also Ronald Walters's *Primers for Prudery: Sexual Advice to Victorian America* (Englewood Cliffs, NJ: Prentice-Hall, 1973; revised 2000); Jayme Sokolow's *Eros and Modernization: Sylvester Graham, Health Reform, and the Origins of Victorian Sexuality in America* (Rutherford, NJ: Fairleigh Dickinson University Press, 1983); Stephen Nissenbaum's *Sex, Diet, and Debility in Jacksonian America: Sylvester Graham and Health Reform* (Chicago: Dorsey, 1980); John and Robin Haller's *The Physician and Sexuality in Victorian America* (Urbana, IL: University of Illinois Press, 1974); Hal Sears's *The Sex Radicals: Free Love in High Victorian America* (Lawrence, KA: Regents Press of Kansas, 1977); John Spurlock's *Free Love: Marriage and Middle-Class Radicalism in America, 1825–1860* (New York: New York University Press, 1988); Joanne Passet's *Sex Radicals and the Quest for Women's Equality* (Urbana, IL: University of Illinois Press, 2003); Carroll Smith-Rosenberg's *Disorderly Conduct: Visions of Gender in Victorian America* (New York: A.A. Knopf, 1985); or G.J. Barker-Benfield's *The Horrors of the Half-Known Life: Male Attitudes toward Women and Sexuality in Nineteenth-Century America* (New York: Routledge, 2000).

160. "*Rekhti* Erotic Poem" is taken from *Same-Sex Love in India*, Ruth Vanita and Saleem Kidwai, eds. (New York: St. Martin's, 2000), 223–25.

Vanita and Kidwai's book includes a good discussion of *rekhti* poetry; see also Carla Petievich's "*Rekhti*: Impersonating the Feminine in Urdu Poetry," in *Sexual Sites, Seminal Attitudes: Sexualities, Masculinities, and Culture in South Asia*, Sanjay Srivastava, ed. (Thousand Oaks, CA: Sage, 2004). On lesbianism in Indian tradition, see Giti Thadani's *Sakhiyani: Lesbian Desire in Ancient and Modern India* (London: Cassell, 1996), or her "The Politics of Identities and Languages: Lesbian Desire in Ancient and Modern India," in *Female Desires: Same-Sex Relations and Transgender Practices across Cultures*, Evelyn Blackwood and Saskia Wieringa, eds. (New York: Columbia University Press, 1999).

161. "Another Kind of Love" is taken from Walt Whitman, *Leaves of Grass* (New York: New American Library, 1955), 112, 122.

There are countless works on Walt Whitman, but some recent studies emphasize the erotic aspects of his life and poetry. See Vivian Pollak's *The Erotic Whitman* (Berkeley, CA: University of California Press, 2000); M. Jimmie Killingsworth's *Whitman's Poetry of the Body: Sexuality, Politics, and the Text* (Chapel Hill, NC: University of North Carolina Press, 1989); Mark Maslan's *Whitman Possessed: Poetry, Sexuality, and Popular Authority* (Baltimore, MD: Johns Hopkins University Press, 2001); or Gary Schmidgall's *Walt Whitman: A Gay Life* (New York: Dutton, 1997). More generally on nineteenth-century American views about male friendship and eroticism, see D. Michael Quinn's *Same-Sex Dynamics among Nineteenth-Century Americans: A Mormon Example* (Urbana, IL: University of Illinois Press, 1996); or Graham Robb's *Strangers: Homosexual Love in the Nineteenth Century* (New York: W.W. Norton, 2003).

162. "Jung on Love" is taken from Carl Jung, *Civilization in Transition*, trans. R.F.C. Hull

(Princeton, NJ: Princeton University Press, 1970), 110–12.

The literature on love and sex that relies on Jungian psychology is endless. On Jung specifically, however, one might read his own writings; or see the chapters on Jung in Janet Sayer's *Divine Therapy: Love, Mysticism, and Psychoanalysis* (Oxford: Oxford University Press, 2003); in Christine Downing's *Myths and Mysteries of Same-Sex Love* (New York: Continuum, 1989); or in Polly Young-Eisendrath's *Subject to Change: Jung, Gender, and Subjectivity in Psychoanalysis* (New York: Routledge, 2004).

163. "Wilhelm Reich and Sex-Economy" is taken from Wilhelm Reich, *The Function of the Orgasm: Sex-Economic Problems of Biological Energy*, trans. Theodore Wolfe (New York: Noonday/Farrar, Straus & Giroux, 1942), xviii–xxi, 336, 341–42, 343.

Works on Reich's life and ideas include Myron Sharaf's *Fury on Earth: A Biography of Wilhelm Reich* (New York: St. Martin's, 1983); Colin Wilson's *The Quest for Wilhelm Reich* (Garden City, NY: Anchor/Doubleday, 1981); W.E. Mann's *Orgone, Reich, and Eros: Wilhelm Reich's Theory of Life Energy* (New York: Simon and Schuster, 1973); Eustace Chesser's *Reich and Sexual Freedom* (London: Vision, 1972); Ola Raknes's *Wilhelm Reich and Orgonomy* (New York: St. Martin's, 1970).

164. "Simone de Beauvoir" is taken from Simone de Beauvoir, *The Second Sex*, trans. H.M. Parshley (New York: Vintage/Random House, 1952), 771–75.

On de Beauvoir's life and ideas, see Toril Moi's *Simone de Beauvoir: The Making of an Intellectual Woman* (Oxford: B. Blackwell 1994); or Mary Evans's *Simone de Beauvoir* (London: Sage, 1996). De Beauvoir also wrote her own autobiography, in five volumes, published in English as *Memoirs of a Dutiful Daughter*, trans. James Kirkup (New York: Harper & Row, 1974; orig. publ. 1958); *The Prime of Life*, trans. Peter Green (New York: Paragon, 1992; orig. publ. 1962); *Force of Circumstance*, trans. Richard Howard (New York: Paragon, 1992; orig. publ. 1963); *A Very Easy Death*, trans. Patrick O'Brian (New York: Warner, 1973: orig. publ. 1964); and *All Said and Done*, trans. Patrick O'Brian (New York: Putnam, 1974; orig. publ. 1972). She also wrote novels, works of existentialist philosophy, a study on the Marquis de Sade "Must We Burn Sade?" in *The Marquis de Sade*, trans. Annette Michelson (London: Calder, 1962), and published the letters between herself and Jean-Paul Sartre. For more on women's rights in modern France, see Joan Wallach Scott's *Only Paradoxes to Offer: French Feminists and the Rights of Man* (Cambridge, MA: Harvard University Press, 1996); Claire Goldberg Moses's *French Feminism in the Nineteenth Century* (Albany, NY: State University of New York Press, 1984); Felicia Gordon and Maire Cross's *Early French Feminisms, 1830–1940: A Passion for Liberty* (Cheltenham, UK: Edward Elgar, 1996); Patrick Bidelman's *Pariahs Stand Up! The Founding of the Liberal Feminist Movement in France, 1858–1889* (Westport, CT: Greenwood, 1982); James McMillan's *Housewife or Harlot: The Place of Women in French Society, 1870–1940* (Brighton, UK: Harvester, 1981); Jean Pedersen's *Legislating the French Family: Feminism, Theater, and Republican Politics, 1870–1920* (New Brunswick, NJ: Rutgers University Press, 2003); Mary Louise Roberts's *Disruptive Acts: The New Woman in Fin-de-Siècle France* (Chicago: University of Chicago Press, 2002); Paul Smith's *Feminism and the Third Republic: Women's Political and Civil Rights in France,*

1918–1945 (Oxford: Oxford University Press, 1996); or Claire Duchen's *Feminism in France: From May '68 to Mitterand* (London: Routledge & Kegan Paul, 1986).

165. "Picasso's Couple" is taken from Edward Lucie-Smith, *Ars Erotica: An Arousing History of Erotic Art* (New York: Rizzoli, 1997), 79.

There are countless collections of modern erotic art, including Lucie-Smith's book, from which this image was taken. On Picasso and erotic art, see R. Rosenblum's "Picasso and the Anatomy of Eroticism," in *Studies in Erotic Art*, Theodore Bowie and Cornelia Christenson, eds. (New York: Basic, 1970).

166. "Jagua Nana" is taken from Cyprian Ekwensi, *Jagua Nana* (London: Heineman, 1961), 166–70.

Ekwensi's sequel, *Jagua Nana's Daughter* (Ibadan, Nigeria: Spectrum, 1986), is something of a variation on Jagua Nana's own story, and would be interesting to read in a history of sexuality, as would the original novel. A collection of essays discuss the author's life and works, of which *Jagua Nana* was the best known; see *The Essential Ekwensi: A Literary Celebration of Cyprian Ekwensi's Sixty-Fifth Birthday*, Ernest Emenyonu, ed. (Ibadan, Nigeria: Heineman Educational Books, 1987). Ekwensi also figures prominently in Gloria Chineze Chukukere's *Gender Voices and Choices: Redefining Women in Contemporary African Fiction* (Enugu, Nigeria: Fourth Dimension, 1995), which also discusses other modern African novels that would be worth reading in a history of sexuality, and in Kenneth Little's *Sociology of Urban Women's Image in African Literature* (London: Macmillan, 1980). For more on women in modern African history, see Catherine Coquery-Vidrovitch's *African Women: A Modern History*, trans. Beth Gillian Raps (Boulder, CO: Westview, 1997); Iris Berger and E. Frances White's *Women in Sub-Saharan Africa: Restoring Women to History* (Bloomington, IN: Indiana University Press, 1999); or Marjorie Wall Bingham and Susan Hill Gross's *Women in Africa of the Sub-Sahara*, 2 vols. (Hudson, WI: G.E. McCuen, 1982). For more on women's economic status, see Margaret Snyder and Mary Tadesse's *African Women and Development: A History* (Johannesburg, South Africa: Witwatersrand University Press, 1995); or, more focused, Judith Byfield's *The Bluest Hands: A Social and Economic History of Women Dyers in Abeokuta (Nigeria), 1890–1940* (Portsmouth, NH: Heinemann, 2002). Other localized histories, centering on African women's changing political and social realities, include Barbara MacGowan Cooper's *Marriage in Maradi: Gender and Culture in a Hausa Society in Niger, 1900–1989* (Portsmouth, NH: Heinemann, 1997); Elizabeth Schmidt's *Peasants, Traders, and Wives: Shona Women in the History of Zimbabwe, 1870–1939* (Portsmouth, N.H.: Heinemann, 1992); Susan Geiger's *TANU Women: Gender and Culture in the Making of Tanganyikan Nationalism, 1955–1965* (Portsmouth, NH: Heinemann, 1997); Marc Epprecht's *"This Matter of Women is Getting Very Bad": Gender, Development and Politics in Colonial Lesotho* (Pietermaritzburg, South Africa: University of Natal Press, 2000); Terri Barnes's *"We Women Worked So Hard": Gender, Urbanization, and Social Reproduction in Colonial Harare, Zimbabwe, 1930–1956* (Portsmouth, NH: Heinemann, 1999); Belinda Bozzoli's *Women of Phokeng: Consciousness, Life Strategy, and Migrancy in South Africa, 1900–1983* (Portsmouth, NH: Heinemann, 1991); Iris Berger's *Threads of Solidarity: Women in South African Industry, 1900–1980* (Bloomington, IN: Indiana University Press,

1992); and Cherryl Walker's *Women and Resistance in South Africa* (New York: Monthly Review, 1991; orig. publ. 1982). A good sampling of local studies are the essays in *Courtyards, Markets, City Streets: Urban Women in Africa*, Kathleen Sheldon, ed. (Boulder, CO: Westview, 1996).

167. "Helen Gurley Brown on Being Sexy" is taken from Helen Gurley Brown, *Sex and the New Single Girl* (New York: Bernard Geis, 1970), 71–72, 83–84, 87–88.

Rodger Streitmatter's *Sex Sells! The Media's Journey from Repression to Obsession* (Cambridge, MA: Westview, 2004) contains a chapter on *Cosmopolitan* magazine. For more on the changing sexual customs in the modern US, especially in the 1960s and 70s, see David Allyn's *Make Love, Not War: The Sexual Revolution: An Unfettered History* (Boston: Little, Brown, 2000); Sheila Jeffreys's *Anticlimax: A Feminist Perspective on the Sexual Revolution* (London: Women's, 1990); John Heidenry's *What Wild Ecstacy: The Rise and Fall of the Sexual Revolution* (New York: Simon & Schuster, 1997); or the essays in *Sexual Revolution*, Jeffrey Escoffier, ed. (New York: Thunder's Mouth, 2003); *Swinging Single: Representing Sexuality in the 1960s*, Hilary Radner and Moya Luckett, eds. (Minneapolis, MI: University of Minnesota Press, 1999); or in *The Family and the Sexual Revolution: Selected Readings*, Edwin Schur, ed. (Bloomington, IN: Indiana University Press, 1964). Many such guides for women were written throughout the twentieth century. Another well known figure in the sexual revolution was Hugh Hefner, founder of *Playboy* magazine in 1953. Hefner's editorials from *Playboy* magazine in the early 1960s have been collected together as *The Playboy Philosophy* (Chicago: HMH, 1963). There are numerous studies on *Playboy* magazine; recent ones include Russell Miller's *Bunny: The Real Story of Playboy* (London: Joseph, 1984); Victor Lownes's *The Day the Bunny Died* (Secaucus, NJ: L. Stuart, 1983). Rodger Streitmatter's *Sex Sells! The Media's Journey from Repression to Obsession* (Cambridge, MA: Westview, 2004) and Bill Osgerby's *Playboys in Paradise: Masculinity, Youth and Leisure-Style in Modern America* (Oxford: Berg, 2001) situate the magazine within a larger historical context. Indexes to and compilations from *Playboy* exist, which can provide sources for study of changing sexual attitudes; see Mildred Miles's *Index to Playboy: Belles-Lettres, Articles, and Humor, December 1953–December 1969* (Metuchen, NJ: Scarecrow, 1970); or *Playboy: 50 Years, the Cartoons*, Hugh Hefner and Michelle Urry, eds. (San Francisco: Chronicle, 2004); or *Playboy Interviews, Selected by the Editors of Playboy* (Chicago: Playboy, 1967); or Ray Bradbury's *The Art of Playboy* (New York: A. van der Marck, 1985); see also *The Twelfth Anniversary Playboy Reader* (Chicago: Playboy, 1965); or *The Twentieth Anniversary Playboy Reader* (Chicago: Playboy, 1974), both edited by Hugh Hefner.

168. "Advertising and the Invention of Halitosis" is taken from Juliann Sivulka, *Soap, Sex, and Cigarettes: A Cultural History of American Advertising* (Belmont, CA: Wadsworth, 1998), 161.

See note 138 on sex in advertising, and note to chapter 12 generally on sex and consumerism. See also Vincent Vinikas's *Soft Soap, Hard Sell: American Hygiene in an Age of Advertisement* (Ames, IA: Iowa State University Press, 1992). Other interesting studies examining the relationship between consumerism and changing sexual patterns in the US include Peter Stoneley's *Consumerism and American Girls' Literature, 1860–1940* (Cambridge: Cambridge University Press, 2003); David R. Wells's *Consumerism and the Movement of Housewives into Wage Work: The Interaction of Patriarchy, Class, and Capitalism in Twentieth-Century America* (Brookfield, VT: Ashgate, 1998); Noliwe Rooks's *Ladies' Pages: African American Women's Magazines and the Culture that Made Them* (New Brunswick, NJ: Rutgers University Press, 2004); and the essays in *On Fashion*, Shari Benstock and Suzanne Ferriss, eds. (New Brunswick, NJ: Rutgers University Press, 1994); or in *Beauty and Business: Commerce, Gender, and Culture in Modern America*, Philip Scranton, ed. (New York: Routledge, 2001). On the history of cosmetics use, see Kathy Peiss's *Hope in a Jar: The Making of America's Beauty Culture* (New York: Metropolitan, 1998); Paula Black's *The Beauty Industry: Gender, Culture, Pleasure* (New York: Routledge, 2004); or Teresa Riordan's *Inventing Beauty: A History of the Innovations that Have Made Us Beautiful* (New York: Broadway, 2004).

169. "The Gay Liberation Front's *Manifesto*" is taken from Lisa Power's *No Bath but Plenty of Bubbles: An Oral History of the Gay Liberation Front, 1970–1973* (London: Cassell, 1995), 316, 320–21, 324–29.

Other writings from the early British gay liberation movement, specifically, from the Gay Liberation Front's newsletter, *Come Together*, have been collected in *Come Together: The Years of Gay Liberation, 1970–73*, ed. Aubrey Walter (London: Gay Men's, 1980). Broader studies of the gay rights movement in Britain include Power's book, from which the excerpt is taken; Jeffrey Weeks's *Coming Out: Homosexual Politics in Britain from the Nineteenth Century to the Present* (London: Quartet, 1977); and *Radical Records: Thirty Years of Lesbian and Gay History, 1957-1987*, ed. Bob Cant and Susan Hemmings (London: Routledge, 1988). Much has been written on the American gay liberation movement: see Margaret Cruikshank's *The Gay and Lesbian Liberation Movement* (New York: Routledge, 1992); Leigh Rutledge's *The Gay Decades, From Stonewall to the Present: The People and Events that Shaped Gay Lives* (New York: Plume, 1992); or Craig Rimmerman's *From Identity to Politics: The Lesbian and Gay Movements in the United States* (Philadelphia: Temple University Press, 2002). Other international comparisons may be helped with the essays in *Different Rainbows*, Peter Drucker, ed. (London: Gay Men's, 2000); or with Denise Thompson's *Flaws in the Social Fabric: Homosexuals and Society in Sydney* (Sydney: G. Allen & Unwin, 1985); Laurie Guy's *Worlds in Collision: The Gay Debate in New Zealand, 1960–1986* (Wellington, NZ: Victoria University Press, 2002); or Tom Warner's *Never Going Back: A History of Queer Activism in Canada* (Toronto, ON: University of Toronto Press, 2002). See also note 153.

170. "S/M Sex" is taken from Charles Moser and J.J. Madeson, *Bound to be Free: The SM Experience* (New York: Continuum, 1996), 14–15.

Different views on S/M, and changes in perspective over the last few decades, may be provided by Michael Grumley's *Hard Corps: Studies in Leather and Sadomasochism* (New York: Dutton, 1977); *Against Sadomasochism: A Radical Feminist Analysis*, Robin Linden et al., eds. (East Palo Alto, CA: Frog in the Well, 1982); *S and M: Studies in Sadomasochism*, Thomas Weinberg and G.W. Lev Kamel, eds. (Buffalo, NY: Prometheus, 1983); Robert Stoller's *Pain and Passion: A Psychoanalyst Explores the World of S & M* (New York: Plenum, 1991); Bill Thompson's *Sadomasochism: Painful Perversion or Pleasurable Play* (London: Cassell, 1994); Gerald and Caroline Greene's *S-M: The Last Taboo* (New York: Blue Moon, 1995); Philip Miller and Molly Devon's *Screw the Roses, Send Me the Thorns: The Romance and Sexual Sorcery of Sadomasochism* (Fairfield, CT: Mystic, 1995); Jay Wiseman's *SM 101: A Realistic Introduction* (San Francisco: Greenery, 1996); Lynda Hart's *Between the Body and the Flesh: Performing Sadomasochism* (New York: Columbia University Press, 1998); Karmen MacKendrick's *Counterpleasures* (Albany, NY: State University of New York Press, 1999); Barbara Nitke's *Kiss of Fire: A Romantic View of Sadomasochism* (Heidelberg: Kehrer, 2003).

171. "A Poem about Bisexuality" is taken from *Same-Sex Love in India*, Ruth Vanika and Saleem Kidwai, eds. (New York: St. Martin's, 2000), 326.

For more on bisexuality in South Asia, see John De Cecco's "Bisexuality and Discretion: The Case of Pakistan," in *Bisexualities: The Ideology and Practice of Sexual Contact with Both Men and Women*, Erwin Haeberle and Rolf Gindort, eds. (New York: Continuum, 1998), along with other essays of a historical nature. See note 181 for more on bisexuality. For more on changing sexual attitudes in India, see Jeremy Seabrook's *Love in a Different Climate: Men who Have Sex with Men in India* (London: Verso, 1999); or the essays in *A Lotus of Another Color: An Unfolding of the South Asian Gay and Lesbian Experience*, Rakesh Ratti, ed. (Boston: Alyson, 1993); or in *Sexual Sites, Seminal Attitudes: Sexualities, Masculinities, and Culture in South Asia*, Sanjay Srivastava, ed. (Thousand Oaks, CA: Sage, 2004). See note 160 for more on lesbianism in modern India.

CHAPTER 15

SEX AND THE USES OF HISTORY

To conclude, I have chosen a set of excerpts from contemporary sources, all of which appeal to history to justify an argument or illuminate a point. The use of history for sexuality, then, and especially for clarifying the relationship between sexuality and identity, is the subject of this final chapter.

Although it is commonly said that studying history can prevent us from repeating the mistakes of the past, that statement makes a number of assumptions that may not be accurate. First, do we know that human beings of the present are so much like those of the past that we will do more or less the same things as they did and react in similar ways? Second, is it true that historical trends or events are close enough in their multiple factors that a past trend or event can be used as precedent for a present or future one? These sorts of questions are not simply idle speculations. All of our decisions about the future are based on our ability to choose the course of action that we predict will give the best possible outcome. The difficulties come in deciding which historical trends or events are the most similar and make the best comparison for future developments, given changing social, political, and economic factors, changing values and attitudes, and so on. It is as true for sexuality as for other aspects of human life.

Despite these difficulties, history is often used to support contemporary arguments about sexuality. Some proponents of the status quo use history to claim that "things have always been this way" and, by extension, should continue to remain so. Advocates of change, if they want to counter such an idea, can dismiss the use of history: "Just because things have always been this way does not mean that they have to remain so." That, however, is not a very persuasive argument, since its advocates must then convince others how human beings can change something that has always been so, even if we wanted to. A better argument is made when lesser known or "hidden" history is brought to bear, showing that some past societies, or some groups within past societies, have thought about or done things differently. The value of history often comes in finding the exception that disproves the rule.

Finding the hidden history of sexuality has been important for many groups in recent decades. Women have studied history not only to support arguments about the oppressiveness of male domination in human history, but also to find those occasions when patriarchy was overturned, even temporarily, or lessened, even to a slight degree. Gay men and lesbians in recent decades have also looked to history to find past societies that celebrated rather than condemned homoeroticism, or at least individuals who created meaningful lives for themselves even amid prejudice. Throughout these explorations, history has proved very useful in bolstering modern identities by showing their antecedents.

The relationship between history, sexuality, and identity became the center of a heated scholarly debate in the 1980s and 90s, one that is linked to the academic theory called social constructionism. Although the debate began in feminist history, it spread from there to gay and lesbian history and beyond. It began as a reaction to the principle that became known as essentialism: a belief that human beings are "essentially" the same, that people in the past lived lives much the same as ours, and that our biological similarity to them explains most behaviors, past and present. Essentialists are common in the academic discipline of biol-ogy, where genetic and physiological factors outside of the realm of historical change are emphasized, but rare outside of it. Social constructionists, in contrast, argued that human beings are products of their historical environment, "constructed" by social and other forces, and that, therefore, labels and ideas about human beings created in the present are not appropriate to use when referring to the past. At its best, social constructionism reminded scholars that we cannot take for granted that the categories through which we understand sexuality have always been the same. At its worst, social constructionism implied that history was ultimately impossible since an unbridgeable gap in understanding separates us from the past.

A few examples will help to demonstrate how influential this school has been in recent studies of sexuality. Patriarchy has long been used to describe men's oppression of women in history, but not all patriarchal societies have been the same. Some past societies permitted women to choose marriage partners, others did not; some allowed women to own property or hold professions, others did not. To group all male-dominated societies as patriarchal is to erase the complicated differences between past societies, and it is often by studying the differences that we learn what is most important in the lessons of the past. It is also to disregard the other types of oppression that existed in past societies: Women of the upper classes could be slave owners, in which case, their oppression was not less than that of the slaves who were exploited by them, just different. To label a society as patriarchal, in other words, ignores the multifaceted power relations of the past.

Another example of the influence of social constructionism has been in the history of homosexuality. Past societies organized same-sex relations in a variety of ways. In ancient Athens, pederasty between adult and adolescent males was socially approved and perhaps almost universally practiced, often by men who were married. Other historical societies organized same-sex relations along this same pederastic model. Nonetheless, some peoples of the past provide much greater evidence for a transgenderal model of homosexuality, in which one partner assumed the appearance, as well as the social and sexual functions, of the opposite sex. Other societies demonstrated more of an egalitarian model, where the sexual partners were roughly equivalent in age, gender role, and other aspects of social status. To lump all of these disparate types of sexual behaviors as being homosexuality is accurate in one sense, since they involve the same basic set of sexual activities, but it downplays the richness of the cultural differences. In the history of homosexuality, in particular, the fact that the word "homosexual" was first coined only in 1869 is seen as evidence that it is a fairly recent category for understanding sexual identity and not much help for historians in understanding premodern peoples.

The challenge posed by social constructionism has been to study and interpret history and historical patterns of sexuality without assuming that we already know the answers as to how past societies were organized. Many historians look carefully at terminology (a trick borrowed from anthropologists) to see how people of the past conceptualized sexual and other behaviors and identities. Historians now also choose their words for sexual customs and concepts more carefully. What is it that makes marriage "marriage," for example? Is it the economic aspect of the arrangement? Is it the consent of the parties to be married? Is it the bond of affection or love between the future married persons? Is it that there are only two persons involved, or that one is male and the other female? In the current global debate about same-sex marriage, it is precisely these

social constructionist-influenced questions that make all the difference. The use of history is again proved in looking at how past people thought about and organized marriage, or even in deciding whether we are bound to follow the past in determining the future of marriage.

Even more recently, in part a reaction to but also an extension of social construction, another set of academic ideas has gained currency in the history of sexuality, namely queer theory, which began with historians of homosexuality. It borrows from sociological studies of deviance and the notion of The Other from Lacanian psychology in looking to history for examples of individuals or ideas judged to be "queer"—somehow different according to the sexual ideals of their own societies, rather than those who correspond to any contemporary categories. Queer theory is still very much in vogue among scholars of the history of sexuality. Its strength lies in permitting the study of past sexual minorities and sexual dissidents without labeling them according to modern standards. Nonetheless, queer theory might be criticized for simply replacing one set of anachronistic terms with another and for collapsing a far greater variety of roles and activities into one homogenous classification.

Where the future of the history of sexuality will go is not knowable. The challenges that social constructionism and queer theory have presented to sexual identities are merely part of a much broader critique of knowledge in our day. That critique, usually called postmodernism, questions the foundations on which knowledge has long been based: ethnic and national customs, religious and philosophical traditions, and the identity of The Self. What new ideas or controversies in sexuality will arise out of that critique cannot be known. I am confident, though, that history will continue to have its uses.

The following excerpts from contemporary writers on sexuality are intended to show the varied uses to which the past is put.

172. MICHEL FOUCAULT AND THE REPRESSIVE HYPOTHESIS

Time: late twentieth century CE
Place: France
Author: Michel Foucault

Michel Foucault made an immeasurable impact on the modern history of sexuality and is often considered the founder of the academic field. Although a few historians before him had dealt with the topic, he asked much deeper questions that linked the history of sexuality not only to the present but also to the perennial issues of human existence. In other words, he was as much a philosopher of the history of sex as he was a historian. This excerpt is from the opening pages of his introductory book, published in 1976, to what was intended to be a series, entitled The History of Sexuality. *He wrote two more volumes, one on ancient Greece and another on ancient Rome, but died of AIDS in 1984 without completing the series. He is often also considered the founder of social constructionism.*

For a long time, the story goes, we supported a Victorian regime, and we continue to be dominated by it even today. Thus the image of the imperial prude is emblazoned on our restrained, mute, and hypocritical sexuality. At the beginning of the seventeenth century a certain frankness was still common, it would seem. Sexual practices had little need of secrecy; words were said without undue reticence, and things were done without too much concealment; one had a tolerant familiarity with the illicit. Codes regulating the coarse, the obscene, and the indecent were quite lax compared to those of the nineteenth century. It was a time of direct gestures, shameless discourse, and open transgressions, when anatomies were shown and intermingled at will, and knowing children hung about amid the laughter of adults: it was a period when bodies "made a display of themselves."

But twilight soon fell upon this bright day, followed by the monotonous nights of the Victorian bourgeoisie. Sexuality was carefully confined; it moved into the home. The conjugal family took custody of it and absorbed it into the serious function of reproduction. On the subject of sex, silence became the rule. The legitimate and procreative couple laid down the law. The couple imposed itself as model, enforced the norm, safeguarded the truth, and reserved the right to speak while retaining the principle of secrecy. A single locus of sexuality was acknowledged in social space as well as at the heart of every household, but it was a utilitarian and fertile one: the parents' bedroom. The rest had only to remain vague; proper demeanor avoided contact with other bodies, and verbal decency sanitized one's speech. And sterile behavior carried the taint of abnormality; if it insisted on making itself too visible, it would be designated accordingly and would have to pay the penalty....

These are the characteristic features attributed to repression, which serve to distinguish it from the prohibitions maintained by penal law: repression operated as a sentence to disappear, but also as an injunction to silence, an affirmation of nonexistence, and, by implication, an admission that there was nothing to say about such things, nothing to see, and nothing to know. Such was the hypocrisy of our bourgeois societies with its halting logic....

This discourse on modern sexual repression holds up well, owing no doubt to how easy it is to uphold. A solemn historical and political guarantee protects it. By placing the advent of the age of repression in the seventeenth century, after hundreds of years of open spaces and free expression, one adjusts it to coincide with the development of capitalism: it becomes an integral part of the bourgeois order. The minor chronicle of sex and its trials is transposed into the ceremonious history of the modes of production; its trifling aspect fades from view. A principle of explanation emerges after the fact: if sex is so rigorously repressed, this is because it is incompatible with a general and intensive work imperative. At a time when labor capacity was being systematically exploited, how could this capacity be allowed to dissipate itself in pleasurable pursuits, except in those—reduced to a minimum—that enabled it to reproduce itself? …

But there may be another reason that makes it so gratifying for us to define the relationship between sex and power in terms of repression: something that one might call the speaker's benefit. If sex is repressed, that is, condemned to prohibition, nonexistence, and silence, then the mere fact that one is speaking about it has the appearance of a deliberate transgression. A person who holds forth in such language places himself to a certain extent outside the reach of power; he upsets established law; he somehow anticipates the coming freedom. This explains the solemnity with which one speaks of sex nowadays. When they had to allude to it, the first demographers and psychiatrists of the nineteenth century thought it advisable to excuse themselves for asking their readers to dwell on matters so trivial and base. But for decades now, we have found it difficult to speak on the subject without striking a different pose: we are conscious of defying established power, our tone of voice shows that we know we are being subversive, and we ardently conjure away the present and appeal to the future, whose day will be hastened by the contribution we believe we are making.

Something that smacks of revolt, of promised freedom, of the coming age of a different law, slips easily into this discourse on sexual oppression.…

Today it is sex that serves as a support for the ancient form—so familiar and important in the West—of preaching. A great sexual sermon—which has had its subtle theologians and its popular voices—has swept through our societies over the last decades; it has chastised the old order, denounced hypocrisy, and praised the rights of the immediate and the real; it has made people dream of a New City.… The question I would like to pose is not, Why are we repressed? but rather, Why do we say, with so much passion and so much resentment against our most recent past, against our present, and against ourselves, that we are repressed? By what spiral did we come to affirm that sex is negated? What led us to show, ostentatiously, that sex is something we hide, to say it is something we silence? And we do all this by formulating the matter in the most explicit terms, by trying to reveal it in its most naked reality, by affirming it in the positivity of its power and its effects. It is certainly legitimate to ask why sex was associated with sin for such a long time—although it would remain to be discovered how this association was formed, and one would have to be careful not to state in a summary and hasty fashion that sex was "condemned"—but we must also ask why we burden ourselves today with so much guilt for having once made sex a sin.

Questions for Reflection and Discussion

In what ways, according to Foucault, do we generalize about the past? What does that generalization say about us in the present? How different are we from our predecessors?

173. THE SPREAD OF AIDS
AND GLOBAL MIGRATION

Time: late twentieth century CE
Place: United States
Author: Gilbert Herdt

Gilbert Herdt, an anthropologist, is the director of the Human Sexuality Studies Program at San Francisco State University. He made his scholarly reputation with the 1981 publication of Guardians of the Flutes *on the sexual customs of the Sambia people of modern New Guinea. Since then, he has received numerous awards and grants for his wide-ranging work on sexuality and anthropology, and on the worldwide impact of AIDS. The following excerpt, from a collection of essays that Herdt edited, situates the current global epidemic of AIDS within a broader historical context.*

There is little doubt that in the time of the modern age, people have traveled to new lands for the purpose of discovery, including the discovery of exotic customs and sexual practices foreign to their own culture's standards. In the first colonial encounters between Western and non-Western in the Pacific, ... the sexual encounter was critical and filled with possibilities of power, exchange, cultural transformation, and the fatal spread of disease. The voyages of Captain Cook thus heralded the negative aspects of the encounters to follow for centuries, from colonial times to the present.

The transition to modernity in Western culture in an earlier historical period and the modernization taking place in many Third World countries today represent similar but unequal processes: the culmination of industrial development and colonial expansion from the West and the inherent changes that internal development and mobility have brought to social and sexual life in the East. Human move-

ment of all kinds played a critical role in both historical transformations. Transnational and internal migration are part of this, but a critical part, since the ability to move and adapt within and across groups is part of our unique species-specific adaptive mechanism, that of culture. Because of their inherent flexibility and ability to move, humans have been better able to survive by taking advantage of the changing opportunities and challenges of their environments. Historically, we have reason to believe that movement typically involves new opportunities for sexual encounters, sometimes resulting in intermarriage and offspring between groups. Indeed, it might be suggested that if change is indicative of the modern period since the later seventeenth century, then change in standards of sexual culture have often proved the vanguard of transformation and modernization in society at large.

Today, however, human mobility is occurring at an unprecedented pace around the world. Its effects are far-reaching and potentially devastating in scope, including the spread of sexually transmitted diseases as studied in this book, such that scholars increasingly think of this flood of migration as a hallmark of human society in the late twentieth century. Crossing cultural boundaries may potentially change the sexual behavior of the agent—either for the lone individual, the married couple, the small refugee group, or the tourist or traveler. The possibilities of new mass media and interactive communication technologies informing and motivating people to move around have also enhanced the globalization that is accelerating movement. Catastrophes (natural or human) sometimes result in mass migration, as we have witnessed many times this century. As the actor's cultural and personal conduct and identity changes in response to these movements, the degree of qualitative change in sexual behavior may also increase, potentially violating beliefs or norms previously thought to be sacred by the individual or the group. Thus, too, the actor may no longer be at ease about "going home," because of the constraints of returning to traditional norms and roles. When the greatest restrictions apply to women, it is understandable that special conditions may apply to the role of women in migration, as a special case of demographic change. The risk to women is greatest.

Sexual practices and identities can serve as the basis for cultural stability—but also of change at the most fundamental level of individual and society. History has shown that a process of inevitable change in matters of sexual partnerships and practices arises from social movement. Change in sex norms go against the grain of many traditional ways of thinking: what seems embedded in the cultural consciousness in terms of sexual thinking—that certain things are "permanent and natural and forever," such as women's roles or the preferred sexual technique (for example, genital-to-genital sexual intercourse, "missionary position")—are subject to revision, and sometimes to quite radical change. Indeed, the pace of change would have been unimaginable before the AIDS epidemic made populations accustomed to sex education campaigns aimed at the explicit change of behavior and cultural attitudes…. Thus the boundaries between peoples, and the lines drawn between ethnic groups and tribes, nations and states, regions and market networks, are breaking down, or being constantly transgressed and built back up again, through human sexual encounters.

The traveler from one culture to another is destined to encounter potential variation in sexual norms and roles. Cultures vary enormously in how they approve or disapprove of sexual behavior, such as sexual play in childhood, or in variations in sexual conduct that include pleasure or non-reproductive fore-play between the married couple. Likewise, significant differences across groups occur in how they approve or disapprove of sexuality outside the context of marriage and reproduction; indeed, a society such as America has seen change within its own ideology, from an emphasis on reproduction to one of pleasure, particularly in the two sexual revolutions of this century. Temporary movement on the part of the tourist is a form of migration that must be reckoned with in the globalization of sexually transmitted diseases….

Consider for instance the differences in cultural attitudes towards the presence or absence of commercial sex and institutionalized sex workers that greet the tourist or traveler to other cultures. Historically, societies differ markedly in their tolerance of commercial sex, from the later Roman Empire—which imposed rigorous rules on sex with slaves—to the nineteenth-century United States with their Comstock Laws intended to regulate prostitution; such variation continues up to the present. Today, groups differ in their received social attitudes and customs about commercial sex, which are often influenced by moral systems and ethical codes, particularly those of the great world religions. But it is precisely these variations in standards that lead tourists and travelers to exotic places, whether Bangkok or Amsterdam, in search of commercial sex that is either illegal or much more difficult to locate and safely enjoy in their home countries.

Sometimes movements from cities to smaller towns or agrarian areas are important to the demographics of movement in the era of AIDS. The shift from rural to urban settings is part of the process. But there is an oscillation, a back-and-forth dialectic, often overlooked in movements that occur from the cities to the rural villages. One of the lessons of the AIDS epidemic and international research on it has been to demonstrate the fallacy of believing that human movement is always a one-way street. Thus, individuals may move to the city, and after a period of life there, perhaps having succeeded financially or failed, as the case may be, they return to the village or smaller town where they expect to find a home and security. The views of commercial sex workers … emphasize the role of reverse migration, and temporary oscillations of movement from towns to cities.

The HIV/AIDS pandemic has fostered a virtual revolution of social change as the education and prevention efforts against the disease have expanded into countries and regions of the world. A vast transformation of sexual customs is occurring in the face of the epidemic, as a recent volume of cultural case studies from around the world has demonstrated.

Questions for Reflection and Discussion

What historical factors have contributed to the scope of the AIDS crisis in the world? How is the impact of AIDS unique in history?

174. PROSTITUTION IN THAILAND

Time: early twenty-first century CE
Place: Thailand
Author: Siroj Sorajjakool

Siroj Sorajjakool, professor of religion at Loma Linda University in the United States, sees a religious imperative behind his efforts to end child prostitution in his native Thailand, where he estimates 800,000 prostitutes are below the age of 16, 200,000 of them younger than 12. His book, Child Prostitution in Thailand, *claims that the legal safeguards set in place to protect children from sexual exploitation are not working, as described in this passage. Elsewhere in his book, he suggests that efforts to improve education and fight poverty will have better and longer lasting effects. He uses the past to predict future developments, even while admitting that such predictions are imperfect.*

The Suppression of Prostitution Act, B.E. 2503 (1960) was intended to wipe out all forms of prostitution in Thailand, which was legalized prior to 1960. This act punished prostitutes more severely than procurers. An arrested prostitute could face imprisonment for three to six months and a fine of 1,000 to 2,000 *baht*, according to the act of prostitution. Prostitutes could be retained for rehabilitation for up to two years. Procurers, on the other hand, faced up to three months of imprisonment and a 1,000-*baht* fine with no rehabilitation. In assessing the 1960 suppression act, Wanchai Roujanavong, Senior Expert State Attorney, Office of the Attorney General, stated: "When prostitutes themselves were targets of suppression and were treated as criminals, they were pushed into protection of procurers who had influence with law enforcement officials. Not only did the Act fail to suppress prostitution as planned, but the Act also encouraged prostitution to be widespread and increased in numbers and forms. Within the period of 36 years the Act had been in use, prostitution had grown and prospered unchecked. Organized criminal rings benefited from prostitution business grew stronger with increasing influence and power."

The present act, which came into effect December 21, 1996, sees prostitutes as victims of poverty and organized crime. Hence, its primary aim is to punish procurers, brothel owners, mama-sans, pimps, customers, and parents who sell their children…. The younger the prostitutes, the heavier the punishment. The punishment becomes more serious when crime against prostitutes turns violent….

The mushrooming of various types of sex industry, such as restaurants and cafes, karaoke, cocktail lounges, and *salaya dong* is, according to many staff workers of various NGOs, partially the result of the Prevention and Suppression of Prostitution Act of 1996. Chitrapom Vanaspongse of ECPAT International, who used to observe young girls walking around in Pattaya soliciting clients, said, "After 1996 you can't find these girls by the street soliciting clients. They are now working in bars or karaokes." It is still about sex, but the form has changed. Owners of these various types of sex business are also circumventing the law, becoming quite creative in supplying sex for cash without getting caught. For example, a restaurant owner will hire a girl to work until midnight or one in the morning. The girl's salary depends on this working hour. However, if a client wishes to sleep with a girl, that client will have to pay the owner 1,500 *baht* to "off" (slang for taking a girl out for sex) her to a motel or hotel. In this way, both the owner and the girl are paid for providing sexual service to the client. Although the girl may be paid for sex, the owner is also compensated for the girl's working hour. It does not matter if the girl leaves the restaurant at 11:00 p.m. or earlier; the same payment is due to the owner. It is understood that none of these girls is paid 1,500 *baht* for two or more hours. The law cannot fault the owner for providing sexual services, however, because the owner does not get paid for providing sex; the owner is compensated for the worker's lost time. As far as the owner is concerned, the sexual negotiation is between the girl and the client.

The second factor driving the change in the sex industry involves the education campaigns by various governmental agencies and NGOs, which have significantly reduced the number of girls from northern provinces entering into prostitution. These programs focus on instilling a sense of pride and dignity among young girls, teaching them that prostitution is not the solution, and offering them alternatives through career training or educational scholarships. These campaigns best explain the phrase I commonly heard while visiting northern Thailand: "Children in our area no longer work as prostitutes."

The final factor behind the change is consumerism, which has fostered a generation of young girls who opt for the life of prostitution to maintain a "better" lifestyle. When products that flood markets dictate lifestyle, society redefines how one ought to live, living by the rules designed by advertising agencies. City girls need to supplement their income so that they can go to school, pay rent, fit in, support their families, and carry mobile phones. According to the research "Factors That Lead Young Girls to Enter Prostitution in Chiang Mai," by Thai Women of Tomorrow, Chiang Mai University, every single girl in their sample population who volunteered her sex services did so because of her level of poverty. If given an alternative, none of them would have chosen prostitution.

Questions for Reflection and Discussion

How do the interconnections of the modern world affect child prostitution in Thailand? What is the lesson of history about prostitution, in Thailand or generally in the world?

175. PORNOGRAPHY AND THE OPPRESSION OF WOMEN

Time: late twentieth century CE
Place: United States
Authors: Andrea Dworkin and Catharine MacKinnon

Feminist writers Andrea Dworkin and Catharine MacKinnon are famous for their concerted and longstanding efforts to raise awareness about pornography and its relationship to attitudes

Some people claim that pornography is irrelevant to violence against women. They say that
pornography is new and contemporary and that
rape, battery, and prostitution are old. They
say that pornography cannot be a cause of violence against women because violence against
women existed long before pornography. This
is not true, but suppose it were. Even if pornography is a cause now, and never was before, we
would have to do something about it now. Think
about environmental pollution. It causes various kinds of cancer (though those who make the
pollution don't think so). Cancer existed long
before the kinds of environmental pollution that
come from highly industrialized societies. But
this does not mean that pollution in our society
does not cause cancer in our society.

In fact, pornography has a long history in
Western civilization (and in Asian and other
civilizations too). Its history is as long as the
documented history of rape and prostitution
(the so-called oldest profession, the misogy-
nist meaning being that as long as there have
been women, women have prostituted themselves). We can trace pornography without any
difficulty back as far as ancient Greece in the
West. Pornography is a Greek word. It means
the graphic depiction of women as the lowest,
most vile whores. It refers to writing, etching,
or drawing of women who, in real life, were
kept in female sexual slavery in ancient Greece.
Pornography has always, as far back as we can
go, had to do with exploiting, debasing, and
violating women in forced sex. Drawings, etch-
ings, and writings were made of or about the

female sex slaves performing forced sex acts.
Women were used in brothels to create live
pornography for men.

The invention of the camera changed the
social reality of pornography. First, it created a bigger market for live women because
live women were required to make the photographs. Someone could make a drawing out
of his imagination or memory. A photograph
turned a living woman into an exploited pornographic commodity. Pornography less and
less existed in the realm of drawing, contigu-
ous with art and imagination, and more and
more it existed in the purposeful and exciting realm of documented sexual violation.
Photographs acquired commercial primacy,
and this meant that pornography required
the sexual exploitation and violation of real
women to exist in a world redefined by the
camera. Second, mass means of producing the
photographs democratized pornography. As
writing, etching, or drawing, or as live shows
in brothels, it had been the domain of rich
men, aristocrats. Now the technology made it
available to all men. Video has remarkably fur-
thered this trend, bringing pornography into
the home, both the product itself and the video
camera that allows the man to make his own
pornography of his wife or lover or child.

The role of written or drawn pornography in sexual abuse before the invention of
the camera was not studied. The rights of
women did not matter. The rights of women
in brothels were not an issue. Violence against
women did not matter. The use of women in
live pornographic scenarios or as models for
pornographic drawings did not matter to the
men who used them or to the society that
allowed these uses of women. If written or
drawn pornography was used in the sexual
abuse of women, prostitutes, or children, it did
not matter. None of them had any legal rights
of personhood.

Questions for Reflection and Discussion

What is the link that Dworkin and MacKinnon claim exists between pornography and the oppression of women? What has changed in the last century regarding this relationship? Would gay or lesbian pornography have the same effects?

176. ISLAM AND WOMEN'S SEXUALITY

Time: early twenty-first century CE
Place: United States
Author: Leila Ahmed

Leila Ahmed, a professor at Harvard Divinity School, wrote the pioneering study Women and Gender in Islam, *published in 1992, and other writings on the relationship between Islam, women, and sexuality. This excerpt, from an essay in* Women and Sexualities in Muslim Societies, *demonstrates her use of traditional religious texts, the Qur'an and hadith, to support her argument for women's equality in modern Islam. She sees herself as working against Islamic fundamentalism by showing historical alternatives. In 1999 she published* A Border Passage *recounting her childhood in Cairo and her education in Cambridge, England.*

All schools of medieval Muslim law ... permitted contraception, though a minority did disapprove of it. The majority also permitted abortion, though there was less unanimity on this matter. With regard to contraception, the legally controversial issue which generated the most debate among jurists was not whether it was permitted, but whether a man may practice it without his wife's permission. The woman's right to practice contraception was not a legally controversial issue and was touched on only in passing in the literature—a point which confirms that it was practiced and was regarded as legally noncontroversial. Some jurists debated whether a wife required a husband's consent to practice contraception, most judging that she did not.

The jurists arrived at these opinions on the basis of what they understood the sacred texts to be saying about the nature of human conception, and about the sexual rights of marital partners. The texts they consulted were in the first place the Koran, and secondly also the *Hadith*—a corpus of literature written down in the course of roughly the first two centuries of Islam (that is the seventh and eighth centuries of the Christian era) recording the acts and sayings of the Prophet Muhammad. Though the *Hadith* were not sacred in the sense that the Koran is, they were revered texts and were drawn on as supplementary to the Koran as sources of legal practice.

The views that contraception and abortion were permissible were based on both Koranic and *Hadith* passages. A verse the jurists quoted on the matter was the Koranic statement, addressed to humanity, "We created you from a single [pair] of a male and a female" (Sura 49:13). This they referred to in their discussions of the nature of male and female contributions to conception, using the verse to counter the Aristotelian and Biblical views of the superior importance of male seed—views which had their proponents ... among Islamic philosophers (as distinct from jurists). The jurists quoted a number of other Koranic passages to argue that neither male nor female seed was in itself important. One such passage, to give an example, reads in translation as follows: "Man We did create from a quintessence [of clay]; then We placed him as [a drop of] sperm in a place of rest, firmly fixed; then We made the sperm into a clot of congealed blood; then of that clot We made a [fetus] lump; then We made of the lump bones and clothed the bones with flesh; then We developed out of it another creature" (Sura 23:12-14).

The passage was read to mean not only that neither male nor female contribution was anything special until the fetus formed, but also that only after a certain point in its development did the fetus acquire a soul—at the point in the verse where, after it states "We … clothed the bones in flesh," it goes on, "then We developed out of it another creature." Abortion was consequently permitted up to that moment—calculated as occurring at the end of the fourth month of pregnancy by some law schools, earlier by others.

Hadith passages were more explicit both with regard to female contribution to conception and to the permissibility of spilling male seed. They make clear to begin with that women as well as men have what is rendered in English as "semen." Thus one *Hadith* reports a number of women as asking the Prophet whether it was necessary for them to wash after having "nocutral dreams" as men were required to do. He replied that, as with a man, a woman should wash if there were any trace of fluid. Another *Hadith* reports a man asking the Prophet whether women had "fluid" or "discharge." The Prophet replied: "Yes … that is why the son resembles his mother." Other *Hadith* state that male and female contribution to conception is equal. Further *Hadith* make clear that male semen is in no way special. In one *Hadith*, for example, a soldier asks the Prophet whether it was permissible to practice withdrawal (a male contraceptive method) with female captives. The Prophet replied that it was, since if God wanted to create something, no one could avert it. In another *Hadith*, the Prophet is told that the Jews believe differently, and he replies that they are wrong, and again states that if God wants to create something, nothing can avert it. On the basis of such

Hadith, al-Ghazali, one of Islam's most influential theologians, categorically stated that female fluid was "a fundamental element," and consequently that male semen could not be regarded as endowed with specialness on emission from the male. It needed to be implanted in the womb and united with female fluid to be considered life-bearing.

It was what the sacred texts had to say on the sexual rights and rights to offspring of marital partners—or what the jurists construed them to be saying on these matters—rather than what they had to say about conception that made the issue of men's right to use contraceptive practices with their wives controversial and, to a much lesser extent, women's right to practice contraception. The reason some jurists thought that men may not practice contraception (the commonest male method was withdrawal) without a wife's permission was, firstly, that they believed it would interfere with her complete sexual satisfaction, and, secondly, that it would deprive her of offspring, to both of which a wife was entitled. Some jurists argued that women and men were entitled to sexual satisfaction from spouses, but not to offspring, and that male withdrawal did not necessarily deprive women of complete satisfaction, and therefore that men did not need their wives' consent. As this might suggest, most jurists regarded the purpose of marriage—which in Islam is a contractual relation between two individuals, not a sacrament—as being primarily that of the sexual satisfaction of both partners, satisfaction that required no justification by reference to procreation.

A number of *Hadith* formed the basis of the jurists' opinion that women had a right to complete sexual satisfaction in marriage. In one such *Hadith* a woman complained to Muhammad that her husband practiced sexual abstinence out of religious zeal, and Muhammad rebuked the husband on the grounds both that Islam did not require or even approve of abstinence, and that he had sexual obligations toward his wife. In another *Hadith*, a woman who had had one husband and was now married to a second, came to the Prophet wishing to return to her first husband and asking to be divorced from the second because of the latter's sexual inadequacy. The *Hadith* reports that others standing by were shocked at her candid speech and rebuked her, but the Prophet, who smiled, responded sympathetically—and his doing so is taken as indicating that women have a right to sexual satisfaction in marriage.

In addition, the Koran may also be read as being sympathetic in its portrayal of female sexual desire. In its version of the story of Joseph and Potiphar's wife, Potiphar's wife, Zuleikha, as in the Bible, desires and pursues Joseph and, when he rejects her, falsely accuses him to her husband; her desire and deceit— again as in the Bible—are then exposed. In the Koran the story continues that when the women of the city learned of Zuleikha's conduct, they gossiped derisively about her. Hearing of this, Zuleikha invited them all to a banquet, and, making sure that each was given a knife, she arranged for Joseph to walk in. The women were so taken with his beauty that quite unawares they cut their own hands – after which they understood why Zuleikha had been overwhelmed by desire. Thus, while Zuleikha's conduct was wrong, it is portrayed as understandable, and the tale does not imply that female sexual desire is in itself evil (Sura 12:24-32).

The laws on contraception and abortion, although liberal even by contemporary Western standards in the amount of control of their own bodies that they gave to women, also were developed from within a perspective which saw male precedence as proper and natural and which further served male prerogative. The ways in which the laws regulating contraception and abortion express that perspective become apparent when one considers the broader legal environment of which these laws were a part and, in particular, when one considers the regulations affecting marriage and sexuality. It was a legal system which permitted polygyny and slave-concubinage, and which furthermore stipulated that men were economically responsible for their offspring from wives and concubines, and (as the Koran explicitly laid down) that once a slave woman had borne her master a child both she and her offspring became legally free and could no longer be sold as property, and also that the child became the man's legal heir along with his "legitimate" children.

It will readily be seen that given these laws it was to most men's economic advantage that women not bear many children—particularly if a man had more than one wife or concubine. And, by the same token, if a wife or concubine did not wish to bear children, this was no particular hardship for the man, since he might legally (a) divorce her and marry another woman, or (b) marry another woman or take a concubine without divorcing her. In the case of a concubine, as long as she bore him no children, he was always at liberty to dispose of her. Consequently, in broad terms, it was to men's advantage to allow wives or concubines to prevent either the conception or the birth of a child. It would have been even more to men's advantage had the law placed the decision for both contraception and abortion exclusively in the hands of men. That this did not become the law was an outcome of the views on human biology and on marital rights embedded in the sacred texts, and reflects also the fact that the principal text that the jurists set out to translate into law, the Koran, is powerfully charged with a sense of the equal humanity of men and women and of the importance of dealing justly with people, so that even a perspective which assumed that the Word of God intended to privilege men could not entirely eradicate that vision. And it attests also to the fact that the men interpreting the texts were genuinely seeking to develop a system which, according to their lights, was just and in accord with the injunctions of the Koran and were not by any means simply seeking to legalize privileges for themselves.

Questions for Reflection and Discussion

What is the value of studying history to women's struggle for sexual freedom, according to Ahmed? How did historical Islam allow opportunities for women's sexual freedom?

177. SAME-SEX MARRIAGE

Time: late twentieth century CE
Place: South Africa
Author: Ronald Louw

Same-sex marriage is currently much in the news, legal now in a few countries and debated elsewhere. In this excerpt from an essay on South Africa, Ronald Louw, a law professor in Durban, describes the issue in its historical context.

More than twenty years ago in a village some distance from Durban in KwaZulu-Natal a young African man by the name of S'bu got married in front of a small circle of friends. What made this otherwise everyday event unusual was that, firstly, he was marrying another man, secondly, the wedding took place in the home of the local Methodist minister, and thirdly, he was marrying the minister! S'bu, a waiter living in Pinetown, told me the story as follows:

When I was 18 years old (in about 1972) the minister called me to stay behind in church one Sunday to count the collection. After everyone had gone he called me into the vestry and told me that he liked me very much and wanted me to be his wife. I was shocked at first but I also liked him. He was about 55 at the time. He had a four-roomed house in the township and I used to spend a lot of time there looking after him and the house. I used to cook and clean and was very happy. After a couple of years he said we must get married. We then had a big party where we invited about 20 guests who were living the same type of life as we were. I had to cook all day for the party in the evening but I had a bridesmaid to help me. Then I got dressed in white: white trousers and a white shirt with big cuffs and I also carried some flowers. I had many necklaces on as well. One of the older people in the church, an old man who was also gay, married us. He also made a speech and said a prayer. We had a wedding cake and people brought presents for me. I also had a wedding ring.

The story of S'bu is one of the many fascinating episodes that I stumbled across in my study of the unresearched history of same-sex desire among African men in KwaZulu-Natal. In this chapter I trace back the origins of the wedding to a moment and a place (Mkhumbane, near Durban), and I argue that specific circumstances made possible new and public expressions of sexuality amongst African men.

It is impossible to talk of homosexual identity in South Africa as a single stable entity. Rather, a variety of homosexual identities have been and still are produced by a set of power relations within the contexts of neo-colonialism, capitalist development, and racial domination. Within these same relations constructions of masculinities have been forged. Homophobia frequently prevented the emergence of alternate masculinities, but it was not all-pervasive or uniform. In specific circumstances and communities homosexual identities could and did emerge. The new spaces of desire had a powerful liberatory capacity for masculine identities. Contrary to dominant images of African masculinity, there emerged in Mkhumbane a thriving and celebrated identity of same-sex relationships....

The episode ... that I recount here is built on a history going back to at least the end of the nineteenth century. In the context of this chapter, the term "marriage" is employed to refer to same-sex relationships that have appropriated to varying extents the discourse of marriage. The first recorded incidents occurred amongst a gang known as the Ninevites. The gang originated as a band of brigands operating in the hills south of Johannesburg but later spread to Zululand. With inevitable convictions following their criminal activities, the gang also began operating in the prisons under the name of the 28s. Under the leadership of Nongoloza, born in Zululand in 1867, the gang openly engaged in sodomy. It was in the prisons that the discourse of marriage became institutionalised. Gang members were divided into two groups, the fighters and the wives or "wyfies." It was this practice of taking wives that primarily distinguished the 28s from other gangs. Achmat points out that "The Ninevites are the only prison gang in South Africa who consciously adopt homosexuality as a creed, and who have a set of laws governing their sexual relations." The "wyfies" are, however, not only sexual partners who are protected from other gangs, but are also subject to the domestic drudgery of marriage of having to wash and care for their fighters....

Other recorded incidents of same-sex marriage among African men occurred on the gold mines. Towards the end of the nineteenth century South Africa developed a booming gold mining industry located initially in the city of Johannesburg. Through a process of various land acts the South African peasantry was forced off the land into wage labor on the mines. Movement to the cities was, however, regulated through influx control laws. Only men with labor contracts were allowed into the cities. Furthermore, they were compelled to stay in single-sex hostels or compounds on the mines and were allowed little freedom of movement. It was in the compounds that there developed the practice of what has become known as "mine marriages." Moodie records that the men or husbands were older men with mine experience who would take a young, new recruit to be their wives. As with the prison "wyfies," the wives were not merely sexual partners but would also have carried out domestic chores for their "hubbies."

Why did homosexual relations in Mkhumbane take on such an unusual form? The answers are to be found in locating the episode in its historical context. For decades prior to these events, Africans in South Africa had been subjected to European colonial expansion and land dispossession. Traditional lifestyles were severely disrupted, and a relatively stable peasantry was forced into wage labor both on white-owned farms and in the cities. In the latter very little of a once more autonomous life remained. Achmat points out that early accounts of same-sex desire among Africans did not develop the notion of a discontinuity giving rise to new sexual practices. He views the emergence of new homosexual practices as ruptures of former social formations which created new historical possibilities and produced new discourses of masculinity. These discourses had their own rules of formation. Achmat argues further that "the compound represented a new space of desire and that it fostered a number of practices, including male homosexuality—practices which irrevocably disrupted social relations in the countryside. In terms of the appropriation of pleasure in the body, a new freedom was created." Could Mkhumbane too represent "a new space of desire"?

Questions for Reflection and Discussion

What does Louw suggest has contributed to the uniqueness of the South African historical experience of same-sex relationships? How might this history affect contemporary discussions about same-sex marriage? What are other historical parallels?

178. OTHER HOMOEROTIC TRADITIONS

Time: late twentieth century CE
Place: Philippines
Author: Jomar Fleras

Jomar Fleras, a playwright and filmmaker with a background in public health, is currently president and chief executive officer for ReachOut Foundation, a group formed in Manila to fight AIDS that broadened to encompass reproductive rights and other public health issues. This passage is taken from his essay in The Pink Book, *a 1993 report of the International Lesbian and Gay Association, based in the Netherlands, on tolerance or intolerance of homosexuality across the world. Fleras contrasts the positive attitudes toward homoeroticism in the historical Philippines with more negative contemporary feelings.*

Before the Spanish *conquistadores* came, the Philippines were populated by Indo-Malayan scattered tribes known as *balangays*. At the head of the tribe was the village chieftain. But exercising more *de facto* power than the chieftain was the *babaylan* or *catalonan*, who was the shaman, the medicine man, the high priest, the overseer of sacred functions, and adviser to the chieftain. Power among tribal people is not perceived as political or economic, but supernatural and paranormal. In most cases, a "man whose nature inclined toward that of a woman," called a *bayoguin*, was assigned the role of the *babaylan*. The ancient tribes believed that the godhead consisted of the interaction of male and female components and that bisexuality or androgyny represented immortality. Thus, the male priest who dressed as a female symbolized bisexuality and, therefore, immortality. A 1738 chronicle of Fray Juan Francisco de San Antonio reports that *hombres maricones* (effeminate men), who were "inclined to be like women and to all the duties of the feminine sex," were "ministers of the devil" or "served as priests to a hermaphrodite god" of the Tagalogs (a Philippine ethnic grouping) prior to the Spanish arrival…. The effeminate *babaylans* were also known to have married men and to have lived with them. It was considered a great honor for a family to have its young son cohabit with the elderly *babaylan*. However, the man-boy relationship would be terminated when the boy was ready to marry; after all, men were still needed to repopulate the tribe….

We do not have colorful accounts of sex between women during pre-Spanish times. But ethnographic accounts and folk legends record the existence of female warriors, chieftains, and shamans. The most famous of them was Queen Urduja, legendary not only for her beauty but also for her strength. It was said that she could do battle with any man. Whether these women were lesbians was never mentioned. They could have indulged in sex with each other, or they could have merely been Amazons who were forced to do the work of men for the preservation of the tribe. With the dearth of written documents, we can only conjecture. What we may conclude from the available documents, is that before the Westernization of the Philippines, sex between people of the same gender was considered normal. Like most ancient societies, the *balangays* did not discriminate on the basis of sexual orientation. Effeminate men and masculine women enjoyed powerful and respected positions in society.

Questions for Reflection and Discussion

What role, according to Fleras, might history play in a reassessment of contemporary attitudes toward homosexuality? According to this approach, does it matter that there seems to have been no historical role for female homoeroticism?

179. CHANGING SEXUAL PARADIGMS

Time: late twentieth century CE
Place: Brazil
Author: Richard Parker

Richard Parker, an anthropologist and professor at Columbia University in New York, has studied sexuality and Brazilian society, and particularly the impact of AIDS and other health issues. This passage, from an article in the collection Latin American Male Homosexualities, *describes the changing ways of understanding sexuality in general and homosexuality in particular in twentieth-century Brazil due to the impact of globalism on local cultures.*

In seeking some understanding of the experience of homosexuality among young people in Brazil, it is absolutely essential to realize that the very notion of homosexuality itself is, in fact, but a rather recent development. In Brazil, as in the nations of the industrialized West, homosexuality has a history. While a whole set of ideas related to homosexuality (and by extension to heterosexuality as well) has recently taken root in Brazilian culture, these ideas have in fact been imported from the industrialized West—modeled on patterns that had already emerged in Europe and the United States. As relatively recent imports, such notions are far from the only, or even the dominant, way of conceiving the sexual universe in Brazilian culture. On the contrary, this modern, more highly rationalized way of thinking about sexual life that was originally developed in the West and only later imported to Brazil co-exists there with what is perhaps a far more deeply rooted set of traditional ideas about the nature of things sexual. Such traditional notions can perhaps best be described as a kind of folk model of the sexual universe....

Within the folk model of sexual life in Brazil, cultural emphasis seems to have been focused not merely on sexual practices in and of themselves, but on the relationship between sexual practices and gender roles—in particular, on a distinction between masculine *atividade* (activity) and feminine *passividade* (passivity) as central to the organization of sexual reality. It is in terms of this distinction that notions of *macho* (male) and *femea* (female), of *masculinidade* (masculinity) and *feminilidade* (femininity), and the like, have typically been organized in Brazil.... The symbolic structure of male/female interactions seems to function in many ways as a kind of model for the organization of same-sex interactions in Brazilian cultures. Within the terms of this model, what is centrally important is perhaps less the shared biological gender of the participants than the social roles that they play out—their *atividade* or *passividade* as sexual partners and social persons. A *homem* [man] who enters into a sexual relationship with another male does not necessarily sacrifice his *masculinidade*, so long as he performs the culturally perceived active, masculine role during sexual intercourse and conducts himself as a male within society. A *mulher* [woman] who conforms to her properly passive, feminine sexual and social role will not jeopardize her essential *feminilidade* simply by virtue of occasional (or even ongoing) sexual interactions with other biological females.

The same cannot be said, however, of the errant partners in such sexual exchanges. On the contrary, the male who adopts a passive female posture—whether in sexual or social interaction—almost invariably undercuts his own *masculinidade*, just as a female, in adopting an active, dominating, masculine posture undercuts her *feminilidade*. By upsetting the culturally prescribed fit between biological gender and social gender, both must sacrifice their appropriate categorization as *homem* and *mulher*. The failed *homem* comes to be known as *viado* (from *veado*, deer) or *bicha* (literally, worm or intestinal parasite, but also, instructively, the feminine form of *bicho* or animal, and thus a female animal) due to his inappropriate femininity, while the inadequate *mulher* is known as *sapatão* (literally, big shoe) or even *coturno* (army boot), due to her unacceptable masculinity....

As a number of writers have suggested, this model seems to have dominated the sexual landscape in Brazil throughout the 19th and early 20th centuries and continues to function, even today, both in rural areas as well as among the lower classes (many of whom are themselves migrants from the countryside) in Brazil's larger, more modernized and industrialized cities. Since at least the first decades of the 20th century, however, and increasingly during the course of the past ten to fifteen years, this traditional system has gradually begun to give way to—or, perhaps, more accurately, to co-exist with—a far more rationalized manner of thinking about the nature of things sexual: a model rooted, perhaps above all else, in the conception of modern science and imported to Brazil from Western Europe and the United States.

Introduced in Brazilian culture, at least initially, through the writing of medical doctors, therapists, and psychoanalysis, and translated only gradually into the wider discourse of popular culture, this new medical/scientific model seems to have marked a fundamental shift in cultural attention or emphasis away from a distinction between active and passive roles as the building blocks of gender hierarchy toward the importance (along European and North American lines) of sexual object choice as central to the definition of the sexual subject. In practical terms, perhaps, its greatest impact has been the creation of a new set of classificatory categories—notions such as *homossexualidade* (homosexuality) and *bissexualidade* (bisexuality)—for mapping out and interpreting the sexual landscape. By the mid-20th century, these new categories had become central to the medical and scientific discussion of sexual life throughout Brazil, and had been fully incorporated into the language of law and government as well. However, until perhaps the late 1960s or early 1970s, their influence seems to have been limited almost entirely to a small, highly educated elite—the same segment of the Brazilian population that has traditionally maintained contact with and been most influenced by European and North American culture....

Precisely at the same time that this new conception of same-sex relations was first making itself felt among the elite, a semi-secretive sexual subculture organized around the same-sex preferences and practices was itself beginning to take shape, principally among the popular classes in such large, rapidly industrializing and modernizing cities as Rio de Janeiro and Sao Paulo. Reproducing the distinction between *atividade* and *passividade* as central to the organization of sexual relations between members of the same sex, and indeed, exaggerating the importance of such distinctions almost to the point of caricature, this subculture seems to have placed less emphasis on a shared identity common to all its participants than on the simple fact of same-sex sexual contacts....

Thus, throughout the early and mid-20th century, two new models for the conceptualization and organization of same-sex desires and practices had begun to emerge in Brazil. These two models seem to have contrasted rather sharply both with one another and the traditional model of same-sex interactions available in popular culture. By the late 1960s or early 1970s, however, as a result of developments both within Brazil itself and in the outside world, the histories of these new models began to merge, ... making possible the progressive formation of what is now probably the most visible subculture anywhere outside the industrialized West. It would be a mistake, however, to view this Brazilian subculture as nothing more than an importation from abroad, a tropical version of the gay community as it exists in Europe or the United States. On the contrary, it has continued to respond in a variety of ways to the particularities of Brazil's own social and cultural context. Perhaps nowhere is this more evident than in its reproduction of such traditional categories as *atividade* and *passividade* in a profusion of sexual categories or types. Terms such as *viado*, *bicha*, and *sapatão* are reproduced, and other even finer distinctions are added. Effeminate *bichas*, for instance, are contrasted with *bofes* (studs or hunks), who are characterized in terms of their aggressive masculinity and their active sexual role. The man-like *sapatão* is contrasted with the more feminine *sapatilha* (literally, slipper), roughly like a butch dyke is contrasted to a femme. In the increasingly prominent world of male prostitution (which is, of course, a function not merely of desire, but also of poverty), a sharp distinction is drawn between the *travesti* (transvestite) and the *michê* (hustler, in this context), between an exaggerated feminine figure who clearly prefers a passive sexual role and an almost equally exaggerated masculine figure thought to be generally available for the active role but unwilling to perform the passive one....

Ultimately, then, what seems to have emerged over the course of the past decade in large urban centers such as Rio or Sao Paulo—and only to a slightly lesser extent in smaller cities such as Porto Alegre, Recife, or Salvador—is a relatively complex sexual subculture that, while surely woven from Brazilian cloth, nonetheless provides a model for the organization of sexual reality that is clearly very different from the more traditional patterns of Brazilian culture. While this new subculture tends to retain much of the fluidity or flexibility of sexual desire that seemed so typical in traditional culture, it organizes it and links it to the formation of identities in rather different ways, and it clearly offers those individuals whose lives it touches a radically different set of possibilities and choices in the constitution of their own sexual and social lives.

Questions for Reflection and Discussion

What has been the trajectory of changes regarding homosexuality in twentieth-century Brazil? How are the differences in slang terminology important in assessing these changes? How exactly does Brazil participate in larger global changes?

180. S/M HISTORY

Time: late twentieth century CE
Place: United States
Author: Charles Moser

Charles Moser, a San Francisco physician with a doctoral degree from California's Institute for Advanced Study of Human Sexuality, has long published on a variety of sexual minorities, often with the express goal of helping others to understand them. At the 2003 annual meeting of the American Psychiatric Association, he argued that sadomasochism, as well as fetishism, transvestism, voyeurism, and exhibitionism, should no longer be classified as mental illnesses and should be removed from the Diagnostic and Statistical Manual of Mental Disorders.

SM behaviors are seen throughout history, dating back at least to ancient Egypt and to the Hindu culture in India where books like the *Kama Sutra* portrayed sexuality as an art form wherein the "erotic arts were not only deemed worthy of respect but were thought to be divinely revealed." Western religion has always taught a receptivity toward certain elements often present in SM: suffering is frequently praised as a purifying force in Biblical literature and is graphically portrayed in Catholic sculpture and paintings of the martyred saints. The dominant/submissive dynamic is explicitly described and praised in a variety of relationships: God/man, King/subjects and husband/wife. Paradoxically, the mainstream religions of the West also profess a specific aversion to dominant/submissive sexual expression. Indeed, the puritan philosophy, a form of religious expression historically part of the American culture, "does not consider any action meritorious," says Theodore Reik in his 1941 book, *Masochism in Modern Man*, "if it is not connected with discomfort [and depri-

vation]." This same philosophical bent can be found at the heart of many religious beliefs including those of Catholicism and Judaism, and some of the societal taboos surrounding SM can be traced to such religious beliefs....

In the late fifteenth century, the first unambiguous case of SM was reported by Pico della Mirandola, who described a man who enjoyed sex only if beaten bloody with a whip dipped in vinegar. In 1516, Coelius Rhodiginus discussed a man who found a severe whipping to be a sexual stimulant, and Otto Brundel in 1534 reported the case of a man unable to have intercourse unless he was whipped. These cases, however, were seen as medical curiosities and not as psychosexual illnesses. Although exploring only the history of masochistic references Roy F. Baumeister states that he finds no record of such activity before 1500 and no historical record until the seventeenth century: "Then, abruptly, in the 18th and 19th centuries, there is abundant evidence of sexual masochism. Thus, sexual masochism is a modern phenomenon. Moreover, masochism is quite unusual in this respect: Most of the modern sexual practices, including many that would be considered deviant today, were familiar to the ancients."

During the late 1800s and the early 1900s, sexologists began exploring all sexual behavior. Many of the European sexologists were Jewish, enabling Hitler to label sexology a "Jew Science," eventually crushing the early sexological movement by imprisoning or killing these researchers throughout Europe, and burning their papers and books. Thus, much early understanding in the area of sexuality—including SM—was lost. While Havelock Ellis saw sadism and masochism as two complimentary emotional states, Sigmund Freud in 1938 introduced the combined term sadomasochism and noted that such states could be found in the same person. Additionally, Freud called this previously unremarkable behavior a "perversion," defining sadism as "an aggressive component of the sexual instinct" and masochism as "a continuation of sadism directed at one's own person," further helping to establish sadomasochism as a clinical entity. As a result of Krafft-Ebing's influence, the categories of sadism and masochism became available as diagnoses of sexual pathologies (disease). The pathological connotations are still evident; both sadism and masochism are defined as paraphilias (aberrant sexual activity) and listed as "mental illnesses" in the American Psychiatric Association's *Diagnostic and Statistical Manual (DSM) of Mental Disorders.*

In their review of sexual attitudes throughout history, Bullough and Bullough conclude: "Sadomasochism is a good example of the way a pathological condition is established by the medical community, for until it became a diagnosis, it received little attention and was not even classified as a sin." Moreover, the sadomasochist was only one of a number of sexual categories that were invented beginning in the nineteenth century; others were "pedophile," "transsexual," "fetishist," and "homosexual." To recognize the historical roots of this classification is to understand that the "sadomasochist" is a socially constructed category…. Such categories perform certain functions. To the public, it makes sense of what appears to be bizarre behavior. Indeed, the term "sadomasochism" is extensively used (especially by the media) to refer to a variety of behaviors that involve sex and violence, e.g., lust murders, rape, and spousal abuse. It is also employed in cases where sex is not involved at all, e.g., referring to a strict drill instructor as a sadist or the wife who stays with an alcoholic husband as a masochist. For professionals, the term reflects the increasing "medicalization of deviance"—that is, defining the behavior as a medical problem or illness.

Questions for Reflection and Discussion

Is Moser arguing that sadomasochism is a sexual identity? How does having a history help that argument? Does Moser assume that S/M existed in much the same way in past societies as now?

181. BISEXUALITY

Time: early twenty-first century CE
Place: Australia
Author: Steven Angelides

Steven Angelides, a historian teaching at the University of Melbourne, is currently working on a history of pedophilia, child sexuality, and child sexual abuse. These passages from his book, A History of Bisexuality, *a project very much influenced by social constructionism and queer theory, question the basis for organizing contemporary sexual categories.*

Doubts about the veracity of bisexuality as an identity are not new. Variously characterized within dominant discourses of sexuality as, among other things, a form of infantilism or immaturity, a transitional phase, a self-delusion or state of confusion, a personal and political cop-out, a panacea, a superficial fashion trend, a marketing tool, even a lie and a catachresis, the category of bisexuality for over a century has been persistently refused the title of legitimate sexual identity. Yet, as is all too familiar to scholars of sexuality, the same cannot be said with regard to homosexuality. Since its invention as a peculiar human species in late-nineteenth-century scientific discourse, the homosexual as a modern identity has been the object of a rigorous, frenetic, indeed paranoid, discursive essentialization. Far from having doubt cast incessantly upon its veritable existence, the homosexual has been mapped, measured, and monitored in what can only be described as an interminable and insane reiteration of the supposed "essence" and "truth" of its being. On a much smaller scale, but with as much scientific zeal, has been the cataloging of myriad other psychosexual "deviations." From the perverts invented by nineteenth-century sexology to the seemingly endless list of twentieth-century paraphiliacs, Western science has placed sexuality in a privileged relation to truth with regard to human subjectivity....

Curiously, however, the category of bisexuality seems to have been spared the rigors of this "never-ending demand for truth." Bisexuality continues, in fact, to represent a blind spot in sex research. This apparent oversight by our all-consuming regime of sexuality is particularly puzzling in view not only of the rather long history of research suggestive of the prevalence of bisexual practices in most human cultures, but also of the emergence, in many Western countries within the last two decades, of burgeoning and highly politicized bisexual movements.

At first glance it would appear, then, that bisexuality has said very little, and has very little to say, to this historical archive. However, I would argue that one of the primary reasons for bisexuality's apparent insignificance might be the fact that the defining mark of gay and lesbian history writing has been a methodological reliance on an identity paradigm. Central to this paradigm has been a distinction between sexual behavior and sexual identity. Constructionist historians, cautious of conflating homosexuality and homosexual identity, have found it useful to examine the history of sexuality through this distinction.... Neither

an act nor a palpable cultural identity—at least until the late 1960s in the case of the latter—bisexuality merely vanishes into the categories of hetero- or homosexuality.

When Alfred Kinsey professed a profound skepticism of the scientific validity of the categories of "normal" and "abnormal" for describing human behavior, he was in fact underscoring their inescapably subjective and thus culturally specific nature. For instance, the term "abnormal," he suggested, may refer to little more than a form of behavior that transgresses "the socially pretended custom." These were more often than not merely descriptive terms of reference for statistical variations of behavioral frequencies on a continuous curve. "One sometimes suspects," he reminded his readers, that normal and abnormal "are terms which a particular author employs with reference to his own position on that curve." Second, Kinsey rejected the widespread notion of separate species of sexuality. "We have objected to the use of the terms heterosexual and homosexual when used as nouns which stand for individuals." Moreover, Kinsey noted, "males do not represent two discrete populations, heterosexual and homosexual. The world is not divided into sheep and goats. Not all things are black nor all things white. It is a fundamental of taxonomy that nature rarely deals with discrete categories. Only the human mind invents categories and tries to force facts into separated pigeon-holes." ...

The work of Evelyn Hooker extended Kinsey's challenge to psychiatry's structuring opposition between the normal and the pathological.... Hooker as a practicing psychologist was able to "address directly the issues of greatest importance to clinicians." Using members and friends of the homophile group the Mattachine Society, Hooker published research that clearly contradicted the psychiatric association of homosexuality and pathology. Via widely used and independently assessed psychological tests, this was demonstrated in an article first published in 1957. Having attained a sample of thirty matched pairs of homosexual and heterosexual men who were not involved in psychological or psychiatric counseling, Hooker argued in "The Adjustment of the Male Overt Homosexual" that homosexuality was not synonymous with social maladjustment. "It comes as no surprise that some homosexuals are severely disturbed," declared Hooker. "But," she went on to say, "what is difficult to accept (for most clinicians) is that some homosexuals may be very ordinary individuals, indistinguishable, except in sexual pattern, from ordinary individuals who are heterosexual. Or—and I do not know whether this would be more or less difficult to accept—that some may be quite superior individuals, not only devoid of pathology (unless one insists that homosexuality itself is a sign of pathology) but also functioning at a superior level." Like Kinsey, Hooker also rejected the psychiatric method of extrapolating from a clinical population of homosexuals to homosexuals in general. So it was that such work was to provide a legitimate scientific basis for gay liberation to critique psychomedical knowledge and deconstruct the notion of binary species of sexuality....

Bisexuality does not therefore explain the existence of the identity or species of homosexual, as Freud and the sexologists assumed.... Rather, for these researchers the existence of homosexuality proves the bisexual potential of human beings.

Questions for Reflection and Discussion

Why does bisexuality challenge the notions of homo- and heterosexuality, according to

Angelides? Why does it challenge the very notion of sexual orientations?

182. THE MEN'S MOVEMENT

Time: late twentieth century CE
Place: United States
Author: Robert Bly

Robert Bly, a poet and storyteller, was instrumental in the popularity of what has become known as the Men's Movement. It is an attempt to find new role models for men, given the general failure of traditional models because of the rapid social change in the modern era. According to Bly, who is inspired by Carl Jung (see source 162), those models should come from ancient mythology, which provides keys to basic human patterns. In this excerpt from his 1990 book, Iron John, *he offers the "Wild Man," or "Lord of Animals" as he also calls him, as a model of healthy male sexuality. It is part of his larger project suggesting that the key to men's and women's future may be found in the past.*

The ascetic attitudes, or the popular longing to repress the libido, which grew so strong at the end of the pagan era, joined in Roman culture with fears of the libertine emphases of the Great Mother [Cybele] to form an antisexual front. A friend once told of his visit to the ancient monastery of Mount Athos in Greece, whose traditions date from the earliest days of Christianity. He sat one evening for several hours side by side with an old monk, looking out over the mountains and sea. He knew no Greek, but longed for a conversation about spiritual matters with the old man. The old monk must have sensed it, and said at last in English the sentence: "Women are evil." That was it. The idea implies that all sexuality is evil. We can sense the dark side of medieval culture in that story, and we can deduce from this instant in the monastery how little support the ascetic wing of Christianity, Islam, or the Sikh would give to a hairy Magdalene or a Wild Man.

Powerful sociological and religious forces have acted in the West to favor the trimmed, the sleek, the cerebral, the noninstinctive, and the bald. Blake said: "Priests in black gowns are walking their rounds, and binding with briars my joys and desires." Women's sexuality has suffered tremendously and still suffers from this tyranny of the bald, ascetic, and cerebral. The goddess Aphrodite, alive inside the female body, is insulted day after day. The same forces have doomed male sexuality to the banal and the profane and the hideously practical.

By contrast the Wild Man's elaboration through Indian imagination into Shiva honors sexual energy. We see statues of Shiva in great sexual glory sitting next to Parvati, whose sexual energy radiates from every inch of her body. Jesus had no wife or children, and the reason for his association with Mary Magdalene does not survive the Gospels. In Christianity, it was Paul who laid the ground for the hatred of sexuality, saying in the First Epistle to the Corinthians, "Let those who have wives live as though they had none." Origen performed the castration operation on himself. Justin reports that Christian men in his time, the second century CE, implored surgeons to remove their testicles; many monks of Mount Athos accepted castration at that time, and later, Gregory of Nyssa said, "Marriage, then, is the last stage of our separation from the life that was led in Paradise; marriage therefore, if it's an ellipsis, is the first thing to be left behind." Augustine said, "A man by his very nature is ashamed of sexual desire," and he, though he acted as a libertine in his youth, changed when he became Christian. Later in life, his sexual member rose, he said, whether he wanted it to or not. He called this "a movement of disobedience" which shows that "mankind since Adam has been entirely corrupt." The Wild Man would take that event to be a charming evidence of spontaneity. We know that inside Christianity, as inside Judaism and Islam, there have been and still remain contrary currents of opinion that defend sexual love....

With thinkers of Augustine's quality on our side, it's amazing that men can make love at all. Young men in contemporary culture conclude quickly that their sexual instinct is troublesome, intrusive, weird, and hostile to spirit. Permissive attitudes of the sort favored by *Playboy* editors miss the battle entirely, because *Playboy* assumes that male sexuality is secular, a sort of play, proper for a playboy. When the Church and the culture as a whole dropped the gods who spoke for the divine element in male sexual energy—Pan, Dionysus, Hermes, the Wild Man—into oblivion, we as men lost a great deal. The medieval Western imagination did not carry the Lord of Animals or the Wild Man on into a well-developed Shiva or Dionysus, and the erotic energy of men lost its ability to move, as they say in music, to the next octave.

Questions for Reflection and Discussion

What are the characteristics of the Wild Man? To what extent is sexual expression a necessary characteristic of male identity, according to Bly? How does he argue against history, as it were?

183. EVE KOSOFSKY SEDGWICK AND QUEER THEORY

Time: late twentieth century CE
Place: United States
Author: Eve Kosofsky Sedgwick

Eve Sedgwick has been called the "Queen of Queer" for her pioneering studies that challenged the usual classifications for studying sexuality. Her own research on modern English literature cham-

AXIOM 1: PEOPLE ARE DIFFERENT FROM EACH OTHER

It is astonishing how few respectable conceptual tools we have for dealing with this self-evident fact. A tiny number of inconceivably coarse axes of categorization have been painstakingly inscribed in current critical and political thought: gender, race, class, nationality, sexual orientation are pretty much the available distinctions. They, with the associated demonstrations of the mechanisms by which they are constructed and reproduced, are indispensable, and they may indeed override all or some other forms of difference and similarity. But the sister or brother, the best friend, the classmate, the parent, the child, the lover, the ex-: our families, loves, and enmities alike, not to mention the strange relations of our work, play, and activism, prove that even people who share all or most of our own positionings along these crude axes may still be different enough from us, and from each other, to seem like all but different species....

In the particular area of sexuality, for instance, I assume that most of us know the following things that can differentiate even people of identical gender, race, nationality, class, and "sexual orientation"—each one of which, however, if taken seriously as pure *difference*, retains the unaccounted-for potential to disrupt many forms of the available thinking about sexuality.

› Even identical genital acts mean very different things to different people.

› To some people, the nimbus of "the sexual" seems scarcely to extend beyond the boundaries of discrete genital acts; to others, it enfolds them loosely or floats virtually free of them.

› Sexuality makes up a large share of the self-perceived identity of some people, a small share of others'.

› Some people spend a lot of time thinking about sex, others little.

› Some people like to have a lot of sex, others little or none.

› Many people have their richest mental/emotional involvement with sexual acts that they don't do, or even don't *want* to do.

› For some people, it is important that sex be embedded in contexts resonant with meaning, narrative, and connectedness with other aspects of their life; for other people, it is important that they not be; to others it doesn't occur that they might be.

› For some people, the preference for a certain sexual object, act, role, zone, or scenario is so immemorial and durable that it can only be experienced as innate; for others, it appears to come late or to feel aleatory or discretionary.

› For some people, the possibility of bad sex is aversive enough that their lives are strongly marked by its avoidance; for others, it isn't.

› For some people, sexuality provides a needed space of heightened discovery and cognitive hyperstimulation. For others, sexuality provides a needed space of routinized habituation and cognitive hiatus.

› Some people like spontaneous sexual scenes, others like highly scripted ones, others like spontaneous-sounding ones that are nonetheless totally predictable.

> Some people's sexual orientation is intensely marked by autoerotic pleasures and histories—sometimes more so than by any aspect of alloerotic object choice. For others the autoerotic possibility seems secondary or fragile, if it exists at all.
> Some people, homo-, hetero-, and bisexual, experience their sexuality as deeply embedded in a matrix of gender meanings and gender differentials. Others of each sexuality do not.

The list of individual differences could easily be extended. That many of them could differentiate one from another period of the same person's life as well as one person's totality from another's, or that many of them record differentia that can circulate from one person to another, does not, I believe, lessen their authority to demarcate; they demarcate at more than one site and on more than one scale. The impact of such a list may seem to depend radically on a trust in the self-perception, self-knowledge, or self-report of individuals, in an area that is if anything notoriously resistant to the claims of common sense and introspection: where would the whole, astonishing and metamorphic Western romance tradition (I include psychoanalysis) be if people's sexual desire, of all things, were even momentarily assumed to be transparent to themselves? Yet I am even more impressed by the leap of presumptuousness necessary to dismiss such a list of differences than by the leap of faith necessary to entertain it. To alienate conclusively, *definitionally*, from anyone on any theoretical ground the authority to describe and name their own sexual desire is a terribly consequential seizure. In this century, in which sexuality has been made expressive of the essence of both identity and knowledge, it may represent the most intimate violence possible.

Questions for Reflection and Discussion

According to Sedgwick, is any categorization of sexualities possible? What would a history of sexuality look like, if it did not assume that the usual categories for studying it were appropriate and meaningful?

SOURCES AND FURTHER READING

Most modern studies about history in general—and there are many of these—will include discussions both of the usefulness of the past and of the difficulties with its reconstruction. The influence of Social Construction on women's history and the history of sexuality has been enormous over the last two decades, as evidenced by such titles as Jill Julius Matthews's *Good and Mad Women: The Historical Construction of Femininity in Twentieth-Century Australia* (North Sydney, Australia: Allen & Unwin, 1984); Ann Waltner's *Getting an Heir: Adoption and the Construction of Kinship in Late Imperial China* (Honolulu: University of Hawai'i Press, 1990); Jay Hatheway's *The Gilded Age Construction of Modern American Homophobia* (New York: Palgrave Macmillan, 2003); just to name a few of the many books and articles with "Construction" in the title, alerting the reader to the author's careful position on avoiding historical anachronism. More theoretical works on the movement exist, include John Money's *Gendermaps: Social Constructionism, Feminism, and Sexosophical History* (New York: Continuum, 1995); and—perhaps for theory in more manageable chunks—the essays in *Feminist Approaches to Theory and Methodology: An Interdisciplinary Reader*, Sharlene Hesse-Biber et al., eds. (Oxford: Oxford University Press, 1999); or in *Theorizing Masculinities*, Harry Brod and Michael Kaufman, eds. (Thousand Oaks, CA: Sage,

1994). A concise but forceful advocacy of Social Constructionism is David Halperin's "Is There a History of Sexuality?" *History and Theory* 3 (1989): 257–74; an equally vigorous opposition to Social Constructionism based on historical methods is Nancy Partner's "No Sex, No Gender," *Speculum* 68 (1993): 419–443. On the Social Construction debates in the history of homosexuality, see the essays in Part 3 of *Same Sex: Debating the Ethics, Science, and Culture of Homosexuality*, John Corvino, ed. (Lanham, MD: Rowman & Littlefield, 1997).

172. "Michel Foucault and the Repressive Hypothesis" is taken from Michel Foucault, *The History of Sexuality*, vol. 1, *An Introduction*, trans. John Hurley (New York: Random House, 1978), 3–9.

Foucault's own writings on the history of sexuality, the introductory volume from which this excerpt is taken, and volumes 2, *The Use of Pleasure*, Robert Hurley, trans. (New York: Vintage, 1985), on ancient Greece, and 3, *The Care of the Self*, Robert Hurley, trans. (New York: Vintage, 1986), on ancient Rome, are all difficult to comprehend. A very readable yet challenging analysis of Foucault's ideas, not only in his *History of Sexuality* but elsewhere, and their compatibility with the work of feminists on gender, sexuality, and the body is Lois McNay's *Foucault and Feminism: Power, Gender, and the Self* (Cambridge: Polity, 1992). See also Sara Mills's *Michel Foucault* (New York: Routledge, 2003) for a more recent overview of his ideas.

173. "The Spread of AIDS and Global Migration" is taken from *Sexual Cultures and Migration in the Era of AIDS*, Gilbert Herdt, ed. (Oxford: Clarendon, 1997), 7–9.

Discussions of the impact of AIDS from a historical rather than a medical or social service perspective include David Black's *The Plague Years: A Chronicle of AIDS, the Epidemic of our Times* (New York: Simon and Schuster, 1985); Mirko Drazen Grmek's *History of AIDS: Emergence and Origin of a Modern Pandemic*, Russell Maulitz and Jacalyn Duffin, trans. (Princeton, NJ: Princeton University Press, 1990); Linda Singer's *Erotic Welfare: Sexual Theory and Politics in the Age of Epidemic* (New York: Routledge, 1993); *AIDS and Contemporary History*, Virginia Berridge and Philip Strong, eds. (Cambridge: Cambridge University Press, 1993); or *AIDS: The Burdens of History*, Elizabeth Fee and Daniel M. Fox, eds. (Berkeley, CA: University of California Press, 1988). See also the American studies in Michelle Cochrane's *When AIDS Began: San Francisco and the Making of an Epidemic* (New York: Routledge, 2004); John-Manuel Andriote's *Victory Deferred: How AIDS Changed Gay Life in America* (Chicago: University of Chicago Press, 1999); or *The AIDS Crisis: A Documentary History*, Douglas Feldman and Julia Wang Miller, eds. (Westport, CT: Greenwood, 1998). See also comparative studies such as *In Time of Plague: The History and Social Consequences of Lethal Epidemic Disease*, Arien Mack, ed. (New York: New York University Press, 1991); *Disease in the History of Modern Latin America: From Malaria to AIDS*, Diego Armus, ed. (Durham, NC: Duke University Press, 2003); *Histories of Sexually Transmitted Diseases and HIV/AIDS in Sub-Saharan Africa*, Philip Setel, et al., eds. (Westport, CT: Greenwood, 1999); *Sex, Disease, and Society: A Comparative History of Sexually Transmitted Diseases and HIV/AIDS in Asia and the Pacific*, Milton Lewis et al., eds. (Westport, CT: Greenwood, 1997); or Jacqueline Foertsch's *Enemies Within: The Cold War and the AIDS Crisis in Literature, Film, and Culture* (Urbana, IL: University of Illinois Press, 2001). See also note 154.

174. "Prostitution in Thailand" is taken from Siroj Sorajjakool, *Child Prostitution in Thailand: Listening to Rahab* (New York: Haworth, 2003), 19–22.

There are many studies on prostitution in modern Thailand. See Heather Montgomery's *Modern Babylon? Prostituting Children in Thailand* (New York: Berghahn, 2001); Thanh-Dam Truong's *Sex, Money, and Morality: Prostitution and Tourism in Southeast Asia* (London: Zed, 1990); Jeremy Seabrook's *Travels in the Skin Trade: Tourism and the Sex Industry* (London: Pluto, 2001); Siriporn Skrobanek et al.'s *The Traffic in Women: Human Realities of the International Sex Trade* (London: Zed, 1997); Ryan Bishop and Lillian Robinson's *Night Market: Sexual Cultures and the Thai Economic Miracle* (New York: Routledge, 1998); Leslie Jeffrey's *Sex and Borders: Gender, National Identity, and Prostitution Policy in Thailand* (Vancouver, BC: University of British Columbia Press, 2002); or Phongpaichit Pasuk et al.'s *Guns, Girls, Gambling, Ganja: Thailand's Illegal Economy and Public Policy* (Chiang Mai, Thailand: Silkworm, 1998). Comparative studies in prostitution can be found in *Global Sex Workers: Rights, Resistance, and Redefinition*, Kamala Kempadoo and Jo Doezema, eds. (New York: Routledge, 1998). Prostitution in Thailand is also described in the documentary film, *Trading Women* (US, Documentary Educational Resources, dir. David Feingold, 2003).

175. "Pornography and the Oppression of Women" is taken from *Making Violence Sexy: Feminist Views on Pornography*, Diana Russell, ed. (New York: Teachers College Press, Columbia University, 1993), 83–85.

On pornography in history, there are various studies, mostly modern, and mostly specific to a time and place. For general histories, see *The Invention of Pornography: Obscenity and the Origins of Modernity, 1500–1800*, Lynn Hunt, ed. (New York: Zone, 1993); or Walter Kendrick's *The Secret Museum: Pornography in Modern Culture* (New York: Viking, 1987) on literature, and Linda Williams's *Hard Core: Power, Pleasure, and the "Frenzy of the Visible"* (Berkeley, CA: University of California Press, 1989), on film. For discussions of modern pornography, see *Porn Studies*, Linda Williams, ed. (Durham, NC: Duke University Press, 2004). On the controversy over Dworkin and MacKinnon's views, see the first few essays in Lisa Duggan and Nan Hunter's *Sex Wars: Sexual Dissent and Political Culture* (New York: Routledge, 1995). For an opposing viewpoint to that of Dworkin and MacKinnon, see Nadine Strossen, *Defending Pornography: Free Speech, Sex, and the Fight for Women's Rights* (New York: Scribner, 1995).

176. "Islam and Women's Sexuality" is taken from Leila Ahmed, "Arab Culture and Writing Women's Bodies," in *Women and Sexuality in Muslim Societies*, Pinar Ilkkaracan, ed. (Istanbul: Women for Women's Human Rights—New Ways, 2000), 55–58, 62.

See the collection of essays from which this excerpt was taken for more studies on women and sexuality in modern Islam, especially Ahmed's essay; Fedwa Malti-Douglas's *Medicines of the Soul: Female Bodies and Sacred Geographies in a Transnational Islam* (Berkeley, CA: University of California Press, 2001); Imam's and Ilkkaracan's essays in *Good Sex: Feminist Perspectives from the World Religions*, Patricia Beattie Jung et al., eds. (New Brunswick, NJ: Rutgers University Press, 2001); see also the essays in *Everyday Life in the Muslim Middle East*, Donna Bowen and Evelyn Early, eds. (Bloomington, IN: Indiana

University Press, 2002). For more on contraception and abortion in modern Islam, see Sa'diyya Shaikh's "Family Planning, Contraception, and Abortion in Islam: Undertaking *Khilafah*," in *Sacred Rights: The Case for Contraception and Abortion in World Religions*, Daniel Maguire, ed. (Oxford: Oxford University Press, 2003). See note 89 for more on contraception and abortion in the Islamic tradition.

177. "Same-Sex Marriage" is taken from Ronald Louw, "Mkhumbane and New Traditions of (Un)African Same-Sex Weddings," in *Changing Men in Southern Africa*, Robert Morell, ed. (Pietermaritzburg, South Africa: University of Natal Press, 2001), 287–88, 293–94.

Most of the discussion about same-sex marriage has taken place in Europe and North America, and that is the subject of most of the writings on same-sex marriage, too numerous to list. See *Same-Sex Marriage: Pro and Con*, Andrew Sullivan, ed. (New York: Random House, 1997) for some of the issues involved and a sampling of the writings for and against it. On the broader issue of changes to marriage, see *Revitalizing the Institution of Marriage for the Twenty-First Century: An Agenda for Strengthening Marriage*, Alan Hawkins et al., eds. (Westport, CT: Praeger, 2002). For a historical discussion of same-sex marriage, if controversial, see John Boswell's *Same-Sex Unions in Premodern Europe* (New York: Villard, 1994). Louw's article is useful for South African traditions of male homoeroticism; for female homoeroticism, see Cheryl Potgieter's "From Apartheid to Mandela's Constitution: Black South Africa Lesbians in the Nineties," in *Ethnic and Cultural Diversity among Lesbians and Gay Men*, Beverly Greene, ed. (Thousand Oaks, CA: Sage, 1997), which also contains some historical infor-mation. Also interesting is the debate about the relationship between homosexuality and colonialism in Africa; on this point, see Marc Epprecht's "The 'Unsaying' of Indigenous Homosexualities in Zimbabwe: Mapping a Blindspot in an African Masculinity," *Journal of Southern African Studies* 24 (1998): 631–51, part of a special issue of that journal on masculinities in southern Africa, and now also his *Hungochani: The History of a Dissident Sexuality in Southern Africa* (Montreal, PQ: McGill-Queens University Press, 2004).

178. "Other Homoerotic Traditions" is taken from Jomar Fleras, "Reclaiming our Historic Rights: Gays and Lesbians in the Philippines," in *The Pink Book: A Global View of Lesbian and Gay Liberation and Oppression*, Aart Hendriks, et al., eds. (Buffalo, NY: Prometheus, 1993), 68–69.

There have been many studies done recently on diversity in gender and sexuality in modern Southeast Asia and the Pacific Islands. On the Philippines, see Frederick Whitam and Robin Mathy's *Male Homosexuality in Four Societies: Brazil, Guatemala, the Philippines, and the United States* (New York: Praeger, 1986); or Martin Manalansan's *Global Divas: Filipino Gay Men in the Diaspora* (Durham, NC: Duke University Press, 2003); or many of the essays in *Filipino Americans: Transformation and Identity*, Maria Root, ed. (Thousand Oaks, CA: Sage, 1997). On New Guinea, see Gilbert Herdt's *Guardians of the Flutes: Idioms of Masculinity* (New York: McGraw-Hill, 1981), his *The Sambia: Ritual and Gender in New Guinea* (New York: Holt, Rinehart and Winston, 1987), or his *Sambia Sexual Culture: Essays from the Field* (Chicago: University of Chicago Press, 1999); or Tobias Schneebaum's *Where the Spirits Dwell: An Odyssey in the New Guinea Jungle* (New York: Grove, 1988). On

Indonesia, see Dede Oetomo's "Masculinity in Indonesia: Genders, Sexualities, and Identities in a Changing Society" in *Framing the Sexual Subject: The Politics of Gender, Sexuality, and Power*, Richard Parker et al., eds. (Berkeley, CA: University of California Press, 2000). On Malaysia, see Tan Beng Hui's "Women's Sexuality and the Discourse on Asian Values: Cross-Dressing in Malaysia," In *Female Desires: Same-Sex Relations and Transgender Practices across Cultures*, Evelyn Blackwood and Saskia Wieringa, eds. (New York: Columbia University Press, 1999). On Thailand, see *Genders and Sexualities in Modern Thailand*, Peter A. Jackson and Nerida Cook, eds. (Chiang Mai, Thailand: Silkworm, 1999); *Lady Boys, Tom Boys, Rent Boys: Male and Female Homosexualities in Contemporary Thailand*, Peter A. Jackson and Gerard Sullivan, eds. (New York: Haworth, 1999); Megan Sinnott's *Toms and Dees: Transgender Identity and Female Same-Sex Relationships in Thailand* (Honolulu: University of Hawai'i Press, 2004); and Rosalind Morris's "Three Sexes and Four Sexualities: Redressing the Discourses on Gender and Sexuality in Contemporary Thailand," in *Circuits of Desire*, Yukiko Hanawa, ed. (Durham, NC: Duke University Press, 1994). On Samoa, see Jeannette Mageo's "Male Transvestism and Cultural Change in Samoa," *American Ethnologist* 19 (1992): 443–59.

179. "Changing Sexual Paradigms" is taken from Richard G. Parker, "Changing Brazilian Constructions," in *Latin American Male Homosexualities*, Stephen Murray, ed. (Albuquerque, NM: University of New Mexico Press, 1995), 242–51.

Richard Parker is a prolific writer, and the collection from which this excerpt is taken is a good starting point for studies on homo-sexuality in modern Latin America. On homosexuality in modern Brazil, see Parker's *Beneath the Equator: Cultures of Desire, Male Homosexuality, and Emerging Gay Communities in Brazil* (New York: Routledge, 1999); James Green's *Beyond Carnival: Male Homosexuality in Twentieth-Century Brazil* (Chicago: University of Chicago Press, 1999); or João Silvério Trevisan's *Perverts in Paradise*, Martin Foreman, trans. (London: Gay Men's, 1986). For comparative studies on gender and sexuality in modern Latin America, see *Male Homosexuality in Central and South America*, Stephen Murray, ed. (San Francisco: Instituto Obregón, 1987); *Family, Household, and Gender Relations in Latin America*, Elizabeth Jelin, ed. (London: Kegan Paul, 1991); Marvin Leiner's *Sexual Politics in Cuba: Machismo, Homosexuality, and AIDS* (Boulder, CO: Westview, 1994); *Machos, Mistresses, Madonnas: Contesting the Power of Latin American Gender Imagery*, Marit Melhuus and Kristi Anne Stølen, eds. (London: Verso, 1996); *Sex and Sexuality in Latin America*, Daniel Balderston and Donna Guy, eds. (New York: New York University Press, 1997); *Chicano/Latino Homoerotic Identities*, David Foster, ed. (New York: Garland, 1999); several of the essays in *Different Rainbows*, Peter Drucker, ed. (London: Gay Men's, 2000); *Gender and Sexuality in Latin America*, Gilbert Joseph and Stuart Schwartz, eds. (Durham, NC: Duke University Press, 2001); *Gender's Place: Feminist Anthropologies of Latin America*, Rosario Montoya et al., eds. (New York: Palgrave Macmillan, 2002); *Changing Men and Masculinities in Latin America*, Matthew Gutmann, ed. (Durham, NC: Duke University Press, 2003); and Sylvia Chant's *Gender in Latin America* (New Brunswick, NJ: Rutgers University Press, 2003).

180. "S/M History" is taken from Charles Moser and J.J. Madeson's *Bound to Be Free: The SM Experience* (New York: Continuum, 1996), 34–36.

See note 170 for more on S/M sexuality. On S/M in history, see *One Hundred Years of Masochism: Literary Texts, Social and Cultural Contexts*, Michael Finke and Carl Niekerk, eds. (Amsterdam: Rodopi, 2000); or Suzanne Stewart's *Sublime Surrender: Male Masochism at the Fin-de-Siècle* (Ithaca, NY: Cornell University Press, 1998). See also the still isolated but intriguing studies for earlier periods of history, such as Suzy Beemer's "Asceticism, Masochism, and Female Autonomy: Catherine of Siena and *The Story of O*," in *Medievalism in Europe II*, Leslie Workman and Kathleen Verduin, eds. (Cambridge: D.S. Brewer, 1997), on a medieval Christian saint.

181. "Bisexuality" is taken from Steven Angelides, *A History of Bisexuality* (Chicago: University of Chicago Press, 2001), 1–2, 6–7, 110–13.

Angelides's book is fascinating but difficult because of its reliance on theory. For more on bisexuality and history, see the essays in *Bisexuality: A Critical Reader*, Merl Storr, ed. (New York: Routledge, 1999); or in *Bisexual Politics: Theories, Queries, and Visions*, Naomi Tucker, ed. (New York: Haworth, 1995); or several of the essays in *Bisexualities: The Ideology and Practice of Sexual Contact with Both Men and Women*, Erwin Haeberle and Rolf Gindorf, eds. (New York: Continuum, 1998). An excellent discussion of many of the issues are to be found in Marjorie Garber's *Bisexuality and the Eroticism of Everyday Life* (New York: Routledge, 2000).

182. "The Men's Movement" is taken from Robert Bly, *Iron John: A Book about Men* (Reading, MA: Addison-Wesley, 1990), 247–49.

Several studies have tracked the recent men's movement, mostly in the United States, including Michael Messner's *Politics of Masculinities: Men in Movements* (Thousand Oaks, CA: Sage, 1997); Kenneth Clatterbaugh's *Contemporary Perspectives on Masculinity: Men, Women, and Politics in Modern Society* (Boulder, CO: Westview, 1997); Michael Schwalbe's *Unlocking the Iron Cage: The Men's Movement, Gender Politics, and American Culture* (Oxford: Oxford University Press, 1996); Clinton Jesser's *Fierce and Tender Men: Sociological Aspects of the Men's Movement* (Westport, CT: Praeger, 1996); *The Politics of Manhood: Profeminist Men Respond to the Mythopoetic Men's Movement (And Mythopoetic Leaders Respond)*, Michael Kimmel, ed. (Philadelphia: Temple University Press, 1995). The US group "Promise Keepers" combines elements of the men's movement with conservative Christianity; on its history, see John Bartkowski's *The Promise Keepers: Servants, Soldiers, and Godly Men* (New Brunswick, NJ: Rutgers University Press, 2004); or Ken Abraham's *Who are the Promise Keepers? Understanding the Christian Men's Movement* (New York: Doubleday, 1997). See also *Women Respond to the Men's Movement: A Feminist Collection*, Kay Hagan, ed. (San Francisco: Pandora, 1992). The large number of magazines published as part of the men's movement can provide interesting primary sources, including *Male View* in Britain, *Everyman* in Canada, and *Transitions* in the US. Of course, there have been other "men's movements" in history, especially for young men, including the Boy Scouts and the Young Men's Christian Association (YMCA); on their histories as men's movements, see

David Macleod's *Building Character in the American Boy: The Boy Scouts, YMCA, and their Forerunners, 1870–1920* (Madison, WI: University of Wisconsin Press, 1983); Thomas Winter's *Making Men, Making Class: The YMCA and Workingmen, 1877–1920* (Chicago: University of Chicago Press, 2002); and John Gustav-Wrathall's *Take the Young Stranger by the Hand: Same-Sex Relations and the YMCA* (Chicago: University of Chicago Press, 1998).

183. "Eve Kosofsky Sedgwick and Queer Theory" is taken from Eve Kosofsky Sedgwick, *Epistemology of the Closet* (Berkeley, CA: University of California Press, 1990), 22, 24–26.

On Eve Kosofsky Sedgwick, see Jeffrey Williams's "Sedgwick Unplugged: An Interview with Eve Kosofsky Sedgwick," in his *Critics at Work: Interviews, 1993–2003* (New York: New York University Press, 2004); or *Regarding Sedgwick: Essays on Queer Culture and Critical Theory*, Stephen Barber and David Clark, eds. (New York: Routledge, 2002). Sedgwick's own writings, of which *The Epistemology of the Closet* is perhaps the best known, are easier to read than most theory. The literature on queer theory is already vast, but see Annamarie Jagose's *Queer Theory: An Introduction* (New York: New York University Press, 1996); or Nikki Sullivan's *A Critical Introduction to Queer Theory* (Edinburgh: Edinburgh University Press, 2003). And already the numbers of histories influenced by queer theory are extensive; to see the range of issues and sexualities incorporated into "queerness," often indicated in their titles, see, for example, Henry Abelove's *Deep Gossip* (Minneapolis, MN: University of Minnesota Press, 2003); Susan Stryker's *Queer Pulp: Perverted Passions from the Golden Age of the Paperback* (San Francisco: Chronicle, 2001); or Jarrod Hayes's *Queer Nations: Marginal Sexualities in the Maghreb* (Chicago: University of Chicago Press, 2000).

BIBLIOGRAPHY

The following list contains only works that are predominantly about sexuality and related topics and those that are mainly composed of historical documents; admittedly, for recent history, the boundary between historical and contemporary documents is not always clear. There are many other collections of contemporary writings about aspects of sexuality; many collections that highlight writers from different periods; many more general collections on various periods that include sections about women, marriage, and the family; and anthologies of modern women's writings, all of which had to be excluded from this list, at the risk of making it too long to be useful at all.

Amt, Emilie, ed. *Women's Lives in Medieval Europe: A Sourcebook*. New York: Routledge, 1993.

Aughterson, Kate, ed. *Renaissance Woman: A Sourcebook, Constructions of Femininity in England*. London: Routledge, 1995.

Awde, Nicholas, ed. *Women in Islam: An Anthology from the Qur'an and Hadiths*. New York: St. Martin's, 2000.

Badran, Margot, and Miriam Cooke, eds. *Opening the Gates: An Anthology of Arab Feminist Writing*. Bloomington, IN: Indiana University Press, 2004.

Beam, Joseph, ed. *In the Life: A Black Gay Anthology*. Boston: Alyson, 1986.

Bing, Peter, and Rip Cohen, eds. *Games of Venus: An Anthology of Greek and Roman Erotic Verse from Sappho to Ovid*. New York: Routledge, 1991.

Birkby, Phyllis, ed. *Amazon Expedition: A Lesbian Feminist Anthology*. Washington, NJ: Times Change, 1973.

Birrell, Anne, ed. *New Songs from a Jade Terrace: An Anthology of Early Chinese Love Poetry*. Harmondsworth, UK: Penguin, 1986.

Bisexual Anthology Collective, ed. *Plural Desires: Writing Bisexual Women's Realities*. Toronto, ON: Sister Vision, 1995.

Blasius, Mark, and Shane Phelan, eds. *We Are Everywhere: A Historical Sourcebook in Gay and Lesbian Politics*. New York: Routledge, 1997.

Borris, Kenneth, ed. *Same-Sex Desire in the English Renaissance: A Sourcebook of Texts, 1470–1650*. London: Routledge, 2004.

Brozyna, Martha A., ed. *Gender and Sexuality in the Middle Ages: A Medieval Source Documents Reader*. Jefferson, NC: McFarland, 2005.

Busby, Margaret, ed. *Daughters of Africa: An International Anthology of Words and Writings by Women of African Descent from the Ancient Egyptian to the Present*. London: Jonathan Cape, 1992.

Castle, Terry, ed. *The Literature of Lesbianism: A Historical Anthology from Ariosto to Stonewall*. New York: Columbia University Press, 2003.

Clack, Beverley, ed. *Misogyny in the Western Philosophical Tradition: A Reader*. New York: Routledge, 1999.

Clark, Elizabeth A., and Herbert Richardson, eds. *Women and Religion: The Original Sourcebook of Women in Christian Thought*, 2nd ed. San Francisco: HarperSanFrancisco, 1996.

Cocalis, Susan, ed. *German Feminist Poems from the Middle Ages to the Present: A Bilingual Anthology*. New York: Feminist Press at the City University of New York, 1986.

De la Haye, Amy, ed. *Fashion Sourcebook*. London: Macdonald, 1988.

De Souza, Eunice, ed. *Purdah: An Anthology*. Oxford: Oxford University Press, 2004.

Dessaix, Robert, ed. *Australian Gay and Lesbian Writing: An Anthology*. Oxford: Oxford University Press, 1993.

Dodd, Kathryn, ed. *A Sylvia Pankhurst Reader.* Manchester, UK: Manchester University Press, 1993.

DuBois, Ellen, ed. *The Elizabeth Cady Stanton—Susan B. Anthony Reader: Correspondence, Writings, Speeches.* Boston: Northeastern University Press, 1992.

Elledge, Jim, ed. *Gay, Lesbian, Bisexual, and Transgender Myths from the Arapaho to the Zuñi: An Anthology.* New York: Peter Lang, 2002.

Faderman, Lillian, ed. *Chloe Plus Olivia: An Anthology of Lesbian Literature from the Seventeenth Century to the Present.* New York: Viking, 1994.

Fairbanks, Carol, and Sara Brooks, eds. *Farm Women on the Prairie Frontier: A Sourcebook for Canada and the United States.* Metuchen, NJ: Scarecrow, 1983.

Feher, Michel, ed. *The Libertine Reader: Eroticism and Enlightenment in Eighteenth-Century France.* New York: Zone, 1997.

Feminist Anthology Collective, ed. *No Turning Back: Writings from the Women's Liberation Movement, 1975–80.* London: Women's, 1981.

Fisk, Earl, ed. *Persuasions to Joy: An Anthology of Elizabethan Love Lyrics.* New York: George H. Doran, 1927.

Flores, Angel, and Kate Flores, eds. *Hispanic Feminist Poems from the Middle Ages to the Present: A Bilingual Anthology.* New York: Feminist Press at the City University of New York, 1986.

Francoeur, Robert, and William Taverner, eds. *Taking Sides: Clashing Views on Controversial Issues in Human Sexuality.* Guilford, CT: Dushkin/McGraw Hill, 1998.

Fraser, Antonia, ed. *Scottish Love Poems: A Personal Anthology.* Edinburgh: Canongate, 1975.

Galloway, David, and Christian Sabisch, eds. *Calamus: Male Homosexuality in Twentieth-Century Literature: An International Anthology.* New York: Morrow, 1982.

Gardner, Jane, and Thomas Wiedemann, eds. *The Roman Household: A Sourcebook.* London: Routledge, 1991.

Gay, Peter, ed. *The Freud Reader.* New York: W.W. Norton, 1989.

Goldin, Frederick, ed. *Lyrics of the Troubadours and Trouveres: An Anthology and a History.* Garden City, NY: Anchor, 1973.

Grubbs, Judith Evans, ed. *Women and the Law in the Roman Empire: A Sourcebook on Marriage, Divorce, and Widowhood.* New York: Routledge, 2002.

Hall, Lesley A., ed. *Outspoken Women: An Anthology of Women's Writing on Sex, 1870–1969.* New York: Routledge, 2005.

Hayes, Alan, and Diane Urquhart, eds. *The Irish Women's History Reader.* London: Routledge, 2001.

Hine, Darlene Clark, and Earnestine Jenkins, eds. *A Question of Manhood: A Reader in US Black Men's History and Masculinity.* Bloomington, IN: Indiana University Press, 1999.

Hodkinson, Keith, ed. *Muslim Family Law: A Sourcebook.* London: Croom Helm, 1984.

Holmes, Richard, ed. *Shelley on Love: An Anthology.* London: Anvil Press Poetry, 1980.

Houlbrooke, Ralph, ed. *English Family Life, 1576–1716: An Anthology from Diaries.* Oxford: B. Blackwell, 1988.

Hubbard, Thomas, ed. *Homosexuality in Greece and Rome: A Sourcebook of Basic Documents.* Berkeley, CA: University of California Press, 2003.

Hyman, Naomi, ed. *Biblical Women in the Midrash: A Sourcebook.* Northvale, NJ: Jason Aronson, 1997.

Jennings, Kevin, ed. *Becoming Visible: A Reader in Gay and Lesbian History for High School and College Students.* Boston: Alyson, 1994.

Johnson, Marguerite, and Terry Ryan, eds. *Sexuality in Greek and Roman Society and Literature: A Sourcebook*. New York: Routledge, 2005.

Karant-Nunn, Susan, and Merry Wiesner-Hanks, eds. *Luther on Women: A Sourcebook*. Cambridge: Cambridge University Press, 2003.

Katz, Jonathan, ed. *Gay American History: Lesbians and Gay Men in the USA: A Documentary Anthology*. New York: Crowell, 1976.

Kauffman, Linda, ed. *American Feminist Thought at Century's End: A Reader*. Cambridge, MA: Blackwell, 1993.

Kaufman, Shirley, et al., eds. *Hebrew Feminist Poems from Antiquity to the Present: A Bilingual Anthology*. New York: Feminist Press at the City University of New York, 1999.

Klinck, Anne, ed. *An Anthology of Ancient and Medieval Woman's Song*. New York: Palgrave Macmillan, 2004.

Kraemer, Ross, ed. *Maenads, Martyrs, Matrons, Monastics: A Sourcebook on Women's Religions in the Greco-Roman World*. Philadelphia: Fortress, 1988.

Krichmar, Albert, ed. *The Women's Rights Movement in the United States, 1848–1970: A Bibliography and Sourcebook*. Metuchen, NJ: Scarecrow, 1972.

Lan, Hua, and Vanessa Fong, eds. *Women in Republican China: A Sourcebook*. Armonk, NY: M.E. Sharpe, 1999.

Larrington, Carolyne, ed. *Women and Writing in Medieval Europe: A Sourcebook*. London: Routledge, 1995.

Levack, Brian, ed. *The Witchcraft Sourcebook*. New York: Routledge, 2004.

Leyland, Winston, ed. *Gay Roots: Twenty Years of Gay Sunshine, An Anthology of Gay History, Sex, Politics, and Culture*. San Francisco: Gay Sunshine, 1991.

Likosky, Stephen, ed. *Coming Out: An Anthology of International Gay and Lesbian Writings*. New York: Pantheon, 1992.

Lim-Hing, Sharon, ed. *The Very Inside: An Anthology of Writing by Asian and Pacific Islander Lesbian and Bisexual Women*. Toronto, ON: Sister Vision, 1994.

Lovell, Terry, ed. *British Feminist Thought: A Reader*. Oxford: B. Blackwell, 1990.

McCarthy, Conor, ed. *Love, Sex, and Marriage in the Middle Ages: A Sourcebook*. London: Routledge, 2004.

McCormick, Ian, ed. *Secret Sexualities: A Sourcebook of 17th and 18th Century Writing*. London: Routledge, 1997.

McKinley, Catherine E., and Joyce DeLaney, eds. *Afrekete: An Anthology of Black Lesbian Writing*. New York: Anchor Books, 1995.

Miller, Paul Allen, ed. *Latin Erotic Elegy: An Anthology and Reader*. London: Routledge, 2002.

Montgomery, Fiona, and Christine Collette, eds. *The European Women's History Reader*. London: Routledge, 2002.

Mudge, Bradford, ed. *When Flesh Becomes Word: An Anthology of Early Eighteenth-Century Libertine Literature*. Oxford: Oxford University Press, 2004.

Murray, Jacqueline, ed. *Love, Marriage, and Family in the Middle Ages: A Reader*. Peterborough, ON: Broadview, 2001.

Nicholson, Linda, ed. *The Second Wave: A Reader in Feminist Theory*. New York: Routledge, 1997.

Norquay, Glenda, ed. *Voices and Votes: A Literary Anthology of the Women's Suffrage Campaign*. Manchester, UK: Manchester University Press, 1995.

Oldridge, Darren, ed. *The Witchcraft Reader*. New York: Routledge, 2002.

Oram, Alison, and Annmarie Turnbull, eds. *The Lesbian History Sourcebook: Love and Sex between Women in Britain from 1780 to 1970*. London: Routledge, 2001.

Osanka, Franklin, and Sara Johann, eds. *Sourcebook on Pornography*. Lexington, MA: Lexington, 1989.

Patterson, Lindsay, ed. *A Rock against the Wind: Black Love Poems, An Anthology*. New York: Dodd, Mead, 1973.

Peacock, John, ed. *20th-Century Fashion: The Complete Sourcebook*. London: Thames and Hudson, 1993.

Peacock, John, ed. *Fashion Accessories: The Complete 20th Century Sourcebook*. London: Thames and Hudson, 2000.

Peacock, John, ed. *Men's Fashion: The Complete Sourcebook*. London: Thames and Hudson, 1996.

Peiss, Kathy, ed. *Major Problems in the History of American Sexuality: Documents and Essays*. Boston: Houghton Mifflin, 2002.

Penelope, Julia, and Susan Wolfe, eds. *Lesbian Culture, An Anthology: The Lives, Work, Ideas, Art, and Visions of Lesbians Past and Present*. Freedom, CA: Crossing, 1993.

Pitt-Kethley, Fiona, ed. *The Literary Companion to Sex: An Anthology of Prose and Poetry*. New York: Random House, 1992.

Plant, I.M., ed. *Women Writers of Ancient Greece and Rome: An Anthology*. Norman, OK: University of Oklahoma Press, 2004.

Press, Alan, ed. *Anthology of Troubadour Lyric Poetry*. Edinburgh: Edinburgh University Press, 1971.

Reade, Brian, ed. *Sexual Heretics: Male Homosexuality in English Literature from 1850 to 1900: An Anthology*. London: Routledge & K. Paul, 1970.

Reynolds, Margaret, ed. *Erotica: An Anthology of Women's Writing*. London: Pandora, 1990.

Rodriguez Matos, Carlos, ed. *PoeSÍdA: An Anthology of AIDS Poetry from the United States, Latin America, and Spain*. Jackson Heights, NY: Ollantay, 1995.

Rowlandson, Jane, ed. *Women and Society in Greek and Roman Egypt: A Sourcebook*. Cambridge: Cambridge University Press, 1998.

Sanders, Valerie, ed. *Records of Girlhood: An Anthology of Nineteenth-Century Women's Childhoods*. Burlington, VT: Ashgate, 2000.

Shelton, Jo-Ann, ed. *As the Romans Did: A Sourcebook in Roman Social History*. Oxford: Oxford University Press, 1998.

Silvera, Makeda, ed. *Piece of My Heart: A Lesbian of Colour Anthology*. Toronto, ON: Sister Vision, 1991.

Singer, Bennett, ed. *Growing Up Gay/Growing Up Lesbian: A Literary Anthology*. New York: New, 1994.

Smith, Susan Harris, and Melanie Dawson, eds. *The American 1890s: A Cultural Reader*. Durham, NC: Duke University Press, 2000.

Stanton, Donna, ed. *French Feminist Poems from the Middle Ages to the Present: A Bilingual Anthology*. New York: Feminist, 1986.

Suggs, David, and Andrew Miracle, eds. *Culture and Human Sexuality: A Reader*. Pacific Grove, CA: Brooks/Cole, 1993.

Sullivan, Andrew, ed. *Same-Sex Marriage, Pro and Con: A Reader*. New York: Vintage, 1997.

Sutherland, Alistair, and Patrick Anderson, eds. *Eros: An Anthology of Male Friendship*. New York: Citadel, 1961.

Thiebaux, Marcelle, ed. *The Writings of Medieval Women: An Anthology*. New York: Garland, 1994.

Tinling, Marion, ed. *Women into the Unknown: A Sourcebook on Women Explorers and Travelers*. Westport, CT: Greenwood, 1989.

Turner, James, ed. *Love Letters: An Anthology from the British Isles, 975–1944*. London: Cassell, 1970.

Varty, Anne, ed. *Eve's Century: A Sourcebook of Writings on Women and Journalism, 1895–1918.* London: Routledge, 2000.

Waelti-Walters, Jennifer, and Steven Hause, eds. *Feminisms of the Belle Epoque: A Historical and Literary Anthology.* Lincoln, NA: University of Nebraska Press, 1994.

White, Barbara-Sue, ed. *Chinese Women, A Thousand Pieces of Gold: An Anthology.* Oxford: Oxford University Press, 2003.

White, Chris, ed. *Nineteenth-Century Writings on Homosexuality: A Sourcebook.* London: Routledge, 1999.

Wilhelm, James, ed. *Gay and Lesbian Poetry: An Anthology from Sappho to Michaelangelo.* New York: Garland, 1995.

Wimbush, Vincent, ed. *Ascetic Behavior in Greco-Roman Antiquity: A Sourcebook.* Minneapolis, MN: Fortress, 1990.

Yohannan, John, ed. *Joseph and Potiphar's Wife in World Literature: An Anthology of the Chaste Youth and the Lustful Stepmother.* New York: New Directions, 1968.

Young-Bruehl, Elisabeth, ed. *Freud on Women: A Reader.* New York: W.W. Norton, 1990.

Sources

Ahmed, Leila. Excerpts from "Arab Culture and Writing Women's Bodies," from WOMEN AND SEXUALITY IN MUSLIM SOCIETIES. Edited by Pinar Ilkkaracan.

Al-Tifashi, Ahmed. "A Woman Criticized Me," from THE DELIGHT OF HEARTS OR WHAT YOU WILL NOT FIND IN ANY BOOK. Translated by Edward A. Lacey and edited by Winston Leyland. San Francisco: Gay Sunshine Press, copyright © 1988. Reprinted by permission of Winston Leyland Publisher.

Angelides, Stephen. Excerpts from A HISTORY OF BISEXUALITY. Edited by John C. Fout. Chicago: The University of Chicago Press, copyright © 2001. Reprinted by permission of The University of Chicago Press and of Dr. Stephen Angelides.

Apuleius. Excerpts from THE GOLDEN ASS: OR METAMORPHOSES. Translated by E.J. Kenney. Harmondsworth: Penguin Books Ltd., copyright © 1998. Reprinted by permission of the Penguin Group Ltd.

As-Salihin, Riyadh of Imam Nawawi. Excerpts from GARDENS OF THE RIGHTEOUS. Translated by Muhammad Zafrulla Khan. London: Curzon Press, Totowa: Rowman and Littlefield, copyright © 1974.

Attridge, Harold W. and Robert R. Oden. Excerpts from THE SYRIAN GODDESS (DE DEA SYRIA). Missoula, Montana: Scholar's Press for The Society of Biblical Literature, copyright © 1976. Reprinted by permission of the publisher.

Bhartrihari and Bilhana. Excerpts from THE HERMIT AND THE LOVE-THIEF. Translated by Barbara Stoler Miller. India: Penguin Books Ltd., copyright © 1990.

Bly, Robert. Excerpts from "The Wild Man in Ancient Literature" and "The Threat of the Wild Man in Europe," from IRON JOHN: A BOOK ABOUT MEN. Reading: Addison-Wesley, copyright © 1980 by Robert Bly. Reprinted by permission of Georges Borchardt, Inc., for Robert Bly.

Bogin, Meg. Excerpts from THE WOMEN TROUBADOURS. New York: W.W. Norton and Company, Inc, 1980. Reprinted by permission of Magda Bogin.

Boswell, John. "An Argument Against Romance," from CHRISTIANITY, SOCIAL TOLERANCE, AND HOMOSEXUALITY: GAY PEOPLE IN WESTERN EUROPE FROM THE BEGINNING OF THE CHRISTIAN ERA TO THE FOURTEENTH CENTURY. Chicago and London: The University of Chicago Press, copyright © 1980. Reprinted by permission of The University of Chicago Press.

Brown, Helen Gurley. Excerpts from SEX AND THE NEW SINGLE GIRL. Copyright © 2003 Helen Gurley Brown. Reprinted by permission of Barricade Books, Inc.

Bryant, Anita. Excerpts from "Appendix III: The Civil Rights of Parents: To Save their Children from Homosexual Influence," from THE ANITA BRYANT STORY: THE SURVIVAL OF OUR NATION'S FAMILIES AND THE THREAT OF MILITANT HOMOSEXUALITY. Old Tappan, New Jersey: Fleming H. Revell Company, 1977.

Castro, Fidel. Excerpts from "Fidel Castro: Speech to the Federation of Cuban Women," from WOMEN AND THE CUBAN REVOLUTION: SPEECHES & DOCUMENTS BY FIDEL CASTRO, VILMA ESPIN & OTHERS. Edited by Elisabeth Stone. New York: Pathfinder Press, copyright © 1981. Reprinted by permission of the publisher.

Chao, Pan. Excerpts from PAN CHAO: FOREMOST WOMAN SCHOLAR OF CHINA, FIRST CENTURY AD, BACKGROUND, ANCESTRY, LIFE, AND WRITINGS OF THE MOST CELEBRATED CHINESE WOMAN OF LETTERS. Translated by Nancy Lee Swann. Copyright © East Asian Library and the Gest Collection, Princeton University. Reprinted by permission of the publisher.

Chaucer, Geoffrey. Excerpts from "The Wife of Bath's Prologue," from THE CANTERBURY TALES. Translated by J.U. Nicolson. New York: Covici Friede Publishers, copyright © 1934.

Chodorow, Nancy. Excerpts from THE REPRODUCTION OF MOTHERING: PSYCHOANALYSIS AND THE SOCIOLOGY OF GENDER. Berkeley: University of California Press, copyright © 1978, The Regents of the University of California. Reprinted by permission of the University of California Press.

Conze, Edward (translator). Excerpts from BUDDHIST SCRIPTURES. Harmondsworth: Penguin Books, copyright © 1959. Reprinted by permission of the Penguin Group Ltd.

Crowley, F.K. Excerpts from MODERN AUSTRALIA IN DOCUMENTS 1901-1939. Melbourne: Wren Publishing, copyright © 1973. Reprinted by permission of Dr. Frank K. Crowley.

Dawood, N.J. (translator). Excerpts from TALES FROM THE THOUSAND AND ONE NIGHTS. Harmondsworth: Penguin Books, copyright © 1954, combined edition with revisions published by The Penguin Group in 1973. Reprinted by permission of the Penguin Group Ltd.

De Bary, Theodore (editor). Excerpts from "Accounts of the Eastern Barbarians – History of the Kingdom of Wei," from INTRODUCTION TO ORIENTAL CIVILIZATIONS: SOURCES OF JAPANESE TRADITION, VOLUME 1. Compiled by Ryusaku Tsunoda, Wm. Theodore de Bary and Donald Keene. New York: Columbia University Press, copyright © 1958, reprinted 1969. Reprinted by permission of the publisher; "Han Yi: Destroying the Family," from SOURCES OF CHINESE TRADITION, VOLUME 2, 2ND ED. Compiled by Theodore de Bary and Richard Lufrano. New York: Columbia University Press, 2000. Reprinted by permission of the publisher.

De Beauvoir, Simone. Excerpts from THE SECOND SEX. Translated by H.M. Parshley. Copyright © 1952 and renewed 1980 by Alfred A. Knopf Inc., a division of Random House, Inc. Reprinted by permission of Alfred A. Knopf, a division of Random House, Inc.

De Sade, Marquis. Excerpts from THE MARQUIS DE SADE: THE 120 DAYS OF SODOM AND OTHER WRITINGS. Translated by Austryn Wainhouse and Richard Seaver. New York: Grove Press, Inc., copyright © 1966. Reprinted by permission of Grove/Atlantic, Inc.

Dimock, Joseph J. Excerpts from IMPRESSIONS OF CUBA IN THE NINETEENTH CENTURY: THE TRAVEL DIARY OF JOSEPH J. DIMOCK. Edited by Louis A. Pérez. Wilmington: Scholarly Resources Inc., copyright © 1998. Reprinted by permission of Rowman & Littlefield Publishers, Inc.

Doniger, Wendy and Brian K. Smith (translators). Excerpts from THE LAWS OF MANU. London: Penguin Books Ltd., copyright © 1991. Reprinted by permission of the Penguin Group, Ltd.

Dowman, Keith and Sonam Paljor (translators). Excerpts from THE DIVINE MADMAN: THE SUBLIME LIFE AND SONGS OF DRUKPA KUNLEY. London: Rider & Co, 1980. Reprinted by permission of Keith Dowman.

Euripides. Excerpts from THE BACCHAE AND OTHER PLAYS: ION, THE WOMEN OF TROY, HELEN AND THE BACCHAE. Translated by Philip Vellacott. Harmondsworth: Penguin Books Ltd., copyright © 1954, reprinted 1969. Reprinted by permission of the Penguin Group, Ltd.

Excerpts from THE HISTORY OF THE TAHITIAN MISSION, 1799-1830. London: The Hakluyt Society, copyright © 1959. Reprinted by permission of David Higham Associates Ltd. on behalf of The Hakluyt Society.

Excerpts from THE NEW INTERNATIONAL VERSION OF THE HOLY BIBLE. The New York International Bible Society, Grande Rapids, Michigan: Zondervan Bible Publishers, © copyright 1978. Reprinted by permission of the publisher.

Ezra, Moses Ibn. "Poem 11," from WINE, WOMEN, AND DEATH: MEDIEVAL HEBREW POEMS ON THE GOOD LIFE. Translated by Raymond P.

Scheindlin. Philadelphia: The Jewish Publication Society, copyright © 1986. Reprinted by permission of the publisher.

Foucault, Michel. Excerpts from THE HISTORY OF SEXUALITY: VOLUME 1: AN INTRODUCTION. Translated by John Hurley. New York: Random House Inc, copyright © 1978. Originally published as *La volonté de savoir*. Copyright © Editions Gallimard 1976. Reprinted by permission of Georges Borchardt, Inc., for the Editions Gallimard and of The Penguin Group, Ltd.

Freud, Sigmund. Excerpts from "The Case of Dora," from FREUD: ON WAR, SEX AND NEUROSIS. Edited by Sander Katz and translated by Joan Riviere. New York: Arts & Science Press, copyright © 1947.

Goitein, S.D. Excerpts from A MEDITERRANEAN SOCIETY: THE JEWISH COMMUNITIES OF THE ARAB WORLD AS PORTRAYED IN THE DOCUMENTS OF THE CAIRO GENIZA: VOLUME III – THE FAMILY. Edited and translated by Jacob Lassner. Berkeley: University of California Press, copyright © 1999, The Regents of the University of California. Reprinted by permission of the publisher.

Gregory of Tours. Excerpts from THE HISTORY OF THE FRANKS. Translated by Lewis Thorpe. Harmondsworth: Penguin Books, copyright © Lewis Thorpe, 1974, reprinted 1982. Reprinted by permission of the Penguin Group Ltd.

Gunther, John. Excerpts from JOHN GUNTHER'S INSIDE AUSTRALIA. Edited by William H. Forbis. New York: Harper and Row Publishers, copyright © 1972 by Jane Perry Gunther. Reprinted by permission of HarperCollins Publishers Inc.

Hammurabi. Excerpts from THE BABYLONIAN LAWS: VOLUME 2. Edited and translated by G.R. Driver and John C. Miles, Ely House. London: Oxford University Press, copyright © 1955, reprinted 1968. Reprinted by permission of Oxford University Press, Inc.

Hardacre, Helen. "The Attainment of Liberation by the Maidservant of Takano Shinuemon," from MARKETING THE MENACING FETUS IN JAPAN. Berkeley: University of California Press, copyright © 1997, The Regents of the University of California. Reprinted by permission of the University of California Press and of Dr. Helen Hardacre.

Hendriks, Art et al. (editors). Excerpts from THE THIRD PINK BOOK: A GLOBAL VIEW OF LESBIAN AND GAY LIBERATION AND OPRESSION. Edited by Art Hendriks, Rob Tielman, and Evert van der Veen, Amherst. New York: Prometheus Books, copyright © 1993 by Art Hendriks, Rob Tielman, and Evert van der Veen. Reprinted by permission of the publisher.

Herdt, Gilbert (editor). Excerpts from SEXUAL CULTURES IN THE ERA OF AIDS: ANTHROPOLOGICAL AND DEMOGRAPHIC PERSPECTIVES. New York: Oxford University Press, Inc., copyright © 1997. Reprinted by permission of Oxford University Press, Inc.

Herodotus. Excerpts from HERODOTUS THE HISTORIES. Translated by Aubrey de Selincourt, revised by A.R. Burn. Harmondsworth: Penguin Books Ltd., copyright © 1954, revised edition 1974. Reprinted by permission of the Penguin Group, Ltd.

Hite, Shere. Excerpts from THE HITE REPORT. New York: Macmillan Publishing Co., Inc., copyright © 1976.

Hooker, Evelyn. Excerpts from "Reflections of a 40-Year Exploration: A Scientific View on Homosexuality." AMERICAN PSYCHOLOGIST 48.4 (1993). Washington: American Psychological Association, Inc., copyright © 1993. Reprinted by permission of the publisher.

Ihara, Saikaku. Excerpts from THE LIFE OF AN AMOROUS MAN. Translated by Kenji Hamada. Boston: Tuttle Publishing, copyright © 1963 Charles E. Tuttle Co., reprinted 2001. Reprinted by permission of Charles E. Tuttle Co., Inc. of Boston, Massachusetts and Tokyo, Japan; Excerpts from THE GREAT MIRROR OF MALE LOVE. Translated by Paul Gordon Schalow. Copyright © 1990 by the Board of Trustees of the Leland Stanford Jr. University. All rights reserved. Reprinted by permission of Stanford University Press, www.sup.org.

Ishimoto, Shidzue. Excerpts from EAST WAY, WEST WAY: A MODERN JAPANESE GIRLHOOD. New York: Ferrar & Rinehart, 1935 and 1936. Copyright © 1935, 1936, 1963 by Shidzue Ishimoto. Reprinted by permission of Henry Holt and Company, LLC.

Jones, Alexander (editor). Excerpts from THE JERUSALEM BIBLE: READERS EDITION. London: Darton, Longman and Todd Ltd. and New York: Doubleday, a division of Random House, Inc., copyright © 1966, 1967 and 1968. Reprinted by permission of the publishers.

Jung, Carl G. Excerpts from THE COLLECTED WORKS OF C.G. JUNG, VOLUME 10: CIVILIZATION IN TRANSITION. Translated by R.F.C. Hull. Copyright © 1964 Bollingen, 1992 renewed. Reprinted by permission of Princeton University Press.

Kalidasa. Excerpts from GREAT SANSKRIT PLAYS: IN MODERN TRANSLATION. Edited by P. Lal. Copyright © 1964 by New Directions Publishing Corp. Reprinted by permission of New Directions Publishing Corp.

Kant, Fritz. Excerpts from FRIGIDITY, DYNAMICS AND TREATMENT. Springfield, Illinois: Charles C. Thomas Publisher Ltd., copyright © 1969. Reprinted by permission of Charles C. Thomas Publisher, Ltd.

Kartini, Raden Adjeng. Excerpts from LETTERS OF A JAVANESE PRINCESS. Edited by Hildred Geertz and translated by Agnes Louise Symmers. New York: W.W. Norton and Company, Inc., copyright © 1964. Reprinted by permission of the University Press of America.

Kinsey, Alfred C. et. al. Excerpts from SEXUAL BEHAVIOR IN THE HUMAN FEMALE. Philadelphia: W.B. Saunders Company, copyright © 1953. Reprinted by permission of The Kinsey Institute for Research in Sex, Gender, and Reproduction, Inc.

Lactantius. Excerpts from LACTANTIUS: THE MINOR WORKS. Translated by Sister Mary Francis McDonald, O.P. Washington: The Catholic University of America Press, copyright © 1965. Reprinted by permission of The Catholic University of America Press, Washington, DC.

Lady Murasaki. Excerpts from THE TALE OF GENJI, VOLUME I. Translated by Arthur Waley. New York: Random House, 1993. Reprinted by permission of The Arthur Waley Estate and of Houghton Mifflin; Excerpts from THE DIARY OF LADY MURASAKI. Translated by Richard Bowring. Harmondsworth: Penguin Books, copyright © 1996. Reprinted by permission of the Penguin Group Ltd.

Leff, Leonard J. and Jerold L. Simmons. Excerpts from THE DAME IN THE KIMONO: HOLLYWOOD, CENSORSHIP AND THE PRODUCTION CODE. Lexington: The University Press of Kentucky, copyright © 2001. Reprinted by permission of The University Press of Kentucky.

Leitsch, Dick. "Police Raid on N.Y. Club Sets off First Gay Riot," from WITNESS TO REVOLUTION: THE ADVOCATE REPORTS ON GAY AND LESBIAN POLITICS, 1967-1999. Originally printed in *New York Mattachine Newsletter*, September 1969. Edited by Chris Bull. Los Angeles: Alyson Books, copyright © 1999.

Li, Yu. Excerpts from THE CARNAL PRAYER MAT (ROU PUTUAN). Translated by Patrick Hanan. New York: Ballantine Books, 1990. Reprinted by permission of van der Leun & Associates.

Ling, P'u Sung. Excerpts from "The Lady Knight-Errant," from RICE BOWL WOMEN. Edited by Dorothy Blair Shimer. Copyright © 1978 Columbia University Press.

Livy. Excerpts from THE EARLY HISTORY OF ROME: BOOKS I-V OF THE HISTORY OF ROME FROM ITS FOUNDATION. Translated by Aubrey De Selincourt. Harmondsworth: Penguin Books, copyright © 1960, reprinted 1971. Reprinted by permission of the Penguin Group Ltd.

Louw, Ronald. Excerpts from "Mkhumbane and New Traditions of (Un)African Same-Sex Weddings," from CHANGING MEN IN SOUTHERN AFRICA. Edited by Robert Morrell. London: Zed Books, 2001.

Lystra, Karen. Excerpts from "Lyman Hodge: untitled poem," from SEARCHING THE HEART: WOMEN, MEN AND ROMANTIC LOVE IN NINETEETH-CENTURY AMERICA. New York: Oxford University Press, Inc., copyright © 1989 by Karen Lystra. Reprinted by permission of Oxford University Press, Inc.

MacKinnon, Catharine and Andrea Dworkin. Excerpts from MAKING VIOLENCE SEXY: FEMINIST VIEWS ON PORNOGRAPHY. Edited by Diana E.H. Russell. Reprinted by permission of Teachers College Press.

Maimonides. Excerpts from THE CODE OF MAIMONIDES: BOOK FOUR – THE BOOK OF WOMEN. Translated by Isaac Klein. London: Yale University Press, copyright © 1972 by Yale University. Reprinted by permission of the publisher.

Malik. Excerpts from MUWATTA'IMAM MALIK. Translated by Muhammad Rahimuddin, Kashmiri Bazar Lahore. Pakistan: Sh. Muhammad Ashraf, copyright © 1980.

Mallanaga, Vatsyayana. Excerpts from THE KAMASUTRA. Edited and translated by Wendy Doniger and Sudhir Kakar. New York: Oxford University Press Inc., copyright © 2002, reprinted 2003. Reprinted by permission of Oxford University Press, Inc.

Martial. Excerpts from THE EPIGRAMS OF MARTIAL. Translated by James Michie. Copyright © 1972 by James Michie. Reprinted by permission of Modern Library, a division of Random House, Inc.

Mascaro, Juan (translator). THE DHAMMAPADA: THE PATH OF PERFECTION. Harmondsworth: Penguin Books, copyright © 1973. Reprinted by permission of the Penguin Group Ltd.

McNeill, John T. and Helena M. Gamer (translators). Excerpts from MEDIEVAL HANDBOOKS OF PENANCE: A TRANSLATION OF THE PRINCIPAL LIBRI POENITENTIALES AND SELECTIONS FROM RELATED DOCUMENTS. Reprinted by permission of Hippocrene Books.

Mencius. Excerpts from MENCIUS. Translated by D.C. Lau. Harmondsworth: Penguin Books, copyright © 1970. Reprinted by permission of the Penguin Group Ltd.

Mirabai. Poems "20," "27," and "151," from THE DEVOTIONAL POEMS OF MIRABAI. Translated by A.J. Alston. Delhi: Motilal Banarsidass Press, copyright © 1980. Reprinted by permission of the publisher.

Muhammad. Excerpts from THE QUR'AN: A MODERN ENGLISH TRANSLATION. Translated by Majid Fakhry and Mahmud Zayid. Reading, UK: Garnet, 1997. Reprinted by permission of Garnet Publishing.

More, Thomas. Excerpts from UTOPIA. Translated by Paul Turner. Harmondsworth: Penguin Books, copyright © 1965 and reprinted in 1974. Reprinted by permission of the Penguin Group Ltd.

Moser, Charles and J.J. Madeson. Excerpts from BOUND TO BE FREE: THE SM EXPERIENCE. New York: The Continuum Publishing Company, copyright © 1996 by Charles Moser and J.J. Madeson. Reprinted by permission of The Continuum International Publishing Group.

Murray, Stephen O. (editor). Excerpts from "Changing Brazilian Constructions," from LATIN AMERICAN MALE HOMOSEXUALITIES. Albuquerque: University of New Mexico Press, copyright © 1995. Reprinted by permission of the University of New Mexico Press.

Neusner, Jacob (translator). Excerpts from THE TALMUD OF THE LAND OF ISRAEL: A PRELIMINARY TRANSLATION AND EXPLANATION, VOLUME 22 – KETUBOT. Chicago: The University of Chicago Press, copyright © 1985. Reprinted by permission of The University of Chicago Press and of Dr. Jacob Neusner.

O'Flaherty, Wendy Doniger (translator). Excerpts from THE RIG VEDA: AN ANTHOLOGY. Harmondsworth: Penguin Books, copyright © 1981. Reprinted by permission of the Penguin Group Ltd.; Excerpts from HINDU MYTHS: A SOURCEBOOK. Translated from the Sanskrit. Harmondsworth: Penguin Books, copyright © 1975. Reprinted by permission of the Penguin Group Ltd.

Philippi, Donald L. (translator). Excerpts from KOJIKI. Co-published by Princeton University Press and University of Tokyo Press, copyright © 1968.

Plato. Excerpts from THE SYMPOSIUM. Translated by Walter Hamilton. Harmondsworth: Penguin Books Ltd., copyright © 1951, reprinted 1983. Reprinted by permission of the Penguin Group, Ltd.; Excerpts from PHAEDRUS AND THE SEVENTH AND EIGHTH LETTERS. Translated by Walter Hamilton. Harmondsworth: Penguin Books, copyright © 1973, reprinted 1981. Reprinted by permission of the Penguin Group Ltd.

Polo, Marco. THE TRAVELS OF MARCO POLO. Translated by Teresa Waugh. London: Sidgwick & Jackson, copyright © 1984.

Pomeroy, Sarah B. "P. Elephantine I … Marriage Contract" and "Tebtunis I 104 – Marriage Contract," from WOMEN IN HELLENISTIC EGYPT: FROM ALEXANDER TO CLEOPATRA. Detroit: Wayne State University Press, copyright © 1984 and 1990. Reprinted by permission of Dr. Sarah B. Pomeroy.

Power, Lisa (editor). Excerpts from "Gay Liberation Front Manifesto – London 1971," from NO BATH BUT PLENTY OF BUBBLES, AN ORAL HISTORY OF THE GAY LIBERATION FRONT, 1970-73. London: Cassell, copyright © 1995. Reprinted by permission of the Continuum International Publishing Group, Ltd.

Pritchard, James (editor). "An Akkadian Hymn – Hymn to Ishtar," from THE ANCIENT NEAR EAST. Princeton: Princeton University Press, copyright © 1958, 1986 renewed PUP. Reprinted by permission of Princeton University Press.

Qian, Sima. Excerpts from RECORDS OF THE GRAND HISTORIANS: HAN DYNASTY II. Translated by Burton Watson, Hong Kong. New York: Columbia University Press, copyright © 1961, revised edition, 1993. Reprinted by permission of the publisher; Excerpts from THE CULTURE OF SEX IN ANCIENT CHINA. Translated by Paul Rakita Goldin. Honolulu: University of Hawai'i Press, copyright © 2002. Reprinted by permission of the publisher.

Reich, Wilhelm. Excerpts from THE FUNCTION OF THE ORGASM. Translated by Theodore P. Wolfe. Copyright © 1973 The Wilhelm Reich Infant Trust. Reprinted by permission of Farrar, Straus and Giroux, LLC.

Robertson, George. Excerpts from THE DISCOVERY OF TAHITI; A JOURNAL OF THE SECOND VOYAGE OF H.M.S. DOLPHIN ROUND THE WORLD BY GEORGE ROBERTSON 1766-1768. London: The Hakluyt Society, copyright © 1948. Reprinted by permission of David Higham Associates Ltd. on behalf of The Hakluyt Society.

Robinson, James M. (general editor). Excerpts from "The Gospel of Philip (II, 3)," from THE NAG HAMMADI LIBRARY: IN ENGLISH, 3RD COMPLETELY REVISED EDITION. Translated by Members of the Coptic Gnostic Library Project of the Institute for Antiquity and Christianity – James M. Robinson Director. San Francisco: Harper and Row Publishers, copyright © 1978, 1988 by E.J. Brill. Reprinted by permission of HarperCollins Publishers and of Koninklijke Brill NV.

Rousselle, Aline. Excerpts from "Oribasius," from PORNEIA: ON DESIRE AND THE BODY IN ANTIQUITY. Translated by Felicia Pheasant. Cambridge: Basil Blackwell Ltd, copyright © 1988. Reprinted by permission of Blackwell Publishing.

Rubin, Eva R. (editor). THE ABORTION CONTROVERSY: A DOCUMENTARY HISTORY. Westport: Greenwood Press, copyright © 1994 by Eva R. Rubin. Reprinted by permission of Greenwood Publishing Group, Inc., Westport, CT.

Saadawi, Nawal El. Excerpts from THE HIDDEN FACE OF EVE: WOMEN IN THE ARAB WORLD. Translated by Sherif Hetata. London: Zed Books Ltd., copyright © 1980. Reprinted by permission of Zed Books Ltd.

Saint Augustine. Excerpts from SAINT AUGUSTINE: CONFESSIONS. Translated by R.S. Pine-Coffin. Harmondsworth: Penguin Books Ltd., copyright © 1961, reprinted 1984. Reprinted by permission of the Penguin Group, Ltd.; Excerpts from SAINT AUGUSTINE: CONCERNING THE CITY OF GOD AGAINST THE PAGANS. Translated by Henry Bettenson. Harmondsworth: Penguin Books Ltd., 1984. Reprinted by permission of the Penguin Group, Ltd.

Sappho. "The Blast of Love," "To Atthis," "Sleep," "The Virgin," "One Night," "A Return" and "Having Refused to Accept the Bitter with the Sweet," from SAPPHO AND THE GREEK LYRIC POETS. Translated by Willis Barnstone. Translation copyright © 1962, 1967, 1988 by Willis Barnstone. Reprinted by permission of Schocken Books, a division of Random House, Inc.

Schapera, Isaac. Excerpts from MARRIED LIFE IN AN AFRICAN TRIBE. New York: Sheridan House, copyright © 1941.

Sedgwick, Eve Kosofsky. Excerpts from EPISTEMOLOGY OF THE CLOSET. Berkeley: University of California Press, copyright © 1990, The Regents of the University of California Press. Reprinted by permission of the publisher.

Solomon, Frank and George L. Urioste (translators). Excerpts from THE HUAROCHIRI MANUSCRIPT: A TESTAMENT OF ANCIENT AND COLONIAL ANDEAN RELIGION. Copyright © Frank Solomon and George L. Urioste, 1991. Reprinted by permission of the University of Texas Press.

Somadeva. Excerpts from TALES FROM THE KATHĀSARITSĀGARA. Translated by Arshia Sattar. India: Penguin Books, copyright © 1994. Reprinted by permission of the Penguin Group Ltd.

Sophocles. Excerpts from THE THEBAN PLAYS: KING OEDIPUS, OEDIPUS AT COLONUS, ANTIGONE. Translated by E.F. Watling. Harmondsworth: Penguin Books Ltd., copyright © 1947, reprinted 1982. Reprinted by permission of the Penguin Group, Ltd.

Sorajjakool, Siroj. Excerpts from CHILD PROSTITUTION IN THAILAND: LISTENING TO RAHAB. New York: Haworth Press, copyright © 2003. Reprinted by permission of The Haworth Press, Inc.

St. Jerome. Excerpts from "The Letters of St. Jerome: Volume 1, Letters 1-22," from ANCIENT CHRISTIAN WRITERS: THE WORKS OF THE FATHERS IN TRANSLATION. Translated by Charles Christopher Mierow, PhD., and edited by Johannes Quasten and Walter J. Burghardt, S.J. Westminister: The Newman Press, and London: Longmans, Green and Co., copyright © 1963 by Rev. Johannes Quasten and Rev. Walter J. Burghardt, S.J., Paulist Press, Inc., New York/Mahwah, NJ. Reprinted by permission of Paulist Press. www.paulistpress.com

Stafford, Peter. Excerpts from SEXUAL BEHAVIOR IN THE COMMUNIST WORLD: AN EYEWITNESS REPORT OF LIFE, LOVE AND THE HUMAN CONDITION BEHIND THE IRON CURTAIN. New York: Julian Press (a division of Crown Publishers), copyright © 1967.

Strossen, Nadine. Excerpts from DEFENDING PORNOGRAPHY: FREE SPEECH, SEX AND THE FIGHT FOR WOMEN'S RIGHTS. Reprinted by permission of the Carol Mann Agency.

Stengers, Jean and Anne Van Neck. Excerpts from "Samuel Tissot: The illness of which the English patients complain …" and "1864 debate of the Surgical Society of Paris," from MASTURBATION: THE HISTORY OF A GREAT TERROR. Translated by Kathryn A. Hoffmann. New York: Palgrave, copyright © by Kathryn Hoffmann, 2001. Reprinted by permission of Palgrave Macmillan.

Suetonius. Excerpts from SUETONIUS, VOLUME I. Translated by J.C. Rolfe. Reprinted by permission of the publishers and the Trustees of the Loeb Classical Library. Cambridge: Harvard University Press, 1913. The Loeb Classical Library ® is a registered trademark of the President and Fellows of Harvard College.

Tilak, Lakshmī Bāī. "Poem CVII. Husband and Wife," from THE HERITAGE OF INDIA: POEMS BY INDIAN WOMEN. Edited by Margaret Macnicol and translated by B.K Uzgare and Mrs. Uzgare. London: Oxford University Press, copyright © 1923. Reprinted by permission of Oxford University Press, Inc.

Tsu-k'uang, Lou (editor) and William Eberhard (collaborator). Excerpts from ASIAN FOLKLORE AND SOCIAL LIFE MONOGRAPHS, VOLUME 55. Taipei: The Orient Cultural Service, copyright © 1974.

Valmiki. Excerpts from THE RAMAYANA OF VALMIKI. Translated by Makhan Lal Sen. New Delhi: Munshiram Manoharlal Publishers Pvt. Ltd., copyright © 1997. Reprinted by permission of the publisher.

Van Gulik, R.H. (translator). Excerpts from SEXUAL LIFE IN ANCIENT CHINA: A PRELIMINARY SURVEY OF CHINESE SEX AND SOCIETY FROM CA. 1500 B.C. TILL 1644 A.D. Leiden: E.J. Brill, copyright © 1961. Reprinted by permission of the publisher.

Vanita, Ruth and Saleem Kidwai (editors). Excerpts from "Kumkum Roy's translation of the Bhagavata Purana: The Embrace of Shiva and Vishnu (Sanskrit)," "Saleem Kidwai's translation of Hakim Muhammad Yusaf Hasan: Do Shiza (Urdu)," "Saleem Kidwai's translation of Shaikh Qalandar Baksh: Rekhti Poetry" and "Vikram Seth: Dubious," from SAME-SEX LOVE IN INDIA: READINGS FROM LITERATURE AND HISTORY. New York: St. Martin's Press, copyright © 2000. Reprinted by permission of Palgrave Macmillan.

Wilson, Edward O. Excerpts from SOCIOBIOLOGY: THE NEW SYNTHESIS. Cambridge: The Belknap Press of Harvard University Press, Copyright © 1975, 2000 by the President and Fellows of Harvard College.

Yü, Upāsaka Lu K'uan (Charles Luk) (translator). "The Realm of the Gods (Devaloka): The Six Heavens of the Realm of Desire (Kamadhatu)," from THE SŪRANGAMA SŪTRA (LENG YEN CHING): CHINESE RENDERING BY MASTER PARAMITI OF CENTRAL NORTH INDIA AT CHIH CHIH MONASTERY, CANTON, CHINA, AD 705. London: Rider and Company, copyright © 1966. Reprinted by permission of the publisher.

Yun, Lu. "Four Letter-Poems Between Husband and Wife," from NEW SONGS FROM A JADE TERRACE: AN ANTHOLOGY OF EARLY CHINESE LOVE POETRY. Edited and translated by Anne Birrell. London: George, Allen & Unwin, copyright © 1982.

Picture Credits

temporal index

Topics are listed by document number. This index includes works drawn from earlier oral traditions or of uncertain date listed under the most recent period by which they were definitely set down in writing. Images are also listed below in the period in which they were created. Items for the nineteenth and twentieth centuries are dated to a specific year, if known.

geographical index

topical index

Topics are listed by document number.

ablution, 64, 68

Aborigines (of Australia), 106, 110, 123

abortion, 89, 90, 101, 112, 142, 155, 176 (*see also* contraception)

Abraham (biblical figure), 12, 84, 85

abstinence (*see* sexual renunciation *and* virgins and virginity)

Abu Nuwas (poet), 75

acting (*see* theater)

active/passive distinction, 6, 179 (*see also* gender inequality)

Adam and Eve (biblical figures), 3, 59, 66, 85, 112, 176, 182

Addams, Jane, 135

adolescents (*see* children)

adoption, 33, 136

adultery (*see* extramarital sex)

advertising, 120, 138, 150, 154, 168, 174

Ahmed, Leila, 176

AIDS, 154, 173

alcohol, 49, 57, 73, 87, 102, 118, 119, 135, 139, 174

androgyny (*see* gender nonconformity *and* transvestism)

Angas, George, 106

Angelides, Steven, 181

Anthony, Susan B., 134

Antigone (by Sophocles), 10

aphrodisiacs, 72

Aphrodite (goddess), 26, 27, 182

Apuleius, 28

Aristotle, 29, 176

army (*see* soldiers)

arranged marriages (*see* marriage: initiation of)

art (erotic), 1, 20, 37, 46, 52, 72, 77, 90, 91, 131, 145, 165, 175

attraction and attractiveness (*see* beauty *and* sexual desire and pleasure)

Augustine (Saint), 18, 31, 66, 182

Augustus (Roman Emperor), 33

autobiographical accounts, 6, 18, 21, 39, 60, 81, 82, 83, 97, 117, 125, 137, 158

Baksh, Shaikh Qalandar, 160

Ban Zhao, 6

barrenness (*see* fertility, reproduction, *and* sterility)

Barret, William, 143

"bawdy house" (*see* brothel)

beachbathing, 151

beauty (female), 1, 2, 4, 13, 25, 26, 38, 42, 45, 50, 76, 77, 78, 85, 89, 100, 101, 104, 106, 111, 120, 169; (male), 34, 42, 78, 82, 89, 169, 170

Beauvoir, Simone de, 164

bestiality, 24, 28, 68, 103, 112

betrothal, 33, 68, 136 (*see also* marriage: initiation of)

Bhartrihari (poet), 4

bible, 3, 12, 13, 24, 25, 42, 55, 56, 57, 58, 59, 61, 66, 67, 69, 81, 84, 85, 107, 176, 180

Bietris de Roman (poet), 83

bigamy (*see* polygamy)

Bira (people of Congo), 111

birth (*see* childbirth)

birth control (*see* contraception)

bisexuality, 16, 86, 90, 91, 128, 171, 179, 181, 183

Bly, Robert, 182

breasts (female), 4, 42, 45, 73, 85, 89, 105, 119, 123, 159, 160, 165, 167; (breastfeeding), 107

bridal gift (*see* marriage: payments)

"bride of Christ," 67

brothel, 86, 119, 139, 143 (*See also* prostitution)

Brown, Helen Gurley, 167

Bryant, Anita, 113

Buddha (Siddhartha Gautama), 50, 52

Buddhism, 50, 51, 52, 70, 71, 72, 78, 79, 129, 130, 142

Bushnell, Kate, 108

Caligula (Roman Emperor), 33

Canterbury Tales, The (by Chaucer), 84

Carnal Prayer Mat, The (by Li Yu), 90

castration, 22, 23, 27, 28, 31, 55, 56, 70, 126, 156, 182

Castro, Fidel, 95

celibacy (*see* sexual renunciation *and* virgins and virginity)

censorship, 145, 146, 172

chaperones, 133 (*see also* dating customs)

Eve (biblical figure) (*see* Adam and Eve)

exogamy (*see* consanguinity)

extramarital sex, 5, 8, 9, 14, 15, 19, 23, 25, 33, 36, 48, 55, 56, 57, 59, 68, 72, 76, 82, 88, 90, 92, 100, 101, 102, 104, 108, 121, 136, 139, 142, 144, 146, 159, 164, 166

Ezekiel, Book of, 25

"fallen women" (*see* prostitution)

family, 6, 33, 85, 86, 92, 93, 94, 95, 96, 98, 106, 123, 129, 136, 139, 156, 158, 172 (*see also* children, fathers and fatherhood, love: familial, marriage, *and* mothers and motherhood)

Fan (people of Gabon), 107

"farmer's daughter," 138

fathers and fatherhood, 6, 10, 41, 68, 90, 97, 98, 101, 117, 128, 136, 156, 158, 166; (in-law), 14, 62

fellatio, 34, 37, 68, 119

feminists and feminism, 95, 164, 175

fertility, 1, 37, 101, 136 (*see also* childbirth, children, reproduction, *and* sterility)

fictional accounts, 38, 76, 78, 84, 87, 90, 92, 100, 129, 130, 142, 166

fidelity, marital (*see* extramarital sex *and* love: marital)

filial piety (*see* love: familial)

films (*see* motion pictures)

Fleras, Jomar, 178

flirting, 39, 162 (*see also* sexual desire and pleasure)

Flower, Benjamin Orange, 144

footbinding, 91, 98

foreplay, 122, 127 (*see also* sexual desire and pleasure)

fornication (*see* extramarital sex)

Foucault, Michel, 172

Franks (people of France), 80

"free love," 162

"French pox" (*see* sexually transmitted diseases)

Freud, Sigmund, 117, 128, 180, 181

friendship, 21, 101, 124, 161, 162 (*see also* love)

frigidity, 122 (*see also* hysteria)

Fryer, John, 103

Galbraith, Anna, 118

galli, 27, 28, 31

Gandhi, Mahatma, 148, 149

gays and gayness (*see* homoeroticism)

Gay Liberation Front, 169

gay pride, 153, 154, 169

geishas, 129, 137

gender inequality, 2, 3, 5, 6, 7, 35, 37, 47, 62, 65, 76, 89, 94, 95, 101, 106, 122, 123, 124, 127, 134, 136, 137, 141, 144, 148, 149, 156, 158, 164, 166, 175, 176

gender nonconformity, 27, 28, 29, 31, 45, 65, 98, 102, 112, 119, 122, 126, 152, 153, 169, 177, 178, 179, 183

Genesis, Book of, 3, 12

genetics, 118, 123, 155

genitals (*see* clitoris, hymen, labia, penis, testicles, *and* vagina)

geniza (of Cairo), 63, 74

girdle, 167 (*see also* corset)

gonorrhea (*see* sexually transmitted diseases)

Gospel of Matthew, 56

Gospel of Philip, 59

Gregory of Tours (bishop), 80

group sex, 36, 90, 91, 103, 110

Gunther, John, 110

hadith, 64, 65, 176

Hahalis Welfare Society and Baby Garden, 110

hair, 34, 85, 101, 119, 123, 131

halitosis, 168

Hammer of Witches, The (by Kramer and Sprenger), 99

Hammurabi, Code of, 9

Han dynasty (China), 6, 22, 23

"Han Yi" (pseudonym), 94

harem, 36

Hasan, Hakim Muhammad Yusuf, 126

Hays Code, The, 146

Heian era (Japan), 38, 39

Hellenistic societies, 13, 21, 27

Herdt, Gilbert, 173

heredity (*see* genetics)

Herodotus, 8, 26

heterosexuality, 128 (*see also* extramarital sex, love, *and* marriage)

hijras, 126

Hinduism, 5, 14, 43, 44, 45, 46, 60, 78, 126, 139, 180, 182

Hite, Shere, 127

Hodge, Lyman, 159

homoeroticism (female), 19, 30, 36, 48, 68, 83, 90, 91, 119, 121, 126, 146, 152, 160, 169, 179, 181, 183; (male), 16, 19, 20, 21, 24, 28, 33, 34, 48, 53, 57, 68, 75, 81, 86, 102, 113, 119, 121, 125, 126, 130, 146, 152, 153, 154, 161, 169, 170, 171, 177, 178, 179, 180, 181, 183 (*see also* love: same-sex, *and* marriage: same-sex)